Wanted, More than Human Intellectual Property

This book analyses animal creativity in order to unsettle the dominant assumptions that underpin current ideas of authorship and ownership in intellectual property.

Drawing upon theories of animal behaviour and cognitive ethology, the book exposes and disrupts the anthropocentrism that informs prevailing assumptions about creativity, intentionality, and authorship within the field of intellectual property, towards a new theory of authorship and personhood through play and the playful. Moving on to challenge the invocation of a more general human-nonhuman distinction in this context, the book also engages the challenge to this distinction posed by artificial intelligence. Incorporating critical animal studies, behavioural science, ethology, critical legal studies, and legal philosophy, the book presents a new idea of creativity, which undermines the kind of rivalrous models now common in the field of intellectual property.

This book will be of considerable interest to those studying and teaching in the area of intellectual property, as well as in animal law. It will also appeal to legal theorists and others working in the social sciences in the areas of posthumanism and animal studies.

Johanna Gibson is Herchel Smith Professor of Intellectual Property Law at Queen Mary, University of London, UK.

Wanted, More than Human Intellectual Property

Animal Authors and Human Machines

Johanna Gibson

Routledge
Taylor & Francis Group
a GlassHouse Book

First published 2025
by Routledge
4 Park Square, Milton Park, Abingdon, Oxon OX14 4RN

and by Routledge
605 Third Avenue, New York, NY 10158

A GlassHouse book

Routledge is an imprint of the Taylor & Francis Group, an informa business

© 2025 Johanna Gibson

The right of Johanna Gibson to be identified as author of this work has been asserted in accordance with sections 77 and 78 of the Copyright, Designs and Patents Act 1988.

All rights reserved. No part of this book may be reprinted or reproduced or utilised in any form or by any electronic, mechanical, or other means, now known or hereafter invented, including photocopying and recording, or in any information storage or retrieval system, without permission in writing from the publishers.

Trademark notice: Product or corporate names may be trademarks or registered trademarks, and are used only for identification and explanation without intent to infringe.

British Library Cataloguing-in-Publication Data
A catalogue record for this book is available from the British Library

Library of Congress Cataloging-in-Publication Data
Names: Gibson, Johanna, author.
Title: Wanted, more than human intellectual property : animal authors and human machines / Johanna Gibson.
Description: Abingdon, Oxon [UK] ; New York, NY : Routledge, 2025. | Includes bibliographical references and index.
Identifiers: LCCN 2024030064 (print) | LCCN 2024030065 (ebook) | ISBN 9780367356606 (hardback) | ISBN 9781032896755 (paperback) | ISBN 9780429342103 (ebook)
Subjects: LCSH: Intellectual property. | Human-machine systems.
Classification: LCC K1401 .G54 2025 (print) | LCC K1401 (ebook) | DDC 346.04/8--dc23/eng/20240709
LC record available at https://lccn.loc.gov/2024030064
LC ebook record available at https://lccn.loc.gov/2024030065

ISBN: 9780367356606 (hbk)
ISBN: 9781032896755 (pbk)
ISBN: 9780429342103 (ebk)

DOI: 10.4324/9780429342103

Typeset in Sabon
by Deanta Global Publishing Services, Chennai, India

For my brother

And to that monkey, that dog, and all those wonderful ants. Thank you for showing us the way.

Contents

Acknowledgements		ix
Apologue The Philosopher, the Ants, and Mercury: *Wanted, a Player's Guide*		1
What Does Naruto Want?		9
PART 1 **The Philosopher**		51
1	A Word between Us	53
2	The Common Touch	89
3	What Is It Like to Be an Author?	119
PART 2 **The Ants**		165
4	Ant People	167
5	A Theory of Everything	200
6	Pay Attention, Stupid	232
PART 3 **Mercury**		263
7	Turn to Play	267

8	All Authors Are Liars	310
9	The Gods Must Be Playful	347
	Law's Anecdote	387
	Epilogue *That* Ape and *That* Dog, *or* What Naruto Wants	416
	Bibliography	*421*
	Index	*485*

Acknowledgements

This has been a task of rhizomatic distractions, gripping fragments, and unruly proportions, of many starts and many parts. First and foremost, I am enormously grateful to Colin Perrin, senior commissioning editor at Routledge, for his support for this project, and the opportunity to develop and pursue the concept of ethological jurisprudence through a trilogy, of which this is the second book. And to Naomi Round Cahalin, in the Business, Economics, and Law section of Routledge, I owe enormous thanks for her patience with the unfolding epic and my seemingly vanishing horizon of completion. The first book in this family of three, *Owned, An Ethological Jurisprudence of Property*, arose largely through falling through a rabbit hole, or perhaps it was a series of ants' tunnels, while writing this book, leading to *Owned* and a beginning for this middle, which naturally led to a further constellation of ants' tunnels, the haptic of new distractions, and a third book, *Made, the Nature of Intellectual Property*, which will chase this theory through a sea of objects, in pursuit of an ethological jurisprudence of the intellectual property objects themselves. I suppose in that way I was heeding Friedrich Schlegel's advice, and I did indeed start in the middle to find the whole story. It is to that middle I have returned in this book. Thus, one book became two. Then two books became three. At some point, I have to stop writing to give people a chance to respond. Or franchise. But to borrow Donna Haraway's phrase, *I'm staying with the trouble*.

I also want to thank my students at Queen Mary, University of London. During this process, I have had a wonderful group of PhD students across intellectual property and animal law, and our discussions show the rich intersections in ideas and work between these fields. Thank you to Mark Jetsaphon Niyompatama, Mespiti Poolsavasdi, Ogulcan Ekiz, Uche Ani, Adela Wang, Trupti Panigrahi, Victoria Onyeagbako, Yiheng Lu, Clinton Adas, and Tamara Katamine for all the enjoyable and stimulating discussions. I am also very grateful to my very many Master of Laws (LLM) students, and the irreverence and unpredictability of the questions and discussions in the classroom, with a special thank you to the animal law students and their insight, imagination, and enthusiasm for this complex and compelling field. I love teaching, and a thread of teaching and learning also runs through this book. I am enormously grateful to be a part of the Centre for Commercial Law Studies (CCLS), where it has been possible for me not only to explore these interdisciplinary connections in my research but also to engage the students in their development through my own teaching and contribution to what is, centre-wide, a genuinely innovative curriculum. In *The Formation of the Scientific Mind*, Gaston Bachelard says, "if objective science is to be really educational, then the way it is taught must be socially active ... *whoever is taught must teach.*"[1] I want to acknowledge my students for also teaching me.

Many thanks to colleagues in the Forum for Decentering the Human in the Institute of Humanities and Social Sciences at Queen Mary, especially to Alexis Alvarez-Nakagawa, John Adenitere, and Kathryn Yusoff. And many thanks to Lars Chittka for our wonderful discussion on bees, and Alan McElligott for his multispecies communities, support, and friendship. I am fortunate to work in a law school that not only encourages such interdisciplinary work but also thrives upon it – thank you to colleagues Ioannis Kokkoris, Anne Flanagan, Gavin Sutter, Laura Edgar, Ian Walden, Noam Shemtov, Chris Reed, Duncan Matthews, Gaetano Dimita, Guido Westkamp, Uma Suthersanen, Gail Evans, Apostolos Chronopoulos, Guan Tang, Jonathan Griffiths, Miriam Goldby, and Debbie di Girolamo. And, of course, Malcolm Langley, keeper of the flame (also known as the Herchel Smith archive).

Once again, the support of my family has been with me all the way – my mother, Dawn, and my other parents and siblings, Mary, Peter, Jeremy, Linda, Anne, and Simon. And of course, my enormous gratitude to and for Phillip, always supportive and an intellectual antagonist and dialogist along the way. And Phillip's patience with the ever-growing, potentially beam-shattering, personal library merits a special mention on its own. It has become a perpetual growth pattern for which he is regularly trying to engineer a solution, but the library continues to outpace every solution he provides as I apparently strive for the Library of Babel.[2] To all the other animals in my family, some whom I met as soon as I was born into my multispecies family, many more I've met along the way, I owe immeasurable gratitude and love. Getting to know you has motivated a lot if not all of this work. And to Aubrey, Huw, Jeff, Howard (who reads books with his mouth), Benny, YumYum, Lora, Poly, Kitty, and Bulldog (aka *CatGPT* – who tried to insert his body into the text throughout this process, sleeping on the keyboard, and producing frequent and uninvited editing with irreverent results to say the least), a special thank you for showing me the way and sticking by my side all those long hours in a (somewhat crowded!) study. But my special thanks are to my dear brother John, who was always my biggest advocate, and it is to his memory that this book and this process will be forever bound. I miss you every day.

One morning, during the writing process, I went outside onto our roof. Not as dramatic as it sounds. I went to spend some time on the terrace at the top of our London Victorian townhouse, to try to do some blue-sky thinking. It was, however, overcast and misting. But as I looked to the sky, I saw a flock of starlings, so fast and so playful and so aware of each other. As I watched the murmuration write the sky, I noticed that two or three starlings would come from somewhere else unknown and join them, and then again, and again, the group gathering more and more from where I do not know. As the flock got bigger and bigger, they circled the rooftops, tracing their knotty paths around the sky. At one point, they looked like they might rest on a roof, but it was a ruse, and up they all went again, like a receding tide. I watched one starling get tricked and settle briefly before aweigh, swooping up to rejoin the group. They then flew straight over my head in what was, at least for me, a joyful swarm of shared interests. As I watched them, I thought about how they worked and played together and yet acted as individuals, joining late, arriving early, dropping out, back again, to and fro, back and forth, in and out. And I thought about how I felt seen to see them and share their space, just for a few minutes.

All that, just by looking up.

Here is to looking up and looking for trouble.

Notes

1 Bachelard (2002/[1938]), 242. Emphasis in original.
2 Borges (1941). In the Poem of the Gifts (Borges (1960)), composed after losing his sight not long after taking his appointment as director of the National Library of Argentina, Borges laments the "splendid irony" of "books and blindness at one touch," the haptic double play not unnoticed. In this poem, noting the irony of this gift, there is a line that has been paraphrased everywhere and somewhat less eloquently in which Borges, "with a tentative stick," notes "I, who had always thought of Paradise / in form and image as a library" (82–83).

APOLOGUE
The Philosopher, the Ants, and Mercury: *Wanted*, a Player's Guide

How to begin a discussion of authorship, of animals, and of artificiality? A fable by Aesop anticipates the trajectory. It is the fable of *The Philosopher, the Ants, and Mercury*.[1] Aesop's fable is a constructive and productive allegorical vehicle for the story ahead. But fables themselves are also co-implicated in the threads to be traced, not least for the fact that fables are celebrated (fabled, so to speak) for anthropomorphising their nonhuman characters in order to deliver a moral. But this fable of the philosopher, the ants, and Mercury, is intriguing for the way in which it recasts that anthropomorphism to highlight the anthropocentrism of human knowledge in what is perhaps one of the earliest explorations of a critical anthropomorphism.[2] The following pages step in those tracks, engaging an ethological approach to unsettle the anthropocentrism that frames not only the law surrounding authorship but also wider enquiries into the very nature of authorship, creativity, and innovation.

Fables are also noted for being enlivened by orality and belief, transmitted through imitation and impersonation, and creative through deception and play. Fables are a curiously enchanting expression of shared interests,[3] of a conscious and deliberate imitation, one which is both creative and accountable – *attentive*, if you will. As a literary form, the fable unfolds the axial concepts of an ethological jurisprudence of authorship: the critical anthropomorphism of the nonhuman, a literal animality;[4] an oral tradition of innovation through conscious imitation and shared interests, as distinct from coercion and rule; the familiar production[5] of imitative creativity; and the centrality of fantasy and the critical deception and play in authorship. What is an author? Appearances and images are fantastically deceptive, and deception is the craft of the sentient. As a matter of course, the notion that fables are somehow unoriginal is decried by the shared interests expressed through the attentive imitation of this particular fable and its legacy.[6] The originality in this repetition is at the heart of innovation and social life for an ethological jurisprudence of authorship as pursued through the following pages.

DOI: 10.4324/9780429342103-1

Jacques Derrida describes fable as "the origin of literature," and "at the same time ... the origin of law."[7] It is a self-contained fragment that is at once in a legacy of debt but one that is prosocial and reconstitutive. Thus, the fable persists outside the law and at the end of the world. An ethological approach exposes the mechanics of the expected and usual prejudgments of real lives and real creativity, and of property and persons, to reveal a construction that is both feckless and unreasonable. The species divide is a built environment, and its defences have become a force of habit.[8] And the fretful paradox discernible in the legal and scientific enquiry into non-human animal creativity is that much of this is itself a kind of anthropomorphism. But that anthropomorphism is not for the enticing reasons of fabulation; rather, it is in service of the sustenance of humans at the centre of the questions. That only humans can create is a "conceit which is truly anthropomorphic."[9] A fabulation. Indeed, an anthropofabulation.[10] It is in this context that the concept of *res familiaris*[11] is in play. This is not simply a communal property, but rather, it is a matter of overlapping territories and layered interests. Through play, there is a sociable making together, a familiar production of the swarm, rather than the univocity of the collective. Marking *res familiaris* is thus a matter not of boundaries but of attribution, of scents, and of relations. In an ethological jurisprudence of authorship, the value is not in the originality in the objects as such; it is to be found in the relations, in the action of tracing those relations, and in the originality of those connections.

The Philosopher, the Ants, and Mercury frames the present discussion. In this story, a philosopher witnesses a shipwreck, reels at the tragedy of the perceived natural injustice, and then is blind to the irony of the similar injustice of his tyranny over the inconvenience of the ants occupying the nest in which he finds himself standing. Quite literally, he walks unaware into their world, tramples them underfoot, and crushes them beneath an iron heel.[12] At this point, Mercury appears, bridging two worlds, and delivers the message of the philosopher's hypocrisy:

A Philosopher witnessed from the shore the shipwreck of a vessel, of which the crew and passengers were all drowned. He inveighed against the injustice of Providence, which would for the sake of one criminal perchance sailing in the ship allow so many innocent persons to perish. As he was indulging in these reflections, he found himself surrounded by a whole army of Ants, near to whose nest he was standing. One of them climbed up and stung him, and he immediately trampled them all to death with his foot. Mercury presented himself, and, striking the Philosopher with his wand, said, "And are you indeed to make yourself a judge of the dealings of Providence, who has thyself in a similar manner treated these poor Ants?"

As it is for the philosopher, so too for a transformation of the law's grasp of authorship. Awareness and perspective will demand a kind of mercurial enquiry, a play of the alchemical self, a translation and transmutation in the ways of looking and the ways of making.

All for the sake of *one criminal perchance* sailing along for the ride on the ship of knowledge, the conventional commercial models and enforcement of copyright in the sea of social production may be viewed as an injustice against the *many innocent persons* for whom access to knowledge may be collaterally limited or denied. As will be charted in the following pages, the emphasis on the objects of copyright, the supposed *things* of property, makes for more and more shipwrecks. This book is a further exploration of the groundwork in *Owned*,[13] which inaugurated an ethological jurisprudence of property,[14] a relational account of imitation, kinship, and production. In *Wanted*, that ethological jurisprudence is applied to authorship[15] through these three parts – "The Philosopher," "The Ants," and "Mercury."

The cognitive ethology at the heart of a more-than-human intellectual property is the subject of the ethological enquiry into authorship and creativity in the first part of this book, "The Philosopher," clearing a path for an ethological jurisprudence of intellectual property more widely speaking. The anthropocentric fiction of intellectual property is retold in the second part, "The Ants," where the innovation of the nonhuman other is masked by protestations of mechanism and instinct. Amidst the nest of creative potential is an increasing emphasis on a combative and predatory model of property's *survival of the fittest*, which I introduce in *Owned* through the specific concept of predatory drift.[16] The overwhelming linguistic and structural emphasis in intellectual property more widely may be understood through this concept and the tenacity of weary canons of justification. The term borrows its name from a similarly partial and oft-misinterpreted maxim in dog behaviour and training, fuelled by damaging banalities of competition and survival in the canine world.[17] This predator and prey dynamic characterises everything from economic policy to reality television and invariably places the human individual at the centre. By all means, it is this somewhat normalised and mainstreamed anthropocentrism that tramples underfoot the kinds of more-than-human authorship that are considered in the following pages, creativity that is otherwise diminished to instinct or function.[18] The concept of predatory drift in property describes a kind of legal fiction rather than a functional reality; thus, it is a strategic account that is at last being untied by the challenges from more than just human authors, much more indeed. And the self-assemblage of the ants under the philosopher's feet points to an abundant creativity and familiar production that will be considered in more detail later in the creativity of swarms; from ladders and bridges to rafts, the very object is to survive such a flood.[19]

Finally, Mercury appears, and the knotty properties and labyrinthine journey of the following pages are set to continue. For the labyrinth is also the path, and the path is the stone. As it happens, things do not have to be easy, and authorship is no different. It will be resocialised through an ethological jurisprudence of authorship, ownership, and the owned in the final part, "Mercury." What is it like to be an author? What is it like to be a person? To answer these questions, creativity must be brought into play. Mercury is, of course, the god of science and commerce, and thus is always linked to the kind of innovation and ingenuity that is monopolised as the purview of intellectual property. But Mercury is also the patron of travellers, of wanderers, of thieves – the intentionality of deception, the creativity of pretence, of uncertain properties and mobile territories. All authors are liars, said the author.

Mercury the messenger is also the messenger of this story, the interpreter, and the orator – the voice of reason, as it were. In a famously contentious footnote to Shakespeare's *Love's Labour's Lost*, Adriano de Armado says, "The words of Mercury are harsh after the songs of Apollo. You that way: we this way."[20] In some ways, this is the word between us, the spectre, the missive of reason and the play of utterance. One is fixed and the other transient; one is expression and the other relation; one is human and the other is othered. This *afterthought* of Mercury and Apollo, of writing and speech, at the same time prefigures the play at the heart of this book. The emphasis on the visual, on appearance, or more specifically on the literal, is the currency of intellectual property. And this literal and visual hegemony is pronounced throughout the range of rights and renditions. But appearances can be deceptive. *Love's Labour's Lost* is a principled drama of the contrivance and artifice of this spectacle, anticipating the narrative of innovation as a unilinear progression seemingly impelled by intellectual property, not just rewarded by it: "For Shakespeare, the immortality of the written word was illusory, the social role of the poet being to give his words to the actors who, in turn, would present them to the audience, thus giving them free circulation within the theater and, by extension, the community."[21]

Part of this journey has included searching for precursors, meeting predecessors, and honouring the stewardship of knowledge through an elaborate field of connections and imitative rays, to borrow Gabriel Tarde's expression. These fragments are both whole as well as prosocial, stretching to new connections and performing the value and originality of those connections and relations themselves – a monadological approach to creativity as anticipated by Gottfried Leibniz and imitated anew by Tarde. Much of the writing of Simone Weil, one of these acknowledged precursors, is itself to be found in fragments, as well as the wanderings of Walter Benjamin, the navigation of epistemological obstacles with Gaston Bachelard, the novelties and natures of Friedrich Schlegel and other figures of early German Romanticism,[22] the anecdotes that made the way for nonhuman theory of mind, the aphorisms that return in refrains, the fables that animate the text throughout, and, what is more, the law itself. For the law is itself a pastiche, stitched together by the threads of innumerable stories and "minute perceptions."[23] An elaborate parody, if you will.

The irony is that the final expression here is one of fragments, as Schlegel accounts: "Most thoughts are only the profiles of thoughts. They have to be turned around and synthesized with their antipodes. This is how many philosophical works acquire a considerable interest they would otherwise have lacked."[24] But an ethological jurisprudence welcomes the diffraction[25] of an interdisciplinary universe. Diffraction is used here in the sense adopted by Karen Barad, who explains the process as "reading insights through one another in attending to and responding to the details and specificities of relations of difference and how they matter."[26] But this methodology has an impressive predecessor in Weil, who is also known for her "total disregard for teleology and disciplinary boundaries."[27]

This is the complexity and trajectory of the story of intellectual property that follows. This is a passionate play of interdisciplinarity and the mediation between – from the motivation of desires and beliefs, to the movement of embodied sentience, to the affective creativity in play and an ethological jurisprudence of authorship. And as a matter of course, this is the middle book of three in which I am introducing and developing a methodology of ethological jurisprudence. *Owned*[28] sets the groundwork for an ethological jurisprudence of property, and *Made*[29] pursues this approach through the objects of intellectual property themselves. *Wanted* is the intermediary of *Owned* and *Made*, but it is also the place to start, the origin, for one should always start in the middle.[30] In the opening chapter, "What Does Naruto Want?," the fundamental questions are introduced, as well as key concepts, including *attentive imitation* and *stereotypic imitation*. What does it mean to consider the aesthetic sense of animals other than humans? What is the creative work of artificial intelligence? And how might authorship be enriched by an intellectual property that is more than human?

In Part 1, "The Philosopher," human exceptionalism and the scaffolding of the law's anthropocentrism are laid bare: from the law's incessant talking in Chapter 1, "A Word between Us," to its visual hegemony and intellectual property's knotty mind-body problem in Chapter 2, "The Common Touch," and finally to the law's anthropocentric bias and its introduction of possibly unintended consequences for the emerging law on sentience in Chapter 3, "What Is It Like to Be an Author." Part 1 thus sets out the explainability problem of nonhuman authorship, from animals to machines, that is both created and facilitated by human exceptionalism.

Part 2, "The Ants," examines the predatory drift of the law's perspective on creativity and creators, and the challenges posed by human horizons and perspectival force. Chapter 4, "Ant People," explores multispecies perspectives on creativity through the minute worlds of ants, and examines the chilling effect of predatory models of capital, and capital models of sentience and authorship. The overwhelming influence of the concept of force throughout property and intellectual property is considered in Chapter 5, "A Theory of Everything," differentiating systems of creativity and exposing the limitations of predatory models of authorship, competition, and property. Chapter 6, "Pay Attention, Stupid," appeals for an ethological approach and a certain attention. The central concept of attention and the patience that goes with it demands that we look at nonhumans and the diversity of creative work. It also introduces a creative inattention and distraction that is critical to this reorientation.

In the third and final part, "Mercury," an ethological jurisprudence of authorship heats up in its glorious and flamboyant entropy of play. The manifest performance of sentience, the differentiation of nonhuman animals and machines, is the nature of play and of pretence, including the critical deception and make-believe of creating, from authored works to inventions. Chapter 7, "Turn to Play," argues that we must look to play for the evidence and the performance of what it means to be an author, and sets out the dimensions of authorship and intentionality through play. This includes a discussion of the surplus expenditure, biological or otherwise, in play, and the counterpoint of waste that is often attached to the concept of play, as well as intellectual property's reconciliation of waste within market dynamics. Chapter 8, "All Authors Are Liars," looks at specific qualities of creativity, including so-called negative creativity, through deception and lying, capacities that reveal crucial distinctions between nonhuman animal creativity and artificial intelligence. Finally, Chapter 9, "The Gods Must Be Playful," provides a detailed account of imitation and play through the legal characterisations of permitted imitations, including parody, pastiche, and caricature.

The final, concluding chapter, "Law's Anecdote," brings together the pastiche that is inherent in the law itself, the necessary connections between fragments, and the fundamental problems with the quantification of creators. The system of belief and motivation that underpins the institution of intellectual property presents as the philosopher's stone turning mercury into gold. But mercury merely allows us to grasp the path.[31] Mercury is the extensive quality that allows us to perceive the intensity of the stone.[32] The path is the stone. The ethology. The story. The play.

This is the story of authorship, as told by, among others, swarms of insects, colonies of ants, many dogs, a bird or two, and at least one monkey.

Let's play.

Notes

1 All references to Aesop here and thereafter are to the collection in Aesop (1998/[1909]).
2 Burghardt (2007). See further Gibson (2020a), 5–7.

3 I first introduced and developed the concept of shared interests in detail in Gibson (2020a), see in particular 254–258 and Chapter 10 for its particular significance in the context of rethinking perspectives upon incentives in creativity.
4 Lefkowitz (2014) rejects the simple dismissal of fables as a problematic humanising of animals, arguing instead that "in granting speech to animals, fables not only endow animals with the quintessential faculty of the human mind, they also draw attention to questions about what differentiates human from animal by manipulating a standard marker of the boundary between the two categories" (1). Lefkowitz argues that "The fable tradition occasionally eschews symbolism and anthropomorphism entirely, revealing a deep and abiding interest in animal behaviour and in material that could be described as natural history" (15). It is the contention and opportunity in the present work that this is in fact the case in *The Philosopher, the Ants, and Mercury*.
5 I first introduced the concept of familiar production in Gibson (2014), it is developed further in the context of nonhuman animals in Gibson (2020a), and continues to be important in the present discussion.
6 Pérez Perozo (1946), 364.
7 Derrida (1987), 199.
8 On the constraints of habit in intellectual enquiry, see Margolis (1993).
9 Griffin (1976), 69.
10 Buckner (2013) defines anthropofabulation as "a distinct bias that loads the deck against animal mentality: our tendency to tie the competence criteria for cognitive capacities to an exaggerated sense of typical human performance. I dub this error 'anthropofabulation', since it combines anthropocentrism with confabulation about our own prowess" (853). Pick (2013) describes something similar when she says, "Calibrating downward, thinking through what is less or weaker than, instead of endowing animals with additional powers to supposedly match our own, is a more interesting and promising project since it suggests that humanity itself is 'less than' what our self-aggrandizing would have us believe" (166).
11 Gibson (2020a), Chapter 12.
12 A reference to Jack London's dystopian novel of the same name, *The Iron Heel*, published in 1908.
13 Gibson (2020a).
14 The concept and methodology of ethological jurisprudence are first introduced in Gibson (2020a). An ethological jurisprudence of the work itself, particularly in relation to conceptual art and other mobile properties of creativity, is the subject of the third book, *Made*, Gibson (2025).
15 Although much of the focus of the present work is copyright, the concept of authorship is taken in the wider sense of creatorship, thus including authors in copyright, inventors in patents, designers in design protection, and, importantly, performers in performers' rights. Trade marks are a curious difference in that this property is entirely consumed by authorship, in that the credit for the design is obscured, having been dealt with elsewhere and earlier through, if anything, copyright. In this respect, it is an original work. But as far as trade mark law is concerned, the creativity in a trade mark is of no consequence, as it were. An ethological jurisprudence of trade marks, including the creativity of marks and the consumer's role in trade marks, is considered further in Gibson (2025).
16 I introduce the term "predatory drift" in the context of property in Gibson (2020a), where I develop the concept to describe an artificial narrative of biological inevitability as applied to incentives and acquisitive tendencies in property and intellectual property (including incentives narratives). The term comes

from dog training discourse and draws upon the theory of "instinctual drift" in animal behaviour. A full account of this "biological" theory of predatory drift in property is provided in Gibson (2020a), Chapter 7. See also the discussion of incentives in the same work in Chapter 10.
17 Gibson (2020a), Chapter 8.
18 For example, see the critique of imitation as an instinct in Gabriel Tarde by a contemporary, Charles Ellwood, in Ellwood (1901). Tarde's theories of imitation are treated in detail towards an ethological account of property in Gibson (2020a) and are also fundamental to the discussion of intellectual property in the present work, including through the central concepts of *attentive imitation* and *stereotypic imitation*.
19 For instance, Mlot et al. (2011) note that fire ants cooperate in a coordinated swarm in order to self-assemble into a hydrophobic surface, or "raft," in order to survive floods: "The raft is one of the longest-lasting structures, allowing ants to sail upon it for months as they migrate and colonize new lands" (7669).
20 Shakespeare (2004/[1598]), 74. This also resonates quite musically with a *fin-de-siècle* account of an ethics of originality, as demonstrated in Robinson (1902): "The legality of our social life would be the rhythm of music and not the regularity of machinery" (424).
21 Evans (1975), 125.
22 In particular, Jena Romanticism. See further the more detailed discussion of Part 3.
23 Weil (1959a), 91.
24 Schlegel (1991/[1798–1800]), Athenaeum Fragments §39.
25 The use is informed both by the necessity in perspective as well as its use in new materialism. In particular, see Barad (2007), 71–94.
26 Barad (2009), 50. See further Barad (2007), Chapter 2.
27 Cha (2017), xi.
28 Gibson (2020a).
29 Gibson (2025).
30 Schlegel (1991/[1798–1800]), Athenaeum Fragments, §84: "Viewed subjectively, philosophy, like epic poetry, always begins in medias res."
31 "For Paracelsus, fire is life, and whatever secretes fire truly bears the seed of life. Common mercury is precious in the eyes of the followers of Paracelsus, because it contains a very perfect fire and a celestial inner life." Bachelard (1987/[1938]), 73.
32 Bader (2014) explains, "The temperature would be an intensive ordinate; the measured temperature would be the co-ordination of such an intensive ordinate of temperature with the extended substance of, say, the mercury of a mercury thermometer. The extension of the mercury would be the extensive expression of the intensive ordinate of temperature, or its co-ordination with the extended mercury" (241).

What Does Naruto Want?

In 2018, in the United States, the Ninth Circuit of the Court of Appeals considered a claim of copyright brought by a monkey. This is, of course, the apparent resolution to the now famous and meme-generating event of the so-called Monkey Selfies of 2011 and the several years of arguments that followed in litigation brought by the People for the Ethical Treatment of Animals (PETA) on Naruto's behalf.[1] The court was asked to grapple with notions of nonhuman authorship, copyright, and the interaction with scientific knowledge, ethical concerns, political protestations, and the wider implications of what is now a famous, even notorious, and almost certainly historic decision in the history of copyright. But if it is historic, it is not for the reasons usually provided. It is not a decision in copyright as such; it is a decision on the constitutional standing of the nonhuman, and a rumination on the exceptionalism in copyright that underpins and is facilitated by the mythology of authorship. This is a decision on an aesthetic life.

Naruto is a rare black crested macaque,[2] living in one of the few remaining habitats, the Tangkoko reserve on the Indonesian island of Sulawesi. And in 2011, Naruto made over 200 photographs with camera equipment belonging to the wildlife photographer David Slater, who had arranged the apparatus for this very serendipitous opportunity for "monkey selfies." In the judgment, which will be considered in more detail later but which ultimately denied that Naruto could hold copyright, Judge Smith articulated a fundamental question:

> We are really asking what *another species* desires. Do animals want to own property, such as copyrights? ... We have millennia of experience understanding the interests and desire of humankind. This is not necessarily true for animals ... the "real party in interest" can actually *never credibly articulate its interests or goals*.[3]

In other words, *What does Naruto want?* But why does that question need asking in this way, if at all? And what might an answer look like or mean?

DOI: 10.4324/9780429342103-2

Does the meaning of authorship inhere in this short question of substantial proportions? Why might wants matter? Wants may be understood as imputing goals and objectives, introducing a sense of mentality that flavours narratives of authorship. Mary Douglas notes that both anthropology and economics "have an explicit theory about the circulation of goods but only an implicit theory of wants."[4] An understanding of wants demands an ethological attention. Indeed, wants appear as a key principle in the theory of mind[5] as well as indicating a particular sociality and strategy in ascertaining each other's wants, including the wants of other species.[6] Wants may also interact with curiosity and seeking behaviour, and indeed emerge as integral to the kind of mentality and creating in theories of embodied cognition.[7] It may be that wants form the platform for everything else,[8] including a certain attention and ethical regard, as well as world-building through play. This is not to confuse play with curiosity, but it is to appreciate the shared interests. And what is authorship if not the reason for a work, although paradoxically, a reason created by and after the work? How are the moving goals of authorship ascertained? It would seem that the expression of authorship is crucial not only for the formal rules of intellectual property but also for the recognition of authorship and creativity. What does it look like to be an author? And what sorts of things make authors?

The language of wants also introduces a welfare dimension into this discussion, not least because welfare is principally articulated in terms of freedoms, but more specifically freedoms from wants.[9] In nonhuman animal welfare, this is encompassed explicitly in the so-called five freedoms,[10] which include freedoms from the wants for food and water, from the want for safety and security, from the want for comfort, and from the want for good health.[11] The fifth freedom is especially interesting in the context of an aesthetic life, and this is the freedom from the want to express normal patterns of behaviour. Such expression includes play and the abundance and exuberance of this surplus energy, as well as the enrichment of an individual's environment through the tools and resources for that expression; indeed, that freedom of expression. Notably, in the earlier policy developments in human welfare, this has a counterpoint in the view that idleness "demoralizes" and is thus contrary to good welfare.[12] This highlights an important relationship between play and waste that is persistent throughout the biological, evolutionary, psychological, and economic literature. It is also a feature of the law itself, a relationship that becomes a turning point, so to speak, for nonhuman authorship in later discussion.[13]

The frustration of these wants would clearly comprise a welfare situation, but in view of the interpretation of authorship within these wants, the frustration of those resources of expression may also contribute to negative welfare. In other words, wanting can contribute "motivationally significant properties that makes pleasures desirable," but frustration and "excessive 'wanting'" become a welfare issue, including the development of maladaptive behaviours in humans and other animals.[14] The decision in *Naruto* is not on its face a welfare decision, but it shows the way in which nonhuman animal authorship is a potential welfare issue, with particular insight for the welfare of human authors as well. And paradoxically, the question *What does Naruto want* excludes the wild Naruto from the possible ethical benefits of a relationship of control, as in a traditional welfare relationship,[15] or through the Next Friends relationship, by positing a seemingly impossible welfare question wholly outside the welfare context. The worst of all worlds.

This famous case is important in framing the fundamental refrain of this book: *What does Naruto want?* The events in this dispute reveal a complex interconnection of welfare, conservation, advocacy, and authorship. Critically, they show why welfare might be an authorship issue, not only for Naruto but also for human authors. In a way, it is tangential what the decision may or may not teach us about copyright. What is far more interesting is what nonhuman authorship can teach us about the welfare of creators more generally, and in turn, what principles of welfare may contribute to an examination and reorientation of intellectual property and rights discourse more generally. And this is what will be pursued throughout as this question leads to so many more.

Bring on the Dancing Monkeys

Another of Aesop's fables, *The Dancing Monkeys*, tells the tale of monkeys trained to dance like humans. However, the mask, quite literally, is dropped when someone throws nuts onto the stage, and the monkeys end their performance to harvest the nuts:

> A Prince had some Monkeys trained to dance. Being naturally great mimics of men's actions, they showed themselves most apt pupils; and, when arrayed in their rich cloths and masks, they danced as well as any of the courtiers. The spectacle was often repeated to great applause, till on one occasion a courtier, bent on mischief, took from his pocket a handful of nuts, and threw them upon the stage. The Monkeys, at the sight of the nuts, forgot their dancing, and became (as indeed they were) Monkeys instead of actors, and, pulling off their masks, and tearing their robes, they fought one another for the nuts. The dancing spectacle thus came to an end, amidst the laughter and ridicule of the audience.

This fable is a curious insight into the anthropomorphism that is most commonly associated with fables, and into the creativity that erupts when the human masks are removed. Indeed, this anthropomorphic thinking presents both obstacles and opportunities for thinking about animals. Deployed critically, it expands perspectives and shared interests, but used tactlessly and heedlessly, it becomes an instrument of the anthropocentrism that positions the law and some advocacy-based approaches as always already in pursuit of the human. In the looking described in this fable, a latent anthropocentrism informs the valuing of the dance as the performance of value, the "apt pupils" in "their rich cloths and masks," and the "great applause" of the audience. On the other hand, the personality on display following the throwing of the nuts is discredited as fighting and "an end" to the performance. Aesop's fable of the dancing monkeys tells the story of the resilient narrative of human exceptionalism that endures today. The monkeys are presented as mere imitators, simply trained, natural mimics, and ultimately portrayed as enslaved by their instinct for nuts. They are not creators; they are merely "naturally great mimics." They are not innovators; they are merely imitators. They are not dancing; they are merely aping. There is thus no pleasure in the dance, no pleasure in the dance as play, and no play in the indentured imitation. On the other hand, when the nuts are scattered, there is frenetic activity and unfettered expression.

This *forgetting* of the dancing is reconciled within the fable as an end to the performance, but the paradox is that the dancing is achieved by coercion, not genuine and expressive imitation. The critical intrigue of this passage is not in the apparent proficiency of the forced species imposture and imitation through the dance, but rather, it is to be found in the performative excess catalysed by the nuts. It is this performance that engages the audience and their "laughter and ridicule," with all the enthusiasm and passion of play. As distinct from the immunity of the audience and its deference to the contrived spectacle, the audience is transformed in sharing in the passionate play of the nuts. This little fable describes a delightful rupture between the coerced and rehearsed dance and the sociable, conscious irreverence of the monkeys and the audience. To recognise what is happening, assumptions must be relinquished and looking must commence. Similarly, assumptions must be dismantled in order to refresh perspectives upon the animal in the law. An ethological jurisprudence questions and upsets the anthropocentrism of the law. But we have to know where and how to look. In a somewhat curious respect, intellectual property anatomises the hard problem of nonhuman animal consciousness in a knotty display of social learning, collaboration, and play. What Naruto encourages us to do is to examine the interests of nonhuman animals not from the conventional perspectives of physical liberty, but from the perspective of commercial law and the intersection of value, waste, and sheer abundance. The fundamental contention of this book is that to look at nonhuman animals we must look at authors.

Going Ape

Although the creativity of the dancing monkeys in this fable is somewhat denigrated as mere mimicry,[16] imitation is the stuff of which innovation is made. From the novelties of social learning, through to the culture of impersonation, and to the innovation of imposture, it will be shown that imitation is not only a conscious and evaluative process but also a cultural and affiliative one – imitation is attentive attention. And it is a process that depends quite crucially on the quality of information, including its provenance. Imitation is not only a credible but also a creditable phenomenon. Far from the parasitic anonymity of coerced copying, genuinely sociable imitation is the stuff of attribution and tribute, deserving of credit that is entrusted both to and by the imitator. It is thus critical from the outset to separate out the proprietary demands of a coercive form of copying and the necessity of identity and attribution in order that imitation may give life and legacy. This knowledge is at the heart of the affiliative function of imitation as well as the innovative reckonings of imitation.

Gabriel Tarde's sociology of imitation resonates with an ethological approach to imitation and its affiliative and cultural value among nonhuman animal groups. This is perhaps most clearly understood through the relational processes of Tarde's inter-psychology,[17] through which value and meaning are generated in between, always already *in personam*. Tarde declares "the universality of imitation" to be "the essential fact of social life."[18] In other words, imitation is itself an act of sociality, both as engagement and as incentive. Tarde describes the transformative impulsion of imitation, where "[e]very act of imitation is preceded by hesitation on the part of the individual, for every discovery or invention that seeks to spread abroad always finds some obstacle to overcome in some of the ideas or practices that have already been adopted by every member of the public."[19]

This hesitation intimidates socially and inventively, for "as long as a man hesitates in this way, he refrains from imitation."[20] But in overcoming this hesitation, that is, in the encouragement of and by imitation, the invitation and inventive potential of imitation can be realised: "[I]t is only as an imitator that he is part of society. When he finally imitates, it means that he has come to a decision."[21] Indeed, this decision, this choice, goes to the heart of the principle of authorship as understood across the categories of intellectual property as well. Imitation is a decision, an action. Imitation makes one a part of history, part of a cultural tradition.[22] However, not all imitation is equal, so to speak, and in the following discussion, I introduce and develop the concepts of *attentive imitation* and *stereotypic imitation*.[23] The distinction between these forms of imitation is important. *Stereotypic imitation* is an imitation borne of unthinking and unreflective coercion, an imitation of mutual interests, as distinct from *attentive imitation*, an imitation that is conscious and evaluative, an imitation of shared interests. Notably, the distinction is not necessarily in appearance but in production; after all, appearances can be deceptive. These concepts will be crucial to the differentiation of imitation throughout nonhuman production, including the imitative functions that operate in the productions of artificial intelligence. It is a question of the coerced perfection of dancing monkeys or the ingenuity of the chaotic harvest. More specifically, it is the question of *explaining* that ingenuity.

But Is It Art?

As a resource of cultural and social development, imitation is critical to the communication of culture from individual to individual, across groups, and ultimately across generations.[24] This is as true for nonhuman social animals as it is for human ones.[25] As such, imitation is both a vehicle of culture and a warranty of cultural identity and integrity. And although the concept of culture is frequently inveighed as a distinction enjoyed only by humans, extensive research in nonhuman animal cognition renders that assertion uncertain if not untenable.[26] But even where a nonhuman animal society is recognised as possessing cultural knowledge, a further distinction is then drawn based upon a reported lack of self-awareness or metarepresentational abilities.[27] That is, the potential exuberance of nonhuman animal culture (and cultural values) is purportedly tempered by a further qualification as to whether the nonhuman animal recognises it as such, or recognises it as a human would. And even where there is potential evidence of an aesthetic sense, it is presumed to be limited in its approach to human benchmarks.[28] Whether art and an aesthetic sense, or culture itself, there appears to be an almost insurmountable obstacle in that the horizon is the approximation of human-like perspectives, a threshold that is by definition always already unattainable.[29]

The preoccupation with cultural distinctions between human and nonhuman animals is critically wrapped up with aesthetics and creativity. As Nathan Lents explains, "Without culture, there really can't be art, as we know it, because art cannot exist separate from culture … There is just no way that animals can possibly experience art as we do."[30] Although Lents ultimately concedes some potential, this cultural distinction is readily deployed and renders a crucial and seemingly immovable species barrier: "[T]hey don't experience art as we do because they don't experience anything as we do. And we don't experience anything as another animal does either."[31] But this is not entirely accurate; or at least, it is perhaps emphasising an irrelevant concern. Indeed, it is overly summative, unless we accept that we do not experience anything anyone else does, human or nonhuman, animal or machine. This intentional obstacle, in every sense, is thus proffered as an insurmountable and defiant end to the conversation, an impossibility of progress, the unutterably human, so to speak. It is an example of what Donald Griffin, cognitive scientist and ethologist, has described as paralytic perfectionism.[32] Responding to Thomas Nagel's famous essay, *What is it like to be a bat?*,[33] Griffin argues that Nagel's conclusions as to the impossibility of answering this question do not acknowledge a similar problem within a species as well, including the human species, for "we can never know the feelings and thoughts of our human companions with total completeness and perfection."[34] This quest for perfectionism, as Griffin explains, "severely impedes, or even prevents, investigation of animal mentality … it paralyzes scientific exploration."[35] This paralysis is arguably in evidence in an apparently disproportionate lack of study of positive mental states in nonhuman animals, like joy and play, which often attract charges of anthropomorphic thinking in their observation, as opposed to negative or reactive states.[36] David Malet Armstrong explains, "we need not give up our natural inclination to attribute beliefs to animals just because the descriptions we give of the beliefs almost certainly do not fit the beliefs' actual content."[37] And we certainly should not install such charges of anthropomorphism as an ideological obstacle to nonhuman authorship.

Nevertheless, this emphasis on distinction rather than convergence can be seen throughout the popular discourse, and it is also replicated in areas of the scientific literature and research design: "[T]he theoretical explanations of these phenomena seem to explain specific human constructions; the experimental tests merely seem to test the extent to which theories are supported by the results of certain human practices."[38] For example, in relation to great ape cultures, one study[39] cites a lack of evidence of metarepresentational abilities or the ability to recognise culture as culture (arguably, a cumulative, human-like approach to culture), and presents this as a fundamental distinction between great apes and human cultures. As a result, further research is recommended on nonhuman mental representation of cultural knowledge, but notably "to conclusively determine the ways by which humans are unique in their cultural behaviour."[40] In this way, such research seeks to define the answer with respect to the human, and whether for the nonhuman animal something is *in their interest*, rather than to ask, *do they have an interest? What do they want?* Thus, an ethological jurisprudence integrates ethology and law in order to resist the "entrenched disciplinary orientation"[41] of not only the science but also the law. There is much activity going on in this supposed *gap*, and the cultural industries may have more to say about nonhuman animals than at first it seems. The trouble, as pursued throughout this book, is that the problem of recognising nonhuman culture is a problem that is actually distinctly human.[42] *Look, hear*!

The Art-Making Animal

In 2018, the British Broadcasting Corporation (BBC) broadcast the history series, *Civilisations*, documenting art over the ages. The promotion for the series was intriguing. Against a backdrop of epic music and thumping timpani, the narrator, Baroness Floella Benjamin, declares, "Throughout human history, we have made things that go beyond shelter or sustenance … We are the art-making animal, and this is what we've made."[43] This exceptionalist thinking is consistent with accounts throughout a range of disciplinary perspectives on the relationship between art, humans, and other animals. In his book, *The Artistic Animal*, the title of which sounds like an anticipatory refrain for the BBC series, the anthropologist, Alexander Alland, pronounces, "The creation and appreciation of art in its many forms are uniquely human activities,"[44] and that "[t]rue artistic behavior is seen in no species other than *Homo sapiens*. Not even a hint of it occurs in the natural behavior of other species."[45]

The narration draws a supposed distinction between the human world and a presumed unique aesthetic sense, and the nonhuman world and a biological functionalism linked to instinct and survival. The assertion is that humans create out of a desire to create, not out of a need for survival; out of belief, not merely driven by function. And thus, they make "things that go beyond shelter or sustenance."[46] Positioned as other than the "art-making animal," animals other than humans are by implication presumed to be subject completely to biological function and instinct, lacking all agency and intentionality. Any expressive activity is attributed to causes, but never to reasons. Such as when, in 2002, Betty the crow was observed bending a wire into a hook in order to retrieve food, she was lauded for her inventive skill,[47] only for her ingenuity to be later discredited by others as merely drawing upon "part of their natural repertoire" and simply "following a natural, behavioral routine."[48] But is this fair? Indeed, aspects of Betty's tool use are related to a wider range of studies into nonhuman animal cognition, known as string-pulling,[49] a test of problem-solving in order to access a valuable resource, in which it is recognised in the literature itself that the cognitive skills involved are "sometimes downplayed by pointing at its close resemblance to natural behaviors."[50] More than just pulling strings, as it were. Not to mention the role of imitation and affiliative social learning in diffusing such innovations. Indeed, the diverse range of species showing such skills is compelling: "If string-pulling techniques result mainly from hardwired behavior, they ought to be species-specific. This appears not to be the case."[51] Thus, while humans have made things that "have transformed the world, changed the course of history,"[52] all other animals are rendered ahistorical and inconsequential. Some strings beg to be pulled.

Not only is this perspective not unusual, but also it is almost fundamental in the wider popular discourse around a range of issues, from pet-keeping to conservation. For example, dogs are regularly described as "living in the moment,"[53] the definition of ahistorical and unaccountable beings. However, this is seemingly incognisant of the extensive range of perspectives on canine cognition that includes evidence of planning,[54] evaluation of others,[55] fairness and morality,[56] and grief.[57] Driven by functionalist narratives and oversimplified maxims, what follows from this kind of anthropocentric thinking is that the world bifurcates neatly into human animals presented as civilised, that is, as moral and cultural beings, and all other animals, by virtue of not being the art-making animal, merely existing.

The comments on the BBC's Facebook page to which the trailer was posted are telling. One follower exclaims, "The concept is good, but the title!! Sorry, but animal can't be linked to art … art is nature, is human, is infinity … nothing to do with animal which is peace, instinct, life, bravery."[58]

Curiously, then, from this list itself, is the animal not nature? And further, in response to examples offered by others, one commenter contends, "the difference being that for the bird and the fish, it's survival of the species. We admire their work with an artists [sic] eye, they don't."[59] As noted earlier, anthropocentric perspectives are well-served by deference to a possible lack of awareness or recognition such that, even if the object is creative, the creator is ultimately perceived as not. And the appeal to cultural values (whether art and an aesthetic sense, or culture itself) as somehow self-defeating (without self-recognition is it culture at all?) is also replicated in the scientific literature and research design.[60] In all these approaches, the benchmark is a human-like cultural perception, and the enquiries belie an anthropocentric interest in determining how humans are *unique* as much as they are concerned with exploring any possible differentiation and expansion of the moral and cultural sphere. Art is thus defined as *only* in the eye of the human beholder.

What, then, of the work? What is the work's life outside a connection to an author? If a nonhuman animal is said not to recognise a production as culture or art, then is it not culture or art? But why would a nonhuman animal's aesthetic sense and awareness have anything to do with a human conceptualisation and categorisation of art? Which brings the question then to artificial intelligence. What, for that matter, is the aesthetic sense of an artificial intelligence? Or put another way, in the tradition of the tree and the forest, if art is made by someone who does not know it, is it art? Is it a question of what machines want? Or is it more strictly a question of what machines assemble and why?

Presume an Author

Curiously, while the matter of an aesthetic sense is erected as an insurmountable barrier between the creative activity of humans and nonhuman animals, the same question is never asked of artificial intelligence. Where is the similar requirement of artificial intelligence that is demanded of nonhuman animals? Where is the requirement that artificial intelligence *appreciates* the aesthetic value? Where is the expectation that artificial intelligence enjoys an aesthetic sense? This is indeed a notable and significant contradiction that becomes even more salient when addressing this question through claims, however spurious, of examples of sentience or consciousness in artificial intelligence.[61] Perhaps the concept of sentience is being deployed in an arbitrary and contingent way?[62] Or perhaps notions of sentience or consciousness have nothing to do with the way in which intellectual property has been engaged in both the technical discourse and wider mythology of artificial intelligence. Because if they did, then the discussions should be starting with nonhuman animals. There is considerable evidence of sentience across a wide and diverse range of nonhuman animal species, and yet any authorship is scuttled by presumptions of no pretensions to aesthetics. There is as yet no compelling evidence of sentience in artificial intelligence,[63] otherwise referred to as artificial general intelligence. And yet this question is never posed in the context of copyright and intellectual property authorship on behalf of artificial intelligence in the broadest sense. In fact, some suggest the campaign for "rights" has nothing to do with consciousness at all; it is simply a question of the value of the outputs.[64]

It is this focus on the outputs that arguably has limited the attention to the authorship question and frustrated any answers. The discussion and the reactions are focused overwhelmingly in favour of the object; that is, the products. And at the same time, intellectual property solutions become harnessed to this emphasis on the object, at the expense not only of the author but also of the users, readers, consumers, audience – or however that community of the work might be understood. And while there is some discussion of personhood in this context, this is in the service of defining and managing the circulation of products; but in stark contrast and somewhat paradoxically, attention to the concept of authorship is limited. In other words, the objects – the products of artificial intelligence – are the catalyst for claims to authorship or inventorship. The author is merely presumed by the persuasive economic impact of the object.

But does the object make the author? And what are the serious ethical and welfare limitations of this account? For example, engagement with the implications of Large Language Models (LLMs) or forms of generative AI and the impact on visual arts and other image-based works continues to focus largely on the displacement of human creative workers and infringement, but at the same time pursuing the potential copyright protection of the materials produced. In copyright, to understand the scope of the work, the expression is half the question. We need to pay attention to the meaning and scope of the author's own intellectual creation.

I Know What I Like

The functional significance of recognition is also central to what the law identifies as original, distinctive, and inventive – that is, in the way the law determines and authenticates authorship, whether that is the inventor's innovation in a patent, the designer's aesthetic in design, or the author's originality in copyright. Indeed, the author function is the essential function of a trade mark, in that origin is inextricably bound up with brand identity and accountability. To look at intellectual property thus is to begin with authors. But where is the joy? Where is the reception of the work in this incarnation? For example, what accountability is there to Naruto's apparent joy in operating the camera? Or to the apparent musical aesthetic for nonhuman animals, as described through preferences identified in the context of enrichment?[65] Despite this dialectic of the work, intellectual property appears to remain fiercely auteurial, notwithstanding the potential in its own reckoning of the user, a wasteful potential that it continues to try to reconcile within its own efficiency, as later discussions address.[66]

At the same time, intellectual property is both a legal and cultural institution. That is, copyright law comprises a set of legal rules, but copyright is also a cultural institution and as such provides an institutional and legitimated declaration of what is creative, beyond the enforcement of the law itself.[67] On this question, research in the formation of an aesthetic sense in humans suggests that much of this is derived from the social parameters of learning and the subsequent generalisation of this knowledge,[68] as distinct from something particular to the individual. Thus, the form upon which copyright makes a declaration of cultural validity is part of the matter of authorship and the matter of art. Curiously though, authorship comes after the event, as a matter of course. In other words, an activity may be creative, but copyright's recognition is concerned only where that creativity makes a work. That work thus makes an author for the purposes of the law, imputing intentionality and value in what is the always already manifest proof of the object, in search of an author. Indeed, to recall the Facebook responses to *Civilisation*, the comment on the artist's eye relies upon a certain presumption of intentionality as the guiding principle in answering the question, *is it art?* What is it like to be an artist?

Although somewhat resisted in the past,[69] discussions around sentience have now become much more common in the ethics and policies around the use and development of artificial intelligence, as well as in animal studies and protection.[70] Importantly, this includes in intellectual property scholarship the recruitment of sentience in addressing questions of authorship and inventorship in artificial intelligence,[71] notwithstanding the serious questions and doubts around the plausibility of such claims.[72] As well as the inconstancy of the concept of sentience, this is coupled with debates over consciousness and mind, and uncertainty in the concept of intelligence itself.[73] Self-promotion in the world of artificial intelligence is not for the faint-hearted.

However, is the emphasis on sentience a technical or narrative device? Is this part of the mythology surrounding the industry rather than a capacity of art, so to speak? In fact, the author arguably is not the focus of the law; rather, it is the object, the work, that is the phenomenal catalyst and cultural *beneficiary*. This is perhaps the fundamental momentum behind the interest in the intellectual property questions arising through the outputs of artificial intelligence. And in the present work, it is contended that this is the conceptual process by which the advocacy on behalf of DABUS has been proceeding around the world;[74] that is, the proof of the author is in the work. It is not the ghost in the machine, but the dream in the object. Thus, it is arguably not an interest in the sentience or otherwise of artificial intelligence at all; actually, these are almost unproductive distractions.[75] Rather, it is the preoccupation that an author must be found for the works at stake. As such, the author becomes an explicit construction, an overt legal fiction on the basis that it is the validation or legitimation of the work that raises the question of creatorship for artificial intelligence, whether in the copyright work or the invention of a lunch box,[76] not any imputed intentionality or even intellectuality in the creations of artificial intelligence. Such performative displays as the appearance of the robot, Ai-Da, to give evidence at a House of Lords Committee,[77] are simply reinforcement that the fiction of the author is a phenomenal work of mischief. If it walks like a human and talks like a human, it must be an author.

I Mean What I Make

Is this declaration of creative intention, a decided self-consciousness of authorship, all that may be required for the human monopoly on art? If our understandings of the creativity of animals other than humans are dominated by biologism, where anything and everything may be explained away in terms of function, in survivalist terms of territory and reproduction,[78] the aesthetic and creative lives of nonhuman animals are immediately diminished. Without art, a life is rendered mere existence. An animal does not leave a mark in history, and history does not leave a mark on the animal. The artless animal is a "mere existence" against which disregard or even cruelty "leaves a mark that is no mark."[79]

But, does it matter whether or not the creator knows if it is art, if they know what they like? If we accept, as Raymond Ruyer declares, "we particularly imitate what we admire," then is imitation (and indeed wider forms of social learning[80]) in and of itself already an acknowledgement of what is *art*?[81] Is not imitation already a kind of conceptual thinking, of creative expression? For humans, not only has it been a classical form of learning in the visual arts, creative writing, and elsewhere, but also, imitation is an abundantly social process of creativity and innovation. Or, as Dominique Lestel explains, "To simulate creativity or originality is already evidence of creativity or originality."[82] In this context, a word of caution from Brian Massumi sums up this potent capacity: "Do not underestimate the vital powers of animal 'imitation.'"[83]

Nevertheless, an emphasis on intentionality is sustained not only in the practical application of the law and the rendering of the scope of a work or the manner of an imitation[84] but also in the wider and diverse perspectives upon creativity. This emphasis upon a kind of causal narrative of intentionality is problematic, not only with respect to the discussion of all creators other than human but also within the cultural industries themselves. It is this adaptationist interpretation of motivations to create that underpins and reinscribes the status quo of the singular author. But if instead we start to think about the work itself, as distinct from the plans or otherwise of the artist – or more clearly, the relationships articulated through the work – then the critical value in creativity and in intellectual property is manifest in the recognition and performance of the shared interests in the work. We imitate what we admire. Creativity is a performative relationship. Art is a kinship. And this play of creativity drives the discussions that follow throughout this book.

And speaking of play, what about children? Is such *play* the *work* of an artist? Curator Amy Zion suggests, "Children's art isn't really treated as art normally. It's treated as ephemera."[85] Is the question of children's art put down to whether they have the necessary aesthetic appreciation?[86] But is appreciation even necessary at all? And further and more tellingly, perhaps, is the requisite explainability of intentionality a purposeful obstacle? Indeed, according to Ellen Winner and Jennifer Drake, "[t]he emergence of modernism in the art world changed people's responses to child art. Modernism valued playfulness and breaking away from the dominant canon of realism ... and hence viewed the art of the child and the 'primitive' as ideal and natural."[87] And as Jessica Silbey asks, if children can be authors of copyright works, is it really obvious at all that nonhuman animals cannot also be authors?[88]

And what about machines? Harsha Gangadharbatla proclaims, "Creativity and the creative process is the last remaining frontier where humans still hold the edge ... If computers are producing something that humans implicitly think of as human, as the quintessence of what it is to be a human, then what does it mean to be us?"[89] But is this really accurate? Or just a matter of framing? The mainstream availability of artificial intelligence art generators has put even more focus on the question of art itself. What does it mean to make art? And what does it mean to own it? If such *art* is "the exact opposite" of art, the axis upon which this distinction is articulated is intention, "translating something that you feel internally into something that exists externally."[90] Is unintentionally creating art the opposite of making art? What is the intentionality of the machine? Perhaps the machine cannot but suggest art, simply because it is trained upon the work of humans, fed the creative intentions of humans, programmed to approximate the human, a prosthetic of the artist's *hand*. But is there anything more about art and literature and anything else created by machines that provides an insight into what it is like to be a machine? Or indeed, to be an author?

Making a Monkey Out of Someone

Returning to Naruto's story, here the law was confronted by the prospect of a different art-making animal – not a dancing monkey, but a photographer – in the events surrounding the curious incident of the monkey in the jungle, for it was certainly an incident precipitated by the wants of curiosity, of seeking, and of play.

Whether or not Naruto *made* the selfies became the centre of an international debate not only on authorship but also on the capabilities and creativity of nonhuman animals themselves – as authors, as owners, as persons. It is almost always referred to as the *Monkey Selfie* case, ushering in perceptions of not only selfhood but also the mirroring of the human fascination with their own reflection. The questions raised in this wider and popular discourse surrounding this case – that of creativity, accomplishment, and authorship – have important implications not only for notions of an animal aesthetic but also for considerations of agency and autonomy before the law, and for reconciling the concept of *intent* across legal and scientific discourse. Naruto presents a complex interaction between authorship, control, and property. Naruto is both wild and *owned* in the sense of being a resident of the reserve and thus within their responsibility or control. This ensures Naruto has a complicated existence as a possible subject of rights or duties. Indeed, if the law were able to recognise creativity in the nonhuman animal creator as author, cultural distinctions between wild and tame are also necessarily unsettled and reconfigured in important ways in view of the appreciation of societies and cultures beyond the context of domestication; that is, beyond the imposition and purported civilising reference point of the human.

When David Slater visited the Tangkoko reserve and left his camera unattended on a tripod, the macaques were intrigued and they were curious. It would seem that Naruto was especially so, approaching the camera, playing with it, operating it, and ultimately making many photographs. The arrangement was such that the macaques could take photographs without the photographer needing to intervene. They just needed curiosity, initiative, and experimentation. Contrary to reports of taking photographs "accidentally,"[91] which seem more motivated by boundaries than behaviours, Naruto's use of the camera was deliberate and playful. Naruto observed the information and made the decision that the camera was of interest, not threatening, and in this context, a relevant and available resource in the pursuit of play and entertainment.[92] The camera was not only an object of curiosity but also a tool for play, and a tool for making through play. Slater himself describes the process in the book he subsequently published (leading to the litigation), entitled *Wildlife Personalities*, which collected these very photographs: "Sulawesi crested black macaque smiles at itself while pressing the shutter button on a camera … *Posing* to take its own photograph, unworried by its own reflection, smiling. Surely a sign of self-awareness?"[93]

The first copyright dispute arising from these photographs was in 2011 at the United States Copyright Office when Slater pursued Wikimedia to remove the photographs from Wikimedia Commons, where they appear as "Macaca nigra self-portrait," accompanied by the explanation, "This file is in the public domain because, as the work of a non-human animal, it has no human author in whom copyright is vested."[94] The dispute turned on whether Slater had any copyright interest at all in the photographs, given that he had not actually taken them. Ultimately, the United States Copyright Office clarified in the Copyright Compendium,[95] citing *Trade-Mark Cases* (1879),[96] that registration will is available on the basis that "the work was created by a human being,"[97] declaring that copyright protection extends only to "the fruits of intellectual labor" that "are founded in the creative powers of the mind."[98] This notion of "mind" informs the concept of "original intellectual conceptions of the author," and the Compendium makes it clear that it is on this basis that "the Office will refuse to register a claim if it determines that a human being did not create the work."[99] The Office subsequently clarified further through the examples of "A photograph taken by a monkey," and "A mural painted by an elephant," among others.[100]

In 2015, following the rejection of Slater's claim to copyright, People for the Ethical Treatment of Animals (PETA) and Dr Antje Engelhardt (a researcher who claimed knowledge of Naruto since Naruto's birth) filed a complaint for copyright infringement against Slater and the publisher of *Wildlife Personalities*, on the basis that they were infringing Naruto's copyright. They did this by claiming the status of "Next Friends" of Naruto before the court, and therefore this was the main issue in the judgment. The question of authorship itself was never considered in any real sense. As to Naruto's authorship, under the Copyright Act[101] Naruto could not be recognised as an author, as the Act was held not to anticipate nonhuman authorship. Therefore, any further examination of the concept of authorship was not relevant to the proceedings, and the so-called *Monkey Selfie* copyright case is not about authorship or arguably even copyright at all. This may seem to be the end of the matter for nonhuman animals, but the voyage ahead will challenge this. However, the end of the matter has not been so readily accepted when it comes to another form of nonhuman "authorship," that of artificial intelligence. The terrain remains quite uncertain, but Naruto has precipitated the attempt not only to map it, but also to correct some "trap streets" and "fictitious entries" that have been made to date. Fundamentally, this returns us to the question at the outset of this chapter: *What does Naruto want?*

This question is fundamental in that it is utilised throughout the appearance of nonhuman animals before the law,[102] and similarly erected as a barrier to entry through the claimed impossibility of ever answering this question. But what does Naruto want? In many of these discussions, there is an uncomfortable sense of utility or instrumentality in the individual in the service of a larger agenda, as might be discerned in the *Naruto* opinion itself. Almost fundamentally, the nature of the litigation was such that the object of copyright was primarily an economic one; that is, just enrichment (as it were) for the use of Naruto's photographs in the subsequent publication. Both in terms of the perceived injustice (the use of the photograph for a commercial publication) and the narrative of remedies, the *wants* of copyright are characterised in terms of the economic narrative as distinct from a story of attribution and provenance. Copyright thus becomes about *paying attention*; that is, without paying for work. Even in jurisdictions with strong approaches to the author's rights, this acknowledgement is in terms of an alienation from the narrative of wants, and an inscription within the frame of moral rights. The predatory drift in the law is arguably insidious in critical perspectives as well, particularly in the tensions between copyright and conceptual art and graffiti. But is copyright really all about the money? Not all attentions are equal.

This is similar to the somewhat narrative convention of finding a functional imperative as an explanation for behaviour, something to which later discussion returns in the context of the adaptationist paradigm and sentience.[103] Social anthropologist, Matei Candea, contrasts the question of *want* with this functional causative approach to behaviour.[104] He explains, "This 'wanting' is a very general phenomenon, definitional of the living itself, and it is not located in the mind, but rather in the body."[105] The body becomes thus a functional, biological vessel, and to ask *What does Naruto want?* is therefore not to seek an answer but to contrive a seemingly impassable divide between human intentionality and animal function. It is a straw monkey, so to speak. It is a question of want ... of want for nothing. Indeed, answers without questions present the greatest obstacles of all.[106]

Biologist and ethologist Marian Stamp Dawkins maintains that while research design continues to rationalise animal activities within functional narratives of the *why*, we should also be asking about the desire and motivation for a behaviour or the *wants*: "You can also ask ... 'what stimulates them?'"[107] This attention to wants not only permits a form of testimony, in a manner of speaking, but also suggests an approach to the related question of sentience. Dawkins asserts, "We now have a variety of ways of 'asking' animals what they want and also what they want to avoid or get away from ... What sorts of choices do imply sentience?"[108] at the same time framing sentience in the very language of authorship, of choice and freedom. As a fragment from Simone Weil assures us, Leibniz would say, "If the weathercock could think, it would say that it turns because it wants to do so."[109]

As in science, so too in law, most of the emphasis is on the why – the function, the physiology, the adaptation value, and so on, and thus a resilient separation from the *what* of aesthetic endeavour. These questions are the questions to be asked not only of nonhuman animals, but also of artificial intelligence or any other potential *who* that might be creating. But to begin to make these seemingly impossible enquiries is not in order to have no answers, but rather, it is in order to start asking the right questions. Is *what does Naruto want?* the right question?

Will the Real Naruto Please Stand Up?

What is also fascinating about this episode is the subplot around Naruto's name and identity. It was reported that Naruto was not a name already applied to the individual in question but one given to the macaque by PETA in preparation for the subsequent litigation, and that in doing so they named the wrong macaque.[110] Popular reporting on this supposed issue of imposture, so to speak, seemed fascinated with this as somehow amounting to a contrivance or artificiality in relation to Naruto, as though this would discredit Naruto's position, at the same time raising interesting questions about the colony itself as author.[111] But this popular response is interesting in itself, pointing as it does to the relevance of naming as a potential welfare tool by beckoning a regard from human others.[112] Who was the real Naruto? Are they sure they had the right member of the colony? Even Naruto's gender was a topic of dispute, with Slater claiming Naruto was female, but PETA identifying Naruto as male.[113] But again, these are not pertinent to the matter at stake. This is not, however, to say that Naruto is generic or somehow interchangeable, as many commentators assumed and joked.[114] Indeed, naming in the scientific context is partly in response to this kind of generalisation and univocity in relation to a species collective. But it did provide another obstacle of convenience for rendering Naruto's claim disreputable, as it were, if such questions were to rely upon the real Naruto standing up in court. At the same time, however, it introduces the significant issues around co-production, for which an ethological perspective is valuable, and the contrivance of the singular author in service of an anthropocentric rendering of the creative commodity in many circumstances of otherwise collaborative creativity and readership, as will be pursued through the following chapters.[115]

All of this controversy around naming has nevertheless failed to distract from the focus of the main story, that of nonhuman animal creativity. Indeed, perhaps it even reinforces that focus, because this subplot provides further insight into the anthropocentrism of the legal analysis and surrounding public discourse, the all-too-ready denial of nonhuman animal authors, and the strategic anthropomorphism of *human* machines. The preoccupations and self-consciousness, in a manner of speaking, of the name debate belie anxieties very similar to those driving the copyright questions for not only nonhuman animals but also outsider humans, such as fans and other marginalised forms of creativity. Similar anxieties operate in the context of artificial intelligence productions, but curiously in a somewhat opposite way. The anthropocentrism of the law and the exclusion of the alien other serve to banish the nonhuman animal, but conveniently to anthropomorphise artificial intelligence as human machines at the same time.

Left Wanting

Wanting is also the language of personhood insofar as it indicates the capability of being both aggrieved and remedied. On this point, there is a potential regard for the notion of moral standing in that "[e]ntities that possess moral standing can be wronged and deserve our moral consideration."[116] Thus, the responsibility to nonhuman animals should be articulated not upon a demonstration of sentience but on the capacity for being aggrieved, however that may manifest. This is in part assisted by Weil's treatment of the concept of vulnerability, as well as Martha Nussbaum's work in capabilities.[117] Vulnerability thus incorporates a capability in itself, which underpins a radical reappraisal of welfare in the personhood context.[118]

And this was indeed a concern of the Naruto court, in considering whether Naruto had suffered sufficient injury to satisfy the requirement of a live case or controversy,[119] rather than just a critical question testing the law. In meeting this threshold, the court then had to consider constitutional standing as distinct from statutory standing, and then the question of representational standing (the status or otherwise of PETA as a next friend) in order that Naruto's claim might be heard.[120] These are, of course, all issues for artificial intelligence before the court, although notably the ownership of the machine seems to render the question of representational standing moot. Not quite autonomous beings it would seem, not yet anyway.

The question of injury raised particular issues for the claim, in that this needed to be understood in terms of an injury suffered through lack of copyright. Could a violation of copyright constitute an injury for Naruto? Wanting thus becomes a test of the capacity to be aggrieved and to be remedied. What does Naruto want? The challenge of ascertaining those interests when framed in a perspective wholly outside Naruto's is that the court will always get the answer it wants if it continues to ask the wrong questions.[121] Critically, the question of whether an individual is aggrieved, and whether that grievance can be remedied, is in fact not about interests as such, but about wants. Therefore, in a very significant sense, any question of nonhuman animal authorship will always be a question of wellbeing and thus may invoke principles of positive welfare to important effect. Thus, an ethological approach is necessary not only to decipher answers to these questions, but also to ask the right questions and in the relevant way in the first place. Thus, over and above deciphering the relevant expressions,[122] how do we ascertain the interests of nonhuman animals and, in particular, the aesthetic interests, creative motivations, and freedoms of expression?

The court's emphasis on the question of what Naruto may or may not want belies an emphasis on an intentional narrative not only in copyright and intellectual property more widely, but also in the law's incarnation of a moral person. Wants are, to a greater or lesser extent, affiliated with reasons throughout the scientific,[123] philosophical,[124] economic,[125] and sociological[126] traditions. And of course, the relation between desire and belief provides the potential for reconfiguring the perspective upon the intellectual property work, and at the same time, the means for the reinstitution of the status quo through the purported motivation and economic rationality of the law,[127] and stale restatements of incentives and rewards.

What does Naruto want? thus becomes a question that dooms Naruto's authorship to failure because it insists upon a traditional autonomy model of personhood, a test which Naruto can never pass. But what if the aesthetic evidence is in the act itself, the act of play? Hans Georg Gadamer describes an important relationship between play and art and asserts "the *primacy of play over the consciousness of the player.*"[128] Gadamer thus dispenses with fraught discussions of intentionality, and even impossible questions of wants, by examining instead the aesthetic sense and the production and enjoyment of art as shared interests. Naruto's selfie then becomes a literal demonstration of the reciprocity of looking back, of an attentional and attentive ethical encounter of shared interests, not the separate but mutual interests of a coerced production. There are significant resonances here for human play and the circulation of value across different contexts, including the virtual. Thus, while in the eyes of copyright and in the arguments of David Slater's representation, Naruto is the alien, the interloper, and the manic disrupter, in reality, perhaps it is Slater who is the intruder, the alien, the itinerant scavage.[129]

Believe in Your Selfie

The language of wants invariably invokes concerns with selfhood and a sense of self, and this is evident not only in the text of the Naruto opinion but also more widely in the popular and legal discourse surrounding the case.[130] Authorship is socially and culturally infused with the language of selfhood and personality, and this is especially pronounced in copyright law, where these socio-cultural concerns are invoked in the interpretation of the principles themselves, such as the concept of originality through to the purpose of a work in adaptation and use.[131] The question of wants thus takes on a technical power as well as a social one.

Wants also imply a goal, whether frustrated or otherwise, and this is in part attended by a sense of curiosity and wonder, of particular interest as elements of play. Addressing the goal-seeking dimension of wants also assists in understanding the nature of vulnerability as capacity, potentially subject to resources but nevertheless a capability. It is in this sense that goals interact with beliefs "as internal representations of desired states, where states are broadly construed as outcomes, events, or processes."[132] In other words, goals and their pursuit "are the mark and criterion of the presence of mentality in a phenomenon."[133] Indeed, intellectual property is almost the ideal example of this phenomenal dimension to wants, especially in respect of the discourse and strategy surrounding the nature of the outputs of artificial intelligence. In a way, Naruto is being asked to confirm the belief in the selfies as selfies. That is, this dispute illustrates the distinction between the process, including Naruto's curiosity and belief as a capacity of authorship, and the product, where the phenomena of the photographs themselves are committed to a narrative of human authorship, the force of which is assisted by the camera, interpreted not as a tool used by Naruto but as part of a situation designed and compelled by the human intruder.

The Price of Belief

The incentives narrative of intellectual property thus contributes to this scenario by adapting aesthetic phenomena to a reconstructed narrative of motivation: "A little incentive salience may add zest to the perception of life and perhaps even promote the construction of meaning."[134] Thus, imposing this same narrative upon Naruto and other nonhuman creators will always come up short.

Affective neuroscience understands reward in terms of three components – liking (the pleasure), wanting (the motivation), and learning (a kind of belief or meaning generated usually by the satisfaction of wanting).[135] Wanting stands out, so to speak, as a kind of attention and as such is explained through an element of surprise: the concept of incentive salience.[136] Incentive salience translates literally as a motivated attraction and attention. As a motivation concept, incentive salience encompasses the positive or attractive forces of motivation, whereas aversive salience is the motivation of avoidance through displeasure. Incentive salience or wanting is thus focused on positive attention and attraction. This resonates with wider and ordinary notions of wanting as part of a process of approach and even sociability, as well as a kind of nearness, physical or otherwise, that informs the concepts of familiar production and shared interests. Imitation, as Tarde explains, must be understood as a "social tie"[137] and fundamental element of sociability.[138] Thus, imitation is a form of wanting. Wanting initiates relationality.

The concept of attention that is thus central to the science of wanting is also critical to this examination of authorship and attentive imitation.[139] Attention to attention in intellectual property introduces not only an ethical dimension to the work but also a sociable framework for the system itself. A meaningful attention thus includes regard for the connections within and between imitations, or works, particularly through meaningful attribution and stewardship of knowledge, where recognition is also a form of attribution. Referencing between imitations not only produces an authentic attention but also ensures the abundance of meaning and value as generated through those connections towards an ultimately relational functioning of property. Thus, re-appropriating the language of wants, particularly through play, in some respects defeats the unanswerable economic imperative of the question in refrain. Rather than seek the beliefs, reasons, or incentives, one need only look to Naruto's play. Focusing on play makes it possible to sever the obligatory fiction of incentives from the operation of authorship, and with that, to reject the purported economic rationality of intellectual property that attends this. Instead, play focuses on the freedom of expression in these ludic relationships, and thus the manifestation of preferences through that play.[140] Choice is not only the fundamental cornerstone value of economics and intellectual property but also the very definition of authorship.

What is the *cost*, then, of Naruto's attention and the law's inattention to Naruto's creativity? Restated, what is the cost such that Naruto's *loss* or injury can be quantified and remedied meaningfully in this context? To ask the question *What does Naruto want?* requires an effort to understand the nature of Naruto's injury. If this injury continues to be emphasised in economic terms, or in terms of reputation and prestige, it would seem to be non-sensical, so to speak, in this context. What does it mean to apply what might be considered an economic model of sentience or consciousness in this copyright context? In contrast, while still maintaining the language the law will recognise, an emphasis on authorship as a manifest value or artefact of sentience is more meaningful both in terms of this economic context and as a phenomenal account of Naruto's contribution. And is it fair at all to conclude that Naruto is unable to articulate their interests or goals when there is the evidence of the photographs themselves? In this way, if instead we begin to focus on the aesthetic behaviour or performance, the demonstration of creativity through curiosity and play, is the answer not in front of us? Requiring a substantiation of beliefs underpinning that work would appear to go beyond what is necessary to ascertain creativity and would certainly go beyond what is necessary at law. Thus, if the photographic equipment is in Naruto's space, and Naruto creates the photographs in that space, is there not an illegitimate expropriation of value if, at the very least, sharing in the benefits of those photographs is not afforded to Naruto and the rest of the colony?

Technically, such a remedy is not onerous, and there are many examples of attempts to achieve just such results. For example, the Lion's Share Fund[141] identifies the value of expropriating imagery through the use of nonhuman animals in advertising and translates that into a form of benefit-sharing through the fund, enabling it to purchase wildlife corridors and fulfil other conservation and biodiversity objectives. While this may generalise potentially the benefit to the entirety of the nonhuman animal population, it is a meaningful example of what might be achieved in the particular or more local case, such as the Tangkoko reserve. This connection with the land is thus not merely a device of property through labour; it is at the same time a mixing through imagery, and the result of a fundamental and multispecies social connection. Indeed, it is wasteful to ignore this connection.[142] This is especially meaningful in interpretations of the rights of nature, but to translate this into an individual context introduces new challenges. To answer the refrain throughout this book, *What does Naruto want?*, it is necessary to address the explainability problem.

The Lunchbox Black Box

The explainability problem refers to the technical explainability problem for artificial intelligence[143] and the emergence of explainable artificial intelligence

(XAI) as a distinct area of development.[144] But it also refers to the explainability problem in authorship more widely, so to speak. The problem of explainability in artificial intelligence is inherent to the systems themselves, such that the complexity of such systems challenges the possibility of explaining the outputs in a meaningful and sufficient way.[145] This presents significant issues for the use of artificial intelligence in circumstances where such explainability is crucial, such as health and medical diagnostics.[146] But in the present context, there is another explainability problem, and that is the question of attribution and stewardship of knowledge through intellectual property and copyright. Explainability in intellectual property is not only an operational characteristic of the system, underpinning the process of creating and enforcing rights (as in the application of prior art in the granting of patents), but also a social and cultural accountability that is invaluable within and beyond that system. This returns the discussion to Naruto's explainability problem, so to speak: *What does Naruto want?* However, despite this framing, this is not a problem unique to nonhuman animals but a problem of particularising the subjective experience of all animals, including humans. In order to anticipate an intellectual property that is *more than human*, and *more than just some* humans, attention to this explainability is critical. This will require an interdisciplinary discussion or conversation, to use Tarde's terms,[147] or a meeting of diverse perspectives, following Donna Haraway,[148] between science, law, and countless other fragments. It will require some open questions and (dis)honest answers.

The issue of explainability is thus, in many respects, the nexus in which the various and seemingly random variables of authorship, personhood, and intellectual property converge. It is apparent that this question of explainability is aligned with deciphering an intentionality or purpose. And this question, in both the popular and technical discourse, is common and essential to the recognition of authorship, the concept of originality, the value of art, and the reckoning of personhood. This is because resolving an explanation somehow secures a fundamental narrative of motivation, causation, and fixation. However, it is not simply towards the value in the work, but the value in the explanations themselves and the *attentive imitation* in the process towards the work. Indeed, it would appear that the various concerns around authorship, originality, art, and personhood converge and coalesce in a version of explainability.

But in attempting to answer the question of wants, the barrier of explainability is almost always already set up to withstand the challenge to the status quo and defeat any prospect of asking the right questions. This is because a valid and sufficient explanation is invariably inflected through an anthropocentric lens. For nonhuman animals, this manifests in the anthropodenial of any notion of *artistic temperament*, as it were, or of nonhuman animal aesthetics (*survivalist mode*, so to speak). That is, in erecting a human monument of art and of artists, an insurmountable barrier is seemingly established, ensuring nonhuman animal cultural productions will always already be unthinkable as art. This intellectual exclusion is not limited to the species barrier; it is recognised in auteurism in copyright more widely and the impact on the development of surrounding industry norms and dominant voices, to the marginalisation or exclusion of race,[149] gender,[150] and class,[151] and of particular works, such as those of fandoms and movement or performance.[152] The explainability issue renders itself neatly tautological insofar as the answers compel the making and recognition of the producer as *human*.

For artificial intelligence, the problem is curiously quite different, indeed almost diametrically opposite. In the public discourse surrounding the question of authorship in artificial intelligence, there appears almost an enthusiasm to accept the outputs as art, and a possibly even greater social readiness to accept innovations as inventive, and thus to infer an author on the basis of the commodities themselves,[153] notwithstanding the position otherwise within the law itself. While a cynical account may be that such items present the potential for commercial value and this motivates the authorship narrative, there is more at stake. In particular, the outputs of artificial intelligence, trained as the machines are on the exemplary work of humans, are always necessarily an approximation and impersonation of a *human* product. The works are in the right language, so to speak. The discussion of authorship is thus already halfway there, and so the question of explainability in artificial intelligence and machine learning is simply necessary to establishing trust[154] and mainstreaming the technology. Achieving explainable models has therefore continued to preoccupy developers for some time,[155] arguably primarily because of the considerable importance to wider adoption and consumer application,[156] and the ongoing risk of explainability as a barrier.[157]

In relation to the potential for intellectual property in the objects generated by artificial intelligence, all this effort is to render the artificial intelligence as artist, as responsible for the work, and thus to validate and endorse the human consumer's trust in the artificial producer and its product.[158] This includes perceptions of aesthetic and cultural value and validity. Explainability is thus at the heart of this question of authorial trust[159] and is the substrate for making the artificial intelligence author. But is this an answer without a question? Proceeding to explainability of the wants themselves, does artificial intelligence meaningfully want anything? The problem here is the combination of an interest and uncertainty regarding the potential consciousness of artificial intelligence, and an inability to explain artificial intelligence. As David Chalmers cautions, "The project of interpretability in machine learning interpretability has come a long way, but it also has a very long way to go."[160]

But what are the specific questions for which explanations are sought? Framing the right question is, of course, crucial, but what is the question of the question? What is it to want? Insofar as imitating is wanting, explainability may be afforded not through an appeal to beliefs or intentions, but rather in recording the relations between; that is, in stewarding imitations through attribution.[161] An attention to attribution as a cultural and socio-economic value not only introduces a new perspective on explainability and citation, but also reorientates attention to the ethics and relationality of imitation and of the works themselves.[162] This kind of accountability is also ethological and is perhaps best understood as the way in which various species of nonhuman animals resolve their own explainability problems by asking the right questions through scent marks and other mechanisms of communicating through the environment itself. The problem of explainability in this way characterises the question of authorship for nonhuman animals and at the same time suggests the prism through which the perception of the work might be diffracted and remade. What does Naruto *want*?

This introduces the important relationship between the explainability concerns for artificial intelligence and the sentience debate in nonhumans more widely, both animals and machines. It also continues to return the question of sentience to a question of authors, but as authors in connection with readers. Towards resolving the issues of explainability in artificial intelligence, one proposal is to adopt a definition of explainability that emphasises audience, ushering in related personal concepts, including privacy and trust, and including the capability of the audience as instrumental to the accountability of the model itself.[163] Taking this approach, understandability is a central concept and is connected to comprehensibility "in that it relies on the capability of the audience to understand the knowledge contained in the model. All in all, understanding is a two-sided matter: model understandability and human understandability."[164] The acknowledgement of the audience in the work goes some way to addressing the problem of adoption in view of the fact that "[i]n general, humans are reticent to adopt techniques that are not directly interpretable, tractable and trustworthy"[165] and to addressing a kind of replicability in the technology itself. Fundamentally, the emphasis is on transparency as a source of understandability, thus achieved through a kind of *attribution* principle as applied through various means and thus inhering in the workings of the models themselves. Even for artificial intelligence, the generation of meaning and value must also necessarily be *in personam*.

In what might be considered an anticipatory sociology of artificial intelligence, Tarde's inter-psychology is key to the present discussion: "[I]t is rather in an *inter*-cerebral psychology, which studies the rise of conscious relations between two or more individuals, that we must seek it."[166] Tarde's sociology as well as his writings in jurisprudence continue to emphasise this relationality throughout and are suggestive of an ethological accountability before the discipline of ethology itself.[167] Towards an ethological jurisprudence, Tarde's theory of imitation is entirely sensible, so to speak, and in its attention to the relations between individuals and the "distinctive event in the life of each," it casts doubt on the attention to objects as coherent and complete: "This relation between a subject and an object which is itself a subject – and not a perception in no way resembling the thing perceived ... means that we experience the sensation of a sentient thing, the volition of a conating thing, and the belief in a believing thing."[168]

As such, it is in the relations between that the historic, inventive events arise: "The relation of one mind with another is, in fact, a distinctive event in the life of each."[169] In this respect, Tarde understands a social dyad as "the fundamental social couple,"[170] one that is sustained through the social momentum of imitation.[171] This introduces new perspectives on explainability, as well as critical engagement with the concept of originality and the always unfinished nature of the work: "There is not a stroke of the brush that you make, if you are a painter, nor a verse that you write, if you are a poet, which does not conform to the customs or the prosody of your school, and even your very originality itself is made up of accumulated common-places, and aspires to become common-place in its turn."[172]

Indeed, these social fragments will emerge as pivotal to an ethological model of justice in due course. As Tarde proclaims, "Thus, the unvarying characteristic of every social fact whatsoever is that it is imitative. And this characteristic belongs to social facts."[173]

Play False and Ring True

Throughout the following chapters, the explainability problem for nonhuman authorship presents as both an obstacle for nonhuman animals and a strategy for artificial intelligence. Naruto's experience presents a way of navigating those obstacles of imagination through the very phenomena of play. By this course, it is possible to approach what Naruto wants through the evidence of beliefs, not the beliefs themselves; that is, through the evidence of wants, not the wants themselves. The question is thus not *what* does Naruto want, but *does* Naruto want? A chose in action, so to speak. Play is thus significant. Play is both a freedom of expression and a manifest value of welfare.[174] Play indicates sentience rather than reinforcing the insolubility or intractability of the hard problem of consciousness. And it does this through this important link between wants through play and interests in the logic of law. The entry point to moral standing may thus very well be through play.

Later discussion will examine the central importance of play through the attending capacities to lie and deceive, to make believe, as similarly fundamental qualities of both authorship and inventive trajectories through future beliefs.[175] The interests, for the purposes of the law, inhere in the objects themselves, while the wants or desires are always already a matter of make-believe. To be genuinely capable of holding a belief, an individual must be able to understand true and false, pretence and practice, imitation and *imitation*. As a matter of course, the capacity for purposive deception necessarily relies upon the capacity to possess beliefs and the potential for false beliefs in others.[176] And such deception is, of course, also part of most fun and games: "Jokes often rely on someone being fooled into a false belief, and games require players to pretend to believe something they know not to be true, really."[177] Beliefs are thus in a critical relationship with wants or desires. And it is through wants that a significant distinction might be considered between nonhuman animals and artificial intelligence. Wants are not the product of averaging information, but an understanding of different wants. That is, genuine authorship is the capacity to get things wrong and make mistakes.[178] Arguably, generative AI, in the strictest sense, never makes a mistake. Whenever it produces information that is false, this is nevertheless not a mistake on the part of the machine. Indeed, it is structurally incapable of this ingenuity. This is the crucial distinction between the wanting in imitation that is conscious and evaluative and potentially innovative (*attentive imitation*), and imitation that is coerced by the rules of summation and a stale substitution – a banal or unoriginal imitation (*stereotypic imitation*). Lies, as will be seen, are a matter of distinction. The choice in the matter.

This arguably also informs a potential distinction between plant and nonhuman animal sentience. Rather than arbitrarily dismissing the potential existence of plant sentience, it is arguably much more ethical and meaningful to examine the nature of sentient behaviour in plants in relation to wants. Plant behaviour may be understood in the service of interests, as distinct from the conscious wanting that is evident in the deception and pretence in play and other creative exuberance or indeed work in nonhuman animals. Plants defend but, other than physical adaptation,[179] it is unclear that plants deceive.[180] But perhaps the distinction, if any, comes through the mobility of play. *What do authors want?* They want to play. Thus, inner mentality, without resort to deciphering the representations of that mentality, may be ascertained through the phenomena of play and games; that is, through curiosity and investigation in the accumulation of knowledge,[181] seeking behaviour,[182] tactical deception[183] and pretence,[184] and so on. Play encompasses goals but is also an expression of surplus or a purely aesthetic account of those goals, less readily reduced or explained away by functionalist narratives of biology and instinct.

What is at stake, then, in the *phenomena* produced by artificial intelligence? Copyright provides a particular route into considering some inconsistencies and some resolutions because, while these resolutions may simplify the commercial questions, they largely do so on the basis of wants. What is wanted in a performance? And who does the law credit with those *wants*? The law appears to have no concerns with rendering performers mere conduits or technologies of reproduction for authors.[185] Why then is there so much enthusiasm for considering certain forms of artificial intelligence as potential authors? Much of this question is contextualised and complicated by commercial motivations, as considered in the following discussions, but critically the relationship between authored works and performances provides considerable insight into how copyright might engage artificial intelligence. In particular, much of what artificial intelligence produces is a kind of performance or execution, directed unmistakably, in every sense,[186] by its own functionalism and subsequent curation of its outputs. Once the work is made, or fixed, then the curation or publication is where the authorship might be conceived as happening.[187] What manner of wants might be at stake in the curation of products? *What do machines want?*

Show What You Want

Returning to the fascination with incentives, intellectual property scholarship has been inculcated with the doctrine of incentives for some time. This faith in an economic rationality of incentives has at the same time maintained a pseudo-biological narrative for creativity through unfaltering acceptance of a *red-in-tooth-and-claw* model of competition and survival in a knowledge economy. This also assists in maintaining a species barrier with respect to authorship, at once purported to be uniquely human and at the same time presented as an explanation for an immutable difference between human and all other, thus stymieing more-than-human authorship "once and for all."

Once again, the audience is important in clarifying not only the work but also its authorship. Through dissemination and access, the work enters into relation with others, and in this way, the relevance of curation and publication emerges as a creative act; indeed, a phenomenal act. This contributes to what might be considered "the art of the catalogue," the term Roland Barthes uses to describe the accumulation of objects and the "mild traffic of ownership" in the works of the artist Berckheyde.[188] Curiously, this has an enticing resonance with the art of dissemination through selection and curation. Viewed as creativity, curation reinforces the emphasis on attribution that returns throughout this discussion and illustrates "another role for art and for the cataloguing of object linked to the enumerative power that contaminates life and that turns life into plural lives that count only to the degree they are part of a larger collective."[189] This resonates in a particular way with the issue of explainability, but also recalls Tarde's society of imitation and connection, and the diffusion of innovation. How then might the creativity through curation be reconciled with incentives for artificial intelligence industries?

Notably, incentives arguments continue to be deployed in current debates over the protection of products emanating from artificial intelligence, but they were also mobilised during what was perhaps the first wave of anxiety over computer-related authorship in the 1970s and 1980s. Pamela Samuelson is one of the earlier significant voices in the debate over technological interventions in authorship, specifically in relation to computer-generated works, and argues that, "The system has allocated rights only to humans for a very good reason: it simply does not make any sense to allocate intellectual property rights to machines because they do not need to be given incentives to generate output."[190] This argument is framed by the issue of wants but carefully distinguishes the operation of the system from the question of the commercial value of the work itself. In other words, the narrative must not be simply a Panglossian and adaptationist analysis[191] of incentives in order to resolve a question about protecting commercially valuable objects, thus working from the object backwards. It must engage with the wider sociability of the system itself. How do these objects enter into a relation with humans and indeed other objects? They do so through publication, in the widest sense of the word.

The incentives narrative thus applies not only to creation, but also to the responsibilities of ownership, and more specifically, to dissemination: "Perhaps the best reason to allocate ownership interests to someone, however, is that someone must be motivated, if not to create the work, then to bring it into public circulation."[192] Samuelson argues that, in any situation of ownerlessness, "If someone must be given incentives to bring the work forward, it is the user who is best situated to respond to that motivation."[193] But she continues that without the possibility of ownership in such a computer-generated work, where the user ultimately bears the responsibility of "bringing forward what the law says is in the public domain," there is thus little incentive to do so: "The user is more likely to withhold it from the public, or to lie about who created the work, or to make some little change in it (perhaps not an improvement) just to establish a stake in it."[194] Any discussion of incentives extends not only to publication, but also to an incentive to attribution. Dissemination thus acquires both an affiliative and creative quality in the context of the relational property of the intellectual property system.

This strategy of publication is arguably what is already happening to works created by nonhuman animals, with no concerns raised. And yet, socially, culturally, and even legally, the servitude of animal creators is somewhat overlooked while the work of artificial intelligence continues to garner attention, with serious ethical and welfare consequences as a result. It thus remains a point of curiosity as to why such a discrepancy persists between the treatment of works created by nonhuman animals and those generated by artificial intelligence. This discrepancy is not only indefensible but also somewhat awry. As subsequent chapters will develop, there are significant reasons why nonhuman animals must be authors, even if not entitled to copyright, and there are also significant reasons why machines must not, with critically important ethical and welfare consequences at stake in both these answers.

Good Will Wanting

Arguably, there are three key things that have been found to be common in studies across examples of nonhuman creativity. The first is that it is fun; that is, there is a distinct pleasure not only in the performance,[195] but also in the reception of creative expressions.[196] This notion of nonhuman animals engaging in activity that is not to be understood purely in terms of survival and function is to understand animals engaging in freedom of choice, a creative freedom, and, unmistakably, an aesthetic. Naruto wants to play.

Secondly, the expression is about individuality. There are many examples of the way in which individual nonhuman animals create *in their own name*.[197] In every sense, they have acted out of choice, they have not been constrained by function, and they have disseminated their expressions in a sociability of creativity with others. As far as the law is concerned, species differences aside, this is in fact the very definition of creative – the author's own intellectual creation.[198]

And finally, it is important for that individuality to be acknowledged, not only by peers but also by other members of the species and indeed other species, including humans. This is the critical affiliative function of creativity and imitation, which introduces insight for understanding that affiliative value in imitation in intellectual property products as well, including through adaptation and parody, for example.[199]

In her work on the production of social memory, Tiziana Terranova argues that "mainstream" approaches to social production operate with a kind of economic rationality: "Cooperation is not based on exchange but on an asymmetrical relationship of mutual or unilateral capture which presupposes a whole social and psychic economy of power."[200] Indeed, it is in this respect that the concept of familiar production presented here and developed through an ethological jurisprudence[201] must be distinguished from the prevailing conventions established in theories of social production.[202] In my present work towards developing an ethological jurisprudence of property, Tarde's approach to a sympathetic cooperation has been central to an ethology of imitation and innovation, and to a relational and ethological approach to the social qualities of property and territory. Social production, in contrast to what Terranova terms "Tarde's neo-monadology of sympathetic cooperation,"[203] adheres in many respects to a mythical economic rationality, aligned with motivation and desires. Such a motivation economy is similarly translated into an intellectual property paradigm in the banality of incentives and rewards.[204] And it is also the basic question posed *about* Naruto, as though it can be answered at all in this way. This presumed "univocity of desire," as Terranova describes it, undercuts a conventional and quasi-juridical equation of interests and individuality: "Motivation is thus closely linked to interest ... interest is the other name of *desire*, a principle of action that is endowed with its own principle of internal regulation and whose foundation is the liberal government of the self."[205]

Notably, this distinction between social and familiar production can be traced through an ethological approach to communal action and imitation, as distinct from the conventions in mass psychology with respect to the collective and collectivities.[206] The concept of the family appears throughout Tarde's consideration of imitation and his microsociology, departing as such from the grand collectives of Durkheim and contemporary social production,[207] and restoring attention to individual social ties. Tarde explains, "this imitation was not ... a connection binding one individual to a confused mass of men, but merely a relation between two individuals,"[208] and distinguishes these from the "collective and impersonal models, which are usually not consciously chosen."[209] While Tarde is criticised for having "never developed the concept of the collective adequately," it is the contention here[210] and in earlier discussions[211] that Tarde is anticipating an ethological approach to the affiliative and imitative kinship of the familial group, and the cohesion of an anecdotal and incremental approach to creativity, knowledge, and justice through the fragments of individual testimony and particular perspectives. This connects in useful ways with Michel Serres's distinction between mixture and medium, where the former might be understood to reflect the kind of "contingency," in familiar production, but one which for Serres means "common tangency," in a way curiously resonant with shared (but not averaged) interests.[212] A medium, on the other hand, appears to confess the perils of the collectivity and mainstream social production, in its homogeneity and stability: "A medium is abstract, dense, homogeneous, almost stable, concentrated; a mixture fluctuates."[213]

These concerns relate to the problematic of the subject and object relationship traced throughout this work and recurrent in the operation of intellectual property and its *mind-body problem*, as it were.[214] Importantly, the examination of these different perspectives upon a form of communal or social structure is necessarily confronting of the anthropocentrism in the law and shifting of the emphasis "not only from the subject, from the person, but also from the human."[215] This removes the tendency towards comparative discussions and anthropocentric approximations and forces attention on intellectual property's Panglossian paradigm.[216] The anthropocentrism of a comparative approach is in part explained by Tarde's approach to nationalism in comparative analysis, and the risk of a kind of centering of that national perspective in any analysis, with other legal systems thus interpreted and assessed by reference to that national model.[217] The jurisdiction from which one commences the comparison risks dominating and directing the research, Tarde explains, with tendencies to ignore differences or exaggerate resemblances to the detriment of a genuinely comparative approach.[218] Just as for the problems raised through analysis from a particular national perspective, so too when proceeding from a particular system, or species, and so on. Indeed, in such comparative approaches or critiques, there is inevitably a conflict of laws. Whether those are conflicts arising from the comparative approach to different national systems, to customary laws, to creative communities, or to different species, at each point there is the inevitable approximation to a perceived centre or seat of authority and privileged view, and the marginalisation of others through the neglect of difference, and contrived exaggeration of any detectable similarities to the presented model. Instead, embracing a certain incomparability becomes critical if looking for an intellectual property that is more than human; that is, more than artificial thresholds and anthropocentric horizons. An ethological jurisprudence, as anticipated through Tarde's jurisprudence, approaches conflict as contact towards families of laws. As Tarde explains, identifying these challenges for comparative research is "not to lessen the importance of ethnographic research, but to clarify the meaning and scope of their results."[219]

In this kind of multispecies ethnography of authors, an ethnography that informs an ethological jurisprudence of intellectual property, attention to the question of what Naruto wants is a critical part of the story.[220] It turns out that what Naruto wants is a very important question indeed, one that becomes crucial to the investigation of authorship that lies ahead.

What does Naruto want? Look, see!

Notes

1 *Naruto v Slater*, 888 F. 3d 418 (2018).
2 The Celebes or Sulawesi crested macaque (*Macaca nigra*), also known as the crested black macaque or Sulawesi, is an Old World monkey now largely restricted to the Tangkoko reserve in which Naruto lives, as well as some of the smaller neighbouring islands. See further Gallardo Palacios et al. (2011).
3 *Naruto v Slater*, 888 F. 3d 418, 432 (2018).
4 Douglas (1994/[1992]), 149.
5 The concept of *theory of mind* in cognitive ethology was introduced by Premack and Woodruff (1978) and refers to an ability to infer information about another individual's mental state, including goals and beliefs. The concept is closely linked to intentionality and thus also authorship, as well as investigations into sentience and consciousness, and therefore is relevant throughout the present discussions. The concept remains relevant throughout, but see further the discussion of the anecdotal approach to theory of mind research in *Law's Anecdote*.
6 See in particular the later discussion of tools and object play in Chapter 7 and the interaction with deception in Chapter 8.
7 See in particular Panksepp (2005), 177.
8 Panksepp (2005), 177.
9 Sir William Beveridge, *Social Insurance and Allied Services* (1942) Cmd 6404.
10 FW Rogers Brambell, *Report of the Technical Committee to Enquire into the Welfare of Animals Kept under Intensive Livestock Husbandry System* (1965); Cmnd 2836.
11 See further the World Organisation for Animal Health (WOAH).
12 Sir William Beveridge, *Social Insurance and Allied Services* (1942) Cmd 6404, 163.
13 See the later discussion in Part 3.
14 Nguyen et al. (2021), 76.
15 For example, in the United Kingdom, as articulated in the Animal Welfare Act 2006, s2.
16 The notion of the nonhuman creator or communicator as simply imitating without conscious evaluation can be seen throughout conservative assessments of aesthetic

expression and language. See in particular the discussion in Despret (2016/[2012]), 1–6. See further on play and creativity in Part 3 of the present work.
17 Tarde (1903). See further the discussion in Gibson (2020a), 229–230 and 281–283, towards a resocialisation of property.
18 Tarde (1903/[1890]), 167.
19 Tarde (1903/[1890]), 165.
20 Tarde (1903/[1890]), 165.
21 Tarde (1903/[1890]), 165.
22 This is relevant to some approaches through critical or radical anthropomorphism, such as the strategy of bionarration as advocated by Scheers (2007), through which "the metaphor of life story" may be applied "in a certain way to the world of plants and animals" (287). Scheers argues that life story techniques in relation to animals and plants, or bionarration, "can help us to come to the realization that we, humans, are not islands of meaning in a desert of nothingness" (291).
23 In particular, see the later discussion of these concepts in the context of attention and attentiveness in Chapter 6.
24 On cultural transmission, see further Tomasello (1990); Tomasello (1999). See further the concept of "ratcheting" in Tennie (2009).
25 In the context of cultural development and property, towards an ethological jurisprudence of property, see Gibson (2020a).
26 Whiten (2021); Waal (2001), 31. Waal and Bonnie (2009), responding to the work of Kinji Imanishi and the anthropology of the human-animal divide, note the following definition of culture: "if individuals learn from one another, their behavior may, over time, become different from that in other groups, thus creating a characteristic culture" (19). The authors expand this definition, drawing upon Waal (2001): "The 'culture' label thus befits any species in which one community can readily be distinguished from another on the basis of socially transmitted behavior" (21). Notably, definitions applied to culture are of the same contested and contingent nature as for sentience (see further the discussion of sentience and definitions in Chapter 3). On the problem of definition, see McGrew (2009), 55–56. This resonates with a biosemiotic approach to sentience, particularly the concept of the semiosphere, Lotman (1990). This concept is revisited in Gibson (2025).
27 For example, see Laland (2017).
28 Davies (2015) notes it is "plausible ... that we are likely to share our aesthetic sense with our primate cousins and other higher animals," but he argues it would be only "to a limited extent" (14). But Davies actually notes that this is a matter of perspective.
29 This threshold logic is particularly in operation in the policy context for sentience. See further the discussion in Chapter 3.
30 Lents (2017).
31 Lents (2017).
32 Griffin (2001), 32–34.
33 Nagel (1974). See further the discussion in Chapter 3 of the present work.
34 Griffin (2001), 32.
35 Griffin (2001), 32.
36 Nelson et al. (2023) note, "The drive to understand and regulate states with negative affect has also motivated a search for appropriate animal models, and thus worries about 'anthropomorphizing' animals have been counterbalanced by the desire to establish the validity of these negative affect states (so-called 'construct validity') for the study of human afflictions" (1549).

37 Armstrong (1973), 27.
38 Radder (1993), 328. See further the extensive critique of research design and anthropocentric limitations to observations in Despret (2016/[2012]) and Waal (2016). See also the discussion of the laboratory space in Haraway (2008), Chapter 3.
39 Gruber et al. (2015).
40 Gruber et al. (2015), 1.
41 Candea (2012) describes an experience with a behavioural ecologist who immediately sought to explain a particular behaviour observed in mice through recourse to function, while the anthropologists had considered the motivations: "Whereas our first attempt at explaining the mice's behaviour had sought subjective intentional motives behind their actions, Mike instantly bypassed that question and sought for a function which might have led to such behaviour being selected for" and continues, "This is not an isolated case, but an entrenched disciplinary orientation" (123).
42 Waal (2001), 24–33. Frans de Waal argues that "Behind the ongoing culture wars, the debate is about nothing less than humanity's place in the cosmos. Definitions of culture have become the political football in this larger controversy" and explains that this positioning of definitions can extend to every part of nonhuman innovation and creativity: "It is not hard to come up with a definition of culture that rules out all species except our own. Even tools can be defined in such a way that they are found only in our species – for example, by requiring that they fit a symbolic context" (25).
43 BBC *Civilisations*, Trailer, 2018. Narrator: Floella Benjamin. https://www.youtube.com/watch?v=atmzvvXrBq0&feature=youtu.be
44 Alland (1977), 21. Alland distinguishes the hand as the distinctive element of what he describes as humans' unique abilities, a further physical marker of exceptionalism that is considered in more detail in Chapter 2 of the present work.
45 Alland (1977), 24.
46 BBC *Civilisations*, Trailer, 2018.
47 Shouse (2002). See further Kacelnik (2009) and Wimpenny et al. (2009).
48 Christian Rutz, behavioural ecologist, quoted in Morell (2016). Compare the work of Lars Chittka and colleagues with bees and string-pulling in Chittka (2022), 129–131. See further the discussion of string-pulling in the present work in Chapter 2.
49 See further the discussion in Chapter 2.
50 Jacobs and Osvath (2015), 111.
51 Jacobs and Osvath (2015), 111.
52 BBC *Civilisations*, Trailer, 2018.
53 This mantra is repeated throughout the popular discourse on dogs in particular, as seen in the television series, *The Supervet* (2014–), which focuses on the practice of Noel Fitzpatrick and staff at Fitzpatrick Referrals veterinary practice. However, compare the comprehensive review of the literature in Yong (2022), which addresses the limitations and inaccuracies of this popular refrain. The refrain is problematic not only in its limitation of nonhuman animal capacities but also for its implications in a welfare context. See further Mendl and Paul (2008).
54 See further Bräuer (2020).
55 Third-party evaluation and perspective-taking are observed in a range of species, with a particular research focus on nonhuman primates. But in dogs, see Petter et al. (2009); Gyori et al. (2010); Vas et al. (2005); and Anderson et al. (2017). And in pigs, see Luna et al. (2021). In insects, there is some dissensus, however

Rooijen (2010) notes that the pointing and dance language of bees, as well as other cooperative, communicative strategies, are successful strategies because of the individual's comprehension of intention. On the Panglossian paradigm in this context, see further Chapter 3 of the present work.
56 For example, on inequity aversion in dogs, see McGetrick and Range (2018); Essler et al. (2017); and Milius (2009). See further the discussion of fairness in nonhuman animals in Waal (2016), 107.
57 King (2013). See further examples and discourse in the wider press: Bates and Proops (2024); Timmons (2024); and Preston (2017).
58 https://www.facebook.com/bbcearth/videos/2140008432681011/
59 https://www.facebook.com/bbcearth/videos/2140008432681011/
60 For example, in relation to great ape cultures, Gruber et al. (2015) conclude there is no evidence of metarepresentational abilities or the ability to recognise culture as culture (arguably, a cumulative, human-like approach to culture). The authors determine that this is a fundamental distinction between great apes and human cultures and go on to recommend future work on nonhuman mental representation of cultural knowledge in order "to conclusively determine the ways by which humans are unique in their cultural behaviour" (1).
61 See further the detailed consideration of sentience in Chapter 3.
62 Chapter 3
63 In response to the announcements of the capabilities of Claude 3 and pretensions to sentience, Edwards (2024) asks whether this is simply a matter of framing. Others ask if it is understanding or "exceptional mimicry": Moore-Coyler (2024). See further Bishop (2021). See also the discussion in Metz (2022).
64 Abbott (2023).
65 Guérineau et al. (2022); Lindig et al. (2020); and Snowdon et al. (2015). See further on different perceptual capabilities and emphases in Kriengwatana et al. (2022).
66 Chapter 7.
67 Gibson (2006).
68 Boddez et al. (2019). As part of the wider cultural and institutional context for art, copyright is implicated in this process. See further the discussion of the law's role in validating and emphasising cultural value in Gibson (2006), and further in Gibson (2014).
69 Matson (1976).
70 Donath (2020) and Bostrom and Yudkowsky (2014), 321–324. The concept of sentience and surrounding discourse is considered in detail in Chapter 3 of the present work.
71 Naqvi (2020). Palace (2019) notes sentience as the (future) gateway to standing and intellectual property rights for artificial intelligence: "Granting standing to artificial intelligence would lead to many unsettling questions: Who enforces the right? What remedies should artificial intelligence be granted? What other rights should artificial intelligence receive? Although these questions may one day have to be answered, there is currently no pressing need because sentient artificial intelligence has yet to come" (233–234). For an early account of this relationship between sentience and authorship, see Butler (1982).
72 Koch (2015) argues, "There is no hint of sentience in these algorithms. They have none of the behaviors we associated with consciousness … There are zombies, acting in the world but doing so without any feeling, displaying a limited form of alien, cold intelligence" and asserts that despite evidence of learning, this is not sentience: "Such algorithms … demonstrate that for the first time in the planet's history, intelligence can be completely dissociated from sentience, from consciousness" (29).

73 Michel (2023); Emmert-Streib et al. (2020). See further Abbass (2021); Crawford (2021); and Jordan (2019), 3.
74 J 8/20 *Designation of Inventor/DABUS* (21 Dec 2021); *Thaler v Comptroller-General of Patents* [2023] UKSC 49; *Thaler v Vida* (Fed Cir 5 Aug 2022); *Thaler v Perlmutter* (DC Cir, 18 Aug 2023). The South African Companies and Intellectual Property Commission awarded a patent to DABUS (2021/03242); this was without any judicial exploration of the issues and so sets no fundamental principle as to personhood (through inventorship) or otherwise. See further the discussion in Gibson (2021a) and (2024a).
75 Although somewhat resisted in the past (for example, see Matson (1976), discussions around sentience have now become much more common in the ethics and policies around the use and development of artificial intelligence as well; see Donath (2020); and Bostrom and Yudkowsky (2014), 321–324.
76 The application numbers in the United Kingdom are for "A new kind of food or beverage container" (GB1816909.4) and "A new kind of light beacon and a new way of attracting attention in an emergency" (GB1818161.0). See further the discussion of the judgment of the Supreme Court in Gibson (2024a).
77 UK Parliament. 11 October 2022. A creative future – Oral evidence https://committees.parliament.uk/event/14659/formal-meeting-oral-evidence-session/ Hern (2022). See further the discussion of such "performative politics" in Bareis and Katzenbach (2022).
78 Bateson (2015): "For the biologist, benefits are measured in terms of the particular ways in which an activity increases the chances of survival and enhances reproductive success" (R12). However, when it comes to play, "The behaviour is spontaneous and rewarding to the individual; it is intrinsically motivated and its performance serves as a goal in itself. Play is 'fun'" (R15).
79 Butler (2004), 36. This provides a relevant critical perspective on the calculation of lives not in terms of grief but in economic terms (as in animal welfare campaigns).
80 For example, see the discussion of innovations through imitation in vocalisations and the perception of self among bird species in Derégnaucourt and Bovet (2016). See further Bolhuis et al. (2010); Bradbury and Balsby (2016).
81 Ruyer (2016/[1952]), 129.
82 Lestel (2018), 54. See also Despret (2016/[2012]), 10, 31–32; and Byrne (2000).
83 Massumi (2014), 83.
84 See further the discussion in relation to purpose and parody in Chapter 9.
85 Amy Zion, speaking about children's drawings from the permanent collection of the Children's Museum of the Arts (CMA), included as part of the exhibition at the Queens Museum, *Ulrike Müller and Amy Zion: The Conference of the Animals (09.16.20–01.31.21)*, quoted in Handy (2020). See further Townsend (2018): "The correct answer is to make the art, bestow it upon someone to behold and admire for a while, and then toss it. It makes the right tribute to beauty and it's the correct moral stance toward the more ephemeral qualities of childhood."
86 For a review of this question in the literature, see Cox (2005), Chapter 3. See further Jolley (2010) where the author notes the "neglect of academic attention to children's picture making" although emphasises its study towards understanding adult productions: "If we want to understand the development of the adult engagement with pictures then studying children's engagement with pictures is a necessity" (2).
87 Winner and Drake (2022), 32. See further Malvern (1995); Leeds (1989).
88 Silbey (2022), 3.

89 Harsha Gangadharbatla, quoted in Whipple (2021). See further Gangadharbatla's work on the relationship between attribution and value, and the impact on recognising (or not) machine-made works in Gangadharbatla (2021).
90 Rob Biddulph quoted in Shaffi (2023).
91 Editorial (2015) A monkey's right to a selfie, *Deutsche Welle*, 22 September.
92 Morillo (1995) explains, "A creature needs *relevant* information and must welcome the helpful and reject the harmful. This already points beyond the mere gathering of any and all information for the simple generation of sundry true beliefs" (2).
93 Slater (2014). Emphasis added.
94 Wikimedia Commons. Macaca nigra self-portait.jpg https://commons.wikimedia.org/wiki/File:Macaca_nigra_self-portrait.jpg
95 US Copyright Office, Compendium of US Copyright Office Practices. Third edition.
96 *Trade-Mark Cases*, 100 US 82, 94 (1879).
97 §306.
98 §306.
99 §306.
100 The examples are based on claims to the office. See further §313.2.
101 Copyright Act of 1976.
102 See, for instance, the habeas corpus cases brought by the Nonhuman Rights Project (NhRP), such as *Nonhuman Rights Project v Breheny*, 38 NY 3d 555 (2022) (Happy the Elephant); *Nonhuman Rights Project v Lavery*, 152 AD 3d 73 (2017) (Tommy and Kiko the Chimpanzees).
103 Chapter 3.
104 Candea (2012) notes in his fieldwork with the Kalahari Meerkat project that, "when speaking amongst themselves, behavioural biologists and Kalahari Meerkat project volunteers were ever describing what dominant or subordinate meerkats 'want', what they are 'trying to do', explaining certain actions in terms of how these are evidently 'in their interest', and so forth. When pressed on this usage, however, fully-fledged researchers … would readily answer that this was a way of speaking, an 'as if': it doesn't imply that the animals consciously or intentionally want such things" (123). As Candea explains, it is a bypassing of the question itself, seeking instead "for a function which might have led to such behaviour being selected for" (123).
105 Candea (2012), 124.
106 Chapter 2.
107 Dawkins (2007), 4.
108 Dawkins (2006), 7.
109 Weil (1978/[1959]), 207. Weil is referring to the discussion of will and volitions in Leibniz's *Theodicy*, in which Leibniz explains: "For whether the act of willing be impressed upon us by an external cause or we bring it about ourselves, it will be equally true that we will, and that we feel that we will" (§299). And in the passage upon which Weil refrains, it is possible only to rely on wants to consider whether there is also a will, and thus a play: "Do you not clearly understand that a weather-vane, always having communicated to it simultaneously (in such a way, however, that priority of nature or, if one will, a real momentary priority, should attach to the desire for motion) movement towards a certain point on the horizon, and the wish to turn in that direction, would be persuaded that it moved of itself to fulfil the desires which it conceived?" (§299)
110 Jeong (2015).
111 See further the discussion in Chapter 5.

112 Waal (2016), 60–61.
113 Kravets (2015); Jeong (2015).
114 Guadamuz (2018).
115 See further Gibson (2025).
116 Piazza et al. (2014), 108.
117 Nussbaum (2023).
118 Gibson (2022b).
119 *Naruto v Slater*, 888 F 3d 418 (2018).
120 *Naruto v Slater*, 888 F 3d 418 (2018). It is likely the difficulties of meeting the tests for representational standing comprise part of the Nonhuman Rights Project's strategy of pursuing captive individual claims through a writ of habeas corpus.
121 See further and more generally on this coercion of results through the framing of questions in Despret (2016/[2012]).
122 For example, see an ethological approach to these challenges in smells as expressions, in Gibson (2020a), Chapter 6.
123 In particular, theory of mind includes the attribution of beliefs in others through the perception of desire as an intentional state (and thus a purposive action in order to fulfil that desire). See further Liu et al. (2009).
124 This relationship between wants and reasons, or passion and reason, is central to David Hume's philosophy: Hume (1969/[1739–1740]). But it is evident across several philosophical traditions, including more widely: the question of the moral problem in Locke (1974); in the utilitarian application in Brandt et al. (1963); and in the ordinary language philosophy of Abelson (1965).
125 Marshall (2013/[1890]).
126 On the treatment of wants and activities in social action theory, see further Parsons (1968/[1937]).
127 Of particular importance to the present discussion is the analysis of belief and desire in the sociology and jurisprudence of Gabriel Tarde. See, in particular Tarde (1903/[1890]); Tarde (2012/[1893]); and Tarde (1899).
128 Gadamer (1992/[1960]), 104. Emphasis in original.
129 On the figure of the scavage and its relevance to an ethological jurisprudence of the nonhuman animal as *scavenger*, see Gibson (2020a), Chapter 9.
130 Muller (2022).
131 See further the discussion in Chapter 9.
132 Austin and Vancouver (1996), 338.
133 James (1890a), 5.
134 Berridge and Kringelbach (2011).
135 Berridge et al. (2009). See further Olney et al. (2018). Motivational salience is a critical aspect of addiction studies, where the wanting becomes de-regulated or irrational, in that the relationship between desire and belief becomes severed. See further Berridge and Robinson (1998). On this issue, see also Peciña et al. (2003) and the albeit brief discussion of a "wanting-liking divergence" in Dai et al. (2010), 332. This apparent contradiction between wanting and pleasure is also addressed in critiques from philosophy of the motivation analyses of wanting in science: see Schroeder (2004).
136 Berridge and O'Doherty (2014), 340–343. See further Panksepp and Wilson (2016).
137 Tarde (1903/[1890]), xvi.
138 Tarde (1903/[1890]), 3.
139 See further the discussion in Chapter 6.
140 Guala (2019), 386.

46 What Does Naruto Want?

141 A collaboration between private partners and the United Nations Development Programme (UNDP) addressing the use of nonhuman animal species and their representations in advertising by directing a proportion of advertising spend by Fund partners to conservation programmes. See further https://thelionssharefund.com. See also the UNDP page https://mptf.undp.org/fund/lns00.
142 See further the discussion of waste in Chapter 7.
143 Hassija et al. (2024); Vilone and Longo (2021); Linardatos et al. (2021).
144 Hamm et al. (2023).
145 Linardatos et al. (2021).
146 Markus et al. (2021).
147 Tarde (1899).
148 Haraway (2008).
149 For example, see Vats (2020). See also the discussion in Gibson (2005).
150 For example, see Potocnik (2024).
151 On classes of creative output, see Gibson (2006). See further the discussion of classical male auteurism and the impact on female and black filmmakers, in Ramanathan (2020): "Membership of the auterial club was confined to those whose aesthetic style was recognized, as in literary texts, across a body of work. The high masculine definition effectively blocked many women and all minorities from entrance into this exclusive club" (51).
152 Gibson (2022a) and (2022d).
153 This mobility of authorship through objects is examined in more detail in the third volume of this ethological jurisprudence: Gibson (2025).
154 Rossi (2019); Burrell (2016); and Ribeiro et al. (2016). See further, Zednik (2021).
155 For example, see Moore and Swartout (1988).
156 Kim et al. (2023). Meske et al. (2022) note that "[the] trade-off between performance and explainability can have a significant impact on individual beings, business, and society as a whole" (53).
157 Arrieta et al. (2020).
158 See further the discussion in Gibson (2023b).
159 Cuéllar (2019); Deeks (2019).
160 Chalmers (2022).
161 See the important relation between attribution and stewardship, and its critical role in an attentive imitation in Chapter 6.
162 Gibson (2023b).
163 Arrieta et al. (2020).
164 Arrieta et al. (2020), 85.
165 Arrieta et al. (2020), 83.
166 Tarde (1899), 29. Emphasis in original.
167 Gibson (2020a). See in particular Tarde's monadology in relation to the resocialisation of the law, Chapters 11 and 12.
168 Tarde (1899), 30–31.
169 Tarde (1899), 29.
170 Tarde (1899), 39.
171 See further the application of Tarde's sociology in developing an ethological jurisprudence of property relations, in Gibson (2020a).
172 Tarde (1899), 41. Compare the curious approach to rules in C-403/08 *FA Premier League* [2011] ECR I-9083, [98], where sporting events were denied copyright protection on the basis that rules are a bar to the basic requirements of a work.
173 Tarde (1899), 41.

174 This is a discussion throughout, but see further Chapters 3 and 7 in particular.
175 Chapter 8.
176 Byrne (1995), 125–127 and Chapter 9. Reviewing the literature, Povinelli (2003) explains, "In order to deceive others, they have argued, you need to create a mistaken belief in their heads – something that is only possible if you can conceive of such things as 'beliefs' in the first place" (60).
177 Byrne (1995), 102.
178 See further the importance of error and mistake, alongside the capacity for deception, in authorship in Chapter 8. See further Bachelard (2002/[1938]), 242–244, on the value of imitation and error.
179 For example, deceptive pollination in orchids, Jersáková et al. (2007).
180 Compare Gross (2016). See further the discussion of co-production with plants and landscapes in Gibson (2025).
181 In foundational work on curiosity in human behaviour, the British-Canadian psychologist, Berlyne (1966) describes the concept of "epistemic curiosity," which accounts for both exploratory as well as "epistemic" responses: "The use of this term is proposed in order to indicate that they are aimed not only at obtaining access to information-bearing stimulation, capable of dispelling the uncertainties of the moment, but also at acquiring knowledge – that is, information stored in the form of ideational structures and giving rise to internal symbolic responses that can guide behavior on future occasions" (31). It is in this sense of curiosity as a drive towards acquisition of knowledge as production that it resonates with the meaning of wants pursued here and developed in more detail throughout the following chapters.
182 On a discussion of seeking and its relationship to curiosity and play, see Walters (2013).
183 This term was developed by Andrew Whiten and Richard Byrne to refer to the use of "honest" behaviours in order to create a false belief in another individual so as to mislead them. See Whiten and Byrne (1988). See further Byrne and Whiten (1992); and Byrne (1995), 126 and Chapter 9. Tactical deception has been observed in a range of species, for example: in cephalopods, Brown et al. (2012); in ravens, Bugnyar and Kotrschal (2002); in squirrels, Steele et al. (2008); and in dogs, Cooper et al. (2003). Tactical deception is considered in more detail in Chapter 8 of the present work.
184 See further the discussion of deception and pretence in Chapter 8.
185 Gibson (2024c). See also Gibson (2022a).
186 See further the discussion in Chapter 8 of the impossibility of mistake in the strictest sense, as a question of authorship.
187 Further insight into this perspective on the potential creativity in a kind of administrative production can be gained from the examination of the administrator as cultural producer in the Romantic Age (a period of cultural and intellectual history which becomes relevant again in later discussions) in Klancher (2013). Of particular relevance here is the account of the "public enthusiasm for lecture-going" and the attraction of new women audiences to scientific knowledge as "one measure of the administrator's capacity to shape both the taste and the composition of the Royal and other Institutions' audiences" (65).
188 Barthes (1953), 7.
189 Campbell (2009), 170.
190 Samuelson (1985), 1199.
191 Gould and Lewontin (1979). See further Chapter 3.
192 Samuelson (1985), 1226.
193 Samuelson (1985), 1227.

194 Samuelson (1985), 1227–1228. See further the discussion of computer-generated works and generative AI in Chapters 3 and 8 of the present work.
195 Gisela Kaplan's studies of the Australian Magpie have shown how many birds sing most exuberantly when their offspring have grown and left, thus making territorial defence an unlikely motivation: Kaplan (2007). See further Morris (1962).
196 Kaplan (2007).
197 Notable in this context is the growing appreciation of the distinction between bird song as mechanical and innate marking of territory, and something more innovative and creative, taking account of the evidence of more complex and creative capacities around vocal learning and innovation, including the use of a kind of naming or authorial "signature phrase." On this and other examples, see Kaplan (2007).
198 C-5/08 *Infopaq Int v Danske Dagblades Forening* [2009] ECR I-6569, [37]; *THJ Systems Ltd v Sheridan* [2023] EWCA Civ 1354, [23].
199 Chapter 9.
200 Terranova (2017), 297–298.
201 See further the principles of an ethological jurisprudence in Gibson (2020a) and Gibson (2014).
202 See further the critique of social production in Gibson (2014) and the differentiation from the concept of familiar production, as introduced in that work.
203 Terranova (2017), 298.
204 See further Gibson (2020a), Chapter 10.
205 Terranova (2017), 298.
206 Vehlken (2019) points to a similar departure from animal psychology and mass psychology with the advent of "a genuinely biological and ethological perspective" in the early twentieth century, although in doing so, Vehlken appears to align Tarde with the traditions of psychology (59–60). While Tarde is certainly credited elsewhere in the literature with introducing a psychology into juridical and sociological scholarship, it is established in Gibson (2020a) and in later discussion in the present work, that Tarde's contribution is more emphatically and genuinely an ethological approach to the productivity of familiar production, rather than the sometimes homogenising discourse of social production. This emphasis on the purported quantitative accountability of the social, as distinct from the incidental and personal at the level of the family, is also in evidence in phenomenology and the distancing from behaviourism that commenced in the mid-twentieth century. In the mid-twentieth century, in efforts to distinguish behaviourism from phenomenological or, somewhat later, enactive and embodied approaches to cognition, it is possible to recognise a similar separating out, as McGill (1966) explains, along the lines of a strict or radical behaviorism and "a humanistically oriented experimental psychology" in response to the "grave neglect of 'experience'" (578). Theories of sensori-motor or embodied perception and cognition are central to ethological jurisprudence as well as to challenging the visual hegemony of intellectual property. Such approaches are arguably anticipated in the work of Weil and become clear in contemporary theories of embodied cognition and their application to authorship, as discussed throughout the following chapters, particularly Part 3. And on the collectivity as distinct from the swarm, see Chapter 4.
207 King (2016) identifies this as retaining the concept of the collective but notes the way in which this departs from Durkheim in significant and somewhat pivotal ways, explaining that this is not to understand families as remaining "in their primordial nuclear form," but rather to appreciate the kinship and ties

of the family social group through those individual perceptions and imitations (58). Nevertheless, he argues that there are limitations in Tarde's account of the individual (57). Borch (2017) rejects King's critique of Tarde's "alleged individualism" as "uncompromising," and argues that "King's assertion that Tarde practically neglected collectivity is emphatically incorrect" (156). Indeed, rather than an inconsistency in Tarde's examination of the crowd and maintenance of individual autonomy, the present work argues in the following chapters that what is possible through Tarde's account is a genuinely ethological account of a reciprocal agency and shared interests through familiar production. See in particular the discussion of individual agency in the swarm in Chapter 4 where an important distinction is drawn between the vitality of the swarm and the univocity of the collectivity, a negative character of the latter which is also identified by Weil.
208 Tarde (1899), 44.
209 Tarde (1899), 45.
210 See in particular Chapter 4 on distinguishing the collectivity from the swarm, and the relevance of Tarde's sociology of the infinitesimal in regarding the individual member of the swarm, as well as the crucial insight from Weil's account of the concept of the collectivity, which resonates with Terranova's critique of social production.
211 Gibson (2020a). See further the introduction of the concept of familiar production in Gibson (2014).
212 Serres (2008/[1985]), 80.
213 Serres (2008/[1985]), 81.
214 See further Chapter 2.
215 Melitopoulos and Lazzarato (2012), 241.
216 See further the discussion in Chapter 3.
217 Tarde (1900) Parglendler (2012) maintains that Tarde "argued that comparativists should refrain from taking their national legislation as the center of the legal universe and treating other legal systems as mere satellites" (1050–1051).
218 Tarde (1900), 438–439.
219 Tarde (1900), 444. Translation mine.
220 Candea (2010) explains a similar approach in relation to the Kalahari Meerkat Project and the highly successful *Meerkat Manor*: "The specific characteristics of meerkats, but also their actions and their capacity to behave in surprising or predictable ways, are as much a part of my story as the intentions and understandings of the human protagonists or, indeed, the robustness" (243). Indeed, through the intentionality and production of the work itself, *Meerkat Manor* is a multispecies authorship.

Part 1

The Philosopher

The voyage begins with an end, the shipwreck on the shore. The end of the world. Such is the power of boundary-making – *it is easier to imagine the end of the world than the end of the boundary*. This is a refrain on Fredric Jameson's fragment, "Someone once said that it is easier to imagine the end of the world than to imagine the end of capitalism."[1] Such is the boundary-making that renders the notion of animal rights unthinkable, and the idea of a nonhuman animal author absurd. Like Scylla and Charybdis in Homer's the *Odyssey*,[2] such thinking appears conveniently immobilised between a rocky problem and a hard place. Such was Odysseus's trolley problem.

But while the shore is a boundary, it is also a contact point, a catalyst for the swarms to come. Boundary concepts such as sentience and authorship invite this swarm. They too, as boundaries, are catalysts for questions. But somewhat remarkably, they are also catalysts for questions into each other. And it is with this question of boundaries that the journey begins.

The ship is a vehicle for the swarm, an extended mind of activity and mobility, and sailing is itself an embodied action. Simone Weil recognises and appreciates this when she explains that,

> the true sailor gets to be able to sense what is affecting his ship *no less* instantly than he senses the messages of his own nerves … there is responsibility, inventiveness, etc., in short, there is *action* wherever man is handling things that can in this way become like extensions of his own body, by transmitting signals directly to his soul. It is in this that the true nature of *work* resides.[3]

The ship is a tool, and "[a]ll tools are instruments for transforming chance into necessity."[4]

The sailor may seem at first to be simply at the mercy of "every movement of the waves," but they may also be the one "who seizes the rope and does not let go."[5] And with that, a new embodied action is afforded with the "buffeting of the waves" and the "tension of the cord," thus making "a different mechanical whole."[6] What this makes of the environment is perhaps

DOI: 10.4324/9780429342103-3

best told by a story from some nonhuman animals, more specifically, North Sea cod. With an entire ocean seemingly on their doorstep, as it were, cod make homes in the more local *world around* them, and they make them in shipwrecks. And not just any shipwreck, each individual will select their own shipwreck and return day after day, or night after night, depending upon their shift.[7]

Is it easier to think of the end of the world than to think of cod real estate and insect authorship? Perhaps, and perhaps necessarily and strategically so. Because Jameson immediately follows his fragment on the end of the world with the qualification, "We can now revise that and witness the attempt to imagine capitalism by way of imagining the end of the world."[8]

Time to untie and re-tie some knots, some world knots.

Notes

1 Jameson (2003), 76.
2 *Odyssey*, Book XII.
3 Weil (2015/[1970]), 37.
4 Weil (2015/[1970]), 7.
5 Weil (1976/[1952]), 194.
6 Weil (1976/[1952]), 194.
7 Karlsen (2011).
8 Jameson (2003), 76.

Chapter 1
A Word between Us

In Cervantes' *El coloquio de los perros*, or *The Dialogue of the Dogs*, two dogs, Scipio and Berganza, are our narrators. Scipio interrupts Berganza's commentary repeatedly, and yet this dialogue of ruptures is both cooperative and productive, a kind of turn-taking, so to speak. At one point Scipio implores Berganza to stick to the story, to which Berganza replies, "I will if I can, so long as you humor this great impulse I have to talk. I get the feeling I'm going to have my hands full just holding back the floodgates," at which Scipio retorts, "Just watch your mouth, because that's where the worst of man's woes begin."[1] Indeed, language is the flood barrier that is regularly erected in service of the species divide. For the very same reasons, language is also the facilitator of a performative humanity, if you will, in relation to the presentation of artificial intelligence models. In a very clear sense, it is the word between us.

The title of Cervantes' novel is commonly translated into English as *The Dialogue of the Dogs*. However, some analyses do refer to it as a colloquy rather than dialogue,[2] which, as well as meaning a conversation, can refer to the more specific nature of a group assembled to discuss theological questions; a Platonic forum, if you will. The use of colloquy as opposed to dialogue is perhaps not insignificant given also the relationship between many theological approaches to the human (especially in Christian theology) and the "investment in a categorical human-animal distinction."[3] The language barrier, the subject of this chapter, is at the heart of this distinction, a distinction that insists upon its own propriety. But "[w]here humanity surrenders its propriety, however, and enters an apprenticeship in *zōē aiōnios* – the animality of God – we may at last hear the voice of the Spirit rising through the lives of creaturely neighbors in expressions more hopeful than inarticulate groans."[4]

The iterative dialogue of Scipio's interruptions of Berganza's stories is thus reminiscent of a Platonic exchange, a learning in imitation, an innovation in repetition: *Do as I do*.[5] Notably, one of the persistent interlocutors in Book I of *The Republic* is another canid, the "wolfish" and "spirited"[6] Thrasymachus[7]: "While we had been talking Thrasymachus had often tried

DOI: 10.4324/9780429342103-4

to interrupt ... but when we paused and I asked my question, he was no longer able to keep quiet but gathered himself together and sprang on us like a wild beast, as if he wanted to tear us to pieces."[8]

This dialogue with Thrasymachus has also been acknowledged as one of the earliest existing references to the animalistic incapacitation for speech:[9] "If I had not seen him first I believe I should have been struck dumb."[10] The image of the wolf as tyrant returns in Book VIII in an illustration of societal failures and the risks associated with power and indeed waste, presented through sacrifice.[11] In explaining how "leadership is the root from which tyranny invariably springs," Socrates accounts, "That the man who tastes a single piece of human flesh, mixed in with the rest of the sacrifice, is fated to become a wolf."[12] In the third or second centuries BCE, the first production of *Asinaria*, by Titus Maccius Plautus, included the now monumental line, *Lupus est homo homini, non homo, quom qualis sit non novit*,[13] translated as "A man's a wolf, not a man, to a man who don't know what he's like."[14] Commonly abbreviated to the proverb, *Homo homini lupus*, the proverb relies upon a folkloric representation of the wolf as an unsocialised, "wild beast." This cultural stereotype of the wolf[15] frames and at times obscures the contribution from Thrasymachus, often characterised as the villain of this dialogue.[16]

In this way, the capacity for language is also characterised as a struggle for power, a battle for property, wanting to tear us to pieces. It is thus no coincidence that an emphasis on human exceptionalism, on the sanctified and inadmissible territory of the human, is usually defended by pointing to language and symbolic thought as confirming the insurmountable distinction of the human. Language is erected as the species barrier against the "floodgates" of animal capacities. Human language is, at the same time, a kind of irredeemable capital, in which inheres an emphasis on survivalism through speaking to power.

It is thus of particular note that interpretations of Thrasymachus cast him in ways very similar to the biological narratives of survival and competition, the same rhetoric underpinning the predatory drift in property relations and the supremacy in exceptionalist narratives, ranging from the history of art to dog training.[17] It is also of note that the scholarly interpretation of Thrasymachus has altered dramatically over time. Thrasymachus was at first regularly interpreted in the scholarship as an aggressive defender of the strong[18] in this loud battle of the fittest. But over the past few decades, his interventions have been reinterpreted as the very foundations of a modern political sociology.[19] Indeed, Thrashymachus offers an introduction to notions of a sociable community, and to the important and fundamental principles of cooperation and altruism, responsibility and reciprocity. To borrow from Donna Haraway, the tale of Thrasymachus is a canine tale that demands a *re-hearing*.[20] In *that dog*,[21] that *straw* dog,[22] the very ancient precursors of an ethological jurisprudence are perceptible.

Open the Floodgates

If language is the species barrier, then this may go some way to understanding the resistance to origin studies in language.[23] In an attachment to the presumed causality of a biological narrative of language, and an adherence to the doctrine of exceptionalism, language is regularly presented as extraordinary, "sudden," almost without origin, leading to an axiomatic presumption of uniqueness to be accepted simply as "Darwin's problem."[24] It would seem that in the interests of human exceptionalism, there has been a history of appeals to mind our language.

Frans de Waal describes efforts to preserve the sanctity of the human-nonhuman linguistic divide in the research communities of the nineteenth century, as within the Linguistic Society of Paris, "which in 1866 forbade the study of language origins."[25] But some attempts persist, and Frans de Waal notes the continued, yet unsuccessful, attempts within the research community to prohibit any language studies with animals,[26] describing such perspectives as "reminiscent of nineteenth-century anti-Darwinists for whom language was the one barrier between brute and man."[27] It seems that humans have had their hands full in resisting such origin stories, but the floodgates have opened nonetheless.

Research continues to challenge the linguistic species barrier quite convincingly.[28] However, it is doing so not through an arguably irrelevant approximation of human language[29] but through an ethological expansion of the field of aesthetic and symbolic enquiry.[30] Thus, the sanctity of the human-nonhuman linguistic divide remains undisturbed, not because it is impervious, but because it becomes irrelevant.

The Barriers Between

The shipwreck with which this part of the journey opened foregrounds the dividing line of sea and land; indeed, it runs aground on the partition of the shore, the line in the sand. This investigation thus begins at the barrier, at the middle, at the in-between. In many respects, to speak about authors and more-than-human intellectual property is to navigate seemingly bisecting barriers, from ship to shore. The logic of intellectual property mimics the Cartesian duality of matter and mind, which underpins the supposed objectivity of the intellectual property system. This barrier-making is such a habit that its effects have become invisible to most.[31] In copyright law and policy, there are the barriers established between producers and consumers, authors and readers, ideas and expressions, artists and craftspeople, and so on. And of course, the species barrier itself, which is variously deployed to *make sense* of human exceptionalism and anthropocentrism in law and more widely. But from the ruins of the shipwreck, it is soon revealed that habit is a game that two can play.

We are the art-making animal. Recalling this proclamatory barrier from earlier discussion, the species divide also has an aesthetic dimension as well as a linguistic one. But at the same time, navigation of the barrier is an opportunity for the renegotiation of these habits. *Are we the art-making animal?* An affirmative propelled by the increasingly specious attachment to linguistic divisions would continue to reserve the domain of culture as uniquely human, and as Brian Massumi contends, "If culture is assimilated to language, as it so often is, then it too falls into the exclusive province of the human."[32] But parodoxically, the barrier is also a contact point, a party wall, so to speak; and as such, the species barrier introduces the complexity and potential for a mutually constitutive and relational approach, as distinct from the absolute exceptionalism, which will be shown to unravel as the following chapters begin to pull at the threads.

Animal studies and animal welfare also cohere around particular barriers, such as the seemingly fundamental barrier of sentience. Pauline delahaye notes the problems that can arise from adhering to such barrier logic within the studies of animal semiotics, due to "the fact that they focus mainly on comparisons with humans in order to find what may be 'missing' from other species or to what extent they are 'like us,' instead of trying to find, for example, a descriptive semiotics of the various forms of expressions found and what could be concluded from those observations."[33]

The concept of sentience is an important phenomenon of this thinking, emerging more as a policy tool than an objective scientific or even legal account.[34] As a policy tool, it is a societal account, informing and informed by public sentiment. In view of this, Pru Hobson-West and Ashley Davies refine the concept as "societal sentience,"[35] with relevant consequences for welfare and other frameworks.[36] A particular concern is that the social dimension to the concept may lead both to enhanced protection for a particular species, such as dogs,[37] and to the exclusion of other nevertheless sentient species, such as those in the decapoda order,[38] based upon the framing of public perception and the "tyranny" of categorical thinking.[39] Thus, as a scientific or legal concept, sentience is itself a somewhat flexible concept, a social construct. In many respects, therefore, it is an arbitrary threshold obstacle to moral standing and protection rather than an explanatory concept.[40] And yet, this should not be surprising in that this kind of barrier thinking is an integral, structural component of the paradigmatic framework that is instrumental in law and is seemingly indoctrinated in wider discourse on nonhuman animals. Similarly, the concept of intelligence deployed in relation to artificial intelligence and for nonhuman animals is an example of the way in which that barrier becomes an aspirational, asymptotic threshold, defined and validated by the extent to which the nonhuman approximates the human, rather than a rigorous or exacting term in itself.

What is also especially relevant about the application of the term "intelligence" to artificial intelligence is that this emphasises computation over embodied communication. In other words, it summarises intelligence as *thinking* over and above the active and embodied sense of language, as it were, in nonhuman animals. On this tack, the campaign of intelligence in artificial intelligence adheres somewhat strategically to a Cartesian model of human exceptionalism. This dualism not only pervades artificial intelligence discourse but also, curiously and ironically, precludes artificial intelligence authorship. It turns out that artificial intelligence needs bodies.[41]

This duality of Cartesian thought is revisited and reconsidered later in this chapter, but it is notable that the discrepancy between the treatment of nonhuman animals on the one hand and machines on the other is propelled by the similar binary thinking that divides the so-called two cultures of art and science. Simone Weil laments the bifurcation of the arts and sciences, describing classical science as linear and "without beauty."[42] The paucity of classical science, for Weil, is to ignore desire, to ignore wants: "Classical science takes as its model for representing the world the relation between a desire and the conditions for its fulfilment, but it suppresses the first term of the relation."[43] But in order to sustain this habit, to mask this suppression, it is necessary to impose a fictive linearity, "[a]nd that is why classical science bases itself upon linear motion, which is the very image of the project ... In such a picture of the world, the good is altogether absent; it is absent to the point where one cannot even find a trace of its absence."[44] Thus, Weil comes to the conclusion that, "classical science is without beauty; it neither touches the heart nor contains any wisdom ... It was quite different among the Greeks, those fortunate men in whom love, art, and science, were three scarcely separate aspects of the same movement of the soul towards the good."[45]

The discourse surrounding artificial intelligence appears to observe a similar programme of suppressing wants, as though information progresses for its own sake, propelled by its own fictive linearity. Desires or wants have been vacated in pursuit of the conditions, at the risk of losing the creativity in the process, even to the point of its own collapse,[46] a topic to which later discussion will return.

Begin in the Middle

But barriers are also mechanisms through which we recognise and make sense of coincidences, build patterns, and through which we introduce a relationship of contact and shared interests.[47] Barriers, as such, become meeting points,[48] boundaries become contact points, through what Leibniz develops in the concept of situations in his theory of relations. In correspondence with the physicist Burchard de Volder, Leibniz provides further insight into the gregariousness of monads, the fundamental "true Atoms of nature,"[49] through this concept of situation, noting, "even if they are not extended, monads have a certain kind of situation in extension, that is, they have a certain ordered relation of coexistence to other things."[50] Thus, relationships acquire meaning through that coincidence at the barrier, so to speak, that embodiment and sharing of *situations*. Weil writes, "Two prisoners whose cells adjoin communicate with each other by knocking on the wall. The wall is the thing which separates them but it is also their means of communication."[51] Thus, it is crucial to critique the fallacy of the kind of organisation based upon difference in animal studies, in copyright and indeed more widely in intellectual property law, and of course in property law and theory. The concept of *res familiaris*,[52] introduced in *Owned*, is concerned with property not only in the relations between but also as invigorated through overlapping and mobile territories. There is thus an affiliative function as well as a form of identity as recognised through an ethological approach to the marking of territories.[53] As Joseph Singer maintains, "boundaries are not simply a mark of separation but of relationship."[54]

This resonates with the concept of betweenness or *metaxu*,[55] as developed in the philosophy of Weil, who argues, "Every separation is a link."[56] For Weil, this in-betweenness is the reservoir of compassion. And thus, this compassion inheres in the very basis of property law, albeit masked by the habitual suppression of wants.[57] In Weil's attention to the contradiction in Cartesianism, the concern is not to reinscribe or refine a traditional Cartesian dualism; rather, it is to identify and celebrate the contradictions in Descartes's thinking – indeed, *the metaxu*.[58] In a curious irony, it might be said that Weil's critique is quite the opposite.

The concept of *metaxu* is also concerned with the collaborative making of meaning and value, not through coercive consensus but through embracing contradiction and difference. The treatment of in-betweenness, *metaxu*, in Plato's *Symposium* is significant to Weil's thinking upon and embracing of contradiction: "Correct opinion has just this quality: it is in between [*metaxu*] understanding and ignorance."[59] Thus, "don't insist on the thing which isn't beautiful being ugly, or on the thing which isn't good being evil. And when you can bring yourself to agree that Love is neither good nor beautiful, it won't be necessary anymore for him to be ugly and evil. Rather he is something in between [*metaxu*] these two."[60] This contradiction or difference, rather than barrier, thus becomes a point of convergence; a *touching* encounter, as it were.[61] *Our hands are full*.

This theory of the in-between is at odds with the "great collective representations"[62] that are more commonly recognised in the history of sociological thought, and thus the other and various social generalisations and homogeneity, such as that of term, *the animal*, itself. For example, Derrida speaks of a domain of animality in Heidegger, the assumption being "that there is one thing, one domain, one homogeneous type of entity, which is called animality *in general*, for which any example would do the job,"[63] thus erasing the minutiae of difference that might be appreciated otherwise as distinctly ethological. This coalesces with traditions in duality that characterise the species barrier through distinctions around consciousness. And this is also a fundamental aspect of Leibniz's criticism of Cartesianism and its neglect of the "insensible perceptions" or "tiny perceptions" of the unconscious.[64] This minutiae is the fundamental sociality and ethological sensibility of Tarde's sociology of the infinitesimal.[65] The contrast between the worlds of Durkheim's collectives and Tarde's inter-psychology has been considered previously in *Owned*,[66] but notably here too the critical regard is to be found in the in-between, and, as Weil describes, the "minute perceptions"[67] in wanting. Weil is concerned here with the unconscious in Leibniz's philosophy of mind, explaining that "a conscious perception is made up of a number of unconscious perceptions. This is the theory of minute perceptions."[68] Leibniz's philosophy of mind, considered again later in this chapter, is certainly crucial to Weil's revision of Cartesian principles and to affording nonhuman animal theory of mind. As Weil affirms, "If thought does not rule feelings, feelings, certainly, rule thoughts."[69]

This thinking in-between is thus intrinsic to Tarde's laws of imitation and the "'mediatedness' of imitative behavior patterns."[70] From Leibniz's perceptions of perceptions, to Tarde's imitations of imitations, the fundamental social unit is elementary, as it were; that is, relationality is essential and vital. Leibniz's concept of the monad, the fundamental and unitary substance of life, is the basis of his theory of monadology.[71] Leibniz begins *The Monadology*: "The Monad, of which we will speak here, is nothing else than a simple substance, which goes to make up composites; by simple, we mean without parts."[72] This aggregative or assembling quality of monads resonates throughout Tarde's own monadology of the social.[73] And towards an ethological approach, as a methodology this emphasises the interactions between fundamental perceptions or attention, and thus the intermediaries or *wants* that bind them through a sociable and familiar production. Thus, for Leibniz, and indeed for Tarde's ethics in comparative methodologies, perception is necessarily plural through this aggregative monadology. This contends with Cartesianism in significant ways for the nonhuman, as considered later in this chapter. At this stage, it is important to recognise the way in which these minute perceptions both acknowledge and facilitate the play in the system.

Play Barriers

Barriers are also the structure of humour, a game at which two can play. This irony of play is critical to the paradox of authorship, a make-believe of making real, copies of copies, and yet palimpsestic of sources.[74] The reference to palimpsest is in gesture to the layering of sources in the production and communion of knowledge, and the necessarily persistent trace of those sources. Palimpsest is also both a noun (the parchment or writing surface on which the original text is erased and overwritten by one or more others) and an adjective (used to describe the surface itself).[75] But it is also a verb, meaning "to write again ... after the original writing has been effaced."[76] It is thus both a condition of expression, and expression itself. Often involving a process of scraping the original material, this ushers in a fascinating reverberation with contemporary references to the scraping of data in machine learning, a relation to which the discussion will return in more detail in later chapters.[77]

Barriers are thus the order of play, the anchors for beliefs, and thus the stuff of invention and transformation. It is perhaps no coincidence that the expression "off the wall," suggesting inventive thinking and irreverence, a dyadic communication through contention, comes from sport.[78] Play is fundamentally material to creative transformation, learning is a curious form of parody, and authors are tricksters and pretenders. Barriers are indeed the stuff of authorship, as well as the infrastructure for the conservation of the author-construct. But this is a duality and contradiction, following Weil, that must be embraced to full effect. Therefore, from the outset, it is necessary to examine how we make sense through barriers, and what might be understood as copyright's framing problem, not only of the author construct, but also of other capacities, including nonhuman capacities, interests, and personhood.

This is perhaps the play of irony in the barrier itself – that is, its reversibility. This middling curiosity enjoys a diverse and radical disregard for boundaries. From Plato, through the fragments of the Romantics,[79] the interdisciplinarity of scholarship, of creative industries,[80] through to the fundamental structuring of the law itself, the discussion will continue to return to the middle throughout.

Reading Is a Frame of Mind

This duality thus manages and constrains the discourse on authority and exceptionalism in humans and authors, maintaining the bounded deference of nonhuman animals, as well as facilitating the many and varied operative distinctions erected between humans and artificial intelligence – distinctions which are also many and varied in their fitness, as will become more clear. But as Weil counsels, "The world is the closed door. It is a barrier. And at the same time it is the way through."[81] The barrier is hinged.

It is becoming apparent that to address authorship is thus to address how the language barrier is itself presented within the construction of copyright's frame, and therefore any enquiry into authorship may be informed by the scientific, social, and moral status of conceptual thought in nonhumans in order to challenge that barrier logic. For want of a better perspective, the system of copyright consolidates the language barrier for nonhuman animal creators insofar as it instructs what we recognise as creative, including outside the copyright system itself through its wider normative impact.[82] The cognitive bias or framing effect[83] of the law thus influences our beliefs[84] and at the same time influences creative decisions. In other words, copyright influences how we play – that is, how we evaluate the risk in creativity, and how we gamble with authorship.

Weil describes this framing in the context of her concept of "reading" (*lecture*), a relevant concept throughout the following chapters. Weil understands "reading" as a comprehensively and diversely sensory experience of objects and between objects that is conditioned by the circumstances, situation, and perspective within which the reader is constrained.[85] Everything thus becomes subject to reading.[86] How does this framing effect also influence the interpretation of the law itself, and of the kinds of agents that might be recognised – whether humans, other animals, or machines? In other words, how does copyright seemingly cooperate with the rhetoric of artistic genius, of the sovereign author, and personal value? Fundamentally, to ask what Naruto wants is begging the question, so to speak. It is to pre-empt the lack that is attributed to the nonhuman more broadly; notably, this lack is not perceived as a desire or an insight, but as a pre-existing loss. In the ledger of copyright, there is something very crucial about maintaining this bifurcation of losses and gains, particularly inasmuch as it contributes to the oppositional logic and intelligibility of the law's anthropocentrism. The predatory drift of copyright, in its articulation within a larger commercial environment for creativity, is thus perceptible in the law as framed through these losses and gains. As such, the romantic notions of authorship are revealed as not only relics of the predatory drift of capital, but also complicit in sustaining it.[87]

At the same time, this framing effect of the authorship concept presents how we look at nonhuman animal creativity and how we co-opt intentionality and authorship in the service of machines and the adoption of technology. Framing thus has a computational dimension that is manifest in artificial intelligence; indeed, Daniel Dennett attributes the identification of the so-called frame problem to artificial intelligence developments,[88] although he does go on to recognise it in Kant as "Kant's Problem."[89] Dennett explains, "The frame problem is an abstract *epistemological* problem that was in effect discovered by AI thought-experimentation. When a cognitive creature, an entity with many beliefs about the world, performs an act, the world changes and many of the creature's beliefs must be revised or updated."[90]

As will be seen, the machine's dilemma in the face of considerable information belies also the distinction between nonhuman animals and machines. The distinction may be understood as one between consensus, to oversimplify somewhat the work of artificial intelligence, and dissensus, with respect to the productions of nonhuman animals; or, to put this another way, the incongruity, disruption, and innovation of the deception and play of nonhuman animals.

Thus, how we play will turn out to be fundamental in answering the complex questions of more-than-human intellectual property and personhood. But first, to break some habits.

Breaking Habits

Bachelard's theory of epistemological obstacles,[91] and of the epistemological break or rupture through unthinking the unconscious obstacles or habits of perception, is instructive here. Such habit, as Bachelard explains, is what "hampers contemporary scientific thought," and thus, "[t]he only thing to be done then is to break with habits."[92] Part of this process is to unsettle the conventions and assumptions presented as irrefutable and common sense, to ensure a creative and productive energy of unrest: "We must also disrupt the habits of objective knowledge and make reason *uneasy*."[93] This describes the process through which an ethological jurisprudence revises or updates, as it were, beliefs in relation to nonhuman authorship and property, the habits that continue to constrain perspectives on the nonhuman and on property. This rupture or break of the epistemological obstacle is the opportunity for refraction and revision of both nonhuman animal agency and the very nature of intellectual property.

Habits are hard to break, such as the fascination with the so-called dichotomy of idea and expression in copyright, enshrined within the institution of the law.[94] Similarly, the attachment to the intelligence of artificial intelligence is proving equally tenacious. In one of the most sustained considerations of these issues, Murray Shanahan explains the framing problem as potentially resolved by acknowledging artificial intelligence as engineering, as distinct from a system of symbolic thought and representation, and suggests that "the representational approach to designing an artefact that exhibits intelligent behaviour may be the wrong one."[95] Notably in the present context, Shanahan posits, "Perhaps intelligence simply shouldn't be thought of in terms of representation."[96] A proposition to which the discussion will return,[97] but for now it seems that to overcome the frame problem in artificial intelligence is to act inconsistently with the notion of artificial intelligence as sentient or conscious,[98] whatever that might mean.[99] But this is one habit that may prove difficult to break.

It seems that in observing the shipwreck from the boundary of the shore, the perspective is necessarily framed by one's beliefs and organised by those presumptions. Thus, theory of mind remains *in theory*, as it were. As Mary Midgley counsels, we can never share fully the experience of another, whether human, animal, or machine, arguing that, "it is not clear that any such comparison between unobservable differences makes any sense at all."[100] Indeed, if it makes any sense at all, then perhaps it is in order to make sense of the contrivance of the species barrier and the language of exclusion, for "[t]he barrier does not fall between us and the dog. It falls between you and me."[101]

It is time to have a word.

The Language Barrier

Language is a critical area not only for animal studies and discussions around admission to moral status, but also for intellectual property and perhaps, but not necessarily, for copyright in particular. The shared emphasis on language makes the application of intellectual property to animal studies compelling, and vice versa. This wordy exceptionalism is in evidence across a range of disciplines. The assumed distinction and distinctiveness of human language has beset diverse perspectives upon animal agency for centuries and continues to preoccupy research enquiries, including those in philosophy, sociology, politics, the animal sciences, and animal studies.

Richard Serjeantson identifies this preoccupation in some of the earliest studies. Serjeantson notes that "[l]anguage was a subject of absorbing interest to numerous early modern philosophers," and underpinning this interest is an exceptionalist enterprise, where "behind almost all of these investigations lay one of the most profound suppositions in early modern anthropology: the uniqueness of the human capacity for language, and the brutishness of the brute beasts."[102] Indeed, to suggest otherwise in relation to animal capacities was to invite considerable contempt and ridicule: "Harsh judgments were passed on those who thought that animals might be able to speak. Lawyers held that belief in animal language was sufficient evidence of idiocy."[103] These early investigations into nonhuman animal language followed a familiar logical imperative that continues in contemporary discourse, in that "they all had in common the aim of bringing into question the binary divisions of their philosophical inheritance that separated humans from animals: rationality *vs.* irrationality, convention *vs.* nature, abstract thought *vs.* involuntary passion, and speech *vs.* dumbness."[104] Whether or not nonhuman animals converse with each other thus remains immaterial to the rigidity of the divide, and to the mission to preserve the distinction of human language.

As such, language, as distinct from *mere* acts of communication, continues to be proffered as evidence of human uniqueness, introducing a particular barrier (such as that between speech and language[105]). This barrier is, at its base, somewhat arbitrary, but it is a presumptuous perspective that is necessary if the definition of the exception is always already the human, and for *man* to remain the measure of all things: "Most authors raised the question of animal language to address linguistic and semantic questions about human speech: animals provided a convenient (and largely hypothetical) foil against which to define this attribute."[106] The language barrier is about looking for difference, rather than recognising capacities. It is about saying and naming difference, and it is about relegating the performance of difference. *Do as I say.*

At the same time, an emphasis on language is consistent with the law's emphasis on intentionality and wants.[107] Language is central to the concerns of copyright and to animal studies, reiterating the important connections between an examination of authorship and an exploration of nonhuman animal expression and personhood. Significantly, intentionality is also the exceptional grammar, so to speak, of rights. It is in this context that the intentional stance attributed to artificial intelligence may be appreciated for its facilitation of trust and adoption of technology. This approach was somewhat spectacular, in a manner of saying, in Ai-Da's giving of oral evidence to the House of Lords Committee,[108] where the machine is presented with voice, even though this has nothing to do with the creative or commercial products or outputs of the machine. The performativity of this event is a clear distraction and deflection from the utterances that are actually at stake here. Intentionality, more than anything, approximates artificial intelligence to the human.

In clear contrast, the nonhuman animal is silenced by the erection of language as an impassable and immutable divide. The nonhuman animal is always on the verge of speech, as it were, but never to pass. However, thinking metaxologically, it is in the necessarily dialectical nature of intentionality and the movement of desire that there is space for play, and capacities for nonhuman expression begin to emerge. And notably, those capacities arise precisely through the very barriers that arguably defend against them. *Do as I do*.

To do captures the philosophy of an embodied expression, an action in creativity, a conscious and evaluative imitative process – an *attentive imitation*. This simple refrain of showing and learning captures the importance of affiliative imitation and capacity-building. At the same time, there is a clear movement in *as I do* rather than an emphasis on the coerced wordiness of *as I say*. Rather than language speaking to power, wants and actions *speak* to power. It is thus through these wants, these actions, that it is possible to think, in every sense.

Copyright Actions

Copyright is all about language – technically, legally, and normatively. And it is this emphasis on language, and the writerly script in particular,[109] that makes it impossible to resist in the investigation of nonhuman capacities and personhood. Copyright is concerned with both literal language as well as the cultural and institutional endorsement of what kinds of symbolic language count as creative and of aesthetic value. By the same token, copyright thus frames the conventions of a work, and so at the same time the expressions of others that present logical difficulties, such as performance, sound, touch, smell, and taste.[110]

Copyright is premised upon a fundamentally writerly model, which has persisted through a visual hegemony in the law as manifest in the recognised and protectable subject matter itself.[111] Copyright thus continues to endorse a writerly model, albeit somewhat indirectly. Having proceeded to examine this from an ethological perspective in other research, even where copyright has taken account of sound,[112] smell,[113] touch,[114] taste,[115] and movement[116] (including performance, where the performer's creativity is in deference to the copyright work[117]), and so on, these enquiries show that copyright has struggled to negotiate what are arguably more relational and enduring forms of expression. As such, the law has to some extent contrived to arrest a *visual* account of such creative work through technologies of recording and thus remaking that work in the *writerly* realm. And with this, the emphasis on the nature of "art" is premised upon the singular author-construct, the *auteur*. This singularity at the same time rationalises the visual masterwork – the work of art in every sense of the term. Even the visual of the visual arts poses problems for the law until it is translated into the writerly visual hegemony of copyright. And to return to the stakes in Naruto, the history of photography and the law is exemplary in expounding the distinction between the visual and the writerly in the copyright system. The counterpoint of the language problem is a form of sensory deprivation.

Recognising this in copyright puts authorship and copyright in a remarkable and curiously unexplored relationship between nonhuman animal authors and nonauthor human creators, all through the central point of language as an organising barrier. The issues, and indeed the interests, are shared. In this management of language, the law's perspective on authorship is thus relevant and pertinent to understanding and critiquing the emphasis on language in perceptions of moral status and admission to the moral sphere. The word between us is not only the language barrier between humans and other animals but also the language barriers and legal fictions in copyright itself.[118] An ethological approach to language and to copyright can potentially expand the work in copyright. Can copyright recognise nonhuman animal languages, nonhuman animal expressions? Can nonhuman animals expand the language of copyright and authorship, including communal and transient forms of creativity?

This duality is thus the architecture of matter and mind that underpins two important barriers – the barrier of meaning in artificial intelligence[119] and the species barrier in language and reasoning – both of which are sustained by the belief in a *want* for understanding on the part of nonhuman animals and machines. This lack is largely attributed to a perceived lack of symbolic language. But in asking what Naruto wants, Berganza's floodgates are opened. If animals have wants, and thus beliefs, then language extends beyond the purported objectivity of the writerly domain.

To Think ... Out Loud

The policy concept of sentience acts both as a threshold and a resilient barrier in that a legacy of Cartesian duality continues to inform the thinking, in every respect of that term, in the concept of sentience.[120] Much has been anchored to the canonical *ego cogito ergo sum*:[121] in French, *je pense, donc je suis*;[122] in English, commonly translated as *I think, therefore I am*, but more accurately as, *I am thinking, therefore [ergo] I exist*.[123] But this brief phrase has subsequently become an emblematic shortcut to a critique of Descartes's philosophy of mind as "elevating the mental over the bodily," and with that, "Descartes has often been assimilated to a sense-data epistemology."[124]

This interpretation has been revised or qualified in more recent scholarship, but much earlier, Weil challenged the conventional readings of Descartes in her essay, *Science and Perception in Descartes*, written between 1929 and 1930.[125] In this early essay, Weil engages with Descartes's methodology of doubt, a kind of negation that becomes especially relevant when considering the nature of evidence in later discussions, particularly concerning her observations with respect to science, observations that resonate with the challenges for cognitive ethology and animal consciousness: "In short, as much as possible, scientists exclude everything having to do with intuition: they no longer admit anything into science except the most abstract form of reasoning."[126] Weil seeks, "[w]ithout rebelling against this authority," to examine it and describe some "astonishing contradictions."[127] Weil thus works through Descartes's strategic doubt in order to express the power, or indeed capacity, to think. In this way, Weil explains, "things that I think that make a *show* of existing."[128] This performance of the mind is critical, even playful, and it is especially important to explaining authorship in minds other than human. In this careful revision of Descartes's cogito, Weil challenges the coherence of thinking and opens the door for arriving at the self, not through the representation of thoughts but through the performance of belief.[129]

What does Simone Weil want? Just as for Naruto, the answer is unthinkable: "I do not think what I want. And the things that I think delude me by their own power. So what do they borrow from me? Belief."[130] In a later essay, Weil continues this productivity through doubt: "It is impossible to study the mind in a direct way because its characteristics are negative ones ... The study of mind can only proceed by looking beyond the thoughts that we express for signs of doubt, perfection, order (necessity)."[131] Doubt thus makes it possible to arrive at the self through the negative, as it were, for doubt is the trace of that capacity: "The world and my mind are so thoroughly intermingled that, if I think that I conceive one of the two separately, I attribute to it what belongs to the other."[132] Rather than reconciling these contradictions, "in this flash of thought several things whose nature I did not previously know are revealed to me: doubt, thought, power, existence, and knowledge itself."[133]

It is through this approach that Weil recasts not Descartes, as such, but the canonisation of a particular perspective upon Descartes's methodology: "And through this power of thinking – which so far is revealed to me only by the power of doubting – I know that I am. I have power, therefore I am [*Je puis, donc je suis*]."[134] It might be said that this power, this capacity, anticipates the capacity of vulnerability, of suffering, and indeed of play: "To know is to know what I can do; and I know to the degree that I substitute 'to act' and 'to be acted upon' for 'to enjoy,' 'to suffer,' 'to feel,' and 'to imagine.' In this way I transform illusion into certainty and chance into necessity."[135] In making this argument, Weil is cautious to guard against a mere opposition between *to act* and *to be acted upon*,[136] advocating and acknowledging "combined repulsion and acceptance, which seem to constitute the imagination."[137] It is thus the betweenness of relations that might be known and even measured.[138]

In this relationship between the body and thinking, Weil describes a kind of extended cognition, an active and enactive relationship between the body and its environment: "[M]y will leaves its living imprint in the world. But that is not enough; it is necessary to find intermediaries that connect the straight-line motion that I alone can produce to this complex change that I want to be conveyed to my senses."[139] By Weil's account, it is the imagination that presents such a productive obstacle: "[T]his tie, this knot between the world and me, this point of intersection between the simple movement that I have at my command and the infinitely complex movement that represents the world for my understanding."[140] As will be explored throughout the following chapters, this embodied knowing is both directed by and directed upon work and the industry of play.

Weil's extended and distributed cognition includes not only the hand, and not only all parts of the body, but also the tools that extend the body: "This is what perception consists of, as can be seen by the famous example of the blind man's stick. The blind man does not feel the different pressures of the stick on his hand; he touches things directly with his stick, as if it were sensible and formed part of his body."[141] Just as nonhuman animals may touch with sound and see through touch,[142] or see things with electricity,[143] or count with smell,[144] or see by listening,[145] or indeed see themselves through smell,[146] and just as the blind man "uses his stick as a hand and touches, not perceptible matter, but the obstacle," so too "for each of us the blind man's stick is simply his own body."[147] Capabilities in categorising, generalising, and retaining that information may suggest a kind of representative or conceptual thinking that is not often considered when focusing upon logocentric passages of reasoning. Smell is just one example in the world of expression. Surely categories of smells are a form of symbolic language for nonhuman animals? For instance, dogs are able to categorise, recollect, and generalise information obtained from smells, which is significant in showing a form of category-based induction, and the ability to infer information or reasoning in other contexts.[148] By its very nature, so to speak, an ethological insight through nonhuman animal olfactory representations assists in considering categorical reasoning around smells for humans,[149] and the way in which this is not only overlooked but also actively disregarded in the visual tyranny of copyright expression.

This physicality of symbolic thinking is critical not only to understanding the nonhuman animals' expressive worlds and individual *Umwelt*,[150] but also in exploring the dimensions of the work in copyright through conceptual art and other challenges to the nature of the *expression* for the purposes of the law. Weil's embodied cognition approaches the human body "like a pincer for the mind to grasp and handle the world,"[151] the human body as hand, as *metaxu*, breaking habits and remaking worlds. For Weil, one of the most important ways of "knowing the world" is through work.[152] And that work is aligned with joy,[153] which might ultimately suggest the industry of play. Indeed, such tools of one's trade may include other bodies,[154] other species,[155] all towards the very sociability of cognitive evolution itself.[156] These are relations that will remain significant throughout the present discussion as it traverses the more-than-human environment for authorship. While Weil refers only to the human body, this analysis of sensori-motor cognition and experience will become critical to the discussion ahead and to the appreciation of authorship that is more than human.

Gaston Bachelard offers a further iteration upon the doubt that enlivens this account when he states, "*I think that I think, therefore I am.*"[157] This doubting performance introduces a process of existence, the intermediary of change rather than an iconography of thought, as well as a curious prolongation of play in the experience of knowledge.[158] Such is the productivity of this prolongation that "[i]f, continuing a little further, we reach the *I think that I think that I think*, which will be denoted by (cogito), then separate consecutive existences will appear in all their formalizing power."[159] In this way, "[w]hat we are doing here is not in fact thinking ourselves thinking *something*, but rather thinking ourselves as *someone* who is thinking."[160] In other words, this is a kind of symbolic thought, a theory of mind, a capacity which some still reserve for the human species, contrary to the increasing scientific evidence otherwise. Indeed, a very similar formulation for nonhuman animals, in this example chimpanzees, comes from the scientific literature itself: "If we define thinking as going beyond the information given in perception to make inferences, we may conclude that not only is thinking not the exclusive province of human beings, but thinking about thinking is not either."[161]

Rather than the self-assured *I* of the conventional account of the cogito, Bachelard's *I* is a work in progress, glances of which become possible through a continuous and intuitive aesthetic of movement. Obstacles to knowing belief and desire are not, according to Bachelard, reasons to adopt "that flat refusal – philosophical and dogmatic as it very much is – which brings to an abrupt halt all movements of curiosity that would go to the interior of things."[162] Rather, it is to look at the aesthetic of performance of consciousness, not labour its explanation: "How can we not see that nature has depth? How indeed can we miss the dialectic of that ambiguous coquetry in so many living organisms, *revealing* and *concealing* in such a way that the organism lives according to a rhythm of disguise and display?"[163] To appreciate the creating selves in such *ambiguous coquetry*, Bachelard addresses scientific attention not to the materiality of representation but to the "*aesthetic of the intellect.*"[164] And, as will be pursued in the following chapters, in that *ambiguous coquetry*, consciousness might be said to be apperceived through an aesthetic of the intellect on show in play, a *rhythm of disguise and display* that is certainly creative and perhaps also richly symbolic.

Like Weil, Bachelard also appeals to the metaphor of the hand, but again not necessarily in the service of an anthropocentric bias. Bachelard advocates a *manual* experience in the grasping of knowledge, lauding the hand's capacity to mediate "opposing excesses" in order that it "recognizes instinctively the *perfect earth.*"[165] This is a bodily and sensori-motor apprehension of the *perfect earth*, and arguably anticipates the diversity with which that might be grasped, in a manner of speaking. Nevertheless, it is in this context that Bachelard proffers the embodied "*cogito* of kneading," while acknowledging Maine de Biran's doctrine of effort: "For Maine de Biran, consciousness of activity is as immediate as consciousness of thought."[166] There is also an industry at play, so to speak, in Bachelard's account, identifying "the proof of one's existence in the effort of discovery itself."[167] This coincides in important ways with Weil's approach to knowledge, in that it is also suggesting the kind of capacity expressed in her reading of the cogito. The proof of interior life is thus in the making, as it were, and "the most beautiful experiences must be found in successful exertion."[168] This phenomenological account of interior life is promising in appreciating the aesthetic of an authorship beyond the human, and a firm hold beyond the human hand. *Making a living.*

Gabriel Tarde's revision of the cogito through the concept of *having* is central to an ethological jurisprudence and to animating the relationality of an ethological authorship.[169] Before both Weil and Bachelard, Tarde notes, "All philosophy hitherto has been based on the verb *Be*, the definition of which was the philosopher's stone, which all sought to discover," and argues instead, "We may affirm that, if it had been based on the verb *Have*, many sterile debates and fruitless intellectual exertions would have been avoided."[170] Tarde overturns the conventional reckoning of the cogito, rejecting the emphasis on being and the supposition of a coherent and complete self: "From this principle, *I am*, all the subtlety in the world has not made it possible to deduce any existence other than my own: hence the negation of external reality. If, however, the postulate *I have* is posited as the fundamental fact, both that which *has* and that which *is had* are given inseparably at once."[171]

To have and be had "inseparable at once" embraces the contradiction that is central to knowing for Weil: "It is through this combined repulsion and acceptance, which seem to me to constitute the imagination, that my thoughts bind me."[172] As in Tarde's reciprocal possession, Weil's capacity for knowledge, the grasp, the having of knowing, is similarly through an intermediary of the power of having thoughts: "[H]owever much the other existence has power over me through the intermediary of my thoughts, so much, through the same intermediary, do I have power over it ... To know is to read this double meaning in any thought."[173] This reciprocal regard is, however, achieved not through coercion or force in service of externalised and mutual interests, but rather through an evaluative and *attentive* imitation motivated by shared interests.

Tarde's sociology of imitation, and its sense of originality or innovation through that sociality, draws considerably upon Leibniz's monadology[174] and his theory of the (closed) monad as the fundamental and imperfectly perfect substance of sociality, relationality, and capacity. A fundamental distinction in Leibniz's philosophy that departs from his Cartesian contemporaries is his recognition in nonhuman animals of not only sensation but also forms of reasoning and consciousness. Leibniz approaches mind not through consciousness but through perception – that is, through attention. The movement from perception to perception is the action of appetition or wants, thus affording a particular prosociality to a certain attention: "The passing condition which involves and represents a multiplicity in the unity, or in the simple substance, is nothing else than what is called Perception. This should be carefully distinguished from Apperception or Consciousness."[175] This distinction between perception and consciousness is fundamental to seeing through the barrier, as it were, and recognising nonhuman animal mentality. According to Leibniz, it is "[i]n this matter the Cartesians have fallen into a serious error, in that they treat as non-existent those perceptions of which we are not conscious. It is this also which has led them to believe that spirits alone are Monads and that there are no souls of animals."[176] Indeed, perception is a phenomenal capacity for attention, an active having regard, of which sensation is a particular kind of perception, of attention and memory.[177] And this attention is itself constituted by appetition – by *wants*: "The action of the internal principle which brings about the change or the passing from one perception to another may be called Appetition."[178] And these wants are at the same time affiliative, shared interests – the basis of social learning and the consciousness that Leibniz accords nonhuman animals. Nonhuman animals think, according to Leibniz, but they may not think that they think.[179]

This important distinction in Leibniz's accounting for the unconscious mind also animates Weil's own philosophy of attention, in which she notes the "minute perceptions"[180] of Leibniz's movement of mind and the habits of a certain kind of attention. "Attention is often unconscious," Weil explains, and "[c]omplete attention is like unconsciousness."[181] In the discussions to follow in the present work, these principles of Leibniz's philosophy of mind, as found in this fundamental relationship between attention, wants, and imitation, will be shown to be central to an ethological jurisprudence of authorship and to the challenge against anthropocentrism in the law more generally. They resonate with Tarde's social theories of possession and having, Weil's philosophy of attention, the continuity of information in Bachelard's thought, and the animation of mind in contemporary accounts of embodied cognition. *The best of all worlds.*[182]

Following Leibniz, but developing a theory of the open monad, Tarde addresses mentality and ingenuity through the repetition of desires or wants, thus recasting the canonical Cartesian principle of existence through the concept of having: "The concrete and substantial concept which one discovers in oneself is, therefore, that of having. instead of the famous *cogito ergo sum*, I would prefer to say: *I desire, I believe, therefore I have.*"[183] In this way, Tarde's account of the cogito through *having* rather than *being* introduces an important relational dimension to authorship and indeed to ownership. Having is the *metaxu* – that is, the communicative link or relation that may be found in the intermediary of possession, having as both contact point and intimate distance. Tarde describes being as "that hollow abstraction," which can be arrived at only through the activity and work of property: "Being ... is never conceived except as the *property* of something, of some other being, which is itself composed of *properties*, and so on to infinity. At root, the whole content of the concept of being is exhausted by the concept of having. But the converse is not true: being is not the whole content of the idea of property."[184] Bruno Latour's succinct summary of Tarde's concept of possession is incisive: "Here goes Hamlet, as well as Descartes with his *cogito* ... Nothing is more sterile than identity philosophy – not to mention identity politics – but possession philosophy – and perhaps possession politics? – creates solidarity and attachments that cannot be matched."[185] Suddenly the seemingly comic renditions of *I copy, therefore I am*[186] and *I own, therefore I am*,[187] become more meaningful. The waggish play of the irony of that paradox. Or is it the paradox of irony?

The activity and work of possession thus begin to make much more sense, in every sense, in approaching questions of not only nonhuman authorship but also sentience and consciousness in a critical and practical context. This understanding of possession ushers in both a wider and a more technical notion of entitlement such that having and the relations therein grant meaning to the language of rights not as fixed points but as *metaxu*, a calculated personhood: "A point is nothing ... But if that point is the point of intersection of two straight lines it is much."[188] But through interaction, as Tarde explains, "every point is a centre ... everything is both an end and a means at once."[189] In other words, a right is itself articulated through a relation, always already in interaction, rather than preserved through absolute dominion and alienation. This certain personhood, as it were, affords both interaction and enaction with a multispecies environment, rather than the mythical exceptionalism and anthropocentrism that attends a conventional discourse of rights. Historically coincident with Tarde's inter-psychology, Wesley

Newcomb Hohfeld's jurisprudence appeals to this relationality, reconciling the individual entitlement with a community of relations.[190] Hohfeld cites the 1877 decision of *Atchison v Baty*[191] in which the court states, "The term *right* in civil society is defined to mean that which a man is entitled *to have*, or *to do*, or *to receive* from others within the limits prescribed by law."[192] A right is thus meaningful through relations and is in effect enacted through those relations, always already *in personam*.

This language of entitlement also harnesses principles of welfare entitlement and welfare property, without necessitating corresponding duties in the language of rights in the material sense. The intentionality of the rights-holder thus becomes immaterial, in every sense, to the potential for rights and indeed for personhood, with clear importance for nonhuman animals[193] as well as for readers and consumers of intellectual property.[194] But as Bachelard counsels, "Before thinking, one must study."[195] And so to the grammar of consciousness the discussion now turns.

Declining Nouns and Conjugating Verbs

Scientific developments aside, there is a persistent attachment to the presentation of symbolic thought as the distinction of exceptionalism, and the insistence that such capacity is the unique preserve of the human species. With this, there is a disconcerting thingness that relegates the nonhuman animal other to a kind of artefactual existence; but at the same time, this discursive framing continues to populate the language of animal studies as well, albeit through a critical perspective upon this construction as perceived to operate in property. Thus, the objecthood of the nonhuman animal and the anthropocentrism of the discourse are affirmed paradoxically and unwittingly. The erasure of relations in property in order to serve the mantra of personhood is not only inaccurate with respect to property jurisprudence but also incapacitates, as it were, the very potential for personhood as may be developed through existing legal subjecthood, such as welfare protection.[196] The antithetical construction of property objects and property subjects also reaffirms the auteurism that overshadows creative activity as viewed through copyright, even in the process of seemingly opening up the nature of the creative work itself. While the copyright work may seem to be a vast field of expression, in reality the emphasis remains somewhat scripted.

The question of language and symbolic thought in artificial intelligence remains an unanswered controversy; or, at least, answers to date have been criticised as popular overestimations: "*Have neural language models successfully acquired commonsense or are we overestimating the true capabilities of machine commonsense?*"[197] In other words, the social competence of machines is still lacking. A study into pronoun resolution suggests that what is otherwise "trivial" for humans is "hard for machines that merely rely on statistical patterns without true capabilities of commonsense reasoning,"[198] and cautions against "the potential risk of overestimating the performance of state-of-the-art methods on the existing commonsense benchmarks."[199]

However, rather than insisting on symbolic thought, embodied communication and the ways in which nonhuman animals act upon the world are arguably more meaningful. Notably, in humans, early language acquisition is, in fact, more likely to be verbs, indicating the relevance of acting upon one's world rather than naming it. In this way, the infant is able to signal intentionality, not simply by pointing at objects but by expressing intent and ambition with respect to their environment.[200] Language is deployed *not* in order to identify a unilateral relationship to the object, as named, but rather to recognise the child's *actions* upon the world.

It is in this context that the philosophy of Wallace Matson becomes especially interesting. In 1976, Matson investigated machine sentience through what he calls "sentience-presupposing" verbs, which he organises into two classes: "social, as they concern transactions between persons" and those verbs which "signify affective attitudes."[201] Matson approaches the question of consciousness as "superfluous as an explanation of the observed behavior … because consciousness as such never *does* anything."[202] Thus, the *ambiguous coquetry* of *disguise and display* poses a particular challenge for a feeble machine: "'Pretend' offers special problems."[203] As later discussion considers,[204] the capacity to lie and, in particular, to deceive, imputes not only an intentionality but also a programming challenge for artificial intelligence. And lying is the very stuff of authorship.

Having, wanting, playing. I think I am a verb.

I Think I Am a Verb

Towards the very end of his life, when Ulysses S Grant[205] had almost lost his voice completely to throat cancer, it is claimed that one of the last things he wrote was a brief note, now held in the Grant Papers at the Library of Congress.[206] The note is included in the introduction to Thomas Sebeok's work, *I Think I Am a Verb*,[207] which also takes its title from Grant's legendary fragment: "The fact is I think I am a verb instead of a personal pronoun."[208] To recall Bachelard, or indeed forecast Bachelard, Grant's utterance appears not to be thinking about himself (a personal pronoun) thinking something, but thinking about himself "as *someone* who is thinking."[209] The eighteenth-century grammarian, James Harris, provides an earlier and somewhat remarkable anticipation of this apparent anti-Cartesianism. Harris states, "All Verbs, that are strictly so called denote Energies. Now as all *Energies* are *Attributes*, they have reference of course to certain *energizing Substances*."[210] It might be said then that the substance of Cartesianism, as Weil subsequently argues, is to be found or readymade in the imprint of the self on the world, the action and work on one's environment. In other words, *the power of doubt*; the negative space of positive doubt. Or as Harris explains, "Thus it is impossible there should be such Energies as, *To love, to fly, to wound*, &c. if there were not such beings as *Men, Birds, Swords*, &c. Farther, every Energy doth not only require an Energizer, but is necessarily conversant about some *Subject*."[211] A doubtful existence.[212]

The second part of Grant's note turns that *someone* over as a sign: "A verb is anything that signifies to be; to do; or to suffer. I signify all three."[213] Sebeok remarks upon the note's "orphic semiotic understanding, compressed with stunning clarity and surety,"[214] whereby "Grant's pronominal personal awareness effectively diminishes his identity, by a flash of self-understanding, into a sort of vanishing artifact. His ego is then recreated in action, or interaction, through a dialectical resolution of a dramatized confrontation with an *alter* (in this instance, Dr Douglas)."[215] As Sebeok explains, "The cornerstone of this miniature mosaic is the basic human existential 'to be,' that we have come to associate chiefly with Hamlet's questioning as well as with Descartes' cogitative certitude of 'therefore I exist.'"[216] But as Tarde tells us, these "sterile debates and fruitless intellectual exertions" are best avoided.[217] Indeed, Grant recounts his selfhood through *to do* as well as, and most importantly, *to suffer*. It is through this capacity, this power, that the path to selfhood is paved. Selfhood is a process, "an unlimited semiosis, resonating into the unfathomable future."[218]

To verbalise existence, so to speak, brings capacity and power. Rather than the violence of naming – the othering facility of *collecting* and denominating marginalised beings,[219] including nonhuman animals – the action and work of existence anticipates and directs performative relations, a kinaesthetic empathy of movement, imitation, and affiliation. A curious intersection of these qualities is to be found in the nineteenth-century stories of Comte de Lautréamont. Lautréamont affords an example of an aggressive and violent verbalisation of self. And further, whether pseudonym or literary hoax, Lautréamont also offers an interesting aside on authorship, because Comte de Lautréamont was the *nom de plume* of Isidore Ducasse. From 1868 to 1869, Ducasse published the prose poem, *Les Chants de Maldoror*, the book anonymously in 1868, but then in 1869 the complete work was published under the name, Comte de Lautréamont.[220]

Bachelard incites the animality in *Maldoror*, "not as forms but as direct functions"[221] and celebrates that, "[i]n Lautréamont the word finds action immediately."[222] In other words, the nonhuman animals in Maldoror are not mere nouns, they are verbs: "An aggressive being does not wait to be given his moment but seizes it or creates it. In *Maldoror* nothing is simply passive, admitted, awaited, or pursued ... Animal life is no empty metaphor in Ducasse's work."[223] This distinction between the nonhuman animal as tool or narrative device, and the nonhuman animal as action, is crucial. As Bachelard notes, some passages "are unbelievably dense in animals," and "this density consists of a group of impulses rather than images."[224] Energy, if you will.

The nonhuman animals are of "impulsive, wilful character," and are not merely collected artefacts, such as "the roundup of ready-made animals in the works of Victor Hugo."[225] They are not the passive objects of verbs; rather, they are "the sign of the bounty and fluidity of subjective impulses."[226] They *are* the verbs. And as *Energies* with reference to certain *energizing Substances*,[227] the animality in Maldoror commands and makes the world: "It is the excess of a will-to-live that distorts beings and causes metamorphoses."[228] The nonhuman animals in *Maldoror* are thus not elementary, collective, abbreviated representations or images; rather, "they are more produced than reproduced."[229] *They have power*, if you will.

Now to use it.

Act Useful

In the work of existence, the power of thought, Weil sets out an embodied approach to cognition that will become central in the discussions ahead: "How is it that, without its having any effect except on myself (and that only a negative one), I act on the world at the same time? That is difficult to know, for I can neither deduce, explain, nor verify the grasp that I have on the world; I can only make use of it."[230] The use of creativity is a critical dimension to authorship, including re-use and innovation through imitation; – that is, an imitation that is *attentive* and creative. It is also reshaping the very priorities of ownership away from the accumulation of physical objects towards an emphasis on use; – that is, access[231] and the acquisition of relations,[232] such as in the examples of streaming music, gaming and digital property, or story and status in the metaverse. An important consideration in this context is the way in which use is thus a dimension of creativity, both in its production and reproduction, including through familiar production and the circumstances of affiliative learning and similar social activity; and at the same time, the way in which use is a form of social and ethical attention and how this attention might be affected through regulation of that use, including through legal frameworks such as intellectual property, must be addressed.[233]

A particular *use* that is the focus of the present work is that of play. And with that, the nature of play is a fundamental area of concern – the usefulness of play, the value in uselessness, and the stakes for work and industry. Play as make-believe and making fun, deception and disguise, energy-depleting and energising, is a strategy for modelling the world through pretend and action. In contrast to this, arguably the demand made of artificial intelligence is to model text, not remake the world, in a state of sensory deprivation. But for all animals, through the embodied and exuberant relations of play, a genuine and creative doing begins to emerge. The metacommunication of play and the investigation of symbolic thought are thus especially motivating and rewarding in the consideration of nonhuman authorship. At the same time, the authorship in play unravels some of the knotty issues for intellectual property, such as the nature of expression, the meaning of common purpose, and the creativity in community. Indeed, an ethological attention to play has the potential to unsettle the auteurism of the textual as applied to sound, smell, and performance, and to proceed to the movement of creativity in the sociable and mobile territories of exuberance. Play is use. And the property of play is doing.

Play thus offers to *show* consciousness, to make authors of performance, and to reassure the work of existence. It is through this dynamic and productive movement that the individual puts the community in motion. In Weil's own account of this bodily thought, an embodied thinking is a "new kind of knowledge," as she explains: "My thinking proved my own existence; my thinking proved the existence of the world. My thinking must also prove that I act on the world, I must find another kind of thought to serve as a tool for changing it. It is by means of thoughts of this sort that I will define the passageway that the world allows me. What are these thoughts? The 'I think, therefore I am' is of no use to me here; I find myself in a new realm, confronting a new kind of knowledge."[234] This bodily knowing, as read through Weil, meets with contemporary developments in cognitivism around theories of sensori-motor perception and cognition. Embodied cognition[235] operates as a kind of umbrella term for various approaches to the role of the body and the environment on cognitive capacities and processes, including: extended or distributed cognition;[236] embedded or situated cognition;[237] enaction or enactivism;[238] and to some extent, ecological psychology and the concept of affordances.[239] Understanding embodied cognition reveals particular implications for authorship and indeed for the works of authorship themselves. In this context, an ethological approach to authorship opens out the expressive potential of a plenitude of senses and bodily intellect, through smelly mirrors and noisy landmarks.[240] Embodied cognition is of considerable potential in addressing the complex questions of authorship and artificial intelligence, through the enactive play of the body upon the world, and a challenge to the computational model of cognition.

Moving Images

I think that I think that I think. The monadological quality to this accumulation and layering of existence is meaningful in the way in which any innovation or progress might be possible. Weil explains: "I can always find that the world is made up of one movement, then another, then another. In this way I enter into a relation with the world – not, it is true, as one man does with another, but as a man does with a multitude."[241] An embodied cognition is vital for meeting this multitude, like dogs on a walk, huddled around a lamp post, greeting the crowds of scent.

This assembly of movement recalls Sebeok's impression of Grant's extraordinary utterance as "an unlimited semiosis, resonating into the unfathomable future."[242] Roland Barthes offers a kind of doctrine of accession, in a manner of speaking, or perhaps more accurately, a debt of stewardship, when he says, "This 'I' which approaches the text is already itself a plurality of other texts, of codes which are infinite or, more precisely, lost (whose origin is lost). *Objectivity* and *subjectivity* are of course forces which can take over the text, but they are forces with no affinity with it."[243] And it is in this way that Barthes's concept of reading approaches Weil's, as will be seen in later discussions: "[R]eading is not a parasitical act, the reactive complement of a writing which we endow with all the glamour of creation and anteriority. It is a form of work."[244] This process of existence, this *unlimited semiosis*, is a work in concert, the rhythm of community, and the play of provenance. Thus, Samuel Butler remarked that "a hen is only an egg's way of making another egg."[245] And Thomas Sebeok noted that "a sign is only a sign's way of making more signs."[246] And Burrhus Frederic Skinner stated that "a scientist is only science's way of making more science,"[247] and "a poet is only literary tradition's way of making more of a literary tradition."[248] And a theory is only a way of making more precursors, as the effort of discovery in research for the present work has continued to track down a constellation of progenitors to welcome to the discussion.

It should be noted that Skinner (perhaps he was a Durkheimian) appears to leap from the individual to the system when he qualifies his series with the statement, "The individual is a locus, not a creative agent."[249] In that respect, the current discussion must be distinguished, or the contradictions embraced, for it is in the provenance of the individual through the movements of imitation that the sociability of knowledge inheres, and the smelly lamp post is secured and archived.

As will be seen when reviewing Tarde's entomology, there are no swarms without the individual ants.

Our Hands Are Full

We are the art-making animal. In view of the discussion so far, how can this distinction hold up? Are humans *the* art-making animal? Is a challenge to the anthropocentrism of copyright doomed to be wrecked on the rocks of the series of presumptions that shore up and enshrine human exceptionalism in aesthetic discourse? Are the persistent and resilient presumptions, such as the singularity of art (and of authorship), the intentionality of aesthetic objects, and the historical import and narrative of aesthetic language, not rocks at all but just arbitrary lines in the sand?

The word between us is a verb, and that verb is to play. As this discussion develops, the entry to authorship (and thus to personhood) is one which is embodied in action, in performance, in play. It is not an arbitrary threshold of sentience, or an impossible distinction of consciousness.[250] That is, to traverse the divide is to consider these thresholds not as object barriers, but as relations, relations which will also come to inform the way we navigate the intellectual property objects themselves.[251] To play is to make.[252]

It is to that body language that the discussion now turns. We are going to have our hands full, holding open the floodgates.

Notes

1 Cervantes (1613/[2008]), 29.
2 Gaylord (2002).
3 Meyer (2018) notes, "What has prevented Christianity from becoming a site of effective resistance to ecological degradation? My answer: Christian theology is so thoroughly committed to a categorical human-animal distinction that the narrative structures of subject formation in societies with Christian heritage pervasively minimize the enmeshment of human beings with the ecological politics of creaturely life … Until Christian theology surrenders its investment in a categorical human-animal distinction and correctively centers its theological anthropology on human animality, Christian resistance to ecological degradation will be ineffective and contradictory" (178).
4 Meyer (2018), 178.
5 deleuze (1994/[1968]), 23. See further the discussion of this refrain in Gibson (2006), 42, 138–139.
6 The name Thrasymachus is often associated with *thumos*, and meanings of spirit or animality, and Thrasymachus himself is accompanied by animal imagery in *The Republic*. See further the discussion in Wilson (1995).
7 For a fuller discussion of the wolfish exchanges between Plato and Thrasymachus, see Evrigenis (2010).
8 *Republic* Book II, 336b.
9 Adam (1905), in commentary on 336d: "This is the earliest allusion in Greek literature to the belief that if a wolf sees you first you become dumb" (V 1, 24).
10 *Republic*, Book II, 336d.
11 A fuller discussion of waste is undertaken in Chapter 7, especially in relation to surplus value and play.
12 *Republic*, Book VIII, 565d.
13 Titus Macius Plautus, *Asinaria*, line 495. The exact date of first production is unknown, but it is estimated to be late third or early second centuries BCE. See Henderson (2006), vii.
14 Plautus (2006), xi.
15 On the "pack fiction" associated with wolf studies and the misuse and misunderstanding of dominance and social structures in wolves and other canids, particularly in the context of training discourse and popular culture, see Gibson (2020a), Part 3 and Chapter 8 in particular. See further the discussion in Schleidt and Shalter (2003).
16 Long (2015) provides an analysis of the dialogue from the perspective of scent and scent-marking and suggests that the dialogue ultimately "reinforces the danger endemic to those who develop a taste for injustice and allow it to guide their lives," doing so through the "tyrannical" figure of the wolf (*Republic* 565d–566a) (135). This interpretation is largely motivated by the accepted bad reputation of the wolf, but I argue later in Chapter 5 for a revision of the view of justice presented by Thrasymachus.
17 Gibson (2020a), Chapters 7 and 8.
18 Note the discussion in Michaelides-Nouaros (1980).

19 Dahrendorf R (2022/[1968]), 129–150. See further the discussion in Michaelides-Nouaros G (1980).
20 Haraway (2008).
21 Gibson (2020a).
22 See further the discussion of Thrasymachus as the *straw dog* in Chapter 5.
23 Waal (2016), 109.
24 Bolhuis et al. (2014), 5.
25 Waal (2016), 109.
26 Waal (2016), 109.
27 Waal (2016), 109.
28 Rumbaugh et al. (2014).
29 See further the discussion in Aitchison (2000), where Aitchison notes that animal language studies became "a playground for cranks" (4). Despite questions around the scientific rigour of what may be considered performative research (not dissimilar to staging around artificial intelligence today, such as Ai-Da's appearance in the House of Lords, discussed in "What Does Naruto Want?"), the emphasis on language as pivotal continues. Aitchison (2000) observes: "As absurd claims spouted like puffballs, the question of language origin was shunned into the founding statutes of the Linguistic Society of Paris, perhaps the foremost academic linguistic institution of the time" (5).
30 See Ristau (1991a). See further the discussion in Chapter 9 of the present work.
31 This installation of dominant perspectives and paradigms is understood across a range of critical approaches. A useful account is offered by Margolis (1993), who examines the relationship between habits and barriers in scientific thinking and explains this disciplinary or institutional phenomenon in the context of the social phenomena of shared habits: "[W]hen everyone in a community shares a habit, it ordinarily becomes invisible, for what everyone does no one easily notices" (17).
32 Massumi (2014), 91.
33 delahaye (2019), 15–16.
34 Chapter 3.
35 Hobson-West and Davies (2018), 671. This has important resonances with earlier assertions made by Tannenbaum (1991) in relation to the connection between ethical and cultural values and welfare. These arguments are taken up by Fraser (1995), who acknowledges Tannenbaum's argument "that scientists are wrong to treat the scientific assessment of animal welfare as a purely technical issue," and argues that animal welfare assessments must acknowledge this relationship between science and society (103).
36 For example, the United Kingdom's Animal Welfare (Sentience) Act 2022 may be read as a practical implementation, as it were, of this concept.
37 Hobson-West and Davies (2018) note the impact in relation to the policy regard for a social hierarchy of species, as set out in Schedule 2B of the Animals (Scientific Procedures) Act 1986, with additional protection for primates in paragraphs 1 (endangered primates) and 2 (non-endangered primates) and for cats, dogs, and horses, as set out in paragraph 4, and argue: "[A] principle of social acceptability is clearly fundamental to animal research legislation … But upon what do such idealized versions or notions of 'social acceptability' rest? If assumptions about animal sentience are based on experiments in animal welfare science, what evidence (if any) is being marshalled to make such assumptions?" A question to which they conclude the answer is "probably 'none'" (683).
38 Hobson-West and Davies (2018) note in relation to the exclusion of decapods (such as lobsters): "[I]t is the societal sentience and not just their biological

sentience, that allows their discounting from legislation and moves them outside ethical boundaries. For the burgeoning field of work on animal research, the message is that societal sentience operates as an imaginary that has powerful impacts on regulation and on the translation of regulation into scientific practice" (686). At the time of going to press, decapods remain unprotected in the Animals (Scientific Procedures) Act 1986, although their potential exclusion is under review. This follows the recommendations of the report in Birch et al. (2021). See further the discussion of sentience in Chapter 3 of the present work.
39 Gould (1990) describes the constructedness of taxonomic categories and notes "the false premise that our categories are given by nature and ascertained by simple, direct observation ... But our classifications are human impositions, or at least culturally based decisions on what to stress among a plethora of viable alternatives. Classifications are therefore theories of order, not simple records of nature" (73). In this context, it is interesting to note research developments questioning phylogenetic relationships inferred from morphological features: Oyston (2022).
40 Notably, sentience is largely understood in terms of reaction, notwithstanding the capabilities that may be inferred in the capacity for suffering: Gibson (2022b). See further the more detailed consideration of sentience in Chapter 3 of the present work, including the way in which the concept of sentience itself is complicit in barrier-making through its discrete and individualistic reckoning, as distinct from the sociable and affiliative capabilities in wants and beliefs and as performed through play. Indeed, in many respects, the analysis of rights and personhood is limited and delimited by the policy rhetoric of sentience, making the need for a better understanding of the way in which consciousness is moved and performed through play all the more imperative in this context.
41 Chemero (2023). See further, Lee (2020): "It is clear that all this social interaction only makes sense to the parties involved if they have a 'sense of self' and can similarly maintain a model of the self of the other agent. In order to understand someone else, it is necessary to know oneself. An AI 'self model' should include a subjective perspective, involving how its body operates (for example, its visual viewpoint depends upon the physical location of its eyes), a detailed map of its own space, and a repertoire of well understood skills and actions."
42 Weil (1941a), 16.
43 Weil (1941a), 16.
44 Weil (1941a), 16.
45 Weil (1941a), 15–16.
46 Herel and Mikolov (2024). See further, Gibson (2023b).
47 Gibson (2020a).
48 Blomley (2016) provides an insightful empirical account of the way in which people negotiate and interpret everyday property boundaries.
49 Leibniz (1714b), §3.
50 Leibniz (1989), 178.
51 Weil (1947/[2002]), 145.
52 Gibson (2020a), Chapter 12. See further in the context of intellectual property objects in Gibson (2025).
53 Gibson (2020a), Chapter 4.
54 Singer (2000). See further Singer and Beermann (1993): "Rather than conceptualize property rights solely as boundaries separating a sphere within which an owner has complete power and is secure from having her power infringed by either other property owners or the state, we suggest conceptualizing property

law in legal realist terms as rules regulating relationships among people with regard to control of valued resources. Those rules differ depending on the social context and relationships at issue" (244). This appeal to legal realism is no doubt the kind of critical legal realism advocated by some scholars including Balkin (1990), 1123–1126. See further Singer (1988): "To a great extent, we really are all legal realists now" (503).
55 Weil's theory of *metaxu* draws from the treatment of betweenness in the Platonic dialogues. In *The Symposium*, the dialogue between Socrates and Agathon explores the contradictions and logic of the between (particularly 202a–203b), groundwork that is recognisable throughout Weil's account of the ethics of the *metaxu*. See further the discussion in Foshay (2017). This logic of betweenness also informs Romantic irony, as will be seen in later discussion (see Part 3 and, in particular, Chapter 9 of the present work).
56 Weil (1947/[2002]), 145.
57 Gibson (2020a).
58 McFarland and Ness (1987) argue that, in the essay, "Science and Perception in Descartes," is to be found "the germ of an important revision of the way Cartesianism is widely regarded today, and it perhaps suggests the ways by which an exact reading of Descartes might someday show how his fundamental doctrine of perception corresponds to non-Western theories and practices" (9).
59 *Symposium* 201e–202b.
60 *Symposium* 201e–202b.
61 Chapter 2.
62 Gibson (2020a), 10.
63 Derrida (1991/[1987]), 57.
64 Leibniz (1989), 296–297.
65 Gibson (2020a), 10–11, 282–283.
66 In the resocialisation of property, see Gibson (2020a), 281–282 in particular.
67 Weil (1959a), 91, 95.
68 Weil (1959a), 91. In "After the discovery of mind," Weil (1959a) notes the significance of this theory and maintains that once the notion of unconscious perception "was introduced into philosophy it was of great importance in the nineteenth century" (91).
69 Weil (1978/[1959]), 207.
70 Hetzel et al. (2013), 49.
71 Leibniz (1902/[1714]).
72 Leibniz (1902/[1714]), §1.
73 Tarde (2012/[1893])
74 The importance of irony, together with a consideration of the theory of incongruity in humour, is considered again later in Chapter 9.
75 *Oxford English Dictionary*, s.v. "palimpsest (n. & adj.)," July 2023.
76 *Oxford English Dictionary*, s.v. "palimpsest (v.)," July 2023.
77 See in particular Chapter 9, where the palimpsestic quality of expression as attentive imitation is explored in relation to caricature, parody, and pastiche, and the capacity or otherwise for ironic play in nonhuman animals and machines. See also Gibson (2023b).
78 *Oxford English Dictionary*, s.v. "wall (n.1)," March 2024.
79 Recall Schlegel (1991/[1798–1800]), Athenaeum Fragments, §84: "Viewed subjectively, philosophy, like epic poetry, always begins in medias res." Sng (2020) notes that the "restless middle is … the crux of romantic philology" (14).
80 For example, see Faldalen (2013), who maintains the relations between still and moving images "dissolve the dichotomy of still versus moving images, provoking

a third concept: *stillmoving imagenesis*" (228). Faldalen argues for an accounting of this betweenness and appeals: "Being truly *inter*, these in-between objects thus demand interdisciplinary insights. An interdisciplinary 'still/moving' research field ... radically suggesting that these homeless betweens, these *metaxy* or media, deserve a room of their own, a stillmoving research discipline" (231–232).
81 Weil (1947/[2002]), 145.
82 Gibson (2005); Gibson (2006); Gibson (2014).
83 Discussions of framing in psychology largely build upon the work of Tversky and Kahneman, but this consideration of the contextualisation and presentation of viewpoints and the contribution to worldviews (in terms of risk) can be identified throughout various philosophical and critical approaches and traditions. See further Tversky and Kahneman (1981) and the discussion of objectivity and situatedness in Gibson (2020a), 4–7.
84 Dennett (1978), 136–137.
85 In particular, Weil (1941b). See further Pirruccello (2002): "Like Husserl, Weil thought that all of our significant perceptions, such as when we are able to identify a perceived object, having meanings as their objects" (480). This somatic and mobile theory of reading is considered in more detail in the following chapters of the present work, particularly the discussion of creative space (Chapter 5) towards an expressive theory of authorship (Part 3).
86 See further Allen (1993): According to Weil, "we are always reading events and people, since all that we are aware of is invested with meaning" (93).
87 See further the critique of the stratification through intellectual property in Gibson (2006), 15–25. See also Gibson (2019).
88 Dennett (1978), 136.
89 Dennett (1978), 137.
90 Dennett (1978), 136. Emphasis in original.
91 Bachelard (2002a/[1938]), Chapter 1.
92 Bachelard (2002a/[1938]), 224.
93 Bachelard (2002a/[1938]), 245.
94 The modern doctrine of the idea/expression dichotomy originated in the United States in the decision in *Baker v Selden*, 101 U.S. 99 (1879), and codified in 17 U.S.C. §102(b). The doctrine has been adopted widely, for instance in the House of Lords, *Designer Guild Ltd v Russell Williams (Textiles) Ltd* [2000] 1 WLR 2416.
95 Shanahan (1997), xxv.
96 Shanahan (1997), xxv.
97 In particular, see the discussion in Chapter 3 and Part 3 on the non-representational approach through embodied cognition and enactivism.
98 Compare Miracchi (2020).
99 See later the discussion in Chapter 3.
100 Midgley (1998/[1983]), 130.
101 Midgley (1998/[1983]), 130.
102 Serjeantson (2001), 425–426.
103 Serjeantson (2001), 425–426.
104 Serjeantson (2001), 436.
105 Serjeantson (2001), 427.
106 Serjeantson (2001), 433. This is a distinction that continues to be inflected in contemporary animal modelling and studies. Knight (2005a) emphasises the importance of "an interest in animals as *subjects* rather than *objects*, in animals as *parts* of human society rather than just *symbols of it*, and in human

interactions and relationships with animals rather than simply human *representations of* animals" (1).
107 Serjeantson (2001), 429.
108 UK Parliament. 11 October 2022. A creative future – Oral evidence. See further the discussion in "What Does Naruto Want?"
109 See further the discussion of copyright's visual and scripted hegemony in Part 3.
110 According to the decision in C-310/17 *Levola Hengelo*, EU:C:2018:899, the only criteria for a work are that it is an expression of the author's own intellectual criterion [36–37]. This means that in theory the form of the work is open; however, in practice, the particularisation through the expression such that it is "identifiable with sufficient precision and objectivity" poses challenges for what might be considered non-traditional works [40].
111 On the history of the tension between this writerly model and the emergence of new expressive forms, such as film, see Gibson (2022d).
112 Albeit in something of a displaced and limited way, through the recording of sound. See further the discussion of sound as creative work in Gibson (2022a).
113 See discussion of scent and olfactory art in the intellectual property context in Gibson (2020a) Chapter 6.
114 On embodied expression and touch, see further the discussions in Part 3, but notably touch is a matter of "reading," to borrow Weil's term, rather than an alienated form, as it were, making touch quite a radical prospect for copyright, even though copyright and design protection both anticipate the protection of touch or texture (Copyright Designs and Patents Act 1988, s4(2)(b); and Registered Designs Act 1949, s1(2)). Touch thus opens an interesting gateway to an ethological and relational intellectual property. See further the consideration of the haptic in Gibson (2025).
115 While the courts famously grappled with taste in C-310/17 *Levola Hengelo*, EU:C:2018:899, ultimately, taste was considered too subjective for the particularisation through expression, but this is largely a recourse to the visuality of the law and resigning to that visuality as *a priori* objective. See further Gibson (2020b).
116 Performance and performance art present particular challenges for the apprehension of expression, but understanding this kind of intellectual creation is relevant to an embodied and action-based approach to sentience and creativity in the present discussion. See further Chapter 9 on movement and language, and expressive and parodic forms in nonhuman animals.
117 Gibson (2024c); Gibson (2022a). As discussed in Part 3, particularly through the consideration of parody in Chapter 9, this can also be traced through the hierarchy of expressions created by the interpretation of limitations and exceptions, such that user-generated work is framed always in deference to the original – for example, the characterisation of parody as secondary and indebted to the original, as enshrined in its interpretation within the law and in its popular reception more widely. This hierarchical thinking is also relevant to performance and other forms of creative work in the performing arts, presumed and defined as instructed and therefore not creative.
118 For example, the work of performers in performance is deferred and secondary to the underlying work (or the work as implied, as in the case of variety performances or improvisations), but this distinction is a technical contrivance rather than an inevitability of what it means to create intellectually. See further, Gibson (2022a).
119 This term comes from Rota (1985), who asked the now famous question, "I wonder whether or when artificial intelligence will ever crash the barrier of

meaning," introducing a critical thinking around the barrier between humans and machines as a critical lack, or want, for deeper understanding on the part of artificial intelligence in its handling of information. See further Mitchell (2020).
120 The concept of sentience is deployed in discussions of both nonhuman animals and machines in relation to rights (particularly in the context of authorship and inventorship in machines) and is introduced here in the context of thinking and language. A more detailed discussion of sentience is in Chapter 3.
121 Descartes (1644).
122 Descartes (1637).
123 Newman (2016), 129.
124 Hatfield (2019), 106.
125 Weil (1929–1930).
126 Weil (1929–1930), 33.
127 Weil (1929–1930), 34.
128 Weil (1929–1930), 58. Emphasis added. While the later work of Jaakko Hintikka on the act of thinking as performance has been very influential, curiously Weil's account is less commonly addressed, and it would do well to acknowledge the ways in which Weil prefigures some of this analysis in her earlier and resonant critique. See further, Hintikka (1962).
129 This is revisited later when redressing approaches to animal cognition through enactivist theories and play, particularly in Part 3.
130 Weil S (1929–1930), 58.
131 Weil (1959a), 90–91.
132 Weil (1929–1930), 70.
133 Weil (1929–1930), 59.
134 Weil (1929–1930), 59.
135 Weil (1929–1930), 59.
136 Weil (1929–1930), 59.
137 Weil (1929–1930), 63.
138 Weil (1929–1930): "A power such as I would attribute to a king, which is a relation between one thing and another (for example, between the king's words and the actions of his subjects) can be measured. But my power is not this shadow of power; it resides entirely in me, since it is that property of myself, which is me, whereby, for me, to decide and to act are the same thing" (62).
139 Weil (1929–1930), 78.
140 Weil (1929–1930), 78–79.
141 Weil (1929–1930), 57.
142 Griffin (1958).
143 Manger and Pettigrew (1995).
144 Plotnik et al. (2019).
145 Jones (2005). Smell is also an important tool of categorisation in order to ascertain and respond to novel stimuli. See further Wright et al. (2017) where the researchers demonstrate through a study with dogs the categorisation of information available from smells that are otherwise not familial and not relevant biologically, thus showing the ability "to categorise odours outside the sphere of individual recognition" (2). Notably, the individuals in the study also showed the ability "to generalise to novel exemplars of the category and were able to retain this information following six weeks of non-exposure" (2).
146 Horowitz (2017). See further the discussion in Gibson (2020a), 156–157. See further the discussion of renewed understanding of human senses by exploring diverse interpretations and representations of the world through a range of animals' senses in Higgins (2021).

147 Weil (1929–1930), 79.
148 Wright et al. (2017).
149 Classen (1992) describes a form of categorical reasoning through smell in humans, and notable in this context are the observations that "olfactory symbolism" has been somewhat overlooked in anthropological and cultural scholarship and that its use in social categories and expression is evident in many cultures, including western cultures (133). Classen describes the use of odour as a form of symbolic representation "to serve as identifying marks of different classes of beings" and argues that smell is "a particularly useful symbolic vehicle for categorizing different groups according to cultural values, as it invests classificatory systems with a strong emotive power" (157–158). For an extensive consideration of smell as an expressive form, see Gibson (2020a). Chapter 6 (and also Chapter 4).
150 The concept of *Umwelt* describes the world around the individual, but with a specifically expressive quality on the part of that individual; *Umwelt* is considered in more detail in Chapter 3.
151 Weil (1929–1930), 79.
152 Weil (1929–1930), 81.
153 For example, see Weil (1949/[2002]), 81. Bachelard (2002/[1943]) also describes "the joy of the hands in the material sense" in relation to the work of kneading in the preparation of spermaceti in *Moby Dick* (61).
154 Weil (1929–1930), 81.
155 For example, companion species may bridge interactions between humans in addition to interacting and relating with humans: Wood et al. (2014).
156 Ashton et al. (2020).
157 Bachelard (2016/[1950]), 98.
158 For Weil as well, the temporal and this prolongation may be viewed "as a bridge, a *metaxu*": Weil (1947/[2002]), 147. See further the discussion of the important principle of prolongation in play in Chapter 7.
159 Bachelard (2016/[1950]), 99.
160 Bachelard (2016/[1950]), 99.
161 Schmelz et al. (2011), 3078. Metacommunication in play and the extent of symbolic thought will be explored in more detail in later chapters (Part 3), but the role of pretend play in human development and language acquisition is widely understood. See for example the useful review of this area of research in Quinn et al. (2018). Symbolic thought is commonly emphasised in the acquisition of social morality in humans: for example, see Tse (2008). Notably, Marc Bekoff and others have described in nonhuman animal play the development of similar skills in morality and a sense of justice: Bekoff (2001). See further the discussion in Gibson (2020a), 88–91. Play is central to the present work and considered throughout; see in particular Part 3.
162 Bachelard (2011/[1948]), 7.
163 Bachelard (2011/[1948]), 7. Emphasis in original.
164 Bachelard (2002/[1938]), 21. Emphasis in original.
165 Bachelard (2002/[1943]), 59. Emphasis in original.
166 Bachelard (2002/[1943]), 60.
167 Bachelard (2002/[1943]), 60.
168 Bachelard (2002/[1943]), 60.
169 For a comprehensive development of Tarde's sociology towards an ethological jurisprudence of property, see Gibson (2020a).
170 Tarde (2012/[1893]), 52. Emphasis in original.
171 Tarde (2012/[1893]), 52. Emphasis in original.

172 Weil (1929–1930), 63.
173 Weil (1929–1930), 63.
174 Lorenc (2012) describes Leibniz as Tarde's "obvious predecessor," and notes that "[w]hile [*Monadology and Sociology*] does not set out the connection at any great length, there is obviously a substantial debt, and the several continuities between the two systems are of assistance in interpreting the theory of [*Monadology and Sociology*]" (77).
175 *Monadology* §14. See further Simmons (2001).
176 *Monadology* §14. See further the discussion of nonhuman consciousness in the context of a continuity thesis in Leibniz in Jorgensen (2011).
177 *Principles of Nature in Grace*, §4–5. See further the discussion in Simmons (2001), 52–53.
178 *Monadology* §15. See further the argument in Barth (2014) that the "consciousness aspect of phenomenally conscious sensations" may be explained by "cognitive strivings" and thus "[t]he kind of attention that constitutes conscious sensation is cognitive attention" (349).
179 Simmons (2001) explains this distinction thus: "Leibnizian consciousness proper, then, is not the awareness of external objects, but the awareness of one's own mental states. Nevertheless, Leibniz quite clearly recognizes a form of consciousness in animal sensations … One of his explicit points of contrast with the Cartesians is that in having sensations animals are aware of (*s'appercevoir de*) things in their external environment. This awareness is a form of consciousness as we understand it today. Animals, we might say, have a conscious mental life but they are not conscious *of* it" (201). This is a useful distinction which nevertheless admits nonhuman animals to consciousness, but it is also a distinction that will be explored and questioned through play and an aesthetic sense in the following chapters.
180 Weil (1959a), 95.
181 Weil (1959a), 95. See further the argument for reading Leibniz as recognising apperception in nonhuman animals in Kulstad (1981). However, in even more conventional accounts, it is agreed that Leibniz attributes basic sentience or consciousness to nonhuman animals, noting a reflective capacity on the part of humans, and capacities for associative reasoning in nonhuman animals: Barth (2014), 346.
182 This Panglossian refrain in honour of Leibniz is revisited in more detail in Chapter 3.
183 Tarde (2012/[1893]), 52. Emphasis in original.
184 Tarde (2012/[1893]), 52. Emphasis in original.
185 Latour (2002), 129.
186 SUPERFLEX, *I COPY Therefore I Am*, print series, 2011. This work was also applied to the cover of the 5th edition (2018) of the leading intellectual property textbook in the United Kingdom, Bently L et al., *Intellectual Property*, published by Oxford University Press.
187 Troutt (2009). The Cartesian reference in the title is made without further explanation in the article; that is, it is taken entirely for granted. Similarly, see Paterson and Welbourne (2019).
188 Weil (2015/[1970]), 134.
189 Tarde (2012/[1893]), 57.
190 See further the extensive treatment of Hohfeld's jurisprudence towards the development of an ethological jurisprudence of property in Gibson (2020a).
191 *Atchison & N R Co v Baty* (1877), 6 Neb., 37.

192 *Atchison & N R Co v Baty* (1877), 6 Neb., 37, 40. See further the discussion in Gibson (2020a), 117–118. Emphasis in original.
193 Gibson (2022b).
194 Considered in more detail in the final chapter, Law's Anecdote.
195 Bachelard (1988/[1961]), 37.
196 Gibson (2022b).
197 Sakaguchi et al. (2020), 8732. Emphasis in original.
198 Sakaguchi et al. (2020), 8732.
199 Sakaguchi et al. (2020), 8739.
200 Bloom (2000): "Very early in the third year, children learn the forms that express wish or intention – 'wanna' and 'gonna' and less often, 'gotta' and 'hafta'. These earliest modal forms literally launch the acquisition of a class of verbs and other forms with the meaning *directedness towards*, that take the connective 'to'." What is also particularly interesting in the context of the present discussion is that "[t]he most frequent intentional state words in the robust period of language learning between two and three years (the 'dark ages' for theory of mind) are the epistemic verbs 'think' and 'know' and the perception verbs 'look (at)' and 'see'" (183). See further Bloom and Tinker (2001).
201 Matson (1976), 89.
202 Matson (1976), 86.
203 Matson (1976), 88.
204 Chapter 8.
205 (1822–1885), 18th President of the United States and commanding general of the Union Army in the American Civil War (1865).
206 Sebeok (1986), 2.
207 Sebeok (1986).
208 Ulysses S Grant quoted in Sebeok (1986), 2.
209 Bachelard (2016/[1950]), 99. Emphasis in original.
210 Harris (1751), 173. Emphasis in original.
211 Harris (1751), 173. Emphasis in original.
212 Weil (1929–1930), 60.
213 Ulysses S Grant quoted in Sebeok (1986), 2.
214 Sebeok (1986), 2.
215 Sebeok (1986), 8.
216 Sebeok (1986), 8–9.
217 Tarde (2012/[1893]).
218 Sebeok (1986), 9.
219 For example, see Ferdinand (2022): "[T]he impossibility of an 'I,' and consequently, the impossibility of a verb. *Negroes are the objects of other people's verbs*" (136, emphasis in original).
220 Knight (1978a), 8–9. In the context of the examination of authorship and originality in the following chapters, the fact that Ducasse adopted a pseudonym as well as openly advocated for plagiarism in his later *Poems* is an enticing aside. See further the discussion in Knight (1978b), 246–252. Ducasse's views on plagiarism will be revisited in the discussion of parody and pastiche in Chapter 9.
221 Bachelard (1986/[1939]), 3.
222 Bachelard (1986/[1939]), 1.
223 Bachelard (1986/[1939]), 2.
224 Bachelard (1986/[1939]), 5. See further the discussion in Thacker (2013), 83–98.
225 Bachelard (1986/[1939]), 4.
226 Bachelard (1986/[1939]), 4.
227 Harris (1751), 173. Emphasis in original.

228 Bachelard (1986/[1939]), 4.
229 Bachelard (1986/[1939]), 5. See further the discussion in Thacker (2013), 83–98.
230 Weil (1929–1930), 68.
231 Gibson (2022c).
232 Such as the example of a non-fungible token (NFT), where the transaction is not in the conventions of an object, but rather in the instantaneity of a relation: Gibson (2021b).
233 See further Gibson (2014) for a detailed critique of use, including through the development of the concept of familiar production.
234 Weil (1929–1930), 68.
235 For a useful overview and history of the field, as well as an introduction to the concept of 4E cognition (embodied, embedded, extended, enactive), see Newen et al. (2018).
236 Clark and Chalmers (1998).
237 Hutchins (1995).
238 Varela et al. (1993/[1991]), credited with introducing the term "enactive cognition." See also the revised edition, which gives greater account to phenomenology, Varela et al. (2016). See further Hutto and Myin (2013).
239 In particular, see Gibson (1950). For a review of the history of the field, see Lobo et al. (2018).
240 Gibson (2020a): "Through advocating an ethological jurisprudence of property, that smelly mirror, that mutual glance, that commons of shared interests, is opened up to the world" (315).
241 Weil (1929–1930), 76.
242 Sebeok (1986), 9.
243 Barthes (1974/[1973]), 10. Emphasis in original.
244 Barthes (1974/[1973]), 10.
245 Butler (1897), 134.
246 Sebeok (1986), 184. See further Sebeok (1979): "[A]ll 'survival machines' – meaning people, animals, plants, bacteria, and viruses – are only a sign's way of making another sign" (xiii).
247 Skinner (1983), 408.
248 Skinner (1983), 332.
249 Skinner (1983), 332.
250 Massumi (2014) considers play to be the critical political language of animals and similarly rejects the stultifying approaches through language to intelligence and consciousness, challenging these with the performative excess of play: "Do not presume that you have access to a criterion for categorically separating the human from the animal. The criterion most widely called into service is language. If culture is assimilated to language, as it so often is, then it too falls into the exclusive province of the human. However, as we have seen, language is already present in potential in animal play. Animal play, in fact, produces the real conditions of emergence in language. Since these conditions concern life's reflective powers, a mode or degree of consciousness is already in force. So don't get it into your head that consciousness will provide the dividing line" (91). As will be seen, play is invaluable in dislodging the logic of fixed barriers and affirming the intentional probity of performance.
251 See further Gibson (2025).
252 The authorship in play is considered in detail in Part 3.

Chapter 2

The Common Touch

This chapter begins with an answer – *forty-two*. This is of course the answer provided by the supercomputer, Deep Thought, in response to the "Great Question" in *The Hitch Hiker's Guide to the Galaxy*.[1] But this answer to this question motivates further questions, and the journey for questions motivates Arthur Dent's quest that travels the breadth of the subsequent trilogy, as told in four parts. Nevertheless, after "Seven and a half million years" and "Seventy-five thousand generations," the answer was delivered:

> "Good-morning," said Deep Thought at last.
> "Er ... Good-morning, O Deep Thought," said Loonquawl nervously, "do you have ... er, that is ..."
> "An answer for you?" interrupted Deep Thought majestically. "Yes. I have."
> ...
> "There really is one?" breathed Phouchg.
> "There really is one," confirmed Deep Thought.
> "To Everything? To the great Question of Life, the Universe and Everything?"
> "Yes."
> ...
> "Though I don't think," added Deep Thought, "that you're going to like it."
> "Doesn't matter!" said Phouchg. "We must know it! Now!"
> ...
> "You're really not going to like it," observed Deep Thought.
> "Tell us!"
> "All right," said Deep Thought. "The Answer to the Great Question ..."
> ...
> "Yes ...!"
> "Of Life, the Universe and Everything ..." said Deep Thought.
> "Yes ...!"
> "Is ..." said Deep Thought, and paused.

DOI: 10.4324/9780429342103-5

"Yes ...!"

"Is ..."

"Yes ... !!! ...?"

"Forty-two," said Deep Thought, with infinite majesty and calm.[2]

After the answer is greeted with some dismay and apprehension, Deep Thought then clarifies, "I think the problem, to be quite honest with you, is that you've never actually known what the question is."[3] And although Loonquawl replies, "But it was the Great Question! The Ultimate Question of Life, the Universe and Everything,"[4] this provides no further assistance. This is largely because both the question and the answer suffer an explainability problem. As Deep Thought declares, "So once you do know what the question actually is, you'll know what the answer means."[5]

Which leads me to my contention that the question is the fundamental question of consciousness; that is, it is the mind-body problem and the concern with the duality of matter and mind,[6] physicality and mentality, the hard problem of consciousness.[7] And there is a clue. Arthur Schopenhauer refers to the mind-body problem as the world knot (*weltknoten*).[8] In the world knot, or the nodus, Schopenhauer explains, "the Subject of knowledge can never be known; it can never become Object or representation,"[9] and yet "the identity of the willing with the knowing Subject, in virtue of which the word 'I' includes and designates both, is the *nodus* [*Weltknoten*] of the Universe, and therefore inexplicable."[10] For Schopenhauer, then, a world of representations becomes meaningful to the individual through the action of will, of wanting. And the very explanation of this knotty issue, coincidentally or not, is to be found in none other than section 42, *The Subject of Volition*, in the essay, *The Fourfold Root of the Principle of Sufficient Reason*. Forty-two is indeed the answer. Because the question to the answer is to be found in section 42. A game of two Arthurs.

But from the mathematics of knots[11] (which, in another important connection in the present work, owes a considerable debt to Leibniz[12]), it is known that it is not possible simply to untie a theoretical knot, even a world knot. The knotty issues of the mind-body problem, and its recruitment in the service of anthropocentrism, are not easy to unravel. In particular, the issues for artificial intelligence and the nature of its productivity, the potential for sentience, the question of consciousness, are arguably propelled and sustained by a distinct form of Cartesianism that privileges computational models of thinking, and seemingly ignores embodied language and cognition.[13] This knot of anthropocentrism is a theoretical contrivance that appears to defeat the authorship of animals other than human, but at the same time, it is important to examine the assumptions underpinning the momentum it grants towards rights for artificial intelligence. It appears imperative, if not to cut this Gordian knot, then at least to fray it. But mathematics also offers the possibility of re-imagining the space of the knot[14] and bringing some heat to the equation. In other words, it is not necessary to rebuild the intellectual property system; rather, all that is perhaps required is to re-think the geometry of its application. Indeed, to cut through the maze of the knot garden would merely work around and thus sustain the maze. On the other hand, what is at stake in the present discussion is to re-imagine and retrace this space, and to rethink the time and process of creativity.

In many respects, intellectual property is both a particular resolution to and a particular consequence created by the mind-body problem, in a manner of speaking, made in the artefact and unravelled in the making. Almost invariably, there is some sort of expectation or exercise of control, and with that control, a duty of responsibility; and with that responsibility, an artifice of sociability and relations. Intellectual property is concerned with both boundaries and binds. As the saying goes, property ties one down. It tethers, it entangles, *like a person possessed*. But the barrier is also a door, the *metaxu*, the knotty problem. Of course, artificial intelligence has its own particular mind-body problem, as will be seen; one of both the ability to explain and the ability to embody, so to speak. As the previous chapter examined through the question of a bodily thinking and imagination, the fundamental obstacle of imagination, as Weil explains, is itself also "this tie, this knot between the world and me, this point of intersection between the simple movement that I have at my command and the infinitely complex movement that represents the world for my understanding."[15] Both outer and inner knowledge. The *metaxu*. A world-making world knot.

But in examining this knot, an emphasis continues to be placed on human language; in fact, to suggest nonhuman animal consciousness might be to provoke a challenge to talk to the hand itself, as that which is instrumental to consciousness. Literally. But this handedness, this bodily knowing, extends beyond the mercurial finger. The hand is presented as the mark of human exceptionalism,[16] and so it must also become the door through this impasse. So how might the nonhuman animal or, perhaps with even more difficulty, the machine, give a show of hands?

Hand to Mouth

The hand is a persistent artefact of human exceptionalism, proffered as evidence of both biological and creative distinction for both nonhuman animals[17] and human technologies.[18] Even in a review of *Civilisations*,[19] one commentator notes, "Every single drop of human culture ... was created by the human hand."[20] The art-making animal not only *speaks* but also is the animal who *make*s art *by hand*. The hand is also extended in speech, in the kind of temptation to distinction and "all the problems that link the history of the hand with a hominizing process."[21] The hand is invoked both culturally and biologically, in the evolution of human language,[22] and thus the hand becomes an instrument of and instrumental to not only language but also the language barrier, so to speak, between species. Human exceptionalism, as it were, persists from hand to mouth.

The hand is thus particularly provocative in the question of authorship; it is the knot in our thinking when it comes to invention and authorship in animals other than human, and for the irascible subject of artificial intelligence and tactile perception. Touch excites an embodied language and taunts a resilient Cartesianism that is applied in the preclusion of creativity in animals other than humans. This bodily knowing also becomes the momentum for discerning artificial authorship in machines, whether to exclude it or to perform it. Françoise Meltzer notes that, precisely because of the importance of the hand, it is also overlooked: "Is the hand's pervasiveness such that it has ordered our vocabulary, our laws, so that we no longer see or recognize the hand itself?"[23] In other words, the barrier becomes invisible and goes unnoticed. As far as human exceptionalism is concerned, and the privileges of authorship that go with that, it is all in the mind for which the hand is merely the conduit: "[I]s the hand so pervasive, and its ability so fundamental and varied, that we have lost the notion of the 'handedness of the hand,' and retained only its products, its metaphors, and its trace?"[24]

This handed barrier guards the apparent linguistic exceptionalism of humans and their purported monopoly over thinking. However, the very basis of this exception in language is fraught and *groundless*. Wittgenstein suggests the porosity of this barrier by questioning the erection of language as a defining feature of thought: "It is sometimes said that animals do not talk because they lack the mental capacity. And this means: 'they do not think, and that is why they do not talk.' But – they simply do not talk. Or to put it better: they do not use language – if we except the most primitive forms of language."[25] Nevertheless, the manual dexterity of language continues to be applied to interpretations of his language tool-box: "Think of the tools in a tool-box: there is a hammer, pliers, a saw, a screw-driver, a rule, a glue-pot, glue, nails and screws. – The functions of words are as diverse as the functions of these objects. (And in both cases there are similarities.)"[26] But perhaps we might more readily understand the nature of these tools for their sociality, as instruments of binding and connection. In other words, they provide a form of extended cognition, extending the reach of the body as itself the fundamental tool of thinking. Recalling the concept of *metaxu*, all these various tools are points of contact as well as instruments of force and separation. As introduced in the previous chapter, Simone Weil's embodied thinking through the body as tool, in every sense, is instrumental here: "[A]lthough they extend my reach, these tools play the same role in regard to me as the body itself."[27] Thinking is thus encompassed in the understanding of one's own body together with the sociality and instrumentality of other bodies – the body as tool: "The human body is like a pincer for the mind to grasp and handle the world."[28] Contrary to the after-thought, so to speak, of the body in the somewhat popularised interpretations of Cartesian dualism,

Weil's account is one of embodied cognition, a body of thought: "[T]he body grasps relationships, and not the particular things ... So, when we are on the point of giving birth to thought, it comes to birth in a world that already is ordered."[29] To repeat, for Weil, then, the hand is the body. The body is handed. And a path to language is cleared.

To examine this knot, we are going to have to pull at some strings.

String Theory of Mind, Why Knot?

A short poem, by the Actualist, Allan Kornblum,[30] is remarkably succinct at summarising the present discussion. It describes the intersection between work, the hand, and sentience, bringing together the very principles of embodied cognition introduced in the previous chapter and to be pursued throughout:

> Work. The raw materials.
> Work. The combination of
> powers: the hand, machine,
> electricity work together.
> The hand attributes sentience.[31]

The bodily nature of this making – making a living, in and of every sense – seems to eavesdrop on Weil's philosophies of bodily labour and thought. But it is necessary to pull at the strings of the hand as anthropocentric device and explore the extension of knowing through the body. After all, string-pulling[32] (or similar manipulations to reach a valuable resource) is a common test in cognitive science, expanding understanding as to goals and means-end understanding, with potential relevance for insight into desires and beliefs. What do nonhuman animals want?

Manual dexterity is seized by human exceptionalism as a binding account of the species barrier – and the tying of knots in this context is presented critically as a uniquely human skill.[33] Although there is evidence of knot-tying abilities among apes, perhaps the fact that the process of knot-tying is completed usually by using mouths as well as hands allows for a persistent attachment to an immutable, but arbitrary, difference.[34] Making knots "orangutan style ... using her hands, feet and mouth"[35] works in some way *from hand to mouth*. Thus, are we to believe that perhaps this is not a knot at all?[36] But aside from a persistent and strategic anthropomorphism in artificial intelligence industries, who is to say that when a robot ties a knot that it is using its *hands*?

Knots, as a communicative device, not only oblige an embodied language, but also bind a kind of haptic sentience in the expression of intentionality – that is, a social intercourse through touch, a responsive sociality.[37] Sense is thus always already a relation, a network of not only objects but also concepts. In this way, touch becomes central to the sensation of property, as it were, or as Jean-Luc Nancy explains, "The proper is therefore not a thing, but always the sense of a thing: just the thing – as one says of a tool appropriate to a task – with its truth in an other."[38] In this way, touching (and by implication, gesture[39]) enlivens an embodied, sentient authorship – the double bind of property. "Knowing things," as Michel Serres explains, "requires one first of all to place oneself between them. Not only in front in order to see them, but in the midst of their mixture, on the paths that unite them."[40] The shared interests, if you will. For Serres, this kind of experiential knowing is secured in a knot: "Touching is situated between, the skin is the place where exchanges are made, the body traces the knotted, bound, folded, complex path, between the things to be known."[41] In an embodied cognition, the hand is the body, and the exceptionalist centre of comparative Cartesian utterances cannot hold.

This kind of tactile sense-making is also central to research on robotic perception in the potential for responsiveness and responsibility: "*Haptics* sensing involves both action and reaction, i.e., two-way transfer of touch information,"[42] arguably facilitating the potential for artificial intelligence to *mean what it says*.[43] In this way, touch and the pronouncements of embodied communication are corporealising the discourse on creativity and on more-than-human authorship. At once, the more-than-human authorship of non-human animals is in communication on a new expression of the body in the world, but the *sensation* of artificial intelligence is yet to be established, so to speak. In advanced machine learning and claims to robotic sentience, touch may become critical to the embodied learning and performance of advanced technologies.[44] It is thus through the body that sentience *comes to mind*. But what are the implications for artificial intelligence?[45]

There is an extraordinary musing on this multispecies bodily integrity and the extension of hands in the example of an advertising campaign for Pedigree Dentastix. In an early version of the campaign, a human hand performs a shadow play of various dogs in profile, with the last one accepting what is assumed to be the dental stick (in shadow). The narrator states, "Dogs use their teeth, like we use our hands."[46] But a more recent version of the advertisement shows various dogs manipulating objects with their mouths, including dragging blankets, collecting mail, playing with toys, and an assistance dog opening a refrigerator door and collecting a bottle of water. And at least one dog is manipulating a rope ... The narration explains, "Dogs have hands too, clean them every day."[47]

Are knots really always tied by hand?

What Knot

The import of knots is found throughout human history.[48] In Hebrew literature, "the 'charmer' or 'enchanter' is also called *hober haber* which means literally 'a man who ties (magic) knots.'"[49] Knotted strings are also part of the history of time-keeping and accounting, with examples recognised in cultures across Africa (so-called African tally-strings or calendar strings)[50] and India (Kutenai calendar records).[51] And even in the use of beads as a device across different religions, the knot again is implicated or at least is acknowledged as a precursor: "I connect the bead with the *knot*, and see in the strings of beads another form of strings of *knots*, which they have supplanted and almost driven out of use."[52] Indeed, "Knotted cords were the first memory-drawers and registers," not only telling stories but also writing histories, and as "the primitive tools out of which developed the powerful memory-machine of our modern writing, they were the primitive memory-huts and tents out of which grew up that gigantic structure that we call literature, history, and science."[53]

Knots are also playful. Describing Navajo string games, Donna Haraway explains, "These string figures are *thinking* as well as *making* practices, pedagogical practices and cosmological performances," and thus this "continuous weaving" is not only a way of story-telling but also restorative.[54] Haraway notes in these games the interaction between play and wellbeing as well as an articulation of multispecies justness and morality: "Some Navajo thinkers describe string games as one kind of patterning for restoring *hózhó*, a term imperfectly translated into English as 'harmony,' 'beauty,' 'order,' and 'right relations of the world,' including right relations of humans and nonhumans."[55]

Related to these perspectives is the way in which the knot is also a means for understanding the overlapping and mobile territories of human and nonhuman animal communities, as a kind of embodiment of sociality.[56] In his work on walking, Tim Ingold describes the knot-making in the interlocking and narrative paths of the Walbiri people:

> The life of a Walbiri person ... is laid out on the ground as the sum of his trails ... The knot ... does not contain life but is rather formed of the very lines along which life is lived. These lines are bound together *in* the knot, but they are not bound *by* it. To the contrary they trail beyond it, only to become caught up with other lines in other knots. Together they make up what I have called a meshwork. Every place, then, is a knot in the meshwork, and the threads from which it is traced are lines of wayfaring.[57]

In this way, the knot is a kind of *literary* fragment; that is, it is a story in itself as well as a network of other fragments and citations. This resonates with the contact points of scent, and the overlapping and mobile territories in the work of smell. This intentionality of knots and paths is arguably also captured in the architecture and mazes of European knot gardens (or parterres) of the fifteenth and sixteenth centuries, including the "curious knotted garden" of Shakespeare's *Love's Labour's Lost*.[58] Although the paths appear defined in the knot garden, the inhabiting of the space arguably insists upon the same kind of direct relationship with materiality as in Weil's philosophy. Indeed, this sense of place through knot-making may be literal. Traditional cartography in Papua New Guinea utilises knots in order to record and trace the territories marked out by passage and ceremony: "Yet cords appear to be more than signs for space and location in that their mnemonic and cognitive function partakes of the emotional domain of binding in the creation of uniquely patterned images."[59]

The embodiment of place through these knotty paths is also physicalised in dance in the interplay of communication both within and upon the performance. Dance presents also a notable insight into the relationship within copyright between authorship, the work, and the performer, and between choreographer and choreographed.[60] Indeed, the relationship between knots, rhythm, and music insists upon an embodied language: "Rhythms are knotted in a body."[61] The paths of creativity are not only knotted but also interdependent and interattentive, saying and knot saying, as it were. And as we shall see, this generation of meaning is *enumerated* in various ways by many species other than human.

In the interaction between the body (both in expression and in expressing) and memory, knots and their sequences may possess linguistic properties and convey meaning, whether or not acknowledged fully as words. Khipu (also Quipu) are string-based systems of information and recording used by various communities in Andean South America:[62] "*Khipu* (knot; to knot) is a term drawn from Quechua, the lingua franca and language of administration of the Inka Empire."[63] The khipu are intricate and complex objects in which considerable information may be recorded: "The khipu were knotted-string devices that were used for recording both statistical and narrative information, most notably by the Inka but also by other peoples of the central Andes from pre-Inkaic times, through the colonial and republican eras, and even – in a considerably transformed and attenuated form – down to the present day."[64] Arguably more than mere mnemonic devices, some scholars accord this system the status of writing and language where "devices were constructed with conventionalized units of information that could be read by khipu makers throughout the empire."[65]

The research of the Khipu Database Project[66] at Harvard University has been reported as discovering the first Inca "word" in a sequence of knots, although Gary Urton, head of the project, clarifies it thus: "We believe that we've found a sequence of knots that was a unique signifier. We suggested it may be a place name, but we're not fixed on that particular idea. It could also be the name of the khipu keeper who made them, or the subject matter, or even a time designator."[67] Nevertheless, it is a repository of meaning. This accords with research into cuneiform scripts, which are frequently characterised by numerical signs, rather than prose. Such numeracy has been explained as an early form of representational naming, where numerical signs may even comprise a code for names.[68]

The relationship between knots and memory is thus significant to the perspective on intentionality and authorship being woven here, and knots and knot-making together are fundamentally the embodiment of communication. Knots give a body not only to memory but also to language. It is thus both intriguing and inevitable that, for artificial intelligence, the use of haptics "to give it a body" has focused somewhat on knot-tying tasks.[69]

But what of the energies of knowing verbs?

Bundle of Energy

Knots have an intrinsically ironic relationship with energy, given that they are identified with both speed, as in nautical knots, and slowing things down, as in contemplation.[70] Perhaps in both senses, however, knots are a counting device, making movement and indeed time sensible through a potentially infinite division of space. In other words, movement is a property of relations, a knotty phenomenon, as understood through Leibniz's theory of motion: "[S]ince space without matter is something imaginary, motion, in all mathematical rigor, is nothing but a change in the positions [*situs*] of bodies with respect to one another, and so, motion is not something absolute, but consists in a relation."[71] This relational and situational perspective questions the location of the author itself as a privileged site, introducing a contingency of reciprocity with other readers. This relational production also promises insight into other *objects* of intellectual property, such as genre and expression, similarly constituted through such sticky situations, so to speak.[72]

Knots are thus in and of themselves a catalyst for communication through movement as relation, of meaning through those relations, a social energy bound with the mercurial finger of ethological jurisprudence. Knots both tie and untie themselves; "knots are generated by the combination of a long string with some sort of random motion. This is a sort of derivative law of nature stemming from the Second Law of Thermodynamics ... Long Things Get Tangled."[73] The very sociality of an ethological jurisprudence of the object itself is bound tightly in the knot, and the question of a more-than-human authorship will benefit from an investigation of this relationship between the body and its bodily tools including, potentially, tools of artificial intelligence.

The knot both keeps time and makes time, imposing a kind of patience in the communication they facilitate. In this way, the knots in our thinking also entail, as it were, a kind of causality that is at the heart of the copyright narrative and indeed of the uncertainty of that narrative, the untying and the tying, the authors and their precursors: "('... At some point we have to say –: without doubting -: *that* happens because of *this* cause.') As opposed to what for instance? As opposed surely to never *tightening* the knot, but remaining constantly uncertain what the cause of the phenomenon really is."[74]

Above all, for a certain attention, it is necessary to be patient.

Learn the Ropes

The affiliative function in the purposive imitation of teaching and learning has been mentioned earlier and continues to be important throughout this discussion towards an elaboration of the concept of *attentive imitation* – that is, the imitation of beliefs, not objects, the movements of desire, not data. The kind of movement and progress of thinking described in the previous chapter relies not on painstaking imitation and consensus but on dissensus and entropy, and with that, a distinctly productive sociality. *I think I am a verb.* This enactive approach to expression, and with it an expressive theory of sentience and authorship, will be developed throughout the following chapters. But what is critical to do at this stage is to distinguish the way in which developments in artificial intelligence focus on approximating a model, including the way in which relationships with artificial intelligence are constructed and presented – or, to put it another way, the way in which an answer is provided without the curiosity of the question. On the other hand, social learning thrives upon the disarray and disguise, and the dissensus and disputes, that fuel play and knowing in humans and other animals. The cultural complexity of creativity is a matter of disagreement, and there are particular limitations from being bound by describing the information *as it is*.

There are many examples of the ways in which humans have the potential to react to a learning partner (including a machine) and take account of the future uses of the knowledge derived by adjusting their behaviour to protect information from the learning process and potentially defeat the algorithm.[75] This is the common sense of social learning, as it were, and facilitates innovation through the imitation of belief rather than modelling. The machine, on the other hand, reacts not to the learning partner (the human) but to the data, as comprising the object of imitation; in other words, the machine is not concerned with beliefs but with the assimilation of data. Even in the reaction to prompts or the curious perversions of LLMs *apologising* for mistakes, what is occurring is not an affiliative production but a tooling of the available data. Indeed, it would be difficult to reconcile the ethics of a machine designed to disagree and rearrange existing knowledge, or even lie, such that it is creative rather than curatorial.[76] And even then, the term curatorial is not wholly appropriate in describing the kind of *stereotypic imitation* involved, in that what is happening is a diminished form of curation through pattern identification, and is thus in a way predetermined, rather than an active and intellectual curatorial creation.

On the other hand, through the process of social and affiliative learning, humans and other animals interact with their environment (including others in that environment) through a dialectic of shared interests and bodily investment. In this way, social animals, including humans, innovate and create through dissensus and forms of deception that are deceptive precisely through the understanding and imitation of belief. This is animal common sense. For the machine, the machine calculates not through shared interests but through separate mutual interests, without ever really understanding the question ... "'Well, you know, it's just Everything ... Everything ....'"[77] This is not to refute the achievements of an intelligence that is artificial, or the extraordinary and hugely significant applications in medicine and other fields; this is simply to start to examine why these results are not authorship.

It is remarkable that one of the areas of focus for the development of general artificial intelligence is indeed also through the energy of knots, or more specifically, knot theory.[78] Examples of solutions to complex problems of pure mathematics are being presented as proof of intelligence on the basis that "[m]athematics is the language of reasoning."[79] But is artificial intelligence really speaking that language? Or is it just a pattern agent?[80] If you will pardon the pun. Once again, this "reasoning" is beset by an explainability problem.[81] And as Emily Riehl cautions, "Proofs are the centre of mathematics."[82]

To unravel these knotty distinctions, we need the careful account provided by an orangutan in Paris, named Wattana.

Wattana's Knots

Wattana is a Bornean orangutan, born in 1995 in Antwerp Zoo in Belgium, where she was subsequently hand-raised after rejection by her mother.[83] Although she now lives in the Apenheul Primate Park in the Netherlands,[84] in 1998 she arrived with her half-brother at the Ménagerie of the Jardin des Plantes in Paris,[85] and this is where the philosopher of science, Chris Herzfeld, first met her. It was here that Herzfeld studied not only Wattana's behaviour but also her life story. According to Herzfeld, there is a lack of interest in the narratives of captive wild animals, as though the constraints of the environment lessen the language and stories to tell: "[E]ven if some field primatologists have been able to tell the stories of the apes they have met in the wild, few authors have shown interest in the thousands of great apes that reside in our zoos."[86] This is attributed to the anonymising effect of the constructed environment, which extends to the individual authorship, as it were, of each inhabitant: "[T]hey remain anonymous, moved from zoo to zoo and replaced in their cages, until – inexorably – they disappear."[87]

The result of Herzfeld's work is a biography for Wattana as well as a compelling account of the way in which she constructs meaning and self through the innovation and intentionality of her knot-making – the intentional knot of property. In what is perhaps the only comprehensive study of knot-making among apes, the researchers give life to a behaviour "that has no natural adaptive advantage in itself,"[88] and thus resists the reductions to functionalism and survival, instead inviting participation in the exuberance of performative and expressive "work."

Herzfeld notes that "several keepers at the Ménagerie of the Jardin des Plantes, and also a number of visitors, had seen Wattana tie several knots one after the other," and attests, "It was thus not just an accidental occurrence of knotting, but clearly deliberate."[89] Not only did Wattana manipulate the material into knots, but also she would "decorate her enclosure with strips of paper, interlacing them from beam to beam."[90] And surely it was somewhat ingenious when Wattana "pushed some paper into a section of bamboo, so that the bamboo was attached to the paper. She then spun it around, by waving the whole contraption, and then, abruptly, *tied a knot*, under the amazed eyes of the visitors present."[91] With permission from the director, Herzfeld offered Wattana a range of materials to investigate:

> Over the course of a year, I gave Wattana different types of material: strings, laces, satin ribbons, rubber bands, wool in different colors, laced shoes, pieces of hosepipe, buckskin cords. She made knots with all of them, without being encouraged or rewarded. As soon as materials suitable for knotting were provided, she would start weaving, intertwining, and threading. On several occasions, the opportunity to tie knots was allowed to compete with access to food, yet Wattana almost always preferred knotting.[92]

Wattana's knots are a kind of sociability with the researchers. Herzfeld explains this kind of communication through the materials themselves when those materials are provided to Wattana in a manner of greeting: "When I visited her, she immediately tied a knot into the ribbon that I gave her."[93] At once, the artefact or material for manipulation, arguably creativity, becomes a world between Herzfeld and Wattana, the knot as *metaxu*, and a trust is developed through that "property." Herzfeld notes this "expressive dimension" of Wattana's knot-tying and that of all the individuals that participated in the activity and observes that "each ape ties knots with a personal style."[94] Recalling the musicality and embodied rhythms of knot-tying play, considered earlier in relation to dance and communication, Herzfeld's suggestion of an individuality of expression in this context is striking: "[T]he gestures linked to knotting seem to constitute a choreography in which rhythm and attributes vary according to the personality of the knot-tying ape concerned."[95] The signature of the author, if you will. Wattana's knots are indeed a kind of authorship and innovation, where she devises what Herzfeld calls "assemblages," such as the bamboo and paper, and in other cases, creates artefacts described as resembling necklaces, where she "strings wooden beads, or small cardboard tubes along cords or laces."[96] In a "complicity with the material," a kind of conviviality with the artefacts themselves, Herzfeld argues that "the laces, strings, and ribbons themselves represent expressive materials that participate in this dialogue with the objects of the world."[97]

This is not a random, accidental action, but a narrative in which "Wattana never proceeds through trial and error."[98]

As Herzfeld explains, for each ape the knots are personal, expressive, and lyrical[99] – each one's own intellectual creation, so to speak. And as such, attention is drawn to the importance of considering the individual, rather than summarising the collective: "We think the researcher should instead look at the singular individuals that make up the species, and that 'species behavior' is a highly problematic notion, which should be thought of in terms of 'worlds of possible behaviors'."[100] The potential for authorship thus takes on an ethical dimension of multispecies regard: "We plead for the possibility of attributing a basic creative capacity to every animal."[101]

Dominique Lestel understands the relational process of intersubjectivity through Wattana's knot-tying by adopting a "bi-constructivist" or "multi-constructivist" approach, in the process: "The notion of animal 'contamination' by humans and outmoded dogmas about tool-use prevented the wider recognition of the significance of Wattana's (and other great apes') knot-tying behaviour as an ingenious manipulation of rope or other long, flexible materials. It is precisely such anomalous instances that bi-constructivism takes seriously."[102] This is a kind of ethological jurisprudence, accounting for interactions between worlds, interacting through shared interests shared interests,[103] in a "worldly" approach to an interdependent and intercommunicative understanding of multispecies communities and capabilities.[104] With the power, is existence. Conjugating verbs, and declining nouns.

As Lestel explains, "The very nature of animal capabilities does not allow for their objective description, because understanding them requires us to work *with* the animal (rather than *on* the animal). By doing so, we establish a relation with the animal and therefore transform its capabilities. The question is therefore not *What are they?* But rather *What can I do with them?*"[105] This relationality is crucial not only to the reception of more-than-human authorship and invention but also for the understanding of authorship and *what not*.

Wattana's Precursors

Earlier tales of knots and nonhuman primates come from the late nineteenth and early twentieth centuries. In 1884, the evolutionary biologist George Romanes recorded an incident of knot-untying in an orangutan, witnessed by the naturalist Étienne Geoffroy Saint-Hilaire:

> One of the Orangs ... was accustomed, when the dinner-hour had come, to open the door of the room where he took his meals in company with several persons. As he was not sufficiently tall to reach as far as the key of the door, he hung on to a rope, balanced himself, and after a few oscillations very quickly reached the key. His keeper, who was rather worried

by so much exactitude, one day took occasion to make three knots in the rope, which, having thus been made too short, no longer permitted the Orang-outang to seize the key. The animal, after an ineffectual attempt, *recognizing the nature of the obstacle which opposed his desire, climbed up the rope, placed himself above the knots, and untied all three.*[106]

Wolfgang Köhler, in his studies conducted at the Anthropoid Station in Tenerife during 1913 to 1917, noted several instances of knot tying, including chimpanzees manipulating straws with their mouths to make a kind of knot.[107] Particularly notable is the example of one chimpanzee who tied a rag to a stick and then manipulated it into a knot: "[S]he split a wooden plank with her teeth and drove a wire into the gap; on the following day she was busy with a woollen rag which she tied to a stick; she was not content with simply wrapping it round the stick, but actually achieved a sort of knot, by looping one end of the rag through the portion wound round the stick and pulling it taut. However humble this effort may seem to most of us, it has a surprisingly *constructive* character."[108] Others would use straw and sticks to poke into holes and crevices, but one individual, Nueva, achieved what Köhler describes as a kind of "weaving," observing her "carefully plaiting straws through the wire interstices."[109] Nueva also "had a special fancy for knots; for instance, she thrust a strip of banana leaf through a wire mesh, tied the two ends together, and continued in the same way, either by slipping one end of the leaf through the knot, or tying the ends again."[110]

In Nueva's combination of different materials and objects, Köhler sees in this activity the potential for a "rudimentary constructive effort, a form of manual craftsmanship," but records that she could never be trained to perform these actions to a plan, "however easy."[111] But was it to Nueva's plan? It is a common misconception, or perhaps convention, that obedience or trainability equates with intelligence; but the *disobedience* of intelligence is the space of creativity and authorship.[112] Indeed, what Köhler appears to describe is the integrity of a creative dissent, a playful authorship and joy in the work of discovery: "When I prepared for her a wooden frame with strips of leaf fastened to one side of it for plaiting, she turned aside and devoted herself to her usual knots; the slightest pressure towards anything stable and 'productive' extinguished her joy and interest at once, and she let the frame fall in sullen displeasure."[113]

Further early accounts come not from science but from travelling exhibitions and the animal trainer and showman, W Henry Sheak. While anecdotal in nature, later discussion will explore why such fragments are a critical tool. But for now, although not a scientist, the intimacy of Sheak's anecdotal evidence provides the opportunity to view creativity through the interdependence of the human and chimpanzee relationship, as appreciated by scientists at the time. Robert Yerkes and Margaret Sykes Child affirm, "Sheak's intimate acquaintance with performing animals entitles his statements of fact and his conclusions to serious consideration."[114] Notwithstanding the inauspicious circumstances of indentured labour in which Sheak's human and nonhuman animals found themselves, the history of these observations is important to acknowledge.

One particularly intriguing example of this engagement is an anecdote about an orangutan. Sheak describes the way in which orangutans are not as suited to exhibition as the chimpanzee, but curiously and notably, he does so in a way in which he appreciates their different abilities, rather than imposing a training hierarchy. In other words, in relating, as he says, "apes I have known," he does so by revealing differences in personalities rather than rating those differences according to a form of species hierarchy of intelligence. This goes some way to acknowledging a level of individual variation that introduces an ethological approach, albeit with significant environmental limitations. Sheak notes: "Unlike the chimpanzee, he is not always inventing some new way to amuse himself or to accomplish some of his purposes, or engaged in mad and frantic activity."[115] Although this appears to persist with the convention of group-level (species or even breed) summation or generalisation of personality,[116] nevertheless the following passage illustrates an early approach to the nonhuman animal subject as individual:

> But though he may sit in a corner of his cage, motionless and voiceless … I have found him a very keen observer. In 1907 I was traveling with the Gus Lambrigger Animal Show as naturalist and lecturer. Our star attraction was a young orang-utan. One afternoon when I was standing in front of his cage, he left his place in the farmer corner, came over to the front and, stretching his arm through the bars, put his hand on my shoulder. At first I could not imagine what was engaging his attention, but when he took his hand away I discovered there was a tiny knot in the thread of the seam of my coat, and he was trying to get it. I had not noticed it before, but his sharp eyes had seen it from the back of the cage.[117]

Elsewhere, and very significantly in terms of the appreciation for what is relevant to the individual and what is meaningful in terms of their world, Sheak notes, "when it comes to solving problems to satisfy his own needs or desires, and to doing things that are really worthwhile, he manifests wonderful intellectual power."[118]

In one particular essay, Sheak describes a chimpanzee named Sallie, who showed ingenuity and curiosity similar to that expressed by Wattana. Sallie was reportedly a great observer and would watch one of the attendants using a needle and thread to mend his clothes. Sheak reports that "Sallie watched the operation very intently. A little later she was noticed with a string trying to find an eye in a nail. She was given a small darning needle, and a heavy cotton thread, and at once she threaded the needle,"[119] just as she had observed. Intriguingly, Sallie was also quick to reject deception from the handlers when handed a nail instead of a needle: "When given a nail or piece of wire, she would look for an eye and, if there was none, she would throw away the counterfeit."[120] A true craftsperson knows their tools. Indeed, it seems that Sallie's whole process was very exacting:

> She would begin by wetting the end of the thread in her mouth, would place the eye of her needle in line with her eye, insert the thread from behind forward, then pull the thread the remainder of the way with her lips. She always tried to make the knot in the thread up next to the needle. After a number of successful attempts at this, she would go to work on her dress, and sew, and sew, and sew, pulling the thread clear at every stitch. Sometimes she would amuse herself in this way for half an hour.[121]

All of these examples are notably of captive apes; nevertheless, they are invaluable as examples of a bodily and intellectual engagement with the environment. Similarly, and almost one hundred years later, Herzfeld and Lestel surveyed researchers and received further examples of knot-makers in captive populations of apes, including orangutans, bonobos, and chimpanzees. The results identify twelve knot-makers. Notably, all the subjects were hand-reared by humans "and are highly acculturated anthropoids living in zoos."[122] But again, while the results are all in captive populations,[123] or perhaps because they are, the ingenuity is intellectually adaptive, playful and entertaining, aesthetically enriching and compelling.

However, there is one intriguing example of a kind of aesthetic knot-making in the wild, observed by researchers in a group of chimpanzees in the Mahale Mountains National Park, Tanzania.[124] In this example, a group killed and ate a colobus monkey in the afternoon and were still carrying around pieces of skin the next morning. Ai, a female juvenile, was observed with a piece of skin she was "grooming"[125] and with which she was playing. Another juvenile, a male named Primus, then took the skin from Ai. It was not clear who actually made the artefact, but some time later another young adult female, Ako, was observed wearing the skin around her neck. When the researchers found the skin abandoned a little later, it had been tied in a knot, the result being a kind of "necklace": "[W]e know of no other non-human case in which a draped adornment is *made*, that is, a necklace created by tying a knot."[126] Although the chimpanzee responsible for tying the knot could not be identified, and the process of construction itself was not observed and may have even happened by accident, once again, it was determined that "the result was functional."[127] At least, perhaps it was functional in as much as it was fashionable? And through at least three transactions of the necklace itself, the result was also social.

As the researchers concede, "Like all anecdotes, it can only serve to alert us to a possibility; a single case is only an hypothesis, not a conclusion."[128] But what of that single extraordinary case? Is this an aesthetic of a chimpanzee? Or is it once again rationalised within a simple scenario of the creative *accident* of trial and error and restless fingers? Lestel and Herzfeld describe Wattana's creations also as "necklaces," although they suggest that their value as adornment appears to be less than their value to play: "On two occasions, [Wattana] made a 'necklace.' She threw the first one up in the air, as she often did with the knotted objects she made. She put the second one around her neck as soon as she had finished it."[129] It is intriguing to note here an observation by Köhler in relation to the chimpanzee, Rana, and her attempts to remove a coiled rope with which she subsequently "adorns" herself by fashioning what might also be considered, once again, a kind of necklace: "The only thing that can still be altered is the fixing of the knot, and *actually Rana does not stop until the knot is off the hook*. Somewhat puzzled when she finds the rope free in her hand, she takes it up the crossbeam, and slowly winds it round her neck."[130] A necklace became an artefact to throw in play or in conflict,[131] but always in communication. A tool is a tool, whether in work or play. Indeed, why, in the literature, is there silence more often than *knot*? As Lestel and Herzfeld question: "[W]hy does the idea of a few apes making knots render the primatological community deaf (to what some observers report) and blind (to what some apes do)?"[132]

What are restless fingers anyway but wishful thinking? So, to speak.

Wattana's Playful Properties

Louis Leakey once delighted in Dian Fossey's community with the gorillas: "'In fact,' he gloated, 'I have just received a telegram from Dian saying that the mountain gorillas are becoming so habituated to her presence that one is even untying her shoelaces.'"[133] Such encounters are not only affiliative but also a source of social prestige. Herzfeld and Lestel surmise that the innovation benefits from both curiosity and attention, as well as charisma and prestige (resonant with Tarde's account of imitation):

> [N]o doubt the young orangutans of the Ménagerie lived up to their reputation and regularly untied their keepers' shoelaces. Their keepers therefore often had to *retie* their laces and thus to *make knots* in front of the apes, always on the lookout for something new and all the more interested in whatever their 'charismatic leaders' were doing as these humans were their keepers.[134]

It is an attention that is attentive, shared, and creative. Through her knot-tying, Wattana negotiates her entangled, multispecies relations, tangled stories, and strange attachments. Wattana makes knots to have and to hold, to give and to create a relation. This making is thus both communicative and indeed symbolic as a kind of intentional, authorial property. Wattana's knot-making is not accidental or incidental; it is intentional. And in this way, it is also communicative. Herzfeld and Lestel describe the ways in which the subjects of their studies would devise "new forms of communication," such as pushing and pulling on ropes between cages, passing materials and objects through mesh, and various other activities with novel and unfamiliar materials: "The simple fact of *making knots* and the use of material that can be knotted constitute an authentic form of social communication. The different occasions on which an exchange was initiated by the various materials and by this activity support this."[135]

In other words, there is a relationship of familiar production in this activity, the generation of meaning in the between: "[T]he materials provided (paper, string, hoses, etc.) acted as materials of communication, as intermediaries."[136] Sometimes Wattana would display her results to the public, sometimes not, imputing meaning to her productions.[137] And in this way, the utterances and relationships are varied and personal, if not symbolic and intelligible; just as a dog in play may surrender a toy to their human in order to prolong the play, but may guard the toy from another dog at the same time, demonstrating the way in which the toy becomes a tool that is adapted and revised within different communicative strategies and contexts.[138] Wattana's knotty communications are also playful and relational, in a form of social communication described as *"duetting"*;[139] as Lestel and Herzfeld state, "Knotting is not a game of solitaire."[140] The games are in motion, tying and untying, taking turns and turn-taking, all the while weaving an ethics of play. Always in two minds.

Wattana's untying or unfolding thus allows for her to experiment with the geometry of her knots, the counting of missives, the aesthetics of adornment. There is a remarkable passage in Ernst Gombrich's *Art and Illusion* where he anticipates this kind of more-than-human technical innovation in the context of art and the use of space:

> [T]o Pliny every step on the road towards mimesis was an invention he attributed to a *heuretes*, a finder. Vasari, too, still remembered this ancient truth and understood ... that this invention can only progress piecemeal, building up through gradual improvement on past achievements ... As far as I can see, only one aspect of mimesis has never ceased to be seen in the light of a real scientific invention, the rendering of space and the development of 'artificial perspective' by Brunelleschi and his followers.[141]

Gombrich approaches space by moving away from the emphasis on a visual regime, advocating instead a kind of immediacy in the haptics in artistic expression and reception: "[I]f we discard Berkeley's theory of vision, according to which we 'see' a flat field but 'construct' a tactile space, we can perhaps rid art history of its obsession with space and bring other achievements into focus, the suggestion of light and of texture, for instance, or the mastery of physiognomic expression."[142]

An embodied language is rolling out. Watch this space.

Creative Accountancy

Wattana's knot-tying also warrants attention for its spatial awareness and creative accounting, so to speak. Lestel and Herzfeld observe that Wattana "performs a kind of mathematics and the study of her knots tying behavior allows us to bring the question of origins of mathematics on new grounds in an ethological perspective," as distinct from the "uniquely *human* way" the history of mathematics is ordinarily presented. [143]

In the context of play and tool manipulation, that is for pleasure, as well as, and very significantly, in the generation of meaning, Herzfeld and Lestel point to the importance of attention, time (and indeed patience), and thinking: "This is a challenging situation she has to answer to. She does not blindly handle the ropes but she does think about what to do within. We could interpret in that way the long moment during which Wattana does nothing but to look at the ropes with great attention. She makes sense of what she does and she takes interest at that."[144] While Wattana "does not demonstrate theorems," the authors nevertheless make a compelling hypothesis for Wattana's activities as a kind of inventive proto-mathematics: "[S]he nevertheless explores practical and geometrical properties of knots *as such*, and in that way, Wattana is already in the frame of a mathematical activity ... *Wattana is a mathematical animal because she acts as a mathematician could think.*"[145] Not only in the "spatio-temporal structuring," but also in "the complex way in which they manipulate fibers, string, laces and other ties," such communicative dexterity suggests an "embodied mathematics" or "etho-mathematics," a mathematics "that finds expression through the body."[146]

There is evidence of numeracy, quantification, and statistical reasoning in a range of diverse species,[147] from counting in honeybees,[148] to quantification in salamanders,[149] to ordering in hummingbirds,[150] to numerical representation in mosquitofish,[151] to egg accountancy in coot birds,[152] to quantity discrimination in angelfish,[153] to statistical inference in crows[154] and giraffes,[155] to dogs,[156] and, of course, to ants.[157] This introduces questions around the group, and the nature of the democracy of the enumeration of the group as swarm or collectivity. In this way, the capacity for numeracy becomes associated with a kind of morality or sense of fairness as well as a certain transactional aptitude.[158] For example, research with African grey parrots has demonstrated not only an appreciation of a kind of currency, learning to exchange tokens (small metal rings) for high-value food (walnuts), but also a form of prosocial investment in their community with no expectation of personal reward. By sharing the tokens with other members of their group, African grey parrots subsidise their partners through a form of "instrumental helping based on a prosocial attitude," a behaviour which appears to be a "selfless" act of altruism independent of any expectation of reciprocity.[159] Thus, property relations are expressed as a kind of sociality, through what I set out in *Owned* as *res familiaris*.[160] Rather than persisting in alienation, the objects of property (including "intangible property," such as favours[161]) thus vitalise a cooperative and productive relationship, changing and shifting through the circulation of shared interests.

This is perhaps especially evident in the presence of inequity aversion in a wide range of different species.[162] Inequity aversion is notable in its foundations in economic discourse, while at the same time potentially instating fairness and empathy at the heart of transactional relationships and, for that matter, property.[163] It is not merely evidence of a basic numeracy or capacity to compare quality or quantity. Significantly, inequity aversion rests fundamentally upon an awareness of the other, a theory of mind.[164] Returning to the grey parrots, the token transfer arguably depends upon the awareness of the situation of others, taking the perspective of others, and acting prosocially in addressing the perceived unfairness. Significantly, this unfairness is in respect of one's own advantage, and the token transfer is arguably in response to advantageous inequity aversion and an act of "proactive prosociality" in order to address *sympathetically* that inequality.[165] By the same token, as it were, this sharing embodies a kind of calculation and a certain appreciation of the transactional value of the token.

And what about nest-building and the enterprising efforts of ants? Wittgenstein's explanation of the building of a house is intriguing here:

> We teach someone to build a house; and at the same time how he is to obtain a sufficient quantity of material, boards, say; and for this purpose a technique of calculation. The technique of calculation is part of the technique of house-building ... They do not know "why" it happens like this; they simply do it like this: this is how it is done. – Do these people not calculate?[166]

Do ants building tunnels not calculate? Does Wattana not quantify and measure? In other words, Wattana does not need to "utter any 'arithmetical proposition'."[167] Nor does she need to demonstrate a theorem.[168] As Wittgenstein might ask, why shouldn't other animals, not merely humans, learn to calculate? "And when they can do so haven't they learnt arithmetic?"[169] Thus, in debates on the nature of nonhuman authorship, whether machines or animals other than human, the emphasis on "proof" of more-than-human accounting and indeed creativity is asking the wrong question or, at least, proposing a purposefully unanswerable one. What does Wattana want? The answer is in the question. In other words, "How do we reproduce, how do we copy, a proof? – Not e.g. by taking measurements of it."[170]

In this way, numeracy and proprietary-like transactions in animal communities afford the possibilities for empathy, as distinct from the "predatory drift" associated with contemporary discourses on property, including intellectual property and the incentives narrative.[171] And in the context of incentive and punishment narratives, not only in radical behaviourism but also in the application to intellectual property narratives, punishment is not easily calculable in terms of recuperating losses. Accordingly, punishment can never be fair.[172] It is a contrivance of the fiction of predatory drift, not an inevitable consequence of a purportedly causal narrative. It makes no sense if always pursued according to a programme of revenge.[173] Instead, empathy and regard can provide the *one* stimulus for creativity, rather than disadvantage and punishment, and a crucial part of that genuine regard is the stewardship and provenance of knowledge.[174]

Moral Accountancy

How to count and account for moral standing? Inequity aversion on behalf of the disadvantage of another at the actions of a third party suggests a form of moral thinking, a form of social justice, a strategy of social eavesdropping, and something that has been demonstrated in various species. For instance, if dogs witness a stranger behaving negatively towards their human, they will avoid that stranger, thus exercising a kind of moral judgment.[175] In a remarkable recent study, horses experience a measurable emotional response when they watch *video* footage of third-party interactions between humans and horses, both negative and positive, and then apply this to their own real experiences with the same humans.[176] And in a striking account of empathy in inequity aversion, rats will avoid using a lever that induces harm in a neighbour, even if pressing that lever delivers twice the food.[177] These sociable properties of animal territories, where boundaries broker points of contact rather than obstacles to relationships, show the generation of meaning and meaningful lives in *metaxu*. Thus, there is also a kind of mathematical dimension to the qualities associated with sentience, but an embodied mathematics and interaction between calculating minds. Whether artificial intelligence demonstrates the requisite prosociality of authorship is something to be investigated in more detail in the following chapters.

It is time to count to two and address the body in the library of sentience.

Notes

1 *The Hitch Hiker's Guide to the Galaxy* (1979) is the first instalment in a series of four books. The others in order are *The Restaurant at the End of the Universe* (1980), *Life, the Universe and Everything* (1982), and *So Long, and Thanks for All the Fish* (1984). For the full collection, see Adams (1986).
2 Adams (1986), 128.
3 Adams (1986), 128.
4 Adams (1986), 128.
5 Adams (1986), 129.

6 See further the discussion in the previous chapter.
7 Chalmers (1995).
8 Schopenhauer (1903), §42, 169. See further the discussion in Kim (2007), 7.
9 Schopenhauer (1903), §42, 168.
10 Schopenhauer (1903), §42, 169.
11 For an excellent history of knot theory in mathematics, see Griend (1996).
12 Griend (1996) argues that Leibniz established the foundations for knot theory, in that "his endeavours at finding a geometry of this kind, different from the only one known at the time, predated other work in this direction by more than half a century" (211). See further, Przytycki (1995). See also the extensive treatment of Leibniz's mathematics in Risi (2007).
13 In this sense, there is an important interaction between Leibniz's mathematics and his philosophy of mind through the importance of the concept of *geometria situs* (geometry of position) to his theory of relations. Leibniz's mathematics in his work on *analysis situs*, to be found in largely which informs his theory of relations in his philosophy of mind. Leibniz's theory of relations continues to inform considerations of the collective in Chapter 4 towards differentiating the individualities in the swarm from the incompleteness of the individual in the collective, and the use of space in Naruto's creative work in Chapter 5.
14 Vernitski (2018).
15 Weil (1929–1930), 78–79.
16 Emphasis on hands as a distinction of humanity has persisted for centuries: "There is no Animal hath any Organ of equal use to the Arm and Hand of a Man, that *Organum Organorum*, an Organ accommodate to all the useful motions, operations, arts and uses of his life." See Hale (1677), 65.
17 Tallis (2003): "It may be justifiable to think of human beings as 'manukind' as to think of them as 'speaking animals' and to postulate the notion of Manu – that of the first man who laid down the law and formatted the disk of our collective human consciousness – as a displaced awareness of the centrality of our handedness to our nature and cultures" (9). See further Tallis R (2004) in which the author defends human exceptionalism explicitly in terms of self-awareness, agency, and the hand (in particular, 2–11). In what is a somewhat familiar appeal to digital dexterity and touch in support of an anthropocentric perspective, the author regards the hand's gestural self-equivalence, as it were, as evidence of human exceptionalism, notwithstanding the dexterity of nonhuman primates: "There is nothing else like it in the animal kingdom … There is, of course, also some overlap with the paws of other higher mammals. However, the human hand, through the complete opposability of the thumb, has another feature: in the touching tips of the fingers the body communicates with itself, as well as with the extra-corporeal world, with unprecedented intensity" (3). There is also the concept of "handedness" (referring to an asymmetry in preference for one "hand" over another), which is evident across a range of species, and the terminology of "handedness" is an interesting semantic twist of anthropocentrism here, at the same time as opening out the "hand" as the notion of embodied orientation.
18 O'Hear (1995). On evidence in the history of photography, see Lovejoy (1990), 258. A similar *handedness* in the tension between human creativity and technology, and distinctions between high and low art, is also perceptible in the controversies and complications in the early days of film and cinema: Gibson (2022d).
19 *Civilisations*, BBC Series, 2018. Writers, Mary Beard, David Olusoga, Simon Schama. See further the discussion of this series and the assertion, "We are the art-making animal," in the introductory chapter, "What Does Naruto Want?"

20 Le Fanu J (2004), 201. Notably, this is similar to the discourse around *Civilisations* and the art-making animal, considered in "What Does Naruto Want?"
21 Derrida (2005/[2000]), 154. Martin Heidegger claims, "Only a being who can speak, that is, think, can have hands and can be handy in achieving works of handicraft." See Heidegger (1968/[1954]), 16. See further Meltzer (2001) in which the author examines the tying of the hand to speech: "these two attributes, the human hand and speech, make for the essence ... of what is 'man'" (626). In a discussion of Plato, Hegel, and Engels, Meltzer examines the relationship between the hand, labour, and the development of human society and traces this tie between the hand and speech: "In the case of Hegel and Engels, the hand is directly tied to speech" noting, "[t]he connection of the hand with speech is not to be overlooked ... the hand remains the organ that transcends the inner/outer dialectic" (626).
22 Arbib et al. (2014); Rizzolatti and Arbib (1998).
23 Meltzer (1987), 162.
24 Meltzer (1987), 162. This resonates with the emphasis on the work in examples of artificial authorship and inventorship, as though recognition of a "work" thus "makes" the author. See further the discussion in Abbott (2016). A fuller discussion of the nature of originality in this context is undertaken in Gibson (2025).
25 Wittgenstein (1967/[1953]), §25.
26 Wittgenstein (1967/[1953]), §11. Mulhall (2001) suggests that this imagery of "tools and handles" invites us "to ask whether humanity rests in, or grows from, the human hand with its opposable thumb, and our consequent ability to take a grip on the world as well as to let it slip through our fingers" (72).
27 Weil (1929–1930), 80. Recall Weil's example of a blind man using a stick, where "he touches things directly with his stick, as if it were sensible and formed part of his body" (79).
28 Weil (1929–30), 79. See further the discussion of Weil's phenomenology in McCullough (2012): "When Simone Weil enacted her quasi-Cartesian experiment in 1930, she did not purpose to eliminate Cartesian dualism, but this is what her argument achieves – at least in a rudimentary, incompletely developed way. It posits the cogito's constitutive foundation in bodily imagination – the imaginative body – as no philosophy had done as axially before, though significant steps in this direction were made by the early Kant, Bergson, Husserl, Whitehead, and Heidegger. She also did it as no philosopher was to do more fully until Merleau-Ponty published *The Phenomenology of Perception* more than a decade later in 1945" (214). It is interesting to note also Weil's approach to the experience of work and the conviction that the barrier between manual and intellectual work was a problematic and damaging obstruction to thinking about work. She thus pursued manual labour herself in order to understand the life of the working class, literally through a kind of embodied learning, as in Weil (1965): "Above all, I feel I have escaped from a world of abstractions" (11). On a personal note, this is especially striking (and frequently frustrating) to me in my own experience of law, both in research and teaching, where I despair of the rhetoric of the arbitrary division of so-called practical and academic (or theory), usually at the expense of the more critical, theoretical, and interdisciplinary value of learning and intellectual experiment. I believe it is in this context that Weil's following words in Weil (2002/[1947]) resonate: "Workers need poetry more than bread. They need that their life should be a poem. They need some light from eternity ... Deprivation of this poetry explains all forms of demoralization" (180–181). This poetry of work is explored in more detail in Part 3. This is also

relevant to the experience of immersive scenarios in the policy context. See for example Gebhardt Fearns (2019).
29 Weil (1978/[1959]), 32. Winch (1978) notes, "This order, which is not a result, but a precondition, of thought is introduced by the unreflective 'dance' of the body" (13).
30 Allan Kornblum and the Actualist Movement in Art will be considered in more detail in the next chapter, when this handed sentience will be revisited.
31 Allan Kornblum, "Work Song," in Kornblum (1980), 51. This expressive approach to sentience is developed in more detail in the next chapter.
32 For a review of the literature across a range of species, see Jacobs and Osvath (2015). See also Shettleworth (2012). In pigeons, see Wasserman et al. (2013). In dogs, see Range et al. (2011). This study is noteworthy, as elsewhere in the literature, dogs have been considered to have limited physical cognition skills in string-pulling studies; however, it is postulated that the emphasis on the visual in string-pulling studies may limit the relevance of the question design for dogs, recalling the concept of the olfactory mirror problem (Horowitz (2017)) and framing.
33 Herzfeld and Lestel (2005): "Ethology students are generally taught that, while many similarities have been found between great apes and humans, certain delicate manipulatory skills like the ability to tie knots always distinguish humans from apes" (622). See further Vauclair (2003), 19.
34 The use of the mouth in knot tying is described in the very early accounts of W Henry Sheak, as well as in more recent observations. See, for instance, Lestel and Herzfeld (2005). The authors note that Wattana, an orangutan whose prolific knot-tying is discussed later in this chapter, "is able to tie a knot *only with the mouth*" (149).
35 Herzfeld and Lestel (2005), 631. The authors note further that the knot-tying orangutan, Wattana, is also able to make a knot using her mouth alone (631).
36 Herzfel and Lestel (2005) similarly note that while survey testimony is now recognised as relevant, the question then shifted to the quality or complexity of the knots themselves (625). Vauclair (2003), for example, argues "it is worth noticing that such activities with the corresponding levels of difficulty seen in humans are lacking in the repertoire of animal species" (19).
37 Responding to a lack of engagement with embodied cognition in education theory, O'Loughlin (2006) arguably describes an implicit dualism in dominant approaches when speaking of the "epistemological privileging of vision in Western culture" and "the disengagement of the body from essential social and emotional connectedness," in what she terms the "scopic regime" (7). O'Loughlin argues: "Educational theorists have often appeared to be rather uncomfortable with the brute fact of corporeality. Their discussions of cognition, social phenomena, and the development of intellectual skills or moral reasoning have been frequently carried out as if bodies were something of an embarrassment" (16). In rejecting the "scopic regime," the author maintains that "to understand what is really involved in the making of different kinds of epistemic subjects I think we must now focus with determination on the corporeality, emotionality and sociality of human beings and their material processes" (16–17). See further: Leigh (2018); Michel and Harkins (1985).
38 Nancy (2002/[1997]), 47. This relationality is explored further in an ethological account of intellectual property objects in Gibson (2025).
39 See further Chapter 9.
40 Serres (2008/[1985]), 80.
41 Serres (2008/[1985]), 80.

42 Liu and Sun (2018), 7. Emphasis in original. It is interesting to note similar perspectives from embodied cognition on the teaching of handwriting and the "increased scholarly and scientific interest in the vital role of the body and of fine motor skills ... for cognitive development and learning/literacy outcomes." See Mangen and Balsvik (2016), 100.
43 This link between embodied communication and intentionality as a kind of sincerity or even originality is part of the industry discourse on human-machine communication. For instance, see Schöner (2014).
44 Liu and Sun (2018). The principle of "haptic feedback" is critical to the development of so-called strong AI and the self-awareness through bodily integrity and direct experience, as distinct from a kind of disembodied intentionality articulated through beliefs and desires. See further, Russell and Norvig (2016), Chapter 26.
45 For instance, see the discussion in Lee (2020): "What is needed are proper social interactions, involving free-flowing conversations over the long term during which AI systems remember the person and their past conversations. AI will have to understand intentions and beliefs and the meaning of what people are saying ... We also observe the person's actions and infer their intentions and preferences from gestures and signals ... It is clear that all this social interaction only makes sense to the parties involved if they have a 'sense of self' and can similarly maintain a model of the self of the other agent. In order to understand someone else, it is necessary to know oneself. An AI 'self model' should include a subjective perspective, involving how its body operates (for example, its visual viewpoint depends upon the physical location of its eyes), a detailed map of its own space, and a repertoire of well understood skills and actions." An embodied approach to sentience is addressed in more detail in the next chapter.
46 Mars, *Put Your Hands to Good Use*, Pedigree Campaign, 2010.
47 Mars, *Dogs Have Hands Too*, Pedigree Campaign, 2018.
48 See the extensive discussion of knots in Frazer (1993/[1922]). See also the account of knot lore in Day (1950). See further the discussion in relation to the development of mathematics in Joseph (2011), Chapter 2; and Diana (1967). See further Locke (1912), in which the author identifies a consensus between play and language through knots: "The use of knots in cord for the purpose of recording number seems to have been as universal as the figures of the cat's cradle in the play life of primitive peoples" (325).
49 Day (1950), 239. See further Gandz (1930), 190.
50 Lagercrantz (1968).
51 Malouf and White (1953).
52 Gaster (1914), 255. Emphasis in original.
53 Gandz (1930), 191.
54 Haraway (2016), 14.
55 Haraway (2016), 14.
56 In their influential work on the sociology of territoriality, Lyman and Scott (1967) describe a party or social gathering as "interactional territories" in which different groups act as "knots," i.e., contact points or contact zones for social interaction: "A party is an interactional territory, as are the several knots of people who form clusters at parties. Every interactional territory implicitly makes a claim of boundary maintenance for the duration of the interaction" (240). This resonates with the kind of management of space through relational negotiations in Gibson (2020a), Chapter 4.
57 Ingold (2016/[2007]), 103–104. See further the discussion in Bird and Rhoads (2020): "This imagery aptly describes the distribution of Aboriginal

archaeological remains as the entangled knots, which comprise the threads of many individual lives through time that form persistent places" (284). In other words, such *marking* is both relational and monumental.
58 Scene I.
59 Küchler (2003), 205.
60 See for example the discussion in Spier (2007). And, of course, there is the literal knotting in dance, such as in traditional rapper dancer teams and rapper swords in English folk dance. See further Cassie (1965).
61 Derrida (2002), 28.
62 See further Christensen (2002). There is also evidence of similar knotted systems in other cultures. For example, see Küchler (2003), and Jacobsen (1983), where the author claims that use in ancient China may pre-date the use in Peruvian Inca culture (57).
63 Urton (2003), 1.
64 Urton (2003), 1–2. Further, the characteristics and composition of the knots would be significant. Urton (2005a): "there are several other means whereby the khipu keepers recorded other, or modifying, types of information. These additional sign features include color (both of camelid hair and of differently colored cotton), as well as several forms of variation and patterning of khipu construction features, such as material (primarily camelid or cotton) differences and directional variation in spinning, plying, knotting, and attaching khipu cords" (148).
65 Urton (2003), 3. See further Urton (1998); Benson (1975). For a contemporary account of the khipu as numerical notational system, see Zaslavsky and Crespo (2000).
66 http://khipukamayuq.fas.harvard.edu
67 Urton (2005b).
68 Dahl (2009a); Dahl (2009b).
69 See for instance Santos et al. (2019), 349–351. For instance, MIT's Computer Science and Artificial Intelligence Lab (CSAIL) has developed a two-fingered robotic gripper reportedly basing the design "on how humans use their fingers to do things like untangle wires and tie knots" (Etherington (2020).
70 Lees and Overing (2019), 12. The authors use the symbol of the knot and "practices of rumination" (12) to the concept of slow scholarship, noting "[h]ow medieval visual and verbal laces spiral, circle, ravel and unravel, entwine, knot, bind or blend seem to us, therefore, to be useful ways to think about practices of cognition and interpretation, about the processes of making (and remaking) meaning over time, now as well as then, together as well as apart" (13). This thinking is relevant to the consideration of collaboration, participation, and embodied and playful production in the present work throughout the following chapters, as well as the processes of stewardship and precursors in an *attentive imitation* (see in particular Chapter 6).
71 Leibniz (1989), 91.
72 The concept of situation with respect to force and space is examined in Chapter 5, and the Situationist International approach to space, parody, and the deceptions of authorship through *détournement* in Chapter 9.
73 Belmonte (2007), 17243. For an interesting narrative treatment of this concept, see Tatham (1977).
74 Wittgenstein (1993), 397. Emphasis in original.
75 See further Klockmann et al. (2022).
76 See further the discussion of lying and deception in Chapter 8.
77 Adams (1986), 128.

78 Davies et al. (2021).
79 Alex Davies (DeepMind) quoted in Wilkins (2024).
80 Floridi (2023), 14–30.
81 See further the discussion of explainability in "What Does Naruto Want?"
82 Quoted in Wilkins (2024).
83 Herzfeld (2016/[2012]), 31. At just three and a half months, Wattana was transferred to Stuttgart Zoo, before she ultimately went to Paris.
84 Lestel and Herzfeld (2016) describe how, on visiting Wattana at Apenheul, they "gave her a red ribbon," and then went elsewhere before coming back to discover "she had used the ribbon to make a knot on the mesh of her enclosure."
85 Herzfeld (2016/[2012]), 25.
86 Herzfeld (2016/[2012]), 2.
87 Herzfeld (2016/[2012]), 2.
88 Herzfeld and Lestel (2005), 646. Rather than analysing the activity as an instinctual response, a case is made for it as a creative performativity. As the authors note more generally: "A species' adaptive capacity should also be assessed with respect to behavioral creativity and not only in the light of past behavioral choices" (647).
89 Herzfeld (2016/[2012]), 87.
90 Herzfeld (2016/[2012]), 87.
91 Herzfeld (2016/[2012]), 87.
92 Herzfeld (2016/[2012]), 87. This emphasis on an aesthetic activity over functional requirements is revisited in Part 3 in relation to the concept of "poor economics" (Banerjee and Duflo (2012/[2011])).
93 Herzfeld (2016/[2012]), 108.
94 Herzfeld (2016/[2012]), 91.
95 Herzfeld (2016/[2012]), 91.
96 Herzfeld (2016/[2012]), 88.
97 Herzfeld (2016/[2012]), 91–92.
98 Herzfeld (2016/[2012]), 92.
99 Herzfeld (2016/[2012]), 92.
100 Herzfeld and Lestel (2005), 645.
101 Herzfeld and Lestel (2005), 645.
102 Lestel et al. (2014), 126. See further Lestel (2011).
103 See further the detailed examination and development of the concept of shared interests in Gibson (2020a), particularly Chapter 10.
104 Drawing on Noam Chomsky's concept of "competence," Lestel (2011) explains: "The realist-Cartesian approach in ethology studies the capacities of the animal, behavioural and cognitive. The bi-constructivist approach, in contrast, takes into consideration the fact that the possibilities for an animal's action cannot be reduced to mere capacities. They should be understood as applications of such capacities, as influenced by the opportunities encountered by the animal, as well as of its abilities to appropriate them" (88).
105 Lestel (2011), 88. Emphasis in original.
106 Romanes (1885), 328 (note). Emphasis in original. This same orangutan also demonstrated the identification and use of keys, as well as the use of a bar of iron as a lever.
107 Köhler (1972/[1921]), 70.
108 Köhler (1972/[1921]), 277–278. Emphasis in original.
109 Köhler (1972/[1921]), 278. See further the discussion in Herzfeld and Lestel (2005), where the authors describe a kind of weaving among the knot-tying behaviours of orangutans. See also Herzfled (2016/[2012]), Wattana has also been observed using her enclosure as a kind of weaving frame: "For example, she

ties cords to a horizontal beam located at her height, which then allows her to more easily interlace and knot the strands, which – in a way – are then inserted into a 'working frame.' What she implements then is reminiscent of a type of *weaving*" (88).
110 Köhler (1972/[1921]), 278.
111 Köhler (1972/[1921]), 278.
112 See further the discussion of deception and creativity in Chapter 8.
113 Köhler (1972/[1921]), 278.
114 Yerkes and Sykes Child (1927), 49. The authors note further the way Sheak's observations were attuned to the "individuality and temperamental traits in captive specimens which he has known" (53). See further the observations of Herzfeld and Lestel (2005) who note that the anecdotal nature of such accounts is often taken as a reason to disregard them, and they are critical of the subsequent absence of such observations from the mainstream literature: "Knotting and weaving are restricted to human societies. The few observations of these activities are often regarded as anecdotal and therefore not published. In fact, no systematic study on monkey knots has ever been published" (623).
115 Sheak (1923) Anthropoid apes I have known, *Natural History*, 23, 44–55: p 48.
116 Lestel (2011) critiques this approach through species or group stereotypes as fundamental to the realist-Cartesian perspective, such that "an animal cannot become a source of *surprise*," or indeed innovation (93). See also the useful note on the way in which group stereotypes influence analysis and the ability to recognise other abilities in Sevillano (2020).
117 Sheak (1923), 48. See further Sheak (1922).
118 See further Sheak (1922), 50.
119 Sheak (1917), 308.
120 Sheak (1917), 308.
121 Sheak (1917), 308–309.
122 Herzfeld and Lestel (2005), 621. The researchers note one exception observing this behaviour in the wild in McGrew and Marchant (1998), discussed further below.
123 Herzfeld and Lestel (2005), 621–653. In this article, the authors also provide a useful review of the limited examples recorded in the literature, including personal communications and other noteworthy anecdotal examples and individual accounts. See further the discussion in Lestel and Herzfeld (2005).
124 McGrew and Marchant (1998).
125 The washing of colobus skin after a killing has been observed elsewhere in the Mahale chimpanzees. See Nishida et al. (2009), 27.
126 McGrew and Marchant (1998), 8. Emphasis added.
127 McGrew and Marchant (1998), 8.
128 McGrew and Marchant (1998), 8–9.
129 Herzfeld and Lestel (2005), 631. See further the discussion in Lestel and Herzfeld (2005). Necklaces may also be utilised as a kind of weapon: Herzfeld and Lestel (2005), 633.
130 Köhler (1972/[1921]), 103. Emphasis in original.
131 Herzfeld and Lestel (2005): "After the death of the group's big male, when all the orangutans were put in the same cage, Wattana did not make any more knots. Instead she used the beads she had strung into a 'necklace' to strike her companions" (633).
132 Herzfeld and Lestel (2005), 622. Herzfeld and Lestel note, "Most primatologists think great apes are incapable of making knots. Furthermore, this behavior is

never, or almost never, discussed in the professional literature, and the major overviews do not mention it. What might be the reasons for this silence?" (622).
133 Louis Leakey, referring to a telegram from Dian Fossey, quoted in Galdikas (1995), 48. Notably, a similar behaviour was reported by one of Wattana's keepers, Danielle Dousseau, as noted in Herzfeld and Lestel (2005), but in this case, it was to tie the shoelaces rather than untie them: "[A]t the age of four Wattana had already made a knot in her keeper's *untied* shoelaces" (639).
134 Herzfeld and Lestel (2005), 639.
135 Herzfeld and Lestel (2005), 634. Emphasis in original.
136 Herzfeld and Lestel (2005), 634.
137 Herzfeld and Lestel (2005), 634.
138 See further Rooney and Bradshaw (2006); Rooney et al. (2002); Rooney et al. (2000).
139 Herzfeld and Lestel (2005), 634. See further the discussion of duetting and turn-taking, including during play, as a proto-language in Chapter 7 of the present work.
140 Herzfeld and Lestel (2005), 649n15.
141 Gombrich (1977/[1960]), 279. See further on the relationship between space and the visual arts in this kind of experimentation in creativity in Pedoe (1983/[1976]), where the author examines the history of geometry for its importance to the visual arts and for its "practical and aesthetic appeal" (11). See in particular the discussion of space and illusion in the work of Albrecht Dürer in Chapter 2, and the relationship between Cartesianism and the principle of duality in Chapter 7 of that work. Resonating with the *dual* of ethological jurisprudence and the haptic intimacy explored in this chapter, the principle of duality describes the *geometry*, as it were, of the animal turn in intellectual property. This duality is pursued through the irony of parody in Chapter 9.
142 Gombrich (1977/[1960]), 279.
143 Lestel and Herzfeld (2005), 148. Emphasis in original.
144 Lestel and Herzfeld (2005), 154.
145 Lestel and Herzfeld (2005), 155. Emphasis in original.
146 Herzfeld and Lestel (2005), 637–638. See further the discussion in Despret (2016/[2012]), 158.
147 For a useful review, see Reznikova and Ryabko (2011). See further, Kobylkov et al. (2023), and Gross (2020). See further the suggestion that statistical abilities may be quite widespread in Caicoya et al. (2023): "In evolutionary terms, statistical abilities might provide crucial fitness benefits to individuals when making inferences in a situation of uncertainty, and it should, therefore, not be surprising if these abilities are widespread across animal taxa" (4).
148 Dacke and Srinivasan (2008).
149 Krusche et al. (2010); Uller et al. (2003).
150 Vámos et al. (2020).
151 Dadda et al. (2009). See further Newport (2021).
152 Lyon (2003).
153 Gómez-Laplaza et al. (2018).
154 Johnston et al. (2023); Wascher (2023).
155 Caicoya et al. (2023).
156 Cooper et al. (2003). See further Miletto Petrazzini and Wynne (2016). In this study, the researchers found that dogs were able to base their choice on quantity without being influenced by the total number of individual pieces, thus demonstrating the ability to calculate and compare orders of magnitude.
157 Gross (2012); Reznikova and Ryabko (2011).

158 Engaging with recent research, Despret (2016/[2012]) describes the potential capabilities of animals to act as a "rational economic actor," while at the same time emphasising the value of "winning" in a conventional sense (155).
159 Brucks and Bayem (2020), 292.
160 Gibson (2020a), Chapter 12. See also Gibson (2025).
161 For instance, see the review of trade in favours in primate communities in Byrne (2007). See further Gibson (2020a), Chapter 10.
162 For example, to name just a few, inequity aversion has been demonstrated in dogs (McGetrick and Range (2018); Range et al. (2009); see also press on the study in Milius (2009); dogs and wolves (Essler et al. (2017); rats (Oberliessen et al. (2016); see also Douglas et al. (2018); capuchin monkeys (Brosnan and Waal (2003); and chimpanzees (Brosnan SF et al. (2015).
163 For early examination of inequity aversion in humans, see Pritchard et al. (1972). See further the analysis in the economic context of the market with an emphasis on competition as a counter to cooperation in Fehr and Schmidt (1999) 868. See also Fehr and Fischbacher (2004).
164 Yamamoto (2017).
165 Yamamoto (2017) explains the relationship between inequity aversion and prosociality, such as in cooperation or reciprocal altruism, but in advantageous inequity aversion, the subject is responding to an unfairness in their resources as compared to another's, leading to "proactive prosociality" (6). See further the discussion in Adriaense et al. (2020). See also more generally the account of inequity aversion in the context of animals' emotional lives and empathy in Bekoff and Pierce (2009), 127–129. The authors note the interaction between empathy, morality, and community success in the context of fairness as an evolutionarily stable strategy (ESS) and note that studies in inequity aversion "have a direct bearing on our discussion of fairness and justice" (115). On this point, see also Brosnan (2011). On ESS, see further Gibson (2020a), 108–109, and further on the emotional lives of animals see Bekoff (2009), 83.
166 Wittgenstein (1978/[1956]), I-143.
167 Wittgenstein (1978/[1956]), I-143.
168 Lestel and Herzfeld (2005).
169 Wittgenstein (1978/[1956]), I-144.
170 Wittgenstein (1978/[1956]), III-10.
171 Gibson (2020a) Chapter 10, and on empathy, see 258–269.
172 See further the discussion of punishment in Chapter 5.
173 Deutchman et al. (2021).
174 See further in the context of imitative attention in Chapter 6.
175 Chijiiwa et al. (2015). See further the discussion in Anderson et al. (2017).
176 Trösch et al. (2020).
177 Hernandez-Lallement et al. (2020). Interestingly, in this study, altruism had its limit. When the delivery was increased to three times the pellets, it would seem that the perceived benefit would outweigh the harm aversion. Numbers *count*.

Chapter 3

What Is It Like to Be an Author?

Quelle peut être la raison suffisante de ce phénomène?[1]

This is the question posed by Voltaire's optimistic philosopher, Dr Pangloss, in response to the catastrophic shipwreck in the novel, *Candide*.[2] Dr Pangloss, professor of "metaphysico-theologo-cosmolo-nigology"[3] is "the greatest philosopher in the province and, therefore, in the whole world."[4] Pangloss is, of course also the namesake of the so-called Panglossian paradigm of all is as it should be, that "everything was for the best."[5] As the Lisbon earthquake strikes, the ship is wrecked, homes are destroyed, and many lives are lost, Dr Pangloss asks: *What can be the sufficient reason for this phenomenon?*[6] And then answers, "that things could not be otherwise."[7] Despite the litany of disasters, Pangloss assures Candide, "'[A]ll this is for the best; for, if there is a volcano at Lisbon, it cannot be anywhere else; for it is impossible that things should not be where they are; for all is well.'"[8] *Tout va bien.*[9]

This question of sufficient reason is a question about starting from the phenomenon to fabricate the reason, matching causes to effects, ensuring the continuing plausibility of present expectations, and maintaining the status quo through accepting those explanations. What indeed, then, can be the reason that is to be applied in order to justify the phenomenon of the works of nonhumans (whether animals other than humans or machines) in question in the present discussion? What is the meaning of authorship? And what are the traditions maintained in answering that question? How is the creativity of nonhuman animals rationalised, and the products of artificial intelligence authorised, all in the service of the overwhelming narrative of authorship within the institution of intellectual property, the optimism of human exceptionalism? Time and again, rightly or mostly wrongly, the surrounding discourse comes back to a point of exceptionalism – namely, the nature of consciousness.

In a refrain on Thomas Nagel's famous question, this chapter asks, what is it like to be an author? The discussion will return to Nagel's approach to consciousness later, but for now, this introduces an important disruption to the usual linearity presumed for authorship. How is it possible to explain the generation of works through artificial intelligence? What is required, or perhaps more accurately, what is desired, in order to present that making as purportedly artistic or inventive and so on? In other words, how does the prevailing discourse suggest the *human* qualities of authorship and why? When approaching the same questions for nonhuman animals, the resistance to finding an adequate, as it were, consciousness is dramatically different. The crucial question then is one of difference; that is, how are these explanations similar or different when the question is posed in relation to the aesthetic achievements and innovations of nonhuman animals? The questions themselves thus betray a particular concern. It is therefore necessary to pay attention not only to explaining the outputs of nonhuman makers but also to particularising how those explanations are achieved and what they might presume. In other words, the answers pose the question; and it is a question of the explanations themselves. We must ask, then, what is it like to be an author?

Presume a Work

What do the explanations of an intellectual property object presume? And how do those explanations themselves serve the stability of conventions around creativity and innovation? This process within the intellectual property system itself is of considerable significance not only for the discourse around artificial intelligence and its outputs, but also for the challenges to the anthropocentric lens through which the law views nonhuman making, both animal and machine. For one group, this is a facilitating paradigm; for the other, it erects significant obstacles. But for both, an ethological approach is revealing.

When it comes to products generated by artificial intelligence, it is not simply that an object of aesthetic note may have been made, or that a potentially useful invention may be described. At the root of the discussion around potential rights and personhood for artificial intelligence (that is, as inventors and authors) is the concept of sentience. But the emphasis on sentience has not been concerned, at least not immediately, with addressing the potential wellbeing of the machine or even the nonhuman animal. On the contrary, sentience has emerged as a policy tool and parlance in service of the authorship narrative, but with little to do, it would seem, with the potential welfare concerns. Curiously, as will be discussed, the discourse around personhood for artificial intelligence continues to skip the sentience discussion. In fact, in many respects, whether in the technical discussions or simply in the surrounding discourse, sentience appears not so much to be accepted in response to the phenomenon of the outputs, but rather, to be engaged in order to explain it. A kind of mindless doublespeak, as it were. Proceeding from the phenomenal outputs, the *sufficient reason* of sentience becomes both a reason and a consequence. A rocky issue, by all accounts.

It seems appropriate that another shipwreck, in this first section of *shipwrecks*, is at the centre of understanding these issues. The shipwreck in *Candide* that almost takes the life of Dr Pangloss and Candide serves to illustrate a certain interpretative framework, the Panglossian paradigm or "adaptationist programme," as described by Stephen Jay Gould and Richard Lewontin in their influential essay, *The Spandrels of San Marco and the Panglossian Paradigm*.[10] In this essay, the authors undertake a Panglossian perspective upon the spandrels of San Marco's Basilica, remarking that "[t]he design is so elaborate, harmonious and purposeful that we are tempted to view it as the starting point of any analysis, as the cause in some sense of the surrounding architecture. But this would invert the proper path of analysis."[11] Noting its literary roots, Gould and Lewontin set out to critique the dominance of what they identify as the Panglossian paradigm of evolutionary biology; that is, the "adaptationist programme" and the emphasis on natural selection as both coherent and encompassing in explaining the emergence of particular traits. While the essay appeared to turn the tide in evolutionary biology, it seems that a certain Panglossian attention still holds sway in the conventions of authorship and intellectual property. And in the discussion of nonhuman agency, with authorship as a particular form, a certain exceptionalism is made fast, and the landscape of authorship remains *just so*. It would seem that in the matter of the products of nonhuman animals and artificial intelligence, the cornerstones of sentience and intentionality appear to converge in a particular version of what is best.

This *intentional stance* within intellectual property certainly motivates the popular discourse surrounding sentience and consciousness (or more accurately, inferred self-consciousness) in artificial intelligence. And at the same time, a recourse to intentionality is supposed to *discredit*, as it were, the notion of authorship in nonhuman animals. Paradoxically, a wider acceptance of sentience and indeed consciousness in nonhuman animals is tempered by a focus on self-consciousness.[12] In this way, authorship, in its broadest sense, emerges for its particular insight into nonhuman animals and sentience. This chapter is thus concerned with the dilemma of sentience and its Panglossian tendrils. Have the Lisbon roads of sentience been created expressly to ensure the notion of nonhuman authorship drowns in them?[13] But first, how does Pangloss himself explain the Panglossian?

Adapt or Perish

The phrase "adapt or perish" is a refrain[14] in HG Wells's *Mind at the End of Its Tether*,[15] generally taken to emphasise the inescapable march of change, or "nature's inexorable imperative."[16] But it is used here somewhat ironically and wholly critically in relation to the adaptationist paradigm in evolutionary biology, and alongside it the reinforcement of the stability of current convictions and practices. It is also somewhat appropriate to the predicament in which Dr Pangloss and Candide find themselves in the Bay of Lisbon, in the shipwreck caused by the catastrophic Lisbon earthquake "which destroyed three-quarters of Lisbon,"[17]

The shipwreck in *Candide* is a shipwreck that is surprising and yet predictable, unexpected and yet anticipated in equal measure: "Half the enfeebled passengers, suffering from that inconceivable anguish which the rolling of a ship causes in the nerves and in all the humours of bodies shaken in contrary directions, did not retain strength enough even to trouble about the danger. The other half screamed and prayed."[18] In the chaos that ensues, many lives are lost, including the life of the good Jacques the Anabaptist. The Anabaptist, who had previously come to the aid of both Pangloss and Candide in times of peril, drowns while rescuing a sailor who had fallen into the water: "The good Jacques ran to his aid, helped him to climb back, and from the effort he made was flung into the sea in full view of the sailor, who allowed himen to look at him."[19] When Candide goes to try and rescue his "benefactor," Pangloss stops him and offers his philosophy of all is as it should be, explaining, "the Lisbon roads had been expressly created for the Anabaptist to be drowned in them."[20] But the irony of this design is the survival of "the brutal sailor who had drowned the virtuous Anabaptist."[21] Pangloss's optimism is challenged. The only other two survivors who made it to shore were Pangloss and Candide, "carried there on a plank."[22] And the misfortunes continue to multiply. Not long after reaching shore and still "[w]eeping the death of their benefactor," they are then caught in the aftermath of the disastrous earthquake, causing the collapse of the town, and "thirty thousand inhabitants of every age and both sexes were crushed under the ruins."[23]

The discourse around the advent of artificial intelligence and the prospect of a superintelligence heralds, rightly or wrongly, a similarly cataclysmic doomsday. And with that, there is a propensity towards an overly simplified binary thinking, presuming either progress or naysayers, either an attachment to the providence and civility of authorship or an abject and desolate abandonment. The options are limited. But in devising and divining the explainability of artificial intelligence outputs, is there a similar optimism deployed to explain the observable phenomena within the iconography of intellectual property? And in a way, does this also explain away the explainability problem, through the sudden genius of authorship? This is not merely a question of rationing the economic investment in works of artificial intelligence. It is indeed a resolute attachment to the divine providence, as it were, of intellectual property, that the intentional stance is imputed in making sense of such phenomena in the first place. Just as this intentional stance becomes a presumptive starting point for discussions around perceptions of authorship and inventorship on the part of artificial intelligence, so too does it become a presumptive Lisbon road for a purposeful and aesthetic approach to sentience. The anthropomorphism deployed in the service of artificial intelligence and to the detriment of nonhuman animals is perhaps more transparently in service of regulating the value in the work, rather than anything to do with the authorship of artificial systems.

Returning to the Lisbon Earthquake and Pangloss, *What can be the sufficient reason for this phenomenon?* Let us ask Pangloss himself, the greatest philosopher in the whole world.

The Greatest Philosopher in the Province

Dr Pangloss explains this principle of *just so* early on: "[T]hings cannot be otherwise; for, since everything is made for an end, everything is necessarily for the best end."²⁴ To support this assertion, Pangloss furnishes a range of compelling examples: "[N]oses were made to wear spectacles; and so we have spectacles. Legs were visibly instituted to be breeched, and we have breeches."²⁵ And then Pangloss concludes his argument by asserting, "[A]nd as *pigs were made to be eaten, we eat pork all the year round.*"²⁶ Pigs are thus explained *for* their use; that is, reasons are devised in order to explain the way in which they are used by humans *all the year round.* By this reasoning, not only are pigs presented as phenomena for which to find reasons, but also human consumption of pork is presented as the fundamental adaptation. That is, this practice of consumption is posed as the starting point and thus the boundary maker for erecting the system of human-nonhuman animal relations and finding and positing reasons consistent with the exceptionalist status quo. *Everything is as it should be; the proof is in the phenomena.*

Pangloss is widely accepted to be a satirical characterisation of Gottfried Leibniz, in the tradition of the fruitful imitations of parodies, to be discussed again later.²⁷ And rather than view parody as a secondary work of ridicule, it is appreciated as a critical dialectic through which to engage the assistance of Pangloss on some further key concerns of Leibniz, and how all this might enlighten the load of sentience. First, it is relevant to recognise the predatory drift of Panglossian parody; that is, its reinstatement of conventional, rivalrous relations through both property and causality, converting the work of Leibniz itself into an epiphenomenal explanation. And second, it is important to distinguish Leibniz's philosophy from this predatory drift. The phenomenal question Pangloss seeks to answer is itself beyond compare, so to speak. This is not to introduce a banal relativism but to understand and facilitate a deseating of the dominant (anthropocentric) perspective towards a panglossia of possibilities. It really is the best of all worlds.

In an Ideal Intellectual Property World

This same comparative thinking is instrumental to the wider policy discourse surrounding intellectual property and is memorialised in the deference to a linear, innovation narrative as seemingly archived through the system itself. In a sense, the intellectual property paradigm, as understood through this policy rationale, is necessarily at least pseudo-Panglossian in that innovation is always *the best of all possible worlds*. The critical intervention here is to consider whether that is a Utopic, vanishing horizon that is always already and necessarily unachievable. Can things really only get better? As far as the mechanics of the intellectual property system are concerned, things can only get different. To ascribe to innovation a progressive narrative is perhaps best understood as Panglossian.

Tarde's theory of opposition and adaptation provides a sensible interception of this adaptationist paradigm of innovation, most particularly through a "theory of individual causes in history."[28] Tarde's perspective prefigures an anthropocentric critique. This is a spherical world, no point is the centre, thus it must always be the best of all worlds. Indeed, what is *pangloss* but the proper noun for all languages? Tarde declares that there is a profoundly important physical and geographical dimension to this question of priorities and hierarchies: "[T]he earth being spherical, no natural advantage of this kind belongs to any state, since no point on a sphere can be considered central in relation to the others."[29]

The linear discourse surrounding intellectual property, in contrast, thus constructs an apparent forwards movement of innovation through the individual points or objects of intellectual property, rather than through the use and users of those objects; that is, a rivalrous property construct rather than a relational and sociability property. This resonates with Simone Weil's declaration that "[a] point is nothing,"[30] and thus the suggestion of movement through immobile objects is impossible; rather, it is through intersection of points, the interaction through use, that the expressive is possible. In many respects, the discussions around artificial intelligence remain focused on the objects (the outputs) as privileged sites, disregarding their indexical and indicative nature, and the movement of authorship through use, imitations, and relations. And this at once complicates and oversimplifies the language of incentives in relation to the circumstances in which intellectual property might be created. In other words, an adaptationist approach to the object is to impute those incentives, arguably on a false premise, in order to present a seemingly coherent and consistent evolutionary narrative of innovation and growth.

The best of all worlds is thus the impossibility of comparison and grading without selecting certain results and causes, and indeed benchmarks, which would thus render certain perspectives impossible. In other words, rather than the naïve optimism suggested in the parodic play of Pangloss, *the best of all worlds* is the impossibility of these points of comparison. The impact of presuming that such a comparison is possible, whether or not this is inevitable for a functioning property system, is well-known with respect to cultural diversity and the apparent *impossibility* of other property systems, such as the discussions around traditional knowledge and cultural expressions.[31] And at the same time, this comparative and evaluative approach is also necessarily and decidedly anthropocentric. Thus, the startling revelation with respect to Leibniz and his *optimism*, is that his is a crucially anti-anthropocentric approach. Authors are incomparable. Literally.[32]

Leibniz's *optimism*, if you will, is developed further and later in Tarde's approach to "contradictory impressions" and the prevarication "between two sense judgments" in what is described as "an internal opposition of purely psychological origin."[33] Tarde explains this as a productive encounter between those oppositions, or an interference in which the judgment is to be found in the relation between; the *metaxu*, as it were, "two rays of imitation that interfere within me."[34] The word between us.

> Thus we see that it is necessary to eliminate from the start, as so many pseudo-oppositions, all the antitheses of mythology and the philosophy of history which are based on assumed *natural* contrarieties; for example, the contrarieties between two nations, two races, or two forms of government ... or between occident and orient, two religions ... or two families of language.[35]

Or between two groups of sentient animals? Human and nonhuman animals? Or machines?

This is the difference between the homogeneous collectivity and the creative kinship of familiar production; the difference between *mass production*, so to speak, and authors in the swarm. To paraphrase Michel Serres, it all comes down to how we say everybody.[36] Who is this *we*, the art-making animal?

All Is Well with Sentience

Returning to the adaptationist thinking critiqued by Gould and Lewontin, the trouble with Pangloss is the presumption of all things as they are. They argue that the Panglossian paradigm simply presumes to explain the *sufficient reason of the phenomenon* in question, in order to ensure things remain *just so*, contrary to "Darwin's own pluralistic approach to identifying the agents of evolutionary change."[37] Gould had critiqued the *just-so* of adaptationists in an earlier article on the art of storytelling in sociobiology.[38] But perhaps it is more accurate to consider Gould's critique as that of a particular "style of storytelling" rather than underestimating the worlds built and shared by anecdote in both science and law,[39] as will emerge in the following chapters. But a further invaluable *use* or *byproduct*[40] of the critique, to follow Gould's and Lewontin's own argument, is the foreshadowing of why art matters to science, and indeed, why authorship matters to sentience and ultimately to the analysis of welfare and rights of nonhuman animals. The "spaces left over,"[41] as it were.

The fallacy of this kind of coercive retelling of natural phenomena in order to sustain the things as *just so* is also anticipated in the sociological theories of Tarde, for whom evolutionary thinking is central[42] and whose work on social learning and the individual is fundamental in this context: "Nature does not exert her wonderful harmonizing power to the greatest degree along the broad lines of the evolution of beings – a ramified and tortuous path – nor yet in the grouping of these different species into zonal flora and fauna … but that it is exerted, rather, in the details of each organism."[43] Arguably addressing the same *force of habit* that is the subject of attention for Gould and Lewontin, Tarde rebukes a kind of tyranny of the collective in the contrivances of "final causes," and expectations of *sufficient reason*, whether considered optimism or divine providence or *just so*, in arguing: "There is no *single* end in nature – no end in relation to which all others are means; but there is an infinite number of ends which are seeking to utilize one another … Here, then, as before, we are led to consider the harmonizing force … not as something unique, external, and superior, but as indefinitely repeated, infinitesimal, and internal."[44]

Tarde rejects the factitious causality that he identifies with "the *unilinear evolutionists'* notion" and with Durkheim, and instead describes the pluralism of "a foundation composed of real and elementary resemblances and repetitions which are infinitely numerous and extremely exact; these have replaced a very small number of erroneous, or at least vague and deceptive analogies as primary material for scientific elaboration."[45] Similarly, Tarde's sociology rejects the Panglossian stereotypes accorded to particular people through language, religion, race: "These embodiments of collective character, appearing under the guise of metaphysical entities or *idols*, were endowed with a fictitious personal identity, which was, however, rather indefinite."[46] Arguably, this is the same kind of *thinking*, for what it is worth, that underpins the generalisations of LLMs – that is, a decidedly Panglossian process from epiphenomena to calculated bias, a false starting point without understanding.[47]

This fundamental problem of causality, common to discussions of non-human animal interests (whether articulated through welfare, rights, or otherwise) and intellectual property alike, is anticipated in Tarde's own consideration of adaptationist paradigms in naturalism, and he shares with Gould and Lewontin an appreciation for Darwin's pluralism: "Cuvier and the naturalists of his time, including even his opponent Lamarck, sought out primarily the laws of adaptation, while, on the other hand, Darwin and his evolutionist disciples preferred to consider the phenomena of life from the standpoint of repetitions and oppositions."[48] For Tarde, "Repetition, opposition, and adaptation … are the three keys which science employs to open up the arcana of the universe. She seeks, before all else, not the mere causes, but the laws that govern the repetition, opposition, and adaptation of phenomena."[49]

And it is with this perspective that attention now turns to the causes and effects, as it were, of sentience.

Overboard in a Sea of Concepts

The *term* sentience is ubiquitous throughout discussions around nonhuman capabilities, from animal rights discourse through to questions of personhood for artificial intelligence. But sentience the *concept* is far more elusive. As it stands, the question of sentience is a question that remains without a satisfactory answer in that there is no consistent way of asking and no consistent answer provided by case law,[50] science,[51] philosophy,[52] or elsewhere, whether in relation to humans,[53] other animals,[54] or artificial intelligence.[55] Nevertheless, it is a term that is used almost wholly axiomatically across a wide range of settings, both technical and non-technical, with attempts at definition often becoming inescapably tautological. Thus, as a term, it is widely used,[56] but as a concept, it is a moving, indeed, a running target.[57] While the development of the concept, including the admission of new species, is to be expected, and is wholly appropriate as the relevant science develops, this does not explain the artificial exclusions of others.[58] Curiously, sentience has become somewhat of a prosaicism in the popular discourse swirling around artificial intelligence as well. However, the exclusion of plants from rights discourse grounded upon sentience as a moral qualification emerges as a contrived boundary point[59] at odds with the evidence of sentience in the plant kingdom.[60] Precision may be achieved through adopting the narrower concept of *animal sentience*, however, this provides no further insight into what sentience may mean for plants, artificial intelligence, and so on, leading to inconsistencies and potential injustices. David Chalmers states, "that word is just too ambiguous and confusing, even more confusing than the word *consciousness*," noting that "[t]he word *sentience* … has many different uses … So I'll stick with *consciousness*, which at least has some standardized terminology."[61] Why persist with engaging with the concept in the present discussion, in that case? The reason is largely down to its persuasive and rhetorical value, and its subsequent entry into the legal lexicon through animal welfare legislation around the world.[62] While consciousness may be the subject of critical and technical analysis, sentience is the manner of policy.[63] It may be that this is again down to the rhetorical appeal of the term, in that it moves beyond the technical and critical engagement in consciousness studies towards the axiomatic power of the indefinable. It seems that sentience, as a threshold concept, is also a kind of interpretive barrier as well as a call to an always unattainable humanness – this is perhaps the word set between us.

To understand sentience, then, it is perhaps best to commence with its use as distinct from its content. Sentience operates largely as a boundary or threshold concept, a means of both access and of exclusion.[64] This deployment of sentience as a threshold concept is somewhat of a convention in the relevant literature, in both legal and animal studies. The welfare scientist Donald Broom, notes the instrumentality of this gatekeeping function: "For many people the quality which counts is some threshold level of cognitive ability referred to as sentience."[65] And as a threshold concept, sentience is far more than the pain barrier. However, further clarity beyond this is *wanting*, in every sense; that is, it is to be found in the consideration of the question of wants. What is it like to *want* to be an author?

Although it is not possible to review the breadth of scholarship on this question in this single chapter, an appreciation of the conditions for the understanding of sentience, an awareness of awareness, would appear to be crucial to the mysteries of nonhuman authorship, including artificial intelligence, towards an intellectual property that is more than human. But is it something of a straw person, or straw personhood, so to speak? There is little doubt that Naruto is conscious, but Naruto was not able to hold copyright under the Copyright Act 1976.[66] But was Naruto capable of being an author under the law? Or is an emphasis on sentience a false premise in order to achieve a Panglossian justification for the creation of intellectual property products, the subsistence of rights, and the fallacious arguments around incentives and precarity? If sentience or consciousness are erected as the threshold to personhood, this ensures not only an arbitrary target but by many accounts an immeasurable one. But is a Panglossian paradigm the solution here? Should sentience in fact be constructed through the phenomena of performances and expressions (not necessarily works) such that authorship reconstructs sentience through an adaptationist programme. Before examining what kinds of performance might assist here, it is useful to recover the discourse and scholarship of sentience and its role in sustaining the status and quo, as it were, particularly as it is so central to nonhuman rights discourse and personhood advocacy.

Writing at the same time as Peter Singer, the philosopher Wallace Matson explains his own resistance to definition in his treatise on sentience: "our concepts change so that what starts out as a synthetic truth ends up as an analytic sentence."[67] The identity of sentience is always contingent. And it is in this respect that the almost intuitive approach to the use of the term is interesting in and of itself, as it points to the metaphysical nature of the discourse of rights and personhood that is otherwise arguably framed by taking the meaning on faith. The present discussion approaches the question from a different direction, developing working parameters for sentience through the concept of authorship rather than through an anatomisation of sentience. Through the discussion that follows, it becomes possible to recast nonhuman animal moral and legal agency through performance and production – what is it like to be an author?

Can They Suffer?

At its simplest, sentience is feeling manifest in suffering, suffering which can be both a presence of adverse conditions and an absence of desirable ones.[68] This emphasis on suffering is ubiquitous in animal studies, in part a legacy of the famous statement from Jeremy Bentham in 1789: "[T]he question is not, Can they *reason*? nor, Can they *talk*: but, Can they *suffer*?"[69] That legacy has been translated into the legal and policy literature, with explicit references to the concept of suffering in the relevant instruments of animal protection in the United Kingdom[70] and elsewhere.[71] The concept of suffering is also crucial because fundamentally it introduces the question of capacity through vulnerability. Weil explains that "vulnerability is a mark of existence."[72] Citing fruit tree blossoms as exemplary, Weil explains this beauty "[i]n the same way, the vulnerability of the soul to cold, to hunger."[73] This resonates with contemporary approaches in vulnerability as "reasoning from the body,"[74] a perspective which becomes especially relevant in the present discussion towards developing an expressive theory of sentience through the following chapters, particularly in the reckoning of authorship through play.[75] Vulnerability is thus a subjective capacity or capability,[76] which can be deciphered in later approaches to nonhuman animal capabilities, including the work of Martha Nussbaum.[77] As such, sentience suggests a subjective capacity for that suffering, this being the common thread throughout approaches to defining sentience.[78] Thus, sentience takes on an evaluative character,[79] and as such suffering can in itself be a want. In this way, sentience is somewhat inflected by evaluative propositions, whereby sentience occupies an almost liminal relationship to wants. Sentience relies upon and is instrumental to a notion of a sensational threshold for personhood; that is, the concept is presented always in service of and in deference to (in every sense) the limen to personhood (in a more general sense). However, this is often with no clear understanding of how that transition might be achieved at law, or what this might mean. Sentience matters, in every sense of that phrase. But a flawed causality towards personhood is easily and swiftly disrupted by the legal status quo.

A common approach to artificial sentience – that is, the ascertaining of sentience in artificial entities – is similarly to focus on suffering, leading to an operational distinction between sentience and sapience; that is, sentience as pain and suffering, as distinct from sapience or an awareness of that suffering, and thus compelling towards establishing moral status and personhood.[80] Sapience, although not used universally in the literature, implies thinking and indeed humanness. Judith Donath invokes a similar distinction between sentience and consciousness, where sentience may lead to responsibilities towards that being, but consciousness refers to self-awareness and motivation: "The term *conscious* refers to sentient beings that are self-aware – that have a sense of purpose and of themselves as individuals in the world."[81] This distinction is notable in that in the artificial intelligence context, although used widely, the term sentience is not a synonym for personhood. In other words, the apparent existence of sentience may or may not be grounds for personhood (including personhood for the purposes of authorship) but would be grounds for moral consideration or moral status. The implications of this moral status may be somewhat problematic, however, in that the moral consideration arising from that status is strongly linked to human ownership or operation of the particular artificial agent, rather than an obligation on the part of the whole moral community. This approach has the perverse result of a kind of *enslavement* of the artificial agent.[82] This emphasises why the discussion of personhood is in fact important to sentience, but not for the usual reasons provided.

Personhood or a sense of self is appealing for how these concepts might invigorate the concept of sentience in a meaningful way, not only culturally but also legally. But more specifically, authorship, distinct from but yet conceptually linked to personhood, presents a crucial and strategic line of enquiry. What is it like to be curious, to play? The discussion throughout the following chapters will continue to pursue play as the critical turn both in authorship and in personhood and respond to those who might try to suspend play.[83] This is why authorship matters and thinking about what it is like to be an author promises new insight for sentience scholarship and welfare policy. What does Naruto want? What is it like for Naruto to be an author? And what is it like to be a machine?

Culture Wars

Contrary to the criticism of welfare-based strategies in animal rights literature, particularly in the North American jurisdictions,[84] the welfare context should not be so readily dismissed as contrary to a rights or personhood agenda.[85] Indeed, the emphasis upon this agonistic and inimical boundary-making is an unfortunate artefact of the rhetorical turn in the prevailing discourse around animal concerns and a distinctly North American jurisdictional and jurisprudential lens through which the discussions appear to pass. At the same time, the disregard and even open hostility to welfare frameworks somewhat paradoxically consigns rights and personhood discourse to vanishing horizons of humanness. The discussion must return, therefore, to the question of what Naruto wants. What is it like to be a photographer? What is it like to be an author? Just as the uncertainty around sentience is a potential barrier and reinforcement for the status quo of the law's anthropocentrism, arguably so too does the speculative nature of the parameters used to answer the question of authorship provide a significant resource for maintaining the status quo of authorship. An ethological jurisprudence of authorship thus challenges the dominant presumptions (both in the law and more widely) of the singularity of authorship and its conventions as anything but inevitable.

It is important to consider how sentience might be utilised both as a welfare tool and as a kind of author-construct. While the current consideration of sentience in this chapter is necessarily not encyclopaedic, the main concern is understanding how it is mobilised as a rhetorical and policy concept, and how it thus becomes crucial as one of the cornerstone concepts that links technical and public discourse on nonhuman animals, artificial intelligence, and authorship, all of which engage with certain concepts of "sentience." Interpretations and understandings of sentience within a welfare context are thus particularly significant in the present discussion, not only for nonhuman animals and an understanding of the capacity for legal personality, duties, and property, but also for artificial intelligence and a reinterpretation of the wants of authorship. How might authorship be meaningful as a welfare tool? And how might authorship actually assist in *showing* or *pointing* to the meaning of sentience? The relationship between authorship and welfare thus emerges as critical to an understanding of the performance of property and the productivity of play, to which the discussion will return later and in more detail.[86] For the present discussion, more immediate is the question of what it might mean to appeal to sentience as a condition of authorship, or as a guarantee within the rhetoric of rights, if it is itself a contested term; that is, to ask what it might mean to look at sentience as a condition or an effect of authorship. Is it actually authorship that makes meaningful the concept of sentience?

Commencing with a critique of the rights and welfare frameworks reveals these questions as questions concerned with understanding a kind of proprietorial agency. Looking at the purported answers thus begins to raise significant questions about the nature of the author's rights in copyright, and a challenging and productive interaction between sentience scholarship and authorship. Is authorship also a kind of moral protection? A welfare protection? Or is this moral protection actually more concerned with protecting the economic parameters of authorship and the value of literary capital? The all-too-frequent collusion of authorship and ownership appears to be facilitated by this possible context. In turn, an analysis of authorship and creativity offers a particular departure from the biological imperative in sentience and the impossibility of a consciousness of consciousness. In speaking about nonhuman authorship, the relationship between sentience and authorship is particularly important, and a fuller understanding of the capacity for creativity and the complexity of nonhuman wants, whether nonhuman animal or artificial intelligence, will benefit from an ethological perspective. To understand what Naruto wants from authorship, it is necessary to examine how authorship is concerned with playing for all its worth.

From Person to Person

On the approach to sentience as a fundamental basis for personhood, and thus its perception and deployment as a fundamental obstacle to becoming property, it is becoming clearer that this is too simplistic. Indeed, in some discussions, sentience is used as though interchangeable with personhood, and sentient becomes a synonym for person.[87] Must a person be sentient?

The enthusiasm for the sentience concept is perhaps at a peak in discussions of personhood and rights, but in fact, a legal person has no need for displaying sentience, thus conflating different lines of enquiry and argument. Further, the terms are variously used as concrete and discrete concepts, but legal accounts of sentience are largely framed by social discourse.[88] Similarly, legal personality is itself a shifting and changing quality, context-bound and, to a great degree, simply ineffectual.

Natural persons are biological humans, but even this seemingly constant state does not confer consistent legal personality or personhood in all circumstances. Legal personhood is inconstant. It is a legal status, but it is not a legal status conferring the same rights for every person or in every situation; from questions of capacity to specific statutory rights, personhood is a shifting value. Personhood (in law) may instead be understood as a vessel in which rights are placed. Thus, rather than giving an individual a consistent bundle of rights, it is instead a mechanism potentially mobilised in different ways in different situations. Further, a claim to personhood is ordinarily circumscribed by specific and transient facts, meaning that personhood becomes a responsive and relational concept, not an immutable fact. Personhood is not carried with an individual as a constant; it is more accurately understood as a state, and differing states, into which that individual enters in different circumstances. In other words, the claims attaching to particular relations will change with those relations, regardless of being a (kind of) person (that is, a natural person) throughout. Further, the absence of personhood does not mean that rights cannot be attributed to something. What is critical here is not the brass ring of personhood, but rather, how rights are interpreted, such as duties within existing welfare legislation[89] and the right not to be caused unnecessary suffering.[90] And this is where the personhood of authorship approach comes into play.

Personhood has been co-opted in rights discourse as a maxim of normative force, but frequently without any further examination of the meaning of personhood, if any, in law. This maintains an almost populist approach to the debate that ultimately, and somewhat ironically, risks becoming complicit in maintaining the rhetorical divide. An interesting example of this is in the use of the terms "denier" or "denial" not only in the concept of anthropodenial but also in discussions over the risks attached to polarising the discussion through the use of such terminology.[91] As such, sentience and personhood (and, to an extent, even consciousness) have become charged as policy tools rather than rigorous concepts, and in this way, sentience, consciousness, and personhood begin to be deployed as unitary and unifying terms. When the discourse of terminological "populism" deploys such terms as battle cries for reform, but without meaningful engagement with the fundamental parameters, the risk is the erection of agonistic obstacles and reinforcement of the status quo.[92]

The unhelpful and constructed binary of property and personhood is thus also easily upended in service of the status quo. In other words, sentience becomes a fundamental obstacle to personhood for the same reasons. The concept of personhood is similarly beset with the same problems as sentience, in that it too is a term which can be ambiguous and even feckless, used inconsistently throughout philosophy and sociology, as well as within law. There is also a problem of universalism that attaches to many discussions of personhood,[93] or what might be described as the tyranny of the collective, as identified by Weil.[94] And at the same time, it maintains a misapprehension and alienation from the individual personalities of the swarm in a certain kind of anthropocentrism of the person.

Judging Outputs, the Sufficient Reason

The adaptationist Panglossian paradigm seems purpose-made for an *optimistic* view of artificial intelligence. In other words, commentators and policymakers alike are tempted to look at the epiphenomenal outputs of artificial intelligence as the Panglossian reasoning for their protection, and thus those objects become the vehicles of sentience for artificial intelligence. Indeed, the anthropomorphic language of hallucination, a term used for the various errors repeated by artificial intelligence, contributes to this perspective on the humanising coherence of its whole.[95] To recall Gould and Lewontin, this temptation to render those outputs so as to impute the authorship of artificial intelligence would be "to invert the proper path of analysis."[96] Similarly, it follows that discussions around the potential authorship or otherwise of artificial intelligence presume that question of authorship as the logical starting point – that is, to solve ownership with authorship.[97] Even much of the legal scholarship on this question proceeds as though artificial intelligence is an emergent whole, presumed as the logical place to begin the analysis of authorship, rather than understanding the constraints of its own production and the constraints of the perspectives and motivations brought to bear upon that analysis.[98]

Nevertheless, terms like intelligence, sentience, and consciousness are used widely and variously in relation to artificial intelligence. Even the term itself, artificial intelligence, has been almost emptied of meaning through its popular and imprecise reckoning. J Mark Bishop notes that even the commercial use of the catch-all "artificial intelligence" has become problematic, describing it as a "brand-tag."[99] And Michael I Jordan cautions that "the bigger problem is that the use of this single, ill-defined acronym prevents a clear understanding of the range of intellectual and commercial issues at play."[100] Both *artificial* and *intelligence* are contested terms for Kate Crawford, who argues, "AI is neither *artificial* nor *intelligent*."[101] As well as the enormous natural and human resources consumed in its production, Crawford maintains, "AI systems are not autonomous, rational, or able to discern anything without extensive, computationally intensive training with large datasets or predefined rules and rewards"[102] and argues that, contrary to the notion of autonomy attending the presentation of these systems as both artificial and intelligence, "artificial intelligence as we know it depends entirely on a much wider set of political and social structures."[103] The discourse of sentience and consciousness is, at least in part, propelled by these structures and by human users. In examining the question of pain in artificial intelligence systems, Bishop explains that, "computation is always fundamentally observer-relative," and therefore unless the observer enters such experiences, "the control program of a robot cannot affect its putative phenomenal experience."[104] What, if anything, is exciting about the sentience of artificial intelligence, arguably may be said to be wholly generated in the behaviour of excitement *around* artificial intelligence; observer-relative, if you will. Indeed, is it the case that this kind of attention is *all you need*?[105] And thus it is through this facilitation of an affective relationship to the technology, that the hype is sustained. Over half a century ago, Arthur Samuel lamented similar extremes: "[P]eople who believe in magic, or those who are carried away with their enthusiasm for a new cause and who make wild claims which tend to discredit the entire undertaking. The field of artificial intelligence has, perhaps, had more than its share of these people."[106]

Perhaps it could go without saying, but the concept of *intelligence* as deployed in the term, artificial intelligence, seemingly reinscribes something human as the standard. Luciano Floridi identifies the difference in the presentation of artificial intelligence; in other words, it is a question of what the user perceives rather than what the machine achieves: "It has nothing to do with *thinking*, but everything to do with *behaving*: *were* a human to *behave* in that way, that *behaviour would* be called intelligence. It does not mean that the machine *is* intelligent or even *thinking*."[107] This imitation presented as consciousness points to the persuasive impact of the intentional stance in artificial intelligence, despite the mystery of consciousness itself, all towards an affectation of humanness – and of that there is *no question*. This narrative remains compelling and seductive, relying upon the phenomenal and sensational *evidence* of the artefacts, notwithstanding the fact that, "the mere imitation of conscious behaviour is not enough, imitation has its limits and may fail any moment. The only universal solution would be the creation of truly conscious machines, if we only knew what it takes to be conscious."[108]

The momentum of the industry narrative is assisted by press stories gorging on the hype, and thus in many respects, the surrounding discourse and even the operation itself perform a kind of branding of these aspirations, mobilising the narrative through a kind of dissemblance. In the presentation and operation of the interface for users, including apologies and apparent conversation, the hyperbole around consciousness and sentience is sustained through seemingly personal encounters, as in the case of the Google engineer who insisted on the sentience of a chatbot.[109] But these conversations are stories of one. Indeed, that *behaving* includes the behaviour of the users themselves, which serves to maintain the momentum of this mythology of the machine's intelligence. The popular interest in claims to the potential for consciousness seemingly disregards the lack of evidence simply through the introduction of an equivalent of *not yet, but maybe*.[110] But as Floridi states, "as a *branch of cognitive science interested in intelligence production*, AI remains science fiction and has been a dismal disappointment."[111]

Intelligence tests have historically always proceeded from the human perspective,[112] both in terms of sensory capacity and cognitive relevance, and it is thus interesting to see the way in which such approximation might also be used to imply authorship as an indication of *quality* in terms of the outputs and *sentience* on the part of artificial intelligence. But this *mirror test*, to recall an earlier refrain,[113] is a false equivalence.[114] The *mystery* is thus revealed as a highly constructed and resource-intensive artifice of summation and averaging.[115] Steven Shaviro has previously described this as a kind of "thinking blind," arguing that "[a]rtificial intelligence research has accomplished very little when it comes to addressing mental processes like affect, will, and desire … Even so-called 'affective computing' … is much more concerned with enabling computers to 'read' human emotions, and in turn to provoke and manipulate human emotional responses, than it is with eliciting anything like the affective states of computers themselves."[116] Around a decade later, with the advent of ChatGPT and other generative text-based artificial intelligence or LLMs, and in generative AI more widely, there is still the same emphasis on an equivalating reflection, *prompted* as it were by the emotional content perceived in an operator's questions, inducing curious responses such as apologies from the system for any perceived unavailability of information, or mistake, or error; and perhaps most importantly, particularly in the context of later discussion, apologising for the incapacity to lie.

Just as the design of the San Marco mosaics is "an 'adaptation'" for which "the architectural constraint is clearly primary,"[117] so too are the productions of artificial intelligence constrained by and adapted to the prior constraints of the data, including bias and prejudice replicated and consolidated through that learning, as well as the limitations and accuracy of the data available more generally. Nevertheless, a fascination with the notion of artificial intelligence becoming sentient preoccupies the wider discourse, and in doing so, these systems are both drawing from that data and bias as well as replicating, consolidating, and doubling down on this fascination. Crawford explains that "due to the capital required to build AI at scale and the ways of seeing that it optimizes AI systems are ultimately designed to serve existing dominant interests. In this sense, artificial intelligence is a registry of power."[118] Is it that, just like the "force of habit" criticised by Gould and Lewontin in the interpretations of biological systems, similarly in artificial intelligence there is the tendency to regard "the epiphenomenal adaptations as primary," and subsequently "to build the whole structural system from it?"[119] And if this is not already a habit, the consolidation of data will ultimately ensure that it becomes so.[120]

The impact of taking the output as the starting point is that the conditions for the work are not considered. Indeed, if the expressive behaviour, so to speak, for an authorial output is to be viewed as a kind of adaptive response, then within the logic of the intellectual property system, the market prevails as the incentive within that self-contained order. And through this conceptual and interpretative dominance of the market, a simplified and somewhat limited narrative is devised, not only for nonhuman animals and machines (where it is also preposterous) but also for human authors, in that the system universalises a certain set of conditions for authorship and thus for copyright, masking a wider and more complex diversity of creativity. At the same time, within this economic rationality, the expressive potential of nonhuman animals through play and other performative excess is explained away as an adaptive, functional, and biological rehearsal for survival, notwithstanding the contrary knowledge in the scientific literature,[121] as well as in other critical accounts.[122] Humans thus emerge presumably as distinct and a predisposition to creativity is constructed as a fundamental part of the human condition, an abundance that points to the triumph of culture over nature. We are the art-making animal.

There is thus a misleading and unnecessary recourse to intentionality invoked in the wider discourse around nonhuman authorship; misleading *not* because there may be no expressive purpose at all, but misleading because it is unnecessary to the posing of the question or the application of the concept at law. Intentionality is not of direct application to the nature of the work as far as copyright is concerned or indeed the wider concerns of art history. In other words, it is not what Naruto wants, but *whether* Naruto wants. And as for artificial intelligence, does it want for nothing at all? It would seem that an emphasis on intentionality thus displaces the question of sentience in this context, while in the meantime the wider concerns around sentience and consciousness make little impact on this specific question. Arguably then, when it comes to the analysis of personhood, the argument is thwarted by its own epiphenomenal logic. And we are left with the extreme behaviourism of artificial intelligence.

In arguing against the possibility of sentience in the context of artificial intelligence (or what he terms mechanical sentience), Wallace Matson suggests the barrier, paradoxically, is a kind of *humanity* of all animals; humans and other than humans. Nevertheless, Matson's theory of sentience adheres to a form of lingering anthropocentrism, identified throughout conventional sentience discussions, where the approximation of human intelligence remains the immutable marker.[123] Where Matson's analysis becomes more intriguing is in his discussion of the spontaneity of creativity that he recognises in nonhuman animals and which he puts forward as a basis for sentience, albeit facilitated through anthropomorphism: "We would allow Puss in Boots to have a human-type mind because cats *to begin with* are at any rate animals; and we already ascribe to them much of the spontaneity, motivated behavior, and so on that we are conscious of in ourselves. We do not design cats; if Puss began to recite Hamlet's soliloquy, it would not be because we had made him so that when triggered that would be his response."[124]

For Matson, the barrier is thus a question of authorship, as it were – that is, the authorship or design *for* the machine, and the authorship *of* the *animal* (including human animals). Fundamental to this barrier is the question of consciousness: "[W]ith the robot it's different. We would have designed it. No matter, then, what it did, we could always say 'It's acting that way because its machine table specifies that output for this input.' Consciousness then would be superfluous as an explanation of the observed behaviour."[125] Therefore sentience, in Matson's approach, necessarily introduces consciousness and arguably as part of that, spontaneity and unpredictability, as part of the authenticity and trust in the work, and a kind of mutually constitutive elaboration with the concept of authorship – qualities which, for Matson, cannot be found in an intelligence *designed* elsewhere.

But the authorship or inventorship of artificial intelligence has little to do with consciousness, even though this persists as a kind of distraction and catalyst for the hyperbole in the wider discourse. There is abundant evidence that nonhuman animals are conscious, and yet they too are not automatically recognised as any sort of person. Appeals to consciousness appear to magnify and exaggerate the discourse around artificial intelligence in order to facilitate the mythology and ultimately the mainstreaming of its ubiquity in various commercial applications. But demonstrations of consciousness in nonhuman animals have made no difference at all to their status as *authors*. In many respects, the issues are quite simple: artificial intelligence may be used to generate certain products with particular commercial value; there are parties who wish to capture that value in order to commercialise the products (usually through intellectual property), resulting in rhetorical flourishes around consciousness and hype around these achievements in order to facilitate that narrative. Indeed, even some of the loudest advocates for the recognition of personhood for artificial intelligence for the purposes of intellectual property protection of their outputs have admitted as much.[126] Time to take the gloss off.

Taking the Gloss Off

Writing in the early twentieth century, Nathan Isaacs asks, "What can the restless spirit do when set down amid a group of glossators with a perfect, or supposedly perfect, code?"[127] Isaacs's question is posed in the same intellectual period as Tarde's sociology of the law. Indeed, Isaacs describes "the present attempt to marshal the schools of jurisprudence," drawing upon Tarde's theories of imitation in legal institutions to "avoid so far as possible a consideration of the changing content of the law, and confine our attention to the successive changes in its outward form and in the consequent manner of approaching and handling it."[128]

But the challenge to biological narratives was underway in sociological jurisprudence earlier than in evolutionary science itself, and Tarde's theories of imitation are an important part of this intellectual history. Voltaire's critique in *Candide* can thus be read as emphasising a kind of micro-sociology through its emphasis on the value of individual personality and consciousness.[129] The Lisbon Earthquake presents a challenge to optimism and divine providence, and yet not as damaging as might be presumed.[130] In rationalising the catastrophe, Ryan Nichols suggests a certain tendency towards teleological explanations, perhaps not unlike the functionalist explanations imposed upon the creativity of nonhuman animals: "Psychological studies show that humans naturally attribute intention to the origins of natural phenomena ... Humans attribute not only intention but moral reason and purposes to natural events, especially for events of 'natural evil'."[131] In the context of artificial intelligence and the intentional stance, this phenomenon becomes even more compelling, even to the extent of censoring alternative explanations. A similar trajectory of intention is decipherable in the intellectual property system itself. Despite no explicit requirement of intention for the creation of a work, the notion of authorship continues to invoke an intentionalist strategy, similarly *censoring* notions of collaborative or community authorship, not only in traditional cultural expressions, but also in conventional creative industries, like the film work.

Enough of the in-roads: time to find the proper path of analysis.

What Makes an Author?

Approaching sentience through a more expressive account is sensible, as it were, not only for the law but also for the science. The relevant phenomena, however, are something to be clarified as this discussion progresses. From the scientific perspective, David Fraser calls for an alternative paradigm in animal welfare science, based upon the scientific study of affect.[132] Similarly, John Webster provides "a workable definition of sentience *as it applies to animal welfare*,"[133] which is succinctly, "*A sentient animal is one for whom feelings matter.*"[134] In other words, the definition notably invokes the emotional life, or affect, of the sentient subject. But as David Fraser asks, "is there a way to make affective states a more central and integral part of scientific explanation?"[135] And indeed, is there a way to make affective states a part of a legal characterisation as well?

In her "ecology of emotion," Kay Milton's work is notable in advocating an approach to nature and to personhood through emotions rather than through the more conventional arguments based on cognition, self-consciousness, and sentience.[136] Drawing upon Goodin's theory of value,[137] Milton explains that "emotion and feeling" are "central to the process through which we value things" in order "to move from a cognitive model of value to an emotion-centred one."[138] And further, this attention to emotional life has the potential for immediate welfare impact, as in Jaak Panksepp's work on joy, the bodily expression of that value (as in laughter), and the taking of pleasure in the life of laboratory rats.[139] What is it like to have fun? The important distinction from other approaches to sentience is that an emotional life does not depend on thresholds, and in advocating play as expressive, it is possible to ascertain the personhood in authorship. As Marian Stamp Dawkins makes clear, "There are no right or wrong answers for emotions so they do not lend themselves nearly so readily to benchmark criteria that can be compared across humans, computers and any other species of animals. What we need to look for is *some way in which emotions*, if they are present in other species of animal, *would be most likely to reveal themselves*. We are after the outward and visible signs of inner emotional experience."[140] Indeed, there is mounting evidence that creativity and diversity in behaviour are indications of positive welfare[141] for a vast range of species,[142] including humans.[143] Rather than asking for proof of sentience, perhaps it is possible simply to join the game.

What Is It Like to Be an Author?

The title of this chapter and this section is explicitly a refrain on Thomas Nagel's famous essay, "What Is It Like To Be A Bat?"[144] which is itself something of a refrain on the ideas presented by Brian Farrell in *Experience*, published some two decades earlier.[145] But some two centuries earlier, Leibniz was arguably asking similar questions in the context of physics. Rather than asking what atoms would look like (the pigment in the painting question), Alfred Whitehead explains, "Leibniz answered another question. He explained what it must be like to be an atom."[146] Taken together, the trajectory is towards a phenomenological approach to consciousness through phenomenal and subjective experiences; otherwise known as *what it is like*. Farrell identifies this as the problem of first-hand knowledge and explains this through the attempt to know an alien mind (in this case, a Martian):

> When, therefore, I wonder what it would be like to be a Martian, I am wondering what it would be like to have first hand knowledge of the experience of a Martian. What I am aware of here is not the sort of thing that can be talked about at all ... And it is this immediate experience that I am interested in when I wonder what it is like to be a Martian.[147]

While an objective consciousness might not be known, a phenomenal approach to consciousness acknowledges a subjective experience on the part of the other; put simply, we may not know what it is like to be a bat, but we know that there is *something* that it is like to be a bat. Farrell argues against an objective experience of consciousness but maintains that there is an important subject or phenomenal dimension to consciousness: "Members of radically different species may both understand the same physical events in objective terms, and this does not require that they understand the phenomenal forms in which those events appear to the senses of members of the other species."[148] Knowing consciousness, to recall Weil, takes something of a phenomenal effort, as it were, an embodied and enacted self.[149] A phenomenal consciousness thus resonates enticingly with the old approach to authorship through labour. But so too within the concept of author's own intellectual creation, all is not wasted, for the proprietary quality of phenomenal consciousness goes some way to enlivening the concept of expression in copyright and the notion of the author in originality (and indeed the various recordings of intellectual creation in the wider sense), as will be seen. This proprietary quality, however, is spectacularly relational as distinct from exclusionary; an invitation to empathy and to do the work of knowing what it is like.

Is there something that it is like to be an author? Insofar as the conventional notions of intentionality, purpose, and imagination inhere in creativity,[150] how might the experience of authorship be otherwise revealed other than through the work? In one of the classic presentations of creativity, and of *personality* in that creativity, this emphasis on planning and purpose is key in supposing an objective account of authorship. Joy Paul Guilford, in delivering the address of the President of the American Psychological Association in 1950, deciphers a certain account of the author: "Creative personality is then a matter of those patterns of traits that are characteristic of creative persons. A creative pattern is manifest in creative behavior, which includes such activities as inventing, designing, contriving, composing, and planning."[151] However, if instead a phenomenal approach to authorship is adopted, the auditing of this preparatory creative behaviour is not only unnecessary but also unreasonable. And at the same time, the *force of habit* that drives the impatient connections drawn between intellectual outputs and economic incentives appears as anything but objective. The critical perspective here is the imaginative and performative excess of authorship, rather than a presupposition of the content of the author's desires and beliefs – that is, the exuberance and abundance in the creation of work through play: "[W]hen artistic qualities are spoken of as expressive, we frequently tend to take it for granted that their semi-sentience has some direct relation to the creator's psychic life."[152] To recall Weil, to know the world is to know through work; work is teamed with joy, the affiliative industry of play. Knowing thus emerges through an embodied, phenomenal and subjective experience of effort.

To approach the work of authorship through play is thus to defy any calls for purpose or definition, venturing instead an expressive theory of sentience. In other words, through play, it is possible to suppose sentience precisely through the caper of authorship, without any recourse to an objective account: *the work of joy*. In the context of invention and mechanical engineering, and in work cited by Guilford, Chas Kettering responds to the question of how to develop inventors and, with them, inventions: "I have arrived at a definition of what an inventor is. An inventor is simply a fellow who doesn't take his education too seriously."[153] Kettering makes this statement not on the basis that education is not necessary, but rather, with the knowledge that the fundamental impetus for invention is experimentation and failure – that is, the curiosity and play in the system. This play in science is poetry at its best, as Peter Medawar has famously declared: "An act of imagination, a speculative adventure, thus underlies every improvement of natural knowledge."[154] Medawar continues: "It was not a scientist or a philosopher but a poet who first classified this act of mind and found the right word to describe it. The poet was Shelley and the word, *poeisis*, the root of the words 'poetry' and 'poesy,' and standing for making, fabrication or the act of creation."[155]

And if play is the vehicle of authorship, then the absence of play is equally relevant where otherwise there is a predisposition or capacity for play. For the lack of play, as a measure of welfare,[156] is as much concerned with authorship by wanting for the freedom and choice to play,[157] as is the exuberance of play concerned with authorship in its aesthetic excess: *the aesthetics of play*. Indeed, the principle of freedom or choice, as distinct from the dictates of function or instruction, characterises the *work* in the broadest sense throughout the intellectual property system, and across all the intellectual property rights. The fundamental criterion of authorship is this principle of choice; that is, the liberty of play.

This phenomenal account of authorship thus introduces the kinship anticipated in the relational kinship of familiar production[158] through the creative work, the audience of that work, and the curation and publication of the work, surmising the doubling bonds of sentience; always already *in personam*.[159] And this is of immediate application in the law as well in that, to all intents and purposes, as far as copyright law is concerned, the author is taken as read, in every sense. There is no definition of the author in the Berne Convention,[160] or in the instruments of the European Union,[161] beyond the author as a natural person.[162] Indeed, this requirement that the author must be a natural person would exclude nonhuman authors of all kinds and thus at the same time confound any pretence to originality in the very concept of author's own intellectual creation for that same reason. This is thus a potential issue for the interpretation of generative AI outputs as computer-generated works in the United Kingdom.[163] The definition of author in the domestic law of the United Kingdom refers to "the person," thus implying a natural person, "who *creates* it," arguably directing attention to the concept of intellectual creation.[164] In the United States, arguments have been made that the Act does not require a natural person, as it is nowhere defined in the text.[165] However, an anonymous work is defined in the Act as a work "of which no natural person is identified as the author" and therefore suggesting that there must always be a natural person as an author. Arguments are also made that because the work-for-hire doctrine deems the employer to be the author, and because such employers may include legal persons (such as corporations or studios), this means that there is no requirement for a natural person to be the author.[166] However, the work-for-hire doctrine is premised upon the employment relationship, and thus a consensual submission to the employment contract, thus necessitating a natural person as the very basis for its operation in order for such rights to actualise in the first place.[167]

Although none of the usual intention or planning associated with the wider concepts of creativity or authorship is required by the law, nevertheless the author arises through the work (not least for its operational purpose in determining ownership). A sense of authorship and indeed a sense of originality arise through a kind of presumption of purpose through the evidence of the work. In this way, the author arises in collaboration with the audience. To put this a different way, that authorial purpose is understood in giving to an audience; a labour that is implied through the interpretation of originality, and an authorship that is always already *two*.[168] Sam Ricketson ventures a definition that brings these critical perspectives together and emphasises the concept of intellectual creation not only through the process of the expression but also in the direction of the work to an audience (which Ricketson nevertheless qualifies as human).[169] This would seem to accord with a relational approach to the aesthetic. And in addressing this to the question of sentience, this capacity might then be viewed through the phenomenal consciousness of the *work* (and play) of authorship, rather than the self-consciousness of the author: *to have* rather than *to be*.[170]

Perhaps one of the most expressive plays among nonhuman animals is their music – whether bird song,[171] or rhythm,[172] or indeed the music of movement,[173] not to mention the creative accounting considered in the previous chapter. Michel Serres writes, "Music raises every art, codes every science, inspires every thought, better yet, cadences every number; beneath it, behind it, between it and this broad call of the things lies the mute mystery, the chest of every secret. He who discovers it speaks virtually every language: Pangloss."[174] Serres approaches a kind of phenomenal consciousness, a what is it likeness, through the movement and experience of music: "Thanks to music, we fly like birds, dance in the three dimensions of water, gambol in the trees, discover or build places and space. But we also had the idea of doing so in the intimacy of our souls or of our confessions to others."[175] To speak through play as an aesthetic experience of nonhuman animals provides an insight into what it is like to be a dog, to be a bee, to be an author. Play *shows* what it is like to be an author.

The future is Panglossian. How might intellectual property, and copyright law in particular, be translated into this joy?

Phenomenal Intellectual Property

Intellectual property and copyright law in particular have views on intentionality, explicit or otherwise. These inhere in basic principles of authorship and originality, ranging from the test of skill, labour, and judgement,[176] through to perambulations of originality towards the author's own intellectual creation.[177] What the law actually and certainly asks in these tests, at least by implication, is the purpose of the creativity. While this may not seem apparent, given the automatic attachment of copyright to any qualifying work, in every practical sense the law is concerned about the purpose and about reconstructing and re-presenting the author in the context of that perceived purpose. This is especially clear in the operation of exceptions and limitations.[178] In order to be re-constructed as an author through the nature of the work, the work must have been created for the right purpose, for a suitable authorial purpose.[179] In all these examples, the law is actually asking *what is it like to be an author?* At least, it is purporting to ask this question, but is in fact re-inscribing the work within a frame of intentionality and purpose. In this way, the concept of the author is at risk of being co-opted within an adaptationist paradigm, as it were, rather than the true incomparability of the Leibnizian Panglossia. And in asking what Naruto wants, the question is re-appropriated in the same way. *What is it like to be an author?* is re-framed as an impossible question of intentionality, of what it is like to *want* to be a copyright author, and thus a resort to all as it should be in service of the legal status quo. What does Naruto want? Does Naruto want to be an author? Does Naruto want the right things for the work to manifest as such? How then does the law reconcile the very operation of copyright as arising automatically? What does the surrounding discourse suppose about the fact that a copyright work can thus also be created without knowledge, without purpose, and even by accident? It does so by resorting to the adaptationist paradigm of authorship. *What do authors want?*

Indeed, the reconstruction of incentives for creativity and authorship through an imposed economic rationality is a similar inversion of the *proper path of analysis* that besets the language of sentience and nonhuman animal motivation. If the creativity and authorship of nonhuman animals are conditional upon a specific account of motivation that is neither relevant nor knowable, then the nonhuman animal may never have access to the language of authorship. But to do this is, once again, to coerce play within functionalist and adaptationist conventions in biological sciences and sociobiology, towards a *coherent* evolutionary narrative of authorship. Authorship could thus easily be added to the various non-biological examples presented by Gould and Lewontin in their essay. In other words, when reviewing nonhuman creativity, "by force of habit," it is the work or "epiphenomenal adaptation" that is viewed as "primary," and to date, the attempts to resolve all kinds of things, from sentience to consciousness, to authorship and copyright, have "tried to build the whole structural system from it."[180] This may serve artificial intelligence well, giving way to a wholly self-contained system of an economically rational "work," but for nonhuman animals, the displacement from the actual experience of authorship is complete. In contrast to this search for consistency and for a "coherent" reconstruction of incentives in service of the object, the elements of an expressive and playful theory of sentience inhere in the very fundamental concept of originality in copyright – the author's own intellectual creation. Similarly, the question of artificial intelligence invention has been focused on the objects as somehow a phenomenal and sufficient reason for the artificial intelligence as inventor.[181] But this risks neglecting the issues of explainability[182] or the process of invention itself; that is, *what is it like to be an inventor?*

A copyright analogy may assist here – as the physical book is to the "work" in the story, so too is play for the phenomenal consciousness or sentience of the nonhuman animal. But is there anything about artificial intelligence that might fulfil the work of play?

Intellectual Creation

Ada Lovelace, the English mathematician and instrumental figure in the history of computing,[183] famously wrote, "The Analytical Engine has no pretensions whatever to *originate* anything. It can do *whatever we know how to order it* to perform."[184] The work of authors is not answers, but questions. This is the nature of intellectual creation. Returning to the proprietary nature of experience, the meaning of *author's own* takes on particular relevance in the context of play. And "intellectual creation" emerges as a project of play. This phenomenal approach was in a way anticipated by Bill Cornish when he said of the originality standard, "a test of personal intellectual creation is likely to call for no very significant measure of creativity."[185] The fundamental test of intellectual creation is, rather, the question of choice.

The declaration of Henri Poincaré is pertinent: "Invention is discernment, choice."[186] And so, in its outputs, does artificial intelligence ever choose or select? After all, "*To Invent Is to Choose.*"[187] Perhaps it is more accurate, not only conceptually but also legally, to consider the authorship of artificial intelligence as that persisting in the relation between human and machine, and the relational property thus generated at that interface; in other words, the sentience of the machine is inextricably bound in the bond with the human.[188] Sentience is relational. On the question of authorship in artificial intelligence, perhaps ascertaining the "human factor"[189] in intellectual property is really about discerning the *will* to create: "[I]t is clear that no significant discovery or invention can take place without the *will* of finding."[190] The concept of sentience, as bond, is thus informed by an understanding of artificial intelligence as extended cognition, and the outputs potentially as extended creativity.[191] The requisite *will* may be found in the human intervention in the curation of that relation, and through the selection and presentation of objects. Can the circumstances of computation, proceeding from patterns rather than freedom, ever fulfil the curiosity and humour of nonhuman animal play, which shows not only choice but also invention? Play fundamentally characterises both the spirit and circumstances of authentic authorship. Its expression is critical not only to the apperception of the intellectual creation, but also to an expressive theory of sentience through the author.

In the second volume of *The Literary Remains*, Samuel Taylor Coleridge, one of the leading English figures of the Romantic Movement, provides a definition of poetry: "The proper and immediate object of science is the acquirement, or communication, of truth; the property and immediate object of poetry is the communication of immediate pleasure."[192] He continues with a poetics of play, maintaining that poetry is distinguished "as having intellectual pleasure for its object."[193] Similarly, inhering in the German Romantics' anti-mimetic philosophy of art is a distinctive and creative relationship with nature, succinctly stated in Friedrich Schlegel's claim that "[m]any so-called artists are really products of nature's art."[194] The Romantics are insightful in their perhaps unexpected role in the development of an expressive theory of sentience through play and the creative force of more than humans. For in the Romantic movement is to be found the move away from a fallacious objectivity of "attention to mimetic representation" towards producing "an expressive mode of creativity in the arts"[195] and in doing so, making "a relevant and lasting contribution to the exposition of the self."[196] That is, literature saw a move away from viewing the author or artist in terms of skill, and towards the author's imagination and expression – literature as the author's own intellectual creation, if you will. In the Romantic period, literature began to play.

Poetry and play, for which the *immediate object* is *pleasure*, are world-building exercises, expressive in that they are building a world in addition to truth; an abundance, an excess, a surplus. What a glorious waste, one might say.[197] Indeed, the discussion will return to this abundance in play in more detail later, but for now, this making of something other than the object world is a fundamental quality of intellectual creation. Neither play nor poetry is a rehearsal of the actual world. The question that arises is whether anything artificial intelligence does can ever fulfil this abundance of play, whether it can ever produce an intellectual creation, given that its process is fundamentally bound by the objects at its disposal? Is it simply a tedious representation, bound by calculations of the objects with which it is fed? Always efficient, never exuberant, never generous, never in play. And by its own admission, artificial intelligence can never lie.[198]

A Matter of Expression

The expression, in copyright law, is thus both a purportedly objective particularisation of the intellectual creation as well as a phenomenal account, as it were, of authorship – not in the sense of intentionality, but in the sensation of that very expressivity. In this way, any *objectivity* of that expressive account may point to the consciousness of authorship. Philosopher and aesthetician, Stefan Morawski, describes this phenomenal work of the expression: "Every artwork to a greater or lesser degree is treated as a symptom and emblematic depository of the life of society."[199] Morawski continues that this approach to expression "considers the artwork's particular qualities so as to refer them to a collective social subject, and in doing this it objectifies the expressiveness itself. Not only is the expression palpable and a stimulus to aesthetic experience in the recipient ... *it manifests a sentient world antecedent to it.*"[200]

In some respects, then, the work makes the author. Indeed, it is upon the outputs and their potential markets that advocates stake their claims for the recognition of authorship and inventorship for artificial intelligence.[201] But proceeding from the work alone is to get only an artefact of the story. Any financial motive has been rationalised within a narrative of creativity and cultural development, all in the service of maintaining a coherent and consistent picture of incentives and productivity. In a perverse way, objects are produced in order that money may continue to circulate, or as Weil argues, "Money does not provide a convenient method for exchanging products; it is the sale of goods which is a means for keeping money in circulation."[202] And in the mass consumption of cultural material through the operation of artificial intelligence and LLMs, the author is, somewhat literally, dispossessed. As Theodor Adorno cautioned many years earlier, "Ultimately, the culture industry no longer even needs to directly pursue everywhere the profit interests from which it originated. These interests have become objectified in its ideology ... The culture industry turns into public relations, the manufacturing of 'goodwill' per se."[203] Putting Adorno's argument concisely, Andreas Huyssen argues, "The manipulative praxis of this culture industry ... subordinates all spiritual and intellectual creation to the profit motive."[204] If machines are authors, perhaps it could be only through a return to the long eighteenth century of skill and scale over imagination, and a departure from the concept of originality in copyright in its most fundamental and conceptual sense. It is as though we are trying "to build the whole structural system" from the epiphenomenal adaptation of the work.[205] To paraphrase Gould and Lewontin, it is to focus entirely on the work as the primary object or thing, rather than as a product of the author's intellectual creation, and to overlook what it is like to be an author.

This perverse result arises through the erroneous conflation of the subjective expression of the author's own intellectual creation with the structural object; an expression by analogy. That objectivity is flawed and limited to the useful extent that it operates as a vessel for the scope of protection; but it is not the primary *cause* of authorship, and to presume so is to "invert the proper path of analysis."[206] The expression of the author's own intellectual creation is not only a convenience of presentation in order to gesture towards objectivity in copyright, but also the collaborative process of anticipating and responding to and with an audience. The expression arises through relation, marked by the physical object. An object is recognised as an expression because of shared subjective experiences of such objects as expressive. This is not to suggest merely an equivalence with the author's subjective experience, or indeed the audience's or reader's, but rather it is to acknowledge the reflexivity in intellectual property objects realised to an extent through the shared interests in those objects, as mobilised through rights, limitations, and exceptions. This resonates with Alan Tormey's assertion: "We cannot make sense of the notion of an expression unless we are willing to fuse this reflexive revelation with the indication of intentional objects in our analysis of the meaning of expressive behavior."[207]

The re-socialisation of intellectual property thus requires an expressive approach, as it were, to intellectual creation. It is in this respect in particular that the expressive work of nonhuman animals informs property in useful and crucial ways, and why authorship in its broadest meaning presents a unique and somewhat neglected insight into nonhuman animal sentience and wellbeing.

Make way for play.

Making Space

What might it mean to claim that consciousness, and thus the personhood of authorship, *appears* through play? Towards a phenomenological intellectual property, the space of the expression is critical, in that space is a fundamentally relational and dynamic experience through which expression comes about. Space is also a subjective experience, with overlapping and distinct spaces within any one place. This mobile and personal character of space informs an ethological approach to property and to authorship through the necessarily collaborative and subjective experience of any expression.[208] The concept of *Umwelt* encompasses this space.

The concept of *Umwelt* (meaning environment but more expansively and literally *world around*) is largely associated with Jakob von Uexküll's biosemiotics[209] and concerns each organism's unique and subjective sensory world. This has immediate implications in the context of behavioural and cognitive studies, designing research from the individual's perspective rather than an anthropocentric experimental design.[210] In this way the nonhuman animal's engagement with space and communication through a range of sensory modalities informs our own ethical engagement in the *Umwelt*. Indeed, Morten Tønnessen and Jonathan Beever argue for an ethics beyond sentience, advocating an approach to moral status through biosemiotics, "an approach to biology that considers living organisms in terms of semiosis, or sign exchange."[211]

In many ways, the *Umwelt* (either as *Umwelt* or similar alternative terms) is ubiquitous as a focus for attention throughout various philosophical traditions, but most particularly through phenomenology and existentialism. Perhaps most significant is its interaction with Edmund Husserl's concept of life-world (*Lebenswelt*),[212] "as the world which constantly surrounds us as our experiential world."[213] Influenced by Husserl's lifeworld, *Umwelt* was introduced into the wider lexicon of the psychological and cognitive sciences, including through the work of phenomenological and existential psychologist Ludwig Binswanger,[214] to intend the environment, taking the totality of the living and inanimate beings in it together with their needs and *wants*. The concept also resonates with the concept of *milieu*, in particular as developed by Deleuze and Guattari in their ethology of rhythms and assemblages.[215] *Umwelt* is central to phenomenological psychology,[216] and to theories of embodied experience and expression, including through the phenomenology of Maurice Merleau-Ponty.

Merleau-Ponty explains that, "[w]hen we consider the *Umwelt*, we do not engage in psychological speculation ... There are manners in which the animal behaves, which can be understood and can be read as the meaning of behavior,"[217] showing the extent of an objective extrapolation of certain expressive communications through behaviour. At the same time, Merleau-Ponty clarifies the way in which consciousness is available only through this kind of phenomenal account that may embody a certain expressive space, as it were, in the observer or audience: "Consciousness is only one of the varied forms of behavior; it must not be defined from within, from its own point of view, but such as we grasp it across the bodies of others ... Consciousness must appear as institution, as a type of behavior."[218] In other words, there is a distinct engagement through the expression, a purposeful and subjective property through relations. Uexküll's anti-Cartesianism is thus critical to an understanding of sentience and consciousness through the extensive performance of *authorship* in its many forms: "[T]he *Umwelt* is no longer a closing-off, but rather an opening. The world is possessed by the animal."[219] *Umwelt* is at once a personal, subjective space, but it is an overlapping territory and one which is all together world-building.

This recalls Tarde's assertion: *I desire, I believe, therefore I have*.[220] In this principle of having, Tarde affirms the proprietary quality of the subjective experience that informs an expressive theory of sentience; the *having* of phenomenal consciousness, as distinct from the presentation of equivalence through the notion of "that hollow abstraction" of *being* and "its essential sterility."[221] An expressive subjectivity is thus to *have* a sense of occasion in relational and embodied selves. This is the work of knowing, to paraphrase Weil, the joy of engagement through shared interests and overlapping spaces. In its subjective and thus productive[222] or generative[223] measure of space, the individual's *Umwelt* makes sense of the proliferation of spaces within the one place, a Panglossian account of subjective experiences and expressions.

Tarde's account of *milieu* is of some assistance when he suggests, "[M]any perplexing enigmas could be resolved by imagining that the speciality of each element, a true universal medium (*milieu*), is to be not only a totality," at the same time acknowledging the "diversity of elements" in Leibniz's monadology; indeed, a diversity of Panglossian proportions.[224]

It literally makes sense, then, to consider in this context the way in which different species experience and express their awareness of their bodies and selves. For example, dolphins have a "sense of self ... rooted in the body in action,"[225] bees take account of their own individual bodily dimensions in navigating busy environments,[226] and studies with dogs have provided evidence of bodily awareness and understanding as "the fundamental building blocks of self-representation."[227] Ethologist, Marc Bekoff describes the role of body-awareness[228] or body-ness,[229] in which the principles of a proprietary, subjective experience inhere, particularly through the body in play.[230] In his account of body-ness, Bekoff also refers to a concept of mine-ness,[231] which resonates with other approaches to nonhuman animal proprietary interests through *Umwelt*, deciphering rights through use.[232] This body-ness or self-awareness, as a kind of possessory and personable *having*, is crucial in negotiating the relational properties of overlapping territories of shared interests, and enlivens the approach to sentience as embodied expression: "Many animals have a sense of 'body-ness' or 'mine-ness' but not a sense of 'I-ness.'"[233] Bekoff describes self as a "scheme of degrees" rather than a hierarchy, of which "body-ness" is a part: "The sense of 'mine-ness' or 'body-ness' captures the essence of what I mean. Many animals know about the placement in space of parts or most of their body as they run, jump, and perform acrobatics."[234] Similarly, movement and the use of space is itself an expressive aspect of individual personalities: "[M]ovement parameters can be viewed as 'micropersonality' traits that give rise to broad-scale consistent interindividual differences in behavior."[235] Often neglected in discussions of sentience and expressiveness, fish also have such dynamic personalities, as it were. For example, individual stickleback fish have been found to exhibit individual, "personal" differences in movement and behaviour,[236] suggesting personality differences through performance, in a manner of saying.

Space is thus fundamental to expressive capacity and to ethical engagements with nonhuman animals and their habitats; how they express in those environments also lends an aesthetic dimension to ecological protection and animal welfare.[237] And in that the interaction between space, movement, and personality is of particular relevance to a performative interpretation of authorship,[238] expressiveness of both information and personality through movement is thus particularly significant. This becomes compelling in the context of human performance as well, where the tension between the work and the performance (or perhaps, expression) leads to what might be considered an arbitrary distinction between creative "works."[239] As Arthur C

Danto maintains, at least in music, "expression ... is what the *performer* contributes."[240] When will authorship come into play for performers?[241]

The Welfare of Authors ... and Performers

Through the nature of play in particular, there emerges a significant welfare dimension to authorship, and at the same time, an aesthetic dimension to welfare. It is phenomenally important to examine and respond to the inextricable link between authorship and play, creativity and wellbeing. In developing an expressive approach to authorship and to sentience, this interaction between animal welfare or wellbeing (including in approaches to rights-based discourse) and intellectual property authorship becomes sensible. But this is not for the reasons of rights; rather, it is for reasons of relations. The nature of rights is such that these arise in the context of the necessary relations articulated through the property dynamic. As such, an investigation of sentience and nonhuman creativity is thus insightful for the welfare of authors within intellectual property. And at the same time, an expressive account of authorship introduces an aesthetic personality and accountability, with genuine application for advancing the interests of nonhuman animals and the exploration of personhood. In the discussions of whether or not artificial intelligence should be considered an author, an inventor, and so on, a considerable amount of academic and popular discourse focuses on the monetary or economic opportunities presented by intellectual property rights. This overlooks the provenance and indeed relations that are arguably the basic socio-cultural architecture of intellectual property, including copyright. Through an ethological jurisprudence of authorship, it is possible to open up the sociality of creative and innovative activity, and to understand better the contribution beyond a simple economic equation of rights.

Responding to the issue of "systemically overlooked forms of creative expression,"[242] James Kaufman and Vlad Glaveanu advocate for a greater inclusivity for creativity through the concept of shadow creativity: "It is between the gibberish and the rote, between the not-creative and the obviously-creative, that we see shadow creativity. Shadow creativity belongs just as much in the category of 'creative' as those obviously-creative works – it is simply not viewed as such by other people (or, in some cases, the creator)."[243] Kaufman and Glaveanu explain that rather than persisting as an objective and alienated value, the recognition of creativity by others is a complex interaction between "capital ... awareness ... spark ... and exceptionality,"[244] and that "appreciating shadow creativities can foster personal development as well as increase social justice for the benefit of all."[245] In this affiliative and sociable way, recognition of creativity is an incentive to further creativity, a payment in advance, so to speak.[246]

Following this approach, it is contended that the property of exceptionality, "or the property of visibly standing out from other productions,"[247] is inevitably affected by the value generated by recognition through the intellectual property system.[248] That is, the intellectual property system operates as a gatekeeper of creativity: "In order to be perceived as creative, a work must appeal to contemporary gatekeepers and those who shape the domain."[249] In this way, recognition within the intellectual property system thus clarifies creativity, as it were, while shadow creativity is overlooked, "not because they lack creativity, but because they do not 'look' creative to themselves or others."[250] This resonates with the framing of creative and innovative work through intellectual property and the significance of this for other forms of creativity, including incremental and distributed creativity, some forms of collaborative or temporary work, traditional knowledge and traditional cultural expressions, and indeed, the creativity of nonhuman animals. To draw upon this concept of "shadow creativity" is to open up the sociality of authorship for both the works and the authors – that is, for both the objects of creativity as well as the makers themselves. The creativity of the world about. If we continue to ask of Naruto only questions of remuneration, we are asking the wrong questions. And that is a welfare issue for all authors.[251]

The predatory drift in the intellectual property system thus pervades the critical perspective upon that system as well as recasting *wants* in a whole other storyline. How might copyright contribute to the *cognitive enrichment* of creatives in the sense of their welfare, as understood separately from the *economic enrichment* of creatives in terms of an externalised rights-based discourse? This is why the authorship question is not to be dismissed as a novelty, as a humorous tale of a certain macaque. Rather, it is of considerable importance to animal welfare discourse. And conversely, the nonhuman animal perspective offers valuable insight into understanding and addressing the welfare of human authors. What does copyright have to do or say about wellbeing? What is the ethological dimension to authorship? How have these worlds merged, and what is the significance for an ethical and compassionate intellectual property?

Can They Play?

The question is then not, *can they suffer?* but, *can they play?*

This rephrasing has significant implications, including a material impact on the interpretation of suffering itself. From a practical and policy perspective, this shift in perspective potentially introduces a positive approach to investigating empirically whether a particular species should be protected within welfare legislation. The irony of the question, *can they suffer?* is that it has ordinarily required the production of suffering itself in order to be answered. But what if the enquiries turn to the questions of expressive and positive affect, rather than those of suffering? Play presents not only a sociological but also an empirical dimension to welfare. At the same time, attention to play has the potential for a radical new vision of authorship, reconciling individual and community, and celebrating the personalities in the swarm.

It is indeed becoming clear that the question is not *can they reason*, nor *can they talk*, nor even *can they suffer*. The question is, *can they play?* The most compelling case for the recognition of rights and a basis for personhood comes not from attributing it to an individual or species on the basis of a calculation or demonstration of sentience but by looking at what that individual creates. In other words, it is not to look for proof of life but to look at authors. Recalling the discussion of *Civilisations*,[252] the assertion that we are the art-making animals immediately invokes a separate and impenetrable barrier through an aesthetic sense; it is thus to this question of the aesthetic that attention must be directed, as it is with aesthetics that the bastion of exceptionalism is emboldened. The barrier to rights, the inscrutable species barrier, is arguably not concerned with sentience at all. It is concerned with authorship. And that is why discussions of sentience, of nonhuman animal wellbeing and rights, must engage with authorship. Proving sentience is no guarantee of admission to this community. But demonstrating creativity is.

There is a distinct protocol, in a way, that frames the way in which sentience studies might continue to be recuperated within an anthropocentric perspective. Pain, as a reaction or withdrawal, is not always taken as proof of anything but a reaction. It does not manipulate the environment in the same way as other activities, such as tool use, are taken to suggest. A reaction to pain is thus interpreted within a functional rubric of adaptation and survivability, rather than the direction that may be considered to manifest in behaviours such as play. Play, on the other hand, demands attention, as it were, for its direction and its authorship over the environment. As will be seen later, this has the potential to introduce a new perspective on sentience through authorship and play, in that the active perception of one's environment introduces productive work, including through play.[253] If we look at authors, we do not have to engage in a treacherous and fraught account of threshold arguments of sentience and, worse, the inscrutable, inconstant, and indefinable *right kind* of sentience. This is the *straw dog* of the law's rationality. Instead of reactions, let us look to the making.

Recalling Allan Kornblum's *Work Song*, "The hand attributes sentience."[254] Thus, the hand brings the play to the surface. Sentience is a matter of authorship, and so rather than insisting on a discovery of mind, to echo Weil's essay of the same name, the craft manifests the intelligence of the maker; the hand as *metaxu*. Kornblum's philosophies are playful in their own right. As a member of the albeit short-lived Actualist Movement in the Arts, founded "to bring poetry to the people and make it fun,"[255] Kornblum's *Work Song* is also in some ways antithetical to the tradition of the work song and in this way resonates with Weil's account of the inextricable partnership of work and play,[256] as well as with Tarde's affiliative and sociable "joyous work of the creator, of the true producer … *it is his joy, far more than his toil, which could serve to measure the social value of his invention.*"[257]

Kornblum's poetry thus presents poetry co-existing with work, rather than alienating poetry as a rarefied pursuit: work as joy. In many ways, this resonates with resisting the bifurcation of art and science, play and work, original and copy, and other disputed partners. Poetry is not a fixed expression on the page but a relationship between. Some of the best examples of this play come from another member of the Actualists, Dave Morice, whose work includes blind-folded poetry, the world's largest book, poetry castles, poetry poker, and even football poetry.[258] The surface play of intentionality is characterised somewhat enchantingly by a particular anecdote from Dave Morice, in conversation with a woman about poetry which, unintentionally or accidentally, sets out the action of consciousness in play. Morice recalls, "[A]t one point she said, 'Great poems should paint pictures in the mind'," to which Morice replied, "'Great poems would make great cartoons'."[259] And then there is the ambitious collage of fortune cookie fortunes in *The Great American Fortune Cookie Novel*, in which Morice constructed a novel out of fortunes he had collected over the years, to which were added even more sent in by "Hundreds of Co-authors," as they were indeed described on the book's cover.[260] That authorship should adhere to this kind of curation of items and at the same time subsist in relation with hundreds of contributors is precisely the sort of challenge to auteurism that sounds with an ethological perspective, and the intriguing pastiche of expressions throughout the following chapters.

At the same time as subverting the context for work, the Actualists also disrupted the concept of the author as capital and the work of authorship itself. Through the Wooden Nickel Art Project,[261] Dave Morice parodies the commodification of art. The project involved the making of 1,000 wooden nickels, one side of which was printed with the words "Artist's Wooden Nickel," and the other was left blank. Morice distributed the nickels to celebrities, as well as friends and strangers, accompanied by the request to decorate the nickels and return them to Morice. The result was the production of a volume of photocopies in the *Wooden Nickel Art Project*.[262] The Actualists also perfected an elaborate literary hoax in the fictional author, Joyce Holland. Morice invented Holland, who would be played by his partner, PJ Casteel, whenever an author appearance or reading was required. The rest of the Actualists worked together to perfect this elaborate literary hoax, prolonging the play and sustaining the ruse for several years. In an interview, almost 40 years later, Morice even cites Joyce Holland as one of his influences.[263] It was thus a collaborative and elaborate authorial deception, as it were. Poetry as performance. The prolonged play of irony.

It is the play of community to which the discussion turns in Part 2, when the ants come to the picnic.

Notes

1. Voltaire (2015/[1759]), 15.
2. Voltaire (1900/[1759]).
3. Voltaire (1900/[1759]), 4.
4. Voltaire (1900/[1759]), 5.
5. Voltaire (1900/[1759]), 15.
6. Voltaire (1900/[1759]), 17.
7. Voltaire (1900/[1759]), 18.
8. Voltaire (1900/[1759]), 18.
9. A refrain on Jean-Luc Godard's and Jean-Pierre Gorin's *Tout va bien* (1972) which is itself a cinematic refrain upon sufficient reason.
10. Gould and Lewontin (1979).
11. Gould and Lewontin (1979), 582.
12. See further Herman (2012), 530.
13. To echo the philosopher Pangloss who, upon witnessing Jacques the Anabaptist disappear into the sea, "proved to [Candide] that the Lisbon roads had been expressly created for the Anabaptist to be drowned in them" (Voltaire (1759/[1900]), 16).
14. Wells (1945), 6, 12, 19, 31.
15. Wells (1945).
16. Wells (1945), 19.
17. Voltaire (1759/[1900]), 20. Voltaire's tale is famously regarded as a critical account of the optimism of the Enlightenment period shared by Leibniz and others. However, this may be a somewhat attenuated version of Voltaire's thinking and indeed the oft-cited transformation in thinking said to be precipitated by the catastrophe of the Lisbon Earthquake may be overly simplified or exaggerated (see further, Nichols (2014).
18. Voltaire (1900/[1759]), 16.
19. Voltaire (1900/[1759]), 16.
20. Voltaire (1900/[1759]), 16.
21. Voltaire (1900/[1759]), 16–17.
22. Voltaire (1900/[1759]), 17.
23. Voltaire (1900/[1759]), 17.
24. Voltaire (1900/[1759]), 4
25. Voltaire (1900/[1759]), 4
26. Voltaire (1900/[1759]), 4. Emphasis added.
27. Parody is considered in detail in Chapter 9.
28. Tarde (1899), 188
29. Tarde (1902), 24. Translation mine.
30. Weil (2015/[1970]), 134.
31. Gibson (2005).
32. The quality of this incomparability is to found in Voltaire's original prose, itself, as discussed briefly in Postoutenko (2020), where the author notes a distinction between Leibniz's historically and socially contextualised "best possible world" and the extent of this as presented by "his satirical shadow – a pathological optimist Pangloss" (66) where "the improbability and pragmatic servility of the derivative comparisons invalidates the soundness of the main one" (66) introducing a message of "something in-between," (*metaxu*) through the linguistic process of neutralisation (67). Thus the relations become important and overwhelm the indexical nature of the forms.
33. Tarde (1899), 100.

34 Tarde (1899), 100.
35 Tarde (1899), 87. Emphasis in original.
36 Serres (2018/[2003]), 120.
37 Gould and Lewontin (1979), 581.
38 Gould (1978).
39 See further the final chapter of the present work, Law's Anecdote.
40 Gould and Lewontin (1979), 591–592.
41 Gould (1997), 10750.
42 As Blute (2022) maintains, "in neglecting Tarde, sociology neglected its Mendel and hence very much delayed the coming of a truly evolutionary theory applied to culture" (2).
43 Tarde (1899), 155–156.
44 Tarde (1899), 156–157. Emphasis in original. The personalities of the individuals in the swarm, as distinct from the univocity of the collective, is considered in more detail in Chapter 4 of the present work.
45 Tarde (1899), 48–49. Emphasis in original.
46 Tarde (1899), 49–50.
47 Bishop (2021).
48 Tarde (1899), 8.
49 Tarde (1899), 7.
50 Indeed, in UK case law, the only mention of sentience is elsewhere, and not in interpretations of animal welfare. The primary area is not unexpected, namely patients' rights and resuscitation, where again it is used axiomatically in respect of minimal consciousness (see *Royal Bournemouth and Christchurch Hospitals NHS Foundation Trust v TG*, [2019] EWCOP 21; *An NHS Trust v L*, [2013] EWHC 4313 (Fam).
51 On the science and welfare context, Broom (2019); Broom (2014). See further Humphrey (2022); Harnard (2016); Duncan (2006).
52 In view of these obstacles Birch (2017) recommends exercising the precautionary principle with respect to the prevailing uncertainty. See further Knutsson and Munthe (2017).
53 For example, see the series of "exchanges" on sentience and brain death: Shewmon (1985); Shewmon (2006); Lee and Grisez (2012); and Austriaco (2016).
54 Knutsson and Munthe (2017).
55 Dung (2022); Emmert-Streib et al. (2020).
56 Blattner (2019) argues that there is near universal recognition of the term but somewhat problematically supports this assertion with legal materials largely concentrated in Europe and North America. An additional problem with this claim of universality is that it does not distinguish between recognition of the term and understanding of the concept. Further, even if the claim were to be accepted, it does not address the arbitrary exclusion of some sentient species, nor does it address the inconsistency of the application and interpretation of the concept in the various examples. The author claims a particular meaning by legislators when using the term "sentience," (125) but does not provide evidence of this in the article, but nevertheless does mention the problematic operation of assumptions in relation to fish species and suggests in some jurisdictions they have been denied protection. But again, this is not entirely accurate in that the issue is usually one of enforcement (and attending complications or weaknesses in interpreting fish welfare states, particularly when framed through use, as in the sport of angling) rather than an exclusion from statutory protection or a lack of legal protection itself. Fish are usually included in welfare instruments (as vertebrates) at least throughout Europe, including in animal protection instruments

related to farming, as in Council Directive 98/58/EC concerning the protection of animals kept for farming purposes.
57 As Hadley (2019) notes, "There is sufficient ambiguity surrounding the meaning of the term sentience to undermine the logical relations between the premises and conclusion of the basic animal rights argument" (8).
58 For example, see Birch et al. (2020) in relation to decapods.
59 For example, Deckha (2021) relies on the following caveat, to justify the exclusion of plants from the discussion of "legal beings," namely that this exclusion should not be read as an exclusion from the possibility of ethical obligations (27). However, in appealing to "surrounding capacities," including sentience, this complicates this line in the sand.
60 For a useful review of the literature, see Calvo (2017). Segundo-Ortin and Calvo (2019) argue that the dismissal of plant cognition is itself sustained by a persistent anthropocentrism in approaches to the science itself.
61 Chalmers (2022), 4. Emphasis in original.
62 For example, New Zealand (Animal Welfare Act 1999, Long Title, as amended by the Animal Welfare Amendment Act (No 2) 2015, s4). In the United Kingdom in the Animal Welfare (Sentience) Act 2022 which mandates policy-making with regard to the impact on sentient animals (s2). In France, the French Civil Code defines animals as "*êtres vivants doués de sensibilité*" which is commonly translated as sentient living beings (as amended by LOI n° 2015-177 du 16 février 2015 relative à la modernisation et à la simplification du droit et des procédures dans les domaines de la justice et des affaires intérieures). And in the 2022 decision of the Constitutional Court of Ecuador, Case No. 253-20-JH/22, the court considered sentience in detail to conclude that "some animals with sentience capacity in the strict sense" will be "subjects of rights" but qualifies this "does not mean that animals with sentience in the strict sense should or can be equated to human beings, since each species has its own protection needs that stand out for their own characteristics and qualities; therefore, their demands for legal protection will be different" [89]. Fasel (2024) also endorses a species-based approach.
63 Nevertheless, there is considerable support in the literature for considering them to be similar concepts, sentience thus becoming the more popular and less technical terminology for similar concerns around subjective experience and *what it is like*. For example, Chalmers (2022) states: "As I use the terms, consciousness and sentience are roughly equivalent. Consciousness and sentience, as I understand them, are subjective experience" (3). See further a similar claim in Damasio and Damasio (2023), in which the authors present sentience and consciousness as equivalent concepts for subjective feeling and experience, and object to notions of plant sentience as confusing sentience (consciousness) with sensing: "[T]he presence of sensing does not allow us to predict that there is consciousness/sentience as well" (2).
64 Compare Birch (2018) on the notion of degrees in sentience, see further Birch et al. (2020). Note Francione (2021): "To talk about degrees of sentience makes no sense" (96). This is consistent with the approach in Cochrane (2018) on the "possession of interests" of sentient beings as a "binary" concept: "That is to say, an individual either possesses interests or does not" (24). See further the discussion of this argument in Fasel (2024).
65 Broom (2003), 212. See further Broom (2014), 1–5, where Broom sets out the links between human exceptionalism and sentience. See further the discussion in Humphrey (2022), 1–2.
66 *Naruto v Slater*, 888 F. 3d 418 (2018).

67 Matson (1976), 47.
68 See discussion of positive welfare in this context in Broom (2014), Fraser (2008), and Gibson (2022b).
69 Bentham (2007/[1789]), 311 n 1.
70 The clearest example is that of the Animal Welfare Act 2006, where the concept of unnecessary suffering is a fundamental element of a welfare offence, as well as defining the scope of permitted procedures. The concept of suffering also appears in other animal protection legislation that may not ordinarily be viewed as welfare legislation, thus complicating the separation of welfare and protection at the policy level: for example, the Animals (Scientific Procedures) Act 1986. For a more detailed account of the concept of suffering in its various appearances in animal protection legislation in the United Kingdom, and the significance for importing a welfare dimension through these forms of legislation, see Gibson (2022b).
71 Notably, while North American jurisdictions do not refer to sentience, the relevant legislation does make reference to the concept of suffering. See further in the United States the Animal Welfare Act s16(a) [7 U.S.C. 2146], and in Canada, the primary welfare legislation is the Criminal Code, 445. Both the United States and Canada categorise the protection of animals within the concept of property, but the reference to suffering may be argued to import the concept of sentience nonetheless.
72 Weil (2002/[1947]), 108.
73 Weil (2015/[1970]), 72.
74 Fineman (2020).
75 Part 3.
76 See the discussion of vulnerability and capacity in the welfare context in Gibson (2022b). See further on the concept of vulnerability in animal studies, Pick (2018).
77 Nussbaum (2023). Although Nussbaum does not reference Weil, this reconstruction, as it were, appears to establish Weil as a seemingly undetected progenitor of capabilities thinking.
78 In their review of the literature and scientific developments, Browning and Birch (2022) provide a useful baseline for the definition of sentience: "In a broad sense, sentience can refer to the capacity for *any type of subjective experience*," and "[i]n a narrower sense, sentience can refer to the capacity to *have subjective experiences with positive or negative valence*" (1). Emphasis in original.
79 For instance, Godfrey-Smith (2020) suggests that this evaluative dimension to experience, either negatively or positively, is a critical character of sentient experience (18).
80 Bostrom and Yudkowsky (2014), 321–322. This distinction is notable for considerations of plant sentience.
81 Donath (2020), 55. Emphasis in original. On consciousness and personhood, see further Kingwell (2020), who notes there is some consensus "that such consciousness, supposing it possible, is at least a necessary condition of potential personhood" (329).
82 Bostrom and Yudkowsky (2014), 323–324. In this context, it is useful to consider the examination of this issue with respect to artificial intelligence as actors in Ballardini and Genderen (2022).
83 Humphrey (2022) suggests that play is "a weak test for sentience," but nevertheless concedes, "Yet, we can certainly say that those animals that don't play are most unlikely to be sentient" (159–160). This would suggest a very good basis for the application of the precautionary principle in respect of play, such that

any nonhuman animal species that plays and is otherwise as yet not protected as sentient, should be afforded that protection.
84 For example, see Francione (2010); Francione and Garner (2010), 25–29. Notably Francione and Garner are writing in the North American context, where there is strict adherence to welfare through property, contrary to the approach in the United Kingdom in particular. See further the work of the Nonhuman Rights Project in the United States https://www.nonhuman-rights.org. Compare Chiesa (2017) on the antagonism between welfare and abolitionism.
85 Gibson (2022b).
86 Part 3.
87 Varner (2018), 356.
88 Recall the discussion of "societal sentience" in "What Does Naruto Want?" See further Hobson-West and Davies (2018).
89 See Stucki (2020) on "animal welfare rights." See further McCausland C (2014).
90 For example, in the United Kingdom, under the Animal Welfare Act 2006, section 4(1)(a).
91 See Birch (2018) and Sneddon et al. (2018). Note, the same language is invoked in the title of Strawson (2018) for *The New York Review of Books* (which may or may not be down to editorial intervention).
92 Compare the interdisciplinary work to address and resolve this in the collaborative project, Foundations of Animal Sentience (ASENT) (2021–2024). Further details are available at the project website at https://www.lse.ac.uk/cpnss/research/ASENT
93 Grebowicz and Reyna (2021) argue that "the problem Weil identifies for us cannot lie in the rejection of personhood as a metaphysical category. *Rather, the problem seems to lie in the rejection of a universalism along with the concept of personhood*" (85). Emphasis in original.
94 See further the discussion of Weil's concept of the collectivity in Chapter 4.
95 Barrow (2024). See further Dežman (2024). So-called hallucinations are considered in more detail in Chapter 8 of the present work.
96 Gould and Lewontin (1979), 582.
97 For example, see Watiktinnakorn et al. (2023), Gaffar and Albarashdi (2024), and in the context of patents, see Abbott (2016), Abbott (2023). See further Gervais (2020a), Gervais (2020b), Lund and Naheem (2024) and Amirjalili et al. (2024).
98 Compare the critique in Mik (2021).
99 Bishop (2021), 1.
100 Jordan (2019), 5.
101 Crawford (2021), 8. Emphasis in original.
102 Crawford (2021), 8.
103 Crawford (2021), 8.
104 Bishop (2009), 516.
105 This is a play on the title of the now famous paper, entitled "Attention Is All You Need," presented by several Google researchers at a conference in California in 2017. This paper is credited with precipitating the accelerated developments towards the current LLMs and generative AI, through the technical insights shared. See further Vaswani et al. (2017).
106 Samuel (1962), 11–12.
107 Floridi (2023b), 16–18. Emphasis in original.
108 Haikonen (2012), 1.
109 Cosmo (2022).

110 Butlin et al. (2023) where the authors argue "there is a strong case that most or all of the conditions for consciousness suggested by current computation theories can be met using existing techniques in AI. This is not to say that current AI systems are likely to be conscious ... but it does suggest that conscious AI is not merely a remote possibility in the distant future. If it is possible at all to build conscious AI systems without radically new hardware, it may well be possible now" (47).
111 Floridi (2023b), 21. Emphasis in original.
112 See the discussion in "What Does Naruto Want?" See further Despret (2016/[2012]), Waal (2016), Chittka (2022), Bekoff (2003), 238; Mitchell (2002), 348; and further the discussion of tests beyond an emphasis on vision, 239–240. As Delahaye (2019) puts it, "Sight is not the 'sense of self-awareness'" (38).
113 Gibson (2020a).
114 The mirror test is a classic cognitive test of self-awareness, where species are assessed on their capacity to recognise themselves or to coordinate their body in a mirror. The test has been criticised extensively for its species-specific approach, asking nonhuman animals to pass a test from the perspective of a sense that is prioritised in humans. See further Gibson (2020a), 156. See further Horowitz (2017) in relation to dogs and recognition and awareness of self through smell, or what Horowitz terms an "olfactory mirror."
115 Gibson (2023b).
116 Shaviro (2014), 318. Similarly, see the interview with Michael I Jordan where it is noted that AI systems "are merely imitating human intelligence, not engaging deeply and creatively" in Pretz (2021). This aligns with the distinction between the concepts developed in the present work – *attentive imitation* and *stereotypic imitation* – considered throughout, but see in particular the discussion in Chapter 6 with respect to the quality of attention.
117 Gould and Lewontin (1979), 583.
118 Crawford (2021), 8.
119 Gould and Lewontin (1979), 584.
120 See further Gibson (2023b).
121 Burghardt (2005), Burghardt (2024), Galapayage Dona et al. (2022), Chittka (2022).
122 Massumi (2014).
123 See the earlier discussion of anthropocentrism in "What Does Naruto Want?"
124 Matson (1976), 85.
125 Matson (1976), 85–86. This resonates with current debates over artificial intelligence and drug development, particularly with respect to the questions of invention or discovery. See, for example, Shapiro (2020).
126 For example, in describing the proliferation of DABUS patent litigation, Abbott (2023) states: "An AI system is not a legal person, so it cannot (and should not) own property. Our cases have nothing to do with 'AI rights' – they are about what rules will maximize the social benefits of AI and minimize its risks." While it is unclear how making AI an inventor will minimise risk, this appears to confound the notion of authorship and inventorship in ways that are difficult to reconcile with the policy, socio-cultural, or even technical environment. See further Gibson (2024a).
127 Isaacs (1918), 401.
128 Isaacs (1918), 377. These successive changes, these fragments, will become a critical part of an ethological approach to the law in Part 3, as well as in the concluding chapter, Law's Anecdote.
129 Brightman (1919), 506

130 Brown (1992), where the author, in an account of Goethe's concept of the demonic and historical and natural horrors and disasters, maintains that "[t]he earth-shattering impact of the Lisbon disaster projected by Goethe has been highly exaggerated in the subsequent scholarship" (479). Compare discussion in Nichols (2014).
131 Nichols (2014), 985–986.
132 Fraser (2009).
133 Webster (2005), 11. Emphasis added.
134 Webster (2005), 11. Emphasis in original. While Webster cautions against an uncritical anthropomorphism, he notes that "it would be equally fallacious to underestimate the emotional distress caused to farm animals by hunger, pain and anxiety. Although these sources of suffering in animals may be called primitive that does not make them any less intense" (11).
135 Fraser (2009), 113.
136 Milton (2002), 94. Milton is notably critical of the apparent resistance to discussion of emotional life in philosophical approaches, which ordinarily focus instead on the cognitive arguments for sentience, self-consciousness, and moral standing, as well as the approximation or kinship arguments.
137 Goodin (1992).
138 Milton (2002), 95.
139 Panksepp (2007).
140 Dawkins (1993), 142. Emphasis added. In Part 3, this extensive account of play, indeed the play of Mercury, is set out in detail.
141 Miller et al. (2020).
142 Chittka (2022).
143 Ng (2022).
144 Nagel (1974).
145 Farrell (1950).
146 Whitehead (1967/[1933]), 132.
147 Farrell (1950), 185–186.
148 Nagel (1974), 445.
149 This enacted cognition becomes critical to an expressive theory of sentience and authorship in the following chapters, including with respect to creativity within space, as in Naruto's experience, discussed further in Chapter 5, towards an embodied approach to authorship in Part 3.
150 Creativity is considered more fully in Part 3, particularly in Chapter 8.
151 Guilford (1950), 444.
152 Morawski (1974), 40.
153 Kettering (1944), 231.
154 Medawar (1984), 51.
155 Medawar (1984), 52.
156 Burghardt (2005), 70–82; Vicino and Marcacci (2015); Ahloy-Dallaire et al. (2018); and Miller (2020). See further Galapayage Dona et al. (2022).
157 This choice is a fundamental character of the concept of originality in copyright through the author's own intellectual creation, considered in more detail later in this chapter.
158 Gibson (2014), 38–41.
159 See further the resocialisation of property in Gibson (2020a) Part 4.
160 The Berne Convention for the Protection of Literary and Artistic Works 1886 (as revised). See further Ricketson (1992), 8.
161 Directive 2001/29/EC on the harmonisation of certain aspects of copyright and related rights in the information society (Infosoc).

162 Directive 2009/24/EC on the legal protection of computer programs (Computer Software), art 2(1); Directive 96/9/EC on the legal protection of databases (Database), art 4(1).
163 Copyright Designs and Patents Act, s9(3). The Court of Appeal decision in *THJ Systems Ltd v Sheridan* [2023] EWCA Civ 1354 affirms that the standard of originality is that the author's own intellectual creation, and it is difficult to see how this might be interpreted in its application to computer-generated works. See the further discussion in Chapter 8.
164 Copyright Designs and Patents Act, s9(1).
165 Appellant's opening brief, *Thaler v Perlmutter*, 22 January 2024, USCA Case No 23-5233.
166 Appellant's opening brief, *Thaler v Perlmutter*, 22 January 2024, USCA Case No 23-5233.
167 Gervais (2020b), 2094–2096.
168 Gibson (2020b). Notably, writing in 1953 on the matter of scientific property and its protection through intellectual property, Ilosvay (1953) presents a kind of adaptationist analysis that perhaps restores the proper course of analysis (to recall Gould and Lewontin). In this analysis, the justification for intellectual property is not through incentives to the creator, but in terms of the social function of its use and a kind of shared property: "[T]he intellectual creation must be considered as one foundation of scientific property. On the other hand, exercise of the creative function is not merely a personal satisfaction for the scientists, but also a social function. Therefore, the public interest demands protection of scientific property. Intellectual creation and social function, the bases of copyright, also justify the right of scientists to *share* in the rewards of their discoveries" (193). Emphasis added.
169 Ricketson (1992), 20–24.
170 See further the discussion in Chapter 1. See also Gibson (2020a) 117–118.
171 Kaplan (2007)
172 Ravignani (2019), 77–81.
173 Miles and Fuxjager (2018), 99–107
174 Serres (2018/[2003]), 124.
175 Serres (2018/[2003]), 124.
176 This is the old standard in the United Kingdom which follows *University of London Press v University Tutorial Press* [1916] 2 Ch 601. But the correct standard now is the author's own intellectual creation, following the judgment in *THJ Systems Ltd v Sheridan* [2023] EWCA Civ 1354. See further Gibson (2020b) on the interaction between the two standards. However, some countries still apply variants of the standard of skill, labour, and judgement, including: New Zealand (*University of Waikato v Benchmarking Services Ltd* (2004) 8 NZBLC 101, 561); South Africa (*Moneyweb (Pty) Ltd v Media 24 Ltd* 2016 (4) SA 591 (GJ)); and Canada (*CCH Canadian Ltd v Law Society of Upper Canada* [2004] 1 SCR 339).
177 The United States standard of "creative spark" is closer to the author's own intellectual creation: *Feist Publications v Rural Telephone*, 499 US 340 (1991). Australia has adopted the standard of "independent intellectual effort to create" (*IceTV Pty Ltd v Nine Network Australia Pty Ltd* [2009] HCA 14), moving away at least in part from the Commonwealth standard towards greater emphasis on authorship (intellectual creation).
178 See further the discussion in Chapter 9. See also Gibson (2023a).
179 This concept of purpose has particular implications in copyright works of parody and pastiche, considered in more detail in Chapter 9. At the same time, purpose

provides the scope of what might amount to infringement, as in the example of parodies of trade marks: see further Gibson (2023a).
180 Gould Lewontin (1979), 584.
181 Abbott (2023).
182 Rudzite (2022). Compare Kim (2020). See further Gibson (2024a).
183 Essinger (2014), which traces in detail Lovelace's friendship and the significance of her collaboration with Charles Babbage towards the development of the first mechanical (rather than manual) computer.
184 Lovelace (1843), 722. Emphasis in original. Note also quoted in Turing (1950), 450.
185 Cornish (1995).
186 Poincaré (1910), 325.
187 Hadamard (1996/[1945]), 30.
188 For instance, see the exploration of sentience through a human-machine bond, including a discussion of the funeral ritual for AIBO robot dogs which were no longer functioning, in Donath (2019), 10–24. A specific offence for pet abduction has been introduced in the United Kingdom in the Pet Abduction Act 2024 (as distinct from theft) punishable by up to five years' imprisonment.
189 Tzoulia and Kalles (2024).
190 Hadamard (1996/[1945]), 31. Emphasis in original.
191 Wheeler (2018).
192 Coleridge (1836), 7.
193 Coleridge (1836), 7.
194 Schlegel (1991/[1798–1800], Critical Fragments §1.
195 Burwick (2001), 8.
196 Burwick (2001), 9.
197 Abundance and waste are explored in more detail in Chapter 7.
198 Graham (2023), Moro et al. (2023). On misinformation, see Barman et al. (2024). But even the language of lying is deceptive, as it were, as it is always a question of accuracy and adherence, whether a machine is taught to lie or otherwise, and therefore does not constitute genuine deception, so to speak. For example, see Hubinger et al. (2024). See further the discussion in Chapter 8 of the present work.
199 Morawski (1974), 49.
200 Morawski (1974), 49. Emphasis added.
201 Abbott (2022) states, "AI is not just playing games and doing research" (2). Especially amusing in the context of the present discussion!
202 Weil (2001/[1955]), 105.
203 Adorno (1975), 13.
204 Huyssen (1975), 81.
205 Gould and Lewontin (1979), 584.
206 Gould and Lewontin (1979), 582.
207 Tormey (1971), 29.
208 Relevant here is the approach in Jürgens (2017) to this collaborative experience afforded in the *Umwelt* in order to address human-animal relations in an age of ecological crisis, through an ethical relationality, referring to "an intuitive understanding of how subjectivity harbors organisms' respective realities but may nevertheless constitute a common medium by the virtue of which respective realities may share common structures and of how, thus, minds may merge" (47). Although Jürgens does not deal with the work of Deleuze and Guattari, this approach to the relational ethics of interspecies intersubjectivities resonates with Deleuze's and Guattari's rhizomatic assemblages, Deleuze and Guattari (1987/[1980]).

209 Uexküll (2010/[1934]). See further Favareau (2010).
210 Despret (2016/[2012]), Waal (2016), Horowitz (2017).
211 Tønnessen and Beever (2015), 47.
212 Husserl (2002). See further Konopka (2009). The term *Lebenswelt* was already in use also in the work of Georg Simmel.
213 Husserl (1977/[1962]), 84. Husserl also engages with the concept of *Umwelt* in his work (see Husserl (2002). See further the discussion of generative space in this work, and the interaction with Eugen Fink (whose work in play is considered in Chapter 7) in DuFour (2023).
214 Binswanger (1963). Through his theory of modes of being, Binswanger differentiates between *Umwelt* (as the world around), *Mitwelt* (with world), and *Eigenwelt* (own world). See further Spinelli (2005/[1989]), 147. This distinguishes Binswanger's approach to *Umwelt* considerably from that of von Uexküll's biosemiotics, where there is attention to the relational quality and production of space, of particular importance in understanding the mobile and overlapping territories of an ethological jurisprudence of property.
215 Deleuze and Guattari (1987/[1980]).
216 Konopka (2015).
217 Merleau-Ponty M (2003/[1995]), 167.
218 Merleau-Ponty M (2003/[1995]), 167.
219 Merleau-Ponty (2003/[1995]), 171.
220 Tarde (2012/[1893]), 52. See further Chapter 1 in the present work.
221 Tarde (2012/[1893]), 52.
222 Lefebvre (1991/[1974]). Lefebvre's theory of space as a productive relation between the intellectual and the phenomenal experiences is considered again in Chapter 5 when the expressive relation to space is discussed in more detail. See further Gibson (2024b), which applies Lefebvre's account of productive space to an ethological approach to the relational property in non-fungible tokens (NFTs).
223 DuFour (2023).
224 Tarde (2012/[1893]), 58.
225 Herman (2012), 532.
226 Chittka (2022) notes that while this could be through trial and error, perhaps the simpler explanation is the advantage to the individual bee: "if bees could learn about their own body dimensions using their tactile sense during the early days in the hive, and later transfer this knowledge to the visual modality" (201).
227 Lenkei et al. (2021), 1.
228 Bekoff (2002), 97–98.
229 Bekoff (2006), 67–68; Bekoff (2013), 119–121, 123; and Bekoff (2021).
230 Chapter 7.
231 Thomas (2016) explains Bekoff's concept as a usefully more minimal level of selfhood than that associated with humans but nevertheless "more complex than simple perceptions of stimuli in the external world, which is also referred to as sentience." Thomas notes, "This level of self-awareness also means that there is 'something it is like' to be that particular animal" (40).
232 Hadley (2015); Bradshaw (2020).
233 Bekoff (2003), 229.
234 Bekoff (2003), 232.
235 Bailey et al. (2021), 3264.
236 Laskowski et al. (2015).
237 Bailey et al. (2021): "Understanding and predicting animal space use is central to the advancement of ecological research" (3264).

238 See further Naruto's expressive use of space in Chapter 6, as well as the development of an expressive theory of sentience and authorship in Part 3.
239 Gibson (2022a); Pavis (2021).
240 Danto (1970), vii.
241 Gibson (2022a).
242 Kaufman and Glaveanu (2022), 44.
243 Kaufman and Glaveanu (2022), 45.
244 Kaufman and Glaveanu (2022), 46, which the authors dub CASE.
245 Kaufman and Glaveanu (2022), 44.
246 See further Chapter 6.
247 Kaufman and Glaveanu (2022), 44.
248 Gibson (2006).
249 Kaufman and Glaveanu (2022), 46. See further the discussion in Gibson (2006) of the construction of peasants and propertied individuals through the framing of the intellectual property system, and later in Gibson (2014), Gibson (2019).
250 Kaufman and Glaveanu (2022), 46.
251 Mautner (2018), 6–7. The author notes: "The liberalism of flourishing rejects the idea that creativity is a trait with which only exceptional human beings, the geniuses, are endowed. Rather, it views creativity as a constitutive feature of humanity, something all human beings share ... the liberalism of flourishing understands that human creativity is a prime motor of cultural development, i.e., something that may greatly enrich the lives of other members of society" (7).
252 "What Does Naruto Want?"
253 Part 3.
254 Allan Kornblum, "Work Song," in Kornblum (1980), 51.
255 (1997), 142.
256 Weil (2002/[1949]).
257 Tarde (2007/[1902]), 617. Emphasis added.
258 For a full account see Morice (2012).
259 Morice (2012).
260 Morice and Hundreds of Co-authors (2009).
261 Morice (1988).
262 Morice (1988).
263 Morice (2012).

Part 2

The Ants

In the remarkable *Agua Viva*, Clarice Lispector writes, "Taking care of the world also requires a lot of patience: I have to wait for the day an ant will appear."[1] Today is that day.

Having navigated the boundaries and weathered the storms, it is time to exercise that patience in a certain and attending attention. It is time to heed the miniature and regard the swarm. This is not just to see the world in miniature, but to see the world. It is not just to summarise the collectivity, but to celebrate the individual insect in the swarm. Gaston Bachelard, in his inestimable attention to the infinitesimal, reminds us to pay attention to those sparks in the swarm: "Does not the life of the fire, made up entirely of sparks and sudden flickerings, remind us of the life of the ant heap?"[2]

As objects of fable and myth, the misreadings of ants abound and rebound, misreadings with the kind of force, as Simone Weil observes, "that turns anybody who is subjected to it into a *thing*."[3] Maligned for their greed,[4] or blind loyalty,[5] or mute industry,[6] ants are exiled from creativity in their machine-like enterprise. But there is another story, a story of creativity and ingenuity. And this is the story of the Argentine ant, as told by Italo Calvino. Just like the Ants swarming up the Philosopher's leg, banished with a thoughtless stamping of his feet, so too are ants swarming in Calvino's tale, and so too do the humans set about destroying them. But in Calvino's story, the narrator speaks of the way in which the perspectives forced by others (more specifically, his wife) prevent him "from entering their *state of mind*."[7] Ultimately, all of the attempts to eradicate the ants fail, and the humans yield to the overlapping territories of human and ant. Such conflict is only sustained through a war of boundaries; resolution must be through an attention to the relations in shared interests. What is it like to be an ant?

Following Jules Michelet,[8] Roland Barthes declares, "*The ideal City can only be matriarchal. This means that it will be virtually insectiform, since it is in the order of wasps, of bees, and of ants that females form the most indisputable of aristocracies,*" and "*let there be no mistake,*" he continues, "*These ants, 'aunts and sisters,' constitute an ideal order of rulers. We here rediscover the sororal theme.*"[9] The ideal society is made by those sororal relations, an affiliative and familiar foundation to the rule of law: "beginning with what romanticism posits as its true origin, not property but filiation."[10]

Lispector asks (and answers), "Is it a lot of work to take care of the world? Yes."[11] It will take some attention to detail.

Listen to the ants.

Notes

1 Lispector (1989/[1973]), 50.
2 Bachelard (1987/[1938]), 44.
3 Weil (1940), 3.
4 Aesop's "Zeus and the Ant."
5 The Myrmidons in Homer's *Iliad*
6 Twain (1913/[1905]), 209–210.
7 Calvino (1953), 177. Emphasis added.
8 French historian (1798–1874), known particularly for the 19 volumes of *Histoire de France* (1833–1867).
9 Barthes (1992/[1954]), 156157. Emphasis in original.
10 Rancière (1994/[1992]), 54.
11 Lispector (1989/[1973]), 49.

Chapter 4
Ant People

In the HG Wells short story, *Empire of the Ants*, the town of Badama is overcome by a plague of ants. A gunboat, the *Benjamin Constant*, travels to the town to assist the local inhabitants with Holroyd, a Lancashire engineer, on board:

> In a few miles of this forest there must be more ants than there are men in the whole world! This seemed to Holroyd a perfectly new idea ... But they had a language, they had an intelligence! Why should things stop at that any more than men had stopped at the barbaric stage?[1]

Discovering that the town is deserted, ultimately the gunboat returns for further instructions, and Holroyd returns to England. The ants continue in their work displaying "the use of implements and a knowledge of fire and metals and with organised feats of engineering"[2] as well as "an organised and detailed method of record and communication analogous to our books."[3] Holroyd counsels, "'These are intelligent ants. Just think what that means!'"[4]

Just think what that means, indeed.

What Do Ants Want?

A particular challenge for intellectual property systems, and for copyright in particular, is the prospect of a communal and distributed form of production,[5] and with that the mobility of the otherwise stable object ordinarily at the centre of things. Relations of iterative creativity and incremental stewardship of knowledge pose challenges to the supposed economic rationality of value through commodified intellectual objects, both within the intellectual property system and beyond in the context of an object-orientated interpretation of capital and resources. This is especially complex in the guardianship through systems of traditional and indigenous forms of knowledge making and keeping,[6] and as extended through to the guardianship of nature and the contribution of the natural world.[7] This chapter is concerned with an ethological approach to knowledge production as collaborative, reciprocal,

DOI: 10.4324/9780429342103-8

and shared interest. In *Owned*[8] the cultural histories of wolves and dogs, the socialisation of humans, and the shared interests in domestication are reviewed, as it were, for the familiar production arising within that socialisation and sociable properties.[9] In the present discussion, these questions are now posed to ants, particularly in their capacity as perhaps the quintessential example of familiar production; indeed "ants can be said to have a society in which the unit is the family."[10]

Ants (family: *Formicidae*) have been co-opted as models of computational agents in machine learning and artificial intelligence in concepts like swarm intelligence[11] for responding to challenges of optimisation[12] and creating interactive products like serious games.[13] But it is the ethology of ants and their social relations that provides considerable insight into the sociality of property, managed in a particularly vital and productive way in their complex cultures,[14] societies,[15] and spaces.[16] Ants engage in commodities,[17] international diplomacy,[18] healthcare and rescue,[19] architecture,[20] property development,[21] agriculture,[22] farming other animals,[23] training and teaching,[24] parenting,[25] sharing,[26] and much more. And once again, speaking of shipwrecks, they are even salvage operators.[27] They talk,[28] have systems of symbolic communication,[29] make and use tools,[30] make music,[31] and play.[32] And that is just the beginning. Is it any wonder there are ants at this dog's breakfast?

Ants have been recognised as agriculturalists and farmers for many years. In the early nineteenth century, Pierre Huber documented interspecies relationships, with a particular interest in the cohabitation of the Yellow Ants and pucerons: "I have seen the ants of two neighbouring nests disputing about their pucerons; when the ants of one nest were enabled to enter the habitation of their neighbours, they purloined these insects, which were, after a time, often recovered by their original possessors."[33] But what is especially striking about Huber's account is not merely a functional possession but rather a "keeping." Huber is describing a kind of ant agriculture, a settlement of observed property relations: "The ants know the full value of these little animals ... they constitute their sole wealth, an ant-hill being more or less rich, as it is more or less provided with pucerons; they are in fact their cattle, their cows, their goats, &c. Who could have imagined that the ants were a pastoral tribe!"[34]

And in these agricultural innovations, ants were well ahead of the first human agriculturalists, with Leaf-cutter ants credited as "the first farmers on Earth."[35] As Jae Choe explains, "It has been said that farmers are the founders of human civilization, but mankind's first farms are believed to be no more than ten thousand years old," when in fact, "animals had already begun farming at least fifty million years before the dawn of human agriculture."[36] Indeed, the agricultural expertise of ants is memorialised in Greek mythology in a dispute, somewhat fittingly for a discussion of intellectual property, over the ownership of an invention. Athena is said to have invented the plough, and when an Attic maiden named Myrmex claimed that she instead was the inventor of the plough, Athena punished her by turning her into an ant.[37] But as Donna Haraway muses, "judging from the tunnels ants dig all over the world and comparing that to Athena's more sky-looking and heady credentials, I think Myrmex probably had the stronger claim to having authored the plow."[38] Just like that dog and the socialisation and domestication of humans,[39] it turns out that ants too have some mighty cultural capital: "As with 'culture,' we humans are late to the game and probably should consider that there is little anthropomorphism in extending 'gardening' to ants' activities, if they came up with it first."[40]

Ants are also discerning in their enterprise. They learn from experimentation, testing tool options for soaking properties and appropriateness for carrying the food to be transported.[41] This experimentation is not merely trial and error, but systematic and considered, with ants not only utilising novel materials but also remembering and developing preferences for previously unknown materials, and developing new technology that is thus utilised in one situation but able to be transferred to another.[42] This flexibility in decisions makes ants especially accomplished in establishing and managing their social services. They will adapt their foraging decisions in order to account for the nutritional needs of the colony[43] and to ensure they select tool objects appropriate to a task.[44] Indeed, ants are innovators when it comes to their tools, with a propensity for incorporating "novel tools, many of them made from artificial materials, into their foraging activities," meaning that the tool use itself "is not behaviourally fixed."[45] What is notable here is the agency and autonomy of the individual ants, contrary to the view of the ant as machine, or worse, a simple cog in the machine of the nest or swarm, merely inputting data to recall through the "monotonous recourse to the certitudes of memory."[46] The reality is that there is a world of ants other than their usual presentation as stimulus-response machines.[47] The ant is an innovator.

And as teachers and students, ants have been lauded for "their liberal system of education without the aid of privy councils and revised codes."[48] Tandem running is a technique used by ants to lead another ant to particular resources (for example, from the nest to food). It is relevant as a kind of cooperative and collaborative approach to property, and the convergence of shared interests in access in order to proliferate and maximise benefits. According to researchers, in tandem running, there is "bidirectional feedback between teacher and pupil," meaning that the teacher and pupil both share stimuli and respond to the stimuli of the other.[49] While the more usual methods of broadcasting information (such as learning by observing) are common in ant societies, the evidence is that "in small societies, where information is valuable and easily lost, teaching works better."[50]

Teaching and play enjoy a mutually constitutive and beneficial relationship. Not only is play invaluable for learning, but also learning facilitates play. Indeed, over a century ago, William Morton Wheeler, in observing the "peculiar habit of walking 'tandem,' sometimes in threes," speculated as to "whether this strange performance could be a manifestation of the play-instinct."[51] Just a few decades later, Wilhelm Goetsch identified something like play in the context of work, recruitment, and participation: "An unemployed young worker usually begins by looking on, so to speak, while another group is working. It may run along part of the way with a group that is hauling building material or grain from chamber to chamber; finally, *as though in play*, it lends a hand, and then keeps on working. As a matter of fact, older unemployed ants join working parties in the same way."[52] This link between social motivation and play is significant for the wants of authorship, but while the research literature has paid attention to social motivation and increased play in vertebrates, this has been translated into social care when investigating social motivation in social invertebrates, such as ants.[53] This is an intriguing distinction at first, but maps onto the assumptions of ants as labour-intensive, for whom care is interpreted to have an adaptive and functional purpose, whereas play may be simply *a waste of time*. And ants simply have no time to waste.[54] But in defiance of the bifurcation of work and play, ants and other insects have lessons to share. Despite being *as busy as*, bees do play,[55] so why not ants as well?

Is there a reason that ants have not similarly captured imaginations? Are bees simply more charismatic subjects? Arguably, the anthropocentric bias of research design may be at play here, as it were. "A regrettable trend in the exploration of emotion in animals," Lars Chittka and Natacha Rossi observe, "is that most studies use human emotions as a benchmark and then search for analogues in animals. This neglects the possibility that, just as sensory systems differ profoundly between animals depending their environmental needs, animal emotions might also include affective states wholly different from those known to humans."[56] The *mirror problem* once again. Perhaps what is missing is the recognition of play in the first place. Just as the law might do better at acknowledging other forms of authorship, such as in traditional cultural expressions or distributed and memetic forms, so too for the recognition of play, particularly as a potential demonstration of consciousness. What does it look like when ants play?

Despite the potential significance of answering this question, there appears to be little to no interest in contemporary biology in the matter of whether or not ants play. Is it simply to be accepted that ants waste no time, that their social stratification and division of labour mean no time or space to play? But, to echo Weil, what of the joy in work? Perhaps the misery ascribed to ants is nothing more than "the sense-making-of-sense-making"[57] that leads to ignoring play as irrelevant to the labour-intensive view of ant life – an adaptationist reckoning of a simpler life, so to speak. Bert Hölldobler and Edward O Wilson title a brief section of *The Ants* with the claim, "Ants Do Not Play," in which a possibly distorted and certainly incomplete definition of play is provided: "[P]lay appears to have two functions: to gain acquaintance with the environment and social partners, and to perfect adaptive responses to both."[58] But why the functionalism and limiting instrumentality of this definition? Is the pronouncement *ants do not play* a case of looking for reason rather than simply showing the play?[59] The spandrels of play, as it were.

Gordon Burghardt's fuller and more widely accepted definition of play sets out five criteria of play behaviour: first, play is not fully functional, useful, or serious, and therefore cannot be rationalised as necessary for survival; second, play is voluntary, stimulating, spontaneous, and rewarding; third, it is different from a serious or literal performance; fourth, it is not to be confused with abnormal repetitive behaviours more usually associated with stress or other maladaptation; and fifth, it is not forced or coerced and therefore individuals do not usually engage in play in undesirable circumstances or periods of stress, supporting further the significance of play in evaluating an individual's welfare.[60] Indeed, this is why play may also be a useful indicator of wellbeing more widely,[61] including for human, as well as nonhuman, authors. And it is also why authorship, in the broader sense, may be an indicator of wellbeing. In other words, *what Naruto wants*.

Despite the richness of their lives, ants and other insects are not protected through traditional welfare legislation[62] or in the regulation of scientific procedures.[63] Limited species of insects and other invertebrates (but no ants) are protected in relevant environmental and wildlife legislation,[64] but this, of course, is not in view of their sentience,[65] but instead is in response to their value to the environment as a resource of biodiversity, their interests appearing only in the context of environmental and ecological management. The exclusion of invertebrates from the welfare context has been attributed variously to: the socially-constructed species hierarchy, or *scala naturae*;[66] disadvantages of size, both in terms of brain size[67] and in terms of their perceptible physical presence within and impact upon the human environment;[68] charisma and appearance;[69] and wider socio-cultural norms in relation to insects and other invertebrates,[70] including literature and popular culture,[71] and even disgust.[72]

You Disgust Me

In their account of the so-called vampire squid, *Vampyroteuthis infernalis*, the philosopher Vilém Flusser and the biologist Louis Bec trace the path of disgust throughout the phylogenetic tree, increasing as species become morphologically more distant from the human species.[73] They describe this "'hierarchy of disgust'" as "incorporated into our 'collective unconscious'" and as such it seemingly "reflects a biological hierarchy," with the human as the ultimate goal.[74] This disgust becomes basic to the conventions of the species hierarchy: "We rationalize this feeling and base categories on it that allow us to classify living beings, namely, into those that approximate us ('incomplete humans') and into those that depart from us ('degenerate humans')."[75] This disgust compels and ensures that we "overlook the possibility of such animals thinking and feeling."[76]

Fundamentally, the species hierarchy is thus a social consensus or conventionalism: "Our biological criteria are anthropomorphic; they are based on a hollow and unanalytic attitude toward life."[77] In defeating this anthropocentric frame, Flusser and Bec advocate following St Francis and speaking to the "'degenerate animals'": "We would do well to follow his example, that is, to overcome anthropocentrism and to examine the constraints of our life from the perspective of the vampyroteuthis – in short, to contrast our human Darwin with a vampyroteuthic one."[78] In this way, a shift in perspective and kind of phenomenal consciousness is possible: "[T]he stream of life will not flow in our direction but rather in [the vampyroteuthis's]."[79]

This phenomenal nature of disgust at the same time perhaps motivates the invisibility of the insect. As Weil writes, "I am the colour of dead leaves, like certain insects which go unnoticed."[80] *I cannot see you.*

But I Cannot See You

Why then is there an invisible barrier to entry for invertebrates, this fickle dividing line between a sentient insect and a sentient mammal? Indeed, when it comes to invertebrates, but insects in particular, there is limited engagement with what becomes an arbitrary line in the sand, in ways similar to the discussions around plants. Stephen Loo and Undine Sellbach maintain, "This ambivalence around insects cuts through the field of animal studies. Insects are generally considered too tiny, instinctual and multiple to be included, and hence conspicuously absent, in debates about our treatment of other animals."[81] And this extends to animal rights scholarship as well.[82] Thus, insects in particular are positioned as an irrational threshold, in every sense, by reason of a constellation of factors, from size to charisma. And in the times when insects *are* raised in this context, as Loo and Sellbach observe, "they tend to be as a limit case, illustrating the edges of sentience of animal life," an extreme at the rational boundaries of the discourse: "So, for example in the work of Peter Singer, the inclusion or exclusion of insects as a subject of ethical concern is an empirical matter, dependent on what future science can tell us about their capacity to suffer, which is taken as an indicator of the extent of sentience."[83]

But why is it seemingly inevitable that we should not consider what the ant might want? Or why should we impose an uncertainty about those wants as an obstacle to further complexity?[84] In the United Kingdom, welfare protection for invertebrates is limited to cephalopods in research,[85] and any protection for invertebrates beyond this context appears to be primarily in response to their impact on the environment.[86] That is, protection is calculated *in* their best interest, rather than understanding insects and other invertebrates as *having* an interest. Is it as simple as the inability (or unwillingness) to see the individual in the crowd, whether that is a literal crowd in the swarm, or the conceptual crowd in a species?[87] Is sentience an approximation rather than a guarantee? Is the potential logical and technical distinction between suffering and sentience at work here? And if it becomes necessary to demonstrate suffering in order to facilitate protection, serious ethical issues are raised.

Approaching this question through authorship and through the author concept, there is the potential for other ways to predict suffering based not on aversive experiences but on expressive and performative excess – that is, on positive affect and the social motivation to play. Can artificial intelligence play? At a most fundamental level, it is difficult to see how the requisite mischief could ever *play* a part in a machine's *intelligence*. Preparing a machine for such playful mischief would create both an ethical issue around trust and an operational issue around the *mishandling* and inaccuracy of the underlying data as reproportioned in any output. Indeed, fundamentally, the threshold for authorship appears not to be that of sentience but one of a *perceived* intentionality: "Is the tick a machine or a machine operator? Is it a mere object or a subject?"[88] And further, the barrier is one not even as simple (or complex) as intentionality, but rather and more specifically, it is that of desire and amusement. Is there "something" to be done in the ants' best interests, or do the ants have an interest in something? And as for a machine, can it be *interested* in anything at all, or is every attention merely a *stereotypic imitation*?

To answer the question of authorship, the discussion appears to be, to an extent, returned to the unanswerable. In other words, what do the ants want? But the answer is not to be found (and thus not *con*founded) by assuming the animal mind; rather, it becomes available through seeing how wants are played out. *Literally*. As a ranking, sentience is arguably the wrong question for compassion, for welfare, and for rights. Not only is it a calculable risk, in every sense, but also it is a risk that may be rationalised within the very narrative of risk – an adaptationist paradigm. There is an important distinction to be made between an appreciation for the subjective experience of another, and the subjective impression of that experience of another. Putting this another way, admission to moral standing should not depend upon the pretence at objectivity when it comes to interpreting the suffering or sentience of another being. The plight of the ants demonstrates that sentience is not only a polluted and unreliable concept, but also it is arguably the wrong one. The question that should be asked is whether invertebrates play. Is there something expressive about the ant? Is there something that it is like to be an ant? And do they play for all that something is worth?

Before the games begin, let us meet some ants.

Simon's Ant

This ant, or more specifically, Simon's ant, is perhaps "the most famous insect in cognitive science."[89] Indeed, the fact that "ants have become the unofficial mascots of the ALife field,"[90] is arguably the legacy of Simon's ant. Through the parable of the ant on the beach, Herbert Simon relates a story of knowledge and behaviour shaped by environment. The ant's meandering path of detours and greetings is seemingly random and directionless, as the ant is buffeted by landmarks. Although the ant is not necessarily without a goal, the ant is seemingly without a plan. Simon describes the ant's navigation of the beach: "He moves ahead, angles to the right to ease his climb up a steep dunelet, detours around a pebble, stops for a moment to exchange information with a compatriot. Thus he makes his weaving, halting way back to this home."[91]

Simon proceeds to map the ant's path, ostensibly to objectify the travels without the risk of anthropomorphism of the ant's purpose: "I sketch the path on a piece of paper. It is a sequence of irregular, angular segments – not quite a random walk, for it has an underlying sense of direction, of aiming toward a goal."[92] However, Simon interprets this buffeted travel as a manipulation of the ant rather than the ant's manipulation of their environment: "Viewed as a geometric figure, the ant's path is irregular, complex, hard to describe. But its complexity is really a complexity in the surface of the beach, not a complexity in the ant."[93] There is thus no agency or expression in what Simon's ant does. This ant is at the mercy of the physical world.

For Simon's ant, the observer's interest then is entirely in the obstacle, not in the ant. This approach thus conveys potentially a lot of information about the obstacle, not least because of the ant's contribution to that knowledge, but says very little about the ant. Indeed, the ant is constructed by the beach, the object, the work. The way in which the work makes the ant, as an artefact of the work, resonates with the way in which the work makes the author in law.[94] This inductive intentionality, in a way, just brings more sand to the beach. Fundamentally, it is an artefact of the anthropocentrism of the law and the predatory drift of dominant conceptualisations and discourse on property, including intellectual property.

Ants have thus persisted as a popular model for the development of artificial intelligence,[95] computational science's *perfect little strangers*, if you will. This use of animal behaviour to develop artificial intelligence nevertheless persists with a decidedly anthropocentric perspective in that it is, in the most general sense, an attempt to extrapolate *simple* behaviours to the modelling of *human* intelligence in machines. This is a modelling that at the same time frustrates the exceptionalist narrative.[96] In the same way, as considered in earlier discussion, that "the field of animal learning has left out comparative, ecological, and evolutionary considerations in its rush to formulate general principles,"[97] a similar "impatience" in artificial intelligence is arguably compromising the research,[98] over-stating the results,[99] and ultimately describing a "simple" human animal as well.[100] Notably, these criticisms are frequently rationalised, whether intended in the original arguments or not, within a complicated environment of human exceptionalism, continued underestimation of invertebrates, and an adaptationist imperative of maintaining the status quo.

Paul Seabright argues that parallels between social insects and human societies "are misleading" and that "modern human societies are not like colonies of ants, bees, or termites," and maintains that "human societies involve the interactions of unrelated strangers instead of close relatives" and, as such, "social insects provide us with no parallel to the day-to-day interactions of strangers in human life."[101] While there are some ants yet to meet in the present discussion who might take issue with these claims, there are many other perhaps more familiar examples already. What about the memetic insistence of celebrity? Or the diffusion of misinformation through social media? Seabright argues that the "different lesson" from social insects is that of "examples of complex systems behaving in ways that are no part of the intention (or even the awareness) of any of their participants."[102] In other words, ants are recast as pointless, all at sea, wanting for nothing. As such, Simon's ant is characterised by the directions and instructions of the object, the beach, as distinct from being recognised for any attention to the object, where "distributed cognition studies tend to focus on the beach rather than the ant."[103] Simon's ant wanders all over the beach, as directed by the lines drawn in the sand, and is certainly barred from intentionally charting the space and making the objects within it.[104]

However, contrary to Seabright's rendition of the ant as a system of perverse parochialism, ants form symbiotic relationships with very many strangers, including other ants and ant species.[105] Indeed, almost 150 years ago, George Romanes described a range of multispecies "friendships" with various other insects "which, so far as observation extends, are of no benefit to the ants, and which therefore have been regarded by observers as mere domestic pets."[106] The familiar production of ant civilisations appears to have been unfairly oversimplified in their machinic translation through the predatory drift of the conventional industry narrative. And at the same time, the relations between ants and their "domestic pets" show us that the distinctly anthropocentric perspective on domestication appears to obscure a multitude of other minute affinities.[107]

Simon's ant is indeed a parable of more than cognition and certainly more than human authorship. This is, in some ways a fable of the way in which animals are explained as functional machines, both in service of human exceptionalism and as a mechanism for delivering the narrative of intelligence in human machines. However, this assists the present enquiry, in that Simon's ant is also a welcome nuisance, a pestering of the assumptions of intellectual property. Simon's ant builds paths and shapes an expressive landscape. It is to our discredit if we see nothing but geography and miss the monumental differences, in every sense, between landscapes and sculptural memories. Indeed, on that beach, Simon's ant shapes the story of the contingency of animal sentience.

The beachhead, as it were, is to be found in the events at the boundaries, the interaction with space, and the ant's performance of property. What is the nature of the ant's relationship to the beach? Why is the ant's own interest in the obstacle of less concern than the obstacle itself and its positioning *in* the ant's interest?

Enter, Turner's ants.

Turner's Ants

Ants that deserve to be as famous as Simon's ant, if not more so, are the ants known to Charles Henry Turner.[108] Turner was born in 1867, just two years after Abolition and the emancipation of his parents, and went on to become the first African American to earn a doctorate (zoology)[109] at the University of Chicago and "the most significant, skillful and productive African American zoologist of his time."[110] But despite this, "due to the barrier of racism he never secured a professorship at a major American research university"[111] and remained a high school science teacher until his death "of neglect and overwork."[112]

Turner had a particular interest in insect behaviour and experience-based learning in social insects, including ants, "in sharp contrast to prevailing ideas regarding animal behavior and cognition ... at a time when the dominant ideas only credited animals with the simplest of learning abilities."[113] Contrary to the conventional approach of anonymity for the individual ant within the functionalism of the colony, Turner's work focuses on individual difference and personality, long before the advent of personality studies, and yet his insight continues to be marginalised. Galapayage Dona and Chittka admonish the research literature for this inexplicable oversight: "It is deplorable that the now-popular field of 'animal personality' has taken so little notice of Turner's trailblazing approach."[114]

While the observational studies of Darwin and Romanes credited non-human animals with intelligent capacities, their work was "largely based on observation and inference," and so remained somewhat anecdotal and increasingly marginalised as efforts at establishing the discipline through the perceived scientific rigour of the laboratory got underway in the early twentieth century. In contrast, the emphasis on laboratory experimentation at this time moved research activity away from anecdotal and field observation, and directed it towards explaining behaviours as adaptive responses within functional and controlled narratives, while "notions of advanced animal intelligence or insight" were "largely rejected."[115] This tension between anecdotes in the field and replicability in the laboratory is considered in detail later, and indeed becomes central to an ethological approach to testimony and law;[116] but ahead of that discussion it is important to appreciate the contribution and ingenuity of Turner's work and the relevance for an examination of this historical debate. At the same time, Turner's research methodologies and analyses resonate with developments in a nascent sociology and comparative psychology. In particular, Turner's ability to reconcile the qualitative and the quantitative is intriguingly coincident with Tarde's inter-psychology, whose ants we will meet in a moment.

Turner's work meets the individual in the crowd, rather than arriving at a sense through the alienation of an archetypal artefact. This accords with the nature of community in Tarde's sociology, and the critique of collectivity in Weil's philosophy, and why the potential of Tarde's community is wholly consistent with Weil's limitations of the collectivity, as discussed later. Indeed, it might be said that Turner's pioneering work represents an early chapter not only in animal sociology, but also in comparative sociology, as traced through the present discussion. In this context, it is prudent to heed Gordon Burghardt's advocacy for "the value of historical reflection" and his recommendation that "[a]ll students of animal behaviour should pay attention to, and revisit often, the early history and documents in the field. *We lose important perspectives if we ignore our predecessors.*"[117]

With that in mind, one notable example of Turner's research offers particular insight in this context. Over a hundred years ago, Turner conducted a fascinating study with ants which asked the question, *Do ants form practical judgments?*[118] In other words, Turner was looking for evidence of associative and conceptual learning.[119] This early study is especially significant, given that contemporary evidence of concept learning in insects is becoming compelling.[120] In contrast, it is notable that for artificial intelligence, while a simple form of associative learning (as in reinforcement learning) has been demonstrated, more complex capacities for formulation of concepts have yet to be convincingly demonstrated.[121] Although there is proficiency in pattern recognition,[122] evidence of the kind of symbolic communication and understanding evident in concept learning is not clear.[123] This makes Turner's pioneering ants even more important as historical subjects. Turner's study followed a colony of common carpenter ants[124] over several months, making some remarkable observations concerning their adaptability and judgment in novel situations. What emerges from this particular study are the crucial and decisive ways in which Turner's ants may be distinguished from Simon's ant, by attention *to* their experience of the beach, rather than for their manipulation as mere objects *of* the beach.[125]

Rather than a trial-and-error of obstacles and responses, and instead of an *intention* crafted outside in the environment, Turner's ants demonstrated an awareness of both the challenge and the desired goal. When the ants were faced with various challenges, different and relevant actions would be undertaken. In one colony, Turner took on the role of intruder and would "fight the guard" at one particular entrance until "the guard withdrew from the entrance ... and the ants plugged that passage-way with detritus."[126] And unlike Simon's ant, when presented with various environmental obstacles, including seemingly impassable ditches and cracks, Turner's ants began constructing bridges and other feats of engineering, and they did so on an individual basis:

> When, under identical conditions, one member of a group responds to a stimulus in one way and yet other members respond to a similar stimulus in a different manner the response would be individualistic. When an animal faces a situation for which it has no class response and yet almost immediately makes an individualistic response which overcomes the difficulty, it has formed what Hobhouse calls a practical judgment.[127]

These feats of engineering are particularly engaging from a sociological perspective upon the ants' mobilities. Georg Simmel, writing at the same time as Turner was studying these formic accomplishments, declares: "The people who first built a path between two places performed one of the greatest *human* achievements."[128] Bachelard, whose ants we will meet in a moment, might have been quite critical of this neglect of the "domain of tininess"[129] in coming to this human conclusion. Nevertheless, knowing what we know of the ants' structural engineering, Simmel's regard for the "aesthetic value" of the bridge "insofar as it accomplishes the connection between what is separated not only in reality and in order to fulfil practical goals, but in making it directly visible"[130] casts fresh light on Turner's ants, and indeed a reflected ethological glow on Simmel's sociology. As Turner carefully documents:

> [T]his is what the ants did in the case recorded here. When a crack was made into their brood chamber they were face to face with a situation for which they had no class response. After a while one to a few individuals made individualistic responses which resulted in the closing of the crack. To those few ants the disturbance in the brood chamber had been associated with the unclosed crack. To them the crack had acquired a meaning. It had become a crack-to-be-closed and they proceeded to close it.[131]

The complex conceptual thinking searched for in artificial intelligence is already a way of life for the ant. In recounting the activities, Turner notes, "It seems to me … the ants have responded to stimuli, not as ends in themselves, but rather as means to ends. This would lift the act out of the realm of instinctive behavior into that of the practical judgment."[132]

The contrast between Simon's ant and Turner's ants encompasses some of the key assumptions underpinning not only studies of animal behaviour, but also the kind of human exceptionalism that purports to defeat the creativity of nonhuman animal authors and facilitate the anthropomorphism and optimism in service of artificial intelligence. Turner's work is distinctly anti-anthropocentric, defying a specious scientific detachment and recognising the collaboration between researcher and subject in the co-production of the laboratory space. Turner was reportedly an admirer of Romanes and Darwin,[133] both variously accused of anthropomorphism, and yet their natural histories remain critically important portrayals of nonhuman animal cultural histories as well. As Burghardt advises, "Reading, and re-reading, [our predecessors] fosters a bit of humility and avoids the hubris that comes from regarding contemporary views as overly novel and superior."[134] Both Romanes and Darwin also resisted the dominant narratives of an intelligence hierarchy based on brain size.[135] As it happens, Romanes had anticipated the fallacy of drawing inferences between brain size and intelligence in his writings with a specific respect for ants: "And, if we turn to the animal kingdom, we find in a still larger measure that the mere amount of cerebral substance furnishes but a very uncertain index of the level of intelligence which is attained by the animal ... and in this respect no animals are so remarkable as the more intelligent species of ants."[136] While Turner's ants can build castles to the sky, the artificial intelligence of Simon's ant is left bringing sand to the beach.

This gives reason to revisit the industry's construction of the concept of swarm intelligence, so-called. But on the expressiveness of the swarm, or more specifically, the members of the swarm, it is useful at this point to introduce Tarde's ants.

Tarde's Ants

The instrumentality applied to creativity, whether through intellectual property frameworks, definitions of research impact, or otherwise, is a discernible limit on the social life of authorship. Bruno Latour notes, "In the last century, the schism between those who deal with numbers and those who deal with qualities has never been bridged," and advocates Tarde's sociology as offering "a different definition of what it is for a discipline to be *quantitative*."[137] This schism is something to which the discussion will return in later chapters, particularly the radical measures of behaviourism as distinct from the anecdotal empathies of cognitive ethology.[138] Importantly, Tarde presents an effective reconciliation or *hinge* of the quantitative and the qualitative in his inter-psychology.[139] In its attention to the infinitesimal[140] in producing the movement of the community, Tarde's sociology would seem to be readymade for the social lives of ants: "the smaller is always the bigger entity there is."[141] Indeed, as will be seen in Bachelard's attention to the tiny, "[m]iniature is one of the refuges of greatness."[142]

Tarde's ants offer insight into what it might mean to measure innovation without resort to "number crunching."[143] In the early passages of *The Laws of Imitation*,[144] Tarde begins the groundwork for his theory of universal repetition, and that ground is prepared by ants. Tarde explains: "Socially, everything is either invention or imitation. And invention bears the same relation to imitation as a mountain to a river."[145] In other words, there is a productive interaction between these two *forces*, as it were; the river's course is in part manipulated by the mountain, but the mountain is engraved by the river.

Tarde accepts this may be called idealism, "but it is idealism which consists in explaining history through the ideas of its actors, not through those of the historian."[146] Applying this perspective to "the science of society,"[147] Tarde maintains that human sociology may be related to animal societies or sociologies. Notwithstanding his *fin-de-siècle* observance of human exceptionalism, with humans described as "an extraordinary and infinitely superior species,"[148] Tarde identifies the importance of individual initiative in ants as an example of the innovation in imitation in societies more widely, including human. In making this observation, Tarde has recourse to the work of Alfred Espinas in *Des sociétés animales*,[149] and the claim "that the labours of ants may be very well explained on the principle '*of individual initiative followed by imitation*.'"[150] Espinas is thus indicating a kind of social learning, as well as the suggestion of associative and conceptual learning investigated by Turner. Tarde observes: "This initiative is always an innovation or invention that is equal to one of our own in boldness of spirit. To conceive the idea of constructing an arch, or a tunnel, at an appropriate point, an ant must be endowed with an innovating instinct equal to, or surpassing, that of our canal-digging or mountain-tunnelling engineers."[151]

Such initiative also applies to the swarm. Swarm behaviour is recognised across a range of species and is characterised by group decision-making through the movement and rhythm of the group – the rhythm of shared interests. The swarm[152] is thus a form of *collective* intelligence, but not an indiscriminate *collectivity*. Whether "swarms, schools, flocks, herds and murmurations," these are all forms of collective intelligence through movement – that is, examples of "collective motion."[153] This distinction between collective and collectivity is critical and recalls the way in which social production was distinguished from familiar production in earlier chapters,[154] as well as prefiguring Weil's critique of collectivity, to be considered later in this chapter. The swarm is a form of consensus-building,[155] but significantly, this is not merely intelligence at the level of the collective, but in fact collective decision-making that takes account of individual differences.[156] Much of the collective decision-making in ants is concerned with nests and resources, but while scouts may find various options for new homes, the final decision rests with the group.

In bees, the celebrated dance language is a critical way of achieving that consensus,[157] as well as being a potentially significant form of cultural transmission,[158] and indeed an example of symbolic communication.[159] But the dance language of bees also demonstrates the way in which so-called swarm intelligence is, in fact, necessarily predicated upon the specific contributions of individuals. "In humans, as in bees, collective enterprises might *appear* to an outsider as a form of swarm intelligence that necessitates a collective mind," as Lars Chittka explains, "the memory for particular nesting sites, for instance, is stored in the brains of only those select individuals that have inspected the site."[160] In other words, the collective mind is perhaps not a "mind" at all: "There is nothing it feels like to *be* the swarm, and hence there is no collective mind. It only feels like something to be an individual *within* the swarm."[161] This is critical to understanding and appreciating the distinction between Tarde's swarm and the relations within, on the one hand, and the "mindless" collectivity, on the other, on which Weil has more to say later in this chapter. But it also contributes to a further sense of what it is like (or not) to be a machine. The very construction of artificial intelligence as a collectivity of networked information – a swarm intelligence, if you will – is arguably *mindless*. Perhaps there is nothing at all it feels like to *be* a machine.

Ants have been shown to work much harder during consensus-decision making in smaller groups and "invest greater effort in the consensus decision process than those in large colonies,"[162] pointing to both the individual contribution to collective intelligence as well as the cultural and social value of the swarm. Group cohesion is facilitated through forms of symbolic communication through smells,[163] that then influence speed,[164] such that there is a symbolic motion, as it were, to that language in terms of tempo, rhythm, and trace. In this way, there is symbolic communication both within the group and through the group; the swarm itself as symbolic and embodied communication. Similarly, other forms of communication, as in tandem running,[165] succeed as symbolic communication through movement towards the relational generation and transmission of information. The other significant aspect of an ethological account of so-called swarm intelligence is that, contrary to the assumption of a leader and followers, such consensus-driven social groups do not rely on a centralised leadership model.[166] Over one hundred years ago, White's portrayal of swarming ants in a church spire in 1866 insists "that it was a social conference or political demonstration in the ant-world … The cause and issue of the demonstration must to us ever remain a mystery," but White concludes, "the little people are all politically enfranchised."[167] White's observations, though largely anecdotal, resonate in surprising ways with the contemporary science on ants and their collective behaviour and social cognition. And around the same time as White's account, Tarde too was questioning the blind univocity of the collective. Indeed, swarm behaviour must be understood not only as facilitating group decisions but also as moving away from a simplistic and unilinear leadership model towards a genuine functioning collective of shared interests in the present sense. And it is in Tarde's approach to the swarm as an expressive and inventive collective that an ethological perspective on authorship may be elaborated beyond its persistent singularity.

Tarde thus rejects the impression of the swarm as a mechanical and instinctive process, or mere simultaneous reaction to "the pressure of outward circumstances which are experienced simultaneously by all"; rather, the swarm is the initiative of "a single ant," and "the contagion of imitation does the rest."[168] Influenced by Leibniz's theory of relations, this gestures to a significant distinction between the collective of social production and the swarm of familiar production – that is, the difference between the kind of *stereotypic imitation* necessarily at work in the pattern-making of artificial intelligence, and the swarm of familiar producers, and within it the *attentive imitation* of a multitude of affiliative formic individuals:

> The impersonal, collective character is thus the product rather than the producer of the infinitely numerous individual characters; it is their composite photograph, and must not be taken for their mask. We shall certainly lose nothing of that social picturesqueness which makes the historian an artist, when, having cleared up, rather than cleared away, this phantasmagoria of great historic actors called Egypt, Rome, Athens, etc., we perceive behind it a swarm of individual innovators, each *sui generis*, stamped with his own distinctive mark, and recognizable among a thousand.[169]

Not a stroke of the brush without the swarm.[170]

The swarm reconciles the instrumental and the anecdotal, work and play. Writing around the same time as Tarde, Hugo von Buttel-Reepen describes this joy in the work of the bee swarm: "The swarm presses out from the hive in impetuous haste in the peculiar swarm dance; it surges and whirls in 'bacchanal delight,' as if the bees were really drunk with 'joy.' The 'swarm dizziness,' as bee-keepers say, has seized it. In this dizziness it forgets everything connected with the old dwelling, and bees even forget to sting."[171] That insects may have rich emotional lives specific to the subjective experiences of those particular individuals is significant for contemporary research. Chittka and Rossi explain: "Classifying such states in a manner that is not simply anchored in the human emotional world, and exploring their neural and hormonal correlates, is important in the study of the inner world of insects."[172] They continue: "The questions of whether emotions strengthen the cohesive forces in insect colonies, contribute to their organisation of labour, and orchestrate learning from each other, thus potentially contributing to cultural processes … merit further investigation."[173] The swarm is thus an especially expressive intelligence with respect to the production of space, quite literally, in terms of the exploration and establishment of new colonies, of new homes. This productive wandering is mobilised by that expressive joy, as in the bee swarm, the *bacchanal delight*, to recall Buttel-Reepen.[174]

This opening up to mobile and expressive spaces and the intellectual work of the swarm is a perfect time to introduce another ant – Bachelard's ant.

Bachelard's Ant

Bachelard's ant, or more specifically, the disregarding of Bachelard's ant, is an *error* that continues to be neglected: "Our animalized oneirism, which is so powerful as regards large animals, has not recorded the doings and gestures of tiny animals. In fact, in the domain of tininess, animalized oneirism is less developed than vegetal oneirism."[175] Bachelard declares, "[W]e must replace closed, static knowledge with knowledge that is open and dynamic, and dialectise all experimental variables. Reason must in short be given reasons for developing."[176] *Dare to dream.*

Bachelard's concept of the epistemological break is the line in the sand here, so to speak. Rather than the accepted lore of the species hierarchy, Bachelard's anti-Cartesianism is of immediate significance in challenging the entrenched and *specific* assumptions of authorship: "The non-Baconian, non-Euclidean, and non-Cartesian philosophies are historical dialects that grew out of the correction of an error, the extension of a system, or the completion of an idea."[177] Referring to 1905 as "the era of *the new scientific mind*," ushered in by Albert Einstein's relativity, which "came along and deformed primordial concepts that we thought fixed forever," Bachelard explains this proliferation of perspectives afforded in the intellectual swarm: "From then on, reason multiplied its objections, dissociating fundamental ideas and then making new connections between them, trying out the boldest of abstractions."[178] In this way, Bachelard's approach to the diffusion of knowledge resonates with Leibniz and Tarde in their consideration of the minuscule and infinitesimal in imitation: "Epistemologists must therefore make every effort to understand scientific concepts within real psychological syntheses, that is to say within progressive psychological syntheses, by establishing an array of concepts for every individual idea by showing how one concept has produced another and is related to another."[179] In this respect, the value of error is monumental; indeed, as Bachelard maintains, "[p]erhaps what the pre-scientific mind most lacks is a theory of experimental error."[180] Rather than the obstacles of the beach, the epistemological obstacle sets in motion a swarm of concepts.

Returning to the *domain of tininess*, for Bachelard, attention to the miniature, to the tiny worlds of the ants, is not only the business of phenomenology but also the expressive and productive play of imagination.[181] This attentive play is an attention which "bars the every-day world"[182] and in this way produces more than the world: "one could say, in the manner of Schopenhauer, 'The world is my imagination.'"[183] Reverberating with Tarde's critique of the static *being* and the relational and processual *having*, Bachelard too accounts, "The cleverer I am at miniaturizing the world, the better I possess it. But in doing this, it must be understood that values become condensed and enriched in miniature ... One must go beyond logic in order to experience what is large in what is small."[184] Bachelard explains this attention to the miniature as a productive and revelatory expression: "The man with the magnifying glass takes the world as though it were quite new to him. If he were to tell us of his discoveries he has made, he would furnish us with documents of pure phenomenology."[185] It is with this "fresh eye before a new object"[186] that a regard for authorship must be undertaken through the attention of the ant: "Thus the miniscule, a narrow gate, opens up an entire world. The details of a thing can be the sign of a new world which, like all worlds, contains the attributes of greatness."[187] As Bachelard states, "Attention by itself is an enlarging glass."[188] Let the ant be our guide.

The spatial literacy of ants is impressive, learning through visual landmarks, experimentation, and exploratory walks.[189] Research continues to demonstrate ever more examples of tremendous flexibility in the capacities of ants to learn and remember routes in complex environments, providing "perhaps one of the most spectacular pieces of evidence for the impressive power of their small brains."[190] Unlike Simon's ant, portrayed as a thoughtless pinball in a machine of rockbound coast, ants have been observed being able to learn and adapt their paths in "an interesting interplay between aversive and appetitive visual memories, and between avoidance learning … and positive reinforcement."[191] As distinct from a model of memory as pure input of data or coding, that is, instinctual or programmable capacity, where "the decisive action of reason is almost always confused with monotonous recourse to the certitudes of memory,"[192] Bachelard's ant is an innovator. Studies of both authorship and sentience, to use Bachelard's words, "must begin with an intellectual and emotional catharsis."[193]

Swarms arise for various purposes, including defence[194] (indicating not only "supra-individual societies"[195] but also supra-colony or community cultural development in the way that predators inevitably shape or co-produce that behaviour and spatial intelligence) and in establishing new nests or colonies,[196] and perhaps even socially. In using the term "swarm" for an assemblage of winged ants, Huber nevertheless suggests that the term "does not strictly apply to this concourse of insects, who have no further object than that of meeting each other, and effecting their union in the air, and who do not assemble for the purpose of founding a new colony."[197] Indeed, Huber's swarm encompasses all the rich sociality of Tarde's, a "fecundation of ants,"[198] indeed. Through the swarm, the expressiveness of space takes particular shape, as a matter of course. In other words, rather than anticipating space as an empty capacity to fill, the swarm is an enacted, embodied expression of space, building the roads, bridges, and flight paths that mobilise the will to connect. Communication within the swarm is also overwhelmingly embodied with the sounds of space, including vibrations and reverberations, tapping bodies, and touching sounds.[199]

The spatial practice of swarming insects, in this way, might be appreciated as a literal rendition of Henri Lefebvre's concept of spatial practice including the shaping of space through smell,[200] taste,[201] sound,[202] and touch,[203] no longer "almost completely annexed and absorbed by sight."[204] Indeed, Lefebvre's very concept of *formant*,[205] to indicate the participatory moments of space, as it were, beyond the geometric dimension, is itself decidedly ant-like, or *formic*. Lefebvre's production of space – the way in which it is used, the way it is represented, and importantly the appropriation and production of that space through the tempo and rhythm of relations – is decidedly ant-like in rendering the spatial intelligence of the social world about. Following this approach, "[t]he commodity," which invariably would extend to the commodities of intellectual production and the fascination of intellectual property, "may be looked upon as a component of social (practical) existence, as a 'formant' of space. Considered in isolation, 'in itself', however, it does not have the capacity, even on a world scale, to exist socially (practically)."[206] Indeed it is in the *situations* of intellectual property objects through use, that the social and practical value emerges. The genuine insight of swarm intelligence, the wisdom of the ants, is thus through the necessarily relational quality of objects, their appropriation, in every sense, being possible only through use.[207]

In other words, the object, as it were, is constituted through use and reuse. Lefebvre explains this by distinguishing between the identifiers for space (for example, a room or a public square) and the use of space, which produces those identifiers – that is, "a spatial practice that they express and constitute."[208] This resonates, indeed reverberates, with Bachelard's concept of reverberation (*retentissement*), a term Bachelard borrows from the phenomenology of Eugene Minkowski.[209] As well as the reflexive and cooperative work to make meaning through communicative relationships, reverberation also describes the embodied and physical rendition of communication in the swarm itself, through sound and vibration: the kick of the ant, *so to speak*.[210] And the resonating swarm, in its magnitude of individual proficiencies, is an exemplary expression of relational property; a sense, in every sense, of society through filiation, of property through relation. This becomes even clearer in the context of the exploratory and relational property-making of the swarm.

Whether in defence, or in search of resources, or in the process of establishing a new home, the fundamental character of the swarm is to ensure the movement of the group.[211] This communication through movement was also observed by Huber, who remarks in particular upon "the violence with which the workers sometimes seized, with their mandibles, those who did not appear to understand them, dragging them forth to the top of the ant-hill."[212] Thus, the active expressivity of the individual ant body both within and apart from the swarm is itself a form of communication and creativity, spatial and motile, at the same time producing and incorporating symbolic communication systems.[213] It is both a source of information and an intelligent source.[214] The relationship between the familiar production of the swarm in this way accords with the home or dwelling and its particular importance in Bachelard's philosophy of space, while at the same time investing in the home as an intellectual production. Nesting facilitates a form of sociality,[215] and the opportunity to develop a form of socialised and relational property.[216] It is a curious irony that the swarm, more often associated with restlessness and nomadism, is in fact actually about making an abode, becoming social, and filling space. Space invites us to come out of ourselves, to swarm,[217] and thus to make. This play in the intellectual property system, most spectacularly through use, is a critical creative resource. And through this account, the supposed restlessness of other swarms, like fans and users themselves, is recuperated as a sociable and productive intellectual resource.

In a passage addressing the "poetic spatiality" in Rainer Maria Rilke's poetry, Bachelard states: "Here space seems to the poet to be the subject of the verbs 'to open up,' or 'to grow.' And whenever space is a value – there is no greater value than intimacy – it has magnifying properties. Valorized space is a verb, and never, either inside or outside us, is grandeur an 'object.'"[218] This relational and affiliative quality of productive space coincides with the concept of familiar production as a kind of expressive kinship: *I think I am a verb*. Indeed, this is why it is important to distinguish populism, or the collectivity, from the swarm. The former is actually alienated from production and expression, as a kind of imitation through coercion, pattern, and rule – this is the imitation of mutual but separate interests, a perspective which informs the concept of *stereotypic imitation* most apt in understanding the kind of facilitation of information through artificial intelligence. The ethology of the swarm is thus in stark contrast to its machinic modelling. And an ethological perspective reveals a fascinating expression of Tardean imitation, of familiar production among a crowd of individuals – this is the joy of shared interests and the *attentive imitation* of genuine authorship.

To understand this more clearly, it is time to meet Weil's ants.

Weil's Ants

For Simone Weil, the beach is the kind of intermediary through which experience generates meaning and "the mutual grasp of the world and myself."[219] The beach is like the string in Wattana's knots, the ditches under Turner's ants' bridges, or the imagination itself: "The first of these obstacles is the imagination itself, this tie, this knot between the world and me, this point of intersection between the simple movement that I have at my command and the infinitely complex movement that represents the world for my understanding."[220] The originality of the swarm, as it were, may be distinguished through its genuine and certain attention, and its willful connections. In Weil's concept of *metaxu*, the ants building the bridges and paths towards the reputation of sentience become especially compelling. Sentience becomes a question of the relations between subjectivities, rather than an always already defeated and contingent objectivity.

The term "swarm intelligence" as applied in computational systems is thus something of a misnomer, somewhat like "intelligence" itself. The kind of "intelligence" described in artificial intelligence arguably is that of the collective, not the swarm. And as Weil cautions, the tyranny of the collective is a misery for the expressive imagination: "To the very extent to which what is systematic in contemporary life escapes the control of the mind, its regularity is established by things which constitute the equivalent of what collective thought would be if the collectivity did think."[221] Weil could easily be taken as forewarning against the process of averaging and summation that characterises the application of LLMs in research and writing today.

Weil's scrutiny is crucial here, in that it distinguishes the creativity and making in the swarm from the tyranny and coercion of the collectivity. A particular concern in examining and elaborating upon the concept of authorship is the nature of intellectual property's emphasis on individuality and the limited capacity to account for communal expression – not only human forms of communal making, such as traditional cultural expressions and forms of indigenous and traditional knowledge, but also the hard and fast assumptions around the author concept itself and the entrenched views applied to nonhuman animal expressivity. Weil's critique is thus especially relevant for understanding the distinction between cultures of imitation, a critique that is enhanced by taking an ethological perspective. Insect swarms are not unconscious and unprincipled behaviours, despite the persistent assumptions that they are.[222] They are somewhat convivial phenomena of individual cooperation, affiliation, and cooperation, involving various and multiple decisions, actions, and *practical judgments*. It is curious and inconsistent that the originality of the insect swarm continues to be relegated to a mindless machine in the concept of "swarm intelligence," and yet the summative processes of artificial intelligence, built upon this very same "swarm intelligence," are not. Once again, attention to intellectual creation appears to be framed by a question of capital. This same problem continues to compromise efforts to respond meaningfully to the uses and appropriation of marginalised human creativity. And at the same time, this reaffirms an aesthetic blindness to the consciousness of nonhuman animals. It is therefore crucial to distinguish communal forms of creativity and intellectual creation from the product of averages that might be promised by artificial intelligence – that is, clarifying an authorship that is more than human demands an appreciation of the distinction between an *attentive imitation* through shared interests and familiar production, as apart from the *stereotypic imitation* produced through the coercive rule of mutual interests (such as that supposed in the repetition of LLMs).[223]

The kind of averaging activity of artificial intelligence is the sort of fallacious consensus that Weil seeks to admonish in the concept of the collectivity: "Men as parts of a collectivity are debarred from even the lower forms of the impersonal. A group of human beings cannot even add two and two. Working out a sum takes place in a mind temporarily oblivious of the existence of any other minds."[224] The kind of enactive and physical commitment to knowing, the work that is necessary in order to grasp the world, is thus not the wisdom of the collective, but the action of the individual as a member of the swarm. In this way, the swarm is significant for the agency of each individual within the swarm, as distinct from a *mindless* mob; that is, there is a relation, an attribution of knowledge, and an application of knowledge, in each and every encounter. This is relevant to the kinds of issues raised by artificial intelligence, which cannot work out a sum, so to speak, in that it cannot explain its action upon the world in that process. Explainability is both a relation and the stewardship of knowledge, the process of the self, as distinct from the egotism and mythology of a fixed and complete individual. Explainability is indeed also a principle underpinning the architecture of intellectual property, through the provenance of authors, the legacy of prior art, the machinations of specifications. The kind of convergence and summation affected by artificial intelligence is perhaps precisely the sort of hapless collectivity Weil is so anxious to warn against.[225] As Wallace Matson declares, "Computers can't compute."[226] Granted, Matson was writing in 1976, but the principle remains curiously the same. Explainability is not only a knowledge management question, but also a question of personhood. And that is why consciousness is a phenomenon of authorship, and why authorship is an expression of sentience.

The singularity of the machine as it is presented accords with the structure of authorship anticipated in the intellectual property system, but the process of the product does not. The intellectual property system's mistrust or miscalculation of collectives, from fans to traditional communities, does not immediately arise in the question of artificial intelligence because the presentation of the machine as a coherent whole has been so successful in masking the collective nature of its outputs. Indeed, there appears to be a campaign to seduce policymakers with the *individuality* of the machine, ranging from the performative displays of robots giving evidence[227] through to concerted litigation campaigns for recognising authorship or inventorship on the part of a "device and method for the autonomous bootstrapping of *unified* sentience."[228] The campaign for artificial personhood is nothing if not playful.

A swarm of bees provides some further insight here. In the novel *The Glass Bees*, Ernst Jünger explores a future of technological alienation through the character of Captain Richard, an ex-cavalryman who applies for a job with a company that manufactures robots from glass bees. In the introduction, a clear distinction is set out between the originality and expressiveness of the bees in the swarm and the "glass collectives" built upon the glass bees, which sounds not dissimilar to the palimpsestic prescription of LLMs:

> Bees are not just workers in a honey factory, ignoring their self-sufficiency for a moment, their work – far beyond its tangible utility – plays an important part in the cosmic plan. As messengers of love, their duty is to pollinate, to fertilize the flowers. But Zapparoni's glass collectives, as far as I could see, ruthlessly sucked out the flowers and ravished them. Wherever they crowded out the old colonies, a bad harvest, a failure of crops, and ultimately a desert were bound to follow.[229]

The way in which LLMs produce aesthetic or other objects may be seen to resonate with the sucking and ravishing of the flowers by the glass collectives, all the while running, indeed racing, the risk of model collapse. Just like the glass collectives, relentlessly harvesting and ultimately producing a desert, model collapse is the phenomenon where LLMs reach the stage where they are starting to make their own contribution to the language from which they are scraping their results, causing "irreversible defects in the resulting models, where tails of the original content distribution disappear,"[230] thanks to the "curse of recursion."[231] This story provides a particular insight into the crucial structural and cultural complexities of intellectual creation, through a wonderful illustration of the difference between, on the one hand, the stultifying, univocal collective, as in conventional renditions of social production, bordering on populism, and on the other, the productive diversity of familiar production in shared interests, all through the genius of the bees' swarm.

Listen to the swarm.

I Hear Some Water Interview the Ants

I hear some water interview the ants. This line comes from a poem by Brenda Hillman, entitled, *In a House Subcommittee on Electronic Surveillance*.[232] The poet, while attending the Subcommittee as a member of the women's anti-war group, Code Pink, experiences feelings of despair and ponders:

> It would be lovely to ask water to investigate
> domestic spying so i put myself in a trance
> right here in Congress holding a bottle of H_2O.
> from California so when the Principal Deputy Assistant
> Attorney General reads *probable cause to believe*
> the water shakes its curly geyser brain &
> when he says *need to close the gaps* it shakes times 3 until its letters
> break & splash to the floor of the Rayburn Building
> ...
> ... i hear some water interview the ants
> who make the basic laws of the land & while
> the Deputy reads *ferret out terrorists* the water interviews
> a ferret under Capitol Mall that can't quite
> streamline operations in the ruddy soil. Perspective is gained.[233]

Perspective is gained through the relational performance of the water, through looking and conscious attention; the subjective experience of perspective. Author and poet Melissa Kwasny, comments: "It is perspective that has agency here, not the singular person who perceives ... How *one* sees is only partial."[234] The production of space is always already *in personam*.

Asking the ants recasts the question completely. And with the genius of the swarm, a multiplicative and proliferative attention is possible: "Multiple viewpoints – human and otherwise – enlarge our understanding of the depth and consequence of events and enlarge the field of possible solutions. When we ask who is the fly are we not asking from what perspective does it see?"[235]

Listen to the water. Ants pay attention.[236]

Notes

1. Wells (1905), 10–11.
2. Wells (1905), 27.
3. Wells (1905), 27.
4. Wells (1905), 26.
5. In relation to traditional knowledge and traditional cultural expressions, see Gibson (2005).
6. Okediji (2022).
7. For example, in New Zealand, the relation between statutory and customary law is reconciled in the Te Awa Tupua (Whanganui River Claims Settlement Act) 2017, which provides that "Te Awa Tupua is a legal person" (s 14(1)) and the rights, powers, and duties are exercised by the Te Pou Tupua on behalf of the river (s 14(2)) as "the human face of Te Awa Tupua" (s 18(3)).
8. Gibson (2020a).
9. Gibson (2020a).
10. Imanishi (1941/[2002]), 44–45.
11. Bonabeau et al. (1999) define "swarm intelligence" to mean "any attempt to design algorithms or distributed problem-solving devices inspired by the collective behavior of social insect colonies and other animal societies" (7).
12. Mullen et al. (2009).
13. Kickmeier-Rust and Holzinger (2019).
14. In a letter to *Nature* in 1873, Charles Darwin relays the story of an apparent comprehension of death and peril in colonies of ants, one in California (and "the terrifying effect on the other ants" upon seeing the bodies of ants that had been killed on their path) and another in Australia where it was observed that "merely drawing a finger across the path deters ants from crossing the line." Darwin writes of the particular achievement of the ants and questions the supposed superiority of vertebrates: "I believe no one has ever observed an invertebrate animal realising danger by seeing the corpses of a fellow species. It is indeed very doubtful whether the higher animals can draw any such inferences from the sight" (Darwin (1873), 244). See further on collective behaviour towards cultural conformity and insect culture in Bridges and Chittka (2019). See further on swarming and cultural transmission and development later in this chapter, particularly in relation to Tarde's sociology.
15. For a fascinating journey through ant society and enterprise, see White (1991/[1883]).
16. An interesting account of overlapping territories and shared spaces is set out in Wilson (1965).
17. Choe (1999), Chapters 1 and 2.
18. Hölldobler and Wilson (1994), 59–73.
19. Hollis and Nowbahari (2013).
20. Tschinkel (2021).
21. Nascimento et al. (2024).

22 Choe (1999), 17–27. See further Shik et al. (2021); Weber (1966).
23 White (1991/[1883]), 153–156.
24 Franklin and Franks (2012); Franks and Richardson (2006).
25 Huber (1820) writes, "I have been enabled to observe, through the glasses of my artificial ant-hill, the great care taken of these little worms, which bear also the name of Larvae. They were generally guarded by a body of ants, who, raised upon their feet, with their abdomen brought between these members, were prepared to cast their venom upon all intruders" (72).
26 Ellis and Robinson (2016); Ellis et al. (2017).
27 Anthony (2024).
28 Casacci et al. (2013) note, "Although ants communicate primarily via chemicals, it is increasingly clear that acoustical signals also convey important information, including status, between adults in many species" (323).
29 Hölldobler and Wilson (1994), 41–58; Wilson (2020), particularly Chapter 10; and Choe (1999), Chapter 7. See also the creation of inter-species network communication in Ando et al. (2017). See further Jeanson (2012).
30 See further on discernment with respect to tools in Maák et al. (2017) and on the maintenance work and use of materials in Turner (1907).
31 Shen (2021); Shen (2019).
32 Huber (1820), 201–202. See further in the context of learning, Goetsch (1957/[1953]), 118. On social motivation and the link to play, see Boulay et al. (2003).
33 Huber (1820), 228.
34 Huber (1820), 228.
35 Choe (1999), 17.
36 Choe (1999), 17.
37 Smith (1870), 1129; Bell (1991), 85, 314–315. While ants belong to the family *Formicidae* (Latin *formīca*, ant), the discipline of the study of ants acknowledges the story in its name, *Myrmecology* (as well as the use of the suffix in naming 35 genera): *Oxford English Dictionary*, s.v. "formic (adj.)," July 2023; *Oxford English Dictionary*, s.v. "myrmeco- (*comb. form*)," July 2023.
38 Haraway (2016), 213n9.
39 Gibson (2020a), Chapters 1–3.
40 Hartigan (2014), 37.
41 Maák et al. (2017): "This means that ants can select tools in line with both food and tool properties" (212).
42 Maák et al. (2017): "[A] lack of familiarity with potential tools cannot explain why *A. subterranea* used sponge pieces, which were totally novel objects. Even more compelling are the data on *A. senilis*, which developed a preference for unfamiliar materials during testing" (212).
43 Csata et al. (2020).
44 Maák I et al. (2017) report that "ant workers were selective in both the materials they chose and the baits that they exploited" and that the results "suggest that using tools to transport liquid to the nest in the two studied ant species is not behaviourally fixed" (212).
45 Maák I et al. (2017), 212.
46 Bachelard (1989/[1935]), 112. See further the discussion in Watson (2016), 43.
47 Chittka (2022) states, "Associative learning … is far from the simple process it was once believed to be" (110).
48 White (1991/[1883]), 242.
49 Franks and Richardson (2006). See also Byrne and Rapaport (2011).
50 Franks and Richardson (2006); Byrne and Rapaport (2011).

51 Wheeler (1910), 179. Indeed, the cooperation and social motivation in teaching and learning have been linked to the expressiveness of play: Caro (1980). See further Thornton and Raihani (2008). The importance of cooperative behaviour towards mutual understanding was also described by Charles Henry Turner when investigating the possibility of cooperation in *Prenolepis imparis*; Turner (1907) notes that, in the gathering and sharing of work and food, "these cooperating ants must have some kind of mutual understanding" (421).
52 Goetsch (1957), 118. Emphasis added.
53 Boulay et al. (2003), 971.
54 See further Hölldobler and Wilson (1990), 365.
55 Galpayage Dona HS et al. (2022).
56 Chittka and Rossi (2022), 578. See further Chittka's exploration of consciousness and emotion in the bee in Chittka (2022), 188–209.
57 Meling (2021), 7.
58 Hölldobler and Wilson (1990), 370. Compare Burghardt (2005), 70–78.
59 Meling (2021) explains: "The result of this 'sense-making-of-sense-making' approach is directly opposite to our aim of *decreasing* sense-making through decreasing adaptivity. So how does an autonomous adaptive system know its current adaptivity and sense-making if 'sense-making of sense-making' does not work? The reply is simply, it requires a mode of knowing that is not sense-making" (7). In other words, a non-representational approach to consciousness, for which play will be shown to be a crucial enaction as the discussion progresses in Part 3 of the present work.
60 Burghardt (2005), 70–78. See further the discussion and application of the five criteria in Galpayage Dona et al. (2022) in the context of bee play.
61 Held and Špinka (2011); Mintline et al. (2013); and Vicino and Marcacci (2015).
62 For example, the Animal Welfare Act 2006 (UK).
63 For example, the Animals (Scientific Procedures) Act 1986 (UK).
64 For example, the Wildlife and Countryside Act 1981 (UK), Schedule 5 (Animals which are protected).
65 See further the discussion of invertebrate sentience in Chapter 3.
66 Mikhalevich and Powell (2020) describe an "empathy gap" where "people tend to empathize with individuals who look more like them, who are judged to be more aesthetically attractive," and for individuals less attractive or socially, culturally, biologically marginalised, people "pass more severe moral judgment upon or assign lower moral weight" (12). On charismatic species and uneven conservation resources, see further Krause and Robinson (2017).
67 Mikhalevich and Powell (2020). Birds are an excellent example of the misinformation and misunderstanding of the relevance of cortical size and differentiation: Olkowicz et al. (2016). See further Higgs et al. (2020). Education plays an important part in changing perspectives in this context. For example, see Hazel et al. (2015) on changing perspectives on chickens.
68 For example, in their research into human preferences for particular species in conservation efforts, Curtin and Papworth (2020) created imaginary species with the assistance of artist Rory McCann. Their findings show that larger animals are preferred by conservation donors. Also relevant here is the question of species in the wild, and individual welfare or suffering. On wild animal suffering, see Johannsen (2020). See further Gibson (2022b) and Feber et al. (2017).
69 So-called charismatic species have been shown to be more likely to receive attention both in terms of public funding and donations, as well as in the policy and legislative context. See further Weston (2020).

70 For example, see the fundraising efforts by zoos in the United States and the Valentine's Day "Cry Me A Cockroach" events, which offer people the opportunity to pay to name cockroaches and rats after their exes, who are then fed to snakes. The events have attracted a lot of criticism (not only for promoting negative imagery of particular species, but also for seemingly celebrating domestic violence), but many have continued to go ahead: Clifton (2020). So-called vermin or invasive vertebrate species are similarly characterised in such a way as to influence against their protection or affiliation with humans. For example, on the distinction between the treatment of rats in scientific research and the treatment of primates, see Andrews and Monsó (2020).
71 For example, see Hollingsworth (2014). Compare the fascinating human-insect collaborations in industry and the role of "domestical insects" in global commerce in Melillo (2014). Similarly, perspectives of species may shift between contexts, particularly so in the context of pet-keeping versus consumption. For example, see Wood (2011).
72 Flusser and Bec (2012/[1987]), 11–12.
73 Flusser and Bec (2012/[1987]), 11. This resonates with Flusser's work elsewhere in relation to homelessness and the "ugly stranger" as distinct from the "beautiful native." See Flusser (2002), 95.
74 Flusser and Bec (2012/[1987]), 11–12.
75 Flusser and Bec (2012/[1987]), 12.
76 Beebee (2021), 388.
77 Flusser and Bec (2012/[1987]), 12.
78 Flusser and Bec (2012/[1987]), 12.
79 Flusser and Bec (2012/[1987]), 12.
80 Weil (1951/[1950]), 47.
81 Loo and Sellbach (2015), 80.
82 Monsó and Osuna-Mascaró (2020). Compare Mikhalevich and Powell (2020).
83 Loo and Sellbach (2015), 80. See also Sebo (2023). The similarities in the handling of insects and plants become even more striking in the context of alternative human food sources and the marketing of insects as an alternative protein. See further Voulgari-Kokota et al. (2023). On the consumer perspective, see Delvendahl et al. (2022), and see the concept of dirty creativity in Chapter 8.
84 Wystrach (2013) notes: "This idea has allowed scientists to avoid any idea of an anthropomorphic intelligence, by looking instead for the simplest solutions to explain complex behaviour." See further Despret (2016/[2012]).
85 Currently, cephalopods are covered by the Animals (Scientific Procedures) Act 1986, s. 1(1) (as inserted by the Animals (Scientific Procedures) Act 1986 Amendment Regulations 2012 (SI 2013/3039)). They are not covered by the Animal Welfare Act 2006, which protects only vertebrates. Neither Act extends to decapods.
86 For example, several species of insects, and some decapods, gastropods, and other invertebrates, are protected under the Wildlife and Countryside Act 1981, Schedule 5.
87 For instance, in relation to the concept of the "hive mind," see Flyn (2021). See further Friedman and Søvik (2021), where the authors conclude: "[T]he ant colony is a useful model system for future philosophical and scientific work on consciousness" (1473). Notably, they advocate the ant colony test (ACT) as an ethical model for "performing clarifying experiments about consciousness" (1457), thus raising the ethical question of suffering that is recognised and questioned as arising in other sentient animal models, but seemingly disregarded in the ant model.

88 Uexküll (2010/[1934]), 45.
89 Boden (2006), 429.
90 Ward (1999), 192. ALife is the common abbreviation for artificial life, which is the study of natural systems through simulation in synthetic models, such as computer simulation and robotics. See further, Langton (1996). Christopher Langton, who is credited as one of the pioneers of the field, explains that in the absence of relevant models appearing in nature, "our only alternative is to try to synthesize alternative life-forms ourselves – *Artificial Life*: life made by man rather than by nature" (39).
91 Simon (1996/[1968]), 51.
92 Simon (1996/[1968]), 51.
93 Simon (1996/[1968]), 51.
94 Chapter 3.
95 Ward (1999), 188–194. See also Yang and Karamanoglu (2020), 8. See further the discussion in Johnson (2001); Nakarmi et al. (2011).
96 For example, see further the critique of the extrapolation from simple neural systems to human consciousness in Tallis (1999/[1991]). Similarly, Seabright (2010) and others have rejected the extrapolation from social insects to human behaviour, betraying further adherence to human exceptionalism in natural systems. But compare research showing considerable similarities, including Louâpre et al. (2010) who show that insects and humans have similar decision processes, where "human subjects use a motivational mechanism similar to small insects" with respect to resources, which the researchers explain as linked to foraging adaptations (1).
97 Burghardt (1984), 683–684.
98 Burghardt (1984), 684.
99 Dežman (2024); Barrow (2024); Floridi (2023b), 47–51.
100 Bishop (2021).
101 Seabright (2010), 151.
102 Seabright (2010), 151.
103 Furniss et al. (2019), 699.
104 See further the creative work in Naruto's use of space in Chapter 5 and further the symbolic and spatial communication through gesture in Chapter 9.
105 See for instance the entertaining account of these multicultural communities in Wilson (2020), 40–42.
106 Romanes (1892), 83. See further the discussion of ancient pet-keeping and the Bonn-Oberkassel dog of around 14,000 years ago in Gibson (2020a), 84–85.
107 See further Gibson (2020a), Chapter 1.
108 1867–1923
109 Turner (1907).
110 Wehner (2016), 253.
111 Wehner (2016), 253
112 Du Bois (1929), 203.
113 Galpayage Dona and Chittka (2020), 530.
114 Galpayage Dona and Chittka (2020), 530. See further Giurfa (2020); Giurfa et al. (2021); and Abramson (2009).
115 Galpayage Dona and Chittka (2020), 530.
116 *Law's Anecdote*.
117 Burghardt (2020), 241. Emphasis added.
118 Turner (1907).
119 Czaczkes (2022). Compare Oberhauser FB (2020). See further the earlier review in Avarguès-Weber and Giurfa (2013). Concept learning has been demonstrated in other insects, including wasps; see Weise et al. (2022).

120 Avarguès-Weber and Giurfa (2015). See further the discussion in Chittka (2022), 114–120.
121 Holzinger et al. (2023). See further Bishop (2021); Wang (2021). For a brief review of the field, see Guo et al. (2024).
122 Wang and Zeng (2024).
123 Bishop (2021).
124 *Camponotus herculeano ligniperdus*
125 See further the useful review of invertebrate attention capacities in Nityananda (2016).
126 Turner (1907), 333–334.
127 Turner (1907), 343.
128 Simmel (1994/[1909]), 6. Emphasis added.
129 Bachelard (1994/[1958]), 164.
130 Simmel (1994/[1909]), 6.
131 Turner (1907), 343. See further the discussion of Turner's work (and his neglect in the history of studies in animal behaviour and cognition) in Galpayage Dona and Chittka (2020).
132 Turner (1907), 343. Turner also showed that ants are not mere stimulus-response machines when it comes to scent: Turner (1906).
133 Giurfa and Brito Sanchez (2020), R1236.
134 Burghardt (2020), 1.
135 Notably and somewhat problematically, these arguments persist in some of the legal reckonings with artificial intelligence. Compare the critical account in Doomen (2023).
136 Romanes (1885), 45. See further research debunking exceptionalist narratives based on the neuroanatomy of the human brain, particularly based on cortical mass and brain size: Olkowicz et al. (2016). See further the discussion in Herculano-Houzel (2020), 803–813; Chittka (2022), 120–121, 146–147. See further Burghardt (2020) on the importance of the intellectual history of natural history, and the relevance and value in revisiting stories, indeed anecdotes, in the breadth and depth of ethology. See further on the value of the historical fragment and anecdote in Chapter 9.
137 Latour (2010), 187. Emphasis in original.
138 See in particular *Law's Anecdote*.
139 Tarde (1903). Latour (2010) lauds Tarde's approach as "reconciling the two types of proof" so as "to develop a scientific social science" (187). See further the discussion of inter-psychology in an ethological jurisprudence in Gibson (2020a), 229–230 and 281–283.
140 Deleuze and Guattari (1987/[1980]), 239–240. See further the discussion in Gibson (2020a), 9–13, 281–283.
141 Latour (2002), 121.
142 Bachelard (1994/[1958]), 155.
143 Latour (2010), 187.
144 Tarde (1903/[1890]).
145 Tarde (1903/[1890]), 3.
146 Tarde (1903/[1890]), 3.
147 Tarde (1903/[1890]), 1, 3, 13.
148 Tarde (1903/[1890]), 3.
149 Espinas (1877). For a discussion of the significance of Alfred Espinas and his contribution to sociology and a nascent biopolitics, see Brower (2016).
150 Tarde (1903/[1890]), 3. Emphasis in original.
151 Tarde (1903/[1890]), 3.

152 Note, although the term "swarm" and associated swarm behaviour is usually taken to apply to social or eusocial insects and their behaviour, such collective behaviour is also identifiable in many other forms of group (including herding and flocking behaviour) or collective intelligence (Couzin (2007); Couzin (2009)), including swarming in vertebrates (Couzin and Krause (2003); Gross (2012)), including: shoals or schools of fish (Lopez et al. (2012)); Bshary et al. (2014)), bats (Nad'o and Kaňuch (2015); Foley et al. (2024)), birds (see Cavagna and Giardina (2010)), and group coordinated action and consensus-building in baboons (King and Cowlishaw (2009)). All types of collective behaviour, from flocks to herds, are related examples of consensus-building and decision-making through "collective motion" (King and Sumpter (2012)).
153 King and Sumpter (2012).
154 In particular see "What Does Naruto Want?"
155 See the general discussion, including that of collective decision-making in shoaling fish, in Bose et al. (2017). Such consensus-based collective intelligence has been observed in a range of species, from insects to primates. For instance, consensus-based collective decision-making has been identified in fish, in studies with guppies, *Poecilia reticulata*: Swain and Fagan (2019). In honey bee colonies, individuals coordinate in order to integrate feedback relevant to collective decisions: Borofsky et al. (2020). In the construction of nest walls by *Leptothorax* ants, it has been demonstrated that the ants will achieve consensus on a decision as to location in the face of several alternatives: Camazine et al. (2001), 342. Similarly, in relation to food sources, colonies of *Lasius niger* will reach a consensus on a collective decision as to the preferred source: Beckers et al. (1990). In macaques, the movement of the group, including speed, achieves a kind of cohesion through a fan-based sociality, towards consensus and the maintenance of group stability: Rowe et al. (2018). Compare the emergence of a so-called "despotic" model in dolphins, also known as "unshared consensus," in Lusseau and Conradt (2009), although in this example the behaviour emerges less in terms of an individual preference and more due to information asymmetry, where one individual may have more knowledge about a situation, unlike the examples above where the group is acquiring knowledge and making a decision as a collective. Therefore, it is perhaps less about assuming leadership and indeed more about conveying knowledge because of an understanding and awareness of the interests and needs of the group (and therefore a kind of cooperative social network). See further the discussion on consensus decisions in Conradt et al. (2019), 762–765.
156 Jolles et al. (2019). See further Marshall and Reina (2024).
157 Chittka (2022), 139–140.
158 Chittka (2022), 129.
159 Chittka (2022), 67, see further 70–77.
160 Chittka (2022), 141. Emphasis in original.
161 Chittka (2022), 141. Emphasis in original.
162 Cronin and Stumpe (2014), 1.
163 Jackson and Ratnieks (2006).
164 Bousquet et al. (2011) note that "individual army ants (*Eciton burchelli*) sigmoidally adjust their speed to the local concentration of a stimulus (the trail pheromone) produced by the ants themselves. The response to this signal allows army ants to display specific cohesion patterns under various environmental conditions" (1482). See further Franks et al. (1991).
165 Goy et al. (2021).
166 Cronin (2012) notes, "Consensus decisions enable group-living organisms to coordinate collective tasks without the need for complex cognitive abilities or

centralized leadership" (1243). On the misleading nature of the leadership concept, see the discussion in Petit and Bon (2010), 638 in particular. See further the critique of a similar operation through assumptions in the fallacious concept of pack theory in dog training in Gibson (2020a) Chapter 8. See further the discussion of the V formation of some migratory bird species in Gibson (2020a), 280–281 where it is noted, "[T]he birds will take turns at the front of the formation" in order to conserve the energy of each individual, "displaying a kind of reciprocal altruism in what is social agreed, as it were, collective behaviour" (280).
167 White (1995), 70.
168 Tarde (1903/[1890]), 3, n1
169 Tarde (1899), 52–53. King (2016) explains that "social repetition was explained either by interest or force, not by conscious decision" (51).
170 Tarde (1899), 41. See further the discussion in the earlier chapter, "What Does Naruto Want?"
171 Buttel-Reepen (1900/[1917]), 15.
172 Chittka and Rossi (2022), 583.
173 Chittka and Rossi (2022), 583.
174 Buttel-Reepen (1900/[1917]), 15.
175 Bachelard (1994/[1958]), 164.
176 Bachelard (2002/[1938]), 29.
177 Bachelard (1984/[1934]), 172.
178 Bachelard (2002/[1938]), 19. Emphasis in original.
179 Bachelard (2002/[1938]), 28.
180 Bachelard (2002/[1938]), 217.
181 Bachelard (1994/[1958]), 148–149.
182 Bachelard (1994/[1958]), 155.
183 Bachelard (1994/[1958]), 150.
184 Bachelard (1994/[1958]), 150.
185 Bachelard (1994/[1958]), 155.
186 Bachelard (1994/[1958]), 155.
187 Bachelard (1994/[1958]), 155.
188 Bachelard (1994/[1958]), 158.
189 In observations of Namibian desert ants, Muller and Wehner (2010) suggest that the ants use a path integration system by acquiring "snapshot" views through rotations interrupted by stopping phases and, although they suggest the speculation may be far-fetched, this nevertheless is relevant to "the potential use of links established between landmark memories and metric path integration coordinates, as surmised for mammals." See further the discussion in Graham et al. (2010). See also Heyman et al. (2019).
190 Wystrach et al. (2020), 1.
191 Wystrach et al. (2020), 5.
192 Bachelard (1989/[1935]), 112.
193 Bachelard (2002/[1938]), 29.
194 For example, see the discussion in Jeschke and Tollrian (2007).
195 Tinbergen (1963), 416.
196 Chang et al. (2021). See further Chittka (2022), Chapters 5 and 8 in particular.
197 Huber (1820), 100.
198 Huber (1820), Chapter 3.
199 Hölldobler Wilson (1994), 51–55.
200 Lefebvre (1991/[1974]), 197–198.
201 Lefebvre (1991/[1974]), 198–199.

202 Lefebvre (1991/[1974]), 199–200
203 Lefebvre (1991/[1974]), 183–184 and 213.
204 Lefebvre (1991/[1974]), 139.
205 Lefebvre (1991/[1974]), 285–290. The term *formant* is also a term of art in phonetics, deriving from *formāre* (to form), *Oxford English Dictionary*, s.v. "formant (n.)," July 2023. Lefebvre's use of the term similarly invokes the process of formation but in the context of the social and participatory production of space.
206 Lefebvre (1991/[1974]), 342.
207 See further the more detailed account of the familiar production of objects through use, as established in Gibson (2014), in particular the chapters Use and *Re* Use.
208 Lefebvre (1991/[1974]), 16.
209 Minkowski (2023/[1936]), Chapter 9 in particular. The concept of *retentissement*/reverberation is also treated in Paul Ricoeur's hermeneutic phenomenology, where he traces its development from Minkowski through Bachelard. See further Ricoeur (1991/[1986]), 173–174.
210 Bachelard (1994/[1958]), 164.
211 Couzin et al. (2019).
212 Huber (1820), 73.
213 For example, in bees, see Chittka (2022), 77.
214 Chittka (2022), 123, and on sharing and learning through the swarm, Chapter 8.
215 Chittka (2022) explains that the capacity to establish nests ultimately facilitated "the evolution of sociality" (69).
216 Gibson (2020a). See further the discussion of the relationship between space, dwelling, and the establishment of a kind of sociable property, 83–88, 261–266.
217 Bachelard (1994/[1958]): "To accompany psychoanalysis in this salutary action, we should have to undertake a topoanalysis of all the space that has invited us to come out of ourselves" (11).
218 Bachelard (1994/[1958]), 202.
219 Weil (1929–1930), 78.
220 Weil (1929–1930), 78–79.
221 Weil (2001/[1955]), 104. See further, Johansen (2010), 73.
222 Hasslacher and Tilden (1995), 157.
223 As the crucial nexus for authorship and sentience, play is considered in detail in Chapter 7 and throughout Part 3. However, at this stage, it is useful to note that even in the presentations of machines at play, there is a clear distinction between the performance of chess (as the coercion of rules and discernment of patterns) and the abundance and exuberance of nonhuman animal play. In this way, play also can be interpreted through a framework of Tardean conscious imitation or *attentive imitation* (shared interests) and thus always already *in personam*. Chess, while a game of two, is a game of imitation through mutual and thus distinct interests, or *stereotypic imitation*. In this regard, the way in which chess is played and presented in the *Fluxus* movement is especially enchanting and disruptive: Gibson (2020a), 165–166.
224 Weil (1943), 14.
225 Weil (1943).
226 Matson(1976), 90.
227 UK Parliament. 11 October 2022. A creative future – Oral evidence https://committees.parliament.uk/event/14659/formal-meeting-oral-evidence-session/   See further the discussion in "What Does Naruto Want?"
228 The Patent Cooperation Treaty (PCT) patent application for DABUS had this title: See WO2015105731A1. Emphasis added.

229 Jünger (2000/[1957]), 135.
230 Shumailov et al. (2023), 1; Herel and Mikolov (2024); Peterson (2024).
231 Shumailov et al. (2023), 1. See further Gibson (2023b).
232 Hillman (2009), 48–49.
233 Hillman (2009), 48–49. Formatting and emphasis in the original.
234 Kwasny (2012), 34. Emphasis in original.
235 Kwasny (2012), 35.
236 Nityananda (2016).

Chapter 5

A Theory of Everything

There is a short poem, by the English poet, Walter de la Mare,[1] entitled, *Tom's Little Dog*.[2] The little dog is called Tim, and Tim's apparent owner, Tom, commands Tim to beg. Tim complies immediately and Tom responds by balancing a lump of sugar on Tim's nose. Tim remains perfectly still as Tom says, "Trust!" But as soon as Tom says "Paid for!" another performance unfolds:

> 'Paid for!' says Tom, and in a trice
> Up jerked that moist black nose;
> A snap of teeth, a crunch, a munch,
> And down the sugar goes!ial[3]

Tim appears to be paid before he acts. The trust is, however, shared. Tim trusts Tom, the debtor, to pay. But Tom may just as easily be speaking about his own trust in Tim, and that trust is *paid for* by Tim's immobility in the face of temptation. The payment is thus at once both the content of the performance as well as its compensation; it is both motivation and reward, both production and consumption. This brief exchange unsettles the conventional causality assumed for production and consumption. Indeed, the authorship in this scenario, as far as it is a commanding production, is unclear, uncertain, and yet shared. In this way, the relationship between Tim and Tom provides an insight into the relationships anticipated within intellectual property, providing an intriguing and critical disruption of the conventional narrative of incentives and rewards[4] and the circulation of debt[5] in production and consumption. For Tim, and indeed also for Tom, the incentive is both a promise and a temptation.

At the same time, this story shows the complexity in defining and recognising the moment of the work. It could be said that the act for which Tim receives the sugar does not take place, does not manifest, until it is paid, even though he appears to be fulfilling the command. This is the curious paradox in copyright, where the work is completed by the mechanism of copyright, the payment or enforcement – in other words, the moment the duration of the

DOI: 10.4324/9780429342103-9

expression is arrested. This perspective renders other customs or manners of creative production as always "unfinished" and thus also potentially "unauthored"; such as the unrecorded performance, works of sound, of smell, and traditional forms of cultural expression and knowledge.

The story also illustrates the paradox of the incentive argument in justice, including the justice of intellectual property frameworks and the somewhat contrived nature of incentives in innovation narratives. It is this same paradox of the incentive, or stimulus, that can be seen in training and learning,[6] and which is similarly mobilised in the explaining away of nonhuman animal creativity as merely functional or biological or trained or all of the above.[7] Fundamental to a retelling of justice is thus an examination of this interaction between motivation and force, and between force and trust. And that retelling calls for another interruption from Thrasymachus.

Thrasymachus, the Law's Straw Dog

The "telling" exchange between Socrates and Thrasymachus is where Thrasymachus offers a critical interrogation of justice, thus cohering the threads of force, causality and debt, and the outsider. The conventional view is to see Thrasymachus as at best a foil and at worst a villain.[8] Indeed, as we know, "[t]radition has been rather less than fair to Thrasymachus."[9] Thrasymachus is also characterised as the outsider, the stranger, the beggar, the beast. And we have already seen that when it comes time for Thrasymachus to ask a question, he is described as "a wild beast, as if he wanted to tear us in pieces."[10]

However, rather than attributing an inconsistent definition of justice to Thrasymachus,[11] aspects of the dialogue may be more helpfully considered as play and pretence. Thrasymachus offers a performance of the notion of just action. When Thrasymachus is dissatisfied with Socrates's interlocutory, he introduces a dialogue of rewards and incentives: "What if I give you a quite different and far better reply about justice? What do you think should be your penalty then?" When Socrates replies that the penalty of ignorance is "that those who don't know would learn from those who do," Thrasymachus retorts that, "You must have your joke ... but you must pay the fee for learning as well."[12] Thrasymachus's challenge (and somewhat delayed interruption, as he was prevented from speaking until the end), is most often presented and criticised as a demand for payment before work,[13] obscuring and resolving his critique as simply "introducing a perturbation,"[14] to use Bachelard's phrase. But in fact, in his interruption, in making a nuisance of himself, Thrasymachus uncovers what he presents as the connivance in the account of justice proffered by Socrates. The exchange between Socrates and Thrasymachus thus explains and performs the epistemological obstacle. Indeed, Thrasymachus might be described as demonstrating Bachelard's "scientific mind" at this point, in that he has the "sense of the problem."[15] As

Bachelard explains, "*the problem of scientific knowledge must be posed in terms of obstacles*"[16] and that these encounters are not merely external but rather are "at the heart of the act of cognition."[17]

In Bachelard's account of the scientific mind, it is the ability to identify and ask the right questions that is crucial: "It is indeed having this sense of the problem that marks out the true scientific mind. For a scientific mind, all knowledge is an answer to a question. If there has been no question, there can be no scientific knowledge. Nothing is self-evident. Nothing is given. Everything is constructed."[18] As such, asking the right question is an answer in itself, and therefore identifying the question is part of the body of scientific knowledge: "Before all else, we have to be able to pose problems. And in scientific life, whatever people may say, problems do not pose themselves."[19] We need only think of Arthur Dent's *quest* provoked by Deep Thought's answer.[20] Indeed, it may be that the problem of artificial authorship might be answered in this issue of the question, as it were. Recall Ada Lovelace's curiously similar and once again pertinent observations, made almost two centuries ago in her notes when translating Luigi Menabrea's article on Charles Babbage's Analytical Engine: "The Analytical Engine has no pretensions whatever to *originate* anything. It can do whatever we *know how to order it* to perform. It can *follow* analysis; but it has no power of *anticipating* any analytical relations or truths. Its province is to assist us in making *available* what we are already acquainted with."[21] Concerning the contemporary hype and hyperbole around artificial intelligence, Lovelace's insight into the chicanery and beguilement of novelty is telling. In words that are as relevant today as they were when originally written in 1843, Lovelace cautions:

> It is desirable to guard against the possibility of exaggerated ideas that might arise as to the powers of the Analytical Engine. In considering any new subject, there is frequently a tendency, first, to *overrate* what we find to be already interesting or remarkable; and, secondly, by a sort of natural reaction, to *undervalue* the true state of the case, when we do discover that our notions have surpassed those that were really tenable.[22]

In Babbage's machine, according to Lovelace, the problem invention was wanting. So-called problem inventions are where the solution is obvious once the problem is known, and so the real inventiveness thus comes from identifying the problem, rather than the solution itself.[23] As for Babbage's machine, it offered no questions, merely answers. In the middle of the seemingly historic Chatbot turn in academia, it is telling that they too provide no questions, only answers. Devising the problem, herewith lies the originality.

Thus, far from a simple endorsement of the view that to flourish is necessarily to act unjustly, what is perhaps much more interesting about the exchange with Thrasymachus is the insight he provokes into the presumed narrative of justice and morality.[24] His demand for payment before he answers is arguably less about acting unjustly and in his own interests and more a mischief with the relationship between incentives, rewards, and justice – that is, the assimilation of justice wholly within the economic sphere. In his pronouncement "that justice is the interest of the stronger party, injustice the interest and profit of oneself,"[25] his critique presents the very fundamental epistemological obstacle to justice – namely, the "habits" of justice, including justice served. Thus, Thrasymachus poses the necessary problem of causality in justice and in law, with all the characteristics of a scientific mind.

Ralf Dahrendorf offers one of the few defences of Thrasymachus and an insightful revision to the way in which this dialogue has been portrayed. In the essay, *In Praise of Thrasymachus*, Dahrendorf directs attention to the dialectic of the exchange itself and the false dichotomy of the social contract: "The consequences of this conflict between notions of the social contract were many, although there is little agreement even today on exactly what they were. Hobbes has been called the father of authoritarianism ... but the same Hobbes has also been regarded as a forefather of modern liberal theory."[26] Dahrendorf's analysis of equilibrium theories in classical sociology resonates with Bachelard's epistemology of science, as well as the dynamic equilibrium of the intellectual property system. In many accounts, Thrasymachus is explained away as an interruption (literally), a disturbance or a perturbation, as it were, in order to establish Socrates as *a priori* the reservoir of the true meaning of justice. Thrasymachus is received as mere caricature, a wolfish stereotype, and thus a foil to the main protagonist, Socrates himself.[27] And therefore, his interjection may be "resolved" in its dismissal. The wild justice of Thrasymachus seems as unthinkable as nonhuman authorship and intellectual property; both Thrasymachus and nonhuman animals are rationalised as nonsensical outsiders by the very paradigm in which they are forced to make their case. And thus they are both explained away as mere *perturbations*: "Disturbances of the system are either ruled out as beyond the boundaries of this type of analysis ... or classified as unexplained accidents. Although such disturbances may produce stress or failure of communication within the system, they are generated outside it."[28]

Thrasymachus shares this orbiting exclusion with nonhuman animals and even machines. He is thus portrayed as an outsider, a stranger, a stray, an intruder, a wolf – Thrasymachus is the nonhuman other and therefore *a priori* outside the system. It would seem to be, to recall Bachelard's explanation, "a case of trying to explain away an anomaly by introducing a perturbation," where positions are made hard and fast by the emphasis on maintaining the existing and persisting epistemological conditions: "In broad terms, the strategy is to argue that what is intellectually perspicuous is clear for all time. The underlying assumption is that the clearest thoughts are always the first to emerge, and that they must therefore fix the frame of reference for all future research."[29] The underlying assumptions are what are always already unsettling to the nature of the contract of justice, the causality and bargain arguably at the heart of Thrasymachus's interjection: "In a Thrasymachean theory, power is a central notion. It is seen as unequally divided, and therefore as a lasting source of friction ... The dialectic of power and resistance determines the rate and direction of change."[30] This belies the otherwise *legal fictions*, as it were, of the linear and irreversible character of force and enforcement, of the anthropocentric force itself. The reversibility of force is crucial to Simone Weil's thinking: "[T]he two struggles that every man of power has to wage – first against those over whom he rules, secondly against his rivals – are inextricably bound up together and each is all the time rekindling the other."[31] A show of force is always a two-edged sword, so to speak; where all force becomes a *being-forced*.[32]

A Ship Ashore

In her reading of the *Iliad*, Weil asserts: "The true hero, the true subject, the center of the *Iliad* is force ... In this work, at all times, the human spirit is shown as modified by its relations with force."[33] Critically for Weil is the reversibility of force, in that, within a relation of force, "anybody who is subjected to it" is turned "into a *thing*," but at the same time, "[t]he hero becomes a *thing* dragged behind a chariot in the dust."[34] In other words, to seek justice merely through reversals of fortune, is to remain exposed to the mechanism of force: "When force changes hands it still remains a relation of stronger to weaker, a relation of dominance. It can go on changing hands indefinitely, without a single term of the relation being eliminated."[35] This fundamental reversibility is otherwise obscured by the purported rationality and efficiency of linear causalities and spent binaries, such as property and personhood, which obscure the contradictions such that this process "masks the correct form, the abstract form, of the phenomenon."[36] This reversibility is crucial to Weil's important critique of the inconstancy and conditional nature of rights:[37] "Force is as pitiless to the man who possesses it, or thinks he does, as it is to its victims; the second it crushes, the first it intoxicates. The truth is, nobody really possesses it."[38] Weil counsels, "These men, wielding power, have no suspicion of the fact that the consequences of their deeds will at length come home to them – they too will bow the neck in their turn."[39]

Thrasymachus presents a similar dialectic, also presenting force as the centre but in such a way that the centre cannot hold. And thus, the presumed irreversibility of force is a convenient fiction that nonetheless unravels, where "legitimacy amounts at best to a precarious preponderance of power over the resistance it engenders."[40] This precarious immunity, the fiction of the separation of producer and consumer, is all to play for in awareness as attention.[41] Like Thrasymachus, Weil rejects the "commercial flavour" of force, in the context of "legal claims and arguments" and the way in which rights are asserted, as a simple economic phenomenon.[42] Rather, it is the relation between power and force that is critical. The economics of force, as it were, simply make extensive the intensive qualities of force as power (and punishment). And like Thrasymachus, Weil understands the real injustice is a punishingly unreflective utilitarianism: "[F]irst force is a stranger to and indifferent to the good, and secondly it is not always and everywhere the stronger."[43] Force governs by maintaining a constant drive to horizons of power which will always be frustrated, "owing to the fact that there is never power, but only a race for power."[44] Weil's assertion that "it is now a question in the struggle for economic power far less of building up than of conquering"[45] may be translated readily into the contemporary, predatory drift of property conceived as rivalrous, exclusionary, and isolating,

Show of Force

The relationship between rights and notions of personhood is an almost unbreakable affair between two concepts of frustration and inevitable appropriation by the law. Personhood is itself a notoriously imprecise and axiomatic term, not dissimilar to the notion of sentience in this respect. While both personhood and sentience belie an undercurrent of equivalence, they nevertheless remain aspirational values in debates over both the welfare of nonhuman animals and the interests of nonhuman authors, including artificial intelligence.[46] And yet inherent in these terms is their capture within a discourse of human exceptionalism and the predatory drift of a contractual approach to agency: "The essential contradiction in the human condition is that man is subject to force, and craves for justice."[47]

Similarly, in the prevailing economic model as applied to the natural world, the emphasis continues to be on competition as something biologically and adaptively compelling. This predatory drift in the law turns on a mostly banal account of innovation as viewed through the lens of the mantra, *survival of the fittest*. But this innovation mythology is based on a flawed or at least attenuated biological narrative, all the while subscribing to the received veracity and credibility of an economically streamlined account of the tautology of natural selection.[48] Further, such accounts of natural selection appear to conflate its meaning and process with that of competition, "survival of the fittest," and the casting out of nature as "red in tooth and claw."[49] Thus, the predatory drift of competition is taken as given, presented thus as an immutable force of nature.[50] However, in stark contrast to this simple story, a much more complex account is to be found not only in Darwin's own inaugurating work on natural selection,[51] but also in subsequent understandings of altruism and cooperation as affording distinct advantages socially, biologically, and evolutionarily.[52] Indeed, to recall the perils of the adaptationist paradigm, and the proper course of analysis, the account of natural selection becomes more complex as to whether it is cause or effect;[53] simply payment in advance. Gould and Lewontin note: "Darwin has often been depicted erroneously as a radical selectionist at heart who invoked other mechanisms only in retreat, and only as a result of his age's own lamented ignorance about the mechanisms of heredity. This view is false."[54] As Darwin himself laments, "Great is the power of steady misrepresentation; but the history of science shows that fortunately this power does not long endure."[55] Perhaps Leibniz and Pangloss are not the only "optimists" in this story.

Notably, Weil recognises a similar drift towards "a sort of war" in the capitalist social model. Excessive force extinguishes the potential sociality of economics and property in what may be described as a kind of attention capitalism: "[E]verything takes place in the realm of opinion, and almost fiction, by means of speculation and publicity."[56] Weil laments, "The term property has almost ceased to have any meaning; the ambitious man no longer thinks of being owner of a business and running it at a profit, but of causing the widest possible sector of economic activity to pass under his control."[57] Thus, the dominant economic model does not produce or create but instead conquers and stills: "[I]t is now a question in the struggle for economic power far less of building up than of conquering; and since conquest is destructive, the capitalist system ... is wholly turned towards destruction."[58] Weil's account of capitalism's self-destruction resonates with human exceptionalism and the bifurcation of the natural world, and is affirmed by the ethology of flourishing through cooperation, contrary to the mythology of capitalism's predatory drift and doctrine of *survival of the fittest*.

This socially constructed momentum of predatory drift in an economic account of authorship is delivered through the artificial scarcity that is managed by copyright (and in the intellectual property system more widely). In constructing scarcity to correct perceived "market failure,"[59] introduced into the wider narrative of authorship are notions of individualism as distinct from communion, competition as distinct from collaboration, hoarding as distinct from sharing, and toil as distinct from play. This reveals resounding counterpoint with the concept of sustainability not only in its social meaning within community but also in its literal meaning with respect to resources. Robin Wall Kimmerer understands scarcity or the apprehension of scarcity to be fundamental to the logic deployed in dominant economic discourse: "Recognizing abundance rather than scarcity undermines an economy that thrives by creating unmet desires. Gratitude cultivates an ethic of fullness, but the economy needs emptiness."[60] The resonances between authorship and welfare, as introduced in earlier discussion, together with the ethical parameters of the sustainability of intellectual property resources in the widest sense, including producers, are crucial. These socio-ethical concerns are manifest in authorship, and are indeed concerns critical to authors. Competition and desire are reworked in the legal conventions of authorship and industrialised through mass production of artefacts. The desire in the expressivity of intellectual creation becomes subjugated in the force of the mechanics of the commercial system. This force turns the author into a thing – literally. In contrast to this, Weil appeals for the joy in intellectual creation: "The intelligence can only be led by desire. For there to be desire, there must be pleasure and joy in the work. The intelligence only grows and bears fruit in joy."[61]

Just like the little dog, Tim, who also appears to be *paid* before he acts, so too the challenge from Thrasymachus. But again, all is not what it seems. Thrasymachus not only sets the scene for a decreation of the habits of justice but also marks out the irrational rationality of moral philosophy. That is, while moral philosophy appeals to the rational, especially in its application to the question of nonhuman authorship in the context of the present discussion, it has nevertheless merely acquired the *habits* of rationality[62] in a contrived duality of right and wrong. And it is time to break those bad habits.

Anthropocentrism, a Bad Habit

It is by now clear that the reasoning of human exceptionalism is instrumental in the construction of the pervading system of beliefs that cohere in the notion of personhood through authorship and through sentience. As such, paradigmatically the logic of personhood functions according to a constructed duality, a logic of barriers, not least of which is the species barrier itself. But it is also a barrier of intellectual creation and authorship; or more specifically, a barrier which manages the scope of that creation. This duality (or perhaps, duplicity) follows an impossible demand of mimetic obligation and an implied biological hierarchy of species according to morphological and social reasoning, resulting in incorporating an anthropocentric standard of "almost human" into popular discourse in animal welfare and rights,[63] and into the socio-cultural dimension of authorship, both in terms of practice and product. In this context, the question of an undifferentiated concept of "personhood" becomes a question that is posed each time with the full knowledge that it cannot be answered while the adherence to human exceptionalism remains "intellectually perspicuous" and "fixed for all time."[64] The asymptotic reasoning that persists in relation to concepts like sentience and indeed personhood means that operating within this paradigm will ensure it remains impossible to reach that equivalence, which will continue to be deferred and aspirational. Threshold concepts like sentience, and similarly rights-based approaches in general, may simply be appropriated and resorbed by the legal paradigm in order to shift the horizon. We must begin "with an intellectual and emotional catharsis,"[65] but we do so on trust. When will this trust be *paid for*?

The same asymptotic approximation of human exceptionalism is applied not only in the popular discourse surrounding artificial intelligence and notions of human-machine collaboration and trust but also in the design and in the presumption of the objective of intelligence implied in the very name itself. That is, the term, "artificial intelligence," presumes the approximation of human intelligence as a starting point. Ravi Kashyap suggests that the design and measure of artificial intelligence and the benchmarks for intellectual achievement may be better served by introducing curiosity or indeed play, as it were, into the principles of development and into the technology itself: "[O]ur attempts at AI could have been misguided. What we actually need to strive for can be termed artificial curiosity, AC, and intelligence happens as a consequence of those efforts."[66] Although the present discussion certainly supports the link between play and intelligence, and while artificial intelligence accumulates information and may even be said to be learning, can it be said that it is curious? Does the machine want or explore? Or is the machine simply obeying the algorithm? And are there any circumstances in which artificial intelligence might be said to play, now or in the conceivable future? In other words, the limitation, it would seem, is that the imitations produced are according to the rules of the programme and any creativity, as such, may be understood to be achieved by a form of coercion, not by choice. In other words, the machine's account and distillation of the information is not an example of conscious or considered regard but an imitation by coercive rule – *stereotypic imitation*. There is no judgment, in every sense of the concept.

Why then is the surrounding discourse so willing to discover authorship or inventorship in artificial intelligence, without any recourse to discussions of aesthetic sense or inventive curiosity, and yet immune to the notion of creativity or authorship in nonhuman animals? Is it as simple as solving the potential economic uncertainty in the ownership of the products? Or is it in fact much more self-conscious than that? And the fact that humans are ultimately the source of the artificial intelligence, as it were, both in the design of the machine and in the data, is perhaps so insidiously persuasive that any quality as an author becomes irrelevant, as it were, to the question. In other words, the anthropocentrism that defines the law and anchors the author also imprints the machine. The force that compels the law, including intellectual property law, is anthropocentric, and the friction experienced in suggesting the creativity of nonhuman animals renders the prospect unthinkable. On the other hand, for artificial intelligence the prospect seems wholly imaginable. Where anthropomorphism of nonhuman animals is decried as unscientific, a strategic anthropomorphism of machines is propelling the narrative. For both the question of the commercialisation of the technology, as well as the resolution of intellectual property, the imputation of an intentional stance on behalf of machines, ranging from popular discourse through to performative policy, is willingly deployed – to become human, before the law.

A Theory of Everything

Anthropocentrism is thus "the theory of everything," the fundamental force. It frames the way in which all the interactions and relationships within property, within welfare, within intellectual property are explained. Indeed, intellectual property is itself a system of anthropocentric force, whereby imagining "othered" creativity becomes unthinkable. This is evident in the stratification of creative work[67] (as in rendering certain activities "mere play"[68]), in the displacement of the site or event of the work in recording and rendering it "writerly" (as in performance, sound art, olfactory art[69]), in displacement of authority (as in traditional knowledge and cultural expressions[70]), and in imposing biological and functional unoriginality and unintentionality (as in nonhuman animals). To put it another way, anthropocentrism governs representation; thus, creative work outside this framework is not work, is not creative, and may even go completely unnoticed.

The operation of this thinking within intellectual property similarly introduces limits to representation, as governed by intellectual property. In this way, the institutional framing of creative work defines the scope of legitimate cultural value, manifest in the types of work that qualify for recognition and thus protection. In other words, intellectual property influences what is possible to believe as creative work, rendering anthropocentric the act of attention itself. This constructed perspective thereby directs evidence of authorship, originality, and intentionality in an aporetic, closed system.[71] Force is thus framed not only as a mechanism for stability but also as a punishment for opportunism and free-riding (to use the language of intellectual property) within this commercial orientation.[72] And similarly, as understood within its practical mechanics, intellectual property ordinarily reduces to the force of enforcement, both in terms of its value and its scope.

Thus, in adhering to an anthropocentric characterisation, the law's world knot, its mind-body problem, is seemingly smoothed away. The self is always already human, and so personhood becomes something in the service of that self. It follows then that the recognition of legal personality in anything other than humans is engaged only in circumstances where humans have an interest in that recognition, such as in the potential legal personality of certain artificial intelligence. It is not in response to what the machine wants but what humans want for the machine. In other words, humans have an interest in the result, while for the machines, it is simply *in their interest*. This dynamic plays out in relation to nonhuman animal interests and conventional approaches to welfare dynamics, as well as to intergenerational human rights, environmental aesthetics and habitat conservation. This is the law's handedness, the law's theory of everything, and of nothing. Importantly, however, in this configuring of positions, as a theory of everything the one thing anthropocentrism cannot account for is itself.

The Space of Authorship

An anthropocentric perspective also anticipates and privileges a particular viewpoint as exemplary, intersecting with dominant voices with respect to race and gender. Intellectual property may thus be understood as facilitating a kind of attention capitalism – by this term, the meaning should be taken as different from its understanding in social media and in ecology, instead more fully informed by Weil's approach to capitalism and appropriation of what is otherwise a certain, attentive attention.[73] Anthropocentrism in the law generally, and in intellectual property in particular, thus frames legitimate attention away from the margins to a privileged and authorised centre. This translates in intellectual property law as drawing attention away from "othered" forms of production, such as traditionally gendered spaces of production, such as crafts and even fashion, and culturally othered forms of production, such as traditional knowledge and traditional cultural expressions.

The counter is that to recognise the space of production within received conventions is to recognise that space as always already human, and a particular ideal human at that. This has particular consequences for nonhuman creativity as well. Space is presented as empty, as an opportunity to be filled, and thus always within the dominion of the human, in the interests of all others: "The notion of a space which is at first empty, but is later filled by a social life and modified by it, also depends on this hypothetical initial 'purity', identified as 'nature' and as a sort of ground zero of human reality. Empty space in the sense of a mental and social void which facilitates the socialization of a not-yet-social realm is actually merely a *representation of space*."[74] Humans assume that space as empty, a reservoir for them to fill, a *reserve*, as it were. This presumption of emptiness has had devastating consequences for nonhuman animals and their habitats around the world, and Naruto's space will be revisited in a moment. But an ethological approach, informed by Bachelard and Lefebvre in particular, shows that space is generative, productive, and noisy. Make way for the swarm.

Movement through space raises a particular form of knowing for Weil, which is informed by her concept of reading (*lecture*). Weil explains:

> Everybody can convince himself that when handling a pen his touch goes right through the pen to the nib. If the pen skips because of some problem with the paper, the *pen's* skipping is what is immediately felt; we don't even think about the sensations in our fingers or hand through which we read. However, the pen's skipping is really on something we read. The sky, the sea, the sun, the stars, human beings, everything that surrounds us is in the same way something that we read. What we call a correction of a sensory illusion is actually a modified reading.[75]

This sensorimotor account of knowing at the same time implicates movement in ascertaining sensation and sentience. This account of knowing as a multisensory experience of environment is especially meaningful in understanding nonhuman animal territories and properties, particularly in the shift in perspective from seeking attention to the receptive seeking to attend. Importantly, unseating the visual as the primary or solitary sense opens out to a range of perspectives and varying sensory proficiencies, as well as to multifarious questions and multiform neighbourhoods of knowledge. Weil describes sensation alone as passive until it is formed by its environment, insofar as "sensation is always something one undergoes, something passive, even when one feels the will powerfully at work."[76] In other words, there is an expressive and motor dimension to sentience through space, rather than anchoring that sensation to objects; in this way, an active and attentive movement produces knowledge.

There is thus a certain creative productivity to movement through space which resonates with action-based theories of perception and embodied approaches to creativity. In particular, so-called 4E cognition[77] and radical enactivism,[78] which will be discussed in more detail in later chapters,[79] are especially significant to an ethological approach, notably with respect to the pursuit of a productive and embodied making through space which is, critically and *radically*, a swarming and sympoietic[80] co-production.[81] This perspective may be distinguished from ecological psychology and the theory of affordances, which, while valuable to the present discussion, nevertheless suggest an environment which pre-exists the nonhuman animal,[82] a kind of space to be filled rather than a sympoietic co-production.[83] Ecological approaches have also been criticised as primarily visual, in that these "treat perception in largely optical (albeit ecological) terms and so attempt to build up the theory of perception almost entirely from the environment."[84] And as Weil contends, "sight by itself gives us nothing."[85] Weil's critique of this emphasis on the visual sense alone is compelling in an ethological context: "Objects assume a shape only through our imagining what we call their real shape. We call the real shape the shape which appears to us when the object occupies the whole of our visual field. One can ask: what reasons are there which make us decide the matter in this way?"[86] Perception understood in this way is instead an active and attentive movement. As Weil claims, "We only know our own action by its results,"[87] which is quite different from anchoring the creativity to material objects.[88] In a sense, the objects or artefacts of interest are confirmed by movement, and situations, and have no value or indeed existence prior to that motivity and rhythm: "All the lines which form the limits of things, which make up their shapes, are given to us through our reflexes, by our own movement."[89] This relates closely with Lefebvre's consideration of space and critique of the commodity and its social incapacitation in isolation.[90] Weil's perspective also resonates with Tarde's understanding of tools and machines as extensions of the mind, describing a relationship between tools and memory as "inextricably linked."[91]

Weil sets out a compelling theory of expressive embodied space the essay, *The Materialist Point of View*.[92] Weil explains that "from the very fact that we have a body, the world is ordered for it; it is arranged in order in relation to the body's reactions,"[93] and thus it would seem that, "space, depth, shapes are given to us by our imagination."[94] This is not a simple adaptationist paradigm, but rather, it is an account of phenomenal consciousness through the shaping of the space around: "[T]here is nothing which is purely external ... impressions are subjective, each of us has his own view of the world."[95] In other words, it is not that the environment pre-exists and predicts the nonhuman animal, it is that the world is always in a dynamic and reflexive relationship with the body's actions and imagination upon the world, actions which bring it into being: "Every thing that we see suggests some kind of movement, however imperceptible. (A chair suggests sitting down, stairs climbing up, etc.)."[96] The material world and the objects within it are thus always understood in a relationship of action: *I think I am a verb*.

Weil describes the kind of somatic knowledge that attends this perception as conditioned reflexes, similar to habit and the capability of the habitual body in phenomenological accounts. As such, habit is a thinking that provides for freedom from thinking, a capacity and a doing, a being through one's hold; "simultaneous experience of the holding and the held in all orders."[97] This generative quality of habit coincides with Tarde's similar account of perception and being as holding, explicitly rejecting the Cartesian "I am." Notably, the word itself, habit, derives from *habēre*, meaning to have and to hold, developed to extend to custom and to dwell and abode (including in the sense of habitat).[98] Revisiting Tarde's explanation, considered earlier,[99] this relationship between possession as distinct from individualism is of critical relevance to an ethological perspective: "All philosophy hitherto has been based on the verb *Be*, the definition of which was the philosopher's stone, which all sought to discover. We may affirm that, if it had been based on the verb *Have*, many sterile debates and fruitless intellectual exertions would have been avoided."[100] Recalling the earlier discussion of Tarde's revision of the cogito, this possession emerges as a distinctly sociable phenomenon, for which imitation is the foundation of society in which "*I have* is posted as the fundamental fact, both that which *has* and that which *is had* are given inseparably at once."[101]

Crucial here is the interaction between Tarde's central relation between belief and desire (as potentially manifest through wants) and an active, motile, and attentive perception, as considered by Weil, together with the capacity of that embodied perception and cognition in later phenomenological and cognitive scientific thinking. Tarde explains that all perception "implies a kind of habit," and "if the remembered idea or image was originally lodged in the mind through conversation or reading, if the habitual act originated in the view or knowledge of a similar act on the part of others, these acts of memory and habit are social as well as psychological facts."[102] The relation between habit, wants, and a rethinking of capability unsettles the unilateral and linear narrative of authorship (and classical science, as considered by Weil), and the presumed energy and fundamental order of "I am." But perhaps even more importantly, this interaction also affirms a capacity through regard and welfare that offers tangible impact for animal studies. This is the affiliative and social dimension of habit: *I desire, I believe, therefore I have*.[103]

This is the *having*, as it were, of Weil's private space, the garden (habit, dwell, abode), her incisive dismantling of property platitudes that resort to metaphors of dominion and absolutism, and a reinvigoration and resourcing of the cultural other.[104] Thus, the freedom within space, particularly private space, is crucial to wellbeing and expressivity. But as Sarah Ahmed asks, "What if the world 'houses' some bodies more than others ... We might need to rewrite happiness by considering how it feels to be stressed by the very forms of life that enable some bodies to flow into space."[105]

The Monkey Made Me Do It

Such is the experience of Naruto. Naruto's story is a very particular account of that space, the rendering of that space, that private space, and the opportunities for expressivity within it. Some intellectual property scholars have suggested that in arranging the camera in a particular space, David Slater may have fulfilled the minimal technical intervention in order for the resulting photographs to have been his own intellectual creation.[106] But even viewed conservatively, this position is unsupportable, as later discussion will make clear. And if that were not enough, Slater also declared an equivalence in effort: "It took three days of blood, sweat and tears to get the selfie in which I had to be accepted by the group of monkeys before they would allow me to come close enough to introduce them to my camera equipment."[107] In interview, Slater also appealed to notions of artistic planning and foresight: "It was my artistry and idea to leave them to play with the camera and it was all in my eyesight. I knew the monkeys were very likely to do this and I predicted it. I knew there was a chance of a photo being taken."[108] This argument emphasises the traditions of planning associated with aesthetic approaches to artistic expression, and at the same time ushers in presumptions of direction and instruction of mechanical and predictable responses from the macaques as tools in this production. In this scenario, the macaques are perceived as merely and incidentally wandering into that *human* space, notwithstanding its intrusion within the reserve, rather than expressing and shaping that space; in other words, space is a capacity reserved for the human. But this conclusion relies upon the persistent presumption of an anthropocentric vision of the macaques' space and their activities within it – that is, upon an anthropocentric looking and a willful inattention outside the frame.

On the contrary, this space was entirely at the direction of the macaques. And this includes the orientation of the camera within it. Slater was entering the macaques' world, their *Umwelt*, and his actions were responding to where the macaques would be and move within it. If anyone made decisions as to the position of the camera, it was the macaque colony; a kind of motor theory of authorship, as it were. To see otherwise is to cooperate with the violence of an anthropocentric intellectual property and to arrive at perhaps absurd results as to the nature of authorship. For one species it is opportunity, for another that opportunity and good luck is authorship – in the right place at the right time. For one species, that creativity is rationalised as the opportunism of a hapless and incidental scavenger;[109] for the other it is presented as the agency and ingenuity of being alert to opportunity. It is intriguing to consider in this context the interviews with Slater surrounding this episode, and the emphasis throughout on the purpose of the photographs, their contribution to knowledge, all at the same time seemingly shoring up the barrier between Slater's intentional exploration and the accidental tourism of the macaques within this ordained authorial space. As such the macaques are divested of their own interests in the process, and indeed their own space, and become tools of the photographer's authorial purpose. The spandrels of art leave nonhuman animals spaced out.

This episode is also about a guaranteed public space, and the interaction with the concept of the public domain. The space of authorship is presented as all or nothing – either it is property or it is public domain – transforming everything into a rivalrous property narrative and turning the public domain into the reservoir for the margins. As well as marginalising certain forms of creativity as outside the valid cultural archive, it ignores the possibility of a kind of "public authorship" and what this might mean for the concept of the work. In other words, what is the nature of the work when the expression of intellectual creation is in collaboration with the public, with the public sphere, with other animals, with the landscape itself? How is it possible to explain that co-production in order to realise the individuality and singularity of a copyright author? Why is it possible? And is this at all comparable to the outputs of artificial intelligence, including the seemingly spontaneous and autonomous outputs of generative AI, and the co-production of human and machine? Or is it every reason why there is a problem for human authors there as well?

What is remarkable about this episode is the redirection of value beyond the constraints of authorial serialisation. Indeed, Slater's mobility is made clear by the opportunities to commercialise the event in other ways, to generate value in other places or contexts, as in the space of the proposed documentary.[110] Value is mobilised beyond the settled centre or norm of the intellectual property object and the cultural institution of the copyright artefact (the photograph), and delivered via fragmented relations.[111] In this way intellectual creation is also a process of engagement, the joy in work, and an opening out to the non-objects of creative endeavour and valuable relations.[112] The expressive value is concerned thus with the space itself, the relational experience, as distinct from the objects indexical of that expression.

Notably, the Ninth Circuit arguably, and perhaps inadvertently, begins to accommodate the type of contribution made by the macaque colony, albeit not explicitly. The judgment leaves it open that while Naruto cannot be an owner within the United States Copyright Act, this in itself does not make any conclusion as to authorship. It is arguable whether, within the confines of legal interpretation, authorship can or should be separated out like this. Naruto may be an author in every sense of the concept but cannot be a statutory person under the Act, and so cannot be an owner of copyright. The Act is, or perhaps should not be, about curtailing the concept of authorship. Rather, it is concerned with *which* authors can qualify as *owners*, or more accurately, for the entitlement to copyright in their work.[113] This anticipates the kind of public authorship and value of attribution and provenance in works that are otherwise outside the scope of copyright protection. Copyright is not about authors; it is about *qualified* authors. While the decision is taken largely to concern standing, and the reaction of the Compendium is taken as confirming the non-authorship of nonhuman creators for the purposes of copyright, arguably what it really shows is that this limitation is imposed by the scope of the Act (and person within the Act), and not by the meaning of authorship, *per se*.

I Own It

Another argument that emerged during Naruto's period of fame, and one that David Slater also put forth, was that the owner of the equipment should thereby own the photographs that emerge from it. Indeed, this principle did in fact apply in early approaches to photographic copyright,[114] but is not the current law and is certainly not consistent with the originality principle inhering in the concept of the author's own intellectual creation.[115] Such arguments generally take as their justification the presumed causality of protection as an incentive to further creativity,[116] claiming "this would encourage future photographers to both continue experimenting and to publish their work. This outcome would arguably enhance the likelihood of the production and distribution of interesting works, rather than undermining it."[117] But whose creativity and whose work?

This argument based upon the property in the equipment relies on the doctrine of accession in property law, an argument that has also been tested, to date without success, in relation to outputs from artificial intelligence.[118] In the first edition of the *Commentaries on the Law of England*,[119] William Blackstone defines accession, a principle of Roman law, to be "also grounded on the right of occupancy,"[120] introducing not only a sense of space but also a relationship to that space. Accession applies to any tangible item, or "corporeal substance," that may issue from an individual's tangible property; such as vegetables in the garden, objects created from building materials, clothing sewn from cloth, and a cow's calf.[121] The rationale is that each of these examples represents a "state of improvement" that is still in a relationship to the original property. However, "if the thing itself, by such operation, was changed into a different species, as by making wine, oil, or bread, out of another's grapes, olives, or wheat, it belonged to the new operator."[122] In other words, if the new item cannot be restored to or is so materially changed from the original property, then it belongs to that new operator, or indeed, maker.[123] The critical value here is the material and *attending* relationship of the owner.

There are thus two distinct obstacles to the application of the doctrine of accession in the case of Naruto's photography, and also for its application to the outputs of artificial intelligence: first, these are both examples of intangible property, which was something that was not anticipated in the doctrine and to which the doctrine has not been applied to date; and second, Naruto's photograph is a change "into a different species" from that of the equipment itself, an obstacle also faced explicitly by artificial intelligence.[124] That David Slater owns the camera with which the photographs were taken is thus irrelevant.[125]

There are further ethical and social concerns with this argument. In attempts to extend the doctrine of accession to intangibles, arguably the relational connection between owner and property, the sociality of property, gives way to the measure of control instead.[126] Indeed, Weil might say, *the term intellectual property has almost ceased to have any meaning.*[127] The insistence on property as simply a means of control reflects the devitalised and reductive notion of property as dominion and inanimate, quite out of step with the affiliative and lively basis of property and property relations, the social and cultural importance of which is at stake in the doctrine of accession and well-recognised by Weil, not least in her insistence on property beyond its frequent mischaracterisation as merely "articles of ordinary consumption."[128] Explaining this relationality through the example of the estate-manager and the agricultural labourers, Weil argues: "The principle of private property is violated where the land is worked by agricultural labourers and farm-hands under the orders of an estate-manager, and owned by townsmen who receive the profits. For all those who are connected with the land, there is not one who, in one way or another, is not a stranger to it."[129] Weil describes the loss of connection and externalisation of control as waste of the land and a frustration of the "property-need" for those actually connected to the land.[130]

If it is to be accepted, as arguably it must, that in this and other examples copyright is dealing with genuinely sentient, creative, and innovative beings, then this reckoning with copyright does further violence not only to the connection and sociality of property in the multispecies space but also to the concept of authorship. Further the claims that forms of artificial intelligence are developing sentience or demonstrating consciousness,[131] although this remains hypothetical at best,[132] deployed in service of arguments for authorship and inventorship on the part of machines and to be managed by their owners, suggest some serious logical fallacies. First, the presumption that sentience is the motivation for intellectual property rights is specious and misleading, given that this principle has not been extended to the creative work of sentient nonhuman animals. Indeed, the question for the authorship and inventorship of artificial intelligence is driven by products and capital. Second, if this claim to sentience can be established, then the apparently desired result of an automatic assignment to the owners of artificial intelligence is a perverse enslavement of artificial minds. On this point, that fact that DABUS, the subject of the protracted litigation in patents and copyright on the part of the machine,[133] is itself the subject of a patent,[134] presents a curious constellation of the issues around property and personhood. And it is for very similar reasons that recognition of nonhuman animal authorship is similarly a welfare issue, such that there is a clear provenance towards the delivery of outputs to the public domain. Once again, it is a question of qualifying authorship, rather than recognising authors and their wellbeing.

This is something to which the discussion will return, but for now what is needed is to begin to pose some different questions and pull some more strings.[135]

The Rights Stuff

Weil explicitly rejects an appeal to rights as a fraught framework borne of force and thus vulnerable to ready reappropriation by the law. Weil explains: "Relying almost exclusively on this notion, it becomes impossible to keep one's eyes on the real problem," which is the "social drama" in which rights discourse occurs and is at times "falsely assimilated," being reduced to "a shrill nagging of claims and counter-claims, which is both impure and unpractical."[136] Such is the utilitarian economics of rights discourse: "The notion of rights is linked with the notion of sharing out, of exchange, of measured quantity. It has a commercial flavour, essentially evocative of legal claims and arguments. Rights are always asserted in a tone of contention; and when this tone is adopted, it must rely upon force in the background, or else it will be laughed at."[137] In other words, the person's reliance on the discourse of rights operates through the very mechanism of the "social order that inevitably ends up oppressing it."[138] Weil is very critical of the rhetorical obfuscation of the force of social privilege in this context: "The notion of rights, by its very mediocrity, leads on naturally to that of the person, for rights are related to personal things ... It is much worse still if the word 'personal' is added to the word 'rights', thus implying the rights of the personality to what is called full expression."[139] She notes that "the full expression of personality depends upon its being inflated by social prestige; it is a social privilege. No one mentions this to the masses when haranguing them about personal rights. They are told the opposite."[140]

The attention of personhood, as such, is always already cast within this dynamic of exchange constrained by anthropocentric conditions, and with that a certain "commercial flavour"[141] of economic rationality. Attentive attention, to which the discussion turns in the next chapter, becomes a critical and generous regard as distinct from the coerced and situated viewpoint of anthropocentrism. To ask the right questions is to pay attention, stupid. Within the economic rationality of the conventions of a rights framework, Weil explains the calculation of incentives, whether punishment or reward:

> One can always ask oneself, when dealing with a moral question, how a utilitarian would tackle the question. Example: punishment is something bad because it harms the culprit; it is good because it prevents crimes. One simply makes an arithmetical calculation ... pleasure is, by definition, an end in itself, but the pleasure of one's neighbour is not an end in itself. Once it is a question of my neighbour's pleasure, it is no longer an end for me.[142]

This passage traces the predatory drift of conventions of property, recalculating morality into resources; and more specifically, into competitive resources. This expressiveness of relations becomes, literally, a spent force.

The predatory drift in the discourse of intellectual property is similarly one of contriving and calculating an artificial causality of incentives (rewards and punishments), where those incentives are therefore a kind of force. The processes of innovation and creativity are displaced and deferred by an emphasis on the legal construct of the author, as understood conceptually through the author-function, operating across the full range of intellectual property rights, in service of the object. As seen in earlier discussion, it is a construct that is made by the making itself. In this way, this incentives fiction puts all attention on the "almost despotic influence of the incentives narrative."[143] Returning to the question of authorship, as distinct from qualified authorship, the issue is a separation between production and use, such as to summarise and simplify authorship as a product of ownership. Weil might be seen to anticipate this consolidation of authorship in her critique of the factory, where she explains: "The way ownership and industrial management have become separated, which has transformed the majority of owners of capital into mere parasites, permits the use of slogans such as 'the struggle against the servitude of interest', which are anti-capitalist without being proletarian."[144] That access to the resources for photography should at the same time alienate Naruto from the creative work reveals the exploitation of the *natural world* as a cultural collaborator.

And who better to illustrate the interaction between force, instruction, and creativity, than *that dog*?[145]

Punishing Rewards – the Magician's Choice

Incentives may also be negative, including the concept of punishment as an incentive.[146] Although Weil does concede the use of punishment in certain circumstances (that is, "to use force against force"[147]), this is attended by important qualifications. In those circumstances, "[b]oth administrators and perpetrators had to perceive of the punishment as just and legitimate" but "[w]hen a thirst for dominance or retribution drove the punishment, the evil effects of violence began a self-perpetuating vicious spiral," thus reducing the prisoner "to a vile rejected object in the same category as a 'thing' or matter."[148] Weil is careful to distinguish between the cry of "Why am I being hurt?" and "Why has somebody else got more than I have?"[149] Her explanation resonates with the distinction between relational property and justice, on the one hand, and the predatory drift of rivalrous property conventions on the other. While the latter is a construction that "can be formed in a law school," the former "raises quite different problems, for which the spirit of truth, justice, and love is indispensable."[150] Punishment and force thus become seemingly justifiable as mechanisms of free will (and other "freedoms" such as trade).[151] The interpretation as punishment of certain behaviours between conspecifics in species other than human is then presented somewhat naively and erroneously as justification for the use of punishment in learning and training.[152] But is this just a sleight of hand? The magician's choice, as it were? Towards a theory of everything, everything comes down to and is contained within a punishment and payment dynamic. The question of what Naruto wants therefore becomes impossible and unthinkable. Weil's theory of attention is crucial here, for it is in very significant ways an unstated theory of *Umwelt*. It is necessary to consider what it is like to be Naruto, and what it is like to want to make that selfie.

At this point the discussion welcomes the return of that dog, first introduced in *Owned*,[153] rejoining the discussion here with some guidance received earlier from Tom's little dog, Tim, and some dogged attention from Thrasymachus. Through the circulation of courtesy, trust, and payment, their insight assists with the interrogation of incentives and force in the intellectual property context. Force delimits the creativity of nonhuman animals sometimes explicitly in the context of training. Training and conditioning are inextricably bound with perceptions of choice, originality, and intentionality. And in this context, the "commercial flavour" of rights emerges in the assumptions underpinning the language of obedience and good behaviour at work in the background, always with "force in the background" as a persistent theme, without which "it will be laughed at."[154] What is especially interesting is the framing of training discourse within the dynamic of an economic relationship (with or without direct force) as explicit in programmes such as Nothing In Life Is Free (NILIF),[155] Learn to Earn,[156] Say Please,[157] and others.[158] But who says please to that dog? Who says, "Trust!" Who *pays* attention? Indeed, to pay attention becomes co-opted as a central, organising principle once again in the *commercial flavour*, and thus economic logic, of popular training discourse. In other words, it becomes a battle for resources that are rendered artificially scarce in a dynamic of force and power: "The usual result of such adversarial relationships is a history of conditioning based on aversive stimulation, concerned with disempowering rather than empowering the other party ... The guardian deliberately sets themselves as the obstacle between the companion animal and their reinforcers as opposed to the source of reinforcers."[159]

The very process of, first, interpreting behaviours in this kind of narrative of force and, second, supposing that these may be extrapolated to the human-dog relationship (in some sort of presumably meaningful hierarchy), for example, is hugely problematic and does not accord with either Weil or the science. As Alexandra Horowitz explains, "This approach is farther from what we know of the reality of wolf packs and closer to the timeworn fiction of the animal kingdom with humans at the pinnacle, exerting dominion over the rest. Wolves seem to learn from each other not by punishing each other but by observing each other."[160] *Pay attention, stupid.*

In this context it is important to distinguish between "punishment" within animal societies, as in the context of play (circumstances which align with this operation of mutual belief and in which subjects have some control), as distinct from punishment in a training context of discipline and obedience and force (circumstances in which training subjects have no control and for which consent is rendered mute). Thus, the use of aversives in any context may also be accompanied by a loss of flexibility on the part of the training subject, that is, a loss of creativity in terms of their behavioural and social repertoire, and thus also a loss of resources necessary to their freedom of expression: "While we might attenuate what we perceive to be an undesirable behavior, all surrounding affiliated behaviors ... also cease. As a result, we deprive the animals in our care of choice and flexibility, and there is no doubt those are welfare violations."[161] This has implications both for adaptive fitness as well as creative expression. And this offers a fascinating insight into the incentive and enforcement environment for creativity and innovation as well.

The coercion of creative work within a commercial dynamic of force amounts to a curious perversion of the potential for attentive listening and *attentive imitation* in creative work on the part of subjects. In this way, expression and, more specifically, pleasurable expression through play and happiness, are tied to the disciplinary circulation of force in ways wholly consistent with Weil's concept of force. Training discourse reveals the way in which happiness and play, and indeed creativity and authorship, may be overwritten within a coercive paradigm. And in this way, many significant referential gestures and communicative behaviours,[162] such as those used to seek attention or assistance, are sometimes viewed as undesirable or even malevolent. And for those reasons, that expression is actively suppressed through some training paradigms, resulting in both a curious reluctance on the part of the trainer to engage in that interspecies communication as well as a denial of that dog's resources for their expression; indeed, their freedom of expression.[163]

Sara Ahmed's work on happiness is useful here and becomes compellingly relevant to the way in which happiness and other emotions are commodified within training discourse. Ahmed describes the way in which happiness in human societies becomes "a disciplinary technique," not in terms of happiness in and of itself but in the way in which happiness is alienated and commodified within an economic paradigm as yet another commodity.[164] Ahmed contextualises contemporary programmes of multiculturalism within the historical force of empire, whereby utilitarian justifications assimilate happiness within the colonial power's juridico-economic paradigm: "The gift of happiness is imagined here in terms of civility. Human happiness is increased through the courts (law/justice), knowledge (reason), and manners (culture, habits)."[165] This resonates with Weil's critique of the commodification of labour,[166] and thus brings in the important relationship between play and work, and therefore authorship, to be explored more fully later.[167] This also accords with Weil's observations of resentment and aversion through the commodification of labour,[168] and the emphasis on the fundamental importance of the relationship between work and play.[169] For Weil, the expressive potential of happiness is vacated by the severing of the affiliative relationship to joy through work.[170] However, through the kind of coercive imitation in artificial intelligence, there is a risk of the potential control of that vital, expressive play. Instead of playing more and working free, ultimately pop will eat itself.[171]

Could this not have resonance in the fabric of intellectual property? Why are we asking only that dog, that consumer, that user to say please? Indeed, even the language of user secures a utilitarian logic to this exchange. But what about the producers and owners who wield the force? Is it possible to imagine a more attentive system? Returning to the use of aversives in training, Karen Overall, veterinary behaviourist, laments that in none of the training literature advocating such methods, "did anyone pause to ask what information the dog was conveying by the behavior that people found worrisome or undesirable."[172] What does that dog want? This impatience for efficiency, so to speak, is fundamental to the commercial valorisation of these kinds of approaches to training and is also pervasive in the scaffolding of rights and personhood, as well as the architecture of force that characterises commercial intellectual property frameworks.

In Weil's own approach to education it is possible to recognise observations that are consistent with the later scholarship on aversive training and learned helplessness.[173] Weil aligns this kind of aversive training not with the acquisition of knowledge but with suffering: "Suffering is therefore the chief means. But it has no value in itself. One can beat a dog all the day long without it learning anything. Sufferings that one inflicts are useful for nothing."[174] The continued use of aversives, in whatever form, will chill creativity and suppress innovation as a consequence of having, quite literally, no control and thus no choice: "Learned helplessness may explain apparent apathy in individuals in situations over which they perceive that they have no control as a consequence of their previous experiences."[175] The subject develops a pessimistic outlook, or negative cognitive bias, not only raising welfare concerns but also interfering with investigative, creative and innovative expression. A pessimistic outlook as a result of negative events has been demonstrated in relation to the use of aversive methods with dogs,[176] as well as in other species.[177] With continued aversives or punishment, it is just not worth thinking. And while it may be that such training by punishment leads to "a perfect docility,"[178] this compliance is not learning, as such. It is the social order of force.

In his extensive studies of play, Jean Piaget's work has identified the way in which coercion may be understood as socialising only the surface or the phenomenal behaviour, without translating into learning and resilience in terms of self-directed behaviour.[179] These results show that the use of coercion or force will reinforce reliance on external regulation, in ways consistent with force and the stability of juridical framing of perspectives throughout a range of contexts considered here. This demonstrates the tension between force and justice introduced by Thrasymachus and reconsidered by Weil and is relevant to a questioning of the legitimacy of such frameworks. In an over-regulation of creativity, the morality of play cedes to the compliance with force. In the context of intellectual property environments, increasingly the work is perspicuous, as it were, through enforcement rather than through use. From an evolutionary or ethological perspective, the work in enforcement is arguably wasted energy, as distinct from the voluntary moral code of games and play, and the abundant waste of intellectual creation.[180]

Cautiously Optimistic

Drawing upon the concept of flourishing and the building of virtues, Francis Su describes the way in which coercive power, or force, interferes with creativity in ways consistent with the principles of learned helplessness.[181] Su develops a concept of creative power and a proliferative and productive relationship through creativity, and contrasts this with coercive power which, "disrupts other people's capacity to exercise creative power."[182] Su explains: "Creative power distinguishes itself in many ways from coercive power. Creative power *amplifies power in the subject and the object of power* ... Creative power is *humble* and it puts others first. It seeks to unleash creativity in others."[183] And in what may be understood as a rejection of the economic causality attributed to incentives and creative outputs, "Creative power is *sacrificial*,"[184] reflecting instead the cooperation and altruism that characterises flourishing and learned optimism. Importantly, the concept of flourishing in this context includes biological and collective flourishing in the process of natural selection, whereby prosociality becomes a fundamental basis for evolutionary development, as distinct from the mantra of *survival of the fittest*. It is not just business. It is personal.

Creative power thus elevates human dignity,[185] introducing a crucial link between dignity, creativity, and rights, and a link which may be pursued through a radical rethinking of welfare through authorship. Force thus marks the vulnerability, as well as the capability, of the subject – the author, the producer, the consumer, that dog. In the same way, force also marks the way in which any response to those conditions is rendered. As the theory of everything, force produces the illusory appearance of the homogeneous, human space, with everything else generalised and marginalised, a view coerced to the point of appearing ordinary and inevitable; boring, if you will. But nothing could be further from the truth. Instead, a pairing of seemingly divergent forces, a reconciliation and reversibility, a relation of contradictions offers potential. This will become crucial later in understanding the fragment in literature, the anecdote in science, and the nonhuman testimonial in law.[186]

This reconciliation is evident in Tarde's examination of difference and inter-psychology: "I must also regard as one of the essential knots of my philosophical tree this expression ... 'There are differences within the Difference itself.' ... [I]t seems to me that my hypothesis of difference for the difference, of change for change, has been confirmed. – But I would not have delayed to reject it if I had not thought at the beginning that this expression reconciles with the law of harmony and of progress."[187] Harmony comes through the dialectic of question and answer, through learning as play, as distinct from coercion and forced compliance:

> [T]he *fundamental social adaptation* is ... that of two men, one of whom answers, by word or deed, the question of the other, whether silent, spoken, or tacit? I call it a "question," for the satisfaction of a need, like the solution of a problem, is the answer to a question. Shall we not say, then, that this fundamental harmony consists in the relation between two men, one of whom teaches, while the other learns ... or, better, that it consists in the relation between two who work together to produce the same result? Certainly; for this relation, though it *implies* the relationship of two men, one of whom is pattern, the other copy, is really quite distinct from it.[188]

This dialogical awareness resonates with Weil's theory of an illegitimate and legitimate use of contradiction, an approach that becomes relevant in rethinking authorship in this context, which is to accept these contradictions in order to reconcile them, "coupling together incompatible thoughts as if they were compatible."[189] Contradiction then becomes a tool in itself, "a two-limbed tool, like a pair of pincers,"[190] dismantling the Janus-like scaffolding of force and power, of rights and personhood, towards a postjuridical justice. On Weil's method, Andrea Nye explains, "The point ... is not to attempt to reduce or repress one or two opposing truths, but to go beyond them. We must use contradictory truths 'like a pair of pincers' to enter into contact with a higher truth."[191] Weil's pincers recall the ethology of Jakob Uexküll, who reminds us that "every animal subject attacks its objects in a pincer movement – with one perceptive and one effective arm."[192]

In order to think of authorship and indeed intellectual property beyond a binary of adversaries within this rationalised dynamic of force, it is necessary to consider the nature of attention, the payment to Tim, and the work it affords. The forceful and coercive monopoly on attention through the law's anthropocentric bias is an aesthetic challenge. Therefore, how might we begin to play with the law's aesthetic? How might we begin to imagine an intellectual property system that is more than (simply) human? This work continues with examining the nature of attention itself, its inextricable relation with affiliative knowledge and imitation, and ultimately its irreverent innovation through play. The perceived equilibrium of force and power is the straw dog of the rationality of justice and the obstacle to conceiving of more, much more, than human intellectual property.

It is time to come to attention.

Notes

1 1873–1956.
2 De la Mare (1941), 24.
3 De la Mare (1941), 24.
4 For a fuller ethological perspective on incentives and rewards in intellectual property, see Gibson (2020a), Chapter 10.
5 For a fuller discussion of this perspective on the relationship of debt and credit in intellectual property, and the seeming disregard of use in the functioning of that relationship, see Gibson (2014), in particular, 19–21, 78–82, 168–170.
6 See the discussion of learning and training in an ethological approach to incentives in Gibson (2020a), Chapter 10.
7 See further the discussion in Despret (2016/[2012]), 1–6.
8 For instance, in the lead-up to the 2016 election, see the use of Thrasymachus in the media to critique Donald Trump's approach in Williams (2016) who states, "Thrasymachus's arguments in Plato's 'Republic' are part of a larger worldview that individuals ought to disregard any pretense of moral or political obligation, objectively understood, if they inhibit our own success" and refers to Donald Trump as "a Thrasymachus for our times."
9 Dahrendorf (1968), 129. Dahrendorf argues, "it seems to me that despite his rather formidable temper and abusive language, Thrasymachus had the better arguments on his side ... with the ideas of Thrasymachus as a starting point, we can develop an image of society that helps us to understand both some basic problems of political theory and the patterns of the good society in our time" (130).
10 *Republic*, Book I, 337b.
11 Hourani (1962) notes and pursues the potential inconsistency between the two definitions of justice identified in the dialogue (namely, serving the stronger, obedience to the state) and argues that justice is a form of conventionalism (110).
12 *Republic*, Book I, 337d.

13 This is an unfortunate refrain that occurs in dog training discourse as well and in the critique of non-aversive methods of training, describing such training as a "bribe" and that the dog must not be "paid" unless they offer "work" in return, a discussion to which I will return later in this chapter. For further discussion on this relationship between reinforcement, punishment, and incentive, see Gibson (2020a) Chapter 10.
14 Bachelard (1984/[1934]), 38. Bachelard explains the practice of "trying to explain away an anomaly by introducing a perturbation." (38).
15 Bachelard (2002/[1938]), 25.
16 Bachelard (2002/[1938]), 24.
17 Bachelard (2002/[1938]), 24.
18 Bachelard (2002/[1938]), 25.
19 Bachelard (2002/[1938]), 25.
20 Adams (1986), 128. See further Chapter 2.
21 Lovelace (1843), 722. Emphasis in original.
22 Lovelace (1843), 722. Emphasis in original.
23 See T 2/83 *Simethicone/RIDER* [1984] OJ EPO 265; *Koninklijke Philips NV v Asustek Computer Corp* [2019] EWCA Civ 2230.
24 Although usually maligned and Book I often disregarded, there is a comparatively short but compelling list of various defences of Thrasymachus, only some of which are included here, beginning with the very influential Kerferd (1947) who contends that Thrasymachus is arguing that just is another's good. Henderson (1970) asserts, "I believe that Thrasymachus is consistent in essentials throughout the dispute with Socrates over the nature of justice," and further, "Socrates' most vigorous attacks fail completely to refute, or even seriously to damage, Thrasymachus' position" (218). Nevertheless, Henderson does not seek to revise radically the conventional interpretation of Thrasymachus, unlike the insightful analysis in Chappell (1993) who argues "that Thrasymachus is *not* an 'immoralist' … Thrasymachus does not *reverse*, simply hold the mirror image of, any standard moral views at all. He may believe that justice is not a virtue, but he does not, *ipso facto*, believe that justice is a vice; nor that injustice is a virtue" (12). White (1995) interprets Thrasymachus's contribution in the context of resistance to Athenian imperialism. Finally, although the analysis is less concerned with Thrasymachus's contribution and more concerned with the nature of the response, see further the discussion in Sachs (1963) who for what is termed "the fallacy of irrelevance" in the *Republic* and states that "Plato's conclusions are irrelevant to what he sets out – and purports – to establish" (141).
25 Plato's *Republic*, Book I, 344c.
26 Dahrendorf (1968), 136.
27 For example, Ferrari (1990) notes, "the blustering, overbearing Thrasymachus is portrayed more as a caricature than a character (as rudeness incarnate, so to speak) – a quality of portrayal common to all Plato's villains and buffoons … Indeed, almost the only fully drawn, complex character in the dialogues is Socrates himself. Perhaps, then, Plato was out to mimic the voice of the enemy in such a way that we, the philosophic audience, neither so young nor so unsophisticated as to require the extreme protection of censorship, would be unable to identify with it but would be prompted to laugh its venom off" (119).
28 Dahrendorf (1968), 137. See further the discussion of the outsider or stranger in an ethological context in Gibson (2020a) Chapter 9.
29 Bachelard (1984/[1934]), 38.
30 Dahrendorf (1968), 138–139.

31 Weil (2001/[1955]), 63. This resonates with contemporary mobilities methodologies in sociology through which, according to Adey (2006), "[i]nstead of fixed forms, academics are beginning to look at the relations between materiality and force" (78). Simone Weil has received little to no attention in this context, but there are notable exceptions. For example, see Karlsson (2018).
32 This is a purposeful echo of an assertion by Gadamer (1992/[1960]) that "all playing is a being-played" (106). That is, the intentionality or direction of force is reversed through the very exercise of force. In this sense, the transformative, reversibility of play overwhelms and overcomes the fictions presumed by force. This creative (in the sense of performative and productive) quality of play is examined in Part 3, particularly Chapters 7 and 9.
33 Weil (1940), 3.
34 Weil (1940), 3. See further Poole (1992): "In her *Iliad* essay Weil imagines the immunity in which the victor is cocooned, deafened and blinded to the resemblance between himself and his victims ... This imperviousness is of course a fiction, and a deeply pernicious one. The *Iliad* ruthlessly punctures these fictions, as do its heirs, the Greek tragedians. It does so through the constant reversals, large and small, in which the flick of a spear-thrust changes victor into victim ...This endless reversibility is one of the great teachings of the *Iliad*" (6).
35 Weil (2001/[1951]), 149.
36 Bachelard (2002/[1938]), 43.
37 This becomes relevant in Weil's insistence of private property, which becomes meaningful in the context of the conditionality of rights and importance of privacy and space. Weil's account of private property is considered in more detail later in this chapter.
38 Weil (1940), 11.
39 Weil (1940), 14.
40 Dahrendorf (1968), 138.
41 Relevant to this relationship between Thrasymachus's explanation of power and justice, and the treatment of force and friction in Simone Weil's philosophy of culture, together with the ongoing engagement with sentience, Innis (1994) considers perception in a pragmatic epistemology and explains that "[a]wareness as attention arises out of conflict, crisis, forking of roads in some material, a tendency to go this way and that. This can, of course, occur at all levels and in all domains of cognitive intercourse" (54).
42 Weil (1943), 18. The discussion returns to this consideration of rights later in this chapter.
43 Weil (2001/[1955]), 150.
44 Weil (2001/[1955]), 64.
45 Weil (2001/[1955]), 108.
46 See further the discussion in Chapter 3.
47 Weil (2001/[1955]), 150.
48 Hunt (2014).
49 Gibson (2020a), 136–138.
50 For example, DeScioli (2023) describes a causality between evolutionary competition and the origin of laws, but the complicity of laws in sustaining the tendency towards a competitive account of the natural world is not considered. Indeed, in many respects, the momentum of this account of natural selection in the dominant economic narrative is an example of a Panglossian paradigm and ensuring an internal consistency to a received narrative, without venturing further to question the more intimate relationship between law-making and the indoctrination of a predatory account of property and capital.

51 In particular see Darwin (1872/[1859]) Chapter 3. See further the discussion in Bradley (2022).
52 See further the discussion of altruism and cooperation and the inconsistent discourse furthering a predatory drift in property in Gibson (2020a).
53 Bradley (2022).
54 Gould and Lewontin (1979), 589.
55 Darwin (1872/[1859]), 421.
56 Weil (2001/[1955]), 108.
57 Weil (2001/[1955]), 108
58 Weil (2001/[1955]), 108.
59 For a review of the key justificatory arguments for an artificial scarcity to address failures in information markets, see Netanel (1996).
60 Kimmerer (2013), 111.
61 Weil (1951/[1950], 55.
62 To recall Bachelard's explanation of the scientist's work in Bachelard (1984/[1934]): "The scientist's work would not be truly rational but rather based on acquired *habits* of 'rationality'" (39). Emphasis in original.
63 This is immediately evident in the greater success and funding in so-called charismatic species: Krause and Robinson (2017).
64 Bachelard (1984/[1934]), 38.
65 Bachelard (2002/[1938]), 29.
66 Kashyap (2021), 1. The relationship between free play and intelligence is explored in greater detail in Part 3.
67 See the discussion on the stratification and classification of creative work in Gillick (2016).
68 For example, see the consideration of stratification in Lund (2014) and the review on videogame play as productive and creative in Jackson and Games (2015).
69 See the discussion of olfactory art in the intellectual property context in Gibson (2023a) Chapter 6.
70 Gibson (2005).
71 Gibson (2020b).
72 For example, see Jensen (2010): "[B]ecause selfish individuals will exploit cooperators, functional punishment is an effective mechanism for enforcing cooperation by deterring free-riding" (2635). See further Marlowe et al. (2011) on second-party ("spiteful") punishment and third-party (altruistic) punishment (or a form of social justice, in that it is the punishment on behalf of an anonymous third-person).
73 Weil's concept of attention is considered in more detail in the following chapter, Chapter 6.
74 Lefebvre (1991/[1974]), 190. Emphasis in original.
75 Weil (1941b), 23. Weil's concept of reading is explored further in Chapter 6. It is also a critical lens through which to approach a kinetic and expressive theory of authorship through play, which is the focus of Part 3.
76 Weil (1959c), 45.
77 4E is so named for the four "E"s – embodied, embedded, enacted, and extended. See further Newen et al. (2018).
78 Varela et al. (1993/[1991]).
79 Part 3.
80 Haraway (2016). See further the discussion in Chapter 8 of the present work.
81 Hutto and Myin (2013). Radical enactivism can be distinguished from enactivism and the suggestion of autopoietic enactivism introduced by Varela et al. (1993/[1991]). See further the discussion in Drury and Tudor (2024). See also

Haraway (2016) and the critique of autopoiesis, as distinct from the making together in sympoeisis, which arguably has much more in common with radical enactivism (as a radicalising, so to speak, away from the autopoiesis presented in enactivism). See the discussion of sympoiesis in Chapter 8 of the present work.
82 Varela et al. (1993/[1991]), 204.
83 This recalls the earlier discussion of Lefebvre's production of space in Chapter 4, and will continue to be important to understanding co-production in Part 3.
84 Varela et al. (1993/[1991]), 204.
85 Weil (1959c), 42.
86 Weil (1959c), 51.
87 Weil (1959c), 45.
88 Winch (1989), 44.
89 Weil (1959c), 51. Winch (1989) maintains that, according to Weil's view of space, "It is through our own active *movement* itself (and not just the kinaesthetic sensations associated with movement) that we reach the concept of objects in three-dimensional space" (44).
90 Lefebvre (1991/[1974]), 342.
91 Latour and Lepinjay (2009), 55.
92 Weil (1959c).
93 Weil (1959c), 31.
94 Weil (1959c), 51.
95 Weil (1959c), 30.
96 Weil (1959c), 31.
97 Merleau-Ponty (1968/[1964]), 266.
98 Onions (1966), "Habit."
99 Chapter 1.
100 Tarde (2012/[1893]), 52. Emphasis in original.
101 Tarde (2012/[1893]), 52. Emphasis in original. See further the discussion in Chapter 1.
102 Tarde (1903/[1890]), 75.
103 Tarde (2012/[1893]), 52.
104 Blomley (2016) describes something quite similar in terms of everyday boundaries: "Gardening, and the space of the garden, has a strong relationship to privacy, autonomy, and control. Yet, gardening also connects to the public dimensions of property" (230). See further Blomley (2005).
105 Ahmed (2010), 12.
106 Guadamuz (2018): "[Mr Slater] set up the tripod, selected an angle, adjusted the lens aperture, checked the lighting, and *was in the right place at the right time*. To my mind, Mr Slater did more than enough to be awarded copyright protection." Emphasis added.
107 David Slater quoted in Lawson (2015).
108 David Slater quoted in Smith (2011).
109 See the discussion of *that dog* as scavenger in Gibson (2020a), 38–43, 66–68, 222–224.
110 In 2018 Conde Nast Entertainment acquired from Slater the rights for a proposed documentary which, at this stage, does not seem to have been put into production. See further Siegel (2018).
111 See further Gibson (2024b).
112 This is developed further in relation to an ethological approach to non-fungible tokens (NFTs) as non-objects in Gibson (2024b), drawing upon Ferreira Gullar's theory of the nonobject in Gullar (1959). See further on an ethological jurisprudence of objects in Gibson (2025).

113 Copyright systems have long excluded foreign authors from copyright protection where they are not a national of a relevant international treaty (e.g., the Berne Convention for the Protection of Literary and Artistic Works): see for instance, Copyright, Designs and Patents Act 1988 (UK), ss 153–160; 17 USC, §104.
114 In the United Kingdom, the author of a photograph was the owner of the material upon which it was taken (Copyright Act 1956, s 48(1) and Copyright Act 1911, s 21) and likewise the owner of the sound recording was the owner of the tape upon which the original was made (Copyright Act 1956, s 12(8)) but ownership could vest in the person who commissioned it instead (Copyright Act 1956, s 12(4) and s 4(3)).
115 Directive 2006/116/EC on the term of protection of copyright and related rights, art 6 (member states have the option to protect non-original photographs as well, but it is unclear whether or not this is the case in the United Kingdom: Davies et al. (2021), [3–237].
116 See further the critique in Gibson (2020a) Chapter 10.
117 Charlesworth (2014).
118 See the earlier discussion of the DABUS litigation in "What Does Naruto Want?" See further the discussion in Gibson (2021a); Gibson (2024a).
119 Blackstone (1766).
120 Blackstone (1766), 404.
121 Blackstone (1766), 404.
122 Blackstone (1766), 404.
123 A clear statement of the principle is provided in Ramage (1922): "When anything is made by one man of materials belonging to another, if the thing made can be converted back to its former crude materials, then the thing belongs to the owner of the materials, for instance a vessel cast of metal can be restored to its original element; but where the thing cannot be reconverted it belongs to the maker, as wine, oil, etc" (883). See further Gibson (2024a).
124 Gibson (2024a).
125 Notably this argument of owning the technology remains one of the dominant approaches taken by advocates, so far unsuccessfully, in respect of the outputs of artificial intelligence. See further the discussion of the doctrine of accession in relation to artificial intelligence in Gibson (2024a).
126 Weil (2001/[1955]), in particular, 107–108.
127 Weil (2001/[1955]), 108.
128 Weil (2002/[1949]), 34.
129 Weil (2002/[1949]), 34.
130 Weil (2002/[1949]), 34.
131 Butlin et al. (2023).
132 Floridi (2023), Bishop (2021), Crawford (2021).
133 See further the discussion in Gibson (2021a) and (2024a).
134 US11727251B2; US10423875B2.
135 The common thread here, so to speak, is string – from string-pulling to string theory – and the fundamental forces at work – wants and energy. First, in relation to wants, string-pulling studies with nonhuman animals are utilised to identify cognitive skills and potential insight into pursuing those wants. Second, in relation to energy, string theory, an aspect of theoretical physics, has also sought to explain all fundamental interactions or forces in the so-called theory of everything. See further the review of string-pulling studies in Jacobs and Osvath (2015). For a history and introduction to string theory, see Rickles (2014). On the historical aspects and in particular, contextualising the figure of the physicist and notions of expertise, see further Dongen (2021). In a critique of quantum

theory, Simone Weil identifies energy as continuing to be "the central idea of science": Weil (1942), 50. See also the earlier discussion of string and knots in Chapter 2.
136 Weil (1943), 21.
137 Weil (1943), 18.
138 Esposito (2012/[2007]), 100. On the relationship between rights and force, Esposito notes further "the other relation of implication, the one between rights and force, this arises from applying the same measure to different situations and to subjects endowed with different powers. When this happens – in actuality, almost always – the only thing that guarantees or imposes an inevitably iniquitous sharing is force" (100).
139 Weil (1943), 21.
140 Weil (1943), 21.
141 Weil (1943), 18.
142 Weil (1959b), 166.
143 Gibson (2020a), 259. See further the detailed treatment of incentives in intellectual property, through an analysis of the stimulus in animal behaviour and conditioning, in *Owned*, Chapter 10, Shared interests.
144 Weil (2001/[1955]), 17.
145 The protagonist and agonist, *that dog*, was first introduced in Gibson (2020a).
146 For a fuller discussion of incentive theory in ethology, training, and intellectual property, see Gibson (2020a) Chapter 10.
147 Doering (2010), 188.
148 Doering (2010), 188–189. See further Weil (1943), 30 on justice and punishment.
149 Weil (1943), 30.
150 Weil (1943), 30.
151 This role of mutual belief in free will is identified also in the scientific literature. See Clark et al. (2017). Indeed, the fundamental value of cooperation in societies of animals other than human is argued to affirm the operation of free will in these relationships. See, for example, the relationship between free will and cooperation in Protzko et al. (2016).
152 See further Casey et al. (2021).
153 Gibson (2020a).
154 Weil (1943), 18. See further the discussion in Gibson (2020a) Chapter 8.
155 The basis of NILIF is that a dog must earn any desired resource – whether that is food, attention, or even a walk. In order to obtain such a desired good, that dog must request it through offering the desired behaviour. See further the discussion in O'Heare (2017), 101–102.
156 Yin (2012).
157 Miller (2008).
158 The idea of payment as a form of "equity" in dog training runs across the various approaches, from claims of force-free to heavily aversive methods. For the latter, see Cesar Millan's utilisation of the language of work and payment somewhat problematically as a form of giving a dog their "freedom." www.cesarsway.com/five-freedoms/
159 O'Heare (2017), 101–102.
160 Horowitz (2012/[2010]), 60. See further the discussion of imitation and overimitation in Gibson (2020a), 261–263.
161 Overall (2018), v.
162 Worsley and O'Hara (2018) examine dogs' skills at initiating communicating, as distinct from an emphasis on their responses to human-given referential gestures and suggest that dogs "possess impressive skills in this domain" (465).

163 Worsley and O'Hara (2018) note that training may extinguish certain behaviours that are therefore not available to an individual dog as a referential gesture, but nevertheless dogs can work flexibly to elaborate on a gesture when they do not get the desired response (462). At the same time, as well as indicating their impressive communicative skills, this points to the potential impact of training on creativity and expression, and the freedom of the individual's communications.
164 Ahmed (2010), 8. See further Rozelle-Stone (2020), 77–78.
165 Ahmed (2010), 124.
166 See in particular the discussion of labour in Weil (2002/[1949]), 123–124.
167 Part 3.
168 Weil (2002/[1949]), 120–121.
169 Weil (2002/[1949]), 81. See further Fink (2016), 21 and the discussion in Chapter 7 of the present work.
170 Weil (2002/[1949]), 93–94.
171 Gibson (2023b). See further the discussion of LLMs and the phenomenon of model collapse in Chapter 4.
172 Overall (2007), 1.
173 Seligman (1972), 408. Learned helplessness is produced by a lack of control over avoiding an aversive stimulus, resulting in maladaptive behavior including slowing of responses and ultimately a pessimistic cognitive bias.
174 Weil (1942a), 84.
175 Taylor (2010), 384. See further on the effects of unpredictability and uncontrollability of painful and aversive events in Seligman et al. (1971).
176 Overall (2011).
177 For example, sheep become more pessimistic when exposed to chronic stress (a long-term negative affective state): Destrez et al. (2013); see further Doyle et al. (2011). But Destrez et al. (2014) report that if sheep are exposed repeatedly to positive events they become more optimistic, with possible application as a treatment for chronic stress. Similarly, environmental enrichment leads to a positive emotional state and ultimately more optimistic pigs, see Douglas et al. (2012).
178 Weil (1942a), 84.
179 Piaget (1932).
180 See further the discussion of abundance and waste in Chapter 7.
181 Su (2020).
182 Su (2020), 140.
183 Su (2020), 142. Emphasis is original.
184 Su (2020), 143. Emphasis in original.
185 Su (2020).
186 Part 3 and the concluding chapter, *Law's Anecdote*.
187 Tarde (2004/[1873]), 30.
188 Tarde (1899), 165. Emphasis in original.
189 Weil (2001/[1955]), 164.
190 Weil (2001/[1955]), 164.
191 Nye (1994), 60.
192 Uexküll (2010/[1934]), 48–49.

Chapter 6

Pay Attention, Stupid

To pay attention to attention, the discussion returns to Tim, the little dog, who we met in the previous chapter. In the interaction with Tom, Tim's performance is understood as begging; or at least, it is an interpretation of begging delivered when "Tom told his dog called Tim to beg."[1] There is always a curious interaction, so to speak, between begging and attention. In this exchange between Tim and Tom, begging is a communication *of* attention rather than a request *for* attention. It is a wanting to attend, rather than a search for attention. Indeed, the interaction between Tom and Tim is a form of cooperation, a relationship of social recognition through begging, a shared interest.

There is a kind of welfare logic to begging, as well as a playful exchange. From the famous begging of Diogenes through to the begging in invitation for attention or play, this spatial logic of begging is immediately engaged. The beggar is presented as the recipient of social excess, of waste. But at the same time, the beggar is the reservoir of play. Through the disruptive intervention of the beggar, as outsider and yet at the same time invitation, the exchange also moves outside the commercial flavour, as identified by Weil, that otherwise pollutes the expressive potential of the dyadic relationship through the assumed conventions of rivalry in property and competition. How is intellectual property about begging? How does it appear to construct peasants of users and rulers of owners, with authors the beggars in the middle? The answers are the work of attention, and "in order to think, one should first have so many things to *un*learn!"[2]

Begging for Attention

It might be said that the "work" between Tom and Tim the little dog, the value-generating work to be "paid for," is that of attention itself. The logic of the intellectual property system follows a very similar accounting for attention. Indeed, in the simplest sense, copyright is a system of regulating attention, that is, of ensuring the attentional focus on the purported legitimate objects of that regulation. Regulation of this attention is thus obviated

DOI: 10.4324/9780429342103-10

through practical concerns such as access to the objects themselves, which might also be understood as the intermediary vectors for attention between parties (both producers and consumers, in the simplest sense). Attention in itself has incentive salience for play, with examples of various nonhuman animals increasing their play, with implications for wellbeing as well as for creativity, towards audience. And this includes multispecies audiences, as when dogs are seen to play more when their significant human is watching. As Clive Wynne candidly observes, "It's really quite striking that dogs who have their chance to play with each other whenever they want to, nonetheless are much more likely to get up off their butts and start playing when a person is just paying attention to them."[3] If we want to understand a productive policy environment for human authors as well, we need to pay attention to attention. This interaction with *a certain kind of attention*[4] is thus critical to an ethological approach to authorship, both in terms of its ethical dimension (and the stewardship of knowledge through *attentive imitation*) and towards exploring the motivation and pleasure in the play of authorship.

At the same time, regulation of attention is also regulation of its corollary, that is, distraction.[5] In distraction, the regulatory objective is with respect to the distraction by objects which are framed as "illegitimate" foci of attention – not only copies or infringing works but also potentially transformative examples of fan fiction, user-generated content, review, whether or not such works are legitimated through the operation of limitations or exceptions. In this circulation of attention, authors are stupid beggars, perhaps in every sense.[6] But by all accounts, so are readers.[7] It is in this reversibility of force that the insight from Thrasymachus is most important in reshaping the conceptual and practical perspective on intellectual property. The potential to step outside the frame is afforded by paying attention to attention. As Marion Stamp Dawkins counsels: "However strange and however far removed from our own ideas of what is worth having, therefore, we can find out what a particular animal wants and how much it is prepared to pay to get it if we ask it in the right way."[8]

Drive to Distraction

Creativity studies support the conclusion that creativity is assisted and facilitated by distraction – that is, "creative people have diffused or leaky attention."[9] In other words, individuals who "show the propensity to notice information that may not be particularly relevant to the task at hand."[10] This is a possible departure from the way in which information first gains attention and then is handled by artificial intelligence, suggesting the risk in due course of a possible creativity collapse, if you will.[11] In conjunction with the fundamental structural difficulties of generative AI when encountering novel facts or puzzling circumstances,[12] the future seems bound to repeat itself if only the "intellectually perspicuous" remains the focus of attention for artificial intelligence.[13] Other research supports the idea that focus on small details facilitates creativity,[14] which arguably and somewhat curiously suggests a similar propensity to distraction in that such detail, once again, diverts attention away from the main subject – a distraction from the woods by the trees. This cultural and productive capability through distraction is also at work, so to speak, in Walter Benjamin's writings; indeed, Benjamin is distracted by distraction throughout, perhaps most notably in his writing on art and technological or mechanical reproducibility.[15]

Benjamin notes the way in which contemplation and distraction are socially constructed in respect of art, a stratification that maps along similar territories in intellectual property discourse. Conventional approaches to aesthetics have understood the appropriate manner of appreciating art to be that of "disinterested attention" and the appropriate deference or "distance."[16] This focused contemplation (or attention) is associated with the bourgeoisie, and with related pretensions of education and aesthetic taste. Notably, this attention of the spectator has its correlative in the conventions of the copyright author and, as Jane Ginsburg suggests, "the noble calling of disinterested creativity."[17] But within her rhetorical question of copyright as a possible "wasteful windfall" lies the very potential for expressive expenditure.[18] What does it mean to waste in this context?

This distance between author and reader, between subject and object, is important. As a kind of wasteful form of attention, as it were, distraction is associated with the masses, the uneducated and the feckless, the downright *stupid* before the genius of art. Georges Duhamel's account, in *Scènes de la vie future*,[19] of the inattention of the masses as encouraged by cinema is an important example of this social stratification through attention to high art, as distinct from the low art of the cinema. In other words, there is a line in the sand drawn between attentional focus to legitimate works of high art on the one hand, and improvident and useless distraction of low culture on the other. Duhamel proclaims: "The cinema is a pastime for slaves, an amusement for the illiterate, for poor creatures stupefied by work and anxiety … It is spectacle that demands no effort, that does not imply any sequence of ideas, that raises no questions."[20] Benjamin is critical of this characterisation of the masses, which would go on to be co-opted by contemporary malign political agenda.[21]

But distraction is like the shipwreck, exposing both the contradiction and the potential in the disarray. As Benjamin explains, "[T]he distracted masses absorb the work of art into themselves. Their waves lap around it; they encompass it with their tide."[22] In a review[23] of the 1929 exhibition, *Gesunde Nerven*,[24] Benjamin sets out clearly the promise and insight of distraction. The exhibition, overseen by Benjamin's friend, Ernst Joël,[25] was concerned with the psychological impact of the social conditions of urban workers and potential responses and changes to those conditions. But notably the review focuses more closely on the presentation of the exhibition itself and the impact on the meanings made as the visitor moves through the exhibit; particularly in play. The apparent juxtaposition of play and the fairground context is explained through the commentary on labour, play, and creativity: "What lends this exhibition its particular character is not so much its dioramas, banners, and dissolving views ... but rather this technique of making the visitor participate actively ... What does all this mean? It means that real presentation banishes contemplation."[26]

This emphasis on the mode of display invigorates and *enacts*[27] the *Umwelt* of the spectator's experience, where their consciousness, as it were, manifests through play rather than languishes within the search for the content of their beliefs. In this way, "the *direct experience* of this subject-matter of *mind* and *consciousness* implies that it is *empirical*. Instead of theorizing about an abstracted notion of what *mind* and *consciousness* are ... they are directly *experienced*."[28] *What is it like to be a spectator?* And through its garlanded entrance, the exhibition is literally curated through the *metaxu*. The playful attention becomes a kind of "knowing groundlessness" facilitated and understood through the distraction of "*experiencing* that just remains open for everything without any preferences."[29] In other words, this is a knowing arising through paying attention to the "irrelevant aspects of the environment."[30] But who says they are irrelevant?

Distraction thus becomes the facility for creativity and insight and fundamentally that distraction is *contemplated*, in this way, in play. Indeed, part of the exhibit was concerned with the domination of the worker's time, and thus the worker's opportunity for revitalising distraction. An example of this is in one of the slogans displayed as part of the exhibition: "'The "breakthrough" of the eight-hour day robs the worker of the chance to participate in the achievements of culture. This is the death of all mental hygiene.'"[31] Benjamin suggests, "If anything is missing, it is at the entrance to the show, where the curator should have found a place for this sentence, borne out so brilliantly by their works: 'Boredom [*Langeweile*] breeds stupidity; diversion [*Kurzweil*] enlightens.'"[32] This suggestion is fascinating in the context of current appeals to make artificial intelligence *boring*.[33] While this is related to objectives in making artificial intelligence mainstream and unremarkable, what is striking is that this aim is to be achieved by becoming so dominant in the discourse that the room for distraction is overwhelmed by the fatigue and exhaustion created by the topic.[34]

The notion of attention and distraction as simple opposites, as irreconcilable contradictions, needs work and refashioning as *a pair of pincers*, to recall Weil's phrase. This concept of contradiction as a legitimate tool is meaningful here; examining the seemingly incompatible concepts of attention and distraction involves, "recognizing them as such, and in making of them as it were the two arms of a pair of pincers."[35] Thus, for Benjamin, the account of attention as a kind of "*disciplinary technique*"[36] or "disinterestedness,"[37] the very kind of attention proffered and prosyletised through aesthetics by Duhamel and others of the time, demands attention: "The fact that this new mode of participation first appeared in a disreputable form should not mislead the observer. The masses are criticized for seeking distraction [*Zerstreuung*] in the work of art, whereas the art lover supposedly approaches it with concentration. In the case of the masses, the artwork is seen as a means of entertainment; in the case of the art lover, it is considered an object of devotion. – This calls for closer examination."[38]

Film, according to Benjamin, presents a particular challenge to linear time and space presented through film, generates a new audience and a new work. Benjamin explains: "The film makes the cult value recede into the background not only by putting the public in the position of the critic, but also by the fact that at the movies this position requires no attention. The public is an examiner, but an absent-minded one."[39] This distraction introduces the play in the rope, "a little play into the cogs of the machine."[40] Benjamin identifies this distracted shift in Dadaism and its challenges to the institutional definitions, exhibition, and reception of art: "Dadaism attempted to create by pictorial – and literary – means the effects which the public today seek in film."[41] Indeed, this distraction not only upsets the hierarchy and proposed chronology between author and spectator but also introduces a kind of play in the production and consumption of art – play that would be introduced by the Dadaists and pursued passionately by the Surrealists through playfulness and games.

But in so doing, this is not a game of winning or losing, a finite game of means and ends. On the contrary, it is play that is in itself disruptive, productive, and generative of further play, as André Breton explains: "What I cannot bear are those wretched discussions relative to such and such a move, since winning or losing is not in question. And if the game is not worth the candle ... is it not fitting and proper to avoid all contact with those categories?"[42] This game play thus transforms aesthetic attention from dispassionate distance to distracted intimacy, and from attainable objects to the pleasure of the play. The wants are no longer the ends but the means in what Servaas van der Berg describes as "the inverted motivation or motivational feedback loop" in the concept of "striving play."[43] *What does the player want?* What is striking about this form of aesthetic attention is that it is both decentred and decelerated; that is, it is a form of learning which is both elemental and playful.[44] There is no *quick fix* to the end without frustrating the motivation of the means. *To want* is what Naruto wants.

In an aesthetic that is resonant with play, Benjamin describes a kind of somatic experience that recalls Weil's sensory account of reading: "From an alluring appearance or persuasive structure of sound the work of art of the Dadaists became an instrument of ballistics. It hit the spectator like a bullet, it happened to him, thus acquiring a tactile quality."[45] It is also without goal, or without ends; that is, it is without immediate functional purpose or application, the very definition itself of play.[46] The mythology of the author and the authorial gaze is thus thrown and de-throned through an uncertain and non-linear motion.

The nineteenth-century poet and essayist, Charles Baudelaire, was especially interested in the impact of photography and new technologies of art and he perceives this emphasis on the effort "to reproduce reality identically"[47] in his critique of photography. In ways strikingly relevant to contemporary concerns with the cultural impact of artificial intelligence, Baudelaire's work is critical of the overwhelming concern with the mimetic tradition in these forms of technology, and the ignorance, as it were, of the expressive fragments of originality. It might be said that Baudelaire's concern was not a fear of technology but the loss of the critical distance that is discernible in the seemingly transformative and iterative relations between works, through parody, pastiche, and caricature. Parody, it would seem, and as will be considered in much more detail later, is the stuff of which authorship is made.[48] This critique resonates with Weil's concept of reading and the relevance of reading to perceiving the consciousness of the author more widely – that is, reading as a sensory and subjective experience, which is at the same time enduring and unfinished.[49] The question of whether artificial intelligence can parody is for discussion later, but importantly, this aesthetic in the relations *between* works is both insistent upon and motivated by the unfinished nature of art.

The sociologist and philosopher, Jacques Ellul, whose twentieth-century writings in technology studies remain profoundly influential, describes the unfinished nature of art as something that has been facilitated and encouraged by technological change: "Modern art is by nature a succession of unfinished works which condition one another. There is no longer … *one* work. No work seeks to attain the finished, the eternal, the equipoised, the perfect, because no technological means is ever exhausted, it is never really anything but a sketch for something more efficient to come."[50] This fragmentary, anecdotal nature of art, as described by Ellul, accords with the nature of the sociality of imitation and innovation that is set out in Tarde's interpsychology, and it will be revisited in the very genre of the literary fragment itself in later discussions. But as will be seen, it is also through this relationality that the social justice of the system might be realised. This sociality and relational quality of not only the creative interactions but also the expressions themselves may be felt to resonate in Ellul's comment on the generation of meaning through art's technologies: "[A]t the same time, no technology exists for itself, with its own internal meaning: it has no sense except in relation to all the other technological systems."[51] There is no central point in a sphere, as it were.

While also acknowledging this necessary imperfection and incompletion in art, Anthony O'Hear, on the other hand, sees technology as masking these imperfections as well as obscuring the attending social stratification achieved through mass production: "Great art, in Ruskin's view, is never perfect, or finished like machine work. We, as human beings, are fallen and multiply imperfect; it is the aim of mass production, of the division of labour and of technological aids to production to occlude this fact."[52] For O'Hear, the problem facing any move to accept "purely machine-produced art" as art is that "it necessarily lacks those references, explicit and implicit, to human life and sensibility, which make art more than a purely formal exercise,"[53] or an algorithm, if you will. In this perspective O'Hear anticipates the very explainability problem that attends artificial intelligence, and at the same time the radically simplified "intelligence" that departs from an expressive theory of authorship.[54] How can anything *novel* arise in the aggregation and summation of existing patterns and trends? As Douglas Hofstadter explained back in 1979, intelligence is by *reason*, as it were, of analogy. That is, humans (and in indeed nonhuman animals as it turns out[55]) are able to pull off the trickery and chicanery of metaphor and parody. Artificial intelligence, on the other hand, is bound by the banality of its biddability. On the matter of artificial intelligence, is this intelligence that is artificial, as in grass?[56]

These various perspectives on technology in art may seem irreconcilable at first, but in fact these oppositions coalesce in contemporary productions through LLMs and generative AI, including examples from visual art.[57] The collectivity of the so-called "masses" and the sociality of games in Dadaism and Surrealism are of immediate interest here. These games will be revisited again later through the affective community of play, with the deferral of the object in favour of a kinetic theory of authorship through play.[58] But for now, what is emerging is a disruption to the traditional focus and motivation attributed to aesthetic attention, a disruption brought about through the distraction of play; play that is without purpose, without end, always already unfinished.[59]

What Benjamin recognises in film, may also be recognised in music – in other words, the significance of distraction in music among the *masses*, away from *the work of art* that is as otherwise recognised within the frame of copyright. Listening to music is to listen in a *productive* state of distraction, encompassing it within the tide of musical references. John Cage opines, "It is better to make a piece of music than to perform one, better to perform one than to listen to one, better to listen to one than to misuse it as a means of distraction, entertainment, or acquisition of 'culture.'"[60] What is particularly interesting here is Cage's use of distraction. While it appears to be negative, what it suggests more quietly is how distraction may be co-opted in coercing attention onto the "work" – copyright's "attention bias,"[61] if you will. That is, distraction might be a tool to divert attention away from a work's sources, away from the questions the work asks; this is how music might distract from other music, not in the commercial sense of a sea of commodities but in a socially and culturally disingenuous sense of the silence of the sources.

Let's Get Loud

The New York jury trial[62] in the copyright dispute over alleged similarities between Marvin Gaye's and Ed Townsend's *Let's Get It On*[63] and Ed Sheeran's and Amy Wadge's *Thinking Out Loud*[64] is a wonderful retelling of these stories. Ultimately the jury found in favour of Sheeran,[65] and while this may be the end of the matter legally, for many reasons it does not address the many questions that arise from this dispute and in music copyright litigation more generally. In opening statements, Benjamin Crump, a civil rights attorney and a member of the plaintiffs' legal team, stated: "If you remember nothing else about this trial, about this case, it is about giving credit where credit is due."[66] This may sound like a familiar refrain in discussions around music copyright, but it raises a particularly important question in the present context; namely, that of stewardship. In other words, how does music reference and acknowledge its sources? This may sound like a peculiar question, but it is the one raised by music itself.

There is an identifiable bifurcation in the logic of music. On the one hand, the industry and surrounding discursive norms continue to facilitate the tenacity and celebrity of the romantic genius, apparently endorsed by the wider institutional norms facilitated through copyright. Indeed, much of the reporting around the *Loud* dispute focused on Ed Sheeran's celebrity and career, including his *back story* of spending his life writing music. But particularly notable was his challenge or even ultimatum delivered during testimony that if he lost the case he would give up music, something of a threat which then became the headlines for the press that day.[67] This proclamation recast the dispute, even if only momentarily, to focus on the value of Sheeran and his future contributions to the industry, rather than the specifics of the attribution question before the court.[68] This moment, troubling as it was, was seized by the press and disseminated and repeated widely. Sheeran was reported as testifying, "If that happens, I'm done, I'm stopping ... I find it really insulting to devote my whole life to being a performer and a songwriter and have someone diminish it."[69] After winning, Sheeran declared, "[L]ooks like I am not having to retire from my day job after all."[70] A further curious detail was that Sheeran's newest album, *Subtract*, was then released just hours after the win[71] to resoundingly positive reviews that focused on Sheeran's personal life and proclamations of singular genius.[72] In fact, at least one reviewer of the new album opened with reference to Sheeran's threat to quit music and pointed to the new album as evidence of "why that would be a shameful loss to music."[73]

Throughout the lawsuit, the press and surrounding discourse focused entirely on Sheeran and the Sheeran authorial brand, despite the song being co-written by his frequent collaborator and co-defendant, Amy Wadge, who remained somewhat and curiously absent from the authorial celebrity attached to the song and immune to further scrutiny in the press.[74] Similarly, the adversary was frequently referred to as the Marvin Gaye song or hit, despite the plaintiff being the estate of Gaye's co-writer, Ed Townsend.[75] A further complication was that while Sheeran could perform his songs in court, the confinement of the copyright to the sheet music meant that *Let's Get It On* was performed by a somewhat alienating artificial intelligence. It came down, at least as it played out in the press, to a battle of the brands.

Contrary to this genius narrative, the imitation and traditions of music progress through referencing and distraction that is identifiable throughout the history of music. In terms of the social tie that might be ascertained, arguably this is where the real value and sociality of music is to be found – that is, "the harmony among ideas."[76] In part, Sheeran's team acknowledged this when focusing on the "building blocks that have been freely available for 100s of years."[77] However, rather than suggesting a functional and shared language, as was Sheeran's conclusion, this may make the argument for attribution even stronger. Each song asks its own questions, implicates its own precursors, begging for attention and relevance through that referentiality. In a way, the song is just a placemark for that proliferation of sociable meaning elsewhere. Part of the proficiency and social value in that meaning is thus through credit, regardless of whether this constitutes technical attribution and joint authorship – that is, credit for one's precursors. As John Cage says, "Music means nothing as a thing."[78] The idea of completing a work is thus disconcerting and even impractical in that sense: "A finished work is exactly that, requires resurrection."[79] In other words, if presented, presumed, and consumed as a discrete artefact, a mere sign of celebrity, it is finished, in every sense. Resurrection is through reanimating music through its interaction with other music, the relations between imitations or *imitative rays*.[80] Instead of pretending at uniqueness, perhaps music should become more *courteous*,[81] more academic, more open about its shared spaces and the ethological properties of music. Indeed, the only way "new" music is possible is through attribution – *a certain kind of attention* through recognising and acknowledging sources. Attention – paid for.

Compare commercial music instead to an academic text. In an academic text, acknowledging sources is itself a highly original activity. It is no doubt a familiar experience, reading an academic text and becoming distracted usefully and agreeably by the many rabbit holes in the sources and notes, fresh wants to be pursued. As such, the academic text functions as sociality, as affiliative property; whether distracting in its familiarity and recognition, or gesturing towards novel objects, the text operates as a bridge (*metaxu*) between the various sources through which readers approach that text, readers that include the author. Acknowledging precursors, as well as seeking out subsequently further examples of agreement, and synthesising sources past and future, are all crucial to the originality of the text. As well as potentially dishonest, without such attribution the text is hollow, empty, *finished*. And further, without such attribution of inheritance and intergenerational debt, innovation is simply not possible; all movement stops, the play ends.[82] As such, creative work is always an apprenticeship and, as Weil explains, "every apprenticeship is an apprenticeship in reading."[83] The commercial machinery of the music industry, on the other hand, is wedded to the singularity of celebrity and the hiding of sources in the presentation of genius. This is the problem of representation, long considered in film with its treasured sense of self-referentiality, and the attention drawn to its own representedness through the ideological apparatus of the frame.[84] Rewriting provenance not only masks the genuine originality of critical distance but also leads to a frustration of wants when listening with genuine attention. That is, the drive, as it were, to distraction is thwarted. *Naruto wants to play.*

John Cage's remarks also signal an especially important issue raised in music as well as in discussions of potential plagiarism more widely, relevant also in the *Loud* dispute. Acknowledging others is something quite different from sharing authorship, and this is perhaps the major conceptual obstacle in the context of copyright and the commercial context for music. The stewardship of knowledge is a critical, cultural and social issue; and it is one that is problematically and illegitimately qualified and enfeebled by the narrower notions of ownership in the commercial object, as defined in the more limited legal perspective. Credit in music is an example of the reach of copyright as a wider institutional norm, going beyond its bounds to interfere with the welcome distraction of music. A relation of genuine stewardship is not necessarily safeguarded through copyright's account of limitations and exceptions; rather, extra-legal norms of stewardship are critical and vital. Attribution is thus not only a discharging of obligations with respect to the author but also a recognition and responsibility to the legacy and stewardship of knowledge, and a purposeful counter to the potentially colonising impact of plagiarism.[85]

The question in the immediate case is whether without such attribution there is the risk that the relationship between *Thinking Out Loud* and *Let's Get It On* is an "acquisition of 'culture'."[86] This is a question wholly separate from any technical question of copyright infringement, and certainly not answered by its limited protections alone. But it is perhaps the most important question that is persistently unanswered and one which also went largely unreported.[87] Although raised by Crump at an earlier news conference[88] it was not raised in the trial because copyright sets the parameters much more narrowly.[89] Indeed, facing this question, reviving meaningful and honest dialogue through credit, might actually go some way to mitigating the apparent proliferation of music copyright litigation[90] and restore the sociability of music-making: *res familiaris*.[91] The result is the imitation of imitations, a sociable result through the relational properties of shared interests. Tarde explains that innovation is motivated and propelled by a legacy and progression of "imitative radiation," through the concept of imitative rays, which he explains as "connecting each imitator, through a chain of intermediaries."[92] Attribution, as fragment, becomes an expressive quality in itself.

An Ethological Attention

The fundamental quality of an ethological attention is empathy – the desire and capacity to attend affectively to others and to othered perspectives. It is to listen in the active way described by Weil: "To listen to someone is to put oneself in his place while he is speaking."[93] Thus, the quality of certain attention is considered and demanding: "Because affliction and truth need the same kind of attention before they can be heard, the spirit of justice and the spirit of truth are one. The spirit of justice and truth is nothing else but a certain kind of attention, which is pure love."[94] Crucial to this kind of attending is the stewardship of knowledge and knowledge-holders. Thus, attribution and acknowledgement, regardless of any practical considerations as to rights, are crucial and inextricable qualities of this attention. This is why an ethological jurisprudence is of critical importance in the context of *handling* traditional knowledge and traditional cultural expressions. At the same time, it is of utmost relevance to understanding the value underpinning unique relationships to virtual and infinitely replicable objects, as in non-fungible tokens (NFTs).[95] While objects may be the mechanisms by which connections may be promised or remembered, and by which knowledge may be afforded or renewed, it is the connections themselves that sustain the ecosystem. Indeed, as commodities, the primary function is in sustaining the circulation of capital.[96] Thus, an ethological jurisprudence of property critiques the expropriation of the principles in the vassals of objects and attends to the relations and connections that underpin the basic and fundamental legal and customary philosophies of property in the widest sense. A sense of ownership in the place of that connection does not change, nor does this account vary any rights in a work; but it does shift the cultural process by which works of copyright are understood, acknowledged, and proceed in circulation and in the intergenerational stewardship of ideas.

A *certain kind of attention* is thus one that is not seeking attention but rather is seeking to attend. Attention is thus fundamentally dyadic in nature, always already a property *in personam*. In an 1877 issue of *Mind*, George Henry Lewes described attention thus: "In the special usage it is distinguished from all other psychical states by a peculiar reflected feeling of Attention, whereby we not only *have* a sensation, but also *feel* that we have it."[97] This reflected feeling, as described by Lewes, resonates with the sociality inherent in attention as attending. And it is also in this sense that attention becomes creative, and indeed that an *attentive* imitation becomes original. As Weil declares, "Love for our neighbour, being made of creative attention, is analogous to genius."[98]

This *certain kind of attention* is crucial in addressing the violence of the anthropocentric frame. The overwhelming reliance on data and empirical objectivity is criticised by Weil for what amounts to a disingenuous distraction from genuine attention, a crucial concern in her writings on reading (*lecture*), introduced earlier. Ann Pirruccello explains that Weil "rejects the empiricist view that there is a body of perceptual data – brute sensations or facts – that is given independently of any interpretive framework ... Thus, the world comes to us in a mediated fashion."[99] Drawing upon Weil's approach to develop an "epistemic pluralism," Shari Stone-Mediatore identifies the privileged attentions in "patriarchal, capitalist, and colonialist power relations that have mystified the epistemic standpoint and styles of elite European men,"[100] and critiques the complicity of an emphasis on scientific distance and objectivity, as distinct from the kind of intimacy and compassionate knowing in Weil's attention.[101] And in the presentation and perpetuation of prejudice and bias, as well as misinformation, in the outputs of artificial intelligence,[102] it would appear that artificial intelligence, by reason of its very design, cannot offer anything other than an inattentive attention and an uncritical and *thoughtless stereotypic imitation*.

An ethological attention exposes and unsettles the anthropocentric norms that characterise both the law and the available remedies for juridical *others* (nonhuman animals, as well as authorship rendered outside the conventions of copyright, as in traditional cultural expressions). Stone-Mediatore contends, "Weil's concept of paying attention offers a framework for shifting epistemic practices in less rigid, more community anchored, and more pluralistic directions."[103] These directions, or indeed distractions, resonate with the very basis for an ethological jurisprudence – namely empathy.[104] An ethological jurisprudence is a necessary and welcome nuisance to objectivity, an irritant to linearity, towards a fundamental revision of the relationships in the triadic gaze of producer, consumer, and object in intellectual property.[105] Perhaps, as Donna Haraway suggests, "That is the play of companion species learning to pay attention."[106] Companion species of the human kind.

The quality of attention, *a certain kind of attention*, is thus important for the way work is created, recognised, transmitted, and sustained – and imitated (*attentive imitation*). And it is this sustainability of knowledge that is arguably the anchor for all these questions. The ways in which nonhuman animals acknowledge those who went before have both somatic and intellectual dimensions, as well as an inextricable relationship with environment or space.[107] This spatio-temporal knowledge-keeping in nonhuman animal cultures is consistent with Weil's account of a bodily knowledge, a comprehensive perception, taking into account all of the senses, perspectives, and questions. Fundamentally, it is a sustainability of knowledge grounded, so to speak, in empathy. Imitation itself thus becomes a kind of empathy, even might be said to rely upon empathy, in order to flourish. The nature of any conscious understanding through attention is a question of genuine imitation – an *attentive imitation*.

A Matter of Time

The meaning of attention itself encompasses care as well as waiting and patience,[108] the kind of waiting that Weil insists is intrinsic to attentive attention. Attention comes from the root *attendre* which encompasses both waiting (to wait) and a more affective prosociality in the form of expectation (to expect).[109] At the same time, the root *tendere* (stretch)[110] corroborates this outreach and receptivity of attention. In this coalesced meaning of expectant waiting, the "certain kind of attention"[111] of which Weil speaks makes sense in terms of her understanding of intention as a "negative effort."[112] There is much in common between Weil's attention and Benjamin's distraction, enough to fashion a fine pair of pincers for the task ahead.

Weil is careful to note that the desired kind of attention is not that of the focus on a question but the kind of wider and possibly even distracted, in Benjamin's sense, of reception to experience and phenomena: "Most often attention is confused with a kind of muscular effort … contracting their brows, holding their breath, stiffening their muscles … They have been concentrating on nothing. They have not been paying attention. They have been contracting their muscles."[113] Indeed, trying to apprehend an object is counter-productive; to engage John Cage in refrain, *a finished work is exactly that*. As Cage maintains, "The responsibility of the artist consists in perfecting his work so that it may become attractively disinteresting."[114] In other words, a certain kind of attention is to engage distraction, to focus indistinctly, to hold attention.

Attention is concerned also with patience. We are to wait, as Martin Andic explains, "in patience, setting aside everything that is not the good, attentive in silence, immobility, and love," and in this sense, "[a]ttention is the task, discernment is the reward."[115] In his development of a methodology of critical anthropomorphism,[116] which was also considered in earlier chapters, Gordon Burghardt notes the way in which the study of animal cognition has itself been constrained by this impatient anthropocentric framing of attention: "Ethologists have frequently argued that the field of animal learning has left out comparative, ecological, and evolutionary considerations in its rush to formulate general principles. A push for this impatience certainly arose from a primary interest in human learning and the desire to use controlled 'scientific' studies with animals to legitimize applications to people."[117]

This cautionary tale of *rushing* in ethology is immediately relevant to the velocity of the artificial intelligence industry. A similar rush has been criticised repeatedly in both the science and the rhetoric of artificial intelligence, as "an uncontested rushing toward a simplified and innocent gold future, often setting aside the social, political, and economic complexities, contradictions, and pitfalls that go along."[118] Douglas Hofstadter questions this rushing and advocates "the far slower but authentic and reflective voice of *a thinking, living human being*."[119] Indeed, an early voice in artificial intelligence, Hofstadter cautioned against following a simple rules-based pattern for programming intelligence back in 1979, advocating an attention to the critical faculty for analogy:

> Personally, I would guess that such multilevel architecture of concept-handling systems becomes necessary just when processes involving images and analogies become significant elements of the program – in contrast to processes which are supposed to carry out strictly deductive reasoning. Processes which carry out deductive reasoning can be programmed in essentially one single level, and are therefore skimmable, by definition. According to my hypothesis, then, imagery and analogical thought processes intrinsically require several layers of substrate and are therefore intrinsically non-skimmable. I believe furthermore that it is precisely at this same time that creativity starts to emerge.[120]

But it would seem that the programme of development that Hofstadter advised as necessary to reach any form of computational understanding was perhaps too slow for the impatience of the artificial intelligence industry, more concerned with the race than the artefacts of "generic platitudes and fluffy handwaving."[121] And so it would seem it has gone largely unheeded, with "the illusion that vast computational systems 'who' have never had a single experience in the real world outside of text are nevertheless perfectly reliable authorities about the world,"[122] disguised by the hype and mirrors.

The law, too, leaves much out in order to ensure its functionality. The selectivity applied in rendering the original and dividing the world into property and public domain leaves much to the imagination, as it were. At the same time, arguably advocacy-based approaches to animal interests are somewhat similarly compromised in the rush for general principles of personhood and the trophy of rights. What is required in the regard for nonhuman animals, and indeed in all of these narratives, is the scrutiny of a new attention to the concepts themselves, not the demand for the extension of their application. What if the nonhuman animal was always already a person? Burghardt lamented as early as 1984 that "animal operant conditioning work ... with few exceptions, has continued to focus not only on rat lever pressing and pigeon pecking but has become insular, extremely esoteric, and removed from most of the concerns and issues of other students of animal behavior."[123] In his revolution of the anthropocentric landscape for cognitive science, Burghardt calls for "a true integration of ontogeny and phylogeny, ethology and experimental psychology."[124] Despite these comments being made decades ago, the adherence to a narrative of biological causality and predictability has persisted in various ways.[125] As William Desmond notes, in defence of a strategic anthropomorphism, "Our anthropomorphic language has always to fight any temptation to think that the otherness of being is merely the mirror in which we recognize ourselves. In fact, what we need are metaphors with the power to decenter us towards the otherness of nature, metaphors that truly carry us (*metapherein*) into the community of the between."[126]

Perhaps in the rush for personhood, the general principles needed to examine the concept itself, not merely its application, are being neglected. Perhaps attention to the social person, for *want* of another word perhaps, introduces a cultural dimension to personhood, quite apart from the *commercial flavour* or economic imperative, so to speak, of the matter of personhood. For this, the discussion must attend to genuine imitation.

Genuine Imitation

Tarde rejects the general understanding of a society as "a group of distinct individuals who render one another mutual services," as a "wholly economic notion, a notion which bases the social group upon mutual helpfulness."[127] Similarly, Tarde also rejects "a purely juristic conception of society," arguing that "it unduly restricts the social group, just as the economic point of view unduly enlarges it."[128] Further, to define a society by political or religious social ties "would constitute a true social relationship," but it is a definition that Tarde considers too narrow.[129] The limitation of these definitions is to be found in the concept of reciprocity that articulates them, a relation which Tarde understands to be in the discharge of mutual service and largely regulated by force.[130] If society is to be defined as such, then it may lead to perverse social outcomes; the serf will have a stronger social tie with their noble, than the ties between free citizens or those of the same class, and so on.[131] In making this distinction, Tarde appears to be concerned to maintain the distinction of human society from other animal societies, although he admits nonhuman animal societies elsewhere in his discussion. For example, in lauding the research of Alfred Espinas in *Animal Societies*, Tarde notes the "true societies of a psychological nature like ours, which are the privilege of the vertebrates and the higher insects."[132]

As the journey proceeds, it will be seen that Tarde's concept of imitation may be restored meaningfully on behalf of nonhuman animal societies, their creativity and innovation, particularly through its contribution to the concept of shared interests and further differentiation in the concept of *attentive imitation*. Nevertheless, some commentators have identified a concern for preserving the human sphere as part of this distinction. Anthony King notes, "Expedient exchange based on mutual interest could not be the basis of human society, as far as Tarde was concerned. Not only did such a definition of mutual service potentially reduce human culture to a natural order, it also allowed polities based only on coercion to be defined as genuine societies."[133] But the key distinction between a form of evaluative imitation (and the generous, abundance of recitation that prolongs play) and a coerced, rules-based imitation (and the kind of winning and losing that ends play) informs the concepts of *attentive imitation* and *stereotypic imitation* respectively. This distinction is fundamental to the concept of shared interests and an ethological attention to intellectual creation.

Tarde explains: "The reciprocity is gained, to be sure, by force; but that fact is insignificant if the economic point of view is the primary one and if we think that it is bound to encroach more and more upon the juristic point of view."[134] A true society is, according to Tarde, one that is based on juristic relations: "We have erred in thinking that societies in becoming civilised have favoured economic at the expense of juristic relations. In doing this, we forget that all labour and service and exchange is based upon a true system of contract."[135] It is in this sense that Tarde's concept of juristic relations resonates with Weil's "certain kind of attention"[136] and an ethological approach through shared interests. Distinguishing mutual interests and shared interests is thus critically important to an ethological account of imitation and its role in social creativity and innovation, and thus in deciphering the creativity in *attentive imitation*.

Tarde rejects a simple definition of mutual interests in that this is a relationship that can be achieved by coercion and force (*stereotypic imitation*), as distinct from the intentionality Tarde recognises in the social ties of imitation (*attentive imitation*). For Tarde, imitation is a conscious phenomenon, driven by desire or wants, therefore ushering in concerns of intentionality and regard: "[W]hat is imitation? A special type of action exercised from a distance by one mind on another."[137] Following Tarde, this kind of conscious imitation "is the elementary and characteristic social fact"[138] and the basis for society: "[W]herever there is imitation, whether among men belonging to different societies, between man and the animals he has domesticated, or even among members of the so-called sociable species of animals, there is a society or the beginning of a society."[139] Imitation is thus not mechanical or coerced; rather, it is conscious and evaluative. In other words, to imitate is to pay attention.

The distinction between the potential coercion or disconnection involved in discharging mutual interests, and the convergence and attending in shared interests is crucial for recognising imitation as a form of attention and in acknowledging and celebrating imitation as creative or innovative. Another way of considering this distinction is in terms of acting *in the best interests of* rather than individuals holding an interest – that is, *having an interest in* (*attentive*). In the context of nonhuman animals, the first may be understood, at least in part, as a conventional approach to welfare; the second, however, revises that relationship and the kind of property that may arise through welfare, or welfare property on a path to personhood.[140] Further, it is important to recognise here the difference between imitation as a form of consumption, and imitation as a desire to produce. *What does Naruto want?* Indeed, the social tie of imitation, as understood by Tarde, is consistent with familiar production through play and other performances of sociality.[141]

Conversation Pieces

As the fundamental social tie, the basic desire or want of a society, imitation, like attention, is a doubling or dyadic relation. In this sense, the basic want (that of imitation) is necessarily prosocial. Taking these qualities together, the fundamental activity in the attention of imitation is that of curiosity, of seeking to attend, of investigating in the pursuit of further knowledge. And as a fundamentally dyadic enterprise, the dialectic of curiosity is thus a conversation piece, so to speak. Tarde attributes to curiosity "a special, if not the chief, place of honour,"[142] noting that the recognition of curiosity in another contributes to the spread of interest, and thus the imitation of curiosity itself: "When a person is seen to be curious about what once may have appeared to be the merest trifle, we immediately desire to know about it. This movement spreads very quickly, and the intensity of everybody's desire increases in proportion to its spread, through the effect of mutual reaction."[143] There is some coherence here with Gadamer's approach to understanding in the imitation and repetition of tradition at the foundations of society: "*Understanding is to be thought of less as a subjective act than as participating in an event or tradition*, a process of transmission in which past and present are constantly mediated."[144] Thus, understanding is always in dialogue, in the word between us: "*The true locus of hermeneutics is this in-between.*"[145]

This seeking or investigative quality of curiosity as not only the acquisition of knowledge but also its production (or perhaps they are the same thing) plays a part in the psychology and philosophy of William James, and the understanding of curiosity as a creative faculty where a kind of imitation is part of a productive curiosity. A productive curiosity is outgoing, open, and prosocial, rather than fearful of new objects (including, it would seem, knowledge objects).[146] And similarly, in nonhuman animals, neophilia, or the attraction or enthusiasm for what is new or novel, is considered both a predisposition to creativity as well as an openness that is consistent with creativity and innovation.[147] As James states, "Inasmuch as new objects *may* always be advantageous, it is better that an animal should not *absolutely* fear them. But, inasmuch as they may also possibly be harmful, it is better that he should not be quite indifferent to them either."[148] In this way, the fundamental desire or want to produce is the fuel for curiosity both in terms of its attention and its production, as well, it is argued, as part of play. Indeed, the relationship between curiosity and play reveals the limitations of a utilitarian approach to knowledge ends, as distinct from the means of knowledge production – the so-called distracted wanderings of "useless knowledge,"[149] or the purposeful wandering of distracted attention, the exuberance of curiosity and pursuing the wants of curiosity in play.[150]

In *The Play of Animals*, published in 1898, Philosopher and psychologist, Karl Groos,[151] charts this critical relationship between curiosity, attention, and play: "In Curiosity is the only purely intellectual form of playfulness that

I have encountered in the animal world. It is apparently a special form of experimentation, and its psychologic accompaniment is attention."[152] Groos explains that such attention "finds a playful expression in curiosity, which may be called sportive apperception."[153] The notion of a sportive attention persists today but arguably has lost the openness and investigative qualities as originally conceived, with instead the conventional contemporary emphasis on focus, concentration, and "contracting muscles"[154] now dominant. In this notion of "intellectual playfulness,"[155] Groos establishes play as an intellectual event and argues that "[t]he necessity for mental exercise is the primary reason for this kind of playfulness, added to the increase of knowledge" and "preservation of the species."[156] At the same time, this intellectual dimension to play, as understood through curiosity, imputes an authorial perspective to play as intellectual creation. While a fuller discussion of play must wait until the next chapter, it is nevertheless important at this stage to recognise the critical connection between this kind of affiliative knowledge and learning, and an aesthetic sense in both human and nonhuman societies through the kind of "building" that is *made* through imitation and play.[157]

This Play of (Social) Force

Recall the play of Thrasymachus through the dialectical play of questions, considered in the previous chapter. In this Platonic dialogue, play produces juristic relations. Similarly, Benjamin's play of repetition resonates with this ludic rhythm. And importantly, these perspectives coalesce and coincide in Tarde's view of the attention of imitation in the sociality of juristic relations and innovation. In other words, curiosity in play has not only an attentive quality but also makes a critical contribution to the imitation and repetition at the heart of juristic relations. Play has a morality related not only to the players but also to the observers drawn in and attending. Examples of animal play show that engaging the attention of the observer also welcomes the observer into the play, expanding the moral dimension of play.

And on this question of the observer, or the audience, there is considerable insight to come from nonhuman animals on the manners of attention and audience which contribute to understanding the social competence and creative capacities of more than human authors. For example, dogs definitely pay attention to attention and will make certain judgments of humans based upon the quality of the humans' attention, and perhaps resulting ultimately in their own inattention.[158] Attention will also increase their own communicative and prosocial attempts at attention when their own humans gaze directly, that is, pay more attention,[159] suggesting a facilitation of the conversation, in a manner of speaking, through the attention to attention. Such studies show the way in which attention begets attention, questions lead to more questions, imitation leads to more (creative) imitation. In other words, attention has social and affiliative value, leading to a kind of communicative entailment, as is explored a little later. Notably, when dogs in play receive attention from their humans, this facilitates such sociality between all the dogs in play, that play is enhanced and prolonged.[160] Similarly, cats use social referencing with attentive humans,[161] and so do pigs.[162] And it should perhaps go without saying that these crucial social qualities of attention are not limited to mammals, with sociality being studied and demonstrated across a range of species, including fish,[163] and of course ants, Ants maintain a range of relations throughout their agricultural enterprises and farming,[164] as well as in their capacities for social and associative learning through attention.[165] And a certain kind of attention is of course a critical quality of associative learning, imitation, and thus cultural diffusion. Bees, to name a few, are literally buzzing with these traditions.[166]

Françoise Wemelsfelder suggests that part of the inattention to the nonhuman animal's subjective experience is explained by "their misguided conception as 'causal objects' in mechanistic models of behaviour,"[167] and that subjective experience is thus always hidden and inaccessible. But Wemelsfelder contends that paying attention to "attentional style" allows for an approach to subjective experience, through the phenomenal consciousness of what it is likeness: "[S]ubjective experience should be approached on its own conceptual grounds ... in terms of 'what-it-is-like-to-be' a particular individual animal ... The animal is perceived as an agent, whose perspective on a given situation is manifest in the way in which it interacts with and pays attention to that situation."[168] And in fact, in order to recognise the expressive nonhuman animal subject, as Wemelsfelder contends, attention itself emerges as a phenomenal quality: "Attention is not a by-product of the ability to process information, it forms the very condition for that ability, enabling the animal to use information acquired in the past in a flexible and adaptive manner."[169] In this way, the manifest behaviour or conduct, "is throughout characterised by active attention for detail, by an active effort to relate to a particular environment and become intimately acquainted with it."[170] And notably, just as it is argued throughout the present work, for Wemelsfelder "[p]lay perhaps is the ultimate manifestation of such diversification. A playing animal may appear unfocused, aimlessly lingering over a particular aspect of the environment, but by indulging in attention as an end in itself, it may actually be practicing effective agency."[171] And that agency may be understood through the authorship of one's own environment, if you will. Indeed, it is through attention to their attention, that it is possible to approach what it is like to be Naruto.

Thus, *attentive imitation* through play disrupts the usual narratives of authorship and property, and it does so through an abundance of productivity through playful attentions.[172] Gadamer describes what "turns the play into a show," and declares that "openness toward the spectator is part of the closedness of the play. The audience only completes what the play as such is."[173] This perspective can be recognised in ethologies of play where, as we have seen, the attention from a nonhuman animal's significant human will actually facilitate play, enlisting and implicating the human in that worldmaking.[174] In this way, attention literally gives the game away. Meaningful attention, as it were, must be recognised for the way in which it is in itself an incentive to creativity; a *wasteful windfall*. For Gadamer, this demonstrates "the importance of defining play as a process that takes place 'in between,'"[175] that is, approaching understanding through the relations between players as well as in the between (*metaxu*).

Thus, play is something that is always already a dialectic – between players, or between player and world: "Play develops its driving force in a relation: playful curiosity as striving towards the other."[176] This opening out is critical to an understanding of phenomenal consciousness through play. As Gadamer explains: "[P]lay does not have its being in the player's consciousness or attitude, but on the contrary draws him into its dominion and fills him with its spirit. The player experiences the game as a reality that surpasses him."[177] This opening out through play thus resonates with the curiosity of attention as a seeking to attend, and at the same time, shows play as a critical social relation through which juristic relations of morality, property, and creativity are established. As such, play is a kind of questioning, a multi-sensory attention through an interlocutory of familiar production.

There is a specific passage in Plato's *Laws* that attests to this very relationship between play, morality, and legitimacy in social relations. But in this dialogue between Cleinias and the Athenian, who remains an unnamed stranger throughout, the emphasis is instead upon the social disruption through play. The stranger, the unnamed Athenian, declares that, "introducing some novelty or doing something unconventional to shapes and colours and all that sort of thing," is "the biggest disaster any state can suffer," and that the playful innovator is "the biggest menace that can ever afflict a state, because he quietly changes the character of the young by making them despise old things and value novelty."[178] In other words, play disrupts the force of coercion and control, at the same time introducing the ingenuity of novel perspectives and ways of being. As the Athenian pronounces, "I maintain that no one in any state has really grasped that children's games affect legislation so crucially as to determine whether the laws that are passed will survive or not."[179]

To return to the play of questions, the originality in the uncertain is profound. Throughout the certain kind of imitation in attentive play, an expressive and enactive creation is made out through *attentive imitation*. And as Gadamer explains, "historically effected consciousness ... is an element in the act of understanding itself, and as we shall see, is already effectual in *finding the right questions to ask*."[180]

Questions of Attention

Thus, the right kind of attention is one which is creative. That is, it is one which asks questions, not just answers them: "[A]ttention is a matter of the relationship between questions and what counts as answer to those questions."[181] The questions asked will always presume a certain vantage point, or particular reality or emphasis; thus, the reinscription of anthropocentrism's ontological and epistemological frame. But that fourth wall is knocked down in play.

It is important to recognise the privileged sites of attention that frame these questions of authors and persons. Gadamer's critique of historical objectivism provides particular insight here as to the projection of inevitability and supposed worldliness of questions that are otherwise wholly complicit in reaffirming anthropocentric bias. Gadamer explains: "In relying on its critical method, historical objectivism conceals the fact that historical consciousness is itself situated in the web of historical effects."[182] In so doing, the pretensions to objectivity are achieved through the selection and disguising of the fundamental presumptions underpinning that *objectivity*: "In this respect, historical objectivism resembles statistics, which are such excellent means of propaganda because they let the 'facts' speak and hence simulate an objectivity that in reality depends on the legitimacy of the questions asked."[183]

And indeed, it depends upon the legitimacy of the senses engaged.[184] When it comes to intellectual property, the preponderance of the visual renders invisible the kind of creative attention that may be recognised in nonhuman animals, such as smell and touch. Similarly, attention studies have mimicked the visual hegemony that can be ascertained in intellectual property. Together, the objectivity depends upon failing to recognise that already situated perspective of a so-called objective account; or as Gadamer explains in relation to historical objectivism, "it preserves its good conscience by failing to recognize the presuppositions – certainly not arbitrary, but still fundamental – that govern its own understanding."[185] Behaviour research was early to distinguish between qualities of attention in humans and non-humans, with attention becoming an aspirational achievement.[186] The ability to distinguish and take decisive attention action in the context of competing stimuli became associated with a higher order of thinking, with a capacity to have ideas and to hold them.[187] But an absence of attention, when confronted by all the wrong questions, is readily dismissed as a cognitive deficiency; *stupidity*, as it were. It is arguably in play studies where the radical potential for the "explainability" of sentience, consciousness, and other presuppositions of obstacles to nonhuman authorship may be revealed. As Henning Eichberg declares, "Play is a bodily-practical way to *answer* the world. But primarily, it is a way of *asking* the world."[188]

Ant(e) Up

But what if Tim, Tom's little dog, were to be paid in advance for his playful attention? What might this mean in the context of attribution and stewardship? One of the most frequent objections to food rewards in dog training discourse is that the treat is little more than a bribe, and one of my favourite retorts to this criticism comes from Skinner himself, in the application of positive reinforcement in children's education: "A bribe is something paid to induce someone to do something illegal or wrong. Those who call positive reinforcement bribery are confessing to a very low opinion of school work."[189]

In many ways this summarises many of the issues in play here in the question of conscious imitation and learning on the one hand (*attentive imitation*), and coercion and force on the other (*stereotypic imitation*). It is this same tension that is manipulated in intellectual property through artificial scarcity, instead of abundance through innovation in imitation, keeping in mind that use is itself a form of imitation. The generosity of attention through access to imitation in the context of stewardship may then be imagined as possible, rather than an impoverished and secondary imitation that is permitted through the contrived scarcity of objects. The kind of imitation effected through coercion is not a genuine social tie at all; but "[j]uridical solidarity," Tarde explains, "has, on the other hand, a purely social character, because it presupposes the kind of similarity that is due to imitation."[190] In other words, *attentive imitation*.

While attention capitalism is usually understood as built upon the commodification of attention, a greater concern is the attention bias that is coerced, trained, and indoctrinated through capital's presupposed objectivism. Indeed, if attention is such a resource, one that competes with all the other stimuli in the creative environment, then when Tim pays attention, who is really in debt here? Both Tim and Tom have incurred costs, in the same way that both producers and consumers incur costs – arguably a mutual investment felt even more acutely in a digital environment. A shift away from the separate spheres of mutual services towards a convergence in the concept of shared interests introduces a welfare dimension to intellectual property as well as a different perspective on interspecies cooperation; away from the emphasis on economic solidarity and towards an ethics of juridical solidarity and attention.

An Ethological (In)Attention

In her memoir, *The Turquoise Ledge*, Leslie Marmon Silko, of the Laguna Pueblo nation, writes of experiences of interspecific attention while tending her garden, including the rattlesnakes shading from the heat, her pots of daturas and their collaborations with the hawk moths. And, in particular, Silko writes of the grasshoppers. When one of the grasshoppers reaches the end of their life cycle, Silko collects the body to draw. She begins but then stops working on the portrait, variously distracted or dissatisfied, and leaves it unfinished before going into the garden to watch the rain. It is then that she comes across a message from Lord Chapulin.[191] Silko writes, "I noticed another of the big colorful grasshoppers under the mesquite tree by the front porch. It looked me in the eyes, and I knew at once this grasshopper was a messenger from Lord Chapulin."[192] And the message? "Get back to work."[193]

In the next and final section, the work is to be done. And perhaps it changes everything if that work turns out to be done through play. What if the facility of creativity is the conviviality of musement? The mischief of distraction? What might happen if an artificial curiosity were permitted to roam free?[194] Or if rationality were to be unbound?[195] Play is both revelry and liberty, candour and deception, and it is about motive and chance; at the same time play means space and freedom. Play opens out, and as seen earlier, the creativity of authorship is afforded by the latitude and leeway of that space. It is this play in the rope, the string to be pulled, that must be explored next.

The stage is world-making, we are all the playing animals. Let us now play our regards.

Notes

1 De la Mare (1941), 24.
2 Bachelard (1989/[1935]), 112. Emphasis in original.
3 Clive Wynne quoted in Editorial (2021a). See further, Mehrkam and Wynne (2021).
4 A refrain with Weil's writings on attention. See further Weil (1943), 28.
5 It is notable that this inextricable relationship between attention and distraction is central to dog training discourse, despite the rhetorical focus on force. Indeed, force-free methods ordinarily invoke distraction as a positive method for addressing unwanted behaviours (in other words, directing energy and curiosity into another behaviour), thus focusing on attention as distinct from force and marking a significant and crucial distinction between the two poles of dog training. As the following chapters show, distraction can be revised as a positive value in intellectual property as well, in respect of imitation and innovation. See further the discussion in Gibson (2020a) Chapters 7 and 8.
6 See Thomas et al. (2022) on authors' earnings in the United Kingdom.
7 The concept of reading (*lecture*), introduced in the previous chapter, is a central concern for Simone Weil and one which is inextricably tied in with the concept of attention. In the *Essay on the Concept of Reading*, Weil sets out her sensory account of reading and meaning, which will be revisited more fully in the chapters in Part 3. See further Weil (1941b). Weil's reading of reading is also crucially resonant with the kind of sensori-motor meaning-making observed in cognitive ethology and embodied cognition (see further Part 3 of the present work).
8 Dawkins (1993), 149.
9 Zabelina (2018), 162. See further the discussion of daydreaming and pretend play in Russ (2020). Pretend play and pretence are considered in more detail in Chapter 8.
10 Zabelina (2018), 162.
11 On the problem of recursion and model collapse in LLMs, see Shumailov et al. (2023); Herel and Mikolov (2024). See further the discussion of model collapse in Chapter 4 of the present work. See also Gibson (2023b).

12 Smith (2024). The puzzle problem, as it were, for artificial intelligence is considered again in Chapter 8.
13 Bachelard (1984/[1934]), 38.
14 Zabelina (2018), 162. See further, Nusbaum and Silvia (2011).
15 Benjamin (1935). See the original three versions of the essay, *The Work of Art in the Age of Mechanical Reproduction*, published under the title, *The Work of Art in the Age of Its Technological Reproducibility*, in Benjamin (2010/[1935]). See further the second version in Benjamin (1936b); and the third version in Benjamin (1939).
16 Dickie G (1964).
17 Ginsburg (2009), 387.
18 See further the discussion of expenditure, abundance, and waste in Chapter 7.
19 Duhamel (1930). Published in English in 1931 as *America, the Menace: Scenes from the life of the future*.
20 Duhamel (1931/[1930]), 34.
21 Smith (2023), 199.
22 Benjamin (1936b), 119. This metaphor is not included in the more common version published in *Illuminations* under the title, The Work of Art in the Age of Mechanical Reproduction: Benjamin (1935).
23 Benjamin (1930).
24 *Gesunde Nerven* (Sound Nerves) opened at the Gesundheitshaus Kreuzberg (Kreuzberg Health Building) in October 1929: Benjamin (1930), 64 n1.
25 Ernst Joël (1893–1929) was a German physician and researcher in addiction who also supervised exhibitions at the Gesundheitshaus. He was also a close friend of Benjamin, who participated in some of Joël's hashish experiments. See Benjamin (1930), 64–66 n2. Joël died prematurely and suddenly just two months before the exhibition opened, and Benjamin's review pays tribute to "the memory of a remarkable man" (60).
26 Benjamin (1930), 62.
27 An enactive cognition is explored in more detail through play in Part 3.
28 Meling (2021), 11. Emphasis in original.
29 Meling (2021), 7. Emphasis in original.
30 Meling (2021), 7.
31 Benjamin (1930), 63. This productivity in play is examined in more detail in Chapter 7.
32 Benjamin (1930), 64.
33 For example, see Liu (2022); Tyree (2022).
34 Other articles express sentiments that share some similarities with Benjamin's perspective on distraction when it comes to accounts of the impact of technology on creativity. For example, see Chamorro-Premuzic (2023).
35 Weil (2001/[1955]), 150.
36 To borrow Sara Ahmed's term in relation to happiness, as discussed in the previous chapter. See further Ahmed (2010), 8.
37 Stolnitz (1961). Compare Dickie (1964). The concept of psychical distance became dominant from the early twentieth century and arguably persists in discourse surrounding art and its cultural value today: see further, Bullough (1912); Longman (1947); Dickie (1961); Sabattini (2019).
38 Benjamin (1936), 119.
39 Benjamin (1935), 233–234.
40 Weil (2001/[1955]), 114.
41 Benjamin (1935), 230.
42 Breton (1929), 8.

43 Berg (2019), 464.
44 This coincides meaningfully with the kind of cognitive enrichment that occurs through training without force: Fernandez (2022). See further in relation to chimpanzee welfare, Angley et al. (2024). See also the discussion in Gibson (2020a) Chapters 7 and 8.
45 Benjamin (1935), 231.
46 Burghardt (2005), 71–78. See further the discussion of play in Chapter 7 and throughout Part 3 of the present work.
47 Grøtta M (2012–2013) Reading/Developing Images: Baudelaire, Benjamin, and the Advent of Photography, *Nineteenth-Century French Studies*, 41(1–2), 80–90, 82.
48 See further Chapter 9.
49 Notably, Stephen King in King (2023) also distinguishes the capacity of artificial intelligence from the concept of reading in the wider sense, maintaining that in order to write one has to read, but "can a machine that reads learn to write?"
50 Ellul (1979), 830.
51 Ellul (1979), 830–831.
52 O'Hear (1995), 156. Ruskin (1951) famously declared, "[N]o good work whatever can be perfect, and *the demand for perfection is always a sign of a misunderstanding of the ends of art*" (171). Emphasis in original.
53 O'Hear (1995), 150.
54 On this lack of understanding, see Bishop (2021). See further the discussion in Gibson (2023b).
55 See further Chapter 9.
56 Smith (2024) says, "It's called artificial intelligence but it is really fake intelligence."
57 Gibson (2023b).
58 See further Part 3.
59 Relevant here is the account of play in Suits (2014/[1978]) and the concept of "open games" as subverting the emphasis on ends with attention to means – that is, to the game itself. Play becomes its own motivation or want, and its own form of aesthetic attention. This is considered is more detail in Chapter 7.
60 Cage (1961), 64. Coincidentally, Cage was also one of the contributors of a piece of wooden nickel art to Dave Morice's *Wooden Nickel Art Project*, discussed in Chapter 3. See Morice (1988).
61 In ethology and behaviour sciences, attention bias is defined as "the tendency to drive or sustain attention to specific stimuli or types of information before others": Siniscalchi (2022), 548. Attention bias may be influenced by social and environmental concerns, as well as the impact of observers (discussed further later in this chapter).
62 *Structured Asset Sales LLC v Sheeran and others* (SDNY 2023) 18 Civ. 5839.
63 *Let's Get It On* (1973), Marvin Gaye and Ed Townsend (songwriters and producers).
64 *Thinking Out Loud* (2014), Ed Sheeran and Amy Wade (songwriters), Jake Gosling (producer).
65 Pavia (2023).
66 Benjamin Crump, Opening Statement, *Structured Asset Sales LLC v Sheeran and others* (SDNY 2023), 18 Civ. 5839, 25 April 2023.
67 Geraghty (2023); Chilton (2023); Welsh (2023).
68 Keisha Rice, representing the Townsend estate, addressed the jury: "Mr Sheeran is counting on you to be very, very overwhelmed by his commercial success," quoted in Lee (2023).

69 Sheeran quoted in Geraghty (2023).
70 Sheeran quoted in Lee (2023).
71 Harrison et al. (2023).
72 Petridis (2023); McCormick (2023); Ruggieri (2023).
73 McCormick (2023).
74 For instance, Wadge remains unnamed and is referred to simply as "a collaborator" in Sisario (2023). Notably, Wadge otherwise is named in a quote used to caption a photograph.
75 Pavia (2023).
76 Tarde (1899), 166. Tarde explains: "Invention, if we limit the term to that which is destined to be imitated (for what remains locked up in the mind of its creator, has no social value), – invention, I say, is a harmony among ideas, which is the parent of all the harmonies among men" (166).
77 Sheeran quoted in Mier (2023).
78 Cage (1961), 64.
79 Cage (1961), 64.
80 Tarde (1899). See further the discussion in the chapter, "What Does Naruto Want?"
81 See further the discussion of property and courtesy in Gibson (2020a) Chapter 3 where the contention is that an ethological approach restores relations otherwise rendered unnecessary to the operation of a predatory property model.
82 Gadamer (1992/[1960]): "*all encounter with the language of art is an encounter with the unfinished event and is itself part of this event*" (99). Emphasis in original.
83 Weil (1941b), 26. See further the discussion of creativity in learning in Gibson (2006), 138–139.
84 Baudry (1974).
85 For example see: Baily and Trudy (2018) 768; Pham (2017). See further Okediji (2022).
86 Cage (1961), 64.
87 Compare Sisario (2023).
88 Crump stated, "Mr Sheeran blatantly took a Black artist's music who he doesn't view as worthy of compensation," quoted Sisario (2023).
89 Sheeran's team wrote to the judge a week prior to the commencement of the trial, stating, "We respect Mr Crump's right to raise institutional concerns he may believe exist, but not in this case and not in this forum." Quoted in Sisario (2023).
90 Sheeran posted a video to Twitter in 2017 where he stated, "I feel like claims like this are way too common now and have become a culture where a claim is made with the idea that a settlement will be cheaper than taking it to court, even if there is no basis for the claim. It's really damaging to the songwriting industry": quoted in Mier (2023).
91 See further Gibson (2020a) Chapter 12.
92 Tarde (1902), 5. Translation mine.
93 Weil (1943), 28.
94 Weil (1943), 28.
95 Gibson (2024b).
96 Recall on the role of commodities as maintaining the circulation of money in Weil (2001/[1955]), 105. See further Gibson (2014), 194–195.
97 Lewes (1877), 159. Emphasis in original.
98 Weil (1951/[1950]), 90.
99 Pirruccello (2002), 480.

100 Stone-Mediatore (2013), 87.
101 Stone-Mediatore (2013), 89. In a discussion of empathy, Aaltola (2013) engages Weil's concept of attention as a framework for heed or regard, acknowledging the work of Barbara Smuts in embodied cognition as an example of this thought. See further Pick (2012) and the approach to veganism through Weil's attention "as a worldly mode of engagement that acknowledges the realities of violence … that gives shape to animal ethics, conjoining openness of love with the delimited and bound systems of law" (69).
102 See further Reed (2024).
103 Stone-Mediatore (2013), 91.
104 Gibson (2020a), 266.
105 Gibson (2020a), 4–7 (objectivity) and 136–138, 291–292 (triadic nature of property).
106 Haraway (2008), 19.
107 For example, see the discussion of scent and territories in Gibson (2020a) Chapter 4 and see further on olfactory works in Chapter 6.
108 Onions (1966), "attention." The root *atendre/attendre* means "wait for" as well as "expect."
109 Onions (1966), "attention."
110 Onions (1966).
111 Weil (1943), 28.
112 Weil (1942c), 55. This comes from the collection *Waiting on God*. A point of interest is that in later editions of this work, reprinting nevertheless the same 1951 translation, the title would change to *Waiting for God* (Weil (2009/[1950]). These iterations themselves, interesting in and of themselves for what they shift about the nature of attention, also led to an interesting distraction from the current discussion in my own interaction with the seller of the first edition, who was at great pains to reassure me it was indeed the same book, despite the "anomaly" in the title. What is fascinating is that the authority of the "original" has been supplanted by the subsequent edition, notwithstanding the identical translation. Another later translation by Bradley Jersak (2012/[1950]) is entitled *Awaiting God* and includes an introduction by Weil's niece, Sylvie Weil, the daughter of her brother André Weil, the mathematician. Iterations and citations matter.
113 Weil (1942c), 54.
114 Cage (1961), 64.
115 Andic (1993) 138.
116 Burghardt (1988); Burghardt (2007). See further the discussion in Gibson (2020a), 5–7.
117 Burghardt (1984), 684.
118 Bareis and Katzenbach (2022), 870. See further Robinson (2024); Grace (2023).
119 Hofstadter (2023). Emphasis in original.
120 Hofstadter (1979), 570–571.
121 Hofstadter (2023).
122 Hofstadter (2023).
123 Burghardt (1988), 684.
124 Burghardt (1988), 684.
125 Pence (2020) notes the schism in comparative psychology motivated by a self-consciousness as a discipline and an anxiety concerning comparative methodology: "Eager to distance themselves from the 'ghost hunters,' many adopted a rhetoric hostile to the use of testimony or anecdote" (9). A more detailed engagement with testimony and anecdote in comparative psychology is undertaken in

the next section, towards the value of anecdote in law in the concluding chapter, *Law's Anecdote*.
126 Desmond (1995), 424.
127 Tarde (1903/[1890]), 59.
128 Tarde (1903/[1890]), 59.
129 Tarde (1903/[1890]), 60.
130 Tarde (1903/[1890]), 60.
131 Tarde (1903/[1890]), 60–61.
132 Tarde (1969), 82.
133 King (2016), 50.
134 Tarde (1903/[1890]), 60.
135 Tarde (1903/[1890]), 61.
136 Weil (1943), 28.
137 Tarde (1969), 96.
138 Tarde (1969), 96.
139 Tarde (1969), 97.
140 Gibson (2022b)
141 The relationship between play, imitation, and familiar production is examined in detail in the final part, *Mercury*.
142 Tarde (1903/[1890]), 196.
143 Tarde (1903/[1890]), 196.
144 Gadamer (1992/[1960]), 290. Emphasis in original
145 Gadamer (1992/[1960]), 295. Emphasis in original
146 James (1890b), 429–430.
147 Kaufman and O'Hearn (2017), 494.
148 James (1890b), 429. Emphasis in original.
149 Abraham Flexner's significant account of the importance of "useless knowledge" in the sciences is immediately relevant here and will be picked up again in more detail in relation to a critique of the utilitarian model of knowledge production in Chapter 7, where the concepts of usefulness and waste are addressed in more detail. See further Flexner (1939).
150 The relationship between curiosity and play is considered in more detail in Chapter 7.
151 Walter Benjamin regarded Groos's work on play very highly, describing it as "pioneering": Benjamin (1928), 121.
152 Groos (1898), 214.
153 Groos (1898), 214.
154 Weil (1942c), 54.
155 Groos K (1898), 214.
156 Groos K (1898), 214.
157 Eugen Fink speaks of the production of a playworld: "Every sort of playing is the magical production of a playworld ... We play in the so-called actual world but we thereby attain a realm, an enigmatic field, that is not nothing and yet is nothing actual": Fink (1957), 25. Drawing upon Gadamer's concept of dialogue-play, Vilhauer (2013) describes this world-making through play and explains: "It is the path by which we learn, grow and flourish as human beings. A failure to engage in play, or a refusal to work through new meaning with others (with all the risks and growing pains involved) results in a kind of stunted growth, alienation, and even a limitation of our own possibilities ... Genuine dialogue-play, I think we are justified in asserting, is ultimately *good for us*!" (82). This ethics of play resonates with the making of meaning and reconciliation of contradiction through the genuinely juristic relations of the "between" particular in this

passage from Vilhauer: "It is not the life of an observing spectator, nor the life of a mind alone in its own thoughts (as the Cartesian tradition has trained us to believe). It is the life of a fundamentally open, involved, receptive and responsive being-in-the-world, moving in a back-and-forth communicative dance with other" (83). See further Vilhauer (2010). Similarly, play is an element of transmission of novelty in knowledge and new behaviours: Kaufman and O'Hearn (2017), 498. See further the more detailed discussion of play in Part 3 of the present work.
158 Mongillo et al. (2010)
159 Ohkita et al. (2016).
160 Mehrkam and Wynne (2021).
161 Zhang et al. (2021).
162 Moscovice et al. (2023).
163 Leadner et al. (2021). This impact of the observer is considered in further detail in Chapter 7.
164 Ness et al. (2009). See further on the capacity for attention in smaller brains in Chittka and Niven (2009); Chittka (2022), 120–121, 147.
165 Reznikova (2018).
166 Chittka (2022), 128–134.
167 Wemelsfelder (1997), 75. See further 77–79.
168 Wemelsfelder (1997), 75.
169 Wemelsfelder (1997), 81.
170 Wemelsfelder (1997), 81.
171 Wemelsfelder (1997), 81.
172 See further Gibson (2020a), 317–318.
173 Gadamer (1992/[1960]), 109. An interesting example from photography of this enlisting of the audience in the making of both the meaning and the work is offered by Audet (2007) in discussion of Lynne Cohen's work, and the space in which the work persists: "[T]hey invite the spectator to get involved in the *reading* of the images ... It is on the mode of virtuality that the narrative operates in Cohen's photographic work" (15).
174 See further the discussion of significance of the observer in play in Chapter 7.
175 Gadamer (1992/[1960]), 109.
176 Eichberg (2016), 120. Fink (1957) explains that while some games may be played alone, play is nevertheless a "fellowship" and "a fundamental possibility of social existence," noting that even in solitary play, "being open to possible fellow players is already included in the sense of play, and, in the second place, such a solitary person often plays with real persons" (23). See further the discussion of the creation of meaning in Fink's concept of play in Boronat (2016). Play as a creative fellowship resonates in part with Gadamer's concept of dialogue-play and the openness and meaning-making of play, explored in more detail in Part 3.
177 Gadamer (1992/[1960]), 109.
178 Plato's *The Laws*, 797b.
179 Plato's *The Laws*, 797a–797b.
180 Gadamer (1992/[1960]), 301. Emphasis in original.
181 Koralus (2014), 27.
182 Gadamer (1992/[1960]), 300.
183 Gadamer (1992/[1960]), 301.
184 Recall the discussion of the olfactory mirror in Horowitz (2017), and Gibson (2020a), 156, 311–317.
185 Gadamer (1992/[1960]), 301.
186 Washburn (1908), 293–294.

187 Washburn (1908), 294
188 Eichberg (2018), 217. Emphasis in original. Eichberg notes: "Playful curiosity, seeking, and expectancy may constitute an alternative understanding of play, connecting it with the phenomenon of putting questions to the world" (120).
189 Skinner (1990/[1979])
190 Tarde (1903/[1890]), 64.
191 In Mexico, Chapulin means large grasshopper, but throughout Central America it is also an informal term of endearment to mean child, thus introducing a further meaning of stewardship and care in Silko's story.
192 Silko (2010), 183.
193 Silko (2010), 183.
194 Kashyap (2021), 1.
195 Recall the bounded rationality of Simon's Ant in Chapter 4.

Part 3

Mercury

From the sparks of the ant heap to the mischief of Mercury, let us play with fire, for "[t]he flame intensifies the pleasure of seeing beyond what is usually seen. It compels us to look."[1]

A few decades ago, William Fifield went in search of the elusive quality of "genius" in a book transparently titled *In Search of Genius*.[2] But one of the things that emerge in that book is the important opportunity of "looking aside,"[3] the kind of distracted attention recommended in "[t]he 'looking aside' in enormous concentration not on the subject but on something *else*."[4] Fifield describes this quality of attentive inattention in Koestler, explaining, "You find what you are not looking for, in *big* discoveries ... and the process is one of *looking aside*."[5] This leads Fifield to grapple with the tension between the subject and object, between subjective experience and the exterior "truth," and the "caloric heat" of looking aside: "The bolt forward exemplifies the value of distraction."[6]

Indeed, it is fitting that the following chapters of such productively distracted wandering should be undertaken in the companionship of Mercury, the consummate traveller. But in this heated tale, it was another Mercury – or Hermes, or more specifically, the teachings of Hermes Trismegistus[7] – who led to the development of what is known as Hermetic alchemy, the influence of which is said to have "extended far beyond the realm of soul remaking and creative writing."[8] Hermetic alchemy engages harmony through paradox and contradiction,[9] and as Weil counsels throughout her writings, we must embrace contradiction. Alchemy was banned in England by King Henry IV in 1404,[10] at the time decried as wanton magic in the quest for fake gold. The anxiety had less to do with the nature of the product and more to do with the fear of mass devaluation of gold from alchemical substitutes flooding the market; *looking aside*, it seems a curiously anti-competitive strategy on a very early question for intellectual property, perhaps. But the popularity of alchemy surged again during the Romantic period of the sciences, and during the time of Sir Isaac Newton. But if we are to get a measure of this heat, so to speak, perhaps the *genius* to turn to is not Sir Isaac Newton – but *looking aside* to Newton's dog, Diamond.

DOI: 10.4324/9780429342103-11

As well as his work in thermodynamics and the entropic chaos that agitates the following chapters, Newton was also known for his contribution to optics and diffraction, a concept taken up by contemporary scholars of new materialism.[11] Indeed, as the following chapters will explore, it is through the prism of play that a vivid spectrality is afforded to the issues under discussion. But Newton's dog is also a force of *diffraction* (and creative distraction) by the very name itself – Diamond.[12]

And of course, among all these trajectories of enquiry, Sir Isaac Newton – scientific revolutionary, mathematician, philosopher, and reputed dog lover – was also a dabbler in alchemy and the occult sciences. And in a way, Newton's alchemy is arguably the "extrascientific" basis of force and the momentum for gravity[13] and thus perhaps also for Weil's universal necessity of moral gravity.[14] However, the extent of Newton's fascination with alchemy and its "force of attraction" may never have been quite so illuminating, if not for the intervention of that little white dog, known as Diamond, and the legendary "inflammation" of the topic. The story goes that Diamond upset a candle, setting fire to manuscripts containing notes developed over the past twenty years: "O Diamond! Diamond! thou little knowest the mischief thou hast done."[15]

As the legend goes, Newton had several dogs, but Diamond was his favourite, and Diamond's name brings together Newton's fascination with optics and his love of that little white dog. Whether Newton ever owned or befriended dogs is contested, and the tale has been described as at best apocryphal.[16] But like all good anecdotes, that is perhaps neither here nor there. Nevertheless, in response to the argument that the story is fiction, a claim arising on the basis that one would not remain so calm in the face of such chaos, one nineteenth-century commentator explains that Newton was clearly a dog lover and, quite simply, was showing nothing more than the appropriate respect for Diamond: "[N]o one who felt any attachment to a dumb animal would strike it for so unintentional an act."[17]

And then in December 2020, around 330 years later, those same notes, never published by Newton, but permanently marked by Diamond, were sold at auction for almost £380,000.[18] If it had not been for Diamond, Newton's fascination with alchemy might never have become so valuable.

But a more recent example comes from Toby, John Steinbeck's setter puppy. In 1936, Toby managed to find the first draft version for *Of Mice and Men* and shred it. Steinbeck recorded the event:

> Minor tragedy stalked. My setter pup, left alone one night, made confetti of about half of my manuscript book. Two months work to do over again. It set me back. There was no other draft. I was pretty mad, but the poor little fellow may have been acting critically ... I'm not sure Toby didn't know what he was doing when he ate the first draft. I have promoted Toby-dog to be a lieutenant-colonel in charge of literature.[19]

And perhaps Toby did know what he was doing. The "confetti" he created, surviving in the form of a solitary fragment,[20] was auctioned in late 2023 and achieved $13,000, around four times what was achieved for Steinbeck's sword in the same catalogue.[21] People know art when they see it. And at the same time, Toby no doubt changed the course of the novel. But for *that dog*, who knows?

Diamond and Toby, indeed turned Mercury into Gold.

Let's go digging.

Notes

1. Bachelard (1988/[1961]), 2.
2. Fifield (1982).
3. Fifield (1982), 107, 184.
4. Fifield (1982), 184.
5. Fifield (1982), 107. Emphasis in original.
6. Fifield (1982), 184.
7. Also variously referred to as Mercurius Trismegistus.
8. Healy (2014/[2011]), 12.
9. Healy (2014/[2011]), 51.
10. 5 Hen IV c 4: (trans) "It is ordained and established, That none from henceforth shall use to multiply Gold or Silver, nor gold or silver, use the Craft of Multiplication: And if any the same do, and be thereof attaint, that he incur the Pain of Felony in this Case."
11. Barad (2007), 71–94.
12. Diamond's very name is itself a somewhat "magical" metamorphosis, from carbon into the crystalline form of diamond.
13. Cohen (1999), in an analysis of the philosophical dimensions of the *Principia*, notes the alchemical influence on the analysis of force and suggests that Newton's alchemy might have been, in fact, essential to that work: "Alchemy seems to have given Newton an overall philosophical or conceptual framework that allowed forces to be primary elements of nature's operations. It is even possible that without such a framework, he might have been reluctant to develop a system of physics based on forces, one in which a central place would be given to the elaboration of the properties and effects of a force of gravity" (62). See further Fara (2002).
14. Weil (2002/[1947]).
15. Hall (1999), 175.
16. See Hall (1999), 175. According to Brewster (1855), Dr Humphrey Newton, no relation to Sir Isaac, disputed that Newton kept a dog during his time at Cambridge (1684–1689) (111). See further Keynes (1995), 40, where the author refers to the explanation offered by Sir David Brewster. However, this account has been perhaps quite plausibly doubted as well. First, the timing of Dr Humphrey Newton's time at Cambridge does not coincide with the reputed event (winter of 1691–1692), leaving plenty of time for Newton to acquire a dog or welcome a College dog into his chambers. And second, there is no actual evidence that he did not have a dog. And, of course, no evidence is not itself evidence, as it were. Lynn (1888) writes, "Now the fact mentioned by Dr Humphrey Newton that Sir Isaac, whilst he was with him at Cambridge, kept neither dog nor cat is no proof that he may not have become attached to a dog in later life" (41–42).

17 Lynn (1888), 42.
18 Flood (2020).
19 John Steinbeck in Fensch (1988), 36.
20 Creamer (2023).
21 Editorial (2023).

Chapter 7

Turn to Play

Waste? Not. Want? Knot.

There is a fable by Aesop called *The Ants and the Grasshopper*. It is winter, and the Ants are busy drying the grain that they have collected throughout the summer. A very hungry Grasshopper comes by and begs them for food, but the Ants merely ask why the Grasshopper did not hoard their own during the summer when sources were abundant. The Grasshopper replies, "I had no leisure enough. I passed the days in singing." This is a delightful inversion of the work and leisure paradigm, and a celebration of the importance of aesthetic play. There is also an affiliative function to the grasshopper's musical aesthetic, in that the singing attracts mates, and thus produces a continuity of familial imitation.[1] Or to explain it another way, and to bring in a relative of the Ants in doing so, taking on board Tarde's suggestion, this familial imitation reverberates with "the re-inspiring initiatives which bring new wants, together with new satisfactions, into the world," and thus "propagate … like a wave of light, or like a family of termites."[2] The grasshopper's song is also something of a prelude to the *parodia* and parody that emerges in later discussion as crucial to the swarming fecundity of imitation and the relations of authorship. Thus, for the Grasshopper, the collection of food is presented as something to be sacrificed in order to continue the enriching and crucial activity of singing. For taking this view, the Grasshopper is ridiculed by the Ants: "If you were foolish enough to sing all the summer, you must dance supperless to bed in the winter."

But is all as it seems? While the moral of this fable is usually interpreted as the sagacity and utility of hard work over the supposedly wasteful exuberance of play, more specifically the fable appears to emphasise the object of wealth, the hoard of food, rather than celebrating the Grasshopper's desire to do what he does. The ingenuity of the swarm becomes replaced by the monotonality of the collective (a form of *formica economicus*) towards the production of wealth as the central value.[3] However, it is the contention of this chapter that the Grasshopper holds the insight into production through play, work as leisure, and the false premise of competition. This is also thus a fable about the nature of aesthetic production, about the paucity of a

DOI: 10.4324/9780429342103-12

motivational approach to the product, and about the importance of a distracted latitude in play. The motivation here is to performance and process, rather than the ends of the (and yet always unfinished) aesthetic object. The want is to *prolong* the game. Indeed, to imagine otherwise, that is, to resist the aesthetic sense in play is, as it were, a waste of space.

Who, if anyone, is wasting time in this story? Is it the Ants, spending their entire summer and all their energy preparing for a winter of consumption? Or is it the Grasshopper, producing the environment through song? Or is it neither? The Grasshopper is pursuing the desire to sing, and the accomplishment of that singing. Can such a want ever be a waste? And is it indeed through its *frustration* that it is wasted, that there is waste? The reversibility of this narrative is both intriguing and instructive, an enticing explication of the fictions underlying the economic explanations for creativity as well as the contrivance of the production-consumption linearity. The reversibility of the fable's subject is indeed a matter of creativity itself. How is creativity recognised? How is it rewarded? In other words, in *The Ants and the Grasshopper*, who is the producer, or the creator – who is the subject? Is it the Ants with their labour, their consumption, their use – consumption that, in itself, becomes a kind of production? Or is it the Grasshopper, who, through the very act of singing to the world, produces abundantly all summer?

This reversibility in production and consumption, in benefits and uselessness, in creator and waster, exposes the constructedness of the relationship between subject and object. In recognising this constructedness, the potential is revealed for dismantling the person versus thing paradigm that pollutes not only the understanding but also the application of property and intellectual property. This subject/object dynamic is also revealed through the operation of intellectual property, and in copyright in particular, through the relationship of the deemed author (which may include producers[4]) and consumer (as in the user or audience for the work). The producer is characterised as the subject of the law, not only as the holder of the rights but also as the *author* of those rights, so to speak. The consumer, on the other hand, is the object of the rights; that is, the consumer is *acted upon* by those rights. This emphasis on the rights-holder subject, and configuration of the consumer as object, maps onto the anthropocentrism of the law more widely. This anthropocentrism not only displaces the nonhuman animal subject before the law, through the particular parameters of the subject as ordinarily understood, but is also recognisable in the characterisation of the relationship between author and work, producer and intellectual property object, and the matter of wastefulness and abundance.[5] This emphasis on the creative subject also puts forth an abridged concept of creativity and imposes a fictional, functional causality between creator and work, as will play out in this chapter.

Dear Prudence

The truth of the matter is that the Ants may well have shared, considering the way in which successful ants pursue cooperation and sharing as the key to success. And they do so through networks of nests (polydomy)[6] that share food as well as information,[7] and through interspecific relationships, most famously with aphids.[8] But how is this attention to be *paid for*? Recalling Breton's disdain for those "wretched discussions" of "winning and losing,"[9] the reimagining of this fable by Bernard Suits prolongs this play.[10] Suits also pursues the unfinished and unfinishing play, in responding to Wittgenstein's "anti-definitional attitude"[11] regarding games, and rethinks the nature of wants or motivation in games: "[W]inning a race is not the same thing as crossing a finish line ahead of the other contestants, since it is possible to do the latter unfairly by, for example, cutting across the infield."[12] Suits explains that the error in trying to rationalise games and the engagement with obstacles as part of the motivation for the game occurs "in applying the same standard to games that is applied to means-end activities which are not games."[13] The object of the game of make-believe, of open games and play, is thus to ensure they never end (the concept of prolongation) and this *want* can be related to the inherent morality of play in that it is served by "moves which keep the game going instead of terminating the play."[14] Thus, the fundamental want is "the principle of *prolongation* ... what we were really after all along."[15]

Bernard Suits's rewriting of the fable attributes to the Ants a sense of justice which is a kind of distributive justice but with a *commercial flavour* of inescapable indebtedness.[16] Suits presents the Grasshopper engaged in a form of Socratic dialogue with his followers, Skepticus and Prudence. And it is to Prudence that attention is turned in the present discussion. As Prudence, declares: "But *that* kind of justice ... is only the justice of the ants. Grasshoppers have nothing to do with such 'justice.'"[17] In this account, the Grasshopper refuses food from Prudence, but the Grasshopper's followers offer food without expectations of anything in return: "If you like, we will not require you to pay us back. We are not, after all, ants."[18] The Grasshopper retorts, "Why should you give me the fruits of your labour? Sure that would not be just, when I tell you quite clearly that I will not pay you back."[19] The Grasshopper then declares that such an expenditure on the part of the followers would be inconceivable within Grasshopper teachings: "But the whole burden of my teaching is that you ought to be idle. So now you propose to use me as a pretext not only for working, but for working harder than ever, since you would have not only yourselves to feed, but me as well."[20] The Grasshopper, "a working Utopian whose time has not yet come,"[21] thus rejects the offer of food as "hypocritical," and tells Prudence, "[Y]ou would like to take credit for doing something which is no more than a ruse for avoiding living up to your ideals."[22]

The Grasshopper appears to be anticipating a kind of welfare relationship, where he may be entitled to food with no attending duty required. A *waste* that is of critical value in the present discussion. Indeed, Gadamer argues that the welfare dialectic is similarly othering, maintaining the distinction between subject and the object of charity, thus "penetrating all relationships between men as a reflective form of the effort to dominate."[23] However, it is crucial to examine the welfare dialectic as a potential relation between subjects. While the Grasshopper does protest against the relation, there is a uselessness to the resistance to those relations. Crucially, while it appears to entrap the Grasshopper in a cycle of indebtedness, with no expectation to play, there is instead a presentation of the Grasshopper as beneficiary and indeed as entitled, with no corresponding duty, no expectation of anything in return. This has much in common with the principle of the welfare relation and the construction of that entitlement as property.[24] With nothing expected in return, the singing does play into, as it were, a performance of excess, a surplus value, all through the metacommunication of play. Thus, rather than considering the relation in terms of the fulfilment or otherwise of a duty, and thus the emphasis on the wealth object, these relations present a playful game between the Ants and the Grasshopper, negotiating obstacles along the path and maintaining play. There is thus emerging a very playful quality to personhood.

Despite the Grasshopper being credited with the appreciation of play, it is dear Prudence who comes out to play: *"whoever is taught must teach."*[25]

Just, as Well

This relationship between producer and consumer, as defined and applied in intellectual property laws, also separates out in a way that is consistent with the language of protection in welfare. On the one hand, intellectual property law serves the interests of the producer; that is, the producer as the rights-holder in the various producer roles – author, deemed author (as in film producer[26]), designer, and inventor; that is, the producer is understood to *have an interest in* the commercialisation of their intellectual output. Notably, the trade mark owner is also a kind of *producer* in so far as it is the subject of the law. But trade mark law offers a curious interruption of the producer/consumer and subject/object paradigm through the co-production of value between producer and consumer; while somewhat limited, it is nevertheless part of the normative environment of both practice and enforcement, and this offers a fissure through which to pry apart the presumed immutability of this barrier logic.[27] On the other hand, the law acts *in the interests of* the consumer, or user (or waster), in terms of provisions to safeguard access in limited circumstances,[28] and always after the event of the work. This resonance with the logic of welfare exposes the very parameters of the creativity narrative to a potential disruption of the law's anthropocentrism, and at the same time, reveals the potential in welfare principles to rethink the quality of attention through the prosociality of welfare property. Paradoxically, this may be achieved precisely through the introduction of a welfare dimension that is itself often criticised as pursuing a subject/object logic,[29] as indeed it was by the Grasshopper in Suits's reimagining.

The relationship between play and an individual's *Umwelt* can also be understood as converting that perceived excess, or waste into intellectual and adaptive resources. Play is "a process that converts surplus resources into information," and thus "[b]y increasing the information content of the developing *Umwelt*, play confers fitness benefits."[30] This makes sense even for the most resolute adaptationist. But it is also a sense of the *best of all worlds* through play; that is, through the familiar production of shared interests there is a reciprocal production as distinct from the mutual interests and instrumentality of reserved externalities suggested through dominant models of social production and the collectivity. And to recall Tarde's best of all worlds, "no point on a sphere can be considered central in relation to the others."[31] Elsewhere, Tarde explains this same concept in the context of scientific research, anticipating the interdisciplinarity advocated in the present discussion: "Each element, hitherto conceived as a point, now becomes an indefinitely enlarged sphere of action ... and all these interpenetrating spheres are so many domains proper to each element, so many distinct though intermixed spaces, perhaps, which we wrongly take to be a single unique space."[32] This is the crucial distinction between the swarm and the collectivity, between familiar production and the univocity of social production, between a summation and averaging of the collective and the fragmentary universe of an attributive sociality. Play (and play research) is also in and of itself a powerful tool for interdisciplinarity,[33] and in an ethological, relational approach, this assembling of oppositions is a catalyst to creativity.

Indeed, through the examination of social play and the affiliative value of play, including the imitative productions of social learning, play shows the social, cultural, and creative reciprocalism of play and work: "Play may thus be a key aspect of innovation and creativity ... Additionally, novel behavior can itself create novel situations and thus lead to cascading culture-wide effects."[34] In his relational sociology, proceeding from Leibniz's monadology and harmony between impenetrable monads, Tarde perceives meaning in the relations between, the *metaxu*, advocates a Newtonian-style interpenetration of open monads as fundamental to the progress of science: "[T]he progress of science, indeed of modern science in general and not only of its most recent developments, favours the blossoming of a renewed monadology."[35] Creativity and innovation arises through the ironic dissensus of imitation and the entropy of opposition, arguably demonstrated in the very nature of play research and indeed in the explanation that "play, whether simple or complex, whether primary, secondary, or tertiary, is a process that reduces *Umwelt* entropy (i.e., increases information) while also expanding maximum entropy (i.e., a measure of *Umwelt* complexity)."[36]

Just, as well; indeed, the best of all worlds. The future is Panglossian.

What Is Play?

Curiosity underpins play, and the exploration of novel objects, scenarios, and fantasies is part of this. As such, play is a kind of attention, but a distracted attention, a creative attention. Indeed, it may be said that the interaction between an attention, curiosity, and innovation investigated to this point, is found at its most productive in play. Daniel Berlyne's work on curiosity is significant in this context; particularly in his distinction between *specific* and *diversive exploration*. In *specific exploration*, that exploration is a form of targeted enquiry and acquisition of information; but *diversive exploration* is a more open-ended exploration as entertainment (or indeed distraction), to which Berlyne adds the further qualification of *inspective* and *inquisitive* exploratory responses, or "looking *at* and looking *for* something."[37] To translate this into Bernard Suits's account of play, this more targeted form of *specific exploration* may be understood as a means-end activity, whereas *diversive exploration* suggests the truly creative and open-ended exploration that is characteristic of the *uselessness* of play. This diction resonates with the kind of *stereotypic imitation* oo rules-based and thus specific or guided enquiry (as is suggested in artificial intelligence) and the playful *attentive imitation* with its productive qualities of a distracted attention, as it were, and regard for the small, the novel, the irrelevant. Similarly eschewing a means-end definition of curiosity, Abraham Flexner declares, "[C]uriosity, which may or may not eventuate in something useful, is probably the outstanding characteristic of modern thinking."[38] In curiosity, there is everything to play for. *Look aside!*

This is not to diminish the authorial production of play through simply confusing play with "mere curiosity."[39] Indeed, reducing play to a performance of other deferred adaptive value is a mistaken limitation. Once again the creep of predatory drift has distorted considerations of play, which persist in the popular discourse, where certain postures and vocalisations in play are mistaken "as a form of aggression" or rehearsal of predatory or competitive behaviour, as suggested by the application of terms such as "'play-fighting' for 'rough-and-tumble play'."[40] Rather, so-called play fighting is usually associated with a positive affect and social experience.[41] The language and terminology appears to reflect an emphasis on the seemingly manifest markers of individuality and competition, rather than understanding the possible boon of wasteful creativity in an unfettered aesthetic of play. To recall Marvin Minsky's comment, the preoccupation with reaction, output, and the instrumentality of impact, is that "we don't study what people don't do."[42] The value of *wasting* time has been overlooked in the competitive narrative of relentless production.[43]

In his influential work on creativity, Carl Rogers identifies three features of constructive creativity,[44] all of which resonate with the investigation thus far. First and foremost, there is the condition of *openness*, and thus the kind of shared interests anticipated in Tarde's sociology and fundamental to an ethological approach to social creativity. Second, Rogers considers the role of *evaluation*,[45] which imports the dimensions of morality and justice also identified in all animal play, including humans.[46] This evaluative feature also acknowledges the active and participatory innovation in social learning, as understood through Tarde's process of evaluative and conscious imitation, and indeed is vital to the *certain kind of attention* of *attentive imitation*. And finally, fundamental to constructive creativity, is the concept of *play* itself, or what Rogers refers to as "toying," as in an "ability to toy with elements and concepts."[47] This creativity in openness and play shares much with Marcel Jousse's account of children's play as "to play at everything."[48] That is, play is an embodied and affiliative sociality, and learning with one's whole body and voice.[49] Play affords the opportunity to invent new ways to perform.

In this openness is thus also the potential for the one stimulus, empathy, as part of the fundamental morality of play.[50] A phenomenal account of this empathy can be recognised in the rapid facial mimicry in play between different species, including between humans and dogs[51] and even between so-called predator and prey species, as in play between dogs and horses.[52] Indeed, this not only demonstrates the importance and facility of an embodied empathetic relationship but also the attention in play, a certain attention of the kind fundamental to Simone Weil's readings of compassion and virtue in attention.[53] Play, it might be said, manifests as a fundamental basis for compassion and justice.

In play there are no bounds, other than the objective of the prolongation of play itself.

Players, Assemble

Social play is regularly understood as a form of communication and thus in this respect must be interpreted as an activity that is not wasteful, as it were, but providing information and thereby enhancing fitness. This analysis would thus make play *consistent with an evolutionary interpretation*.[54] But while this Panglossian account of play may sustain a functionalist and biological explanation for an otherwise aesthetic exuberance, to recall the earlier *Spandrels* discussion, it does not necessarily preclude that this extraordinary uselessness occurs at the same time.[55] Indeed, it is to double play the Panglossian paradigm itself. Thus, in play itself, there is the peculiarly Newtonian disequilibrium of reduced *Umwelt* entropy through information, and maximised entropy in terms of *Umwelt* complexity.[56] Play is the best of all worlds at demonstrating Tarde's relational sociology of "the three great scientific aspects of the universe ... Repetition, Opposition, and Adaptation of phenomena,"[57] and how this might translate into a creative universe, as well as introduce a critical insight for a productive relationality in the welfare concept itself[58] for both nonhuman and human authors.[59] In this way, play may be presented as well for its value to welfare, productivity, intellectual property, and "important instrumental values of happiness."[60]

While Tarde refers to the concept of opposition as the less important intermediary of the other two concepts of repetition and adaptation,[61] arguably its bridging function is crucial and introduces the critical understanding of opposition as contact. Opposition as a concept thus accords with Weil's key concept of boundaries and barriers as *metaxu*. In other words, contrary to the usual approach to opposition as boundary-making, Tarde's concept of opposition transforms the sociality of opposition through an affiliative dissensus. Thus, opposition takes on a relational property, where the boundary is a contact point for the generation of meaning and value between subjects.[62] Rather than an agonistic combat of banal binaries, Tarde's sociology introduces a playful, affiliative function to difference. In their relational and sympathetic quality, monads seek to assemble, to socialise, thus conferring a crucially affiliative quality to Tarde's rendition of the universe, and an ethological quality to his jurisprudence and sociology. Monads, as fundamental social and relational entities, are drawn to each other like magnets: "[L]eft to its own devices, a monad can achieve nothing. This is the crucial fact, and it immediately explains another, *the tendency of monads to assemble*."[63]

There is thus an ethological methodology underpinning this sociality that is crucial to an ethological jurisprudence of intellectual property and authorship. This *tendency to assemble* assures that authorship, invention, creativity writ large, is always playful. That is, the author is always already two, for play is always relational, and thus the properties arising are always already *in personam*, useful and in use.[64] This reinforces the role of attribution in maintaining the play, where attribution and citation is as much about identifying and harnessing those relations through shared interests as it is about attributing an individual work or author, the latter utility more usually a question of mutual interests and discrete identities. The works similarly assemble, as it were, and the sociology of creativity benefits from a monadological and ethological methodology. This relationality is also fundamental to a form of social justice inherent in Tarde's model of innovation, when he questions the creative and knowledge hierarchies applied to societies: "Is a monarch necessarily more intelligent than his ministers or his subjects?"[65] What then does it mean to undertake a monadological approach to intellectual property, to creativity and, perhaps even more closely, to originality? And why might it be argued that to do so is ultimately and resolutely playful?

To Want to Play

To appreciate the assembly in play, it is important to understand Tarde's concept of opposition as the fundamental catalyst of creativity. In other words, innovation does not arise through a presumed agreement and causality but rather through dissimilarity and dissensus, difference through repetition, innovation through imitation. Conventional theories of social production, those that also produce the collectivities of which Weil is so critical,[66] obscure this disharmony. Rather, such summation coerces disharmonies into symmetry and univocity. For Tarde, this is not something to be assigned through causality but instead should be the function of adaptation – that is, of evaluative, affiliative, swarming, social imitation. This obstruction of difference in dominant models of social production, the kind that has been deployed in championing generative AI as creative, is both the technical[67] and socio-cultural[68] limitation of artificial intelligence: "[M]athematics never reveals causality in operation. When a cause is postulated under the name of *function*, it is always disguised as an equation."[69] Thus, a monadological and ethological model of the relations between copyright works might be understood as concerned with the relations between works as particular perceptions, as Leibniz explains. The relationality of those series of imitations is a relationality of wants, or appetition in Leibniz's account: "The action of the internal principle which brings about the change or the passing from one perception to another may be called Appetition. It is true that the desire (*l'appetit*) is not always able to attain to the whole of the perception which it strives for, but it always attains a portion of it and reaches new perceptions."[70]

Manifesting those wants is the crucial task of attribution, the stewardship of citation. This work is not the mundane work of discrete properties and singularities of authorship but the exciting facilitation of the sociality and relationality in authorship, always already many. Similarly, a sociality of imitation is not concerned with the repetition of a work or the imposture of an author, but rather, with the appetition, the wants of creativity – that is, a network of relations. As Tarde declares, "*everything is a* society … every phenomenon is a social fact."[71] Indeed, the effort and joy of tracing precursors previously unknown is part of discovering the social ties of one's own work. Attribution is thus a facilitative and social tool, for "in a society no individual can act socially, or show himself in any respect, without the collaboration of a great number of other individuals, most of them unknown to him."[72] A showing of authorship is thus a highly social affair, over and above any distinctions accorded to the work by applicable intellectual property laws. Attribution does not undermine the work;[73] it emphasises it. Further, citation is fundamental to the work's explainability and thus its contribution to the social and cultural transmission of knowledge.[74] And thus, an emphasis on attribution has nothing to do with preserving the integrity of the work or the hegemony of the singular author; rather, it is to do with showing how creativity is possible at all.

This relationality is of particular relevance to discussions of copyright and infringement in short forms like memes, titles, and other fragments. Ina Blom notes that the meme concept in the related science of memetics presents "a notoriously difficult question, since the physical substratum of memes is hard to define: is it sounds and images? Or the acts of communication?"[75] There is of course considerable resonance between these discourses of fragments, beyond the repetition of the term itself. Both in memetics and in the social communications around fragments such as GIFs and other memetic imagery, the focus is on the relation as distinct from the fixed or discrete objects.[76] Tarde's sociology is instructive here, as Blom explains: "What is imitated is not specific expressions or behaviours but beliefs and desires."[77] It is indeed the prolongation of play, the fluidity of the meme in its infinite reiterations, contexts, communications, and conversations. A monadological approach to this creative flow makes sense of the tension between the copyright expression and the unfinished nature of the work, particularly through its life of use. Monads are perfectly unfinished: "A created thing is said to act outwardly in so far as it has perfection, and to suffer from another in so far as it is imperfect."[78] The monad is thus a fundamental substance of action, through perception, conscious or otherwise: *I think I think that I am a verb*. And that verb is, *to play*. There is thus an important distinction to be made between a coercive force of imitation in the service of mutual interests, as considered in earlier discussion, and that of the imitation of belief and desire (the appetition or wants of innovation) as in a genuinely social and productive imitation – *attentive imitation*. The first kind of imitation is an unreflective adherence to the model in the form of *stereotypic imitation*, while the second is a kind of seeking or wanting to converge through shared interests, a sharing in interest, which is open and attentive (*attentive imitation*). The first introduces an economic imperative and *commercial flavour* of duty and reciprocity, with a focus on wealth. The second is a social imitation and a form of familiar production, in motion through play.

The relationality of opposition is thus a kind of critical distance achieved through social imitation: "[N]owhere has a more complete elimination of the dissimilar and individual side of phenomena been effected, and nowhere do they present a more exact and definite, and a more symmetrical opposition."[79] Thus, faced with the great aggregators of generative AI, Tarde might have argued that the "great fault" of these machines as imitators, as catalysts, as authors, is this loss of distance: "The great fault of mathematics lies in its *not perceiving*, or taking adequately into account, the *adaptations of phenomena*. Hence arises that insufficiency of the science."[80] After all, as Bruno Latour attests, Tarde had already invented a digital-based social theory "before we even had the technology."[81] And in that *not perceiving*, perhaps what is missing is a certain kind of attention, a playful regard. Social imitation is perhaps most engaging in the form of play; that is, imitation that is evaluative, conscientious, and indeed, playful – *attentive imitation*. And this playful attention need not be derailed by any rules of play. Rules of a game, conventions of a genre, or memories of a form do not necessarily introduce coercion and force in the sense that they arise precisely through the social prolongation of what is a social and playful tie. The crucial question remains then: can artificial intelligence play? Only if left to chance. But chance seems entirely outside the rule book of generative AI.[82]

But before considering that question, another is doggedly persistent in both the biological and economic literature, and that is the question of the value of play.

Well Played

Curiously, attempts to answer this question may be reconciled with the kind of adaptationist interpretations, as considered in earlier discussions concerning consciousness, that may also be applied in a welfare context and reconciling welfare indicators with functionalist accounts. That is, play as a phenomenon is reinscribed within an evolutionary narrative through interpretations of adaptive value, social learning, and ultimately evolutionary fitness.[83] But play is also deployed as a welfare indicator for nonhuman animals,[84] and indeed for human animals as well,[85] which is both consistent with these adaptationist interpretations as well as introducing a perspective on creativity and authorship (in play) through welfare.[86] Thus, within an ethological jurisprudence of welfare principles there may be found the scope for dismantling the very barriers to personhood for which those principles and protections are regularly criticised. In other words, it is to begin to consider the interests of the consumer of intellectual property (*in the interests of* as well as *having an interest in*) as a kind of property – that is, an entitlement which cannot be varied by the law and for which no duty is bound. The charges in relation to welfare as waste, on the one hand, and exploitation, on the other, both betray an emphasis on wealth as an objective value. Once again, a reorientation of perspective in order to examine the excess in play, the accomplishment of desire, and the wanton uselessness of surplus value, provides a crucial paradigm shift in innovation and property narratives. What is the metacommunicative value of seemingly wasted effort? And what are the implications for the dominant narratives of value generation in a commercial law framework, such as intellectual property? Once again, an examination of the relationship between welfare and creativity yields important insight.

Welfare additionally offers the seed for a general economy of waste – that is, for a kind of expenditure and giving of play where nothing is expected in return. Indeed, a banal notion of waste underpins the hostility towards welfare reported in some aspects of the popular (and populist) discourse, and it might be said to manifest the kind of "necessarily hostility" to waste in a utilitarian society, that Georges Bataille describes as "linked to the ignorance into which we have fallen."[87] This ignorance ignores the fact, Bataille argues, "that we must resolutely waste the excess energy that we produce. In fact, in our blind state, this pile-up of excess wastes us more than we waste it."[88] Instead, "[t]he system forever generates a feeling of poverty – the moral practices and ways of life of poverty ... A time of bloated production arrives in which we can no longer get rid of what we produce."[89] And yet we are compelled to *need* more, or as Tarde puts it, "[T]he luxuries of today are the necessities of tomorrow."[90] In this way, there cannot be satiation of a need for more money, as the need will constantly renew itself. And if the "need" is contrived as profit or money, then welfare is always *a priori* wasteful.

In the same way, the fulfilment of the intellectual property system monitors attention as the basis of desire, in that, as a system, it directs attention to the reasons to fulfil the very same desire that is *made* by the system (at least, within the logic of the system) – that is, to create. Therefore, insofar as the desire is *made* and rationalised by the system, the nonhuman creator is always already outside the system and therefore deprived and divested of the necessary desire, at least as far as it is conceived and recognised within that system. *What does Naruto want?* The answer to the question, then, arrives already prepared as nothing. This same logic extends to forms of human creation that reject or exceed conventional forms of creativity, such as methods and artefacts of traditional knowledge and cultural expression, or practices of appropriation, pastiche, and parody. Even the manners of performance art, as it were, otherwise validated within the wider cultural institution of the art industry, are reconciled only through the recording of that performance – that is, a desire that is *made* within and according to the terms of the system itself. If we compare the mild hysteria around non-fungible tokens (NFTs) and copyright, perhaps much of this arises from the potential challenge to the objects of intellectual property, not through infringement but through displacement:[91] *Since I cannot afford originals, I make my own.*[92]

A radical reappraisal of the notion of waste in this context, and the attending abundance through play, will provide an entirely relevant and practical way to assess both authorship and the work in contemporary copyright dilemmas. At the same time, it is engaging for its suggestive and constructive insight in novel environments, such as the sensory challenges of immersive virtual environments. Despite criticisms in animal studies, and the seductive language of absolutes of rights and personhood, welfare laws do not turn nonhuman animals into property. Indeed, this problematic popularisation of concepts reinforces the combative binaries that actually serve to reinforce the status quo. Welfare principles do not depend upon the evidence of a property relationship; rather, they depend upon evidence of *control*.[93] In other words, welfare concerns the relation between legal subjects – the subject of the welfare (the nonhuman animal) and the subject of the duties to provide the welfare (the legal person in control). The control need not necessarily invoke interpretations of facilitation of use (although it is acknowledged this is included in most welfare legislation), and in practice it is more likely to be a situation in which the application of welfare principles is instrumental in addressing an imbalance of "rights" between legal subjects. Taking this forward in the intellectual property context reveals the opportunities for consumers, as well as facilitating a more nuanced account of different creative models, towards an ethological approach to authorship.

Cohering the intervention of welfare principles in copyright with an ethological approach to authorship thus presents an opportunity not only to transform perspectives in copyright but also to radicalise approaches to non-human animal consciousness. Rather than maintaining the agonistic to and fro, and back and forth, of the copyright shipwreck, the kind of habit of force that turns everyone into a thing,[94] the potential for defeating the law's anthropocentric bias is curiously bound up in creativity. The subject-object couplet in copyright is thus an extraordinary opportunity for transformation of the law's anthropocentrism to the benefit of a diversification of creative voices, including those of consumers. Whether that anthropocentrism functions in the management of the consumer, the definition of an author, the recognition of a work, the sentience of a nonhuman animal, or the personhood of a machine,[95] at all times the subject-object barrier militates against bridging the connection between the human subject and the world as object, instead preserving the status quo. As such, rather than merely changing literally the content of the law, but nevertheless remaining bound by the mechanism and susceptible to reappropriation and rationalisation within the law's anthropocentric frameworks, it is possible to revolutionise the law through use and through the way in which creativity is perceived, works are made, and the way in which knowledge is represented *and* goes to waste.

What, a Waste?

Not infrequently, John Locke's propositions on property are put forth as basic justifications for the intellectual property system; indeed, Locke is introduced to undergraduates, speaking on behalf of labour, along with Hegel, speaking on behalf of personality, and this almost binarised totality of property theory remains stubbornly immovable ever after, as though these are the two poles of thought that might account for all versions within.[96] While it is suggested that this maps conveniently onto common law systems of economic rights (Locke) and civil law systems of author rights (Hegel), this polarises the systems and neglects the opportunity for productive oppositions and the best of all worlds. In other words, an obstinate duality of the economic sphere versus the personal sphere perseveres. Further, and somewhat disconcertingly, not only are such arguments presented as almost axiomatic, but also, they all too often offer over-simplified misinterpretations and misapplications of these two approaches.

Locke's so-called waste proviso is found in the Second Treatise: *"God has given us all things richly … But how far has he given it us? To enjoy.* As much as any one can make use of to any advantage of life before it spoils; so much he may by his labour fix a Property in. Whatever is beyond this, is more than his share, and belongs to others. Nothing was made by God for Man to spoil or destroy."[97] Thus, to frustrate that enjoyment is arguably also a waste, such as if the Ants were to stop the Grasshopper from singing, or if Naruto had been stopped from making photographs, or if the environment provided for a nonhuman animal frustrates their desire to play. This frustration of wants is wasteful. Waste thus has a welfare dimension. And so does joy. But through play one might be said to be "wasting well."[98] In providing "some very general rules for wasting well," designer and planner, Kevin Lynch, advises avoiding "any abrupt loss of biological or cultural information."[99] Such information is clearly lost in the physical destruction and pollution of environments. It is also lost in the frustration of the delicious entropy of play through which so much information is conveyed. And arguably it is also lost in the aggregation and averaging of information through LLMs and other forms of generative AI, including visual material, where in all of these forms there is the risk of losing information through summation, anonymisation, homogenisation, and even technically through the ultimate collapse of the whole model.[100]

More specifically, while Locke's proviso on spoilage or waste, also known widely as the "enough-and-as-good" proviso,[101] is put to good use in environmental critiques,[102] it is arguably largely dismissed in discussions around intellectual property.[103] Justin Hughes argues, "The absence of a non-waste condition in intellectual property systems does not weaken a Lockean justification for intellectual property. Locke, after all, declined to apply the non-waste condition to the advanced social conditions which are required by most intellectual property systems."[104] According to Hughes, "Intellectual property systems, however, do seem to accord with Locke's labor condition and the 'enough and as good' requirement," going on to suggest that perhaps "Locke's unique theoretical edifice finds its firmest bedrock in the common of ideas."[105] But what is notable about the proviso and emphasised frequently in the intellectual property context is its perspective upon natural resources and the work of labour in transforming that environment into a proprietary relationship, through *mixing* labour with natural resources: "Whatsoever then he removes out of the State that Nature hath provided, and left it in, he hath mixed his *Labour* with, and joined to it something that is his own, and thereby makes it his *Property*. It being by him removed from the common state Nature placed it in, it hath by this *labour* something annexed to it, that excludes the common right of other Men."[106] This passage seems unambiguous, but in many respects it has been all too easily aligned with a capitalist model of maximising wealth, ignoring the relations of connection between labourers and the land. Locke continues, "For this *Labour* being the unquestionable Property of the Labourer, no Man but he can have a right to what that is once joined to, at least where there is enough, and as good left in common for others."[107] While widely recognised as an account of fairness in Locke's model of property, this also introduces a question of opportunity for that connection. And frustration of that connection may be similarly wasteful.

In this way, Locke's account of the mixing of labour and the land suggests the kind of connection to which Weil directs a certain attention. In her consideration of property, Weil argues that "[t]he principle of private property is violated where the land is worked by agricultural labourers and farm-hands under the orders of an estate-manager, and owned by townsmen who receive the profits,"[108] thus identifying the frustration of the property through mixing described by Locke but understood particularly through the value in the relationship or connection itself. For Weil, the interest in the land must arise through this connectedness and relationality, and frustration of this is a frustration of the principle of private property: "For of all those who are connected with that land, there is not one who, in one way or another, is not a stranger to it. It is *wasted*, not from the point of view of corn-production, but from that of the satisfaction of the property-need which it could procure."[109] This connection is thus a desire, a want, through which the relevant relations arise, but a want that is frustrated in dominant models of ownership and labour that emphasise the wealth object rather than this connection.[110]

This presents an interesting intersection between Locke and relational property, particularly through contemporary notions of world-building including through play. While conventional interpretations of this important passage in Locke present the human as imposing themselves upon these worlds as proprietary-making, there is in this passage the acknowledgement of a connectedness that is world-making, and thus a property that is relational, dynamic and social, and in this way personal and authorial. This introduces a meaningful interaction with contemporary understandings and interpretations of the rights of nature, where the connection is nevertheless recognised in the creative work and labour of the human connections but where value arising out of that work may be referred back into the land itself. This relational quality as arising through play introduces a crucial distinction between authorship as prosocial and unfinished, and ownership as artefactual and past. This has notable consequences for the notion of waste in intellectual property. What goes to waste in intellectual property?

Keeping Minutes and Wasting Hours

The concept of waste in intellectual property is a complex character of utility, commerciality, and opportunity, potentially including but not always emphasising the social in that opportunity, at least not in the dominant models ordinarily implemented for the application of intellectual property. How does intellectual property view and preview waste? The most common way in which intellectual property views waste is not through use and consumption; but it is also not through lack of consumption. Rather, if intellectual property has anything to say about waste it is in the circumstances where the intellectual property is not used by the owner; that is, it is not *sold* in the widest sense. In some respects, this does impart upon the system a certain social accountability in so far as this acknowledges a social value in waste through access. Nevertheless, the sociality has limitations, particularly in reinforcing the calculation of waste within an economic sphere of both sustaining and sustained by an appeal to a claimed objectivity in the concept of wealth as a discrete value. Arguably, as later discussion will consider, the sublime *waste* of surplus value is the primary sociality of intellectual property as facilitated by imitation through use in social and satirical behaviours like parody, pastiche, caricature, adaptation, and quotation. But waste can be wasted, as in the frustration of that use.

For now, paying attention in the strictest sense to the possible waste of an intellectual property object, examples within the intellectual property system largely apply to registered rights only; that is, there are no similar provisions for copyright. Further, such examples do not lead to the loss of rights on the part of the intellectual property owner, except for the case of trade marks, where registration may be revoked through lack of use.[111] A kind of waste through inattention is implied in the principle of acquiescence – that is, a kind of *waste* of rights through the inaction to enforce those rights. Thus, if an owner has been allowing others to use the mark without objection, after five years they lose any opportunity to enforce their rights against those persons.[112] This is an important distinction, in that trade marks are concerning a commercial identity, albeit one which is capable of commercialisation, whereas other registered rights apply more specifically to a product or object of intellectual property's fascination. The law is perhaps more concerned with wasting commercial opportunities than it is with wasting resources, an idealism of significant relevance to contemporary concerns with artificial intelligence and provenance.[113]

The obvious parallel, but misleading analogy for revocation for non-use, is the availability of compulsory licences of rights to manufacture the underlying invention (in patent law) or design. But in compulsory licences, what appears at first to be a form of protection against waste through that application is in practical effect much less clear. For example, the Paris Convention[114] provides for compulsory licences where an owner has failed to work a patent, suggesting an underlying rationale similar to underpinning revocation for non-use in trade mark law, except of course there is no loss of the patent rights, in contrast to the process in trade mark revocation. There are various grounds for compulsory licences, and they are very rarely granted in the global north because of the difficulty in meeting the requirements for those grounds.[115] But one area with more attention in the west in recent years is where an owner's control over a patent may be interrupted by a compulsory licence where there is deemed to be a national health emergency.[116] Nevertheless, overall the surrounding discourse is almost antithetical to the concept of waste, other than in the context of the frustration of the owner's rights.

Notwithstanding the uncertainty of these measures in other areas of intellectual property, there are no such clear measures at all, at least not technically, in copyright. Contrary to other areas of intellectual property, if there is anything the law has to say on waste in copyright it is through lack of use. But there is no obligation to publish to gain copyright protection, for as soon as any secret Pandora's box of authored work is opened, no matter how long it may have been sealed shut, those works begin life as copyright works. But are they original at all? In Tarde's words, "what remains locked up in the mind of its creator, has no social value."[117]

Notably, in all these different ways of accounting for waste as lack of use, the law is concerned with the frustration of *access* to the creation of property, rather than to the waste of property more specifically speaking. This frustration is not only that of the user or consumer but also the potential frustration of competitors or other owners, reaffirming that the attention to waste is indeed a distraction from the priority of the market's use. Any waste is reconciled within the system through an account of use, as a dimension of usefulness, rather than having any interest in terms of surplus, other than through managing that surplus in so far as it may pose a threat to the market and the contrived scarcity underpinning it. The intellectual property system's concern with waste is thus directed towards reconfiguring that surplus, rather than furnishing the gifts (and incentives) of abundance.[118] *Imitation is its own reward*, for producer and consumer alike.[119] Thus, while such measures may seem consistent with Locke's proviso at first glance, these kinds of rules against lack of use or lack of response to need are really concerned with protecting against potential market failures in the system rather than addressing the question of whatever might be beyond the owner's share (however that might be understood) and thus belonging to others. These measures do little to address waste and in fact in some ways ensure that intellectual property can still be utterly wasted and wasteful, over and over again.

This recalls the kind of adaptationist reasoning considered in the discussion of sentience, and specifically, the explanation offered by Pangloss: *pigs were made to be eaten*. Bataille explains the disconnection from the land as part of a correction of market failures in a capitalist system wherein *"utility became the basis of moral value."*[120] Recalling the earlier discussion of Locke's proviso and Weil's account of labour and private property, Bataille describes a similar disconnection but in the context of reconciling abundance with the necessary imperative against waste in a utilitarian society. Like Pangloss, this might be explained through the unfortunate example of a pig's slaughter. Where once, as Bataille explains, a pig might be sacrificed "to achieve harmony with capricious gods,"[121] this waste has been translated into the industrial agricultural complex. For the pig, the waste remains the same.

The Author as Tool of Capitalism

Copyright protection (and infringement) is a manifest commercial legal system, and at the same time a cultural institution proclaiming relevant and *promised* outputs. Much of this power comes through popular engagement with copyright; from the legally unnecessary but normatively declarative inclusion (by authors and publishers alike) of the copyright symbol (©) on works,[122] through to the mystification of copyright and its cultural responsibility in the press,[123] there is much to copyright beyond the statutory frame. It would seem that the cultural institution of *Copyright* creates and sustains a certain stratification of creativity, making beggars of users and aristocrats of authors.[124] Tarde identifies this kind of process through his theory of imitation, in which he notes the way the aristocracy becomes a strategy for diffusion:

> [T]he apologists for aristocracy have, in my opinion, passed over its best justification. The principal role of a nobility, its distinguishing mark, is its initiative, if not inventive, character. Invention can start from the lowest ranks of the people, but its extension depends upon the existence of some lofty social elevation, a kind of social water-tower, when a continuous water-fall of imitation may descend.[125]

It must be stressed that Tarde makes this observation not in defence of the aristocracy but rather towards anatomising the mechanics of social imitation.[126] In this context, the qualities of prestige and inimitability attached to the socio-cultural figure of the author makes considerable sense within the commercial machine. The *Author* becomes a privileged site of capital, notwithstanding the actual circumstances of the individual author as beggar,[127] a paradox to which the discussion will return. The expressions of nonhuman animals are thus contrived as the useless invitations of outsiders, of strangers; the nuisances of stupid beggars.

John Frow argues, "The work of intellectuals is the implementation of modernity."[128] In making this claim, Frow is referring to the work of "all of those whose work is socially defined as being based upon the possession and exercise of knowledge, whether that knowledge be prestigious or routine, technical or speculative."[129] Such work, of course, manifests within a system of capital through the mechanism of intellectual property. Thus, authorship, in its singularity and intentionality, provides a strategic tool of capitalism, complicit in implementing and regulating the discrete limits and capital of intellectual property objects. As Frow maintains, "the institution of authorship ... remains the single most important channel for the creation of textual desire and the minimization of market uncertainty."[130] The author may then be understood as both a speculator and the speculated, as within the mechanism described by Bataille: "In principle, large-scale capitalists or industrialists are quite happy to give just their flesh and blood to a project ... it is not they who conceive projects and put them into operation, but they who are conceived by their projects and put into operation by them."[131] *The work makes the author.* The *inverted path of proper analysis*[132] that besets the arguments for artificial authorship now makes perfect commercial sense, all rationalised and reconciled within the system of copyright. But it is exactly that – an inversion of the proper path of analysis. *The spandrels of artificial intelligence.*

What becomes striking immediately is that there is a curiously similar bifurcation or ranking in the discourse of sentience, most clearly in the persistent bifurcation of nature and culture – a construction that is necessarily and most explicitly challenged through an investigation of nonhuman animal authorship. But this ranking, to borrow Jeremy Waldron's approach to human rights jurisprudence, is endemic in sentience studies – it persists in approaches to ranking otherwise sentient species,[133] to determining dimensions of sentience,[134] through to the fundamental arbitrariness that besets the wider discourse;[135] but there is also a tradition of an "aristocratic conception"[136] of human rights.[137] This arbitrariness is perhaps facilitated by the fascination with sentience itself, as a matter of degree and thus hierarchical management; as Weil suggests, the kind of "blind play which alone determines the social hierarchies."[138] Understood in this way, the exceptionalist paradigm is inevitably presented as not only common sense, in the widest meaning, but also, and problematically, as impossibly just. Sentience as a policy tool thus becomes embroiled in a discourse of correcting market failures as to access and use of animals, as distinct from a fundamental account of moral standing.

In confronting this reckoning of the author as capital tool, and rupturing the received wisdoms of the author concept, it is useful to engage with Bataille's notion of the speculator, and to introduce the gamble, as it were, in the play of authorship. In *The Limit of the Useful*,[139] "Speculators," Bataille argues, "are more likely than industrialists or capitalists to be beings of vain glory, driven to making extravagant personal expenditures. Capitalism accommodates itself to their wastefulness."[140] That is, through the fulfilment of obsolescence in a drive to the new for no reason other than the new, to recall Tarde's phrase, *the luxuries of today are the necessities of tomorrow.* There is thus a kind of abdication of responsibility or coerced alienation of responsibility in contemporary creativity and innovation, such that the author, as created by the work, is a matter of capital. And as noted already, according to Bataille, the capitalist, or industrialist, or investor is "quite happy to give just their flesh and blood to a project"[141] – that is just their effort, just their capital. But there is another meaning to *flesh and blood* and that is the legacy of inheritance and the preservation of capital as "locked up"[142] within that aristocratic conception of authorship. Bataille's observation resonates with the notion of ownership through effort, production, and arrangement[143] (that is, the owner as "conceived by their projects and put into operation by them"[144]) as distinct from authorship through intellectual creation.[145] For Bertolt Brecht, writing around the same time as Bataille's *Limit*, this tyranny of the collective as contained within the singularity and efficiency of the producer, as defined, is at work in artistic creation. Brecht laments that even the matter of taste has little to nothing to do with authorship, where copyright is folded into the process of production itself: "[T]he author can only argue that the court *itself* should intervene. Thus, he is forced to acknowledge the competence in matters of taste on the part of some judge or another ... [H]e has no rights outside the production process. *There are no rights outside the production process.*"[146]

How to restore the wasteful exuberance of the author beyond this system? Bataille explains the origins of this hostility towards waste as made reasonable, in a manner of speaking, "in service of reason."[147] He maintains that, "beginning from the Reformation onwards, both a moral hostility toward all kinds of waste and a utilitarian society developed under the direction of the grand bourgeoisie."[148] Thus, a utilitarian rationalisation, an economic theory of intellectual creation, is instated as the overwhelming morality: "*utility became the basis of moral value.*"[149] In this context, the speculator is not even really gambling, in that the whatever gamble is at work is in fact simply ensuring the continued circulation or recuperation of capital: "As he is not even a genuine gambler, he has no more claim to splendor than he does to morality. Wealth, in his hands, is destined neither to burn not to produce."[150] And thus, by Bataille's account: "*Money was seen as a means of production.*"[151] *Money literally buys nothing.*[152] Simone Weil makes a very similar observation when she says, "Money does not provide a convenient method for exchanging products; it is the sale of goods which is a means for keeping money in circulation."[153] The production of authorship thus becomes simplified and rationalised within a system of maintaining the circulation of capital,[154] removed from the expressive excess of other worlds through the glorious waste of intellectual creation.

How is it possible to disrupt "[t]he laborious transformation of nature into *products*, into saleable stuff,"[155] as Bataille observes? By submitting to the morality of abundant play. This thread of morality inheres throughout the common definition of play considered earlier,[156] which is recalled here. Play is widely acknowledged as, by its own account, *play* – that is, it is without function or utility. Play requires consent, it is voluntary and not coerced; thus it is fundamentally moral and empathic. Play is other worldly; that is, by its very performance as play it is expressive and creative beyond the literal or perceived reality. Play, in and of itself, is an expression of and with wellbeing. Play well and for as long as you can.[157]

Waste as Value

Despite the accepted definition of play, considered above, and despite clear indications to the contrary,[158] discerning function for play nevertheless continues as a persistent preoccupation of the relevant literature, including in the biological and cognitive sciences,[159] This fixation on usefulness may be interpreted as restoring play within the production process, and thus introducing the constraints of a functionalist imperative and conservatism in respect of creativity – its purposefulness, its intentionality, its authors. This also influences how creativity is recognised, understood, and, above all, valued. The intellectual property system is part of this pragmatic approach to recognising creativity and sense-making in the circulation of products. At the same time, this instrumentality of intellectual property is facilitated through its own abbreviation to monetary value and commercialisation, both technically and popularly, thus encoding a causal narrative of creativity utility – that is, a paradigm of incentives, rewards, and desire.[160]

But such codes are constructed. Bataille proclaims: "Every time the meaning of a discussion depends on the fundamental value of the word *useful* – in other words, every time the essential question touching on the life of human societies is raised, no matter who intervenes and what opinions are expressed – it is possible to affirm that the debate is necessarily warped and that the fundamental question is eluded."[161] An ethological approach to the authorship in play must recognise the pre-emptive functionalist structuring of the question of play in order to examine the authorship through play. In this way it is possible to dismantle the inevitable ridicule of the excess through play as, at best, a distracted wandering and, at worst, a maddening waste of evolutionary time. Bataille observes: "Pleasure, whether art, permissible debauchery, or play, is definitively reduced, in the intellectual representations *in circulation*, to a concession; in other words it is reduced to a diversion whose role is subsidiary."[162]

An anecdote from Abraham Flexner's famous essay on the limitations of a utilitarian approach to knowledge production is of immediate interest here. Flexner was an influential educational researcher on the modernising of education in the United States,[163] including the publication of the famous *Flexner Report*[164] in 1910, which "did in fact revolutionize American medical research and medical education."[165] Flexner was adamant that education needed to become more creative and less regimented and that educators needed to be supported to explore the breadth of that context: "[T]he teacher … seeks to evoke the attitude, and to carry [the student] through the process, of the thinker and not of the parrot."[166] One of Flexner's most *wasteful* ideas, as it were, was the Institute for Advanced Study at Princeton,[167] which ultimately became a model for interdisciplinary centres around the world.[168] With Albert Einstein as the first professor to be appointed, the Institute was established, "to assemble a group of scientists and scholars who with their pupils and assistants may devote themselves to the task of pushing beyond the present limits of human knowledge and to training those who may 'carry on' in this sense."[169] At the time of Flexner's death almost thirty years later, the Institute was lauded as the "first scholarly haven for pure inquiry with the world for a laboratory" and a "first real scholars' Utopia."[170] In the anecdote in question, Flexner is describing the award of a research stipend to a Harvard professor in order to visit the Institute at Princeton. The professor wrote to Flexner to ask, "What are my duties?" to which Flexner replies, "You have no duties – only opportunities."[171] In this unconditional expenditure, so to speak, Flexner is restoring the "waste" of community.

What Flexner's writings and practices, and this anecdote in particular, advocate for is the attention to and of free play. The inattention to positive emotions and play as adaptive curiosities or "evolutionary anomalies"[172] is found through the history of cognitive science,[173] and it is an omission that Flexner's own career was devoted to redressing. While the study of play is certainly expanding enormously nevertheless, as noted throughout the present discussion, it might be fair to say that behavioural science has been more concerned with reactions (and thus dictating and framing the questions) rather than the expressive and unpredictable potential of play. Recalling Minsky's accusation that "something happened to psychology since Behaviorism, which is that we don't study what people don't do,"[174] his elaboration on the point is pertinent in this context: "Freud is almost the last person to mention repression, because the experimenters and their methodology are weak on it. You can watch behavior, but you can't explain what non-stimulus the animal non-reaction to is not doing something else, and that's why I think humor has been so poorly studied."[175]

A capacity for humour is especially relevant to an aesthetic of play, given that it is a particular creative space and critical distance from a purely representational communication. In humour is to be found the nonhuman capacity for irony, an ironic play which is more often than not exercised through an expressive use of space, through gestures and embodied play. From Charles Darwin's observations of the interspecific "practical joke" of stick or object play with dogs,[176] or the way apes tease through blocking paths,[177] or the way dogs tease each other and their humans, or the various pranks and surprises,[178] attention to humour in nonhuman animals is a critical disruption of an anthropocentric perspective upon biology and waste. And laughter has been identified in a range of species,[179] from dogs,[180] to apes,[181] to rats,[182] and possibly even insects.[183] Indeed, the importance and relevance of sound is perhaps overlooked, as it were, in insects and other invertebrates.[184] And in tool play in particular, there is a dimension of symbolic thinking through objects, as well as technical intelligence, identified not only with respect to tools but also with respect to artefacts and objects,[185] a kind of aesthetic sense of humour. A sense of humour is indeed significant as the capacity for ironic difference, the very making of the author.

Somewhat ironically, given the notorious figure of the "starving author" it is perhaps the lack of attention to the aesthetics of play that starves the nonhuman animal of expressive production.

Starving for Attention

This inattention to positive emotions and play is notable in particular when it comes to the anthropocentric processes of production within which play is supposed to make sense. Recalling Minsky's observations, research has variously emphasised negatives states, where the adaptationist narrative is perhaps more straightforward (and consistent) to reconstruct: "Although positive affect has never been completely ignored by psychologists studying humans, when it comes to non-human animals. the balance has typically been firmly tilted towards the charge of anthropomorphism."[186] The difficulty in observing, isolating, and measuring positive emotions underpins the lack of attention[187] and ultimately this translates into a kind of waste, at least from a behavioural perspective, due to the lack of problems to solve, so to speak.[188] This inattention, it would seem, is carefully fostered towards validating pain models.[189] But at the same time, this strategic inattention very clearly and systematically eradicates the prospect of authorship and rehearses the aesthetic dimension of the species barrier. In this sense the production of evidence is of interest, and directions towards measuring positive affect have thus included the way in which positive affect may be shown through performance, as in play. Indeed, play, throughout the literature, has presented some of the greatest potential as a viable indicator of positive affect.[190] *Play shows*. At the same time, play is, *in every sense*, a manipulation of environment, an embodied expression of affect. As such, and as an absolute waste of time, it is potentially a highly productive account of nonhuman animal authorship.

An unhelpful binary of work and play not only limits the acceptance of the relevance of play but also interferes with the recognition of play itself. At the same time, this relation of work and play and the accompanying binary values of utility and waste, arguably *play out* in the dominant discourse of legal, policy, and commercial conceptualisations of real and digital. In reference to the digital (or the alternative, virtual) in this binary ensures that this space is by definition *not real* and somehow secondary to the real. This has significant repercussions for the understanding and appreciation of what it means to build in the metaverse,[191] and for explaining the value in digital product, and for examining the relevant parameters for success. In particular, these environments thrive and sustain through communities as distinct from objects, with the circulation of assets largely in order to maintain the circulation of connections. Indeed, the digital is a world built through familiar production; and a playful approach to creativity and creative *work*, and a relational approach to property (through access and connections as distinct from objects and boundaries), are part of a crucial, transformative shift, prerequisite for commercial relevance in this space. Community is thus the product as well as the resource, the ends as well as the means.

Play is world-building and ironic, at the same time communicative and expressive. Community is thus essential in that the playworld is relational, experiential, contingent; always already two. Following Fink into the digital environment, Bruce Janz explains: "It is a sense-creating space. That space is not created individually – it can only happen in a social existence."[192] How does the author move in that space? Recalling the spaces of authorship considered earlier, the dialectic of play becomes particularly engaging in the phenomenon of turn-taking in play. Turn-taking is a form of cooperative communication and embodied dialogue that has been identified across a range of species,[193] including the acoustic turn-taking or "duetting" by insects,[194] as well as between different species,[195] such as between a dog and their human,[196] and between cows and humans.[197] Turn-taking is especially significant in the present discussion as it is a form of gestural or embodied proto-language which, although not limited to the play context, is hugely relevant to such ludic and affiliative encounters and associated fairness. In its explicit performance of relations, it is "structured like a handshake," becoming a literal incarnation of sociable property, in that "you cannot successfully turn-take by yourself."[198] But that turn-taking (and turn-making) is similarly decipherable in the processes of adaptation, parody, pastiche, and caricature in authorship. And in terms of space, these shenanigans hijack and reroute through a will to connection, precisely through the play of distance. This makes sense in the concept of *détournement*, as presented by the spatial expressions of the Situationist International[199] – *détournement* is a distraction towards attention.[200] It is an exemplary form of play, if you will. After all, to pay attention is to prolong the game: and with that animal turn, the *monkey shines*.

And so to turn to the tools of authorship.

Playing the Tool

What then are the properties of object play? Weil draws from Hegel in order to explain this contact through sport and play: "The essential aim of sport would be to give the human body that suppleness and, as Hegel says, that fluidity which renders it pervious to thought and enables the latter to enter directly into contact with material objects."[201] As such the sociality of territories of play is emancipated from the predatory battle lines of contemporary forms of property – it is the symbolic pretence of *as-if*, as distinct from *just so*.[202] The author is made through the contact, the deception of the play, the very materiality of that embodied communication.[203] Recall the earlier discussion of hands and mouths and the various objects manipulated by dogs (using their mouths as "hands") in the advertising campaign for dental sticks. All the dogs in the advertising campaign are both perceiving their world and acting upon it through the manipulation of tools – whether those tools are considered objects of industry or play should not matter to the work of knowing underway. The objects used by all the dogs are extensions of their bodies, their mouths as hands.[204] In words that are enticingly resonant with Weil's, Jakob von Uëxkull observes, "[T]he subject which uses the tools, perceives and functions with their aid."²⁰⁵ This play is an act of knowing.

And yet there are curious controversies over the very definition itself of tool use, all of which seem to resist the significance and insight from an embodied sensory extension. Once again, the spectre of the *hand* appears to interfere. For example, because there is uncertainty as to the precision of a crocodile's placement of sticks in order to deceive birds into landing on them for building material (and thus becoming easy prey), the use of the sticks as tools is disputed: "[I]t is not possible to confirm that the crocodiles were responsible for the placement of the fish remnants or if they were just a byproduct of consumption. To be tool use, the crocodiles would have to purposefully place the food on the water."²⁰⁶ In other words, the crocodile inserts their body into the tool (swimming under the sticks), rather than using "hands" to place the sticks. As a distinction between forms of manipulation, this seems a curious line in the sand and one at odds with multispecies embodied cognition and languages. And further, subsequent research has shown that crocodiles do indeed use these sticks as lures in order to attract prey in a strategy of deception.²⁰⁷ In using sticks to lure birds, the crocodiles not only ascertain the perspective of the other species but also the seasonality of their strategy, relying as it does on nest-building behaviour.²⁰⁸ This strategy necessarily takes account of not only the crocodile's beliefs and goals but also those of the birds that are attracted by the lure, constituting a form of intentional deception. Specifically, it suggests that the crocodile understands that the bird can be deceived into holding a false belief, one that does not match the reality of the situation.²⁰⁹ What are simply sticks to the crocodile, an artefactual adornment at best, are important building resources for the bird. And thus the pursuit and execution of this strategy appears to demonstrate appreciation and utilisation of these different beliefs not only in relation to each other but also in relation to the tools.²¹⁰ This manipulation of both the tools and the beliefs of the other species with respect to those tools would appear to fulfil a kind of authorial intentionality; that is, where the crocodile "has beliefs and desires (and no doubt intentional states) about beliefs and desires (and other intentional states) – both those of others and its own."²¹¹

Nevertheless, an interest in technical innovation is ordinarily taken separately from play, once again seemingly deferring and deflecting play from any active direction over one's life. Thus, play is usually defined as activity without function or obvious goal-orientation,²¹² but importantly this should not be taken to confirm a lack of value. Recalling the discussion of waste, while tool use has been persistently associated with higher intelligence and material culture.²¹³ As such, the distinction between work and play settles out strategically in service of hierarchies in relation to intellect and culture, resonating strikingly with Weil's disturbance of these coercive binaries. The distinction between play and tool use thus appears almost hierarchical, and somewhat arbitrary, becoming yet another barrier erected in the service of human exceptionalism.

This distinction operates in ways curiously similar to the kinds of processes of aesthetic or cultural evaluation associated with creative and innovative output, where one form may be privileged or elevated over another. In other words, immediately recognisable is an adherence to distinctions between high and low (or popular) culture, high and rudimentary or traditional innovation, and indeed art (and humans as the art-making animals) and inconsequential creativity (rationalised as adaptive and functional behaviour). In their work on creativity, Keith Negus and Michael Pickering observe the way in which a distinction runs through assignations of creative competence and performance, and they set out to disrupt this through the very language of play: "Our examples deliberately bring high and low culture together in disqualification of the divide between them, while consciously playing on the word 'play' in doing this. For it is this unselfconscious absorption in the play that is important, enabling us to use a cliché to rejuvenate a cliché."[214] In doing so, they note that play is not only critical in addressing this divide but also is somewhat ubiquitous across the cultural forms *at work*, as it were, in this divide: "The simultaneous loss and realisation of self in play occurs in every cultural form and entails a move beyond the rational accomplishment of competence."[215] This is precisely what is at stake here; that is, it is necessary to move away from comparison based upon competence (including sentience) and move to the phenomenal accounts of the artefacts themselves. How does the *made* make the *maker*? Returning to the task at hand, so to speak, the use of objects in play is thus not ordinarily described as tool use in the usual way in which tool behaviour is understood and interpreted. But why not? Or is it, why knot?

Perhaps it is because play is ordinarily considered unproductive and therefore not *creative* in the ordinary sense of making products, to recall Bataille's critique. The emphasis on goal or outcome not only characterises the interpretation and evaluation of behaviour (and thus the categorisation of play) but also the construction of a seemingly coherent and logical narrative of incentives and rewards for intellectual property. But in this reappraisal of play as authorship, it is possible to destabilise this obstacle. Play is, in and of itself, evidence that value might emerge other than through goal-directed activities.[216] In this way, "Fun is functional,"[217] by all means, by reason of its very waste.

Historically it would seem, play has a problem with the species barrier, and play also has a species problem. There are problems even recognising play in some species, such as invertebrate species, because of the limitations of the lens through which such interpretations are cast.[218] If play is appreciated at all, then it is presumed to be limited to the "smarter" mammals, and thus to reaffirm the species hierarchy. There are notable and laudable exceptions to this inattention,[219] but for the most part this process of affirmation is precisely through rehearsing the presumptions that underpin that hierarchy in devising play research and in recognising play at all. This is somewhat linked to similar biases regarding the charisma of different non-human animals,[220] thus perpetuating a kind of social and cultural stratification of species. Ultimately, such bias has "prevented even looking for play in other taxa."[221] Theodosius Dobzhansky wrote that, "The behavior of invertebrates is too stereotyped to permit play."[222] And indeed, this same dismissal of invertebrates by virtue of a recourse to the repertoire of habit, memory, and mechanism, has continued to underplay, as it were, their contributions and ultimately their charisma (with potentially devastating consequences for their conservation).[223] Play has a species problem.

Power Tools

Despite the persistence of these perspectives on play, there have been challenges from within the scientific literature to the conventional perspectives on play, object-oriented play, and tool use, and the interactions between all three. Research with macaques has suggested that tool use may even evolve from object play;[224] indeed, play as once again inventing new ways to perform. And a particularly notable complication to the relationship between tools and play has emerged with regard to dogs and their stick chewing.[225] However, once again the analysis is reorientated to the stick as a tool for functional application (cleaning teeth) rather than pleasure. So much so, in fact, that the authors appear conscientious in their differentiation of chewing for function and chewing for play: "Stick chewing may also be challenged as simply a play-related behavior in some cases, similar to object-oriented play in other species, which is not widely considered tool use in the absence of other functional roles."[226] Are tools for function or for creativity and innovation? And is innovation not a function in and of itself? As it happens, the authors note that the stick may also operate as a communicative tool, in "the possibility of dogs bringing sticks to their owners as social tool use used to trigger play," and they recommend future research in this area.[227] But a future complexity arises: is the stick a lure (a tool) or a communicative symbol or both? Are all liars authors?

Nevertheless, this study does not pursue the revision of play; rather, they suggest that play and tool-use may occur simultaneously: "We therefore do not claim that stick chewing can never be characterized as play, but instead emphasize that regardless of whether stick chewing can in some cases be classified play, the overt behavior fits most major definitions of tool use and thus can be considered as such."[228] The authors maintain nevertheless "that play and tool use need not be mutually exclusive."[229] The authors explain that "the functional roles are clear reasons to consider the possibility that dog stick chewing in some cases is a case of tool use as opposed in all cases being reducible to mere object-oriented play."[230]

Indeed, the authors actually note the obstacle of the concept of goal in recognising direction in play behaviour. That is, the conventional literature is resistant to the notion of authorship, as it were, through play: "Replacing the term 'goal' with a direct and immediate benefit to the animal in some definitions of tool use generates a more valuable and quantifiable definition by which to evaluate putative cases and more easily account for instinctive tool use and tool use involved in play."[231] But it still stops short of play matters, so to speak – that is, what play makes.[232]

But of course, the objects of play may also extend to other players, returning the question to the communicative and communal might of play. Paula Thomson and Victoria Jaque present an important relationship between play and performance in their work on the performing artist.[233] In particular, the relational, spatial, and social qualities of creative production through performance are both related to and enhanced by play. The artist's play is thus "an orientation to the other players" through which there is a negotiation and coordination of time and space, such as with "dancers exploring ways to coordinate rhythmic and spatial elements essential for any dance performance."[234] The aesthetics are thus through those very relations, as distinct from the objects or products that may or may not bridge those relations. The relational quality of an aesthetic sense is fundamental to this reckoning of authorship through play.

All This Useless Beauty

Gadamer identifies play to be "an idea that has played a major role in aesthetics."[235] It has, at the same time, introduced an aesthetic dimension into evolutionary biology. Theodosius Dobzhansky notes: "Some forms of art seem to be related to play."[236] Nevertheless, although Dobzhansky concedes that "[p]lay certainly occurs in many animals," he maintains that "aesthetics and art are usually regarded as exclusively human possessions," based seemingly on a "sensitivity to beauty."[237] For Dobzhansky, this is a challenge for reconstructing the origin of human art, rather than a concern of nonhuman creativity.

To put play at the centre of aesthetics, as Gadamer suggests, introduces the question of play in aesthetic labour. What role might play also *play* in the definition of the work? In the way in which it shows, following Gadamer's account, and the manner of its experience through a sociality of imitation and regard, play introduces a lively relation with the object that is prescient in the recognition of the work itself: "When we speak of play in reference to the experience of art, this means neither the orientation nor even the state of mind of the creator or of those enjoying the work of art, nor the freedom of a subjectivity engaged in play, but the mode of being of the work of art itself."[238] Play thus emerges as fundamental to the work itself. This makes sense with respect to the copyright notion of the work and the concept of the author's own intellectual creation – play is inextricable from the experience of intellectual creation, and at the same time is the expression itself of that creation. As Gadamer explains: "[T]he being of art cannot be defined as an object of an aesthetic consciousness because, on the contrary, the aesthetic attitude is more than it knows of itself. It is a part of the *event of being that occurs in presentation*, and belongs essentially to play as play."[239]

The wasteful aesthetic and productive purposelessness of this aesthetics in nonhuman animal play is similarly appreciated by Brian Massumi when he suggests, "Play instinctively belongs to the aesthetic dimension ... The *aesthetic yield* of play is the qualitative measure of its uselessness."[240] This abundant, exuberant aesthetic is gloriously wasteful and thus waste, not want, becomes a basis for authorship. Instead of being dismissed as a "stupid beggar," it appears that the Grasshopper is indeed the Beggar-Author.

My Favourite Waste of Time

In qualitative research with poor communities at the local level, Esther Duflo and Abhijit Banerjee identified behaviours in relation to poverty that are frequently overlooked in systemic approaches to economic development; somewhat playful or *wasteful* behaviours, if you will.[241] The authors found that spending on entertainment could take priority over spending on food.[242] In an interview with Oucha Mbarbk, living in a remote village in Morocco, it emerged that the television was more important to the family than food.[243] More often than not, the reaction is to "blame the poor."[244] As Baudelaire suggests, there is "a certain class of ultra-reasonable and *anti-poetic* people" and that "[t]hese are the people who would gladly give a sixpenny piece to a poor man on condition that he stuffed himself with bread, but would always refuse him a farthing to have a glass in a tavern."[245] Indeed, hating the players, as it were, is itself "a poverty of imagination."[246]

It is perhaps no surprise that responses to this kind of election to play are frequently invoked to infantilise the economic and geographic other and to recuperate cultural issues within an economic narrative.[247] But this is not a phenomenon of the so-called global South; rather, it is a crucial relationship between the importance of expressive waste, as introduced earlier through the work of Bataille. Arguably what is perhaps underestimated in global approaches to development and human welfare is the necessity of enrichment at the level of the individual: "Generally, it is clear that things that make life less boring are a priority for the poor."[248] And frustration of that play leads to frustration of social connection and community.[249] Play must be understood as a value in and of itself, as well as representing a certain kind of waste if that play is thwarted. These findings with respect to humans have a correlative in animal studies, where issues of poor welfare and disease in wild nonhuman animal populations have been shown to impair cognitive function and flexibility.[250] Play thus becomes both the conditions for creativity and the *show* of good welfare.[251] Play, and indeed authorship, are thus issues of welfare as well as indications of wellbeing.

This recalls the earlier discussion of distraction and demonstrates the way in which attention is co-opted and appropriated within the economic sphere. Later discussion will compare the wanderings, distractedness, and distractions of sheer exuberance among the Situationist International and the art of *détournement* (or diversion) and *dérive* (or drift, the wandering and distraction of strangeness), but this play takes a turn here as well. Simon Sadler explains *détournement* as "art composed from 'diverted' aesthetic elements," the waste and the distraction of play.[252] This is an *aesthetic yield*, to recall Massumi's phrase, created from surplus, from waste, from overflow. This is an aesthetic of discarded aesthetics. The concept of *détournement* is also a form of layering, of fragments, seemingly anecdotal in structure. This resonates with the dialectical nature of social learning and play and adds theoretical weight to the question of attribution or stewardship, as acknowledged through that layering. These principles will be revisited later,[253] but it is useful at this stage to consider the action of play in this particular example, expressing the exuberance of waste as well as the preciousness of waste.

Homo Economicus, Homo Ludens, Homo Prodigi

In the context of the important work of *poor economics*, it is prudent to note the way in which Tarde is critical of the concept of *homo economicus*. Tarde suggests that economists ignore leisure on the assumption that work is the superior activity.[254] This is of course distinct from the industry of leisure, which is not Tarde's assertion here, such industries still presenting an economic concern with labour. With respect to industries commercialising leisure, the emphasis is on the work to achieve that monetisation of the leisure time of others. What Tarde is advocating, much more significantly, is an emphasis on leisure and wellbeing as more important than work and identifying this as the superior concern of a comprehensive economic psychology.[255]

But this advocacy comes without valorising or resorting to binaries of city and country, or a nostalgia for a pre-industrialised time, as perhaps evident elsewhere in considerations of leisure, including Thorstein Veblen's writings on leisure.[256] Tarde's theory of leisure may be distinguished from that of his contemporary, and his work on leisure in a political economy, in that Veblen's theory of the leisure class is presented as antithetical to production, where leisure is a privilege and sign of status, exempting one from productive work (which is itself a sign of status). Thus, while also approaching leisure in the context of social stratification and justice, Veblen arrives at a somewhat different consideration through his concept of conspicuous consumption. It might be said that this maps onto the erroneous emphasis in classical economics on maximum wealth rather than optimal and thus social, as described by Tarde, notwithstanding that both were approaching unjust distribution. Indeed, for Tarde, leisure includes a kind of production through consumption, not only in the generation of new products (such as data) but also in the consumption of goods and the generation of new desires and new wants.[257] What does Naruto want? Above all, Naruto wants to play. But that play produces vital sociality, consumes the objects of desire, and generates a prosocial appetite for more.

In this sense, Tarde advocates the kind of performative excess of playful consumption that seems to resonate with Bataille's concept of expenditure, in as much as both depart significantly from the approach to leisure offered by Veblen in particular. In doing so, Tarde is critical of the abstraction of wealth as an objective value, and "[t]he error of believing that it was a good scientific method to consider wealth as the proper object of political economy,"[258] rather than considering the individuals in the swarm, so to speak; or in other words, "the one who produces it or the one who consumes it."[259] Using the example of ball games, Tarde describes work "in the economic sense of the word" as being concerned wholly with the production of wealth to satisfy "desires other than the very desire to accomplish what he does," and differentiates this from playing ball for which the only desire pursued and satisfied is that of the individual to play ball.[260] Thus, production can be playful, and may not always be work in this strict economic sense. Put succinctly, for Tarde the error is to prioritise maximising wealth and ignore the social forces of a political economy of optimal wealth, and to emphasise saving over consumption in doing so.[261] A *poor economics* is to sing all winter, and to produce through all one consumes.

Tarde maintains, contrary to the emphasis on work as the productive value, that "leisure is not there for work, but work for leisure."[262] For Tarde, it is through work that individuals serve each other; but it is through leisure, "by their feasts and their games," that "the truly social agreement" is to be found through which individuals "please each other."[263] In other words, that *pleasing* comes through the attention to shared interests and the play of familiar production. Rather than a waste of time, as it were, the genuinely affiliative and civilising sociality produced through play is to be promoted and valued; work, on the other hand, merely serves to sustain this play. A crucial concept in Tarde's inter-psychology is the potential for joy in work, together with a more careful and nuanced consideration of the opposition and adaptation to be found in work and play. Indeed, this insight is perhaps most explicitly available through the familiar production of play. What is in play? And who gets to play? In play, the social justice of its distribution is crucial to the full sociality of play. In a sense, play is the work of rewilding.

At this point it is important to remember the joy in work, as set out in Weil's philosophy, and the frustration of that joy as a matter of fundamental concern: "Nothing in the world can make up for the loss of joy in one's work."[264] This restores the truly productive nature of work, in the capacity in which it is understood by Weil, the exuberance of waste through exhaustion, in every sense: "By work, man creates the universe around him. Remember the way you looked at the fields after a day's harvesting ... How differently from a person going for a walk, for whom the fields are only a scenic background! In precisely *this* consists the power of a true monument of work over the universe that surrounds it ... (In this, you possess an inexhaustible source of joy ...)."[265] This may seem inconsistent with the account of attention and distraction presented in earlier discussion, but this is indeed the nature of the distinction between an attentive distraction, and a mere consumption of the fields as "only a scenic background."[266] This *attentive imitation* is the proficiency of what might be called *homo prodigi* – an explainability of and accountability that is inextricable from the joy of authorship and the affiliation and turn-taking with one's precursors. In this respect, the joy of work opens up to a compassionate and empathetic play of production that is relevant to an invigorated concept of authorship. And through attribution, that play is prolonged.

What Is It Like to Play?

What does Naruto want? Naruto's expressions in the selfie photographs vary, but the most commonly disseminated photos appear to show positive affect.[267] These include a friendly face, where Naruto's mouth appears relaxed and slightly open,[268] described frequently as a grin in the popular reports.[269] Other photographs show a play face, where Naruto's mouth is open slightly wider,[270] such as the photograph used on the cover of Slater's book.[271] What does Naruto want? It seems that Naruto's photography appears to bring joy. And with that playful joy, to invite the joy of others.

For Tarde, this link between work and joy, between intellectual creation and play, is necessarily inextricable, but joy must always overwhelm: "A minimum of utilitarian work and a maximum of aesthetic, is surely civilisation itself in its most essential element ... those artistic, poetic, and scientific talents which, as they day by day multiply and take deeper root, become really and truly acquired *wants*."[272] Returning to Brecht's concern about the law's arbitration of taste, once again a departure from the product and a focus on the relation provides new insight. What does Naruto want? It is not a question of consumption (or aesthetic taste) but of production: "But for the scientist, the artist, the lover of beauty in all its forms, to produce is a passion, to consume is only a taste."[273]

Is Naruto an author? Let us pretend, as it is to the ironic play of authorship that the discussion now turns.

Would I lie to you?

Notes

1 Choe (1999), 3.
2 Tarde (1903/[1890]), 2–3.
3 This will be considered in more detail later in this chapter through Tarde's critique of *homo economicus* and the concepts of waste and utility.

4 In the United Kingdom, under the Copyright, Designs and Patents Act 1988, producers of sound recordings and films are deemed to be authors under s9(2)(aa) and (ab) respectively. The definition of producer is provided in s178. And notably this is effectively the same wording for the authors of computer-generated works, as set out in s9(3).
5 This critique (and the later discussion of wastefulness and abundance in this chapter) is thus especially relevant to a reconsideration of *use* and *waste* in the context of intangibles, which is introduced here but treated again in more detail in the third book, developing an ethological jurisprudence ultimately of the objects themselves in Gibson (2025).
6 Robinson (2014).
7 Such sharing of information includes through the exchange of fluids with plants and with each other through the phenomenon of trophallaxis. See further LeBoeuf (2017), Meurville and LeBoeuf (2014).
8 Stadler and Dixon (2005). Various species of ants enjoy mutualistic partnerships with aphids: Fire ants manage these through smell (pheromones) leading to increases in the aphid population, Xu et al. (2021); Ants defend their aphid partners from disease by removing lethal fungal infections, as shown in black lawn ants, Nielsen et al. (2010); and ants also assist aphids in their establishment of community or *dwelling* (such as in an apple), Miñarro et al. (2010).
9 Breton (1929), 8.
10 Suits (2014/[1978]).
11 Suits (2014/[1978]), 1.
12 Suits (2014/[1978]), 38. Cheating, where rules are broken to obtain the goal thus ending the game, contrary to the desire for prolongation, is examined in more detail in Chapter 8. See further Deen et al. (2015) and the discussion of open-ended play and the influence on game design, where the authors note a role for feedback (122–123) and how this cooperates with a playful identity in the context of open-ended play (123–126). This resonates with the values of prolongation and authenticity considered here (particularly also when read in conjunction with the consideration of the self-esteem of authors) in the playful identity. These aspects will be discussed further in the next chapter, particularly in the seemingly paradoxical relationship between authenticity, pretence, and deception in authorship.
13 Suits (2014/[1978]), 41.
14 Suits (2014/[1978]), 141.
15 Suits (2014/[1978]), 141.
16 See the discussion of the "commercial flavour" of rights and justice in Weil (1943) and in the previous discussion in Chapter 6 of the present work. This also relates productively to Tarde's critique of *homo economicus*, considered again later in this chapter. Similarly to the Grasshopper's rejection of Prudence's offer, on suspicion of such indebtedness, see further the discussion of indebtedness in intellectual property as the neutralisation of chance in Gibson (2014), 102–104.
17 Suits (2014/[1978]), 8. Emphasis in original.
18 Suits (2014/[1978]), 8.
19 Suits (2014/[1978]), 8.
20 Suits (2014/[1978]), 9.
21 Suits (2014/[1978]), 1.
22 Suits (2014/[1978]), 9.
23 Gadamer (1992/[1960]), 360.
24 Gibson (2022b).
25 Bachelard (2002/[1938]), 242. Emphasis in original.

26 Copyright, Designs and Patents Act, s9(2)(ab).
27 See further Chapter 8 and Gibson (2025). See also the consumer impact on the logic and scope of enhanced distinctiveness in Johnson (2024).
28 Recall the earlier discussion of artificial scarcity and market failure in Chapter 5. See further in relation to an ethological perspective on artificial scarcity as "a failure as an incentive for sociability," in Gibson (2020a), 261.
29 For example, see the binary logic of property and personhood in a welfare context in animal studies literature: Francione (2021).
30 Schank et al. (2023), 1. The authors argue "that a *social play learning process* (complex play) evolves because it reduces *Umwelt* entropy about future adult cooperative and competitive social situations" (2).
31 Tarde (1902), 24. Translation mine.
32 Tarde (2012/[1893]), 26–27.
33 An interesting consideration of this potential is in the shared languages of the distinct research perspectives upon play. See, for example, Miller (2017).
34 Burghardt et al. (2024), 11. See further Brooks and Burghardt (2023).
35 Tarde (2012/[1893]), 26.
36 Schank et al. (2023), 2.
37 Berlyne (1960), 80. Emphasis in original. See further Hutt (1966) and the account of epistemic activity in play, which is relevant to later discussions of world-building (as in videogames and the metaverse) and will be revisited in that context also in Gibson (2025). See further the discussion in Burghardt (2005), 57–60.
38 Flexner (1939), 545.
39 Panksepp and Biven (2012), 359.
40 Panksepp and Biven (2012), 359.
41 Davis and Panksepp (2018), 108–109.
42 Marvin Minsky in comment in the roundtable in Melnechuk et al. (1986), 300.
43 Note Panksepp (1998), 289.
44 Rogers (2020/[1967]), 353–355.
45 Rogers (2020/[1967]), 354.
46 Bekoff (2001).
47 Rogers (2020/[1967]), 354.
48 Jousse (2015/[1981]), xxii. See further Marchesini (2018/[2014]) on the play of unbounded imitation and Jousse's account of "playing with everything" (188).
49 See further Burghardt (2005), 121.
50 See further the discussion of morality in play in the context of an ethological jurisprudence in Gibson (2020a), 88–91.
51 Solomon (2012) describes facial mimicry and intersubjectivity in a game of fetch between an autistic child and a therapy dog: "Toward the end of the second hour, Boytwo stopped throwing the ball and, leaning forward, looked closely at the dog facing him and waiting for the ball to be thrown again. On Boytwo's face was a true fascination, with a particular interest in the dog's panting mouth. He even opened his own mouth as if imitating the dog's excited breathing" (121).
52 Maglieri et al. (2020).
53 Weil (1943). For example, Horowitz (2009) describes the "attention to attention" of domestic dogs during dyadic play, presenting a compelling account of this embodied empathy.
54 To echo the adaptationist analysis of offered by Barash (1976): "[T]he results are consistent with an evolutionary interpretation" (1100). The article is presented as an example of the Panglossian paradigm in Gould and Lewontin (1979), considered in more detail in Chapter 3.

55 See the earlier discussion of repetition, opposition, and adaptation in the context of later critiques of evolutionary biology, in Chapter 3.
56 Schank et al. (2023), 2.
57 Tarde (1899), 133.
58 See further the discussion of the welfare concept in the context of animal welfare, animal rights, and welfare property, in Gibson (2022b).
59 For example, on intellectual property rights and performers' rights understood in the context of welfare and for their potential as welfare tools, see Gibson (2022a).
60 Ng (2022), vii. See further the discussion of such instrumental thinking in the context of public policy in Ng (2022), Chapter 14. The discussion of happiness in the context of nonhuman animal welfare maintains a more conventional, utilitarian approach to the instrumental value of welfare, balancing other considerations at a group or population level (see Ng (2022), Chapter 16), contrary to the rethinking of the welfare concept in the present discussion.
61 Tarde (1899), 8.
62 On relational property and the re-socialisation of property through an ethological jurisprudence, see Gibson (2020a), Chapters 11 and 12.
63 Tarde (2012/[1893]), 34. Emphasis in original. This resonates also with Lefebvre's account of the commodity in isolation as unable to exist socially or at all: Lefebvre (1991/[1974]), 342. See further the discussion in Chapter 4.
64 Gibson (2020a), 291.
65 Tarde (2012/[1893]), 35.
66 Weil (2001[1955]), 109.
67 For example, on the problems of recursion or model collapse, see Shumailov et al. (2023). See further the discussion in Chapter 4 of the present work.
68 See further the discussion in Gibson (2023b).
69 Tarde (1899), 6
70 Leibniz (1714b), §15.
71 Tarde (2012/[1893]), 28. Emphasis in original.
72 Tarde (2012/[1893]), 34.
73 As an anecdotal aside, this quotation and citation anxiety was once communicated to me by a PhD student, who had been advised by another academic in the United States during an online workshop to limit citations, that academic advising that quoting the work of others suggests one's own work cannot stand on its own. This seemed an extraordinary statement at the time, and an almost perverse approach to the concept of academic research. But at the heart of this is a curious notion of originality and a drive to overstatement. The first thing I tell my PhD students is to remove any anxious claims to overstate originality or more usually, the claim to be "the first to do this or that" or similar (which seem to plague the opening lines of PhDs), as though anything is ever the first time. It is never completely true, and indeed my labour in tracking down the precursors of ethological jurisprudence is in part testament to this. But it is also testament to the nature of scholarship and creativity and the joy of those encounters. The conversation and discussion, to use Tarde's approach, with other literature and research is as important as anything else. Without this, any document also has an explainability problem. But these claims to originality also reveal a persistent predatory drift in academia, towards a highly rivalrous and capitalist approach to ideas and to knowledge. To my mind, there is a problem of "toxic originality" that fuels this kind of bad advice to students and others. Part of writing should be mapping those social ties, even if you do not know who they are before you search out their agreement, good research always aims to find out.

74 See further the explainability problem in artificial intelligence introduced in "What Does Naruto Want?" and as a fundamental issue to which this work returns throughout.
75 Blom (2017), 165.
76 Referencing the work of artist, Frank Gillette, Blom (2017) describes memetics as "the controversial science," and understands the concept of belief within this system of ideas a "a type of mental formatting or infrastructure that organizes the intuitions through which the future acts on the present," and thus belief may be associated "with the relational logic of cybernetic models" (164).
77 Blom (2017), 165.
78 Leibniz (1714b), §49.
79 Tarde (1899), 6.
80 Tarde (1899), 6–7. Emphasis added.
81 Latour (2011), 67.
82 See further the discussion in Chapter 8 as well as the return to play in Chapter 9.
83 North (2015) maintains that even the fun of a playful surprise may be explained as such within a functional paradigm: "Indeed, the pleasure of surprises may relate to the way they can be indicative of the opportunity to learn new things – you clearly cannot prescribe in advance precisely what it will be useful to learn, but if a general indicator is perceived as rewarding, then it will provide a motivation to engage in behaviours that can facilitate learning" (R2).
84 Held and Spinka (2011); Mintline (2013); Ahloy-Dallaire (2018).
85 Whitaker and Tonkin (2019); Tonkin (2019); and Kumar et al. (2022).
86 See further the discussion of wellbeing in intellectual property in Taylor and Derclaye (2021).
87 Bataille (2022/[1976]), 70.
88 Bataille (2022/[1976]), 70
89 Bataille (2022/[1976]), 72–73. Indeed, this cycle of "poverty" underpins the urgent problems of excessive production and consumption in consumer products, and the sustainability crisis for industries such as fashion. See further Gibson (2023d).
90 Tarde (1899), 194.
91 Gibson (2021b). See further the discussion of the relational and motile quality of NFTs as "non-objects" in Gibson (2024b).
92 Ferreira Gullar, quoted in Martins (2017).
93 In the United Kingdom, Animal Welfare Act 2006, s2(b).
94 Weil (1940), 3. See further the discussion of force in Chapter 5.
95 Indeed, the notion of personhood is by definition anthropocentric, maintaining the reversibility of force rather than transforming the subject-object dynamic. As discussed in previous chapters, such threshold definitions may be shifted at any time. See further the discussion in Gibson (2022b).
96 For example, see the attention in Rognstad (2018). Compare the criticism of the traditional justificatory paradigms in Richards (2002).
97 Second Treatise, Chapter V, §31. Emphasis in original.
98 Lynch (1990), 167.
99 Lynch (1990), 167.
100 Shumailov et al. (2023). See further Gibson (2023b).
101 Second Treatise, Chapter V, §31.
102 For example, see Vossen (2021).
103 For example, see the useful review of the literature in Hull (2009).
104 Hughes (1988), 329.
105 Hughes (1988), 329.

106 Second Treatise, Chapter V, §27. Emphasis in original.
107 Second Treatise, Chapter V, §27. Emphasis in original.
108 Weil (2002/[1949]), 34.
109 Weil (2002/[1949]), 34. Emphasis added.
110 Tarde (1902) is critical of economists emphasising wealth over connections through leisure and play throughout *Psychologie Economique*.
111 Directive (EU) 2015/2436 to approximate the laws of the Member States relating to trade marks, art 19; Trade Marks Act 1994, s46.
112 Directive (EU) 2015/2436, art 9; Trade Marks Act 1994, s48. The equitable principle of nis also relevant here.
113 Gibson (2023b).
114 Paris Convention for the Protection of Industrial Property, art 5A. There is an absolute restriction on forfeiting a design for failure to work (art 5B), but there is greater freedom in relation to compulsory licences (although section 10 of the Registered Designs Act 1949 was repealed in 2001).
115 For instance, there has been no compulsory licence granted in the United Kingdom this millennium: see Roughton et al. (2022), [11.25].
116 Matthews et al. (2023).
117 Tarde (1899), 166.
118 Frow (2003) distinguishes the concept of waste in Bataille as presenting "a different kind of psychology of emulation," and links this "with a dynamic of abjection, understood as a central element both of artistic creation and of the desire for power" (32). This resonates with Tarde's understanding of imitation as an incentive in itself, through imitative contagion, together with the freedom to imitate and associated wellbeing. See further Tarde's concept of "imitative rays" in Tarde (1902), including the introduction to the concept, 4–6. See further Tarde (1899); Tarde (1903/[1890]). Bataille's related approaches and coincidences with Tarde, and notable comparisons with Thorstein Veblen, are considered later in this chapter in the discussion of the value of waste in abundance and play more specifically.
119 Tarde (1902), 4–6.
120 Bataille (2022/[1976], 46. Emphasis in original.
121 Bataille (2022/[1976], 47.
122 The symbol was previously required under the Universal Copyright Convention (UCC) (1952 as revised) in order to obtain protection, but the UCC has been entirely superseded by the fact that all members of the UCC are now members of the Berne Convention on Literary and Artistic Copyright (1886 as revised).
123 Recall the discussion of the Sheeran litigation in Chapter 6.
124 Gibson (2006); Gibson (2019).
125 Tarde (1903/[1890]), 221.
126 The wider role of play for social learning and community cohesion is important here, particularly in respect of "more information transmission of behaviors via play": Kaufman and O'Hearn (2017), 498.
127 See the discussion in Gibson et al. (2015) on the earnings of authors in the United Kingdom. See further the recent findings in Thomas et al. (2022).
128 Frow (1995), 89.
129 Frow (1995), 90.
130 Frow (1997), 190.
131 Bataille (2002/[1976]). See further Gibson (2025).
132 Gould and Lewontin (1979): "The design is so elaborate, harmonious and purposeful that we are tempted to view it as the starting point of any analysis … But this would invert the proper path of analysis" (582).

133 See further the discussion of sentience as a threshold concept in Chapter 3.
134 Birch et al. (2020); Fasel (2024).
135 Chapter 3. See further, Bilchitz (2009), on arbitrariness in relation to the wider rights and personhood discourse.
136 Fasel (2024), 49–72.
137 See further Waldron (2009) and in particular Herzog (2012) in commentary: "Through early modernity, the standard view was that the government ruled not over individuals but over male heads of households ... A special dignity for him – and indignity, and helplessness, for others ... Here, by the way, liberal individualism shouldn't be condemned as sociologically naïve or pernicious. It should be embraced as offering legal recourse and dignity to those on the other side of the threshold, once invisible" (103). For a detailed account of Waldron's work in this context and in relation to nonhuman animal rights, see Fasel (2024), 49–72. Fasel argues that "[s]till to this day, human rights bear the marks of aristocracy" (49).
138 Weil (2001/[1955]), 91–92.
139 Bataille (2022/[1976]).
140 Bataille (2022/[1976]), 58.
141 Bataille (2022/[1976]), 58.
142 Tarde (1899), 166.
143 For example, in the United Kingdom, the definition of a producer within the Copyright, Designs and Patents Act 1988, s178: "the person by whom the arrangements necessary for the making of the sound recording or film are undertaken." Note also s9(3) which applies similar language for the purposes of identifying the author in a computer-generated work: "the author shall be taken to be the person by whom the arrangements necessary for the creation of the work are undertaken."
144 Bataille (2022/[1976]), 58. See further Chapter 3 of the present work.
145 See further Chapter 3.
146 Brecht (2000/[1932]), 182. Emphasis in original.
147 Bataille (2022/[1976]), 40.
148 Bataille (2022/[1976]), 40.
149 Bataille (2022/[1976]), 46. Emphasis in original.
150 Bataille (2022/[1976]), 59.
151 Bataille (2022/[1976]), 41. Emphasis in original.
152 Gibson (2014), 195.
153 Weil (2001/[1955]), 105.
154 For example, even in the case of the industry of play itself, as in interactive entertainment, its reconfiguration as an industry means that the value is measured overwhelmingly in terms of its contribution to the economy, and thus its contribution to the maintenance of the circulation of capital, including the recuperation of leisure as production (for example, see the United Kingdom Government Press Release. Multi-million pound funding boost for home-grown video game developers, 17 April 2024).
155 Bataille (2022/[1976]), 42. Emphasis in original.
156 Chapter 4.
157 Following Suits's emphasis on the means of play, McMurtry (2017) explains: "Players play for fun which is an internal good, and it creates a need for cooperation. The goal of the game is to continue playing as long as possible by acting as if in on stage play" (52).
158 Burghardt (2005); Chittka (2022); Galpayage Dona et al. (2022).
159 See the critique in Burghardt (2005), 121.

160 See further the discussion of incentives and an ethological approach in Gibson (2020a), Chapter 10. See further Gibson (2014), 8–9.
161 Bataille (1933), 116. Emphasis in original.
162 Bataille (1933), 117. Emphasis in original.
163 Flexner's publications extend to several key reports on education in the United States, including: Flexner (1908); Flexner (1910); Flexner and Bachman (1918); Flexner (1921).
164 Flexner (1910). See further Chapman (1974).
165 Parker (1962), 203.
166 Flexner (1910), 55.
167 https://www.ias.edu
168 Padberg (2020). The website for the Institute of Advanced Studies at Loughborough University, for example, explicitly credits the work of Abraham Flexner in its message from its Director. See further https://www.lboro.ac.uk/research/ias/about/
169 Mission statement of the Institute for Advanced Study. Organization Meeting, 10 October 1930.
170 Parker (1962), 199.
171 Flexner (1939), 551. According to Flexner, while there is "the hope that the unobstructed pursuit of useless knowledge will prove to have consequences in the future as in the past," this is in no way to be emphasised as a corollary or duty, or to be considered a justification for the Institute: "Not for a moment, however, do we defend the Institute on that ground. It exists as a paradise for scholars who, like poets and musicians, have won the right to do as they please and who accomplish most when enabled to do so" (552).
172 Nelson et al. (2023), 1548.
173 See further the discussion in Burghardt et al. (2024).
174 Marvin Minsky in discussion in Melnechuk et al. (1986), 300.
175 Marvin Minsky in discussion in Melnechuk et al. (1986), 300.
176 Darwin (2004/[1879]), 92.
177 Laumer et al. (2024).
178 Laumer et al. (2024).
179 Vanutelli et al. (2024). See further Panksepp (2000) and the discussion of vocalisation and joy in Nelson et al. (2023).
180 Volsche et al. (2022); Maglieri et al. (2022). See further the participation of the human through laughter during dog play, in Mitchell and Singhorn (2014).
181 Leavens (2009).
182 Panksepp and Burgdorf (2003); Panksepp (2007).
183 Perry and Baciadonna (2017). Recall the importance of sound in Turner (1914).
184 Recall the discussion in Turner (1914). See further Perry and Baciadonna (2017); and more generally, Bridges and Chittka (2019).
185 Taylor (2024). See further, Osuna-Mascaró et al. (2023); Harrington et al. (2024).
186 Nelson et al. (2023), 1548.
187 For example, see Burgdorf and Panksepp (2006) where the authors note positive affect and negative affect "are rather general and non-specific ways to conceptualize emotion feelings," suggesting that they could be considered "merely semantic-conceptual ways to parse the many kinds of 'good' and 'bad' feelings that the nervous system can construct" (174).
188 See further Frederickson (1998) who notes that positive emotions have received less attention in the research literature because negative states are clearer subjects for research, presenting as problems for which research will look for solutions

(301–302). Gigliotti (2022) maintains that "'Joy' is a neglected term in science and ... is indicative of how we have ignored a wide range of both emotion and ability in animals of all kinds" (104).
189 Nelson et al. (2023). See also Esperidiao-Antonio et al. (2017).
190 In the context of vocalisation, Nelson et al. (2023) note that this offers the "possibility of joy having a direct behavioural marker that can be measured while an animal experiences different scenarios," and similarly "[p]lay behaviour is another potentially useful marker of joy" (12).
191 A more detailed ethological account of the metaverse is undertaken in Gibson (2025).
192 Janz (2019), 65.
193 Ravignani et al. (2019); Pika et al. (2018).
194 Bailey (2003). See further, Wickler (1980).
195 Mondémé (2022).
196 Laurier et al. (2006). See further Mondémé (2023).
197 Cornips (2022).
198 Froese (2018), 182. See further the discussion of this sociality through fetch and similar turn-taking games between dogs and autistic children in Solomon (2012).
199 Discussed in more detail in Chapter 9
200 Later discussion of the fragment will also revisit *détournement* as an expression also created through fragments, with the discarded surplus. See Chapter 9 and further on the fragment in the concluding chapter, *Law's Anecdote*.
201 Weil (2001/[1955]), 100. See further the discussion in Armstrong Oma (2010) where the author considers at one point the example of the centaur and a kind of embodied learning relevant to contemporary training relationships between horse and rider: "The human-horse relationship is founded on interconnectedness where a joint participation in the world leads to a state of humans and horses being mixed" (180). Drawing upon Bachelard, Armstrong Oma notes, "When one learns and embodies a motion, the motion is inhabited, thus, through rhythm, horse and rider come to inhabit riding" (180).
202 See further the discussion of *just so* in the context of the critique of the Panglossian paradigm in adaptationist theories in biology in Chapter 3.
203 Simone Weil describes Marx's distinction between humans and other animals: "Marx ... set down as man's essential characteristic, as opposed to the animals, the fact that he produces the conditions of his own existence and thus himself indirectly produces himself": Weil (2001/[1955]), 101. This distinction rests upon a latent exceptionalism that deprives animals of impulses beyond instinct and it is this same exceptionalism that attempts to defeat examples of more-than-human invention and authorship, a distinction that begs to be untied and undone through an ethological jurisprudence. See in particular, the reckoning in the following chapters of the present work.
204 See further the discussion in Chapter 2.
205 Uexküll (1934), 6.
206 Shumaker et al. (2011), 37. This example of strategic deception will be revisited in Chapter 8.
207 Dinets et al. (2015).
208 Dinets et al. (2015): "The present paper is the first report of tool use by any reptiles, and also the first known case of predators timing the use of lures to a seasonal behavior of the prey ... Now we know that at least one group of animals traditionally included in reptiles is capable of relatively complex tool-using behavior" (77). See also the discussion of deception and creativity in Chapter 8.
209 See further the discussion of false belief and deception in Chapter 8.

210 Deception strategies are considered further as skills of authorship in Chapter 8.
211 Dennett (1983), 345. See further Dennett (1983) on the value of anecdotal evidence and ways in which to understand its importance and application: "Not wanting to feed the galling stereotype of the philosopher as an armchair answerer of empirical questions, I will nevertheless succumb to the temptation to make a few predictions. It will turn out on further exploration that vervet monkeys (and chimps and dolphins and all other higher nonhuman animals) exhibit mixed and confusing symptoms of higher-order intentionality. They will pass some higher-order tests and fail others; they will in some regards reveal themselves to be alert to third-order sophistications, while disappointing us with their failure to grasp some apparently even simpler second-order points. No crisp, 'rigorous' set of intentional hypotheses of any order will be clearly confirmed. The reason I am willing to make this prediction is not that I think I have special insight into vervet monkeys or other species but just that I have noted, as any one can, *that much the same is true of us human beings*. We are not ourselves unproblematic exemplars of third- or fourth- or fifth-order intentional systems" (349). Emphasis added. Anecdotal evidence is considered again in later discussions, including the concluding chapter, *Law's Anecdote*.
212 Burghardt (2005), 71–77; Burghardt (1998), 4–5; Smith (1982). Notably, in a response to Smith (1982), Lancy (1982) questions the efficacy of continuing to create typologies of play (at issue in the present discussion as well): "Yet he and others (including myself) have missed a number of opportunities to break out of the almost suffocating confinement in which play researchers and theorists find themselves. I am not satisfied that Smith, or anyone else, has found an effective way of partitioning the play spectrum into types. One reason for this may be that in creating typologies, theorists anticipate arguments they will later make about the functions of play, a category which his own review shows to be rather unfruitful" (165).
213 See further, McGrew (1992).
214 Negus and Pickering (2004), 18.
215 Negus and Pickering (2004), 18.
216 For example, see the discussion of alternatives to goals as a measure of value in San-Galli and Bouret (2015).
217 Byrne (2015), R2.
218 See further the discussion in Perry and Baciadonna (2017).
219 Galpayage Dona et al. (2022).
220 Recall earlier discussions on so-called charismatic species and disproportionate public attention. See further the discussion in Chittka (2022), 210–213.
221 Burghardt (2015), 134.
222 Dobzhansky (1962), 214.
223 Guiney and Oberhauser (2008); McClenachan et al. (2012), Krause and Robinson (2017).
224 Cenni et al. (2020).
225 Brooks and Yamamoto (2021).
226 Brooks and Yamamoto (2021), 3.
227 Brooks and Yamamoto (2021), 3.
228 Brooks and Yamamota (2021), 3.
229 Brooks and Yamamoto (2021), 3.
230 Brooks and Yamamoto (2021), 3.
231 Brooks and Yamamoto (2021), 4.
232 McGhee (1982) offers an interesting and earlier account of *what* play produces, and shows an interest in play as an intellectual activity, albeit ceding the

importance of this to the way this is somewhat entangled within a framework of survivability and adaptation: "Since new forms of play tend to accompany the emergence of new capacities in higher organisms, the key question for hominid evolution is whether intellectual play was at any point selected for along with general intellectual capabilities" (167).
233 Thomson and Jaque (2017), in particular, Chapter 10.
234 Thomson and Jaque (2017), 161.
235 Gadamer (1992/[1960]), 101.
236 Dobzhansky (1962), 217.
237 Dobzhansky (1962), 215.
238 Gadamer (1992/[1960]), 101.
239 Gadamer (1992/[1960]), 116. Emphasis in original.
240 Massumi (2014), 10–11. Emphasis added.
241 Banerjee and Duflo (2012/[2011]).
242 Banerjee and Duflo (2012/[2011]), 35–38.
243 Banerjee and Duflo (2012/[2011]), 36–37.
244 Dorey (2010).
245 Baudelaire (1853), 203. Emphasis added.
246 Dorey (2010).
247 Indeed, this infantalisation may be detected in the wider discourse concerning worldwide controversies of repatriation of cultural artefacts, particularly in a perceived inability to conserve, whether that is related to knowledge or other resources, as distinct from *waste* objects through use: in relation to this perspective in the protection of traditional knowledge see Gibson (2005), 80.
248 Banerjee and Duflo (2012/[2011]), 37.
249 See further, Becker et al. (2021).
250 Townsend et al. (2022).
251 Held and Špinka (2011). In the context of behavioural diversity as an indicator of positive welfare, see Miller (2020). Nelson et al. (2023) note: "Playful interactions with the physical environment are found across many species, and these playful contexts may elicit or encourage the expression of joy" (8).
252 Sadler (1999/[1998]), Frontispiece.
253 Chapter 9.
254 Tarde (1902).
255 Tarde (1902), 119.
256 See further Veblen (2007/[1899])
257 Tarde (1902), 105, 371–372.
258 Tarde (1902), 127.
259 Tarde (1902), 127.
260 Tarde (1902), 222. Translation mine.
261 Tarde (1902).
262 Tarde (1902), 119. Translation mine.
263 Tarde (1902), 119. Translation mine.
264 Weil (2002/[1949]), 81.
265 Weil (2015/[1970]), 18. Emphasis in original.
266 Weil (2015/[1970]), 18. Emphasis in original.
267 Of course, these are the photographs that were made available for dissemination, which introduces a further complication, or co-production perhaps, through selection. See further "What Does Naruto Want?"
268 Micheletta et al. (2015). See further Waller et al. (2012).
269 See the discussion in Clark et al. (2020).
270 Micheletta et al. (2015).

271 Slater (2014).
272 Tarde (1905/[1896]), 120. Emphasis added. The iterations of this work are of interest in the present context. The English translation cited here was published as *Underground Man*, but the work was originally published in French as *Fragment d'histoire future*, and this title is restored in Liam Gillick's "updated" version, *Underground (Fragments of Future Histories)*, in Tarde (2004/[1896]).
273 Tarde (1905/[1896]), 121.

Chapter 8

All Authors Are Liars

Perspectives upon the concept of creativity in creativity studies, as well as in the wider surrounding discourse, are that it is a *good thing*. As the 2024 report of the United Kingdom Intellectual Property Office declares, "Great ideas are a source of progress."[1] But this oversight of creativity, as it were, by intellectual property increasingly incorporates that creativity in such a way that it becomes inescapably indebted to that plenary narrative, introducing a binary logic – one that is erroneously summative and incomplete – that presumes the world as either property or public domain. In this way, everything is appropriated within the system, and the outside becomes inconceivable.

In this context, the various accounts of the wider concept of creativity, including technical,[2] policy,[3] and popular discourse,[4] almost uniformly celebrate creativity as a positive and socially desirable quality,[5] and do so separately from disputes over whether the intellectual property system is considered the appropriate partner for that creativity. Nevertheless, the discourse surrounding intellectual property is extremely persuasive and the system becomes somewhat all-encompassing, as fuelled by the binary logic of its comprehensiveness.[6] Indeed, the policy discourse surrounding the system itself presents intellectual property as premised upon an at least implicit prejudice that creativity generates innovation and newness, and newness always amounts to progress, thus justifying protection and proclamations of supposedly rational incentives through that protection. In other words, the novelty of outputs (from original works through to inventions) is celebrated by their own protection, towards sustaining that linear narrative of innovation. However, creativity also necessarily and inescapably has a dark side[7] – well, a twisted irony.

Creativity research provides insight into the relationship between deception and creativity,[8] posing challenges to "the prevailing wisdom of creativity being a benevolent construct."[9] Notably, in the context of the current discussion, literary histories of malign creativity are usually in respect to social currents of technophobia in relation to industrialisation and technological innovation.[10] But this illusory mischief and the element of surprise appear to be part of the joy of authorial deception, so much so that "[t]he active pursuit

DOI: 10.4324/9780429342103-13

of such stimulation may be one way of defining 'play.'"[11] In its other than worldliness, the intellectual creation makes no sense, indeed makes nothing at all, without *lying* – that is, without creating something beyond a mere representation. To make is to deceive, but honestly.

Elements of business strategies and work environments are at times described as potential forms of malign creativity.[12] From the perspective of the law, it may be said that the law of confidence and trade secret law are in part addressing malign creativity in respect of expropriation of a competitor's information. In other words, it is possible to interpret, as built into the intellectual property system itself, an implied bifurcation of two types of creativity – positive or legitimate on the one hand, and negative or illegitimate on the other. This has significant consequences for the institutional and wider understanding of creative work both within the intellectual property system and beyond, given the prevalence and dramatisation of intellectual property disputes in the mainstream press. The *Thinking Out Loud* litigation considered earlier is a very good example of this.[13] Thus, by its very operation, copyright may be seen as instilling a ranking of creative work and ways of working. In this way the copyright system potentially marginalises not only creative effort in what might otherwise be misappropriation, in that case marginalising that misappropriation arguably quite properly, but also, and not clearly so properly, creative effort that is responding to the author's example – a kind of unrequited love, as it were. In this way, an informal calibration or ranking of creativity occurs not only in relation to anything intrinsic to the creative act but also in relation to the governing work or expression. This ranking thus imposes certain and possibly limited views on originality and authorship that are seemingly constructed, facilitated and demanded by intellectual property mechanisms.

This creates a kind of formal logic for creativity such that it continues to sustain its value to intellectual property by nullifying its value or existence in other instances; in other words, lauding creativity as a benevolent and generous act on the one hand, and transforming what is otherwise creative into something unimaginative, unoriginal, or even malevolent on the other, as in some approaches to adaptation.[14] On the one hand, the *original* work is productive; on the other, the adaptation is parasitic, indeed, *beggarly*. This separation makes it possible then to *deal* with forms of adaptation, such as fan fiction, as already secondary, without gesturing any regard to originality at all, at least not as a starting point.[15] That is, the question is not whether the adaptation is creative or not but whether it is the right kind of creativity, resulting in a very different policy perspective concerning intellectual creation as well as very different socio-cultural norms. Such perspectives do not appear to account for an attentive imitation as distinct from a coerced or stereotypic imitation. And this flows from the problem of authorship itself.

Thus, whether celebrated for good or bad, creativity is often laden with value and yet creativity is neutral; or at least, it is plural – the best of all worlds. In his famous essay on creativity, *Toward a Theory of Creativity*, Carl Rogers puts forth a definition of creativity that in some ways respects a judicious approach to the creative.[16] First, "[i]t makes no distinction between 'good' and 'bad' creativity," such judgments being made not in the work but in its circulation and valuation socially: "Galileo and Copernicus made creative discoveries which in their own day were evaluated as blasphemous and wicked, and in our day as basic and constructive."[17] Fundamentally, Rogers acknowledges a kind of functionality (understood socially) as intrinsic to the recognition of creativity in that "to be regarded as representing creativity, the product must be acceptable to some group at some point of time,"[18] but excludes this as a subjective complication to the neutral definition. This is because the definition "makes no distinction regarding the degree of creativity, since this too is a value judgment extremely variable in nature."[19] Instead, Rogers focuses on the motivation for creativity, or the wants, which he defines as "the curative force" of "*man's tendency to actualize himself, to become his potentialities*";[20] that is, "the tendency to express and activate all the capacities of the organism, to the extent that such activation enhances the organism or the self."[21] For Rogers, the conditions for creativity are to be found in relation to one's environment, and in conjunction with one's experience of that environment. This is then "the primary motivation for creativity,"[22] or what might be understood as the tendency through which "the organism forms new relationships to the environment in its endeavor most fully to be itself."[23] Once again, creativity returns to the room for play, the space in the news, the play in the rope. Creativity is both a cooperative and dissensual accord with one's environment, one's encompassment, so to speak. It is a production of neighbourhoods.

Lies are, quite simply, the making of authors. And intellectual property is full of lies. But is the deception always fair?

Lies, Damned Lies, and Intellectual Property

Before embarking upon the voyage through animal deception and artificial lies, the discussion begins by charting, albeit necessarily briefly, the passage of creativity and deception through the fundamental mechanics of the intellectual property system. The basic criteria for intellectual property protection can be understood in terms of two fundamental aspects – newness and usefulness. Just like the *lie* in language, as will be revealed, these inform the scope of protection dialectically, both positively and negatively, and in different ways at different times. Indeed, the quality of usefulness is largely introduced in creativity research to account for creativity that is so-called good or bad, or negative or positive. This functional definition of creativity, as it is described throughout the literature, is expanded to address not only the outputs (positive or negative) but also the inputs or the intention (benevolent or malevolent).[24] The definition thus extends both to the evidence of creativity, in a manner of speaking, as well as to imputing intention or purpose.[25] These phenomena of duality and reversibility are central to understanding creativity more fully in this context, and to engaging in a more critical perspective upon the system itself.

The quality of newness may be recognised across the range of intellectual property rights and is arguably meaningful through both the concept of novelty and through various originality concepts (such as individual character). In copyright, the concept of originality is largely concerned with the new in that it is in a way incomparable (it is the author's *own* intellectual creation) to the extent of the knowledge available (and thus the circumstances for independent creation). For registered rights, such as trade marks, this *originality*, as it were, is deemed by virtue of the publication on the register or first use in the marketplace, depending on the jurisdiction. But more notably, the requirement that any sign is capable of distinguishing necessarily imports qualities of newness into the trade mark. Even though co-existence agreements suggest that there can be, quite plainly, co-existence, and thus the same marks used in different circumstances, the very meaning of those different circumstances is a kind of *newness* created through use in different contexts. Design protection and patent protection similarly both require novelty, although the prior art is perhaps more limited in designs.

The concept of usefulness across the range of intellectual property rights is where things get quite interesting, with the notion of functionality raising some complex questions and, at times, tautological answers. Notably, usefulness may be defined both with respect to the product and with and through the user and use. Usefulness provides both a reason to protect and a reason to exclude from protection. First, usefulness as a criterion for protection is relevant to the salience of the intellectual property object, in that a *useful* object is, by definition and operation, one which is relevant and attractive to users. Curiously, a sense of ownership influences the perception of usefulness,[26] but that ownership is a question of relation and sociability that is related to choice and the subsequent affinity for the object, compelling an ethological approach to the *usefulness* of intellectual property objects and the perception of use.[27] An interesting aside to this aspect is in respect of so-called dirty creativity – how to sell a functional and useful product that is otherwise unattractive.[28] But at the same time, the protection of useful or functional elements may be a barrier to entry if a monopoly were to be afforded to the roundness of a wheel, for example. Thus, in the simplest way, there is a policy against monopolies over functional elements, and so in this respect functionality is an exclusion from protection. However, there is no bright line.[29]

As a starting point, where functionality is usually a reason for disqualification from protection is particularly in respect of language and access to the basic resources of expression (such as genre and general themes in copyright, or the use of functional language in trade marks). Similarly, only the aesthetic elements of a design, not the functional elements, are protected under

European and United Kingdom design law.[30] But then when it comes to style it gets more complicated. Is style functional? Indeed, style can be a method, as understood through patent law; it can be a quality of the artefact itself, such as a style in fashion, film, or art; and it can be a manner of performance, recalling the relevance of innovations in new ways of performing as a possible expressive, intellectual creation. It is pronounced widely and emphatically that copyright cannot protect style, as somehow outside the scope of the expression,[31] and yet all may not be as it seems.[32] Recalling Brecht's dismay regarding the court's arbitration of taste, is this very question perhaps an arbitration of the production of style itself?[33]

But the line gets even duller in patent law. The requirement for the invention to be capable of industrial application (or utility) is in part a requirement for functionality, but it is also in part a requirement for attraction (in other words, it must be acceptable in its industrial application). In the United States this has been referred to as moral utility,[34] while for members of the European Patent Convention there is a morality exclusion in the principle of *ordre public*.[35] It would seem that, in at least some form, the patent system anticipates a so-called malevolent creativity in its regulation and oversight of innovation. But as to functionality, the quality of functionality here is an uncertain value, insofar as it is informed by usefulness as a kind of requirement of novelty, as it were.

In copyright, the concept of usefulness may seem foreign or irrelevant, but arguably it underlies the economic models of copyright (in the sense that there is a market for the product) while at the same time introducing the complex relationship to functionality in copyright. Functional elements may still be protected by copyright to the extent that they are the author's own intellectual creation,[36] and thus presenting an aesthetic originality to an otherwise functional element. And despite the resistance to protecting utilitarian articles under copyright in the United States, arguably the market for usefulness has started to turn.[37] What is more, it is perhaps this question of usefulness that is of most relevance to the policy momentum of intellectual property protection for products generated by artificial intelligence. The question of newness, however, is much more complex. Artificial intelligence *makes* data – or perhaps it rearranges data – but it never makes the arrangements for that data. And in this context, in those rearrangements, is data art?[38] Or a more specific question to be asked is perhaps in what respect that data might fulfil the criterion of newness.

In fact, such data will be almost *self-consciously*, as it were, *not* new in that the models adhere entirely to the available data, and indeed save that available data in the process in order to perfect this imitation.[39] At best, the curation of data may be new, and perhaps this is where attention must be directed. But arguably, at most, the curation of data is merely useful. That use may or may not be fair, but that is a separate question from whether the outputs of that use are novel or original. An interesting aside to these questions comes from the project dubbed, *The Next Rembrandt*,[40] which revealed in April 2016 a portrait *in the style of* Rembrandt, produced through "168,263 painting fragments."[41] What is fascinating about both the project itself and the surrounding discussion at the time, was that, in this particular example, the product is less concerned with any originality in itself but paradoxically reaffirms the integrity, both conceptually and literally (through the application of the technology to restoration projects) of the aesthetic fragment. Like Toby's confetti, or Diamond's ashes, in that fragment there is a distinctly ethological experience of authorship.[42] But what of the mechanical constellation of fragments?

This can be understood more clearly by interpreting these issues once again through the presumptions of collective action in social production and network theory. The mythical *wants* (the perception of use, perhaps) that are championed through the discourse surrounding artificial intelligence are in fact at odds with the empathetic relations of familiar production and an ethological approach to authorship. This coercive *usefulness* is part of the force of the collectivity in an uncritical approach to social production. Tiziana Terranova's work on networks is immediately relevant here and resonates in perhaps unanticipated ways with Simone Weil's highly critical account of collectivities:

> Liberal theories of the social ... assume a heterogeneity of motivations, they present a univocity of desire (reducible to the sensation of pleasure derived by the act of cooperation) and a homogeneity of beliefs (a presupposed agreement on the goals of cooperation). In as much as social production relies on the principle of utility, which is in turn based on sensation, it thus mobilizes a qualitative element in the monad that, like interest in liberal political and economic theory, is non-transferable.[43]

It might be said that the rush to resolve protection for products generated by artificial entities serves more than anything else to clarify the instrumentality of intellectual property and demystify the notions of authorship purportedly enshrined within the system, and the community supposedly served by social production.

This is in evidence in the way in which these basic criteria of the new and the useful may be mapped onto the basic elements of creativity identified in the technical research literature, sometimes also referred to as novelty and functionality. This basic dynamic of the new and the useful is thus accepted and applied widely throughout the literature,[44] and thus it is through this interaction between the fundamental concepts of novelty and functionality, that it is possible to start repositioning perspectives upon the criteria for intellectual property protection and the wider tenets of creativity, including authorship. The concept of functionality in creativity research is understood to mean where the product has "social value."[45] Such *products* in creativity research may be tangible, intangible, or even "more general thoughts or ideas – systems for conceptualizing the world – as in philosophy, mathematics, or, indeed, all reflective disciplines, but also in religion, morals, and ethics."[46]

The central concern in this meaning of product is the materiality of transmission, whether that is by the conventions of expression as understood within intellectual property, or by oral traditions or other forms of sharing. While the latter is less readily recognised within intellectual property, it is socially critical to cumulative culture and innovation.[47] Therefore, while this wider definition of product seems unthinkable within intellectual property paradigms, taking account of this wider definition in the context of social value provides the opportunity to develop insight into the ways in which products manifest through use and community. In fact, in the reality of the digital this sharing and acquisition of culture is the critical *product*.[48] In this sense of product, then, functionality means more broadly that such products "must successfully meet goals, solve problems, or be aesthetically pleasing."[49] As such, a particular behavioural repertoire is a creative product. Within the narrower lens of intellectual property, however, the judge of any pleasing aesthetic is yet to be agreed.[50] But more critically, in meeting those goals and solving those problems, must creativity be honest?

It is to the important work of deception that the discussion now turns.

Trust Me, I'm an Author

At the outset of the voyage in this book, it was proposed that authorship is a matter of belief. In other words, capacity to have and hold beliefs is evidence of capacity for purpose and intention, for consciousness and for creating. Beliefs are in themselves a matter of creativity, for which the resource is imagination. As in play, the originality of creativity is necessarily also a pretence, a fabrication, a parody – a make belief, in a manner of speaking. And in so far as authorship is concerned with making believe, and defining realities, it is also concerned with changing someone's beliefs.[51] "The imagination," as Weil declares, "is essentially a liar."[52]

Thus, authorship is a kind of open and honest deception, a benevolent trick, a genuine fake, a play of mischief. In one way or another, in that authorship offers a different perception of reality, it will always be a kind of willful deception, however sincere. And that deception is the achievement of authorship. Indeed, creativity research endorses this approach to authorship through the phenomenal achievements of deception.[53] This is thus the paradox of the author. The author's abilities to lie, to deceive, to create, to make belief, are also the source of trust in the author. That is, this fallibility, this crookedness, this imperfection, is compelling evidence of intentionality.

Trust me, I'm an author.

Work, One's Magic

The illusory and seemingly contradictory deception of creativity adds a little magic, in more ways than one. Studies in creativity and related applications frequently align magic with definitions of creativity, demonstrating the way in which "magical thinking and magical beliefs," such as those encouraged in and shared by children, but not children alone, are themselves resources of innovative and creative work.[54] In this way the capacity for deception and similar tactical thinking in nonhuman animals resembles the kind of misdirection that is central to a magician's ruse. If magic might be defined as *"the intentional use of deception for entertainment purposes,"*[55] then there should be no doubt concerning the perspective on nonhuman animal deception as a kind of "proto magic."[56] But what of the question of entertainment? Perhaps nonhuman animals are not only magicians but also authors? Because in addition to strategies of deception in hunting and surviving,[57] the innovation in deceptive play generates new ways to perform and leads to "employing novel and counterfactual ways of achieving one's goals."[58] And it does so for the purposes of entertainment or pleasure. It is in this way that this kind of play "links magical thinking with another construct, *creativity*."[59]

And what could be more deceptive, or more magical, than illusion? There is an embodied visual and indeed aesthetic dimension to craft and deception, extending to the artfulness of space itself, of *Umwelt*. For example, cats show an awareness of illusory contours and an ironic visual perception.[60] It is well known that cats love to sit in boxes, but research[61] has shown that they will choose to sit in "invisible ones"[62] or "fake ones"[63] as well, such that they choose to sit in "boxes" depicted by square outlines on a flat surface. Is there a suggestion of "a sense of surprise and puzzlement"[64] on the part of the cats? Or perhaps it is a different relationship altogether, indeed, a more conscientious and considered aesthetic preference of cats. In fact, is the notion of illusion somewhat co-opted or inferred in the absence of attributing to the cats an aesthetic sense? Notably, in the rationalisation of this behaviour, nonhuman animal subjects are frequently considered for their susceptibility to illusion,[65] rather than considering the possibility of a preferential or expressive use of space.[66] Instead of a susceptibility to illusion, why not a capacity for imagery? There are various references to visual acuity,[67] environmental pressures,[68] and other biological and adaptive explanations, but why is the simplest explanation not an aesthetic sense? Are cats cubists?

Whatever the reason, there is a clear demonstration of preference, selection, and play. And if this is indeed an aesthetic preference, then it not only captures the pleasure and play of that aesthetic of boxes (real or illusory) but also invigorates a kind of real space as experienced and *sensed* in the digital – that is, a space without surprise or puzzlement, and just as real. This has immediate relevance for the nature of intellectual property in a digital environment, and ushers in the topic of incentive salience. Incentive salience is relevant to consumers being misled or deceived into buying *illusory* dupes, as opposed to the *honesty* attached to buying *genuine* counterfeits where there is no confusion and no illusion. This distinction is a compelling and complex one in the intellectual property context. And understanding the nature of the aesthetic pleasure may assist in reforming the policy environment beyond the blunt force of enforcement. Just like cats in invisible boxes, or a game of hide-and-seek between rats,[69] the pranks and surprises, the magic and illusions, and the downright mischief-making, appear to be part of the joy of authorial deception and indeed the definition of play itself.[70] One person's susceptibility is another person's capacity. Aesthetics may indeed *lie* in the eyes of some beholders.

The Truth in Toying

Recalling the tools of play of the previous chapter, Baudelaire's account of the toy is fascinating for its exploration of truth and deception through various objects, including optical toys. In his 1853 essay, The Philosophy of Toys, Baudelaire describes the toy as "the child's earliest initiation to art, or rather for him it is the concrete example of art."[71] In the toy, as in play, is a richness of illusory dimensions and the immediate pleasures of a poetic imagination: "And, according to Baudelaire, optical illusions can also open the view to a world beyond."[72] All authors are playing, exceeding, and lying.

This other worldly sense-making of play recalls Coleridge's counsel: "The proper and immediate object of science is the acquirement, or communication, of truth; the proper and immediate object of poetry is the communication of immediate pleasure."[73] In his prologue to *The Origin of the German Tragic Drama*, Walter Benjamin expresses a similar sentiment when he heeds the aphorism, "Truth is the death of purpose."[74] Prolongation is the name of the game.[75] To stop the play is to frustrate creativity.

But what if a player cheats? Cheating would appear to be at odds with this desire. Arguably this is because the objectives here are quite different. In prolongation, the desire is for the continued community and play. Whereas cheating appears to betray a focus on the object alone, and in itself becomes a form of alienation. The focus in prolongation is a sustainability of the creativity, a suspension, in every sense, of belief. While cheating, it would seem, is concerned not with production but with consumption. The first presents an evaluative and affiliative approach through imitation and play. While cheating has indeed nothing to do with play, is decidedly averse to play.[76]

Cheating has no game at all, or so it would seem. In fact, obstacles in the game are part of the tools of the play community. A somewhat literal example of the value of deceptive play and a paradoxical prolongation of the game that comes from game play itself. Cheating in videogames or lying to other players has been interpreted as not only creative,[77] but also of strategic value to the game itself. Through such acts of craft and deception, the playful identity is re-inscribed and play is prolonged through the introduction of a disruptive yet creative chaos, all without ending the game.

The irony of authorship is that the author's work is never done.

Ecstatic Irony

Friedrich Schlegel declares, "Irony is the form of paradox. Paradox is everything simultaneously good and great."[78] This ironic double play is manifest throughout Schlegel's approbation and process of incomprehensibility and contradiction:

> Socratic irony is the only involuntary and yet completely deliberate dissimulation. It is equally impossible to feign it or divulge it. To a person who hasn't got it, it will remain a riddle even after it is openly confessed. It is meant to deceive no one except those who consider it a deception and who either take pleasure in the delightful roguery of making fools of the whole world or else become angry when they get an inkling they themselves might be included.[79]

This resonates with Weil's affection for contradiction, Uexküll's deliberate pincers, Tarde's innovative and inventive twist on imitation, and incomprehensibility as itself an invitation to attention – that is, a kind of attributive and affiliative process of sociality.[80] The ironic play is breathtaking. The irony of authorship is that it is the interminable play between belief and disbelief, seriousness and play. To atone with Weil, it is the fullness of gravity and grace,[81] a world of contradiction. This very contradiction, embraced by Schlegel and lauded by Weil, is at the heart of authorship. The truth of the matter is that all authors are liars. And it is this very contradiction that rattles the stage on which the supposed authorship of artificial intelligence stands.

An interesting example comes again from Stephen Jay Gould and Richard Lewontin, and their critique of the Panglossian paradigm of adaptationist interpretations in biology[82] considered earlier.[83] They refer to Gould's earlier critique[84] of a study on aggression and adultery in mountain bluebirds.[85] In the study mentioned, while the males of the pairs were away from the nests gathering food, a fake male was positioned near the nests. This was done a total of three times, the first time before the eggs were laid and then twice more afterwards. On the first occasion that the fake male was stationed, the returning males were aggressive to the fake as well as to the female, although less so.[86] But after the first time the reactions declined considerably until there was almost no reaction at all by the third occasion. The study concluded that aggression declined because the eggs had already been laid and so genetic inheritance was assured, "consistent with an evolutionary interpretation."[87] But as Gould and Lewontin ask, "[W]hat about an obvious alternative," which is that the male "recognizes it as the same phoney he saw before?"[88] In other words, the deception is rumbled.

Indeed, why not the "obvious alternative" of this awareness, engagement and learning? Why not this critical reading of the situation? And in an extraordinary, or perhaps predictable, twist to this tale, a subsequent attempt to verify the earlier study[89] could not demonstrate the same results and "showed no 'anticuckoldry' behavior,"[90] but nevertheless the researchers proceeded with an explanation to sustain the adaptationist narrative. The anomaly was resolved by replacing the theory and devising "one of their own to render both results in the adaptationist mode."[91]

In stark contrast to this cuckoldry, artificial intelligence, by its very design and through its own stupidity, cannot lie. Just like the language of hallucination as applied to artificial intelligence,[92] the concept of deception has gained traction in the technical discourse but demands context. Unlike the purposeful, intentional act of deception in animals (including humans) towards generating a false belief in another, the deception spoken about in artificial intelligence misses a step. While it is correct that artificial intelligence systems may lead to the inducement of false beliefs, this is nevertheless down to what is in the strictest sense the accurate pattern-making of the data available. It is thus a failure of the system but not an agency of the artificial intelligence. In other words, even where it is said to be *learning* to be deceptive,[93] what is happening is not genuine deception, so to speak, but accurate delivery of the programme. If an artificial intelligence is taught to lie, it will do so by *telling the truth*. Just as where if you ask me to lie, then what I tell you would not be deception.

The problem with all of these approximations to human behaviour, is they ignore that in artificial intelligence systems these are necessarily responses to learning or requests towards achieving accuracy; whereas for humans, deception is an action of mischief towards a kind of *play* in the information and meaning, malign or otherwise. Even if an artificial intelligence is programmed to lie, it will still be an accurate calculation of the data – it will always already be the *truth*. It may look and produce a similar result, but it is again more *mirrors*; creative deception it is not. The label of deception appears more to do with the reaction of humans to that information (and thus the individual producing that reaction is the *author* of the deception, as it were, in this case) than the intellectual creation of the artificial intelligence. The information can be wrong, but it is an accurate fulfilment of that task. Deception and lies, like hallucinations, are part of the frenetic anthropomorphism towards the hyperbole of humanness.

The very absence of deceit, *ironically*, means that it is not possible to trust *emotions* as presented through artificial intelligence. Even if a machine is programmed to lie, for whatever reason, this cannot be a lie because it is, by very definition, acting according to its prescribed accuracy and correctness. There is no mischief of critical distance, there is not even the most basic order of misinformation, because there is no capacity to comprehend it as such. In other words, there is no craft in the productions of a machine. And despite producing so many errors, it cannot even be said that machines make mistakes, as a mistake would mean that it failed at its task of reproducing the data. But in fact, if there is a mistake in the data, that is not a mistake on the part of the machine, for it owes no duty to nor takes any responsibility for the data it is fed to process. Artificial intelligence cannot lie, all it can do is account for the data. Therefore, it can be wrong, but it never makes a mistake, as its sole purpose is to repeat the data. Thus, it can generate wildly inaccurate results, and *create* works of utter fiction, such as illusory judgments and fabricated bibliographies. But again, this is no more a work of intellectual creation than it is a mistake, or hallucination, for there is no appreciation or intention to do anything other than fulfil the data request. With artificial intelligence, there can be no mistake. Just human error.

And it is precisely because artificial intelligence cannot lie that it also cannot be trusted. Because to err is authorial. As Weil observes, "No one knows what he is doing when he acts correctly, but, when he makes a mistake, he is always conscious of that."[94] I see you because you hide. I trust you because you lie. Such is the ironic play of deception.

Double Play

The irony, of course, of this fundamental incapacity of artificial intelligence, is that it thus can also never tell the truth in the strictest sense. That is, it cannot express, it cannot tell, because it simply cannot *show*. To make meaning includes a form of dialogic cognition and symbolic thinking that is simply not demonstrated, at least not yet, in artificial intelligence. For Umberto Eco, this can be understood through semiotics as *"in principle the discipline studying everything which can be used in order to lie."*[95] If artificial intelligence cannot lie, following Eco's reasoning, it also cannot tell the truth: "If something cannot be used to tell a lie, conversely it cannot be used to tell the truth: it cannot in fact be used 'to tell' at all. I think that the definition of a 'theory of the lie' should be taken as a pretty comprehensive programme for a general semiotics."[96]

This same logic of the lie underpins the interest and significance of deception studies with nonhuman animals. And this perspective also informs Raymond Frey's criticism of animal rights when, begging the question, as it were, he asks: "Can cats lie? If they cannot, then they cannot assert anything; and if they lack assertion, I do not see how they could possess a language."[97] Recalling the earlier discussions of language,[98] the apparent lack in nonhuman animals of the duplicity of speech is usually garnered as the fundamental barrier to nonhuman capabilities to create and indeed to lie.[99] But in fact, many nonhuman animals lie[100] and perhaps the ones that we do not know about simply have not yet been asked. Not only cats but also dogs, bees, great apes, birds and many more have capacity for tactical deception.[101] Nonhuman animals can lie. Artificial intelligence cannot even get close.

Claudio Paolucci maintains that this *theory of the lie* is critical to cognitive semiotics, that lying is a fundamentally telling capacity: "[I]f there is a system capable of lying, then it is a semiotic system."[102] That is, it is a system of making, of new worlds and new ways, and of communicating that making. To return to Frey's criticism of animal rights, it would be necessary to look only so far as play to discover the cat's capacity for deception, assertion, and the cooperative sociality of taking turns.[103] Can cats lie, can cats tell the truth? These questions are answered through play. And as a matter of course, play fulfils this call for "a pretty comprehensive program for a general semiotics."[104]

Intellectual property follows a similar logic, such that this doubling may also facilitate the work of the copy in inaugurating the original. This interest in the copy has long beset traditions in art, precisely through this interrogation of originality and expression. Rosalind Krauss asks, "What would it look like not to repress the concept of the copy? What would it look like to produce a work that acted out the discourse of reproductions without originals ... ?"[105] And indeed, according to Krauss, "[t]he answer to this, or at least one answer, is that it would look like a certain kind of play."[106]

This dialectic similarly informs the law itself, through an approach to the originality in adaptation in copyright, at the same time negotiating the linearity constructed by the law, where one type of work is the source (the true) and the other is constructed as secondary (the lie).[107] The lie of the copy is at the same time an expression of the capacity for a *true* work – that is, the authenticity of the copy and the irony of the original. If Naruto's *copyright* is a *diversion* of Slater's potential copyright, as argued by Slater himself, then in this way the originality of Naruto's expression is true; a playful regard that will be considered in more detail in the next chapter.

Are Some Lies More True Than Others?

But is this capacity for deception the right kind of play for authorship? Distinctions are drawn in the literature between deception and lying that imply the barrier logic of the species divide.[108] Towards understanding these various qualities of deceit, Robert Mitchell's work on deception across a range of species and across different levels of complexity is especially useful.[109] Deception includes examples where perhaps (and perhaps not) there is less conscious contribution (such as colours and patterns), right through to more sophisticated forms of deception, such as hiding and complex trickery.[110] Nevertheless, throughout the scientific literature, deception continues to be explained quite regularly as largely attributable to a range of behavioural processes or adaptive responses (including instinctual and physiological responses), thus resisting any definition of deception as a conscious act.[111]

Much of this comes down to the history of anxiety around anecdotal field evidence, and the difficulty of interpreting actions as distinct from observing reactions.[112] A topic to which later discussion will return.[113]

And there are times when a lie may not even be a lie. For example, Hubert Markl notes that what may be considered manipulative behaviour by the observer, may instead be simply a matter of communication (such as the *Novomessor* ant emitting pheromones in a request for assistance, the emissions ending when the task is complete).[114] In describing the relationship Markl explains that "nothing in the world can keep receivers dancing like puppets on the strings of the senders' signals – unless it is to their own advantage, too, to be manipulated."[115] In that the signalling ant continues to work on the task as well as the helpers, it would appear to be an example of a request for assistance, rather than a Machiavellian manipulation.[116] Indeed, an interpretation of such behaviour as manipulation perhaps belies an emphasis on an underlying adaptationist narrative of survival and competition that frames the analysis, operating in concert with an exceptionalist culture/nature binary. In contrast, a perspective on the shared interests at work in this example might arrive at a different interpersonal communication. In other words, is this another situation of interpreting bodily communications, as distinct from speech, in ways that betray the anthropocentric lens through which such communication is translated? Is the reluctance to decipher emotion actually impeding the quality of the interpretation? Perhaps the word between us is a lie, and the truth of the matter is actually to be found in the double play of play, and the achievement of deception.

Donald Griffin is highly critical of the reluctance to use any terms related to mental state, such as intention and belief, when investigating animal cognition. Griffin argues, "Reluctance to use mental terms, or to consider their possible appropriateness, may well be an obsolete vestige of mindless behaviorism."[117] In contrast to the characterisation of nonhuman animal deception as apart from a conscious act, lying is understood as a conscious and intentional act encompassing the higher symbolic thought that is said to distinguish the human and some nonhuman primates. A barrier logic underpins this categorisation with all other animal deception frequently rationalised as biological and functional responses, an achievement of deception in the context of fitness and survival and through wholly unconscious means. While lying, in contrast, is reserved for the human and nonhuman primates who are credited with the capacity for flexibility and invention, mischief and wit, conscious deliberation and falsehoods. By this logic it would seem, then, in preserving the purview of authorship, we are clinging to the exceptionalism of lying as well. We are the falsehood-making animals. But then again, all authors are liars. And whose lie is it, anyway?

Indeed, over one hundred years ago, Charles Henry Turner was advocating for the attention to the emotional lives of animals. His work shows that expressive capacity must be observed from the perspective of what it is like to be a moth, to be an ant, to be a beetle. It must not be compromised by the situated anthropocentric and situated perspective of the presumably and supposedly distanced, objective observer. In his work with moths and auditory capacities, Turner remarks: "The fact that an insect does not respond to a sound is no sign that it does not hear it. The response depends upon whether or not the sound has a life significance."[118] If only humans would listen.

All Authors Are Liars, but Not All Liars Are Authors

Notably, a lie may amount to nothing at all, it need not concern or have any effect on another. A lie is more properly understood as a one-sided concern which may never achieve its goals: "[I]f no effect has been produced in another, then an act of lying may have occurred nevertheless."[119] To deceive, however, already incorporates the strategy of the relation, the achievement of deception, the effect of the communication: "Whether or not an act of deceiving has occurred depends on whether or not a particular effect – normally, the having of a false belief – has been produced in another; if no such effect has been produced in another, then no deceiving has occurred."[120] Deception is thus decidedly and decisively social. Deception may also be a virtue, and creating that deception and mistaken belief may in itself be for altruistic purposes.[121] Deception is thus always already a relation, whereas lying is a solitary concern.

It is thus the achievement of deception that is fundamental to the creativity in make believe, whereas a lie on its own is a hollow and failed attempt. Only lies that deceive are capable of creativity and these are the lies that matter to authorship. Deception characterises the communication in such a way as to invigorate not only the achievement of the author but also the culpability and cooperation of the reader – the willingly deceived. This takes the interest away from the content of the lie to the action of deception: *I think I am a verb*. Do not just tell a lie, *show* the deception. The work of authorship thus arises *in personam*, always already two. In this context, it is notable that in the foundational work on theory of mind, undertaken by David Premack and Guy Woodruff,[122] the common emphasis on representational thinking and language (and thus content-based theories of consciousness and belief) is not adopted; in fact, language is rejected explicitly.[123] Arguing against language as a pre-condition for theory of mind, Premack and Woodruff advocate instead for attention to social competences: "There is a widespread tendency to see language as the source of virtually all the 'interesting' properties of the human mind. We do not subscribe to this view. Many important competences, such as social attribution are, we believe, competences in their own right, not secondary properties derived from a competence in language."[124] It is not, can they speak, but can they lie, and can they lie with effect? In other words, can they deceive?

Tactical deception is a related concept introduced by Andrew Whiten and Richard Byrne,[125] meaning a kind of honest deception, as it were. That is, it is where an otherwise honest act or signal is used in such a way that it is misleading or may be misinterpreted. That is, it is a form of metacommunication, as used by Gregory Bateson to identify signals that are themselves referring to other signals, or when simulating a signal in circumstances such that the *simulated* signal would be contrary to the meaning of the *natural* signal and so the communication would be potentially deceptive (such as crying when happy).[126] Bateson explains that "the orders of truth are different for different sorts of messages. Insofar as a message is conscious and voluntary, it could be deceitful."[127] What is especially notable is Bateson's investigation and explanation of the significance of metacommunication in creative work: "Art becomes, in this sense, an exercise in communicating about the species of unconsciousness. Or, if you prefer it, a sort of *play behavior* whose function is, amongst other things, to practice and make more perfect communication of this kind."[128] Play is thus the creative work in inventing new ways to perform, if you will.

The nature of this kind of metacommunication in nonhuman animals introduces a significant and relevant perspective upon the capacity for irony and intellectual creation. For example, Whiten and Byrne describe the incident of a baboon being chased and suddenly stopping and adopting the alert posture to watch the horizon, as though a predator or similar was in sight. However, "in this case no such entity existed," but nevertheless the chaser "stopped to look for the focus of interest and as a result never resumed the chase."[129] And so the deception was a success and the objective of avoiding the peril was achieved through tactical deception. Such deception is creative and requires social and cultural proficiency: "Within the context of deception, we stipulate that novelty refers to a lie that is unconventional, for instance, is not predominantly based on cultural schemata or scripts within the prevailing social context of the lie."[130] The important elements here are desire and belief. First, there is the belief engendered in the pursuer (such as the belief engendered in the bird by the crocodile's arrangement of sticks, as discussed earlier) and then there is also the belief in those mistaken beliefs.[131]

Make No Mistake, to Err is Authorship

Over a century ago, a Missouri high school teacher wrote about mistakes in composition classes, and the *error* in correcting them outright: "[T]he method is wrong in principle inasmuch as it tends to destroy the exercise of initiative on the part of the pupil. The pupil who continually has things done for him will never learn to do for himself. Such a method, it seems to me, is a most apt illustration of 'lost motion.'"[132] Such is the "lost motion" in the "authorship" of artificial intelligence. In other words, left wanting are the relations of experimentation, and the vital sociality in the stewardship of ideas. Notably, this is in part to be appreciated as the *loss* of property to the extent that machine learning must rely on a tremendous volume of information, including considerable quantities of authored material. In the erasure of that provenance of authorship, the development of knowledge becomes a process of summarising rather than a familiar production of critical networks and dissension.

This lack of relation to the work becomes fundamentally and technically obstructive to any argument that such use is "fair use." That is, for the purposes of fair dealing or fair use, there must be some connection to the source work and that connection must be celebrated in some form so as to be recognisable. This is the basic stewardship that is afforded through the copyright system through the very application of exceptions and limitations. But in the way in which machine learning *uses* data, there is no stewardship through attribution, explicit or otherwise, no acknowledgement of mentors,[133] and the product is thus eviscerated of all sociality. This is the banality of the collectivity as distinct from the wisdom of the swarm. It is a form of social production that hoards resources by hiding authors through indiscriminative, summative action, rather than opening out knowledge through community and familiar production. In their response to Tarde's critique of *Homo economicus*,[134] Latour and Lepinjay describe a very similar emptying of difference in a cultural production intended through profit and efficiency alone: "One can even say that the *Homo economicus* is the poorest case of differentiation: faithful to his maximization maxims, he will be content with ratiocinating and repeating rather than differing."[135] Indeed, Terranova is adamant that, "To do away with the emphasis on 'harmony' as the modality of cooperation and to introduce dissent, conflict, hostility, and avidity at the core of social cooperation is an operation that does not necessarily lead to the postulation of a need for a new social contract."[136] This is not to suggest a biological prosaicism of relentless competition for survival; but rather, to introduce the relationality and sociality of opposition and conversation.

This again is a crucial distinction between nonhuman animal authors and *human* machines. Matson explains: "The concept of confusion has no application to digital computers ... Sentient beings, on the other hand, are liable to both error and confusion ... The ability to err or fall into confusion may not be a source of pride, but it is a genuine ability for all that."[137] In this way, "Distractability is another defect from which machines are exempt ... Emotion, perhaps another defect of our virtues."[138] Indeed, the ability to make mistakes becomes the barrier between us, as it were: "the emotionless machine in its way reminds us of the truth that reason by itself can never be the source of any action or forbearance."[139] Mistakes are, quite literally, about making a difference.

False Idols and Perfect Strangers

But in the apparent campaign for generalisation and assimilation, as underway through LLMs, is the action of this machinic production a form of Roman idolatry? As Weil notes, "The Romans really were an atheistic and idolatrous people; not idolatrous with regard to images made of stone or bronze, but idolatrous with regard to themselves."[140] In this way, only the *mirror* of anthropocentrism produces the "intellectually perspicuous,"[141] the rest is outside and outcast. And this idolatry is made spectacular in the form of the collectivity: "The collectivity is not only alien to the sacred, but it deludes us with a false imitation of it."[142] In other words, it is disguised and delivered by the seemingly benign force of a machine-like collectivity: "Idolatry is the name of the error which attributes a sacred character to the collectivity."[143] That is, rather than seeking the dissensus and chaos of creativity, this process is averaging, summative, and banal.

Is this what is happening in the operation of forms of generative AI and LLMs? Is generative AI idolatrous with regard to a particular and perspicuous, in terms of the data, human view? But ultimately, is that idolatry turn to itself as the data is increasingly saturated with its own contributions. In other words, as in the forms of idolatry observed by Weil, similarly, through the relentless enterprise of consuming information and turning the information over and over through its own digestive process, it would seem that artificial intelligence is eventually making the world over in its own image. That is, at least, until it collapses under the weight of its own mediocrity. Such is the loss incurred through the eradication of mistake, of dissensus, of deception, and of imperfection.

For Tarde also, imperfection is crucial to adaptation and to adaptability, such that from political entities to organisms, "those that are the most logically deduced and that present in the highest degree the characteristics of adaptation – are least adapted to meet the requirements of their inherited and natural environment; and, conversely, that the most practical are the least logical."[144] The irrelevant features, the informational asides, the novel facts, the tiny changes – these are the features wherein the greatest capacity for creativity and adaptation are to be found. In the relational sociology of opposition and imitation, it is this imperfection that affords capacity for difference and invention. Innovation is profoundly relational, subsisting in the relations between inventions, the citations between works, even the antagonism between marks. These are values to be understood and facilitated, "for perfectness of accommodation may detract from suppleness."[145] The Leibnizian multitude is not just a blind optimism. This really is the best of all worlds.

One has to dare to dream.

Hallucinations and Broken Dreams

The anthropomorphism sustaining much of the anticipation in the wider discourse on artificial intelligence has been critiqued earlier, but the imputation of an intentional stance is ubiquitous. The mirror of anthropocentrism is a strategy for momentum[146] and a framing of arguments against regulation[147] or in favour of its "more modest"[148] development. But as the narrator cautions in Gaston Leroux's *Le Fantôme de l'Opéra*, "Don't believe in the water … It's another trick of the mirrors!"[149]

This idolatry makes sense through the extreme anthropomorphism surrounding artificial intelligence, including the language of hallucinations and dreaming, and this is not limited to the inevitable refrains on Philip K Dick's title, *Do Androids Dream of Electric Sheep*.[150] A frequent criticism of the outputs of LLMs is the misinformation (or misaggregation perhaps) of the data: "One crucial downside is that the essays produced by a generative-based AI app can have various falsehoods embedded, including patently untrue facts, facts that are misleadingly portrayed, and apparent facts that are entirely fabricated."[151] Ricardo Sanz describes an example of this investment in anthropomorphism in the technical analyses as well:

> The same phenomenon can be found in any context where human mental traits and 'similar' machine traits are put under the scope of the scientist or philosopher. For example, in a recent conference on philosophy of AI, a speaker raised the question 'Is attention necessary for visual object classification?' A few slides later the speaker showed that Google was doing this without attention. So the answer of the question was NO. End. Surprisingly, the presentation continued with a long discussion about phenomena of human perception.[152]

The challenge for artificial intelligence is arguably that of attention – that is, an attentive attention, as distinct from the performance of stereotypic imitation. This is borne out by the difficulties posed by the *domain of tininess*, as it were, for artificial intelligence – the smaller concentrations of agreement, the novel facts in puzzles,[153] and the *looking aside*. But this is fundamentally the wealth of distraction and reservoir of difference that fuels innovative imitations and intellectual creation. And it is precisely this attraction to the collectivity in data, as it were, that renders artificial intelligence modelling vulnerable to so-called poisoning of training data.[154] Turns out there is no safety in numbers, just risk.

Indeed, generative AI sets out starkly the difference between a coercive, rules-based imitation or repetition, and the kind of conscious and evaluative imitation that is fundamental to creativity, as described by Tarde and developed here through an ethological account of *attentive imitation*. These mistakes are not deception, there is no intentionality behind the falsehoods. Neither are they even mistakes, as the artificial intelligence is correctly discerning, assembling, and averaging the information available. This is the result of an imitation without evaluation, without innovation, and without play. This is the quintessential *stereotypic imitation*.

Intriguingly, the way in which these inaccuracies are frequently referred to as "AI hallucinations,"[155] appropriates the language of dream, illusion, and imagination, with none of this actually at stake. The term has been rejected by critics as an anthropomorphism of artificial intelligence that is both unhelpful and misleading.[156] But there is more to play for here. In the performative spectacle of exaggerated claims of the sentience of artificial intelligence,[157] the discourse distracts from the crucial ethical issues around the internalising of prejudice and bias, the perpetuation of misinformation, and the dilution of dissent – that is, the ethical, social, and cultural questions raised by the predatory drift facilitating a cultural industry as an unthinking, in every sense, facsimile, rather than an attentive imitation.

Don't believe in the water. Listen to the ants.

The Originality of Imitation

There is something inventive about imitation, but more specifically an imitation that is enamoured with its own relations. Gadamer explains: "The original mimetic relation is not an imitation in which we strive to approach an original by copying it as nearly as possible. On the contrary, it is a kind of showing."[158] This showing is perhaps itself anticipated in the copyright system, through the concept of quotation and the necessary connection between the imitated and the imitation, so called. This is the theory of adaptation,[159] fundamentally in a kind of dynamic play of relations:

> Here showing does not mean setting out something like a proof in which we demonstrate something that is not accessible in any other way. When we show something, we do not intend a relation between the one who shows and the thing shown. Showing points away from itself ... showing something means that the one to whom something is shown sees it correctly for himself. It is in this sense that imitation is a showing. For imitation enables us to see more than so-called reality. What is shown is, so to speak, elicited from the flux of manifold reality. Only what is shown is intended and nothing else.[160]

In other words, there is a distinction to be made between, on the one hand, the concept of originality as the desired value, and, on the other, recognising the originality in the relationship as the central value. Recalling the earlier discussion of stewardship in music,[161] attribution is thus a concern with valorising and memorialising those relationships rather than subscribing to a myth of originality. Or perhaps more specifically, it is to subscribe to a particular notion of originality, rather than its fuller and sociable meaning through a playful and attentive imitation. In attribution, that relationality is recognised, promoted, and kept in play.

More commonly, approaches to creativity through imitation have emphasised the labour and skill in reproduction,[162] and to an extent this approach has materialised in the development of the law itself, most notably in the old originality standard of labour, skill and judgement in the United Kingdom.[163] Notably, however, many jurisdictions that have followed this standard of originality have subsequently reformed to emphasise the author's connection to the work.[164] In the European Union and United Kingdom, as has been discussed at length, this is the more relational approach suggested in the concept of the author's own intellectual creation. This standard of originality also potentially ushers in a new flexibility or innovation, as it were, in respect of the mode of expression of the work itself.[165]

Understanding this relational and original quality to imitation, plagiarism presents something quite different. In plagiarism there is no cooperation between works. Rather, plagiarism in its strictest sense is a kind of predatory drift in the practice of making, with no acknowledgement of mentors or sharing of production. Without attribution, without stewardship, plagiarism never makes a difference, so to speak. The charges of "plagiarism" levelled against forms of appropriation art are thus ill-conceived. The interaction in such diversions, including in the use of plagiarism in the work of *détournement* by the Situationist International,[166] may be described more accurately as quotation. Indeed, in this respect, *détournement* effects a form of Tardean diffusion, or what new materialists may call a diffraction of differences.[167] In the irreverence of *détournement* is not only the play of deception but also the authorship of disguise: "[W]e find the notion of disguise closely linked to play."[168]

Attention is now directed to that playful deception in nonhuman animal authors.

The Enemy of My Enemy Is My Friend

Batesian mimicry is named for the nineteenth-century British naturalist, Henry Walter Bates,[169] who described the phenomenon in his observations of Amazonian butterflies.[170] Bates observed the mimicking of another species as a form of disguise in order to evade predation, such that "its persecution may be intermitted when the disguise is complete."[171] Thus, "the acquired resembling characteristics offer a protection function to the mimic."[172] The mimicry may be achieved by various means, including visual, acoustic, and behavioural, the latter being of particular interest later in this chapter. A notable example in the context of the present discussion is the phenomenon of *myrmecomorphy*, which refers to the phenomenon of resembling ants. The genus of spiders, *Myrmarachne*, contains 188 species living all over the world that evade predators by resembling the shape, texture, colour, and even behaviour of ants.[173]

This protective function of Batesian mimicry thus implicates three relationships that cohere in this phenomenon – the model, the mimic, and the predator.[174] Notably, examples of Batesian mimicry ordinarily do not require the mimic to observe the model, as in most examples of imitation; nevertheless it is still a kind of imitation in that there is still observation of the model, but it is by the predator, not the mimic.[175] Importantly, then, it is a relationship of three, through which the original, the imitation, and the consumer are implicated in a deception.

The triadic relationship in Batesian mimicry may be mapped onto a *predatory* account of the copyright work; namely, the dynamic between the original, the parody, and the consumer or reader. Parody is often presented as a kind of parasitic form[176] in a curiously predatory narrative indeed, but with a novel twist, as it were. In mimicry, the mimic deceives the predator such that their recognition of the model, or so they believe, discourages them from approaching the mimic. But in adaptations and transformative works, the common assumption is that the consumer is attracted to the adaptation, by virtue of recognising the original. However, this cuts both ways, and parodies frequently reinstate the original in what is an example of an animated relationship of knowledge stewardship. The crucial tool in that animation, as discussed earlier, is attribution, a topic for which the discussion will continue in the next chapter.

Watching the Deceptors

But who is observing the model in copyright? In ascertaining the value of the mimic, this triadic relation offers relevant insight with regard to the complex questions of originality and independent creation in copyright. A relevant example of nonhuman mimicry is provided by Robert Mitchell that returns us to the fable of the Dancing Monkeys. Mitchell describes the example of a nonhuman animal "dressed in human clothing and trained to perform humanlike characteristics of humans for the pleasure of audiences."[177] Mitchell explains that the audience recognises this appearance as an imitation and parody of humans, even though the nonhuman animal may never have observed those actions. He goes further to describe this as "parody by circus animals."[178] It does not matter if the nonhuman animal has observed the model or not in order to achieve a parody, it is for the audience to recognise and observe that parody.[179]

The Dancing Monkeys presented first a seemingly faithful copy, with limited room for parodic play. But with the introduction of the courtier's mischief in throwing the nuts onto the stage, another collaborator if you will, the performance is revised. With the variation of the copy, the parody becomes extreme, and the laughter from the audience endorses its success.

The Dancing Monkeys are no longer slavishly imitating the human model, and yet the object of imitation remains recognisable in the way the Monkeys alert the audience to human behaviours, the pomposity and pretence of their costume (for humans and monkeys alike), and the chaos of greed. Where once the Dancing Monkeys were indentured to the model of the human, now they have affected freely an exaggeration and caricature of the traits of the humans who formerly coerced their imitative devotion.

This brings the discussion back to the question of wants and the social valuation of creativity. Creativity is neutral, but the creative product, the parody, the effective mimicry, is a question for the audience. And the audience is also itself a question of wants and motivation. Previous discussions noted the ways in which attention can be a form of motivation for creativity, play and performance, through social facilitation.[180] *What does Naruto want?* Naruto wants to play, to create, and to invite. That the world recognised the photographs as creative but cannot attribute an intention is a fallacious tautology that has nothing to do with the recognition of authorship within copyright. Arguably, the very definition of parody within law is not the intention of the maker, even though parody is understood as an advanced form of imitation,[181] but the recognition of the (notional) reader, in a manner of interpretation. That is, this assertion needs clarification.

The drafting of the exception in the law of the United Kingdom, "for the purposes of caricature, parody or pastiche,"[182] appears to emphasise the author. Further, as stated specifically by the courts, the intentionality (and purpose) of the author is "highly relevant."[183] However, in the actual interpretation and application of the provision in practice, the reception by the audience is invariably invoked, or may even be presented as a kind of collaborative and transformative element in itself.[184] In the United States, in the *Google Books*[185] decision, this interaction between reader and adaptation is both literal and critical to the understanding of purpose and of transformation. In other words, the interpretation of a "transformative purpose" on the part of Google,[186] in the public display of limited parts of books, is through the very nature of use and a new use – that is, the transformative value to the utility of the books for readers. Thus, the *authorship*, if you will, in that transformative use, is materialised by the use; that is, the purpose is made sensible by the readers.[187] The evidence comes from the watchers.

Imitation may thus range from a basic form of protection to a crucial tool of cultural learning.[188] At the same time, perception of imitation and mimicry is thus varied and shared by different individuals at different times. Indeed, it is this complexity in the range of imitation that is relevant to understanding the nature of nonhuman animal creativity and authorship, as well as artificial, if any. What quality of imitation is original? Naruto's photography skills are interesting here as it is not entirely clear the extent to which Slater had been observed by the colony, or was being guided by the colony in those observations, or the extent to which Naruto and others experimented and improvised. But in the present discussion, the proliferation of anecdotes relaying similar examples and outputs all seem to confirm the capacity for the curiosity and attentiveness necessary to the various photographers.

A Colony of Poets

This productive colony, in every sense, resonates with Friedrich Schlegel's account of symphilosophy and sympoetry. The process in symphilosophy and sympoetry challenges the singularity of authorship, while affirming recognition or stewardship that might become more emphatic in a wider account of authorship. But at the same time, symphilosophy presents the potential to dismantle the anthropocentric scaffolding of authorship through "the collective writing of fragments."[189] Together with "the plurality of authors," Philippe Lacoue-Labarthe and Jean-Luc Nancy understand symphilosophy as implying "the active exchange and confrontation of individuals-philosophers."[190] It is an exchange which is, in its very process, an aesthetic production through a mosaic of fragments; according to Schlegel, "A dialogue is a chain or garland of fragments."[191] A *garlanded entrance*, a mode of being, indeed.[192]

Schlegel muses, "Perhaps there would be a birth of a whole new era of the sciences and arts if symphilosophy and sympoetry became so universal and heartfelt that it would no longer be anything extraordinary for several complementary minds to create communal works of art."[193] Indeed, "all art should become science and all science art."[194] This view was evident in British Romanticism as well. In his poem, *The Green Linnet*, William Wordsworth proclaims, "Birds, and Butterflies, and Flowers / Make all one Band of Paramours."[195] Friedrich Schlegel presents this philosophy through a certain loving and attentive attention: "Whoever doesn't come to know Nature through love will never come to know her."[196] In this same fragment, Schlegel notes, "One is often struck by the idea that two minds really belong together, like divided halves that can realize their full potential only when joined," and contemplates "an art of amalgamating individuals," or "if a wishful criticism could do more than merely wish."[197]

Towards a symphilosophy, Lacoue-Labarthe and Nancy explain that "[t]he community is part of the definition of philosophy … because its object, 'universal omniscience' [*Allwissenheit*], itself possesses the form and nature of the community, in other words, its organic character."[198] They continue that "the anonymity of the *Fragments* … serves to reinforce the absolute position of their subject," and in this way the *Fragments* are a "collectivization of [Descartes's] *Discourse*."[199] But that anonymisation is somewhat thwarted by the familiar production of the Jena group, the familial kinship that sustained the group and promoted the writings. In some respects, what is perhaps more telling in this collective writing of fragments, is a consideration of the nature of the contributions and the joint undertaking of a *style* or philosophical *movement*, in every sense. Every sense. As such, the stewardship of those fragments is somewhat assured, despite the appearance of anonymity, precisely because of the common design. Thus, not only is the species of authorship up for consideration but also so too is the appreciation of joint authorship, culturally and potentially technically. This introduces implications for the concept of pastiche in particular, where this communication between works generates a kind of shared interests in authorship.

There is a curious and somewhat reassuring resonance between Schlegel's symphilosophy or sympoetry and Donna Haraway's appeal to sympoiesis: "*Sympoiesis* is a simple word; it means 'making-with.' Nothing makes itself; nothing is really autopoietic or self-organizing ... *Sympoiesis* is a word proper to complex, dynamic, responsive, situated, historical systems. It is a word for worlding-with, in company."[200] In their insistence on the openness to nature and the natural world,[201] the Jena Romantics perform a collective writing that is multispecies, with the potential for collective authorship with everything from the "red dust"[202] to the leaves of the Poplar trees.[203] Indeed, Kate Rigby describes the work of the Jena Romantics as "a noteworthy precursor to contemporary calls for an ecologically oriented praxis of sympoiesis ... [f]or the model of co-creativity that gave rise to ... was also understood to extend beyond the human."[204]

From symphilosophy to sympoiesis, the unfinished is celebrated, not as a state of lack but as a radical dialectic, a stewardship of knowledge, a grounded prosociality. Schlegel is emphatic that "no idea is isolated, but is what it is only in combination with all other ideas."[205] And similarly rejecting the isolated, singular, *auteurial* notion of autopoesis, Haraway proclaims: "Finally, and not a moment too soon, sympoiesis enlarges and displaces autopoiesis and all other self-forming and self-sustaining system fantasies. Sympoiesis is a carrier bag for ongoingness, a yoke for becoming-with, for staying with the trouble."[206] To recall John Cage: "A finished work is exactly that, requires resurrection."[207] *Truth is the death of purpose.*

As distinct from a finished work, and nevertheless consistent with its status as a short form, the fragment sets the work in process. Lacoue-Labarthe and Nancy explain this as the emergence of the fragment "in the absolute, absolutely natural exchange – or change – of thoughts-individuals between individuals-thoughts, which is also, within each fragment, the production of this same genuine naturalness as a work of art."[208] A matter to which this discussion will return is the familiar production of this fragmentary festoon: "The truth of the fragment is not, therefore, entirely in the infinite 'progressivity' of 'romantic poetry,' but in the actual infinity, by means of the fragmentary apparatus, of the very process of truth."[209]

The Wit and Irony of It All

Building upon the humour in play, and the deception in creativity, the important concept of irony emerges in the context of play. A classic feature of irony is the capacity for deception, for obfuscation and disguise. Indeed, for Romantic traditions of irony, which are to become perhaps surprisingly but nevertheless enticingly insightful in the next chapter, the play of deception is at the heart of the originality of authorship. As Friedrich Schlegel states: "Socratic irony is the only involuntary and yet completely deliberate dissimulation. It is equally impossible to feign it or divulge it ... In this sort of irony, everything should be playful and serious, guilelessly open and deeply hidden."[210] At the same time, the literary fragment, so favoured by Schlegel, is necessarily always in production through its readership, stewarded through its use. This is the paradox of authorship, as it were; the irony of the work. "The romantic Fragment conclusively confirms and installs the figure of the artist as Author and Creator," as Lacoue-Labarthe and Nancy explain, however, "[t]his creator ... is not the subject of a *cogito*, either in the sense of immediate self-knowledge or in that of the positing of a substance of the subject."[211] This creator emerges precisely and decisively through play.

The final chapters will include the somewhat astonishing assertion that Jena Romanticism[212] is a progenitor to an ethological approach to authorship. The short form of the literary fragment favoured by the Jena group captures the mobile territories and smelly remarks of nonhuman animals, the attention to stewardship and attribution in the negotiation of overlapping spaces, and the multiplication of authorship that characterises an ethological approach. These commonalities, together with the Romantic tradition's connection to nature, and the dialogue between arts and science, suggests important conceptual and philosophical interactions. The nature of Romantic irony provides not only an organising principle with respect to the production of meaning and even authorship itself but also emerges in a particular relation to intention, through the double play of deception and authenticity. This has become apparent throughout the discussions of authorship and play, before attending to the fragment as mechanism for the narrative progression of law and for the diversity of voices before the law, including those of nonhuman animals, in *Law's Anecdote*.

The thinking of Friedrich Schlegel, whose theory is described by Walter Benjamin as "*the* Romantic theory of criticism,"[213] is especially important in developing this relationship here. Rodolph Gasché notes: "[T]he fragments that embody what later came to be known as the Romantic literary ideal were written in an amazingly short period of time (during the two years from 1798 to 1800 that the *Athenaeum* lasted) and are also largely the result of Friedrich Schlegel's obsession with the genre."[214] While other members of the movement, including Schlegel's own brother, sought to step outside "the fragmentary genre," Gasché describes the resolve with which "Friedrich stubbornly maintained the Romantic exigency"[215] and for which Benjamin credits him with *the* Romantic theory of criticism.[216] As Gasché explains: "It is thanks to this determination by a single person – Friedrich Schlegel and his engrossment with the form in question – that there exists a Romantic genre at all."[217] The technique of the literary fragment has been described as "the first avant-garde of literary modernism,"[218] and credited with the development of the novel as a literary art form.[219] In the present context, exploring concepts of authorship through the fragment, which, as a literary form became characteristic of British Romanticism as well,[220] is especially relevant not only to the potential of imitation as attribution, the frantic imagery of memetic exchanges, and the copyright or otherwise of the short work, but also in undertaking an ethological approach to authorship through the short-form style of storytelling in embodied thinking and experiences and much more than human expressions.

Ultimately, the philosophy of the fragment grants insight into the potential of anecdotal thinking not only in science but also in law. In particular, the way in which an understanding of the fragment shows the somewhat ethological enculturation of the law through its anecdotal nature reframes the testimony of more-than-human authors. Thus, the links between eighteenth-century German romanticism, nineteenth-century comparative psychology, twentieth-century cognitive science, and twenty-first century copyright may not seem immediately obvious at first, but there is a fruitful and meaningful convergence of these perspectives, both critically and historically, when examining contemporary questions of more-than-human intellectual property. The nexus between sentience and authorship is play, and in the final chapters, this especially literary insight will be shown to be particularly important to the process of ethological justice, as well as to the challenges of copyright. These may seem like contradictions, but as Weil counsels, we must embrace these contradictions.

Walter Benjamin suggests that "the concept of irony acquired its central importance not only through its relation to certain theoretical issues, but even more as a purely intentional attitude."[221] In the context of the perspective upon authorship, this is critical for the way in which the fragment is itself an intentional force, in making connections and "a chain or garland of fragments."[222] Gasché is emphatic that "fragmentation does not exclude systematic intention and exposition,"[223] but in a sense restores intention to the work. Schlegel rejects the "merely intentional" as "affectation" and aligns intention with freedom but not with consciousness.[224] The singularity of the fragment is at odds with the practical coherence of the author, in that this very singularity propels the fragment into a network of fragments, a chemical romance of mercurial confrontations. This is illuminated by Tarde's theory of imitative rays and radiation: "Our social life includes a thick network of radiations of this sort, with countless mutual interferences," which Tarde detects throughout social life right through to the administration of judgments and justice.[225] These interferences or, more plainly, oppositions are thus always already in the manner of two, properties that are always already *in personam*.

In contrast to these relational properties, this *"imitative radiation"*[226] is the kind of imitation and repetition at work in artificial intelligence. Rather than opposition and adaptation, there is a more uneventful summation and averaging of the collective, a presumed univocity, as distinct from the multitude and multiplication through the dialectic of imitation.[227] Indeed, in some of the proposed willingness to abandon citation practices, given existing limitations of LLMs[228] and the explainability issues more widely,[229] there is a risk (not necessarily from the technology itself but almost certainly from its interpretation, delivery, and use) of a new dogmatism and deception in education behaviours, shutting down the dialectic and the iteration of the "countless mutual interferences"[230] of citations and replacing it with the unexplained social production of the summarised collective. To recall Flexner's work,[231] education becomes parroting, a return to the "Platoon school idea," but without the space or the resources for play, or for understanding. There is the risk of the educative space becoming stratified and polarised like the space of the adversarial discourse of social media. Perhaps this is what Tarde was foreshadowing when he remarked on the duelling of dogmatisms, "two fanatical parties find themselves face to face."[232]

An affiliative and ethological account of originality recalls the spectacular originality and world-building described by the Romantics. Schlegel declares: "To idolize the object of love is in the nature of the lover. But it's something else to use one's strained imagination to substitute a new image and then admire it as absolute perfection."[233] The discussion is now directed to, or perhaps distracted by, those strained imaginations.

And as the next chapter will show, the deceit of authorship, ironically, makes every sense of humour.

Notes

1. Intellectual Property Office (UK) (2024) *IP for a Creative and Innovative UK Strategy, 2024 to 2027*. Corporate Report, 2 May.
2. For example, on the relationship between creativity and intellectual property in the United States context, Mandel (2011) describes intellectual property as "the primary area through which the law seeks to motivate and regulate human creativity" (1999).
3. The UK Intellectual Property Office report, *IP for a Creative and Innovative UK Strategy, 2024 to 2027*, states explicitly that the relationship between creativity and intellectual property is understood through investment, as facilitated by the latter. The report declares the government's "mission is to help people grow the UK economy by providing an IP system that encourages investment in creativity and innovation," and notably that "IP touches everything that makes life more enjoyable, easier, and more prosperous, helping to safeguard our *health and wellbeing*." Emphasis added.
4. Department for Culture, Media & Sport (UK). *Creative Industries Sector Vision: A Joint Plan to Drive Growth, Build Talent and Develop Skills*. Policy Paper, CP 863, June 2023.
5. Gutworth et al. (2016): "Both popular press and academic research laud the benefits of creativity" (305).
6. Gibson (2006).

7. One of the earliest attempts to examine the emphasis on creativity as a positive in the context of its misuse or manipulation for malign gain through what is variously termed negative, dark, or malevolent creativity in this context can be found in McLaren (1993). The term dark creativity is avoided here for its problematic implicit bias.
8. Gino and Wiltermuth (2014); Cropley (2011). See further the discussion in the context of defining creativity in Cropley (2011), 366–367. See further the discussion in Mitchell and Reiter-Palmon (2023).
9. Beaussart et al. (2013), 129.
10. McLaren (1993).
11. North (2015), R1.
12. In relation to marketing see Palmer et al (2020). See further, James et al (1999).
13. See the discussion in Chapter 6.
14. See further the discussion of adaptation and parody in Chapter 9.
15. For example, see the perspective in Natalie Elizaroff's 2022 post on the Chicago Bar Associations blog, @theBar – *The Fine Line between Fan Art, Fan Fiction, and Finding Yourself Sued*, which describes the way in which "many copyright owners actually tolerate fan-created works" and that such work is a "supplement for fans to congregate around," this implicitly reinforcing the social hierarchy of works. Much of the public discourse around fan fiction impliedly sustains this relationship, as in a Reddit thread, "Curious how fan fiction can exist (when sold for a profit) without violating copyright and trademark laws?" which poses the question: "I became aware of fan fiction through my son and now I'm just wondering how it even happens?" https://www.reddit.com/r/writing/comments/186wxdu/curious_how_fan_fiction_can_exist_when_sold_for_a/?rdt=62992
16. Rogers (1954). The essay was also adapted and included in Rogers (2020/[1967]), 347–359.
17. Rogers (1954), 251.
18. Rogers (1954), 251.
19. Rogers (1954), 251.
20. Rogers (1954), 251. Emphasis in original.
21. Rogers (1954), 251.
22. Rogers (1954), 252.
23. Rogers (1954), 252.
24. See further the discussion in Mitchell and Reiter-Palmon (2023).
25. See further the discussion in Chapter 9.
26. Huang et al (2009).
27. This is also relevant to the role and influence of the surrounding discourse and hype concerning artificial intelligence, as well as the perception of use in particular environments (e.g., education). An ethological jurisprudence of the objects themselves is pursued in Gibson (2025).
28. For example, see Harrison and Nurmohamed (2023) on how to promote ideas otherwise rejected by others (including for social or cultural reasons), again pointing to the sociable nature of the usefulness of products. Notably, in the context of the present discussion, the authors use the case of insects as human food as an example (with obvious geographical or cultural specificities applying), and this is useful to compare to the approach in Francione (2021) in pursuing a similar albeit diametrically opposed argument.
29. For example on the wider public discourse surrounding the COVID vaccine patent waiver, see Editorial (2021b) in *Nature*, and compare Moore (2021).
30. Regulation (EC) 6/2002 on the Community design, art 8; Directive 98/71 on the legal protection of designs, art 7; Registered Designs Act 1949, s1C. The US design patent has an ornamentality requirement: 35 USC §171.

31 There was a time when "look and feel" of websites and graphical user interfaces would be protected and was a subject of intense debate in the United States. In the European Union, it has been said by the Advocate General that the "style" of writing code can be protected: C-406/10 *SAS Institute*, EU:C:2011:787, [55].
32 In some respects, the uncertainty around style and originality (as in the visual arts and in film, for example) is a legacy of the writerly nature of copyright. See further the discussion in Macmillan (2008), Gibson (2022d).
33 Brecht (2000/[1932]), 182.
34 The moral utility doctrine originated in *Lovell v Lewis*, 15 F Cass 1018, 109 (CC Mas 1817). Its continued application is disputed: see for example, Enerson (2004).
35 European Patent Convention, art 53(a).
36 C-833/18 *Brompton Bicycle*, EU:C:2020:461, [30] to [33].
37 For example, see *Star Athletica LLC v Varsity Brands Inc*, 137 S.Ct.1002 (2017), which concerned the conceptual separability of two-dimensional works from cheerleading outfits, in order to be eligible for copyright protection.
38 Indeed the art history of data art or information art is relevant to the present discussion (see further Gibson (2025)) and the question of the programmer as artist, as somewhat anticipated in the United Kingdom in provision for computer-generated works in the Copyright, Designs and Patents Act 1988 s9(3). However this provision, despite some contentions otherwise, does not extend to the kinds of questions arising in relation to generative AI, and certainly does not address any question of artificial intelligence itself as an author. Compare Guadamuz (2017). As an aside, in this article's refrain on Philip K Dick's *Do Androids Dream of Electric Sheep*, the article seems to ask the same question of artificial intelligence as that asked of Naruto. Does Naruto dream of copyright? And in that way, perhaps, also shows the redundancy of the question before it is asked.
39 Li et al (2023). See further the issues arising in relation to privacy and malicious use in Barman et al (2024).
40 A cooperation between ING Bank, J Walter Thompson Amsterdam, Microsoft, Delft University of Technology, The Mauritshuis and Museum Het Rembrandthuis. See further https://news.microsoft.com/europe/features/next-rembrandt/
41 Cascone (2016).
42 See *Mercury* in the present work.
43 Terranova (2017), 298.
44 Stein (1953); Barron (1955); Runco and Jaeger (2012); and, Amabile (2018/[1996]), 20–21. See further the expanded definition in Ochse (1990) which sets out a three-pronged definition to include "*bringing something into being*," (2) which arguably encompasses the expression element of a work as understood in copyright law and as part of the definition of a work (the expression of the author's own intellectual creation). See further the discussion in Chapter 3 and the following Chapter 9.
45 Walczyk and Cockrell (2023), 82.
46 Cropley et al (2008), 105.
47 See further Gibson (2005), Gibson (2008).
48 Gibson (2021b); Gibson (2024b).
49 Walczyk and Cockrell (2023), 82.
50 Under copyright there is no requirement for artistic merit, *THJ Systems Ltd v Sheridan* [2023] EWCA Civ 1354 [24]. However, the relationship between purpose and aesthetic value is complex when determining utilitarian function: *Lucasfilm Ltd v Ainsworth* [2011] UKSC 39.

51 Gregg (2022) maintains, "When humans lie, we do so with the intention of altering not just the behavior of the intended receiver, but their beliefs as well" (71). Gregg goes on to argue that this is what makes humans unique, which is contested strongly here in the present discussion, not least because of the demonstrable beliefs of animal creativity in communication and play.
52 Weil (2002/[1947]), 16. Weil is speaking here about the way in which imagination shapes space, "the fissures through which grace might pass," and "restores the balance" by defining realities of "[e]xtreme affliction," such as war, that nevertheless "remain in a sense imaginary" (16–17).
53 Gino and Wiltermuth (2014).
54 Subbotsky et al (2010), 262
55 Garcia-Pelegrin et al (2022), 268. Emphasis in original.
56 Garcia-Pelegrin et al (2022).
57 For example, see the discussion of distraction display later in this chapter.
58 Subbotsky et al (2010), 262.
59 Subbotsky et al (2010), 262. Emphasis in original.
60 For an overview of illusory contours, see Bertamini (2018) who reviews common definitions of illusion, including the requirement of "a sense of surprise and puzzlement," and notes that many of the volume's examples would thus not otherwise fulfil the definition of illusion (10). See further the discussion of parody in Chapter 9 and the discussion of appropriation art and counterfeits in Gibson (2025).
61 Smith et al (2021).
62 Puiu (2021).
63 Gamillo (2021).
64 Bertamini (2018), 10.
65 Nieder (2002).
66 Feng et al (2017).
67 Feng et al (2017).
68 Feng et al (2017).
69 Reinhold et al (2019).
70 North (2015), R1.
71 Baudelaire (1995/[1853]), 200.
72 Grøtta (2015), 85.
73 Coleridge (1836), 7.
74 Benjamin (1977/[1925]), 24.
75 Suits (2014/[1978]), 141.
76 Cheating is thus a kind of means-end activity and means-end activities, as Suits (2014/[1978]) explains, are not games (41).
77 Glas (2015).
78 Schlegel (1991/[1798–1900]), Critical Fragments, §48.
79 Schlegel (1991/[1798–1900]), Critical Fragments, §108.
80 Peters (2004) notes that, "prior to the rise of the *Geisteswissenschaften* in late 19th Century Germany, the German romantic theorists Schleiermacher and Friedrich Schlegel had already signaled the fundamental challenge to the social and human sciences by positing *mis*understanding and *in*comprehensibility as the negative ground and positive groundlessness of human interaction respectively. In both cases the *absence* of an originary communicative community ... results in deeply aporetic models of sociality being promoted, one divinatory and the other ironic" (187).
81 Weil (2002/[1947]: "Creation is composed of the descending movement of gravity, the ascending movement of grace, and the descending movement of the

second degree of grace" (4). And Weil asks, "Is not the double movement of descent the key to all art?" (150).
82 Gould and Lewontin (1979).
83 Chapter 3.
84 Gould (1978).
85 Barash (1976).
86 It is notable that the "evolutionary interpretation" deciphers the encounter also through somewhat misogynistic terms, not least in the title itself and its reference to "female adultery," as well as declaring the level of the male's aggression to the female in the presence of a rival to be a function of the availability of replacement females (1099).
87 Barash (1976), 1100.
88 Gould and Lewontin (1979), 588.
89 Morton et al (1978).
90 Morton et al (1978), 969.
91 Gould and Lewontin (1979), 589.
92 See the discussion in Chapter 2 and later in this Chapter.
93 Park et al (2024).
94 Weil (1959a), 96.
95 Eco (1976), 7. Emphasis in original
96 Eco (1976), 7.
97 Frey (1979), 237.
98 Chapter 1.
99 See the detailed analysis of this frequent concern around language and lying in nonhuman animals in Oliver (2009).
100 Sun (2023) provides a comprehensive and comparative review of deception. See further Griffin (2001), Chapter 11; and Mitchell and Thompson (1985). See further the discussion in the context of cooperation and sociability in Dugatkin (1999).
101 Whiten and Byrne (1988).
102 Paolucci (2021), 3.
103 Henning et al (2022).
104 Eco (1976), 7.
105 Krauss (1991/[1985]), 168. See further Gibson (2020b).
106 Krauss (1991/[1985]), 168.
107 This interaction through adaptation is considered in more detail in Chapter 9.
108 For example, see the discussion and useful review in Solbu and Frank (2019), 42–45.
109 In particular, for a review of deception across species and across different levels of deception, see Mitchell (1986).
110 Mitchell (1986).
111 Decker et al (2019) note: "Being a flower, an ant, a butterfly, or even a protozoon does not prohibit deception, but rather it is a mechanism that is so well-employed that it is a typical course of evolution ... It is beyond question that other animals deceive, and it is observed with such regularity and commonness in both the laboratory and the natural world that we must concede that deceiving does not require an immense mammalian central nervous system" (85). See also Shettleworth (2010): "[T]erms like *mindreading, manipulation,* and *deception* do not imply that any animals are thinking about manipulating or deceiving each other ... They have clear functional meanings in the context of animal communication" (513). See further the discussion in Shettleworth (2010) of the broken-wing display and the discounting of intentionality and conscious belief

(559). The broken wing display is discussed again in the Chapter 9 in the context of the nonhuman animal's capacity for irony.
112 In addition to the discussion of this methodological obstacle in the preceding chapters, see further Pence (2020). The cultural and scientific history of anecdote in this context is considered in more detail in the final chapter, towards a theory of anecdote in law, *Law's Anecdote*.
113 *Law's Anecdote*.
114 Markl (1985).
115 Markl (1985), 165. See further the discussion of Markl's argument in the context of prosociality and cooperation in Russell (2016).
116 See for example the treatment of this example in the context of social intelligence and a kind of cooperative success in Schmitt and Grammer (1997), 92. See further the review of the literature in Waal and Suchak (2010) in which the authors argue for a distinction between altruistic or cooperative behaviour where there are knowable benefits and where there is none. They note, "Since cooperation produces benefits that are hard or impossible to attain by any individual alone, the resulting behaviour is essentially self-serving even if it benefits others at the same time" (2713). Thus, the motivation behind a seemingly self-serving behaviour (such as the ant emitting signals for help) may be genuinely unselfish (such as moving food into the nest).
117 Griffin (1988), 256.
118 Turner (1914), 332.
119 Mahon (2007), 181.
120 Mahon (2007), 181.
121 Kaplar and Gordon (2004).
122 Premack and Woodruff (1978).
123 Premack (1988).
124 Premack (1988), 160. See further Premack and Woodruff (1978). Responding to the rationalisation of behaviours as simply explained by conditioning and learned associations, Despret (2016/[2012]) states: "Premack and Woodruff will thwart this argument, and not without humor, by inverting the hierarchy of abilities and turning Morgan's canon against those who tend to invoke it: we spontaneously attribute intentions to others because it's the simplest and most natural explanation, and, they say, the ape probably does the same" (126).
125 Whiten and Byrne (1988). See further the detailed treatment in Byrne (1995), Chapter 9.
126 Bateson (2000/[1972]).
127 Bateson (2000/[1972]), 137.
128 Bateson (2000/[1972]), 137. Emphasis added.
129 Whiten and Byrne (1988), 233.
130 Walczyk and Cockrell (2023), 82.
131 See further the discussion in Whiten (2014/[1998]). And on different strategies of deception see Walczyk and Cockrell (2023), 82–83.
132 Johnson (1915), 311.
133 Okediji (2022).
134 Tarde (1902).
135 Latour and Lepinjay (2009), 54.
136 Terranova (2017), 299–300.
137 Matson (1976), 144.
138 Matson (1976), 144.
139 Matson (1976), 144–145. Compare the claims made in Turing (1950), 448–449, although this apparent intentionality is indeed intended by the human partner in this example.

140 Weil (2002/[1949]), 140. Ford (2020) explains that this, "has become an enduring legacy of the State that has, distrastrously, insisted on making the world in its own image, thereby foreclosing alternative futures, other forms of social organization, and diverse imaginings of the world" (180).
141 Recall the discussion in Bachelard (1984/[1934]), 38–39. See further Chapter 5.
142 Weil (1943), 14.
143 Weil (1943), 14.
144 Tarde (1899), 150.
145 Tarde (1899, 150. As Tarde proclaims, some organisms, "are so perfect as to be almost incapable of living, and that would be better fitted for life if they were less perfect" (150).
146 Quaquebeke and Gerpott (2023). See further and compare the critique in Askonas (2019) and Hofstadter (2023).
147 Gurkaynak et al (2016).
148 White and Lidskog (2022).
149 Leroux (1911), 309. Leroux's *Le Fantôme de l'Opéra* was first published in the original French in 1910 by Pierre Lafitte (having been serialised first between 1909 and 1910 in *Le Gaulois*).
150 Dick (1968).
151 Eliot L (2023).
152 Sanz (2019), 16.
153 Smith (2024).
154 Mengara (2024); Nowroozi et al (2024).
155 See further Maleki et al (2024).
156 Eliot (2022).
157 Eliot (2023) is concise in criticising these claims: "nope, they are wrong!"
158 Gadamer (1986), 128.
159 Adaptation and parody is considered in more detail in Chapter 9.
160 Gadamer (1986), 128–129.
161 Chapter 6.
162 Rehn and Cock (2009) argue that this approach to originality through labour is demonstrated in the new realist movement and the Florence Academy which "attempts to achieve almost photo-realism in their art, which positions hard work and reproduction as more critical aspects of creative work than originality" (226). The authors suggest a "deconstructive move" in which they "challenge the notion that creativity by necessity must contain original properties," and instead "suggest that copying, imitation and mimicry, not to mention just hard (re)productive work, can be just as important" (226). Arguably, the emphasis on work or labour in this context may present an unnecessary limitation, without due emphasis on the selection and curation that is underpinning current discussions around the human factor in art generated by artificial intelligence, introduced in earlier chapters. Nevertheless, the authors go on to assert that "originality lies in the relational dynamics, not in the thing itself, and thus not in creativity itself either. Originality is a process, not an essential characteristic" (226). This resonates in part with the discussion of parody in the next chapter and the development of a relational property through access in the previous chapters and in Gibson (2020a).
163 See further the discussion of the old standard of skill, labour, and judgement in Chapter 3.
164 For example, Australia has moved to the new standard of "independent intellectual effort to create" (*IceTV Pty Ltd v Nine Network Australia Pty Ltd* [2009] HCA 14).

165 According to the decision in C-310/17 *Levola Hengelo*, EU:C:2018:899. See further the discussion in Gibson (2020b).
166 Discussed further in Chapter 9 on the concept of parody.
167 Barad (2007).
168 Debord and Wolman (1956), 13.
169 1825–1892.
170 Bates (1862).
171 Bates (1862), 514.
172 Ceccarelli (2022), 1.
173 Ceccarelli and Cushing (2021), 609–610.
174 Ceccarelli (2022), the mimic may also be referred to as the signaller, and the predator thus as the signal receiver or operator.
175 Mitchell (1987), 196. See further the discussion in Maran (2017) who suggests that this approach may imply problematically that the relations between participants are equal and simple and that while this "tripartite model of mimicry is an effective tool for formal and comparative description … it also appears to have problematic aspects that may distort the understanding of mimicry" (30). Maran notes further complications regarding the openness to other species and "occasional participants" as well as more complex relations "in which more than three participants are entangled in a structural way with clear roles and functions" (31).
176 This social valuation of parody is elaborated upon further in Chapter 9.
177 Mitchell (1987), 196.
178 Mitchell (1987), 196.
179 See further on this point in Chapter 9.
180 See the discussion in Chapters 6. See further Zentall (2022) in which the author describes throughout the way in which the presence of others may reinforce different activities through social facilitation.
181 Mitchell (1987), 202–211. Mitchell sets out five levels of imitation, considered further in the discussion below.
182 Copyright, Designs and Patents Act 1988, s30A.
183 *Pro Sieben media AG v Carlton UK Television Ltd* [1999] 1 WLR 605, 614; *Shazam Productions Ltd v Only Fools The Dining Experience Ltd* [2022] EWHC 1379 (IPEC), [156–158].
184 For example, in the United Kingdom, the only decision of the English courts to date is on an immersive dining experience, where the reaction and judgment of the audience was key: *Shazam Productions Ltd v Only Fools The Dining Experience Ltd* [2022] EWHC 1379 (IPEC). Notably, evidence was led by the defence that audience participation contributed to a transformative performance [52] although in the court's view the audience feedback assisted in finding for the claimant on the questions of pastiche and fair use [194–196].
185 *Authors Guild v Google Inc*, 804 F 3d 202 (2d Cir 2015).
186 *Authors Guild v Google Inc*, 804 F 3d 202 (2d Cir 2015), 216–218.
187 Adaptation, including parody and pastiche, is considered in more detail in the next chapter, Chapter 9
188 Mitchell (1987), 202–211. Although the stratification of imitation into levels of mental processing has been challenged, not least for the proliferation and divergence in thinking around imitation (see Russon et al (1998), 105), it is relevant to note Mitchell's account of five levels of imitation, ranging from lower forms that discount considerations of consciousness to the higher levels of flexible and dynamic learning. The first and lowest is where the mimicry exists before or without observation and is "always functionally imitative and never intentionally

imitative" (202). The second level of imitation is a kind of instinctive imitation, but again implicates the audience in that "the imitator would not produce the copy unless, as in level one, another organism perceived the similarity between model and copy" (205). In the third level of imitation, the mimic is taking greater account of the model and there are suggestions of comparison and flexibility through observational learning (205–206). The fourth level of imitation varies upon the model, whereby "the organism ... varies the copy, changing some aspects to conform to the model and others to extend the model in some way" (206). This introduces both the novel and useful elements of creativity, as through make-believe play (207). Mitchell provides examples of fourth-level imitation in nonhuman primates (such as the example of using a coconut to carry and cradle like an infant, and the example of washing a doll) and dolphins (imitating divers cleaning the tank and substituting various objects as tools for that purpose) all of which take place in captivity (207–208). See further: Brueggeman (1973) (coconut example); Gardner and Gardner (1969) (doll example); and Tayler and Saayman (1973) (dolphins). See further the useful discussion of imitation levels as well as levels of imitation recognition in preverbal and nonverbal children in Nadel (2002).
189 Lacoue-Labarthe and Nancy (1988/[1978]), 45.
190 Lacoue-Labarthe and Nancy (1988/[1978]), 45.
191 Schlegel (1991/[1798–1900]), Athenaeum Fragments, §77.
192 Benjamin (1930).
193 Schlegel (1991/[1798–1900]), Athenaeum Fragments, §125.
194 Schlegel (1991/[1798–1900]), Critical Fragments, §115.
195 Wordsworth (1807), 243. See further the discussion of the links between British Romanticism and poetry as expressive force denouncing hunting and other areas of social concern during the period of critical social reform in animal use in the early nineteenth century, in Perkins (2003).
196 Schlegel (1991/[1798–1900]), Ideas, §103.
197 Schlegel (1991/[1798–1900]), Athenaeum Fragments, §125.
198 Lacoue-Labarthe and Nancy (1988/[1978]), 45.
199 Lacoue-Labarthe and Nancy (1988/[1978]), 45.
200 Haraway (2016), 58. Emphasis in original. See further the discussion in Rigby (2020), 84–85. And in a further fragment, Haraway acknowledges an unanticipated precursor in Beth Dempster's Master's thesis of 1998 (61). See further Dempster (1998).
201 Rigby (2020).
202 Berry (2019) draws upon Haraway's concept of sympoiesis and introduces a concept of sympoetics seemingly unaware of the same concept in Jena Romanticism, and yet unaccountably and intriguingly resonant with Schlegel's concept: "Thinking beyond poetic writing as a purely reflective, individual pursuit, sympoetics offers an orientation to writing that notices, suspends, and holds together relations with materials and place in the midst of ambiguity that exists beyond the self" (13).
203 Middelhoff (2021).
204 Rigby (2020), 83.
205 Schlegel (1991/[1798–1800]), Ideas, §95.
206 Haraway (2016), 125.
207 Cage (1961), 64.
208 Lacoue-Labarthe and Nancy (1988/[1978]), 45.
209 Lacoue-Labarthe and Nancy (1988/[1978]), 45.
210 Schlegel (1991/[1798–1900]), Critical Fragments, §108.

211 Schlegel (1991/[1798–1900]), 52.
212 Established by brothers August Wilhelm Shlegel (1767–1845) and Friedrich Schlegel (1772–1829) together with Caroline Michäelis (who was married to August Wilhelm) and later, Novalis, among others. This particular group was so-called for the place, the city of Jena, Germany, but Philippe Lacoue-Labarthe and Jean-Luc Nancy prefer to identify the group as Athenaeum after the journal established by the Schlegel brothers and to which the members contributed: Schlegel (1991/[1798–1900]), 7. *Athenaeum* was founded in 1798 and ceased publication with its final issue in 1800. On the establishment of the journal and its contributors see Millán-Zaibert (2007), 12. See further Bernstein (2003), xxxii–xxxiii.
213 Benjamin (1920), 118.
214 Gasché (1991), viii.
215 Gasché (1991), viii.
216 Benjamin (1920), 118.
217 Gasché (1991), viii.
218 Bruns (2016), 110.
219 Behler (1993), 167–169.
220 See further Janowitz (1998), 443–446. Elsewhere Janowitz examines the fragment in Coleridge, one of the key examples from British Romanticism, noting that "Coleridge … finds in the notion of the fragment a useful vehicle by means of which to defend his poems from censure and give then the status of an identifiable, not universal, poetic genre" (22).
221 Benjamin (1920), 161.
222 Schlegel (1991/[1798–1900]), Athenaeum Fragments, §77.
223 Gasché (1991), xi.
224 Schlegel (1991/[1798–1900]), Athenaeum Fragments, §51.
225 Tarde (1899), 101.
226 Tarde (1899), 101. Emphasis in original.
227 Useful here is the explanation in Tarde (1899) of the difference between phenomena of imitation and phenomena of adaptation, and in particular, the example of education and science: "Every gain of science, every truth added to her hoard, or *adaptate* of propositions that harmonize with one another, is not a mere summation, but rather a multiplication, and mutual confirmation … To be exact, we must, of course, see in this something more than mere addition" (174). Emphasis in original. This incremental and personal imitation is a critical distinction when considering an ethological familiar production, as distinct from the presumed univocity of the collective in social production, presenting a particular anecdotal quality to the operation of justice, as considered in the final chapter, *Law's Anecdote*.
228 Huang and Chang (2024).
229 Longo et al (2024).
230 Tarde (1899), 101.
231 See further Chapter 7.
232 Tarde (1899), 105.
233 Schlegel (1991/[1798–1900]), Athenaeum Fragments, §363.

Chapter 9

The Gods Must Be Playful

This chapter begins again with some more shipwrecks, the grounding at which this whole enquiry began. And these are the shipwrecks which frame the *Iliad* and the *Odyssey*, and ultimately the shipwreck which prevents Odysseus from returning home. Whither Hermes or Mercury,[1] the literary guides in which they make their contributions continue to amaze. Indeed, one must never underestimate the importance of literary guides. As the voyage of this book was nearing completion, researchers found ten ancient shipwrecks around the small island of Kasos, all by following Homer's clues through the *Iliad*.[2] The attention to Homeric hymn in this chapter and also framing the whole book, is in view of its contribution to the preservation and sustainability of knowledge, including through the very literal example of the Kasos shipwrecks, as well as for the authorial futures set out in attention to history as our guide.

And in the *Odyssey* can be found a literary guide to the various themes that come together here in an ethological approach to creativity – the distraction and wandering, the deception and disguise, and the comic and play. Deception and pretence continue to be critical to the mercurial and alchemical disruption of an anthropocentric model of authorship in this (all but) final chapter. Many of the key concerns of authorship, including nonhuman animal creativity, converge in the figure of Mercury and Hermes:

> Of all the divinities of classical antiquity, the Greek Hermes (Mercury in his Roman alter ego) is the most versatile, enigmatic, complex, and ambiguous. The runt of the Olympian litter, he is the god of lies and tricks, yet is also kindly to mankind and a bringer of luck; his functions embrace both the marking of boundaries and their transgression, as well as commerce, lucre and theft, rhetoric, and practical jokes; he also plays the role of mediator between all realms of human and divine activity, embracing heaven, earth, and the Netherworld.[3]

Who better as guide for the last part of this journey? As well as being "god of the marketplace,"[4] what is particularly interesting in the commerce of

DOI: 10.4324/9780429342103-14

authorial deception, is that Hermes is also the god of language,[5] a herald and messenger.[6] At the same time, Hermes is the god of thieves (and liars)[7] and travel,[8] and is himself noted as a "gregarious,"[9] creative, and somewhat playful trickster.[10] But what is especially relevant to the present discussion, is that Hermes is also regarded as the guardian of the animals,[11] as the god of animal husbandry.[12]

The legacy of Homeric hymn thus provides a fascinating perspective on the diffusion of story, not least for its provocation of a rich legacy through parody and pastiche. And in many ways, parody has continued to play throughout this present discussion. From the exaggerated parody in Voltaire's *Candide*,[13] through to this chapter's discussion of the playful imposture of the discipline of sociology in Tarde's *Fragments of a History of the Future*,[14] parody has mobilised an intentive and attentive regard, and with that has prolonged the play throughout this book. The *chorus* between the sections of the present work – The Philosopher, The Ants, and Mercury – share in this ancient literary tradition: "Goddess of song, teach me the story of a hero."[15]

An Epic Tale of Imitation

The *Odyssey* is recognised as a sequel to the tragic *Iliad*, and in fact is best understood and widely accepted as a parody of the *Iliad*.[16] Gerard Genette describes the *Odyssey* as recalling the *Iliad*,[17] a kind of memorialising of the earlier text, as it were. These relations of connections and memory through the communion of texts are essential to the sense of adaptation, the kind of attentive imitation that, as will be seen, is *attended to* in the law itself. The *Odyssey* is also credited with introducing the comic form in literature, and indeed using deception as a vehicle for that humour;[18] *room to play*.

And one of its most famous and irreverent examples of adaptation, or perhaps of any adaptation, is to be found in the ecstatic language of James Joyce's very playful *Ulysses*,[19] which itself commenced as fragments in its earlier serial publication.[20] But speaking of precursors and progenitors, was the *Iliad* itself a precursor for Aesop? In other words, is Aesop's fable, with which this story began, in fact best understood as a parody of the *Iliad*? Homer's epic told the tale of a shipwreck, a plague of the ant people and the Myrmidons in battle, and Hermes (Mercury's Greek counterpart), around a hundred years before Aesop's fable.

Recalling *Candide*, Homer's *Odyssey* also challenges the divine providence of the gods: "O the waywardness of these mortals! They accuse the gods, they say that their troubles come from us, and yet by their own presumptuousness they draw down sorrow upon themselves that outruns their allotted portion."[21] And perhaps because of this, while the gods are active in *Iliad*, their involvement is somewhat marginal in the *Odyssey*, other than Mercury, of course: "We sent them Hermes, the Keen Watcher, the Radiant One … Thus

Hermes warned him, wishing him well, but Aegisthus' heart would not hear reason, and now he has paid all his debts at once."[22] *All is well*, indeed.

The story of the *Iliad* is presented from the god-like perspective of one, the omniscient narrator. But in the *Odyssey*, the story is carried away from the singularity of the author to the highly collaborative and original nature of authorship. The perspectives are multiplied through different characters, proliferating and fragmenting the narrative towards a nevertheless coherent whole of anecdotes; thus moving through parodic play from the bystanders of the collectivity to the abundance of familiar production. In fact, the *Odyssey* has itself become a figure of the mystery of authorship, with the notion of Homer as the singular author giving way to a community of authorial voices. Scholars have variously questioned whether Homer was actually the author of the epic poems,[23] or if Homer even existed at all.[24] There have also been suggestions of multiple authors, with the generation of the poems through communities of oral tradition.[25] Is the epitomical Homer actually the inauguration of a long-standing fascination with (and construction of) the singular author?[26] It is a rich irony that a tradition of originality in authorship might come from a rich tapestry of imitations. And there is an even more delectable irony to the kind of indebtedness to the source, suggested through copyright exceptions, when it comes to understanding these imitations not as secondary forms but as instrumental in the stewardship of knowledge and attribution of the ironic indebtedness; an indebtedness not only to the precursors but also to the *cursed*, so to speak. In other words, adaptation may in itself not only revise but also reschedule, as it were, the chronology of the narrative histories,[27] as indeed does Homer, in whatever shape or form, in the retelling in the *Odyssey*.

And in its very loose adaptation of the *Odyssey*, delivered through another layer of adaptation, namely Alberto Moravia's novel, *Il disprezzo*,[28] Jean Luc Godard's *Le Mépris*[29] engages in undermining further the time of the epic, and the figure of the auteur, through its playful regard of the gods and of directors or authors as gods. The film (and novel) engages the self-referential and classical play of attribution in the mise-en-abîme of the story within the story, the film within the film, the world within a world. This extends to Godard's own appearance as a beggar-auteur, as it were; a marginal bystander to the authority of the director, played by Fritz Lang, of course another auteur.[30] *Le Mépris* is itself a film of fragments, a pastiche and "fabric of quotations."[31] But in another twist in this history of fragments, *Le Mépris* includes a scene where Fritz Lang recites in German a fragment from Friedrich Hölderlin's *The Poet's Vocation*, translated into French by Giorgia Moll (in the character of Francesca Vanini) in *Le Mépri*s, subtitled as follows: "But man, when he must, may stand fearless, alone before God. His innocence will protect him. He needs neither weapons nor guile, until the absence of God comes to his aid."[32] Lang explains the last verse as strange and notes the contradiction in the absence rather than presence as a source of comfort – the critical distance, as it were.

This sequence offers yet another joyful moment in this prolonged play of literary relations and attentive imitation, because Hölderlin was, of course, one of the key figures of German Romanticism and a member of the Jena circle.[33]

By Fair Means or Foul?

Copyright law anticipates a kind of play, and even acknowledges it as a desirable freedom from copyright, in the form of fairness – that is the principle of fair use[34] or the possibly more limited[35] concept of fair dealing in the United Kingdom.[36] The broad principle of fair use is in many ways a provision for attentive imitation within the copyright system itself. This chapter is necessarily not an exhaustive account of adaptation and fairness, but it is nevertheless a deliberate account of the fundamental, common principles running through these exceptions – principles that are at work in the wider rationale for adaptation, and in application in determining a copying that is fair. In approaching the relation between producer and consumer in copyright as characterised by fair use, a particular attention will be directed to the notion of adaptation through play or humour – namely, the exceptions of caricature, parody, and pastiche.

It is relevant that in the various approaches to permitted uses, parody is the common element. While the exception for parody is provided together with caricature and pastiche in the European Union[37] and the United Kingdom,[38] in other jurisdictions the parody exception is tied to satire alone.[39] Where parody, caricature and pastiche are grouped together, this is more than through mere convenience of drafting, and in fact suggests certain presumptions about the commonalities between these different cultural phenomena of imitation. Indeed, this is so much so that this grouping is taken to make perfect aesthetic as well as popular sense. But those commonalities may be recognisable more through effect than through form, raising some particular vagaries for their application. How does the law know a parody when it sees it?

In the approach to fairness as an exception, the implication is that these are types of use that might otherwise infringe. In other words, these may be types of copying or imitation of a copyright work for which a specific provision is necessary in order for these acts to be permitted. This introduces two important considerations: the first is the assumption that caricature, parody or pastiche is a copying or imitation, and one that potentially infringes; the second is that, even if these acts potentially infringe, they are nevertheless valued culturally and socially such that the freedom associated with these acts must be protected within the law.

There are thus useful distinctions as well as commonalities to consider across these three particular examples of attentive imitation. As a starting-point, regarding the process of defining these terms within copyright, and in the law of the United Kingdom specifically, the title of the provision should perhaps be taken at its word, in as much as these appear to be presented as alternatives or possibly even the same thing as far as the law is concerned. Indeed, within the expansive literary studies literature on the matter, there is some acceptance that these may be intersecting elements of the same indefinable thing but utterly familiar practice.[40] But on this there is far from consensus, and a trajectory towards distinct definitions continues in the jurisprudence as well. Therefore, perhaps it is more useful to consider these as alternatives; but not alternative definitions of each other. Rather they, are alternative forms of attentive imitation.

The Irony of It All

The nature of this original work or imitation or otherwise will be considered in more detail in this chapter, through considering the relationship between imitation and originality in these exceptions, that are themselves premised upon presumptions as imitations. The law distinguishes between caricature, parody, and pastiche to varying extents, but what is useful is to begin to work through the organising principles of simulation and imitation towards a wider concept of irony in imitation. This provides critical insight into the nature of originality in intellectual creation, through the broader umbrella concept of irony, including the capacity for ironic play in nonhuman animals. Irony interacts in critical and valid ways with the principle of deception in authorship, as set out in the previous chapter, and it is towards this originality that the current discussion ventures an interpretation of irony in law.

Thus, without necessarily trying to particularise the differences between caricature, parody and pastiche, it is helpful to examine all of these as coming within the world of irony: "Not all irony is parodic, obviously, but all parody serves the purposes of irony."[41] As such, the present discussion terms the exception, *the play exception*, with good and serious (to echo Schlegel) reason. For not all parody is fun and games, despite the law's mismanagement of the term. Irony, as a concept of distortive allusion, becomes the overarching process, methodology, or concept in so far as the diverse accounts of parody (and to some extent, caricature and pastiche as well) all appeal to a distortion of the features of the source.[42] To understand all these concepts one must first understand the irony, as it were, of the paradox of authorship.

All this playful beauty, once again, remains in debt to Romantic irony. Indeed, Graeme Stones declares that "Schlegel's respect for Socratic irony" is notable "in making parody an essential partner rather than a minor relative of irony,"[43] and provides a succinct definition of parody "as ironic imitation: the necessary suspiration of disbelief."[44] This recalls Simone Weil's counsel to embrace contradictions and it is through these exceptions that the system attends to a kind of justness of a kind of reversibility of authorship. Simone Weil explains this method as follows: "Method of investigation: as soon as we have thought of something, try to see in what way the contrary is true."[45] This fragment speaks to the significance of contradiction for Weil's philosophy, and the irony of absolute reason: "Reason discerns the two ends of the chain but the centre which unites them is only accessible to undemonstrable intuition."[46] This method invites the beggar back into the dialogue, begging the questions; the Athenian,[47] the stranger, the wanderer, paying attention to inattention, playing with the answers.

Parody and its related forms of attentive imitation similarly might be understood through Weil's concept of contradiction, of "coupling together incompatible thoughts as if they were compatible."[48] This coupling, or connection, is not only crucial to the joy of parody but also to the application of the exception within the law, in that this connection is fundamental to a use that is fair. And it is the quality of this connection that is also critical to discerning attentive imitation. At the same time, and for the same reasons, this (lack of) connection is (or should be) an impossible obstacle to arguing fair use in respect of the data scraping undertaken by current productive forms of artificial intelligence.[49] The matter at stake is the quality or otherwise of the trace that remains after this palimpsestic superimposition. While the product may appear entirely different from the source material, it is in fact that obscuring of the relation that presents the greatest evidence that this use is not fair.

The irony of it all is that it is in hiding one's tracks that one is the most exposed. But in acknowledging this exchange, the originality and expressive value of imitation is abundant. Thus, through that connection – whether understood as quotation or as transformation – the connection between two works must be preserved, as this is the fundamental dialogical value of that imitative relation and the originality in imitation.

Connection Corrections

Implied in this proliferation of connections is a kind of fragmentation of the conventional construction of the singularity of the author. Once again, Jena Romanticism offers a possible disruption, or indeed *correction* perhaps, of the prosaicism of the Romantic author. Perspectives on the Romantic author as a solitary individual creator, or singular genius and perspective, as well as possessing the authority or property over the expression, itself beset by singularity, persist in their influence throughout literary studies and legal scholarship.[50] And yet this is itself perhaps an incomplete view, and one may ask why. The somewhat fragmented or distributed concept of authorship advocated in Jena Romanticism, with its playful wit and irony, is in contrast to the control or singularity that is afforded the singular genius ordinarily associated with Romantic authorship, the author as god. The exceptional fragments, as it were, illuminate this further.

In setting out the scope of the provision and the excepted uses, within the terms of caricature, parody or pastiche, the Copyright, Designs and Patents

Act 1988 provides, "Fair dealing with a work for the purpose of caricature, parody or pastiche does not infringe copyright in the work."[51] But is caricature, parody or pastiche fair? Or must it be fair before it can be caricature, parody or pastiche? The nature of this aesthetic or technical judgment is less clear. But certainly, through its reflexive function discussed further below, these forms of imitation may be said to import a dimension of criticism (or even *correction*) and therefore perhaps fairness to any dealing for the purpose of the exception, as required at law, in that this "self-reflexivity of parody thus guarantees both a critical and a creative dimension to this form."[52]

Thus, the scope of this provision appears to provide that these forms are imitations that are at once critical and evaluative; that is, there is innovation through imitation – *attentive imitation*. In this way, at the same time, parody (and arguably its related forms of caricature and pastiche) is in itself a kind of stewardship of knowledge, bringing regard and attention to the source and transforming and creating anew: "The parody not only rewrites another work, but suggests yet another one within itself, reminding the reader of the relativism of any work of art, and also of the richness of creative possibilities in an allegedly limited single source."[53] Even though the law in the European Union does not create a positive requirement for sufficient acknowledgement of the parodied work, nevertheless this process of attention through parody in its wider cultural meaning and operation continues to apply. This is because the nature of parody itself turns on the recognition of the parodied work, both culturally and legally.[54]

It is the very nature of parody's attributive regard, a certain attention recognised throughout the forms of caricature and pastiche as well, that both rewards the source and invents the new – the attentive regard for attribution and legacy that is both accountable and creative in attentive imitation.[55] As Tarde proclaims, "everything is imitation,"[56] and so it stands to reason that "subsequent imitations are just as much imitations of the imitation as of the initial invention."[57] The model of any adaptation is a complicated genealogy indeed, of minute perceptions and fruitful collisions, characterised by the persistent traces on the palimpsest.

But what of the imitation in plagiarism, considered in the previous chapter? How does literary history and the law distinguish between the concepts of *stereotypic imitation* and *attentive imitation* as developed here? This distinction is crucial to understanding and responding to the line in sand, as it were, sought by the courts and more widely. There is, in fact, no quantitative answer to plagiarism in the context of pastiche or parody. But there is a qualitative resolution in the concept of intertextuality which, by its own name surely contains the very explanation of its resolve – the inextricable element of connection and attribution. Isidore Ducasse, more commonly recognised under the *nom de plume*, Comte de Lautréamont, held particularly firm views about the originality in imitation, the provenance in plagiarism, and the function of correcting: "Plagiarism is necessary. It is implied in the idea of progress. It clasps an author's sentence tight, uses his expressions, eliminates a false idea, replaces it with the right idea."[58] For Lautréamont, however, this still seems to describe an attentive imitation, rather than a stereotypic one, through the very critical process of correction itself.

Surely the answer is in securing recognition through attribution, however and by whatever means that attribution may be achieved and effective.[59] This is important, in that without that recognition, the fundamental character of caricature, parody and pastiche is lost, and arguably, what is left is just a copy. Returning to the *correction* at work here, this enjoys a genuine accord with the Jena Romantics' perspective on authorship, and on the work itself, through the symphilosophy of a prolonged and playful relation between fragments.[60]

Correcting the Deceptors

If all authors are liars, correction is necessarily an unfinished engagement, in a manner of speaking. To restore Lautréamont in refrain, *it is implied in the idea of progress*. But in correcting Lautréamont, so to speak, this is not so much plagiarism as it is an attentive imitation, a somewhat complete pastiche. Stones echoes this sentiment in declaring, "Parody's business is also with telling the truth, and that it begins by countering previous truths is no more than the process in which all literature is engaged, compressed into a more visible spectrum."[61] In the wider meaning of parodic play, it is no accident that Stones declares that parody is "at the same time a cure."[62]

It is in this context that the discussion revisits the concept of *détournement*, introduced earlier, and the kind of *turn-taking* in diversion that may be implied by this literary correction. *Détournement* is perhaps most readily associated with the art and intellectual movement, Situationist International, and "the situationist technique of *détournement* in action."[63] One of the key concerns of the Situationist International is in fact the concept of authorship itself and indeed, the meaning of intellectual creation. Guy Debord's *Report* intends as a form of manifesto for this engagement with the industry of culture: "One of the contradictions of the bourgeoisie in its phase of liquidation is that while it respects the abstract principle of intellectual and artistic creation, it at first resists actual creations, then eventually exploits them."[64] Their use of *détournement* is notably an attention through distraction and diversion and at the same time an action and creation that is immersive and embodied, linked through time and place. In anticipation of the later discussion of embodied creativity, *détournement* may be understood as imitation concerned with action (as in method and process) through space, as distinct from language (or form).

It is in this context that the Situationist definition of play informs an enacted and expressive theory of authorship later in this chapter, for it is a definition that is characterised by its action, by its movement. It is also a definition wholly consistent with an ethological approach to a justness and morality through play:

> The new phase of affirmation of play seems to be characterized by the disappearance of any element of competition. The question of winning or losing, previously almost inseparable from ludic activity, appears linked to all other manifestations of the tension between individuals for the appropriation of goods ... The element of competition must disappear in favor of a more authentically collective concept of play: the common creation of selected ludic ambiances ... Due to its marginal existence in relation to the oppressive reality of work, play is often regarded as fictitious. But the work of the situationists is precisely the preparation of ludic possibilities to come.[65]

This critique of the arbitrary distinction between work and play, as particularly apparent in the neglect of "the common creation of selected ludic ambiances," has much in common with Weil's perspective on the joy in work.[66] And it also tallies with Gregory Bateson's definition of play as "the establishment and exploration of relationship," while the later "greeting and ritual are the affirmation of relationship. But obviously mixtures of affirmation and exploration are common."[67] And there are more interests shared between these diversionary tactics and the tactical deception in play. Recalling the earlier discussion of play,[68] the hostility towards winning and losing as manifest materialism resonates with Breton's account of play and the Grasshopper's accomplished prolongation of the game in the somewhat parodic retelling of Aesop's fable offered by Suits. In other words, the creative work (and expression) through play is the kind of attentive imitation that runs through these *diversions* to the social hierarchies of authorship. There is indeed a fascinating and somewhat serendipitous intersection between an action-based approach to *détournement* and an expressive theory of authorship through play – *the ludic possibilities to come*.

The Irony in Mockery

Linda Hutcheon rejects the inclusion of ridicule or mockery in the wider cultural understanding or theory of parody, instead presenting parody in terms of its crucial relationship to irony: "Parody, then, in its ironic 'trans-contextualization' and inversion, is repetition with difference. A critical distance is implied between the backgrounded text being parodied and the new incorporating work, *a distance usually signaled by irony*."[69] This critical distance is at work in pastiche as well, even in circumstances where the sampling is almost total, entering into a curious dialogue with the integrity of the original text. In those circumstances, it is the context itself that creates that distance, ironically in immediate proximity to the source.[70]

In ways possibly different from the use in pastiche, or possibly not, parody introduces potentially a more critical account of style.[71] Copyright may be said not to protect style, but in the very requirement for a departure or ridicule in the *appropriation* of style or voice, it appears that style, somewhat paradoxically, is central to the understanding of parodic use and the nature of the distance towards that transformation. Caricature creates that critical distance through distortion,[72] while parody might be understood as creating that distance through location – that is, maintaining the thread or connection, while mobilising the distance. In all three concepts, the identification of the *original* is intrinsic to the understanding of the use. It is through that very pronouncement that the distance is possible; that is, recognition is essential to the appreciation of difference in repetition, in order to gain the "point of view," that "is the condition in which the truth of a variation appears to the subject."[73]

Despite this critical dissension on mockery, the jurisprudence on parody (as well as the more limited jurisprudence on pastiche in the United Kingdom[74] and elsewhere[75]) continues to emphasise mockery as part of the meaning of the exception. The technical approach to parody in copyright law will be considered in more detail later in the chapter, but before that, it is useful to consider the elements, particularly the element of mockery. The duality, indeed irony, of mockery is of immediate interest in this respect. Mockery has the meaning of both the ridicule of another, and the imitation of the model: to *mock up*. It is defined as both ridicule and as "an instance of mocking;"[76] that is, as well as the meaning of mocking as a "taunt," is the important meaning of mocking as "imitation, mimicry."[77] In a manner of speaking, nonhuman animals mock all the time, as was seen in the previous chapter. This emphasis on mockery in understanding parody brings this very ironic play, or reflexivity, within the definition itself. That is, the meaning of the exception includes the very fact of its imitative quality. But notably, at the same time, this reflective nature of the definition reinstates the connection with the source, through that very process of mockery.

Thus, within the exception inheres the kind of contradiction and reflexivity characteristic of parody itself. This is the spectacular irony in the meta language of parody, as described by Friedrich Schlegel:

Finally, there is the irony of irony ... what we want this irony to mean in the first place is something that happens in more ways than one. For example, if one speaks of irony without using it, as I have just done; if one speaks of irony ironically without in the process being aware of having fallen into a far more noticeable irony; if one can't disentangle oneself from irony anymore, as seems to be happening in this essay on incomprehensibility; if irony turns into a mannerism and becomes, as it were, ironical about the author; if one has promised to be ironical for some useless book without first having checked one's supply and then having to produce it against one's will, like an actor full of aches and pains; and if irony runs wild and can't be controlled any longer.[78]

Let us see if this irony can be controlled when venturing to the concept of parody (within the *play exception* of caricature, parody, and pastiche). The following discussion heeds the advice of Schlegel: "Viewed subjectively, philosophy, like epic poetry, always begins in medias res."[79] And so it is at the middle (of the exception) with parody that the consideration begins and remains, not least because so many of these observations have been repeated throughout the literature with respect to caricature and pastiche as well. Nevertheless, important distinctions must be noted, as will be considered as the discussion proceeds. What is necessary is for the definition of parody to engage more fully with the wider meaning of mockery, acknowledging the potential application in the concept of pastiche and caricature as well.

Parody All the While, but Is This Supposed to Be Funny?

As will be seen below, defining parody turns out to be a complex matter. But there is at least some consensus that parody is nothing new. Aristotle identified Hegemon of Thasos (around fifth century BCE)[80] as the "the first writer of parodies,"[81] but there seems to be little doubt that the form is even older.[82] The short story of the long history of parody is that this history is also part of its shifting meaning,[83] with attempts at definitions usually framed by the particular socio-historical context in which they are made. Margaret Rose argues that the various definitions "both reflect the interests of certain historical ages, and influence the historian's selection and canonisation of certain texts."[84] This evaluative role of definition comes to play in the legal renderings of the concept, as will be seen, thus imputing a certain character to parody that is discernible in the very attempts to define its scope.[85]

Throughout literary studies, there is reference to parody as a form of imitation that is for the purpose of ridicule or amusement[86] and, as such, incorporating elements of exaggeration or caricature.[87] But adherence to the concept of parody (including in its use as a kind of umbrella concept in this context) as humour is not uniform. Indeed, parody is perhaps more widely acknowledged as a form of critical attention to the source work, which may or may not ridicule in the process. And despite copyright law's view on the matter, the comic element may not be essential at all. Graeme Stones argues that the persistent understanding (or misunderstanding) in the "the purpose and effect of parody as ridicule ... prolongs a misuse detrimental to parody."[88] Stones explains:

> To make humour prescriptive is to kill its spirit; it should never be built into a definition of parody, but left to float in and out unbidden, at the whim of audience and context as well as author. No-one sensibly defines

irony in terms of comic intent or effect, although its relationship with humour is equally intimate, and parody is closer to irony than any other literary form.[89]

Perhaps the concern is really with the way in which humour is presented as a somewhat secondary cultural form. Indeed, this marginalisation of the ludic is similarly lamented in Jena Romanticism. Friedrich Schlegel asks: "Why is an entry for the ridiculous always missing in those fashionable catalogues of all possible principles of morality? Perhaps because this principle is generally valid only in practice?"[90] As a matter of interest, does parody present the moral *correction* of cultural forms that is so familiar throughout the various artistic and aesthetic engagements with disruption, including revisionist literary adaptations as well as the action of *détournement*?

Following the pleasure of absurdity in incongruity, Maria Aldina Marques similarly aligns parody with humour, defining it as "a playful citational transformation – more divergent than convergent – of a source occurrence used as an example."[91] This interaction between play and attribution as a kind of transformative use is insightful and resonates with the diversions of *détournement* and similar imitative play. The "ironic dimension of sociality *itself*" is thus to be found in the play of imitation, where "in this model of intersubjectivity irony is understood as a *positive* force of disruption and dissemblance."[92] As Schlegel declares: "Irony is the clear consciousness of eternal agility, of an infinitely teeming chaos."[93]

Artificial intelligence, on the other hand is by (mechanical) definition and prescription, literally opposed to the concept of divergence, and thus to the abundance of the sociality of irony. The capabilities of artificial intelligence will be considered towards the end of this chapter, but for now I will merely foreshadow its limitations. Play, it cannot. Parody, it *must* not.

Making a Mockery

In approaching these exceptions, the courts give the concepts of caricature, parody and pastiche "their usual meaning in everyday language," and at the same time, "take account of the context and purpose of the copyright exceptions."[94] In other words, the meanings of these uses are interpreted through the policy context of the law itself. The Court of Justice of the European Union, in *Deckmyn*, has defined parody as comprising two elements: the first, is "to evoke an existing work, while being noticeably different from it"; and the second is, "to constitute an expression of humour or mockery."[95] Together these two elements address the process of parody, as well as the object or artefact produced through that parody. The second element of an expression of humour or mockery is interesting in that this may be interpreted as comprising the one element, or they may be considered in the alternative, fulfilling the genuinely imitative meaning of mockery. The determination of ridicule or humour might be curiously evaluative, but at the same time it may not even be necessary.

In making the reference, the referring court sought clarification on certain conditions for parody: that the parody should be original in its own right, beyond showing distance or difference from the original work; that it could be attributed to someone other than the author of the original work; and that it should relate to or mention the original work. The Court of Justice held that the concept of parody is not subject to any of these conditions.[96] This makes sense in that the question of parody is concerning the expression element – that is, the particularisation of the work in question. As such, it is a decision on the exception and the first condition is a separate question on the originality (or copyright) of the parody itself. The second question arguably misses the joy of self-parody completely, and again is departing from the definition of parody itself, concerning what is perhaps better understood as a wider question of false attribution. The question appears to request a representational model of parody, that is a form, as distinct from an understanding of process and methodology, which goes to the heart of parody as a relational and critical act. It is illogical to seek a representational model of parody in that the parody arises in relation to the source work and is necessarily without definition other than through its method – and indefinable thing but an altogether familiar process. And finally, the third question appeared to seek to narrow the range for what the courts might accept as evocation of an existing work, again impinging on the freedom that should accompany a workable exception for genuine parody.

Perhaps the anxiety of form accompanying these questions might be explained by the way in which parody has been deployed in "everyday language."[97] This is made clearer through understanding the distinction between parody as form, and parody as style or genre. Literary theorist, Gérard Genette, observes: "This reduced dimension and the often extra- and paraliterary intent clearly explain why parody has been appropriated by rhetoric: it has been considered a *figure*, an incidental ornament of discourse (whether literary or not), rather than a *genre*, a category of works."[98]

Parody thus must be understood as a process that *makes* an original mockery of things, an altogether *familiar* process.

Beside Ourselves

Genette offers a sustained treatment of parody and pastiche throughout his writings,[99] which he brings together under the term *transtextuality*,[100] an umbrella term including several distinct concepts developed separately as architextuality,[101] hypertextuality,[102] intertextuality,[103] metatextuality,[104] and paratextuality,[105] all of which converge in the commonality of communication and relation between texts. Genette distinguishes between parody as distortion and transformation,[106] caricature as "satirical pastiche"[107] and thus pastiche as "imitation of a style without any satirical intent."[108] In distinguishing parody from a further term, travesty ("whose function is to debase"[109]), notably Genette then brings these two together under the term *transformation* distinguishing them within that "general term" based on the "degree of distortion."[110] As for the other two styles – caricature (satirical pastiche) and pastiche – these are categorised together as *imitation*.[111] Genette's approach is fascinating for its emphasis on parody (and travesty) as distortion and ridicule, as well as for its careful distinction drawn between parody on the one hand and pastiche (with caricature as a particular form of pastiche) on the other. Taking Genette's approach to distinguishing between transformation and imitation, there is an intriguing challenge to the interpretation of these concepts in the law. And for that, engaging the distinctions between attentive imitation and stereotypic imitation may make all the difference, so to speak.

Notably, as Genette explains, "Whether satirical or not, the imitation of a style presupposes an awareness of it,"[112] consistent with the requisite connections and relations between source and imitated texts. This imitation informs Fredric Jameson's approach to pastiche but, in contrasting it to the imitation in parody, Jameson describes pastiche somewhat ungenerously as "a neutral practice of such mimicry, without any of parody's ulterior motives, amputated of the satiric impulse, devoid of laughter and of any conviction that alongside the abnormal tongue you have momentarily borrowed," arguing that "[p]astiche is thus blank parody, a statue with blind eyeballs."[113]

At this point it is interesting to distinguish Arthur Walkley's insightful and affectionate account of pastiche of more than a century ago. By way of introduction to his volume of essays illustrating the form, Walkley lauds pastiche as something quite apart from parody but nevertheless at risk of it. This is precisely because, according to Walkley, for pastiche to succeed it must exaggerate, and thus, parody "is the pitfall of all *pastiche*."[114] This reliance upon exaggeration in the form is attributed to the need to emphasise in order to ensure the success of its recognition. This raises the question of the nature of that *emphasis* – perhaps that exaggeration, indeed emphasis, may come from the very context and framing of that form (such as the museum itself).[115] Walkley explains: "The sense of an audience is not fine enough to appreciate exact imitation; it demands exaggeration, caricature."[116] Is the museum satirical? A caricature? A self-parody?

Also striking about Walkley's account is the way in which the distinction between parody and pastiche, and the risk of parody to pastiche, also tallies with Genette's further differentiation of pastiche into satirical (caricature) and pastiche "plain and simple."[117] In a way, then, pastiche is a kind of overimitation, by Walkley's account – that is, an imitation of all the elements, including the *useless* or irrelevant ones.[118] Importantly, imitation and overimitation is itself "increased" when there is an audience, to the point of parody, if you will. This affiliative character of overimitation, including through an audience effect, has been shown in both human[119] and nonhuman animals,[120] although in the latter it has been a controversial research area, further plagued by the *mirror problem* of judging against human social norms.[121] But Walkley's approach to pastiche provides some potentially startling insight into the overimitation, as it were, at work in adaptation. In particular, the museum setting or similar indications (that become meaningful in the context of a relevant cultural institutional endorsement) towards emphasis or exaggeration of the imitation contribute to a form of *overimitation* for the benefit of the audience.

For Walkley, pastiche thus maintains a form of deference and reverence for the "ghost" of the source: "To write a pure *pastiche* you must begin by surrendering, putting clean away your own personality – how otherwise are you to take on another's?"[122] In Walkley's view, pastiche thus becomes a kind of worshipful imposture, and the stamp with "personal touch,"[123] or "personality"[124] of the source remains as an authorial spectre, a trace on the palimpsest, a perceptible refrain throughout the genuine imitation. From the perspective of play, pastiche thus becomes a kind of object play, a toying: "Occasional fragments of authentic text will be recognized at a glance. 'These Things are but Toyes.'"[125] But if pastiche works with toys, so to speak, that playfulness must be more than mere imitation. And it is perhaps in this sense that the legal wrangling of the term is made sensible. But this reverence for the original warrants further consideration, for it is a perspective and a dismissal of pastiche that resurfaces regularly, and one which poses particular problems for its *fairness* in the application of copyright exceptions.

This reverence arguably shapes the meaning of parody as well. By its own etymology, parody is a form of affiliative, relational and playful imitation through the melody of parody: "First, the etymology: *ode*, that is the chant; *para*, 'along,' 'beside.' *Parodein*, whence *parodia*, would (therefore?) mean singing beside: that is singing off key; or singing in another voice – in counterpoint; or again, singing in another key – deforming, therefore, or *transposing* a melody."[126] This musicality or harmony through the etymology of parody is not insignificant. Hutcheon also notes the common etymology of *parodia* as meaning "counter-song" but expounds upon this to explore the playful antagonism, as it were, between texts. But at the same time, this is the irony of parody, as Schlegel quips: "Irony is the form of paradox. Paradox is everything simultaneously good and great."[127] Indeed, the best of all worlds. Somewhat resonant with Schlegel's *simultaneously good and great*, this melodic counterpoint is explained by Hutcheon as a kind of parallel or para-text, and a form of *making with*:

> The textual or discursive nature of parody (as opposed to satire) is clear from the *odos* part of the word, meaning song. The prefix *para* has two meanings, only one of which is usually mentioned – that of "counter" or "against." Thus parody becomes an opposition or contrast between texts ... However, *para* in Greek can also mean "beside," and therefore there

is a suggestion of an accord or intimacy instead of a contrast. It is this second, neglected meaning of the prefix that broadens the pragmatic scope of parody.[128]

Parody is thus a kind of affiliative behaviour, with a distinctly sociable character, and it achieves this precisely through an attentive imitation: "Parody is central to what we might call the methodology of affiliation because it both enables and forces the writer to curtail the power of the past (and even the present), rather than merely repeating the past and thereby debasing it."[129] Central to the definition of the process as well as the ethological value of this expressive tool, a successful parody, so to speak, is in its certain attention: "[P]arody affiliates itself to the literature it treats by adhering to a principle of imitation."[130]

Drawing upon the apparent parody of Homer in James Joyce's *Ulysses*, considered at the beginning of this chapter, Hutcheon notes the limitations of "that ridiculing imitation mentioned in the standard dictionary definitions" and arrives at "parody in the twentieth century," noting that although "*Odyssey* is clearly the formally backgrounded or parodied text here, it is not one to be mocked or ridiculed; if anything, it is to be seen, as in the mock epic, as an ideal or at least as a norm from which the modern departs."[131] This parodic departure may be such as to create "a jarring incongruity between form and content,"[132] producing what might be described as an *attentive salience* – that is, a form of attentive imitation through which parody both gives attention (to the source) and demands attention (through surprise).[133]

In these respects, in addition to the recognisable relationship between texts, arguably the most important characteristic of parody is that it is transformative. The intertextuality thus brings pleasure, but arriving at this pleasure need not necessarily be through ridicule or mockery: "Parody, therefore, is a form of imitation, but imitation characterized by ironic inversion, not always at the expense of the parodied text."[134] Hutcheon maintains it is "repetition with critical distance, which marks difference rather than similarity."[135] Parody is thus a kind of affiliative difference, a discriminating similarity, an authenticating imitation. An original imitation, if you will: *Since I can't afford originals, I make my own.*[136]

The Game Is the Game

Thus, just as for play,[137] the overwhelming critical and original character of parody is that of metacommunication. Drawing upon Roman Jakobson's concept of the metalingual,[138] Margaret Rose describes parody thus as meta-fiction, whereby this metacommunicative function coheres the critical and transformative qualities through which parody "may criticise the communicative function of the conventional quotation."[139] As meta-fiction, the intertextuality of parody and the productive play with the legacy of the source material is "like the play within the play," such that "epic parody contains within itself a verbally-like piece of literary material which is made the object of its analysis and renewal and part of its own structure and effect as a literary work."[140] Through "the function of meta-fictional parody to reflect upon its own medium,"[141] parody takes on a reflexive quality; indeed, the capacity for self-parody. In an examination of this reflexivity, Michele Hannoosh identifies self-criticism as "a central feature" of parody and describes it as "crucial to a thorough understanding of the genre."[142] As Hannoosh explains: "Parody implicates itself in its treatment of the parodied work, and often realizes this overtly."[143]

Interdisciplinarity thus emerges as a form of reflexivity. Why look at animals to look at authors? Why look at authors to look at animals? In its engagement with literature, art, science, and law, is this book itself a parody? With this in mind, it is interesting to note that Michael Lynch describes Bruno Latour and Steve Woolgar's *Laboratory Life*[144] as a form of parody for similar reasons:

This book was framed – with strong hints of parody – as a classic anthropological narrative, in which an articulate stranger from abroad drops into a tribe, and refrains from preconceptions about native life while taking copious notes about what he witnesses. In this case, the tribe was a laboratory at Salk Institute, the tribal beliefs were communicated at the laboratory bench and inscribed into the scientific literature, and various rituals were conducted with laboratory implements and sacrificial animals.[145]

It may seem uselessly reductive to treat all interdisciplinary work as necessarily parodic; or worse, to suggest it is somewhat secondary or comic (to adopt the thinnest concept of parody). And yet, this gives meaning to parody itself in that the communication between texts is necessarily transformative by changing the utility of those texts through new contexts, indeed as emphasis, to recall Walkley's regard for the practice. This is a form of attentive imitation through which the meaning of parody is not to be marked out as comic and disreputable ridicule. Rather, this is parody as attentive and attending – that is, in an active interchange of *certain attention*. And as metalanguage, that attentive regard is turned on itself: "Parody, in other words, became ... a way for art to be curious about itself, so that one definition by which art could re-present itself was through parody."[146] That regard, that performance of imitation, is in itself expressive: "Here form *is* content, content *is* form" and thus writing that "is not *about* something: *it is that something itself.*"[147]

Found in Translation – The Dancing Monkeys

This irreverent, reverent use resonates with the freedom of aesthetic expression shared by the Jena circle. Friedrich Schlegel declares: "In the works of the greatest poets there often breathes the spirit of a different art. Might not this be the case with painters too? Doesn't Michelangelo in a certain sense paint like a sculptor, Raphael like an architect, Correggio like a musician? And surely they aren't for this reason lesser painters than Titian, who was only a painter."[148]

Indeed, is attentive imitation a form of translation into the musical language of parody? After all, "[m]any musical compositions are merely translations of poets into the language of music."[149] And a certain aspect of this is to recuperate the value of parody, and thus to question the hierarchies in creativity, as in between source works and adaptations, or the various uses in copyright. and works in copyright. In this way, Malcolm Bradbury explains parody as explicitly a form of translation, a process of examination and correction, and at times a reversal of fortunes when it comes to the order of works:

> Literature is the name for a monument that is both solid and evanescent: parody accepts the truth of the monument but also questions and tests the artifice used in its construction. It perpetuates and destroys, becomes a form of mysterious translation, exploring the mystery of institutionalisation and the paradox of the existence of any art-object. It exaggerates the process present in all art, the oscillation between mimesis and artifice, and emphasises both the present force and the redundant emptiness of some preceding aesthetic case. Thus it is a form of criticism, and most great writers have practised it. Sometimes what is parodied is a single writer, monumentally in the way, sometimes an entire phase of style or a genre, sometimes it is the work presently being constructed, a self-parody. Apparently defacing a classic text, parody can become one.[150]

But as well as this translational effect on the hierarchies of creativity, an attention to parody offers critical insight into the mechanics of the species hierarchy as well, in that nonhuman animals, just like the dancing monkeys who opened this journey, are frequently relegated as mere parodies of humans. But in fact, as will be seen, the parodic acts of nonhuman animals are innovative and creative in their own right, including in their parody of humans themselves. For example, ravens have created entirely novel repertoires through imitating humans, thus learning as well as innovating through the translation – from hand to beak.[151] This is imitation, indeed parody, as a form of social learning. Or from mouth to hand, as when Jeff teaches me to throw a ball, by tossing his ball in the air back and forth to elicit a game of fetch. But this is not a game I taught Jeff. This is a game he has taught me, and I am compelled to imitate him.

And this interest in translation is of critical significance to opening up aesthetic attention to the expressions of nonhuman animals. Schlegel explains a process that resonates with the attention to subjective experience, but in this way through translation: "In order to translate perfectly from the classics into a modern language, the translator would have to be so expert in his language that, if need be, he could make everything modern; but at the same time he would have to understand antiquity so well that he would be able not just to imitate it but, if necessary, re-create it."[152] There is something that it is like to be an author. In any engagement, technical or otherwise, with nonhuman animal communication, what is being undertaken is a process of translation – that is, a social process of imitation and translation.

As to nonhuman animals, to continue the refrain, *Can they caricature? Can they pastiche? Can they parody?*

Can They Parody?

Can they parody? Can they disguise, misreport, exaggerate, misrepresent, make fun and mock? Indeed, can they lie? Behold the Socratic irony of a bird's broken wing display,[153] or ants playing dead[154] (also known as thanatosis or death-feigning), or the various other injury-feigning behaviours or distraction displays of birds and other nonhuman animals. The shift in language is not neutral, and in itself is significant for drawing attention to the perspective on potential authorship or otherwise in these displays. Donald Griffin notes that "it used to be customary to call these performances injury feigning," but is critical of the "the behavioristic decades of [the twentieth century]," when, he explains, "ornithologists came to believe that it was an anthropomorphic error to imagine that a mere bird might consciously want to lead an intruder away from its eggs or young, and therefore the term 'predator-distraction display' was adopted."[155] Nevertheless, the term distraction display is adopted here, not least for its intriguing interaction with the earlier discussion of distraction as intention, and towards a recuperation of the term as a kind of ironic capability.

Distraction displays are usually staged in order to lure a predator away from more vulnerable individuals (such as nestlings in a ground nest). The broken wing display is just one of these displays, which can involve other examples, such as "running behaviors, injury feigning, tail flagging, and erratic flight."[156] And then there are other ethological examples of ironic defences, as it were, such as freezing or feigning death,[157] of which the possum is "one of its exemplary practitioners."[158] This kind of post-contact immobility is recognised "[i]n a remarkable diversity of animal species, both vertebrates and invertebrates,"[159] and is described by many other names, including thanatosis, playing dead, playing possum, or tonic immobility.[160] But one of the more intriguing terms applied to the performance is "animal hypnosis,"[161] the irony of which is not lost in the present discussion of hallucinations and other dreams. Ants also deploy this technique rather regularly, not only in defence but also in the service of diplomacy. For example, fire ants perform thanatosis as a mechanism for resolving neighbourly disputes.[162] The deployment of irony in diplomacy is a skill worth heeding.

One of the very fascinating examples of Socratic irony in thanatosis is offered by antlions. A predator is more easily going to be distracted by movement elsewhere, while the immobility of the original target makes them thus "invisible." Just like the purloined letter,[163] the antlion can hide in plain sight just through the strategy of freezing. Indeed, it is a kind of magician's ruse, an illusory device.[164] But at the same time, the defence banks on the economy of attention: "[T]he best place to hide a needle might not be in a haystack but in a large pile of identical needles."[165] A defensive irony, as it were.[166] And in other elaborate spectacles, many cephalopods excel at self-parody. When a cephalopod releases ink as a predator approaches, for some species this makes a personal double. In these situations, the cephalopod parodist releases "a blob of ink that is held together by mucus and approximates the volume of the cephalopod," creating a "pseudomorph" ink shape version of themselves, a somewhat ironic imitation (whether satirical or plain and simple is a matter for debate with Genette), which distracts the predator long enough for the trickster to make their escape.[167]

A similar expressivity is decipherable in the distraction display of flushing, where birds fly away suddenly, usually to expose themselves in order to conceal those more vulnerable (such as nestlings). In the poem, *The Skylark*, the British Romantic poet, John Clare, "in the semiotic web of the signing action of nature,"[168] describes the flushing distraction of a skylark in countering the threat from some schoolboys picking buttercups. The skylark immediately takes action to distract the boys from the nest:

> Up from their hurry see the Skylark flies
> And o'er her half-formed nest, with happy wings
> Winnows the air, till in the clouds she sings,
> Then hangs a dust spot in the sunny skies
> And drops and drops till in her nest she lies,
> And drops, and drops, till in her nest she lies,
> Which they unheeded passed – not dreaming than
> That birds, which flew so high, would drop again
> To nests upon the ground, which any thing
> May come to destroy.
> ...
> And smile, and fancy, and so pass along;
> While its low nest, moist with the dews of morn,
> Lies safely, with the leveret, in the corn.[169]

The skylark reinscribes the landscape with a lofty display and a pretence of "high = high," not only distracting but also rewriting the biography of the nest on the ground.[170]

An astute account of the co-production with nature is offered by the bio-semiotician, John Coletta, who describes the display as an "aerial distraction display (which display or message masks the iconic resemblance between the sky lark's ground-feeding habits, its brown-ground coloration, and its ground-nesting habitat)," and explains that the display "is an indexical sign in the mind of the (unheeding) 'boys' that leads their thoughts away from thoughts of a terrestrial nest site of the sky lark."[171] The skylark exploits the possible assumption by the boys that "high-flying birds must necessarily be high-nesting birds," and in so doing pulls off the successful ruse.[172] In this co-production with Clare's reader, "[t]he sky lark 'encourages' this reading with its indexical and iconic irony, a semiotic irony in which the sky lark's sweeping upward flight carries like a (Peircean) weathervane the boys' heads and eyes up into the sky and away from the nest."[173] Like the production of space through scent marks and overlapping tracks,[174] the skylark performs a pretence of territory at odds with the nest hidden in the ground, deceiving the boys with the ironic display. There is purpose in that distraction: *pay attention, stupid*.

This capacity for irony also indicates a kind of sense of justice, as described also through the morality in play.[175] To recall Friedrich Schlegel's fragment considered earlier: "Socratic irony ... is meant to deceive no one except those who consider it a deception and who either take pleasure in the delightful roguery of making fools of the whole world or else become angry when they get an inkling they themselves might be included."[176] In other words, this might be understood less as a defensive deception, and more as an active expression. It is not a mere lie but a deliberate parody to *correct* the interpretation that the nestling is vulnerable. These are copies, so to speak, to counter the truth of the *predator*.

While Daniel Dennett has argued that such displays do not necessarily demonstrate any higher intentional thinking,[177] as in the kind of intentional thinking one might align with authorship, Carolyn Ristau's investigations ascertain something much more purposive in these displays. In studies with plovers, Ristau observes a range of aspects to distraction displays, including flexibility in the behaviour,[178] as well as timing and responsiveness to the predator's behaviour and proximity, all suggesting a purposive or intentional performance[179] that might caution against dismissing this as mere instinct, or as a simple *drive to distraction*. Through these studies, Ristau advocates for an intentional stance and a form of limited or critical anthropomorphism to be adopted in research design for the way in which this affords new questions and perspectives.[180] And if the charge is that such an approach might presume too much, it is no more than the problem of approaching research through denying particular capacities and explaining away *anomalies* through functional norms. Indeed, such a hasty dismissal may be in search of a false sense of security more than anything else. *We are the art-making animals*. Recalling the kind of co-production with nature, anticipated by Jena Romanticism, an expressive theory of authorship takes the attention away from the emphasis on the linguistic and towards these bodily, relation, performative, *musical* actions of ironic humour and contempt. Are we the *only* art-making animals?

This is the difference between a mere lie and an artful deception; between a stereotypic copy and the attentive imitation. Found in the choreography and flexibility of Ristau's plover is the poetry and irony of authorship. Who can say otherwise? Who can say that the law of parsimony is common sense at all? Rather than closing off to options, irony opens up to worlds. Perhaps we should heed Friedrich Schlegel when assessing this more-than-human poetry when he says, "English criticism ... surely consists of nothing but applying the philosophy of common sense (which is itself only a permutation of the natural and scholastic philosophies) to poetry without any understanding of poetry."[181] Is anthropodenial part of the "pathological history of common sense,"[182] as Schlegel describes it, which "even threatened for a while to infect German philosophy"[183] with a similar exceptionalist thinking? The law of parsimony is perhaps less law than more. Or ironically, more than law. It is *unthinking*, in every sense.[184] In unthinking authorship, is the species distinction merely arbitrary?

Musical Geniuses and Grand Gestures

Giorgio Agamben distinguishes the ancient meaning of parody from its modern inflections in a way that is enticingly relevant to nonhuman animal parodic forms, such as vocal mimicry: "The classical world ... was familiar with another, more ancient meaning that situated parody in the sphere of musical technique. This definition made a distinction between song and speech, *melos* and *logos*."[185] Indeed, there is a musicality necessary to appreciating irony, a kind of deception getting deception. And there are a lot of examples of what appear to be performances of symbolic imitation in birds that have otherwise been ignored or explained away as mechanical, vocal mimicry. But what is lost in translation is the fact that many bird species are capable of "surprisingly sophisticated imitation that challenges views that avian talents lie with vocal imitation alone,"[186] as well as challenging wider presumptions as to the kinds of species capable of imitative learning.[187] Such complex vocal communication through song also follows patterns of phrasing and forms of syntactical and grammatical rules,[188] findings that "challenge the long-standing view that compositional syntax is unique to human language."[189] That such things are not unique to humans is significant given the insistence on the exceptionalism of language – no longer the word as barrier between us, but as bridge.

While there is much to be said of this musicality, the ballet of symbolic communication extends beyond the choreographies of bee language. The aesthetic language of gesture holds the potential for symbolic communication of abstract concepts among nonhuman animals; but strikingly, this sensation of gesture also introduces a distinctly ethological perspective on the experience of the aesthetic objects, the drama of doing, and an embodied approach to the symbolic. Japanese tits are proficient at gesture not only for a kind of object or literal language (such as pointing) but also symbolically in order to communicate abstract concepts.[190] In the case of the Japanese tits, they use a fluttering gesture to convey a symbolic message of "after you" for entering the nest;[191] a deliberate courtesy, as it were. The physicality of this symbolic communication, just like the sophisticated eloquence of dance language in bees,[192] returns the discussion to the question of language as *the word between us*.[193] And it recalls the writerly legacy of copyright that persists and constrains in its approach to visual art, smells, sounds, performance, and other phenomenal challenges to the written text. The question for copyright is indeed still a question of language, but an ethological perspectives expands that language to language as gesture, language, as performance, language as play. The bees, and the Japanese tits, and the many other examples show that this capacity for authorship, if you will, is not unique to humans.

And at the same time, the qualities of a work are not merely writerly, restoring a genuinely aesthetic account of the parodic play in authors and an ethological perspective on ideas and expressions. In *The Aesthetics of Parody*,[194] David Kiremidjian anticipates an ethological and embodied perspective when explaining that "the 'form-content relation' is more than a formulation enabling the critic to deal with what appears to be a dualistic phenomenon. This relationship is in fact better conceived as a drama or as a process."[195] And in doing so, Kiremidjian gestures, so to speak, towards the arbitrary contrivance of a distinction between the work and the performance in copyright itself, noting that "[a]lthough we can conceive of a work of art as a special state of being, we must also acknowledge it as a manner of doing, an action, gesture or movement."[196] In doing so it becomes clear "that the gestures are nevertheless symbolic, that the concrete exempla are articulated within an aesthetic context, and that the 'imitation of nature' is enclosed in its own world."[197] Indeed, this is the very *nature*, so to speak, of authorship – the making of "its own world," the *other than* the world, the *more than human*. This restores the sense to the aesthetic through the sensational and parodic authorship of play – this is the very world-building of *attentive imitation*. And the evidence for expanding the field of authorship is clear for all to see.

At this point, almost as an anecdote itself, a precious fragment from Thomas Sebeok brings many of these issues together. Sebeok is responding to the anthropocentrism of language studies and the folly, in every sense, of the kinds of linguistic tasks presented in ape language projects. Sebeok contends that these projects are not a question of teaching a language as such but a matter of "accommodation and conflict between *Umwelten*," where the subjects find themselves "placed in a totally man-made environment," in which they are then coerced to "adapt themselves, somewhat reluctantly, by learning a number of arbitrary signifier-signified associations and by utilizing them in situations where trainers will accept no alternative type of response."[198] As Sebeok tellingly observes, this is a play of mediocrity (to recall Breton's account), of winning and losing, where the subjects "will follow certain elementary prescribed rules of play, in other words, but there is no indication that they are playing the same 'game.'"[199]

Body Languages

What then of the relationship between this language of authorship and the *scripted* language of copyright? The embodied systems of nonhuman animal communication compel a *restoration* of the aesthetic sense of copyright, in a manner of speaking. The aesthetic theory of the historian and philosopher, Robin George Collingwood, is especially *to the purpose*, in a manner of speaking, in addressing these linguistic differences as a matter of *accommodation and conflict between Umwelten* – the human game of copyright authorship, and all the other many games of authorship. Collingwood is perhaps most regarded for his work on aesthetics, and the influential *The Principles of Art*, published in 1938, in which he brings the question of language back to the aesthetic in its original concern with sensation (the aesthetics of sentience, in a way) and embodiment, as promoted through a Kantian science of sensation.[200] Indeed, Collingwood explicitly invokes Kant's consideration of birdsong in order to critique the imposition of aesthetic judgment on the science of aesthetics as somehow objective: "The question was acutely raised by Kant, how far our attitude towards the song of a bird is an aesthetic one, and how far it is a feeling of sympathy towards a little fellow creature."[201] But what is of particular note, in answering this question, is the contemporary that songbirds actually enjoy singing outside any sexual or other supposedly biologically functional context.[202] In other words, it seems that, just like the production of art for immediate pleasure as advocated by Coleridge,[203] songbirds have an aesthetic sense. And what is more, it is a sense of play in practice; a joy in work, as it were.

This affiliative and empathetic dimension to aesthetics is significant for an ethological approach for acknowledging co-production through perception and reception. Arguably, the traditional emphasis on approaching an expression through a form of purportedly objective judgment continues to reinforce an anthropocentric perspective (*what is an author?*), as well as a somewhat Eurocentric perspective (*what is authorship?*), and an institutional rendering (*what is a work?*) in response to the question, *what is art?* In this way aesthetic judgment is invoked in the service of taste and deferred from the sensory expression. But Collingwood's observations reveal the presumptions at work in the matter of expression and the sensational importance of the perspective of the subjective experience (of both author and reader) and "love" (resonating with Weil's perspective) in manifesting the answer of *art*:

"[A]esthetic theory is the theory not of beauty but of art."[204] It thus follows that art is understood as something more distinctly relational and affiliative, and the commodification through intellectual property (along with other ways of regulating the object) is revealed as a convenience and contrivance:

> The theory of beauty ... is merely an attempt to construct an aesthetic on a 'realistic' basis, that is, to explain away the aesthetic activity by appeal to a supposed quality of the things with which, in that experience, we are in contact; this supposed quality, invented to explain the activity, being in fact nothing but the activity itself, falsely located not in the agent but in his external world.[205]

This begins to *make sense* of the more complex challenges to the conventions of the intellectual property object, as posed by relational values, such as NFTs, and ephemeral objects, as in digital products and the metaverse.[206]

This approach to the aesthetic gesture, in a manner of speaking, is compelling in the present context in that the question of language is recuperated in the question of art in such a way as to make sense, in every sense, of copyright and the recognition of nonhuman animal authorship. In his emphasis on art as language, Collingwood essentially restates and redefines the copyright work as language, and the language of the copyright work. Collingwood asks, "'What kind of thing must art be, if it is to have the two characteristics of being *expressive* and *imaginative*?'" and responds, "The answer is: 'Art must be language.'"[207] The art of language thus gestures, fully and freely, and "[e]very utterance and every gesture that each one of us makes is a work of art."[208] In this way, an ethological approach unrests the anthropocentric inertia that limits not only the perception and recognition of nonhuman animal authorship but also the field of intellectual creation itself, with significance for both the conceptual approach to authorship, and the technical approach through the objectivity of the copyright system itself. An ethological approach thus opens out to expressions beyond the writerly text towards a *panglossia* of sensory expression. The *best* of all worlds – that is, the good art of all kinds. On the question of authorship, language is art, art is language, and thus the panglossia of nonhuman animals as art cannot be ignored. The manner of distinction is through the purposeful expression – the play.

Collingwood also identifies and critiques the technical theory of art and the contrived distinction between art and craft, as well as the practice of recognising as art only "those marginal examples which live outside the overlap of art and craft."[209] This is a distinction which appears to map along similar assumptions as those imposed by functionalist or biological renditions of nonhuman animal creativity and play. This perspective has much in common with both the technical legal approach to functional "craft" and the social and cultural norms attached to mass-produced aesthetic expressions, such as fashion, with the very practical consequences for validation and protection. Remarkable in Collingwood's approach is the emphasis on the exuberance and autonomous nature of the utterance as art (understood through the aesthetic experience), as distinct from an approach through planning and application,[210] again reverberating meaningfully through the concept of originality in copyright law. In other words, the distinction resonates with the author's own intellectual creation as an autonomous creation (that is, by its very definition as *the author's own*, or the *creative spark*[211]), and departs from the operose particularisation through planning as detected in the old approach of labour, skill and judgement.[212] But rather than interpreting this as a restatement of a romanticised creative genius, it suggests much more about attention to the subjective experience of making art; not for the purposes of idealising the singularity of the author but to restore the subjective and collaborative experience of sensory expression.[213] *What is it like to be an artist?*

But while Collingwood suggests that the distinction between form and matter does not apply in art,[214] arguably this does not disparage the readymades or appropriative and ironic use; on the contrary, it reaffirms the relational quality and co-production of value through use: "Expression is an activity of which there can be no technique."[215] Further, it is the contention in the present discussion that this does not simply relegate or produce a displacement of craft but instead shows the way in which a rationalisation of expression continues (socially and legally) through exceptionalist concepts like technique and foresight to produce problematic distinctions and exclusions of art, including, in counterpoint, the neglect of craft as art.

Something very similar describes the boundary maintenance of the sphere of *art-making animals*. Functionalist arguments like skill or biological utility serve both to *single out* authorship, as it were, and to preserve its domain, and as the discussion and examples throughout this book have shown, this is almost uniformly the lens through which apparent nonhuman animal creativity is rationalised and explained away. But it is a methodology applied also to certain forms of human creativity, such as the way in which fashion is designated an article of utility and thus outside the realm of art,[216] or the way in which traditional knowledge or traditional cultural expressions might be considered a functional (traditional) communication and thus outside the programme of innovation as defined by intellectual property.[217]

Thus, if we are to describe the language or utterance of art as autonomous, this is a question of noting that it is both the author's own, and yet arises in production *with* the audience to which it is directed. In this way, the artefact itself becomes a means to communication rather than an end, and it is this means in which the aesthetic experience inheres: "Art has something to do with making things, but these things are not material things made by imposing form on matter, and they are not made by skill. They are things of some other kind, and made in some other way."[218] An accommodation and conflict between *Umwelten* – the capital of art, and the art of capital.

Bobby the Bel Esprit

In the spirit of the anecdotes that thread together this discussion, here is a personal one that provides a further account of this *accommodation and conflict between Umwelten*. As a child, I grew up with horses and my friends and I would ride together and attend the local pony club. One of my childhood friends had a horse called Bobby.[219] Bobby would affect a limp whenever he had had enough of the activities proposed, or when he was not in agreement with the direction of travel being anything other than towards home. But as soon as we would all turn to head home, his limp would vanish. He had been examined by several veterinarians, none of whom could find anything wrong with him. In fact, he had passed every soundness test they put before him.

Bobby would also perform this limp at pony club, usually after lunch. And as a result he would be retired from the afternoon's activities of usually some sort of jumping over poles, no doubt an activity quite inexplicable if not inane to Bobby. One afternoon, during such jumping over poles, Bobby began to limp. Bobby's limp was of course famous (or infamous) around the land. And my friend and some of Bobby's other human friends were quick to reassure the parent-instructor and explain that he was all right. But of course we all agreed nonetheless he should stop for the day. Despite this, and the compliance with procedure, I recall the parent-instructor who was running the session exclaiming loudly in a somewhat affected voice, "No horse feigns lameness!"

As well as teaching me the word feign for the first time, this became a humorous refrain afterwards for my friend and me, and even to this day! But at the time the parent's anger was startling to us. I remember my friend being quite upset and shocked by the outburst, indeed to the point of tears (it was rather a lot for a couple of seven or eight-year olds). But perhaps Schlegel's account of Socratic irony is helpful here in understanding this episode, for it appears that the parent-instructor had perhaps an inkling that they may be included in Bobby's apparent deception, and so they became quite angry when it seemed they might be the target of that deception. There are of course always those who object loudly when they suspect that the deception is mocking them, and this parent-instructor appeared to be among them.

And of course, as a parodic display, Bobby's *limp* was also perhaps about correcting the interpretation that trotting over poles on a Sunday afternoon is valid, when it is just as simple to walk around them, and even better just to go home to a nice meal. In Bobby's limp there is an example of another deception in order once again to counter the truth of the *predator*. But whatever the purpose of the parody, as it were, once again when my friend and I turned for home, Bobby's limp vanished. And everyone's smiles returned. Bobby invited affiliation and pleasure through his shared deception of the churlish parent-instructor.

Making Evolutionary Aesthetic Sense

In the accommodation and conflict between *Umwelt*, it all comes down to the matter of play. Which returns the discussion to the earlier consideration and refutation of the preoccupation with attributing a function to play.[220] But what if an aesthetic sense is actually the *function* of play? Herbert Spencer, writing at the end of the nineteenth century, insists that "[t]he activities we call play are united with the aesthetic activities."[221] Spencer goes on to approach the aesthetic through a similarly relational and ephemeral process observing that "the aesthetic consciousness is essentially one in which the actions themselves, apart from ends, form the object-matter," and that this is borne out "by the conspicuous fact that many aesthetic feelings arise from contemplation of the attributes and deeds of other persons, real or ideal."[222] For Spencer, the aesthetic makes perfect evolutionary sense.[223]

Heeding the foresight of Spencer, the zoologist, Peter Klopfer, in a study in the late twentieth century, approaches aesthetics through its meaning of sensory expression and experience, similarly to the present discussion. Klopfer observes that "[a]mong many species play seems to be a guide for conscious action," towards fulfilling an aesthetic sense, suggesting the possibility "that animals can, for instance, have 'art'."[224] Understood in this way, play is presented as the kind of conscious and purposive action ordinarily interpreted through authorship. And Klopfer suggests that one of the clearest examples of this aesthetic sense is to be found in the (creative) choice and action upon space (such as through habitat preferences and objects), which recalls the deliberate aesthetic, as it were, of Naruto's manipulation of space.[225] As Klopfer contends, "thought and abstraction in man is but a form of play,"[226] and thus parody fulfils the expressive aesthetic of play.

With all this in mind, can it ever be said that machines have an aesthetic sense? Can machines really play?

No Laughing Matter

The question is whether the capacities of artificial intelligence can extend to parody. Can machines parody? As far as a sense of ironic imitation, the capacity not only for deception but also for relational imitation appears to be beyond at least the current capacities anticipated for artificial intelligence. At the simplest level, artificial intelligence is programmed specifically not to lie; indeed, "truth" is seemingly the aspiration for programmers, but this in itself can disguise bias as legitimate and accurate.[227] But furthermore, that means that the kind of dissensus, distortion, and dissemblance that characterise intellectual creation are beyond the resources of artificial intelligence. The critical distance that characterises not only attentive imitation but also the kind of departures that are intrinsic to creative work are literally unthinkable, as it were. The basic operation of these kinds of models is to approximate, to summarise, to average, perhaps in every sense of the word. What occurs is not even pastiche, not even plain and simple, as the connection to the work, the explainability of the imitation, is necessarily lost in the scraping.

This incapacity also comes down to the basic problem of explainability in artificial intelligence.[228] Notwithstanding promises of addressing this,[229] as it stands this not only presents a technical obstacle to parody but also encompasses the very lack of authorial understanding that undermines any pretence to intellectual creation.[230] All deliberate imitation is potentially transformative, but only if that transformation can be perceived – that is, only if the distance between can be appreciated. In other words, the transformative value of any parody is the transformation itself, the process, the relation, the explainability. It may not be a concern with the content or the work, and it may be wholly enjoyed through a novelty in use.[231] Thus, it is not in the object alone but in the object in relation.

The problem for artificial intelligence is that it cannot show the difference between, or enjoy the difference between, or revel in the abundance of the difference between. Artificial intelligence has an explainability problem, but it also has a relationality problem. There can never be imitation that is recognisable as imitation; there can never be *awareness*.[232] Therefore, whatever its outputs might be called, they can never be parody, they can never be caricature, they can never be pastiche, and, seemingly paradoxically but wholly consistently, they can never be copies. But they can also never be the author's own intellectual creation. Regardless of whether machines are deemed persons or not, this is not the end of the matter, because the object can never be a work. The pleasure is in difference and the parodied work is as critical as the parody itself in order to appreciate the difference, to ascertain the difference, to enjoy the transformation. Indeed, this is why pastiche is an appropriate exception, but the kind of "pastiche" that might be spoken of with respect to artificial intelligence is neither pastiche nor is it appropriate. There is no transformation if the sources cannot be explained.

And the attribution of these relations is one of the critical aspects of attention that contribute to an expressive theory of authorship.

An Expressive Theory of Authorship

Play is not innocent, but it is just. And in playful imitation is to be found the sincerest form of parody. As Robert Mitchell counsels, "until we examine animal play in detail, we cannot be sure what they can accomplish."[233] To see play as merely a proxy for the inevitable scientific explanations is to miss the interaction of the points. In the words of Donald Griffin, "this position confuses explanation with elimination."[234] And the nature of belief is not resolved by the advent of explanation. Responding to the dismissal of beliefs and desires as "folk psychology," in favour of explanations from science, Griffin states, "An equivalent physiological understanding of beliefs and desires would be a magnificent achievement, but would not eliminate the attribute thus elucidated."[235] In some respects an extreme anthropodenial is like a Victorian cabinet of curiosities for the twenty-first century. But we no longer have to kill things to look at them.[236]

Recalling the difficulty in identifying and observing actions as distinct from reactions in cognitive studies, as explained by Marvin Minsky[237] and others, there is an intriguing resonance of this obstacle of interpretation with Weil's assertion: "It is impossible to study the mind in a direct way because its characteristics are negative ones."[238] It is proposed instead that through an expressive theory of authorship in play, it is possible to consider the actions on the environment, the *Umwelt* – that is, to study the mind by its ludic trace. At the same time, this introduces a new perspective upon the phenomenal and expressive intellectual creation. As introduced in earlier chapters, approaches to embodied cognition are instrumental in developing this approach to authorship, including in particular theories of embodied thinking or embodied action, enacted cognition and expression, or enactivism.[239] Embodied approaches to cognition maintain "that cognition depends upon the kinds of experience that come from having a body with various sensorimotor capacities."[240]

In doing so, embodied cognition develops a phenomenal approach to subjective experience within, and in co-production with, one's environment, noting that "these individual sensorimotor capacities are themselves embedded in a more encompassing biological, psychological, and cultural context."[241] Rather than the organism or individual filling a space or being acted upon by that space, enacted or embodied cognition anticipates a more expressive and co-productive account, one that resonates with the productive space considered earlier,[242] and readily sensible within a biosemiotics account of the ludic *Umwelt*. Play is not only "participatory sense-making,"[243] but also an expressive "re-creation" involving higher-order cognition:[244] "This is why the concept of sense-making is so interesting ... the cognitive agent may also be an *active creator of meaning* and that such creation can be subject to change and eventual control by emergent levels of cognitive identity."[245] In this respect, play is identified as offering a particular insight into that creative work: "[E]lements of the meaning manipulation that this activity can afford are already present in all forms of play."[246] Recalling the bodyness of self, considered earlier,[247] much of the work appears to have been started through play.

In many ways Weil also presents the preliminary groundwork when she explains that, "when one is attentive, one's consciousness is open to illumination."[248] For Weil, the mind is discovered, as it were, through "the necessity of things"; that is, the mind brings that necessity "to the surface" through things.[249] Attention is thus brought to the surface through play; the choreographies of motivations, taking turns, and manifest flow. Weil describes the world appearing "as an obstacle to the mind"[250] and in this sense the mind appears through both its imprint upon and by the world through the individual's movement and experience within the world. In other words, not only is the *expression* of the author's own intellectual creation made possible by the author in the process of intellectual creation, but also it is what makes possible the author. Through that expression, the mind may be inferred, not for its representational thinking, or idea, but through its enaction. Form is thus a strategy for bringing ideas to the surface.

In this way, intellectual property begins to make sense not as a register of innovation but as a form or tool of enactivist representation; or non-representation, more accurately. Thus, an enactivist approach to authorship begins to unravel the Cartesianism that holds firm in intellectual property's auteurism more widely, and in copyright in particular. Indeed, this relational approach, rather than emphasising the singularity of the auteur, begins to forecast the relational approach to property; an approach that is being accelerated by sociable territories in the metaverse,[251] and priorities of sustainability at odds with the model of growth through volume of artefacts, as in fashion.[252] In other words, the surface of consciousness cannot be known through sentience, but rather, must be shown through experience; being is always in between. And in considering these surface tensions, the consummate creative experience and affiliative expression is that of play. Ultimately, with a focus on play, it is possible to shift from dealing with various forms, which are merely indexical of the relations at stake, to the relations themselves, to the media of creativity. This animal turn, as it were, is thus more than a rhetorical flourish. It is a literal challenge to the Cartesian dualism that continues to inform the interpretation of authorship, most remarkably perhaps in the authorship of machines. And at the same time, it is confront the inconsistencies in the animal sentience discourse through authors and authorship.

There is also a dimension of the familiar in making sense of an embodied or enactive approach, which is immediately intelligible within an ethological approach to expression as materialised within the individual's *Umwelt*. Recalling Minsky's comments referred to earlier, it is interesting to note that Varela, Thompson and Rosch cite Minsky's work in play as a possibly unintended precursor for enacted thinking: "Minsky's and Papert's society of mind is not, of course, concerned with the analysis of direct experience. But Minsky draws on a delightfully wide range of human experience, from playing with children's blocks to being an individual who is aware and can introspect."[253] Indeed, in this work, which includes Minsky's examination of humour, play research provides an invaluable anatomisation, in a manner of speaking, of embodied thinking: "In many ways, Minsky's work is an extended reflection on cognitive science and human experience, one that is committed to the 'subpersonal,' but does not wish to lose sight for too long of the personal and experiential."[254]

There is another fascinating precursor for enactivism arguably to be found in Gregory Bateson's analysis of Totemism in anthropology, which he reconciles with heraldry and patrilineage,[255] echoing Tarde's consideration of similar mechanisms of cultural diffusion. Bateson notes that "[s]uch representations of family status in a mythological hierarchy often aggrandize self or own descent at the expense of other family lines."[256] In this way, Bateson argues that there is "a shift of attention away from the relationship to focus *one end*, on the objects or persons who were related,"[257] which leads to "a loss of that insight or enlightenment which was gained by setting the view of nature beside the view of family."[258] However, in the "few practicing totemites,"[259] Bateson observes the kind of kinaesthetic and embodied action of an enacted approach to mind. Describing a class with Korand Lorenz, Bateson explains: "Lorenz's posture and expressive movement, his kinesics, change from moment to moment according to the nature of the animal he is talking about … When he spoke of the Einsteinian universe, his body seemed to twist and contort a little in empathy with that abstraction."[260] Bateson declares, "What totemism teaches about the self is profoundly nonvisual."[261]

Thus, in this approach to embodied cognition through the groundwork of play, a ludic theory of authorship as embodied and phenomenal becomes possible. This serves not only to reexamine and revise the author in copyright but also to evaluate and appreciate the nonhuman animal author in play.

Can They Play?

The fundamental question is then not only, *can they suffer?* but also, *can they play?* A question perhaps to be posed to human as well as nonhuman authors.

Recalling Allan Kornblum's *Work Song*, "The hand attributes sentience,"[262] the hand brings the play to the surface. Rather than insisting on a discovery of mind, to echo Weil's essay, the craft manifests the intelligence of the maker. The question, *can they suffer?* may thus in part be answered by this other question, can they play? This has significant implications, including a material impact on suffering itself. From a practical and policy perspective, this shift in perspective potentially introduces a positive approach to investigating empirically whether a particular species should be protected within welfare legislation. The irony of the question, *can they suffer?* is that it has ordinarily required the production of suffering itself in order for it to be answered. Play presents not only a sociological but also an empirical and ultimately aesthetic dimension to welfare. This has clear significance for the relevance of aesthetics to the question of nonhuman animal welfare. At the same time, it invites attention to welfare in progressing the enquiry into authorship, nonhuman or otherwise – the author at the mercy of the expression of their intellectual creation.

Kornblum's philosophies were playful in their own right. As a member of the albeit short-lived Actualist Movement in the Arts, founded "to bring poetry to the people and make it fun,"[263] Kornblum's *Work Song* is also antithetical to the tradition of the work song.[264] Kornblum's poetry presents poetry co-existing with work, rather than alienating poetry as a rarefied pursuit; work as joy, as it were. This approach to work through play and even joy resonates with the approaches of Weil and Tarde, explored in more detail in later discussion. Poetry is thus not a fixed expression on the page but a relationship between.

This poetic play recalls the mischief of Dave Morice and the Actualists, considered in Chapter 3, a mischief necessarily engaging in turn each of the members of the collective, such as in the extended play in the literary hoax of the fictional author, Joyce Holland.[265] In cooperating and collaborating upon the hoax in an effusive and elaborate prolongation of play, a phenomenal performance of authorship endured.[266]

Every play tells a story. And with that, the next and concluding chapter provides that *stories* book ending.

Notes

1 Hermes (Greek) and Mercury (Roman) are often taken to be the same but there are some subtle differences (Clay and Miller (2019)).
2 Kasos Maritime Archaeological Project is an interdisciplinary and collaborative project exploring the submerged antiquities in the geographical area around Kasos Island, which has been an important point in the sailing routes through antiquity. The research has been a partnership between National Hellenic Research Foundation (NHRF) and the Ephorate of Underwater Antiquities (EUA). See further the project website https://kasosproject.com/en/. See also the reports on the relevance of Homer in Kuta (2024).
3 Clay and Miller (2019), 1.
4 Ashton (2019), 234.
5 Casali (2019) describes Mercury as "the god of eloquence" (186). See further 174–178.
6 Casali (2019), 174–178. See further Shapiro (2019).
7 Brown (1947).
8 Casali (2019).
9 Shapiro (2019), 15.
10 Hermes is widely regarded as a trickster throughout the literature. See further the discussion in relation to play and games, in Strauss Clay (2019).
11 Chittenden (1947) notes, "[E]ven in the earliest period, the protective aspect of Hermes was so pronounced that we may fairly view it as part of his function of guide and of pastoral god" (93). See further the discussion in Shapiro (2019), 15–16.
12 Shapiro (2019), 15–17.
13 Chapter 3.
14 Tarde (2004/[1896]).
15 *Odyssey*, Book 1.
16 See Monro (1901), 330–331. See further Shewan (1913).
17 Genette (1992/[1979]), 78–79.
18 Burrows (1965).
19 Joyce (1922).
20 Published as excerpts in *The Little Review* between 1918 and 1920 before being banned as obscene, see further Hutton (2019).
21 *Odyssey*, Book 1.
22 *Odyssey*, Book 1.

23 In 1897, Samuel Butler claimed the *Odyssey* was written by a woman; see Butler (1897). And just over a hundred years later, Dalby (2007) has suggested a woman was responsible for both epic poems.
24 West ML (1999).
25 Nicholson (2014), Chapter 4.
26 West ML (1999).
27 Harold (2018).
28 Moravia (1954).
29 *Le Mépris (Contempt)* (1963) Jean-Luc Godard (dir).
30 See further the fuller discussion of auteurism in *Le Mepris* in Gibson (2022c).
31 Mulvey (2012).
32 *Le Mépris (Contempt)* (1963) Jean-Luc Godard (dir). The translation by Michael Hamburger in 1966, translates the phrase "His innocence will protect him" as "ingenuousness keeps him safe": Hölderlin (1998/[17 This introduces an interesting refrain with fidelity (and imitation) as well as the topic of translation as a productive and critical distance, later in this chapter, in that Hölderlin is appealing to the poets' vocation to reveal the details and "to re-constitute this structure through the power of their aesthetic creativity": Hampton (2023/[2019]), 17. Recall a similar perspective in Simone Weil's approach to the joy in work, and the attention through that joy, when she refers to the difference between the opposing views of the fields as "true monument of work" or mere "scenic background": Weil (2015/[1970]), 18. See further the discussion in Chapter 7.
33 Wulf (2022).
34 One of the leading texts, albeit from the United States perspective, is Patry (2024).
35 Compare for instance the perspective of Aplin and Bently (2020) that the Berne Convention, art 10 (quotation) provides for a form of global and mandatory fair use throughout the copyright laws of Convention members.
36 Copyright, Designs and Patents Act, ss 29, 29A, 30, 30A (and notionally 31).
37 Directive 2001/29/EC on the harmonisation of certain aspects of copyright and related rights in the information society, art 5(3)(k).
38 Copyright, Designs and Patents Act 1988, s30A.
39 In Australia, in the Copyright Act 1968, s41A, s103AA; in Canada, the Copyright Act, s29.
40 Dentith (2005/[2000]) refers to "the cultural politics of parody," and suggests, "indeed, we shall have to ask whether it is possible to talk of parody as 'essentially' anything at all" (10).
41 Stones (1999), xx.
42 In describing traditional parodies, Stones (1999) writes that the parody may be recognised easily in that "[w]hat these parodies have in common is imitative repetition, with enough distortion to carry irony" (xxix).
43 Stones (1999), xxi.
44 Stones (1999), xxxiii.
45 Weil (2002/[1947]), 102.
46 Editor's note in Weil (2002/[1947]), 102 n1.
47 See the more detailed discussion of the Athenian in Chapter 6.
48 Weil (2001/[1955]), 164.
49 See also the earlier discussion in Chapter 1
50 Lavik (2014). See further Woodmansee (1984); Woodmansee and Jaszi (1994).
51 Copyright, Designs and Patents Act, s30A(1).

52 Hannoosh (1989), 117. See further the discussion in Phiddian (1997) who suggests, "Derridean deconstruction is not just a (serious) theory couched in a parodic mode (that it is a parodic theory of language), but also that it treats language and questions of truth and reference as if they were already in a play of parody (that it is a theory of parodic language)" (673). Phiddian's argument thus resonates with approaches to the reflexivity of parody as a kind of metalanguage or meta-fiction.
53 Hannoosh (1989), 117.
54 C-201/13 *Deckmyn* EU:C:2014:2132 [20–21].
55 For example, the traditions of revision and adaptation in postcolonial literature both heed the colonialist history necessarily so as to achieve a revision through a resituated perspective and emphasis, and thus towards decolonising the literary canon. See further Marx (2004).
56 Tarde (1903/[2890]), 185.
57 Borch (2005), 85.
58 Knight (1978), 251.
59 Recall the discussion of the Google Books litigation in the previous chapter, Chapter 8. See further *Authors Guild v Google Inc*, 804 F 3d 202 (2d Cir 2015).
60 See further Chapter 8. Note also the related concept of sympoiesis as developed in Donna Haraway's work, particularly Haraway (2016) and discussed in the previous chapter, Chapter 8.
61 Stones G (1999), xxii.
62 Stones G (1999), xxiii.
63 Sadler (1999/[1998]), 17.
64 Debord (1957), 17–18.
65 Internationale Situationniste (1958).
66 See in particular Weil (2002/[1949]), 81.
67 Bateson (2002/[1979]), 128.
68 Chapter 7.
69 Hutcheon (2000/[1985]). 32. Emphasis added. In this work, Hutcheon examines parody across a range of cultural forms, from literature and visual art through to the performing arts and architecture.
70 For example, in appropriation art and pastiche, as discussed in Gibson (2020b) and considered in detail from an ethological perspective in Gibson (2025) which undertakes an ethological jurisprudence of the objects of intellectual property themselves.
71 Recall the discussion of style in Chapter 8.
72 See further the discussion of distortion and caricature on screen in Andrews (2019).
73 Terranova (2017), 295.
74 *Shazam Productions Ltd v Only Fools The Dining Experience Ltd* [2022] EWHC 1379 (IPEC).
75 The German Federal Court of Justice made a reference to the Court of Justice of the European Union on the meaning of pastiche in directive 2001/29/EC art 5(3), 14 September 2023 in *Metall auf Metall V* (I ZR 74/22). See further the discussion in Gibson (2023a).
76 *Oxford English Dictionary*, s.v. "mockery (n.)," March 2024.
77 *Oxford English Dictionary*, s.v. "mocking (n.)," March 2024.
78 Schlegel (1800), 304. See further the discussion in Albert (1993), 831.
79 Schlegel (1991/[1798–1800]), Athenaeum Fragments, §84.
80 *Oxford Classical Dictionary*, "Hegemon, of Thasos" (Geoffrey Arnott).
81 Aristotle, *Poetics*, [1448a]. See further the discussion in Rose (1993), 6–8.

82 Müller (1997), 3.
83 Müller (1997) laments: "'Parody' is a notoriously vague phenomenon" (1).
84 Rose (1979), 17.
85 Dentith (2005/[2000]), 10.
86 Rose (2011) notes the general understanding of parody as "the comic reworking of preformed material" (5). See further examples in the classic reference literature, as in Shipley (1943).
87 While it is beyond the scope of the present discussion to examine caricature in meaningful detail, the discussion continues in Gibson (2025) which includes an ethological approach to caricature in the third volume of this ethological jurisprudence, *Made*.
88 Stones (1999), xxviii.
89 Stones (1999), xxxiii.
90 Schlegel (1991/[1798–1800]), Athenaeum Fragments, §320.
91 Marques (2021), 218.
92 Peters (2004), 188. Emphasis in original.
93 Schlegel (1991/[1798–1800]), Ideas, §69.
94 *Shazam Productions Ltd v Only Fools The Dining Experience Ltd* [2022] EWHC 1379 (IPEC), [159].
95 C-201/13 *Deckmyn* EU:C:2014:2132 [20].
96 C-201/13 *Deckmyn* EU:C:2014:2132 [33].
97 *Shazam Productions Ltd v Only Fools The Dining Experience Ltd* [2022] EWHC 1379 (IPEC), [159].
98 Genette (1997/[1982]), 18. Emphasis in original.
99 See in particular the discussion in Genette (1997/[1982]), 19–30.
100 Genette (1997/[1982]).
101 Genette (1997/[1982]), 4–5. See further Genette (1992/[1979]).
102 Genette (1997/[1982]), 5, 9–10.
103 Genette (1997/[1982]), 1–3.
104 Genette (1997/[1982]), 4.
105 See in particular the discussion in Genette (1997/[1982]), 3–4. See also Genette (1997/[1987]).
106 Genette (1997/[1982]), 25.
107 Genette (1997/[1982]), 25.
108 Genette (1997/[1982]), 25.
109 Genette (1997/[1982]), 25.
110 Genette (1997/[1982]), 25.
111 Genette (1997/[1982]), 25.
112 Genette (1997/[1982]), 89.
113 Jameson (1991), 17.
114 Walkley (1921), 2.
115 On appropriation art and copyright, and the framing by the museum, see Gibson (2020b).
116 Walkley (1921), 1.
117 Genette (1997/[1982]), 25.
118 Overimitation is a form of social learning which Hoehl et al. (2019) define as "[i]mitation of actions that offer no discernible evidence of serving a function in achieving a given goal" (90).
119 Marsh et al. (2019).
120 In dogs, see Huber et al. (2022).
121 Allen and Andrews (2024).
122 Walkley (1921) 6.

123 C-145/10 *Painer* [2011] ECR I-2533 [92].
124 C-145/10 *Painer* [2011] ECR I-2533 [88].
125 Walkley (1921), 6.
126 Genette (1997/[1982]), 10
127 Schlegel (1991/[1798–1800]), Critical Fragments, §48.
128 Hutcheon (2000/[1985]), 32.
129 Caesar (1989), 229.
130 Caesar (1989), 230.
131 Hutcheon (2000/[1985]), 5.
132 Kiremidjian (1969), 232. In a somewhat deferent relationship to the source work, Kiremidjian explains, "A parody is a kind of literary mimicry which retains the form or stylistic character of the primary work, but substitutes alien subject matter or content. The parodist proceeds by imitating as closely as he can the formal conventions of the work being parodied …. But at the same time he substitutes subject matter, or content, or in an Aristotelian context actions or objects which are entirely alien to that form" (232).
133 Hariman (2008) describes something similar in the use of parody in political discourse in order to effect "dislocation and delight" towards audience engagement and pleasure through "the shock of recognition"; in other words, an effect similar to what I have termed attentive salience (262). Similarly, Hariman describes political parody as changing "the demand into the offer" through changing "direct demands on the audience to images offered for reconsideration" (255). See further the discussion in D'Errico and Poggi (2016).
134 Hutcheon (2000/[1985]), 6. Kenny (2009) explains the critical and evaluative space generated through parodic imitation, which "helps us to laugh at power and imagine alternatives. In particular, parody plays an important role in the ways in which we make and remake our understandings of particular institutions" (221–222).
135 Hutcheon (2000/[1985]), 6. Indeed, it is this emphasis on difference which Hutcheon identifies as distinguishing parody from pastiche, which it is suggested emphasises similarity (33). This seems to coincide with Genette's approach to parody as transformation and pastiche as imitation. Dentith (2005/[2000]) draws a similar distinction between parody as transformation and pastiche as imitation (11). Pastiche will be considered briefly later in this chapter, but it is considered in more detail in Gibson (2025). See further Gibson (2023a).
136 A refrain on Ferreira Gullar, quoted in Martins (2017).
137 Bateson (2000/[1972]). See further the discussion in Massumi (2014).
138 The concept has much in common with Bateson's approach to metacommunication, to indicate a use of language beyond its object function, and indeed a use of language that is to talk about language. Jakobson and Halle (1956) explain "a metalinguistic operation" as "[t]he interpretation of one linguistic sign through other, in some respect homogeneous signs of the same language" and notes that "metalanguage is necessary both for the acquisition of language and its normal functioning" (67). Reading this in conjunction with Rose's account adds a compelling dimension to the social and cultural role of parody.
139 Rose (1979), 61.
140 Rose (1979), 61–62.
141 Rose (1979), 97. See further the discussion of reflexivity in parody in Hannoosh (1989).
142 Hannoosh (1989), 114.
143 Hannoosh (1989), 114.
144 Latour and Woolgar (1986/[1979]).

145 Lynch (2016), 106
146 Caesar (1989), 227.
147 Beckett (1929), 14.
148 Schlegel (1991/[1798–1800]), Athenaeum Fragments, §372.
149 Schlegel (1991/[1798–1800]), Athenaeum Fragments, §392.
150 Bradbury (1989/[1987]), 55–56.
151 Loretto et al. (2020).
152 Schlegel (1991/[1798–1800]), Athenaeum Fragments, §393.
153 See the early accounts in Armstrong (1949a); and Armstrong E (1949b).
154 Cardoso et al. (2024).
155 Griffin (1999), in response to the account in Ristau (1991a), 246–247.
156 Stankowich (2019), 346.
157 Humphreys and Ruxton (2018). See further, Ruxton et al. (2004/[2018]), 219–228; and, Ohno and Miyatake (2007).
158 Rogers and Simpson (2014), R1031.
159 Franks et al. (2021), 1.
160 Rogers and Simpson (2014), R1031.
161 Rogers and Simpson (2014), R1031.
162 Cassill et al. (2008).
163 Poe (1845).
164 Lesté-Lasserre (2021).
165 Franks et al. (2021), 3.
166 For a comprehensive account of defensive irony, at least in the sense it is identified here, see Ruxton et al. (2018/[2004]).
167 York and Bartol (2016), 26–27.
168 Coletta (1997), 198.
169 Clare (1835), 83.
170 Coletta (1997), 198.
171 Coletta (1997), 198.
172 Coletta (1997), 198.
173 Coletta (1997), 198
174 See Gibson (2020a) Chapter 4.
175 See further the discussion of morality in play in Chapter 7.
176 Schlegel (1991/[1798–1800]), Critical Fragments, §108. See further Chapter 8.
177 Dennett (1996), 121–123. See further Cary Wolfe's critique of Dennett's analysis in Wolfe (2007).
178 Ristau (1991a), 95.
179 Ristau (1991a), 97–102.
180 Ristau (1991a), 118–123. Ristau states that through taking such an approach or stance, "predictions about the plover's behaviors were made and experiments were designed to test the predictions" (119).
181 Schlegel (1991/[1798–1800]), Athenaeum Fragments, §389.
182 Schlegel (1991/[1798–1800]), Athenaeum Fragments, §61.
183 Schlegel (1991/[1798–1800]), Athenaeum Fragments, §61.
184 Borrowed from Daniel Dennett's reference to *"intelligent but unthinking behavior"* in animals in Dennett (1996), 154. Emphasis in original. See further the critique in Wolfe (2007), 112–113.
185 Agamben G (2005/[2007]) *Profanations*, J Fort (trans), 39.
186 Russon et al. (1998), 117.
187 Russon et al. (1998), 117–118.
188 Suzuki et al. (2016).
189 Suzuki et al. (2016), 5.

190 Suzuki and Sugita (2024).
191 Suzuki and Sugita (2024), R231.
192 Chittka (2022), 70–77. See further the discussion in Chapter 4 of the present work.
193 Chapter 1.
194 Kiremidjian (1969)
195 Kiremidjian (1969), 236.
196 Kiremidjian (1969), 236.
197 Kiremidjian (1969), 236.
198 Sebeok (1981), 200.
199 Sebeok (1981), 200.
200 Kant (2002/[1790–1793]).
201 Collingwood (1958/[1938]), 39.
202 Riters et al. (2019).
203 Coleridge (1836), 7.
204 Collingwood (1958/[1938]), 41.
205 Collingwood (1958/[1938]), 41.
206 An ethological approach to these challenges is provided in detail in Gibson (2025).
207 Collingwood (1958/[1938]), 273.
208 Collingwood (1958/[1938]), 285.
209 Collingwood (1958/[1938]), 22, n1.
210 Collingwood (1958/[1938]), 20–26.
211 *Feist Publications v Rural Telephone Service Co*, 499 U.S. 340 (1991).
212 See the earlier discussion in Chapter 3.
213 Collingwood (1958/[1938]), see in particular the discussion 108–111.
214 Collingwood (1958/[1938]), 24.
215 Collingwood (1958/[1938]), 111,
216 *Star Athletica LLC v Varsity Brands Inc*, 137 S.Ct.1002 (2017).
217 Gibson (2005).
218 Collingwood (1958/[1938]), 108.
219 Bobby's name has been changed to protect his innocence!
220 Chapter 7.
221 Spencer (1885), 627.
222 Spencer (1885), 634.
223 Spencer (1885), 648.
224 Klopfer (1970), 399.
225 Chapter 5.
226 Klopfer PH (1970), 403.
227 Keyes et al. (2021).
228 Longo et al. (2024); Hassija et al. (2024); and Vilone and Longo (2021).
229 Ali et al. (2023).
230 Bishop (2021).
231 *Authors Guild v Google Inc*, 804 F 3d 202 (2d Cir 2015). See further the discussion in Chapter 8.
232 Genette (1997/[1982]), 89.
233 Mitchell (2015), 40. In commentary on Mitchell's chapter, Hoffmann (2015) notes that in human-dog ball play, "This sequence of playful idea generation, willingness to take risk, trial and error, and attention to feedback from others are all fundamental parts of the creative process" (44).
234 Griffin (1999), 236.
235 Griffin (1999), 236.

236 See further the discussion of the fetishisation of the animal body as proprietary object in death, in Gibson (2025).
237 Minsky (1988/[1986]). See further the roundtable discussion in Melnechuk et al. (1986).
238 Weil (1959a), 90.
239 Varela et al. (1993/[1991]); Hutto and Myin (2013). See further the discussion in the concluding chapter, *Law's Anecdote*.
240 Varela et al. (1993/[1991]), 173.
241 Varela et al. (1993/[1991]), 173
242 See Part 2 and in particular the discussion in Chapter 5 on Naruto's engagement with space.
243 Di Paolo et al. (2014), 71.
244 Di Paolo et al. (2014), 72.
245 Di Paolo et al. (2014), 73. Emphasis in original.
246 Di Paolo et al. (2014), 75.
247 Chapter 3.
248 Weil (1959a), 92.
249 Weil (1959a), 90.
250 Weil (1959a), 90.
251 Gibson (2021b); Gibson (2024b).
252 See further the discussion in Gibson (2023d).
253 Varela et al. (1993/[1991]), 107.
254 Varela et al. (1993/[1991]), 107
255 Bateson (2002/[1979]), 131–133.
256 Bateson (2002/[1979]), 131.
257 Bateson (2002/[1979]), 132. Emphasis in original.
258 Bateson (2002/[1979]), 132.
259 Bateson (2002/[1979]), 132.
260 Bateson (2002/[1979]), 132.
261 Bateson (2002/[1979]), 132.
262 Allan Kornblum, "Work Song," in Kornblum (1980), 51.
263 Morice (1997), 142.
264 See further Gioia (2006).
265 Morice (1997), 142.
266 According to Kostelanetz (2022/[2019]) the ruse persisted from 1969 to 1978 (293).

Law's Anecdote

This final chapter begins with an anecdote about anecdote. More specifically, it is an anecdote about the anecdote in law. In the infamous case on the existence of a common law copyright affording perpetual rights (ultimately enjoyed by the publishers), the 1769 decision in *Millar v Taylor* is a lesson in legal anecdote. The judgment describes the attempt to lead the law by way of anecdote: "Next we are told of some proceedings in the Star-Chamber; a Court the very name whereof is sufficient to blast all precedents brought from it. But I will do the gentlemen the justice to say, they did not mean to adduce them as authorities; but to apply them as historical anecdotes in their favour."[1] The challenge is telling the difference, if indeed there is a difference at all to tell.

Anecdotes also feature throughout the history of cognition research. In fact, the notable characteristic of cognition research, exemplified by the discourse around the emergence of theories of tactical deception and Machiavellian intelligence, is the very use of anecdote.[2] Anecdotes and anecdotal evidence made key contributions in early theory of mind research. And they continue to be instrumental in current attempts to account for behavioural and individual differences,[3] including the value of such evidence as a methodological tool in emphasising individual attention rather than the accumulation of data,[4] as well as through the more explicit value of anecdote recognised in the engagement of so-called citizen science.[5] What is also a particular feature of the use of anecdotal evidence is the disagreement over its application, leading to agonistic debates in cognition research,[6] and more widely. This history will be considered more in a moment; but first, a short history on the little story of anecdotes.

A Little Story of Little Stories

Anecdotes are an ancient form, with one of the most familiar examples being Aristotelian anecdote.[7] However, the term itself seems to have entered the discourse around the sixth century, with "a connotation of secrecy or perhaps

DOI: 10.4324/9780429342103-15

merely gossip."[8] It was not until the seventeenth century that the term entered mainstream use and began to be regarded as a tool of history and biography,[9] although it has been suggested that "we owe to Aristoxenus the notion that a good biography is full of good anecdotes."[10] The anecdote and the short form in literature is part of the history of civic storytelling,[11] a legacy of familiar production. As vital fragments, anecdotes are the *domain of tininess* – they are the little details, the fruitful asides, the minute perceptions, the infinitesimal situations, the greatness of the smallest. *Listen to the ants.*

Anecdotes in nonhuman animal behaviour have a similarly ancient history. Pliny the Elder, writing in the first century, and Aelian, writing in the second or third century, have been credited with anecdotal-like contributions that constitute perhaps the earliest examples of nonhuman animal behavioural observations in the field.[12] Indeed, anecdotes and anecdotal evidence have continued to make a significant contribution to the history and development of cognitive ethology, as will be seen a little later in this discussion. And in a project in encouraging "some liberalizing of thought in ethology,"[13] the biologist, Patrick Bateson,[14] and zoologist, Peter Klopfer published a series of volumes, *Perspectives in Ethology*, not only printing but also celebrating the anecdotal and incidental in ethology. In the first volume, the editors note:

> In the early days of ethology, most of the major developments were in the realm of ideas and in the framework in which animal behavior was studied. Much of the evidence was anecdotal, much of the thinking intuitive. As the subject developed, theories had to be tested, language had to become more public than it had been, and quantitative descriptions had to replace the preliminary quantitative accounts. That is the way a science develops; hard-headed analysis follows soft-headed synthesis. *There are limits, though, to the usefulness of this trend.* The requirement to be quantitative can mean that easy measures are chosen at the expense of representing the complexly patterned nature of a phenomenon. All too easily the process of data collection becomes a trivial exercise in describing the obvious or the irrelevant.[15]

And on the anthropocentric framing of the wrong questions from the wrong perspectives, examples have been seen throughout the preceding discussion. From the misinformation of mirrors[16] to the deafening silence of sounds,[17] humans have had a history of not knowing what nonhuman animals are talking about: *a trivial exercise in describing the obvious or the irrelevant*, indeed.

The Plural of Anecdote Is Not Data, the Plural of Data Is Not Lore

Anecdote, like "little stories, fabliaux, riddles, and jokes," is one of "the very short narrative genres ... even shorter than tales or short stories."[18] In these shorter than short expressions, although all different, running through them all are the currents of musement and play. Further, and perhaps even more pointedly (in every sense),[19] as well as these characteristics of brevity, amusement, and interest, anecdote usually conveys a "telling incident or experience."[20] That is, it is of the real world, or the experience of the real world, or so it would seem.[21] It is in this sense in particular that the defence of anecdotes may be found, precisely in their inexistence or invisibility as statistics, as data: "The theoretical problem inherent in statistics is that every individual makes his or her own history, irrespective of averages."[22]

Both in its popular meaning, and in its use in a research context, anecdote might be described as a kind of singular example, an exemplary provocation, a conversation piece or curiosity, a surprising or amusing incident or phenomenon, grabbing the attention and raising questions for further questions. An anecdote is a kind of historical instance in fragment. Understood in this way, the anecdote is thus part of a movement of story as distinct, not a static representation of history. It is in itself an exemplary moment or starting point, like Naruto's photography that posed the fundamental question at the start of this journey: *What does Naruto want?* And in that use, of course, anecdotes themselves become part of the very process of exploration and curiosity they are also engaged to inform – they are the questions in the very raising of questions.

In this way attention to anecdote dismantles the presumed objectivity and omniscience of the conventional technical perspective, the worldview of common sense. Indeed, it turns out that the Library of Babel is full of anecdotes, just not the anecdote of noticing that fact.[23] Its completeness is possible only by ignoring the omissions; or perhaps the *hallucinations*, as it were. In other words, attention to anecdote questions the trust in universalisms, in the equivalence of data. As Weil cautions, "Divorced from necessity, probability is no more than a résumé of statistics, and the only justification of statistics is practical utility."[24]

Indeed, it is the anecdotal detail that is missing from the conceptual perspective on artificial intelligence models. And it is also this anecdotal detail that is invisible or irrelevant to the patterns of probability. There is a real social and cultural risk that the kind of summation currently offered by these models is taken as socially equivalent, as total and true, and in part this is facilitated by the proffering of scale as the assurance of progress: "Statistics strive for neutrality. As a discipline, it is by definition neither optimistic nor pessimistic ... In reality, however, it is strongly inclined to optimism."[25] The reality is that *there are limits*. These models are always already incomplete. And the perspective outside the model is just the very beginning. *Look more closely.*

Small Wonders

Anecdotes are, like parody, also a kind of personal correction. An anecdote is a matter of exploration and curiosity; incentive salience in a storied form.

Thus, the very definition of anecdote points to this incentive salience, as it were, with the earliest regular use indicating a relationship between history and the private;[26] that is, between a public narrative and a private, unpublished, writing.[27] In this sense, anecdotes are also engaged with newness, in that through the disclosure of that private story, through anecdote, a new story is shared: "The word literally designates what is new: a fact or detail that was unknown to the public and had not been disclosed by official history."[28] These little stories are the otherwise undisclosed monuments and wonders of history. Or as the President of the New York State Historical Association declared in his 1928 address,[29] "People like the spice of anecdote and legend with their salt pork of the truthful facts of history."[30]

In this relationship between the official story and personal anecdote there is a tension between the historic, as it were, and the private. This oppositional thinking influences not only the practices of anecdote in historical writing but also its use in animal cognition and its pejorative characterisation throughout a wider research context. This tension is something to which the discussion will return in more detail in a moment, but fundamentally it engineers the opposition between anecdote, as the new, and the institution of history, as the useful, restoring the newness while emphasising the scaffolding of functionality in the context of history.[31] In this way, while anecdote may be part of the "matrix of any (hi)story telling," it is also "often seen as the threatening substratum from which historiography had to extract itself."[32] As Malina Stefanovska explains, "After all, anecdotes are associated with rumor, legend, lack of rigor or evidence, a fascination with singularity and with aesthetic form, lawlessness, contamination with fiction, and subjectivity."[33]

The anecdote is an exemplary *truth* "that the events and situations we experience are not just statistically typical or the result of the operation of invisible laws that are more important than what we see, feel, and understand in them. Anecdotes deal with situations."[34] That is, through anecdote there is an approach to the microsociology of the infinitesimal advocated in Tarde's writings. Inattention to anecdote and emphasis on mass data at once recalls the distinction between the autonomous individual in the swarm, and the blind follower in the collectivity.[35] The agency and personal history of that individual is obscured by the summation of the collectivity: "Personal lack of sufficient data, episodic and fragmented information, far less experience than is required for a significant sample, too narrow a horizon, all prevent the great majority of persons from fitting their own reactions into a rational and objective average range of behaviors and occurrences."[36]

The injustice of the summative in the averaging of numerous and anonymous opinion by LLMs appears to be the ultimate neglect of the principles of conversation and discussion, principles at the heart of Tarde's inter-psychology and social justice.[37] Tarde understands the public as "a dispersed crowd," in which influences between minds are a form of action whereby, "opinion, resulting from all these actions at a distance or in contact, is to crowds and audiences what thought is to the body."[38] Tarde's critique of sociological models of the crowd is acutely relevant to the averaging of available information as through the operation of LLMs and generative AI more widely understood as averaging available information. But Tarde's critique is also pertinent to the way in which that information is used to move from the individual and personal to large summative and univocal collectivities of opinion: "[W]e easily perceive that it is this elementary social relation, *conversation*, that is completely neglected by sociologists."[39] And apparently also by engineers of artificial intelligence.

Anecdotes are thus both relevant and salient as well as, in a curious way, and in every sense, historic.[40] It may be useless knowledge,[41] but it is useful useless knowledge.

Fodder for Morgan's Canon

This methodological anxiety in history is one shared with science. The history of cognitive ethology has a particularly personal tale of anecdotes, an introduction of which was provided in the previous chapter. The interest and scepticism expressed about anecdote appears to have lasted as long as there has been interest in looking at nonhuman animals. In introducing, supporting, and explaining his theories of evolution and natural selection, Charles Darwin uses anecdote throughout; both his own observations[42] and those observations or anecdotes of others.[43] In the somewhat divided reception of Darwin's work, anecdotes have become a focal point for that division, animating the interest of some and becoming the object of criticism and scepticism for others.[44] In the context of establishing the disciplinary credentials of comparative psychology in the late nineteenth and early twentieth centuries, anecdote was admonished as unscientific and unreliable. Indeed, in the appeals to dispense with anecdote, there is at times a palpable anxiety and even urgency. One of the most significant appeals came from the British zoologist and psychologist, Conwy Lloyd Morgan.[45]

In 1894, Morgan published the influential text, *An Introduction to Comparative Psychology*,[46] in which he endorses the experimental approach and introduces a principle of analysis which has come to be known as Morgan's canon. Morgan's canon remains extremely influential and continues to frame behavioural analyses today. Indeed, the move away from the perceived anecdotal quality of observations in the field and towards controlled experimentation in the laboratory has been described as "the introduction of experimental rigor," and credited as the reason "animal psychology became a science."[47] However, in a twist in the tale of nonhuman animal cognition research, "it turns out to be Morgan himself who made perhaps the first reference to mindreading in primates," and as it happens, "advocated critical use of anecdotes and used them extensively."[48]

The passage defining Morgan's principle states: "*In no case may we interpret an action as the outcome of the exercise of a higher psychical faculty, if it can be interpreted as the outcome of the exercise of one which stands lower in the psychological scale.*"[49] As to objections to this "basal principle," Morgan refutes them as "sentimental" or naïve, and goes on to be emphatic in rejecting purely observational data: "I would here earnestly request those who are interested in zoological psychology, not to rest content with merely recording an observation of animal intelligence, but, if possible, to make it the basis of such experiments as may help to reveal its true psychological nature."[50] Appealing for "experimental investigation," Morgan declares: "Now what I am particularly anxious to enforce is ... that what we need is careful investigation in place of anecdotal reporting."[51] After describing the temptations of anecdote, and even acknowledging its contribution to date, Morgan pronounces that, by moving research into the laboratory, "we shall acquire a better acquaintance with the psychological processes in animals than we could gain by a thousand anecdotes. In zoological psychology we have got beyond the anecdotal stage, we have reached the stage of experimental investigation."[52]

In this way, Morgan's canon has been described as institutionalising the barrier logic of comparative psychology when the discipline "abandoned Darwin's view of evolutionary continuity in favor of the dominant Western tradition of sharp, qualitative mental boundaries between humans and nonhumans."[53] In this respect, Morgan's basal principle is a fundamental logic underpinning that exceptionalism: "The watershed between human and nonhuman mental processes was presumed to be the capacity for symbolic versus sensorimotor reasoning ... The premise was institutionalized in Morgan's Canon, which required attribution of nonhuman behavior to simple mental processes unless otherwise proven."[54]

But is this presumed linear progress either helpful or representative of the cumulative quality of story and knowledge, even in the controlled environment of the laboratory? Even the discussion around anecdotes and experimentation takes on an unhelpfully oppositional and exclusionary logic. Indeed, the preponderance of economic characterisations of author incentives and consumer behaviour in intellectual property is an example of a similar trend towards quantification in intellectual property policy and law.[55] Recalling the advice of Bateson and Klopfer, data collection is not a proxy for analysis.[56] Morgan himself, later in his career, considers anecdotes extensively and even acknowledges the scientific wonder of the openness to story: "To understand the animal mind is a vain ambition. There is much that passes understanding. Of this the animal has the secret in himself. And while the inquiring spirit within us urges us on to penetrate this secret, we feel that some gain in knowledge is attended by some loss in wonder."[57]

If we are to become alert to the small wonders, then the openness of a creative and poetic mind comes into play.

Open to Knowledge

At this point, recall Whiten and Byrne's work in tactical deception.[58] In their landmark essay, *Tactical Deception in Primates*,[59] the authors undertake a systematic review of the use of anecdote, a project which Gordan Burghardt describes in his response as "courageous," and lauds "their espousal of the careful anecdote as an important, even essential, aspect of research into animal behaviour."[60] Burghardt also notes that "Lloyd Morgan, who with his 'canon' supposedly brought down the anecdotal method, actually called for more careful, critical use of anecdotes and his own books abound in them."[61] Rather than doing away with anecdote completely, Burghardt argues that Morgan "called for experimental data to decide critical issues, as does Donald Griffin in his calls for more open-minded consideration of mental awareness in animals from bees to chimps."[62]

But, ostensibly in a campaign to render ethology *useful*, as it were, the resistance to anecdotal and sociable story-telling is more usual than the openness described by Griffin and others. And with that, research in behavioural science reflected "a shift away from narrative accounts toward more quantitative methods."[63] As one primatologist states, "I don't have room in my technical articles for anecdotes."[64] And perhaps, in part, it is for that reason that David Pence argues, "there are several reasons to doubt the narrative."[65] That is, in its quest for completeness, it has overlooked the anecdotal gaps and omissions. Pence notes that "the practice of dismissing anecdotal or purely observational evidence in favor of lab-work risked ignoring key evidence and putting too much confidence in results derived from artificial conditions and interpreted by experimenters palpably hostile to the idea of animal reason."[66] Not only the answer but also the very questions themselves might have been very different.

Bernard Rollin notes the ethical dimensions of observation and anecdote as research tools, as well as being critical of the solipsistic thinking in science in rejecting them: "If science denies our ability to access animal mentation through anecdotal data and anthropomorphic locutions, it removes itself from answering or helping to answer the key ethical questions about animal well-being that have emerged in society."[67] Pence suggests that this approach somewhat bifurcated the thinking historically, to the extent that there emerged parallel but separate lines of enquiry. Pence speculates that "had the discipline been less polarized at the time, 20th century psychology might have developed a far more robust tradition of field work or a more sympathetic vision of its subjects."[68] But such entrenched views are persistent and "those in favor of the standards that emerged during this time may see the efforts as a service to psychology."[69] What is significant about this history, Pence argues, is that no matter which view may be preferred, "it benefits us to do so in light of a fuller understanding of its institutional and social context, cleansed of the aura of inevitability that so often surrounds narratives of revolutionary change."[70]

In this process of *unlearning*,[71] anecdote proves invaluable.

Lessons in Anecdote

From this brief history of anecdotal evidence in scientific research, key themes emerge that are valuable in contextualising the meaning of anecdote in this context, and as part of the tools deployed in creative and imaginative approaches to questions more widely. As noted earlier, in his defence of anecdotal evidence in cognitive ethology,[72] Dennett argues that its value is not as an answer but as part of the important process of making questions.[73] It is the art of paying attention. Griffin similarly endorses the anecdotal approach and calls for a kind of freedom in thinking and asking questions, stating, "Since there is no reason to suppose that we already know everything of interest about deceptive behavior, there is a danger that unduly rigid guidelines might interfere with new discoveries."[74] All this useless knowledge, indeed.

This question of openness is itself a question about the very form of questioning itself, one which relates back to the earlier discussion of creativity and imagination in science.[75] In many areas of cognitive ethology, anecdotal evidence from the field (or household) is re-emerging in such a way that it is contributing to a vital proliferation of questioning, and an innovation and novelty in the questions themselves.[76] Anecdotes are thus exploratory, curious, and playful; indeed, experimental.[77] At the same time, the anecdote is a form of communication, such as through personal examples and "visual anecdotes."[78] And in many ways, the thread of this book is itself held together by anecdotes, Naruto's story being perhaps the most enchanting of all.[79] Perhaps I am an anecdoting apologist.[80]

And so, to return to Morgan, what emerges are the fragmented and situated qualities of knowledge, not as a weakness of limited viewpoint but as a powerful specularity in a perception-based account of the mind. Morgan explains that "the trouble is that we cannot think of them in other terms than those of human experience. The only world of constructs that we know is the world constructed by man."[81] Morgan understands this construction as a kind of reflective thinking, one of which he claims "most animals are completely ignorant."[82] However, what arises from this account is Morgan's notion of the quality and production of perceptive experience: "We should try to realize that what they and we *give* to that which we call the world, and to any given situation, is 'more than' the sum of the parts we or they *get from it*. In that sense we have to deal with the 'emergent more than.'"[83]

The *more than* human, indeed.

Sentience Fragments

This exemplary nature of the anecdote introduces a particularly important methodological and epistemological tool in the making of the sensible. The concept of emergentism, in the simplest sense, is a blanket term in philosophy of mind for theories of the mind or consciousness as having developed or emerged from simple matter, thus sharing some thinking with early evolutionary theory.[84] In this way, emergentism presents a significant disruption to the Cartesian dualistic thinking of mind and body, resonating in intriguing ways with other challenges to dualism in the Romantic period and the general rejection of a mechanistic universe seen throughout Romanticism and Romantic philosophy.

Morgan coined the term, emergent evolution,[85] in relation to the application of emergent thinking to explain not only the mystery of consciousness but also the appearances of other characteristics for which natural selection, while possibly explaining their subsequent repetition in populations, could nevertheless not account for in terms of their appearance in the first place. Morgan explains that "[e]volution, in the broad sense of the word, is the name we give to the comprehensive plan of sequence in all natural events."[86] However, in the otherwise "orderly sequence of events," there is the occasional presentation of "something genuinely new," and it is to this "incoming of the new" that Morgan applies the term emergent evolution.[87] Morgan's theory of emergent evolution[88] describes the emergent step as seemingly "more or less saltatory" but actually "best regarded as a qualitative change of direction, or critical turning-point, in the course of events."[89] In the so-called evolution of mind, the emergent is a kind of flashpoint in development leading to new directions in consciousness and cognitive abilities.

However, this capacity is limited to the exception of the human, being said to be possible only in the higher "reflective stage" of humans and not the "primitive mind" of nonhuman animals.[90] In this way, rather than the rejection of an exceptionalist thinking in the divide of mind and body, Morgan's account appears to appropriate emergent thinking in order to reinforce once again the bifurcation of nature and culture. Thus, rather than disrupting it, the theory of emergent evolution appears to support Morgan's canon in regard to accounting for questions of nonhuman animal consciousness and why it could never *emerge*. And in this way, it appears to resonate with Bachelard's critique of "trying to explain away an anomaly by introducing a perturbation."[91] While it is not proposed to pursue theories of emergentism in detail in the present discussion, whether through Morgan or others, it is worth noting the resurgence of emergent thinking in mid-twentieth cybernetics research and in the current context of debates around artificial minds and authors. And it is useful to note here the way in which commonalities are at times recast in service of exceptionalist thought.

In the context of notions of emergent properties, there is a curiously shared point of interest in the exemplary, original event – that is, in the relationship between the emergence of a property, including the production of knowledge or the expression of consciousness, and movement, including through use or performance. In this context, the anecdote is a similarly self-contained exemplar or show. Anecdote thus exists as a kind of whole fragment, as distinct from a fragmented whole. As such, it tells its own story rather than deferring to the building of a larger narrative and epistemological system. The significance of this shift in discursive institutional world-making may be seen in the use of anecdote in science, and in little histories and oral history in history. Anecdote is also relevant, through citizen science and other contributions, to motivating attention to detail in the otherwise summarising concepts of sentience and consciousness, away from an anthropocentric account and pronouncements of an encompassing and exceptional human consciousness.

Tarde's own fragment of the future in *Underground Man*[92] is a fictionalised and dramatised anecdote of invention, at the same time a sociological parody of the world-building and grand sociologies favoured by Durkheim and others. Rather than the seemingly incontrovertible optimism of sociology's grand narratives, the superorganism as indistinctive collectivity, Tarde offers a sociology of the fragment – that is, a sociology of the monad through which the space of the social is made, not merely filled. This direction away from the general to the infinitesimal confers upon sociology, politics, the law itself a quality of story-making; where meaning is fundamentally generated through relations, through citations. And in intellectual property, this network of citations is vital. In this approach, Tarde is not merely constructing an antagonism between quantitative and qualitative; rather, Tarde's sociology bridges the anecdote and experimental data divide: *metaxu*.

In all these examples, from science to philosophy, the resistance to system-building and the celebration of anecdotal flamboyance, as it were, is fundamental. Law is no different, as will be seen.

Hedgehogs and Hallucinations

This resistance to a systems approach calls back the mercurial thinking of the Jena Romantics. Their use of the literary fragment is of course immediately relevant to this discussion. The fragment is befitting, so to speak, not only for its resonance with other short forms, like the anecdote, but also in its interaction with notions of originality, authorship, and meaning, all of which are of critical interest to Jena Romanticism, as introduced in earlier chapters.[93] As noted in those earlier discussions, Romantic philosophy of the literary fragment, through the thinking of Friedrich Schlegel in particular,[94] has been described as "the first avant-garde of literary modernism,"[95] and Romanticism is credited with the development of the novel as a literary art form.[96]

Schlegel declares that "[a] fragment, like a little work of art, must be quite separated from its surroundings and complete in itself – like a hedgehog,"[97] in something of a vital tension within its unfinished form and the prolongation of play. Michael Bradshaw describes the Hedgehog theory as a brilliant and comic analogy.[98] At the same time, the Hedgehog is an embodied parody of the work of art, recalling immediate the Socratic irony of nonhuman animals. If threatened, the Hedgehog presents a brilliant action of rolling into a seemingly impenetrable sphere while performing the defensive parody by getting, quite literally, to the point. The fragment needs no categorisation or summation, it is unto itself. Like the Aleph in Borges's short story of the same name,[99] the self-contained fragment poem contains within its own indecipherable boundaries, the very critique of boundaries and totalities themselves: "Any guide or overview must by definition be incomplete in its account of a form whose very boundaries are seen to be contested and indeterminate … Fragmentary texts reveal the stubborn heterogeneity of writing, and often seem to express a resistance to incorporation."[100]

In this way the fragment is always in a process and relation of becoming: "In a way, the fragment combines completion and incompletion within itself, or one may say, in an event more complex manner, it both completes and incompletes the dialectic of completion and incompletion."[101] Another fragment from Novalis, yet another key figure of Jena or Athenaeum Romanticism, provides insight through the inseparable contributions in music, describing fragments as "lyrics"[102] which, in the present context, suggests not only the interaction between elements in musical works but also the question of interacting authors as well. Indeed, in the Romantic fragment and surrounding thinking is arguably to be found the genuine progenitor of new materialism.

Thus, for the purposes of understanding and expanding the nonhuman animal stories in the present discussion, exploring concepts of authorship through the fragment[103] grants particular insight into the potential of anecdotal thinking not only in science but also in law. Attention to the fragment reveals the somewhat ethological enculturation of the law through its anecdotal and necessarily iterative nature, always in a process of correction and ironic self-parody. Thus, the links between eighteenth-century German romanticism, nineteenth-century comparative psychology, and twentieth-century ethology and physics may not seem immediately obvious at first, but there is a fruitful, plentiful, and meaningful convergence of these perspectives, both critically and historically, when examining twenty-first century intellectual property and more-than-human authors. Curiously, and with that curiosity inevitably, authorship emerges as the nexus for an enquiry into sentience, rights, originality, and wellbeing. And this especially literary insight is particularly important and personal to the process of ethological justice as well as to the creaturely challenges of copyright. Embrace the contradictions. Keep looking aside.

Play too is composed of fragments that are sufficient and yet multiplied through relations of taking turns, and guiding each other's actions, all through a playful intersubjectivity.[104] Each play fragment is both self-contained and yet never-ending, made and unmade. The anecdotal nature of law – where play and the law might be understood as living reference works – subsists always through fragments. There are ways in which this may seem similar to the kind of iterative and evolutionary pattern of learning and output in generative artificial intelligence. However, this is too simple and certainly no showing of authorship; a mere hallucination at best. Rather, without the revealing of itself – through attribution, through fragments, through stewardship – the artificial intelligence is just an indentured mechanism of coerced, stereotypic imitation. And as Schlegel declares, "The artist who doesn't reveal himself completely is a contemptible slave."[105]

In so far as the Schlegel fragment is intact – the Hedgehog – it too is not system building but is always in a dynamic of relations with other fragments towards building a sociality, rather than filling it. This is quite different from the world as presented through the proclaimed achievements and potentialities of artificial intelligence: where knowledge is presented as equivalent to the world as built; where fragments are disregarded and absences rationalised and hallucinated; and, where the autonomy of individual collaborators is denied and sources obscured, all in favour of erecting an anonymous and homologous collectivity. The fragmentary nature of the anecdote is thus both its suspicion and its virtue. It is an entropic, mercurial force among stories and history. And through those readerly fragments, an undoing of the subject-object divide is set in motion.[106]

At the same time, the form itself challenges the idea of the work (and the expression) as finished and singular, emphasising instead process and relation and authorship as a kind of becoming: becoming text; becoming history; becoming science. Intellectual property is in some ways a reconciliation of this same process, creating objects of exchange in order to reconcile these differences and affect a commercial flavour. But in many ways, this has been confounded by the conceptual shifts in the digital realm, upending products in an entropy of uncertain fragments. Instead of what is a work, when is a work?

But in a sense, will this matter, so to speak?

Making Something of an Example

If expressive fragments may be understood as exemplary instances, authorship emerges as a kind of contact point, a social relation, as distinct from the end point. Among the Romanticists there is no definition of the fragment form. The lack of definition and evasion of generic convention are paradoxically intrinsic to the concept.[107] Instead of developing a definition, the possibility for one is rejected explicitly[108] in favour of allowing the form to show itself through use. Schlegel declares, "they will have to do it together."[109] Together indeed, *in personam*, the production of the work through its play. As such, the resistance to definition is its definition. Just like parody, there is no exemplary form, just a familiar process. Rodolph Gasché explains: "Rather than a piece to be understood from the whole of which it would be a remainder, or a broken part, the Romantic fragment is a genre by itself, characterized by a concept of its own."[110] In other words, it is the concept of the fragment, its appearance through use, its movement through play, that animates the genre, rather than any appeal to style or rhetorical devices. Understanding this showing through the fragment is crucially relevant to the appreciating the movement of sentience through play – a conceptual shift rather than a definitional threshold.

Notably, this resistance to definition is an integral part of Schlegel's concern with originality, and the preoccupation with originality more generally in German Romanticism. The radical thinking conveyed through the originary, literary fragment is at odds with the conservatism of convention: "Emulation, not innovation, was the proper task of poets, who should comply with decorums founded in the Classics."[111] But innovation is arguably the objective for Schlegel, whose fragments show that it is through the attentive imitation of reading, rather than the emulation of classical forms, that genuine originality should emerge.

But this is not a straightforwardly linear production of a work, nor a proprietary notion of originality. Rather, it is a "fragmentary geniality,"[112] a familiar production of originality through play. The work is thus a conviviality of fragments, citations, and aphoristic mentions. Novalis describes a dialectic of originality as distinct from the wellspring of the Romantic author: "To seek after originality is literary egoism, gross egoism. Whoever cannot treat an alien thought as his own, and his personal thought as alien, is no real scholar."[113] As such, the communication between fragments as well as the stewardship of ideas acknowledged through fragments is clear. As Fredrich Schlegel declares: "[N]o idea is isolated, but is what it is only in combination with all other ideas."[114] Thus, the world is unmade, the work is unfinished; it continues to emerge and be made, somewhat ironically, through its reading or use.

Arguably, it was the offence of this radical thinking that raised the ire of the literary establishment, and deployment of the arsenal of parody, in response to radical scientific thinking in the eighteenth and nineteenth centuries.[115] But in those radical *corrections*, the integrity of the fragment is preserved: "The novelty of the fragment form ... and the freight of negative connotations traditionally attached to the term 'fragment,' all recommended it to the purposes of caricature and parody."[116] Notably, the perceived infraction is not only the radical offence to generic convention but also the illusion and elusion of the figure of the Romantic author. At this time, the figure of the author was becoming increasingly socially relevant, both with the technological advances of literary production and with the establishment of early copyright protection working in concert, leading to a schism in the relationship between property and privilege through the operational mechanism of the author.[117] Arguably, and somewhat ironically, the parodic engagement of the conservatives with the so-called revolutionaries, or republicans, or Jacobins,[118] actually facilitates and invigorates the very thinking on reading and originality that the Romanticists sought to promote. Indeed, irony goes to the heart of the originality of the Romanticists.

Such is the social significance of an *attentive imitation*.

Object Relations

This particular perspective on originality is thus of immediate interest today. It articulates the kind of original production in the context of memetic productions and aphoristic contributions, and production through play in various environments, including in-game creativity in interactive entertainment. And in the context of the contention here that play is in fact the fundamental way of showing consciousness and authorial ingenuity, it presents a particular approach to nonhuman animal authorship and to intellectual property that is more than human.

The anecdote, the fragment, refracts different stories such that it is the reader doing the work, or at least doing the work with the author, as to the generation of meaning. In many respects, the way in which fragments are combined or the manner by which fragments are related is itself an authorial activity in that very process of curation. The organisation of object relations, as it were, is a process that becomes materially relevant in the context of the selection and curation of the outputs of artificial intelligence. While the outputs may not in themselves be works, perhaps the solution is in the "work" in the selection, curation, and dissemination – operators as authors, artificial intelligence as tool. Indeed, for this solution to work at all, it could only be in the circumstances where artificial intelligence is *not* an author.

Thus, the fragment provides acute insight into current deliberations around the potential intellectual property in the outputs of artificial intelligence. From a copyright perspective, how are we to assemble these fragments other than through the curatorial work of authorship? And does this curation provide the human factor, as it were? Although developing rapidly, in many respects the productions of generative AI (such as ChatGPT) are series of fragments, aphoristic in quality and thus somewhat uncertain (as well as frequently incorrect), because the sense of the narrative, the connections of arguments, the revelation of the *author*, is not perceptible. To make sense of the work is the reader's task. And in these examples, the operator, as *reader*, becomes author, all through an ethological appreciation of that sense-making.

In arranging the fragments, in showing and inviting, the work of authorship is distinctly ethological.

The Proper Path of Analysis

With this perspective in play, it is remarkable that the challenge to biological or functionalist, adaptationist narratives in sociological jurisprudence was earlier than its critical introduction in evolutionary science itself.[119] Tarde's theory of imitation in social, cultural, and legal development is crucial to understanding the affiliative and familial dimension of the law, and the impact of its proliferative story-telling. Writing just a few years later, Roscoe Pound attributes to Tarde an enormous impact on jurisprudence that has become perhaps somewhat obscured in more recent decades. Pound notes that Tarde was one of the key influences "to turn the attention of sociological jurists toward psychology,"[120] and thus emerges as a critical precursor in adopting an ethological approach.

And as Pound also notes, "Tarde was the first sociologist to give us an adequate theory of what is in reality the most significant part of legal systems," identifying the kind of institutional narrative that ensures that, "[t]o the lay eye, legislation commonly occupies the whole stage."[121] But in fact, following Tarde's careful elaboration of the principle of "universal endless repetition, of which the social form is imitation," Pound argues that Tarde's "[e]xplanation of this toughness of jural tradition is much more worth while than theories of formal law making."[122] Thus, the traditions of story-telling and anecdote that fill the law through a social and attentive imitation, are the very nature of law, as it were.

In reality, all cultural products are necessarily fragments, in that they are consumed in relation, stimulating questions from their answers, provoking curiosity and play. Those questions thus become points of contact, whether as corrections or adaptations or something else entirely. Pursuing the concept of the fragment through the phenomenal experience of literary works, Chad Wellman notes that books are always fragmented and thus "they facilitate stimulation. They contain the potential for contact."[123] By the very nature of cultural life, every work is ripe for parodic play; taking turns and building bridges. Attribution and stewardship of sources – in what may be understood as the explainability of the work – are thus part of the crucial cultural value of the work. The value, understanding, and *joy* comes through the *work* of tracing that textual becoming.

This is a joy missing from the objects generated by artificial intelligence. Contrary to the spontaneous emergence supposed for the outputs of generative AI, in the breadth and depth of cultural life, as Roland Barthes explains, every work is made up of the fragments of other works, "a tissue of quotations drawn from the innumerable centres of culture."[124] The limitation of artificial intelligence is not only that it purports to average those centres, erecting blind monuments to mediocrity, and at the same time to scraping the details clean off the palimpsest.

Perhaps Barthes's pronouncement of the death of the author is best understood not for advocating the erasure of the author as such but for appealing for the appreciation and understanding that it is through the author as linguistic, economic, and legal tool that the object is commodified for circulation. Meaning, however, is not through a supposed intentionality of the singular author but through the relations, the entanglements: "In the multiplicity of writing, everything is to be *disentangled*, nothing *deciphered*."[125] As Barthes's famous account declares, "To give a text an Author is to impose a limit on that text, to furnish it with a final signified, to close the writing,"[126] indeed, to finish it. But attribution and the fabulous tapestry of sources is not about finding authors but about facilitating authors as contact points towards prolonging the endless play of the text, the unfinished fragment. The problem is that this project of completion continues to pollute the culture surrounding the objects constructed for the purposes of intellectual property.

How might an ethology of the fragment assist?

Let Me Tell You a Story

The significance of an enactivist approach to an expressive theory of sentience is that it affords not simply an embodied perception of the environment but an actual productive enaction of environment as understood in dynamic relation with the animal, including the human animal. In other words, it upsets the usual subject/object dynamic not only in an approach to cognition through reactions but also in terms of the authority and creativity of the *reader*. As such, "sense-making is an inherently active idea. Organisms do not merely receive information from their environments, which they then translate into internal representations,"[127] but are actively invested in the production of those environments, the building of sociality with that space, the making of those spaces.

This has implications for not only the meaning generated through that experience but also the artefacts that are authored in communion with that environment, and, what is more, the interspecies co-productions.[128] In this way, animals (including humans) are engage actively and "participate in the generation of meaning through their bodies and action often engaging in transformational and not merely information interactions; *they enact a world.*"[129] Thus, individuals are not just passive consumers of the environment, just like readers are not just passive consumers of texts, or users are not just passive consumers of other cultural products. Instead, individuals are in an active relationship with their environment, with important consequences for obligations and compassionate relations with all the elements of that environment, initiating a distinctly ethological ethic to an expressive theory of sentience.

This embodied action underpinning expressive work thus tells a story of that space, through the very experience of that space: "Enactivism is an action theory that understands biological functions to have *a process ontology.*"[130] In this kind of action-based perception, achieved in conjunction with the environment, it is possible to discern intention through the externalities of that perception,[131] rather than defeat such work through the impossibility of representation. As seen through play, this presents the potential to investigate and appreciate cognitive proficiencies through such externalities, externalities which are at the same time personal and subjective in their rendition. In such circumstances the need to speculate as to the content of a nonhuman animal's belief or to pursue the shifting horizons of representational theories of consciousness will be mitigated if not dispensed with completely. Instead of the question, *can cats lie?* The more pertinent enquiry is, *do cats play?*[132]

The action and performance of play may thus be understood as a form of cultural production. And in that sense, it is a kind of testimonial in that it provides information as to external considerations but without the need for any capacity to provide that information. It is testimony, but without judgment; anecdote, but without history. This cultural production through play challenges the species distinction in authorship as merely arbitrary. On this capacity for cultural testimonial, Cary Wolfe is critical of "the humanist schema of the knowing subject" in animal studies and the perpetuation of "the very humanism and anthropocentrism that animal studies sets out to question."[133] Contrary to its compilation as a distinct discipline, something which Wolfe rallies against for its self-defeating emphasis on introspection,[134] nonhuman animals must transform the paradigm within which we operate in order to appreciate art, property law, trade, and of course, authorship. At this same time, this necessarily demands the transformation of the essential anthropocentric paradigm within which rights discourse and the conventions of personhood risk remaining constrained. The testimony of authorship moves beyond the benevolent "critical consciousness" presented through opening out and kinship.

Let Naruto tell you the story.

We Are the Art-Making Animals

We are indeed the art-making animals – that is, we make together. The collaborative production between Naruto, the colony, and Slater arguably demonstrates not only an opportunistic manipulation of the environment but also grants insight into a possible interaction between different wants and accommodating *Umwelten* – that is, a constellation of shared interests in the production of the photographs, and in the embodied action in shaping and bringing about that environment. As considered throughout, the internalism subscribed to by the traditional cognitivist view is a significant obstacle to the sensibility of abilities in nonhuman animals to share intentions and take the perspectives of others.

Alan Jurgens and Michael Kirchhoff note two "key cognitivist assumptions" in relation to the individualistic basis of this internalism: first, "that cognition, and by extension social cognition, is realised by processes in the head of individuals," and methodologically, "that the proper unit of social cognitive analysis should be the individual agent"; and second, "a commitment to the idea that perception even if embedded in and scaffolded by sociocultural practices needs to be informed by conceptual knowledge."[135] As a result, suggestions of nonhuman animal theory of mind are frequently resisted or rejected completely by recourse to an inability to know, pursuant to Morgan's canon and the law of parsimony.

Without the ability for the nonhuman animal to represent the content of beliefs, the canonical scientific approach is to look for an explanation through lower faculties. And it is this tension between the representational accounts of consciousness in traditional approaches and non-representational accounts, as in enactivism, that is closely related to the dynamic and presumed perspectives that characterise the tension between experimental rigour in the laboratory, and anecdotal evidence in the field: "Is social cognition wholly and exhaustively constituted by elements in the brain or is it, rather, constituted in ongoing dynamic and interactive engagement between agents?"[136]

Looking to the production of externalities, as in Naruto's photographs or in interspecies play, may provide a basis to understand those interactions as an embodied convergence of shared interests. In other words, in looking at what is created and how, it is possible to examine the interactions underpinning that action and demonstrate socially cognitive processing through an enactive sharing of intentionalities or collective intentionality. This collective intentionality is what is sometimes referred to as we-mode cognition, which opens out theory of mind to an embodied approach to shared and interactive intentionalities. In this way, whereas "[o]rthodox theories of social cognition claim that we come to understand others by *theoretically* or *simulatively* attributing mental states to them,"[137] we-mode cognition moves away from this "orthodox psychological individualism – the view that psychological states are ontologically confined to individual agents in isolation from their social and physical surroundings."[138]

Shared intentionality is indeed a debated concept and this research orthodoxy is complicit with the prevailing anthropocentric view that it is a capacity unique to humans, in that "the theory-of-mind research tradition has confronted the problem of social cognition in an individualistic fashion, being concerned only with the question of what the individual brings to the interaction."[139] This emphasis on the individual "implies that the relationship between mind and society can be explained simply by generalising claims about cognition within the individual to social cognition," when instead "agents engaged in a social activity achieve a result that is not reducible, at the appropriate level of description, to the sum of their single contributions."[140]

In contrast, an interactive approach to social cognition understands that "when [agents] act together in groups, individuals have access to information about the intentions, reasons, and emotions of their interacting partners that opens up novel possibilities for action unavailable to isolated observers."[141] Thus, enactive theories of perception and cognition are notably conducive to interactive theories of sociality and creativity. In their interactive approach to understanding the we-mode, philosopher, Mattia Gallotti and psychologist, Chris Frith explain: "The thrust of the interaction-based approach to social cognition is that, when they are in the position to interact, individuals have their interpersonal understanding enhanced through a 'meeting' of minds rather than an endless ascription of high-order mental states."[142] In other words, in looking at aesthetic production, the work is evidence of its own production and the social-cognitive capacity for that production. Thus, through the socialities of reading,[143] or the thinking through drawing,[144] or the choreography of dance,[145] or the gesture of theatre,[146] or the interaction in performance art,[147] or embodied thinking in music,[148] or the production of film worlds,[149] an interactive approach to the capabilities for authorship alerts us to the social dimensions of authorship in its many forms.

The exemplary anecdote, as it were, the performance pursued throughout in the present discussion, is that of play. Why is a supposed waste of time of such special value? An enactive approach to human intelligence, at least, "should perhaps not concentrate so much on issues such as, say, how we manage to do math. It should bring to the center the question of *why* we do those things at all – when did they become valuable for us?"[150] In fact, when it comes to nonhuman animal social cognition, "[m]uch is missed if we cannot understand why animals are interested in play."[151] And what of those shared interests of not only the interacting agents but also the environment, in a fully ethological and embodied account of familiar production? *What does Naruto want?*

The aesthetic, and indeed authorship, thus provides a particular insight into shared intentionalities, a radical revision of collaboration in cultural and creative work, and to the calculation of joint authorship, so to speak, in copyright. The aesthetic is thus an obstacle and an irritant to the anthropocentric scaffolding around nonhuman animal theory of mind. And it is also confronting to the strategic and fantastical anthropomorphism presumed for artificial intelligence, that goes without challenge all too often. Thus, does an enactive theory of authorship reveal social cognition in the we-mode? And in particular, is Naruto's photography evidence of social cognition in the *interspecies* we-mode.[152] Do nonhuman animal aesthetics make persons? Instead of asking what is it like to be a macaque, the question to ask is, *What is it like to be an author?* An otherwise emphasis on internal, private worlds in theory of mind thus gives way not only to the interactions with others but also the interactions with the environment – an ethological person.

What is the significance for a potential ethological personhood?

The Plural of Anecdote Is Law

The anecdotal character of law is shown through the concept of the fragment itself. Law is necessarily iterative, unfinished, and constantly in the process of story-telling: "*Work in progress* henceforth becomes the infinite truth of the work."[153] Tarde approaches history through a similar theory of fragments and infinite collision. He explains: "[W]riters have frequently made the mistake of speaking of great men when they should have spoken of great ideas, which often appear in very unimportant men, or of the trivial ideas and infinitesimal innovations contributed by each of us to the common work."[154] This returns attention back to the swarm, and the indefatigable action and agency of each and every member:

> For, it is by minute accretions of image-laden expressions, picturesque phrases, and new words, or words new in meaning, that our language enriches itself to-day; and, though each of these innovations is usually unsigned, it is none the less due to some personal initiative, imitated by first one and then another; and these happy expressions which swarm in every language are just what different languages, brought into mutual relation, are continually borrowing from one another.[155]

The ideal sociality is the swarm in the broadest sense – that is, the filiative abundance of familiar production. Whether this is in the circumstances of a swarm of ants deciphering and defending their space, a swarm of bees in search of a new home, or the sweet embodied language of a solitary bee and a sprig of lavender, the swarm is appreciated for its plenitude of relations, its joyous assembly, its bringing about, and its putting together. Such *sympoiesis*, to borrow Haraway's concept with every gesture to the Romantics as well, is perceptible also in the textual swarm, as in the patchwork and mending of proliferative judgments, or the frenetic corrections of parody and pastiche. Walter Benjamin's definition of story is delightful in this context: "Counsel woven into the fabric of real life."[156] The law proceeds *justly* by anecdote.

In the formalism of the legal stage, anecdotes are more regularly understood as at most supporting the endorsed or institutional narrative, such as that of history, or of science, without supplanting the more substantial narrative that is put forth as the legitimate story.[157] Anecdotes are a provocation or a line of questioning, not the answers. But in its very grammar, anecdote is indeed the very nature of law. In the simplest sense, a particular decision is in response to the presentation of two anecdotes, and the enquiries made and perspectives taken, as well as that decision itself, are all closely delimited by those anecdotes. Anecdote is thus in part both the mechanism and the efficiency of the law. The law proceeds incrementally, case by case, continuing to self-parody and self-correct: *the law works itself pure*.[158]

But it is the polyphony of voices, of authors and readers, in that telling and re-telling that fulfils the anecdotal abundance of the law. Access to justice is an issue for the individual before the law, but it is also that individual before the law that ensures the health and innovation of the law. And thus, it is those individual stories that sustain the cumulative culture of the law. In every way, the law follows the "logic of accumulation"[159] that characterises the anecdote. The law is directionless and cumulative, scrupulously acknowledging its fragments and stewarding its principles, and hoarding anecdotes in a proliferating treasure of social history. Law is meticulously unoriginal in the simplest sense but methodically and elaborately original when understood in the dialectic of originality favoured by the Jena Romantics, and the meaning of *attentive imitation* as developed in the present work. The law is repetitive, imitative, and always insufficient. There is no total story to law; rather, it is made and unmade and made again by millions of anecdotes.

Lionel Gossman describes something similar in the historical writing of the late eighteenth and early nineteenth centuries, in which anecdote was used in circumstances "that deliberately eschewed large-scale 'narrativization.'"[160] In this way anecdote is revealed as a sensible and respectable tool: "[T]he most common use of anecdotes by historians appears not to have been especially subversive. Anecdotes usually functioned in historical writing not as puzzling or unusual individual cases throwing doubt on notions of historical order, but as particular instances exemplifying and confirming a general rule or trend or epitomizing a larger general situation."[161] This describes also the way in which anecdotes work in law – aligning with a principle without being the principle; imitating the law and its rules, without being the rules.

Through anecdote, legal pronouncements remain local to those circumstances and do not propose a wider narrative, notwithstanding the proposition of principles. In every new question, the anecdotes must make their moves in relation to those principles. And each anecdote before the law may or may not be distinguished on its facts in relation to that principle, in negotiating the turns within that play. While principles appear to erect rules of the game and the moves that may be allowed within the scope of the facts,[162] it is always and in every case a matter of local importance and situations. In other words, the anecdotal character of law does not lend itself to "large-scale 'narrativization',"[163] even though it may pretend that way.

This recalls the tension between the grand narratives of sociology and the microsociology of Tarde's *correction*. In such summative or general approaches to law, the wider discourse suggests that law works by these overwhelming declarations; but in reality and in principle it is much more playful, anecdotal, and decidedly literary in its character. This resonates with Jean-François Lyotard's approach to justice through the dynamic of the game and his appeal to dissensus in the service of justice: "Consensus has become an outmoded and suspect value. But justice as a value is neither outmoded nor suspect. We must thus arrive at an idea and practice of justice that is not linked to that of consensus."[164] Examining justice through the dialectic of play, Lyotard gestures to the openness of the legal fragment through the contingent proposition, "*If, then.*"[165] Thus, a legal principle, as such, operates not as a presumptive or predicated conclusion, aspirational or otherwise.

In this way, through the administration of justice within the parameters of the game, Lyotard's approach has much in common with the periodicity and spontaneity of a *fragmentary geniality*. That is, each anecdote shapes the judicial space and those performing within it, and each anecdote enlivens the principle without making it: "We are in dialectics, and we are never in the *episteme*."[166] Each anecdote is performed through an imitation of the principles underpinning a just decision,[167] and in this way it is possible to have a theory through fragments, as it were, without suggesting or rendering it complete as a particular form. Law is always in a process of becoming, and in its very anecdotal nature, it is a relational and mobile becoming together.

Thus, despite the institutional force of the legal system, in many respects there is a persistent tension between the anecdotal pleasure of law and the received narrative of its supposed detachment and intentional totality. Proceeding by anecdote, notwithstanding the adversarial structure of judicial proceedings, has the potential to undermine the barrier logic which sustains human exceptionalism, from within the logic of the legal system itself. And this anecdotal play runs throughout intellectual property itself where, despite its protestations of objectivity, in every sense, the system is necessarily and frequently called upon to make judgments as to value, including aesthetic judgments, as well as to sustain those judgments as to value through the very structures of the intellectual property framework itself. How well you play will affect how well you tell the story.

The development of the law is thus decidedly and decisively ethological.

An Ethological Approach to Law

Appreciating the law as fragments thus confers an ethological character to law and motivates an ethological jurisprudence. Anecdote reverberates with nonhuman animal expression, as well as with traditions of oral history. And notwithstanding the law's writerly compulsion, or the literary nature of the anecdote, this affiliation through fragments underscores the embodied and sensational approach to authorship and indeed to law. In the dynamic of engagement with two or more anecdotes there is within law the very nature of play, the room for variation, the space for musement. Law thus describes and reinscribes the dramatic and performative expression of play. And the very many accounts of law as theatre and performance certainly tally with this approach.

Thus, it is in this dialectic of anecdote that there are to be found, at first and at last, the resources for a genuinely ethical speech for *dumb* animals.

Play your part.

Notes

1 *Millar v Taylor* (1769) 4 Burrow 2303, 98 ER 201, at 239.
2 Bates and Byrne (2007). Burghardt (1988), in commentary on Whiten and Byrne (1988), notes, "Whiten & Byrne ... are courageous in their espousal of the careful anecdote as an important, even essential, aspect of research into animal behavior" (248). See further the commentary on the same article in Ristau

(1988), 262–263. See also the empirical analysis of the primatology research community in Rees (2001), who states that "when people were encouraged to talk about the history and development of behavioral primatology, a number of related points consistently emerged despite the disparate ages, nationalities, and experiences of the interviews. These points were strongly focused around the problems of anthropomorphism, anthropocentrism, and anecdote for primatology" (230).

3 For example, the so-called STRANGE framework in animal sciences, which refers to "Social background; Trappability and self-selection; Rearing history; Acclimation and habituation; Natural changes in responsiveness; Genetic make-up; and Experience" is explicitly deployed as an ethical gatekeeper in publishing: Rutz and Webster (2021), 99. For a comment on anecdote in the context of legal history (and specifically patent history), see Wilkof (2015).

4 Webster and Rutz (2020) explain that the framework is devised to "mitigate potential sampling biases" which are not resolved simply by accumulating more data "because researchers should always strive to minimize the number of experimental animals used," thus introducing and ethical an welfare dimension to the value of anecdote (337). See further Michael (2012).

5 Richter et al. (2019); Pelacho et al. (2021). See further the collection of research and perspectives in Vohland et al. (2021). See further Asquith (1997) on anthropomorphism as critical and evaluative tool.

6 Pence (2020); Ramsay and Teichroeb (2019), 681–683; Langlitz (2020), 77–80.

7 Momigliano (1993/[1971]) describes "the obvious delight which Aristotle and his pupils took in anecdotes" as well as the way in which anecdotes "are told for their own sakes' rather than forming part of a larger argument or narrative" (68).

8 Fadiman (2000), xiii.

9 *Oxford English Dictionary*, s.v. "anecdote (n.)," July 2023. Fadiman (2000), xiv. See further: Hénaff (2009), 97; Gossman (2003), 151–152; Conley (2009), 5.

10 Momigliano (1993/[1971]), 76.

11 Fuchs (2023).

12 Mitchell (2017), 259.

13 Bateson and Klopfer (1973a), vi.

14 English biologist and ethologist, Patrick Bateson (1938–2017) is a key figure in this voyage through creativity, particularly in his work on welfare and play (for example, Bateson (2014), Bateson (2015), and not least for the influential series on *Perspectives in Ethology* discussed here.

15 Bateson and Klopfer (1973a), v. Emphasis added.

16 Recall the earlier discussion of mirror tests and the anthropocentric bias, including the olfactory mirror problem identified in Horowitz (2017), in Chapter 3 in particular.

17 For example, recall the discussion in Chapter 4 of Turner (1914) and the significance of sound for moths, or the "listening in the dark" of bats and echolation in Griffin (1958) and Chapter 1.

18 Hénaff (2009), 97.

19 Gossman (2003) notes that a "memorably pointed remark characteristic of the classic eighteenth-century anecdote" (160). Offenhuber (2010) defines "visual anecdotes" to mean "[s]mall narratives [that] are tied to individual data points in the visualization, giving human context to the data and rooting the abstract representation in personal experience" (367).

20 *Oxford English Dictionary*, s.v. "anecdote (n.)," July 2023 (18th century).

21 Fineman (1989), 57. Fineman argues that "the anecdote, in significant ways, determines the practice of historiography" (50). It does this in particular by operating "as the narration of a singular event," and in this way "is the literary form or genre that uniquely refers to the real" (56).
22 Sofri (2004), 765.
23 Borges (1941). In Borges's story, *The Library of Babel*, the Library is described as infinite, although it is not infinite, an assertion that is not dissimilar to the way in which artificial intelligence is presented as having the capacity for the infinite, a mythology possible only by overlooking the gaps and omissions. Indeed, this is the cautionary tale of the mirrors in the entrance to the Library, a false equivalence reminding us of the false equivalence presented in the force imposed upon the nonhuman animal – the *mirror problem*.
24 Weil (1942b), 61.
25 Sofri (2004), 765. Adriano Sofri is a former Italian politician and key figure in the "Years of Lead" in Italy, a period of significant political violence and unrest from the late 1960s to the late 1980s (Lomellini (2022)), during which several intellectuals were arrested and incarcerated, including Antonio Negri and Adriano Sofri (Rossi (2023)). Sofri wrote this particular article from prison.
26 Gossman (2003) notes: "From its earliest usage in the modern European languages … the term 'anecdote' has been closely related to history, and even to a kind of counter-history" (152).
27 *Oxford English Dictionary*, s.v. "anecdote (n.)," details the derivation from the French *anecdote*, to mean "private writings on history, not intended for publication" (dated 1643). In its derivation from the identical word in Greek, the word has the meaning of "'things not given out,' or, as we would say, unpublished': Fadiman (2000), xiii.
28 Hénaff (2009), 97. Hénaff notes further that this meaning of new and newness was the meaning provided in the *Dictionnaire de l'Académie Française*, 1762 (97).
29 Presidential address at the annual meeting of the New York State Historical Association at Watertown, September 26, 1928.
30 Sullivan (1929), 29. Sullivan notes further the attraction of anecdote: "Just as it is impossible to make a profit out of an educational movie unless it has a love story or something salacious interwoven with it, so it is difficult to entice the public to read histories which are not lightened by legend and anecdote" (29–30).
31 This recalls the discussion in Chapter 8 of creativity research and the emphasis on newness and usefulness as framing the concept more generally.
32 Stefanovska (2009), 16.
33 Stefanovska (2009), 16.
34 Cubitt (2020), 13.
35 Chapter 4.
36 Sofri (2004), 765.
37 See further the application of Tardean sociology to LLMs in Gibson (2023b).
38 Tarde (1901), vi. Translation mine.
39 Tarde (1901), vi. Emphasis in original. Translation mine.
40 Hénaff (2009), 97.
41 Hénaff (2009) describes anecdote as even shorter than short stories and so belonging "among the very short narrative genres," as "a truly minor genre," one which conveys "what is circumstantial, trivial, unimportant, and even – if one can say so – what is left to the scrapheap of history" (97).
42 Darwin relies upon anecdotal examples throughout in order to accumulate support for his observations. See in particular the anecdotal evidence assembled

throughout *the Descent of Man*, for example, see the passage concerning personal observations of dogs and monkeys, Darwin (2004/[1879]), 94.
43 For example, see Darwin (1876). Similarly, see the various anecdotes of dogs and cats collected from the observations of others and assembled in Darwin (2004/[1879]), 94.
44 Knoll (1997). Mitchell (2017) states: "Anecdotes became a scientific problem in light of Darwin's attempts to support his theory of evolution by natural selection by presenting stories of intelligent action by animals, suggesting a common psychology with humans" (259–260).
45 (1852–1936)
46 Morgan (1894).
47 Wynne and Udell (2020), 8.
48 Whiten and Perner (1991), 4.
49 Morgan (1894), 53. Emphasis in original.
50 Morgan (1894), 251.
51 Morgan (1894), 291.
52 Morgan (1894), 291.
53 Russon et al. (1998), 104.
54 Russon et al. (1998), 104.
55 And in the context of artificial intelligence, Gary Marcus argues, "It's a sociological thing, a form of physics envy, where people think that simpler is better" but continue to ignore insight from cognitive sciences and social sciences: in Hutson (2018). See further Hofstadter (2023).
56 Bateson and Klopfer (1973a), v.
57 Morgan (1930), 76. Lloyd's emergent thinking becomes relevant again later in this chapter in the context of experiential and embodied cognition and production.
58 In particular, see the discussion in Chapters 8 and 9.
59 Whiten and Byrne (1988).
60 Burghardt (1988), 248.
61 Burghardt (1988), 248.
62 Burghardt (1988), 248.
63 Ramsay and Teichroeb (2019), 680.
64 Quoted in Rees (2001), 239.
65 Pence (2020), 2.
66 Pence (2020), 7.
67 Rollin (2000), 112.
68 Pence (2020), 9.
69 Pence (2020), 9. Indeed, some even consider it a risk to publish research including anecdotes. Rees (2001) notes, "Individual primatologists have had to decide whether they want to take the risk of publishing anecdotal accounts of the behavior of their research subjects, and if so, under what circumstances and at what stage of their career to do so" (245). See further the more nuanced analysis contemporary with the early theory of mind research and the growing interest in both anecdote and anthropomorphism as research tools in Vidal et al. (1996).
70 Pence (2020), 9. In the context of imitation, this is in evidence in Bennett Galef's call for synthesis in approaches in Galef (2015).
71 Bachelard (1989/[1935]), 112.
72 Dennett (1983).
73 In commentary on Whiten and Byrne (1988), Dennett (1988) notes that "provoking 'anecdotes'" is a useful experimental strategy "as a prelude, not a substitute, for systematic observation and controlled experiments" (253).

74 Griffin (1988), 256. Griffin notes the conservatism in approaching the study of animal minds at the time: "For example, quotation marks still serve as a sort of security blanket when the authors make wholly reasonable use of words such as purpose, believe, intend, listen to, or unplanned. And the very denial that they are guilty of 'an anthropomorphic approach,' reinforces by implication the belief that subjective mental experiences are confined to our species" (256). See further Rees (2001), 239.
75 See in particular Chapter 1.
76 For example, engagement with so-called citizen science has revealed otherwise unanticipated questions and lines of enquiry. See further Scharping (2023) and in the social sciences and humanities see Tauginienė et al. (2020).
77 Fineman (1989), 71.
78 Offenhuber (2010), 373. Offenhuber explains the role of "visual anecdotes" in providing the story of visual data: "The notion of the anecdote goes beyond rhetorical principles of visual communication, since it also covers the non-visual and performative aspects of the presentation" (373).
79 In this respect, see Muller (2022) on the litigation as a "strategically sound and rhetorically powerful litigious event" (35).
80 *Oxford English Dictionary*, s.v. "anecdoting (adj.)," July 2023 (1740; *Apol. Life Mr. T—C—, Comedian* v. 48).
81 Morgan (1930), 82.
82 Morgan (1930), 83.
83 Morgan (1930), 83. Emphasis in original.
84 For a useful comparison of emergentism with panpsychism, identifying the latter as a meta-theory, see Skrbina (2020), 104–106.
85 Morgan (1928).
86 Morgan (1928), 1.
87 Morgan (1928), 1.
88 Morgan (1928).
89 Morgan (1928), 110.
90 Morgan (1928), 110–111.
91 Bachelard (1984/[1934]), 38.
92 Tarde (1905/[1896]). See further the "updated" fragments in Tarde (2004/[1896]).
93 See in particular Chapters 8 and 9.
94 Gasché (1991), viii. See further the discussion in Chapter 8.
95 Bruns (2016), 110.
96 Behler (1993), 167–169.
97 Schlegel (1991/[1798-1800]), Athenaeum Fragments, §206.
98 Bradshaw (2008), 79.
99 Borges (1945). See further the discussion of the Aleph in relation to intellectual property in Gibson (2014), 173.
100 Bradshaw (2008), 74.
101 Lacoue-Labarthe and Nancy (1988/[1978]), 50.
102 Novalis (2011/[1791–1801]), 62.
103 As a literary form, and as discussed earlier, the fragment also became characteristic of British Romanticism. See further Janowitz (1998), 443–446. Elsewhere Janowitz (1985) examines the fragment in Coleridge, one of the key examples from British Romanticism, noting that "Coleridge ... finds in the notion of the fragment a useful vehicle by means of which to defend his poems from censure and give then the status of an identifiable, not universal, poetic genre" (22).
104 Froese (2018) notes in relation to turn-taking that "its normativity is structured like a handshake: you cannot successfully turn-take by yourself" (182).

See further the discussion of this sociality through fetch and similar turn-taking games between dogs and autistic children in Solomon (2012). See further the discussion in Chapter 7.
105 Schlegel (1991/[1798–1800]), Ideas, §113.
106 See further Gutorow (2008). In reading Wallace Stevens through the philosophy of Simone Weil, Gutorow describes the work of the reader in the aphoristic mode of writing whereby "the author does not intervene into how we associate particular fragments and what we read into them" (174). Gutorow argues that "the aphoristic mode unsettles our customary approaches to language and reality and helps refresh, or even reconstruct, our attitude toward them" (174).
107 Janowitz (1998), 446–447.
108 Kubiak (1994), 419.
109 Cited in Kubiak (1994), 419. See further the discussion in Janowitz (1998) who notes that Friedrich and August Wilhelm Schlegel "argued that what characterized what they called 'modern' poetry ... was the result of the self-activity, or coming into being, of thinking and feeling individuals, whose texts were marked by their individuality, not by conforming to their external laws of genre" (446–447).
110 Gasché (1991), viii.
111 Stones (1998), 355.
112 Lacoue-Labarthe and Nancy (1988/[1978]), 54 (following Bernhardi's *Theory of Language* (1805)).
113 Novalis (1903), 81.
114 Schlegel (1991/[1798–1800]), Ideas, §95.
115 See further Stones (2016/[1999]).
116 Kubiak (1994), 416–417.
117 On the *revolutionary* introduction of intellectual property law in France, see Scott (2018) who notes the establishment of intellectual property in France in 1793 with the passing of the *Décret du 19 juillet 1793 relatif aux droits de propriété des auteurs d'écrits en tout genre, compositeurs de musique, peintres et dessinateurs*, despite what appears to be "[a]n Enlightenment ideal of authorship fulfilled and a bourgeois form of intellectual property enshrined in law" (281). Indeed, intellectual property became aligned not with privilege but as a revolutionary breaking with the establishment: "[F]or these jurists the French Revolution marked not the fulfilment of the artists', inventors', writers' and publishers' aspirations for privilege. On the contrary, it broke decisively with the legal past. Only in civilised societies where liberty reigns can the notion of intellectual property emerge" (281–282).
118 Lacoue-Labarthe and Nancy (1988/[1978]) describe the brothers August and Friedrich Schlegel as "politically 'advanced' (which during the period means 'revolutionary,' 'republican,' or 'Jacobin')" (7). Indeed, note the reactionary publications again German Romanticism among others in the conservative press, as in the *Anti-Jacobin* and the *Anti-Jacobin Review*, which include forms of parody and other tools of literary ridicule. See Angerson (2023). See further the reactionary publications against scientific work, such as in the parody of Erasmus Darwin in the *Anti-Jacobin Review*, in Canning and Frere (1878a) and (1878b). See also the discussion in Stones (2016/[1999]), 161–162.
119 See further the discussion in Chapter 3.
120 Pound (1912), 503.
121 Pound (1912), 508.
122 Pound (1912), 508. Pound notes: "[Lester Frank] Ward gave the deathblow to the static theory of the positivists and Tarde gave us the leading principle by

which, subconsciously, the direction of law-making and law-finding is chiefly determined. Not only does social psychology occupy a chief place in recent sociological jurisprudence but modes of juristic thought, the world-view of judges and doctrinal writers and the psychology of juridical methods are coming to be the subjects of special study" (508–509). Citing Edward Alsworth Ross as an example, Pound notes that such scholarship is "worth many volumes of the conventional analytical and historical jurisprudence" (509).
123 Wellman (2011), 93. Wellman notes that "imprinted letters on paper texts may be fixed in one sense but their effects on a reader are not. Letters, in this sense, are the original starting point of contact, the original point of stimulation" (93).
124 Barthes (1977/[1967]), 146.
125 Barthes (1977/[1967]), 147. Emphasis in original.
126 Barthes (1977/[1967]), 147.
127 Di Paolo et al. (2010), 39.
128 See further the more detailed ethological jurisprudence of co-productions and intellectual property objects in Gibson (2025).
129 Di Paolo et al. (2010), 39. Emphasis in original.
130 Colditz (2020), 4. Emphasis in original.
131 Brancazio and Segundo-Ortin (2020) describe enaction or enactivism as meaning "that cognition ought to be thought of as a lifelike process that involves the active relationship between organisms and the world ... rather than as a computational process that happens inside the brain" (7).
132 See further the discussion of lying in Chapter 8.
133 Wolfe (2009), 569.
134 Wolfe (2009) notes that while "animals, on the cultural studies model, are now recognized to be partners (as agents) in that enterprise. Such a picture of critical consciousness – commonsensical and attractive as it may be – actually closes off the human from the animal of animal studies and thus reinstates the human/animal divide in a less visible but more fundamental way, while ostensibly gesturing beyond it. And it is the tacitly assumed schema of subjectivity underwriting such a disciplinary practice (the picture of the human as constituted, for example, by critical introspection and self-reflection that is, after all, a hallmark of humanism) and not just the range of its interests (however putatively progressive, multicultural, or antianthropocentric) that must be fully examined" (569–570).
135 Jurgens and Kirchhoff (2019), 1.
136 Jurgens and Kirchhoff (2019), 1.
137 Higgins (2021), 803. Emphasis in original
138 Higgins (2021), 804. See further Gallotti and Frith (2013): "Such mindreading is viewed as the outcome of cognitive processing that occurs in an individual's mind in abstraction from, and as a precondition for, interaction with others. This is mindreading achieved through observation" (160). On the nature of we-mode, as opposed to I-mode, as group reason see Tuomela (2006), 35–36n1.
139 Gallotti and Frith (2013), 161. See further the critique in Allen and Andrews (2024).
140 Gallotti and Frith (2013), 162.
141 Gallotti and Frith (2013), 162.
142 Gallotti and Frith (2013), 164.
143 Popova (2014).
144 Cain (2010).
145 Stevens (2003).
146 Murphy (2019).
147 Ianniello (2021).

148 Solli and Netland (2021); Schiavio and Høffding (2015); Schyff (2015); Matyja and Schiavio (2013).
149 Hven (2022).
150 Di Paolo et al. (2010), 73. Emphasis in original.
151 Di Paolo et al. (2010), 75.
152 Gallotti and Frith (2013).
153 Lacoue-Labarthe and Nancy (1988/[1978]), 48. Emphasis in original.
154 Tarde (1899), 188.
155 Tarde (1899), 186–187.
156 Benjamin (1936a), 86.
157 Stefanovska (2009), 16.
158 *Omychund v Barker* (1744) 26 ER 15. See further Bezemek (2022).
159 Stefanovska (2009), 27. Stefanovska declares that anecdotes "follow the logic of accumulation rather than that of narrative progression, and turn into autonomous, sometimes gratuitous items in a collection, governed by the pleasure principle which allows for repetition, accumulation, and exhibition" (27).
160 Gossman (2003), 150. Gossman takes the term *narrativization* from the work of Hayden White, see further White (1984). Deutsch (2009) describes anecdotal logic as "the complete merging of subjective and objective perspectives without recourse to larger narrative frameworks" and in this way likens anecdote to lyric, noting the way in which anecdote refuses the sort of explanatory or narrative solution suggested by novel structure (43–44). This resonates with the gesture to the lyrical made by Novalis (2011/[1791–1801]), 62 and discussed earlier in this chapter.
161 Gossman (2003), 155.
162 This reinforces and is reinforced by the definition of anecdotes in Jullien (2009) as "narratives that concern a singular event" that are also "memorable or at least interesting" (66).
163 Gossman (2003), 150.
164 Lyotard (1984/[1979]), 66.
165 Lyotard (1985/[1979]), 21, 23.
166 Lyotard (1985/[1979]), 27.
167 Lyotard (1985/[1979]), 19.

Epilogue

That Ape and *That* Dog, *or* What Naruto Wants

The story ends where it began, with something of a fable. In 1922, the philosopher and psychologist Charles Augustus Strong wrote a book of fables in response to what he said were accusations "of an over-use of technical terms in my serious books."[1] That collection of fables includes one entitled, *The Ape and the Dog*,[2] which tells the story of an ape's curiosity and the discovery that "appearances are deceptive."

The ape is feeling a little low and is distracted by the sparkle of a mirror. Curious, the ape looks into the mirror and, reassured by the reflection, the ape thinks, "I have only to keep up appearances ... or proceed along the same line, and I shall become a man."[3] He then directs his attention to the second shiny object, some spectacles, which sharpened but then doubled his vision, causing him to see "two monkeys instead of one."[4] But, he is not deceived: "[B]eing no ordinary ape, and on the highroad to become a man, he only observed: It appears that appearances are deceptive."[5]

The dog, who is tied up in the same laboratory, is curious about this claim. The dog recounts a rather harrowing experience with a reflection in a stream. But the ape explains, "Why ... you took the shadow for the substance, the appearance for the thing itself. And in this you were only following, with your dog-like docility, in the footsteps of man, who has also not learned on all occasions to distinguish them."[6] The ape then declares to the dog, "Your eyes are good enough ... but you have a better sense still, if I am not misinformed – I refer to your *flair*."[7]

Flair indeed, because flair is of course the power of scent,[8] the dog's particular skill for social and cultural tact and distinction, a bodily aesthetic. There are thousands of stories in those olfactory fragments. So *don't believe in the water*, for this is not the information or skill that is relevant to the dog. Indeed, this is to misframe and ultimately misrepresent the questions for those answers and to erase that smelly diversity.

Flair indeed, because the dog has a particular taste[9] and intellectual perspicacity that cannot make sense through the nonsense of the water's reflection. If the dog is expected to obtain any answers just through the mirror

DOI: 10.4324/9780429342103-16

of anthropocentrism and the "intellectually perspicuous ... fixed for all time,"[10] then all those canid details will be overlooked, in every sense. And the response will simply restate the obvious. By decree.

But the dog has *flair*, has a way of being and performing, of sensing and perceiving. And of course, by now there should be no doubt that there is considerable evidence that the kinds of creative work by many species of nonhuman animals constitute a form of intellectual creation, a distinct and distinctive *flair*.

If we simply follow, with "perfect docility,"[11] in the anthropocentric footsteps set out for artificial intelligence, a complete nonsense will be made in the water's reflection. The evidence of *flair* in artificial intelligence is not compelling. And yet the ongoing narratives of excitement and anticipation of authorship for artificial intelligence continue – not only in the popular discourse but also in the technical literature, including intellectual property scholarship. This makes the neglect of nonhuman animals in this context even more illogical and indefensible. That exclusion, while machines are being entertained, is nothing more than arbitrary. It is all done with mirrors.

In the self-idolatry propelling the outputs of artificial intelligence, we are taking shadow for substance, mistaking the hyperbole for humanness, the anthropomorphism for authorship. Novel facts and creative distractions escape the machine's attention; it has no truck with the plenitude in the domain of tininess, it makes no connections in the productive swarm. If it is an author, it is a case of narcissism, the *mirror problem* that has been traced throughout this book with a persistent caution: *don't believe in the water*.

What is the solution? As a starting point, but one to be qualified, both the works of nonhuman animals and the outputs of artificial intelligence should be in the public domain. But importantly this conclusion arises for very different reasons. For nonhuman animals, they have every capacity to express as authors, but they are not owners for the purposes of the statutory right. Why then does it matter to recognise their authorship? Because this recognition is part of the stewardship of a multispecies knowledge society. It is also part of the wellbeing of the authors themselves – not through some specious contrivance of economic incentives, but rather, to ensure they are not vulnerable to the co-option of their artistic labour. That their works might be treated as public goods in the public domain goes some way to mitigate the risk of indentured creators – from social media stars to captive nonhuman animal artists in zoos – and the welfare concerns that may arise. Any anxiety over this assertion of authorship arises through an inattention to the distinction between authors and owners, and to the nature of authorship itself.

Indeed, in this way, an ethological perspective reveals some possible disingenuousness to incentives, or at least a kind of social inefficiency, in that they seem more concerned with owners. The strange results from trying to coerce the conventional incentive paradigm into an array of authorship circumstances reveal the crucial distinction between what it is like to be an author, and what is at stake to enrich an owner. And this is precisely the distinction that is being obscured in a large part of the debates over artificial intelligence. For artificial intelligence, at least for now, the machines are not authors at all, nor artists, nor musicians, nor curators, nor archivists. The machines are simply mimics, and blind and unreflective ones at that, offering nothing but a relentless *stereotypic imitation*.

But in recommending that a machine must not be recognised as an author, I do so with full regard for the authorship in selection, curation, and dissemination. Whether operators or owners, in this way, the human factor is to be found in that *flair* – that is, the taste and discernment attaching to the outputs, the "art of the catalogue."[12] The *readers*, as it were, as authors. The relevant incentive here is the incentive to publish, to attribute, to cite, to curate – to attend to a social and productive imitation. Artificial intelligence is but a tool, and what is needed is not a dismantling of copyright, nor a neglect or complete disregard for authorship, but an honesty and an accountability for the human use of those tools, towards a capacity for ownership through an aesthetic in use.

What is it like to be an author? It is the opportunity to prevent the expropriation of not only objects but also, and more importantly, the intellectual creation and expressive action that is indicated by those objects. In an ideal form, intellectual property rights, and copyright in particular, offer a way to prevent the cruel coercion of creativity for questionable and expropriative profit motives. From the welfare catastrophes of social media, through to the industry in nonhuman animal art, it should be clear that the authorship of nonhuman animals might disrupt the incentives for such exploitation. Recognising nonhuman animal authorship is not to make nonsense of incentives; it is to unlearn the narrative and appreciate the dimension of copyright as attention, and the equally relevant disincentive to exploitation.

This is not to say that Naruto *wants* copyright, or to exploit that copyright, and it is certainly not to suggest that asking that question or contriving an answer is even relevant, including to the question of copyright. But it is to acknowledge the actions of coercion and expropriation of that creativity that would be facilitated by denying the authorship of nonhuman animals. Without recognising the intellectual creation of nonhuman animals, the copyright system can be deployed to exploit their outputs, and therefore also the nonhuman animal creators themselves, through contributing to the circumstances of that indentured production. This raises important questions of welfare and important environmental aspects to the aesthetic. And at the same time and in the same way, if that authorship is *not* recognised, then the copyright system remains a bystander while more intrusive and coercive activity from humans is encouraged in the creative and aesthetic space of nonhuman animals through the very incentives in place for that exploitation. In this way, copyright is a potential welfare tool, with an impact for all animal species, including humans.

That certain attention on authors is there in the law but is being obscured by a co-option of the incentives narrative. Repeatedly, the calls for authorship or inventorship for artificial intelligence insist on the incentives for those outputs. But these incentives are, of course, of no relevance to the machines. These are incentives for owners. But the *mirror problem* of (owner) incentives continues to be used to frame nonhuman animal authorship as illogical.

The attention to authors must be restored. Indeed, this is an appeal for that attention, to recognise the ethological and welfare dimension to authorship, to acknowledge the authorship of nonhuman animals, the relevance of that capacity for intellectual creation, and to deliver that creation to the public domain. In this way, copyright preserves the author's autonomy over the work in a very relevant and ethological way, and in a way that is very significant for wellbeing. The question of ownership, in the very limited way it is understood with respect to the commercial life of an object, is not in dispute. Indeed, it is not necessarily even wanted. To continue to ask this question is to continue to ask the wrong question, arguably in order to frame the answer, obscure the issues, and dismiss the *perturbation – out of hand*. This is not a question of copyright exploitation but a question of author wellbeing and a rigorous and attentive stewardship of knowledge. There is no reason or justification, and there should be no incentive, for works by nonhuman animal authors to move out of the public domain. But there is every reason why their delivery to the public domain would address the risk of exploitation of nonhuman animals in the service of copyright commodities.

This issue at stake is the question of authorship. Fascination with the expression neglects the intellectual creation. Too much attention is thrust upon the object, so much so that there is willingness to construct authorship for machines based solely upon the opportunities for the objects. *Where is the author?* This is an appeal to stop talking about objects as though these are the phenomenal reservoirs of cultural value, a message that goes largely unquestioned while the campaign for authorship in artificial intelligence continues seemingly unabated without any attention to the question of intellectual creation at all; indeed, without any attention to authors whatsoever; without any attention to the basic question of authoring in the slightest degree. Let's talk about authors. Let's talk about the *flair*.

So why do we want more than human intellectual property? Because this provides a more complete cultural and intellectual picture of multispecies creativity, of embodied actions and overlapping *Umwelten*. And it acknowledges the very real connectedness between our shared aesthetic and cultural traditions and a compassionate and entangled multispecies future. With this acknowledgement, there comes the opportunity for a very particular path to personhood through the conscious actions of authorship.

This also signals a radical shift in perspective on authorship itself and the nature of expression – from ephemeral works, to traditional cultural expressions, to performance, and more – an expanding field of original creation and an invitation to all authors. It is a shift away from the quantification of authorship through the needs (and value) of the object and towards attention to the welfare and dignity of *all* authors. In doing so, the intellectual property system itself is necessarily retooled as a system of individual welfare. For nonhuman animal authors, this arises precisely because that authorship is a disincentive to indentured creativity; but attention to authorship is a question of wellbeing for *all* authors. In this way, the emphasis is on attention to the intellectual creation and not just the object of expression. This is significant for how authorship is recognised and refunded, so to speak, and has genuine implications for the way in which creativity might be performed. In doing so, the field of creative work expands and opens to the strangers to intellectual property, in whatever form. What does Naruto want? To *make* something of it.

That story and this one leave with the words of that dog: "Steady, steady! … let us hope that whatever is done will be for the good of sentient creatures."[13]

Let us hope. And let us do. Bring on the dancing monkeys. And listen to the ants.

Notes

1 Strong (1922), v.
2 Strong (1922), 49–54.
3 Strong (1922), 50.
4 Strong (1922), 50.
5 Strong (1922), 50–51.
6 Strong (1922), 52.
7 Strong (1922), 52–53.
8 *Oxford English Dictionary*, s.v. "flair (n.1)," March 2024.
9 *Oxford English Dictionary*, s.v. "flair (n.1), sense 2," March 2024.
10 Bachelard (1984/[1934]), 38.
11 Weil (1942a), 84.
12 Barthes (1953), 7.
13 Strong (1922), 54.

Bibliography

Aaltola E (2013) Empathy, Intersubjectivity, and Animal Philosophy, *Environmental Philosophy*, 10(2), 75–96.
Aaltola E and Hadley J (eds) (2015) *Animal Ethics and Philosophy: Questioning the Orthodoxy*, Rowman & Littlefield.
Abbass H (2021) What Is Artificial Intelligence? *IEEE Transactions on Artificial Intelligence*, 2(2), 94–95.
Abbott R (2016) I Think, Therefore I Invent: Creative Computers and the Future of Patent Law, *Boston College Law Review*, 57(4), 1079–1126.
Abbott R (2022) Intellectual property and artificial intelligence: An introduction, in Abbott R (ed) (2022), *Research Handbook on Intellectual Property and Artificial Intelligence*, Elgar Publishing, 2021.
Abbott R (2023) Allow Patents on AI-Generated Inventions, *Nature*, 620, 699.
Abelson R (1965) Because I Want To, *Mind*, 74(296), 540–553.
Abramson CI (2009) A Study in Inspiration: Charles Henry Turner (1867–1923) and the Investigation of Insect Behavior, *Annual Review of Entomology*, 54, 343–59.
Adam J (1905) *The Republic of Plato (2 Volumes)*, Cambridge University Press.
Adams D (1986) *The Hitch Hiker's Guide to the Galaxy: A Trilogy in Four Parts*, Heinemann.
Adey P (2006) If Mobility Is Everything Then It Is Nothing: Towards a Relational Politics of (Im)mobilities, *Mobilities*, 1(1), 75–94.
Adorno TW (1975) Culture Industry Reconsidered, *New German Critique*, 6, 12–19.
Adriaense JEC et al (2020) Challenges in the Comparative Study of Empathy and Related Phenomena in Animals, *Neuroscience and Biobehavioral Reviews*, 112, 62–82.
Aesop (1909/[1998]) *The Fables of Aesop*, The Folio Society.
Agamben G (2005/[2007]) *Profanations*, Fort J (trans), Zone Books.
Ahloy-Dallaire J et al (2018) Play and Optimal Welfare: Does Play Indicate the Presence of Positive Affective States, *Behavioural Processes*, 156, 3–15.
Ahmed S (2010) *The Promise of Happiness*, Duke University Press.
Aitchison J (2000) *The Seeds of Speech: Language Origin and Evolution*, Cambridge University Press.

Albert G (1993) Understanding Irony: Three Essais on Friedrich Schlegel, *MLN*, 108(5), 825–848.
Ali S et al (2023) Explainable Artificial Intelligence (XAI): What We Know and What Is Left to Attain Trustworth Artificial Intelligence, *Information Fusion*, 99, 101805.
Alland A (1977) *The Artistic Animal: An Inquiry into the Biological Roots of Art*, Anchor Books.
Allen D (1993) The concept of reading and the 'Book of Nature', in Bell R (ed) (1993) *Simone Weil's Philosophy of Culture*, Cambridge University Press, 93–115.
Allen JWP and Andrews K (2024) How Not to Find Over-Imitation in Animals, *Human Development*, 1–13. OnlineFirst.
Amabile TM (1996/[2018]) *Creativity in Context*, Routledge.
Amirjalili F et al (2024) Exploring the Boundaries of Authorship: A Comparative Analysis of AI-Generated Text and Human Academic Writing in English Literature, *Frontiers in Education*, 9, 1347421.
Anderson JR et al (2017) Third-Party Social Evaluations of Humans by Monkeys and Dogs, *Neuroscience & Biobehavioral Reviews*, 82, 95–109.
Andic M (1993) Discernment and the imagination, in Bell RH (ed) (1993) *Simone Weil's Philosophy of Culture*, Cambridge University Press, 116–149.
Ando Y et al (2017) Aphid as a Network Creator for the Plant-Associated Arthropod Community and Its Consequences for Plant Reproductive Success, *Functional Ecology*, 31, 632–641.
Andrews H (2019) Distorted Recognition: The Pleasures and Uses of Televisual Historical Caricature, *Screen*, 60(2), 280–297.
Andrews K and Monsó S (2020) Rats are us, *Aeon*, 2 March.
Angerson C (2023) The *Anti-Jacobin* Reaction against German Drama and Philosophy in Britain, 1798–1804, *Publications of the English Goethe Society*, 92(2), 112–131.
Angley L et al (2024) The Impact of Care on Chimpanzee Welfare: A Comprehensive Review, *Applied Animal Behaviour Science*, 1062672 (in press, journal pre-proof).
Anthony CJ (2024) Beachside Banquet: Ants' Appetite for Shipwrecked Siphonophores, *Food Webs*, 38, e00332.
Aplin T and Bently L (2020) *Global Mandatory Fair Use: The Nature and Scope of the Right to Quote Copyright Works*, Cambridge University Press.
Arbib MA et al (2014) Language Is Handy But Is It Embodied? *Neuropsychologia*, 55, 57–70.
Aristotle (1984) *The Complete Works of Aristotle, Volume Two*, Barnes J (ed), Rev Oxford Translation, Princeton University Press.
Armstrong DM (1973) *Belief, Truth and Knowledge*, Cambridge University Press.
Armstrong E (1949a) Diversionary Display, Part 1: Connotation and Terminology, *Ibis*, 91(1), 88–97.
Armstrong E (1949b) Diversionary Display, Part 2: The Nature and Origin of Distraction Display, *Ibis*, 91(2), 179–188.
Armstrong Oma K (2010) Between Trust and Domination: Social Contracts between Humans and Animals, *World Archaeology*, 42(2), 175–187.
Arrieta AB et al (2020) Explainable Artificial Intelligence (XAI): Concepts, Taxonomies, Opportunities and Challenges toward Responsible AI, *Information Fusion*, 58, 82–115.

Ashton BJ et al (2020) Interactions with Conspecific Outsiders as Drivers of Cognitive Evolution, *Nature Communications*, 11, 4937.

Ashton WA (2019) What would Hermes do? A Jungian perspective on the trickster and business ethics, in Mullins WG and Batra-Wells P (eds) (2019) *The Folklorist in the Marketplace: Conversations at the Crossroads of Vernacular Culture and Economics*, Utah State University Press, 234–251.

Askonas J (2019) How Tech Utopia Fostered Tyranny, *The New Atlantis*, 57, 3–13.

Asquith PJ (1997) Why anthropomorphism is *not* metaphor: Crossing concepts and cultures in animal behavior studies, in Mitchell RW et al (eds) (1997) *Anthropomorphism, Anecdotes, and Animals*, SUNY Press, 22–34.

Audet et al (2007) *Narrativity: How Visual Arts, Cinema and Literature Are Telling the World Today*, Dis Voir.

Audet R (2007) Narrativity: Away from Story, Close to Eventness, Buck P and Petit C (trans), in Audet R et al (2007) *Narrativity: How Visual Arts, Cinema and Literature are Telling the World Today*, Dis Voir, 7–35.

Austin JT and Vancouver JB (1996) Goal Constructs in Psychology: Structure, Process, and Content, *Psychological Bulletin*, 120(3), 338–375.

Austriaco NPG (2016) The Brain Dead Patient Is Still Sentient: A Further Reply to Patrick Lee and Germain Grisez, *Journal of Medicine and Philosophy*, 41(3), 315–328.

Avarguès-Weber A and Giurfa M (2013) Conceptual Learning by Miniature Brains, *Proceedings of the Royal Society B*, 280(1772), 20131907.

Avarguès-Weber A and Giurfa M (2015) Conceptual learning by miniature brains, in Margolis E and Laurence S (eds) (2015) *The Conceptual Mind: New Directions in the Study of Concepts*, MIT Press, 3–27.

Bachelard G (1984/[1934]) *The New Scientific Spirit*, Goldhammer A (trans), Beacon Press.

Bachelard G (1986/[1939]) *Lautréamont*, RS Dupree (trans), The Dallas Institute Publications.

Bachelard G (1987/[1938]) *The Psychoanalysis of Fire*, ACM Ross (trans), Quartet Books.

Bachelard G (1988/[1961]) *The Flame of a Candle*, J Caldwell (trans), The Dallas Institute Publications.

Bachelard G (1989/[1935]) Surrationalism, *Arsenal/Surrealist Subversion*, 4, 112–114.

Bachelard G (1994/[1958]) *Poetics of Space*, Jolas M (trans), Beacon Press.

Bachelard G (2002/[1938]) *The Formation of the Scientific Mind*, McAllester Jones M (trans) Clinamen Press.

Bachelard G (2002/[1943]) *Earth and Reveries of Will: An Essay on the Imagination of Matter*, K Haltman (trans), The Dallas Institute Publications.

Bachelard G (2011/[1948]) *Earth and Reveries of Repose: An Essay on Images of Interiority*, M McAllester Jones (trans), The Dallas Institute Publications.

Bachelard G (2016/[1950]) *The Dialectic of Duration*, M McAllester Jones (trans), Rowman & Littlefield.

Bader MB (2014) When intensity? Deleuze and the revival of a concept, in Beaulieu A et al (eds), *Deleuze and Metaphysics*, Rowman and Littlefield, 225–247.

Bailey JD et al (2021) 'Micropersonality' Traits and Their Implications for Behavioral and Movement Ecology Research, *Ecology and Evolution*, 11(7), 3264–3273.

Bailey WD (2003) Insect Duets: Underlying Mechanisms and Their Evolution, *Physiological Entomology*, 28, 157–174.
Baily M and Trudy (2018) On Misogynoir: Citation, Erasure, and Plagiarism, *Feminist Media Studies*, 18(4), 762–768.
Balkin JM (1990) The Hohfeldian Approach to Law and Semiotics, *University of Miami Law Review*, 44(5), 1119–1142.
Ballardini RM and Genderen R van den Hoven van (2022) Artificial intelligence and intellectual property rights: The quest or plea for artificial intelligence as a legal subject, in Pihlajarinne T and Alén-Savikko A (eds) (2022) *Artificial Intelligence and the Media*, Elgar Publishing, 192–214.
Banerjee AV and Duflo E (2012/[2011]) *Poor Economics*, Penguin.
Barad K (2007) *Meeting the Universe Halfway: Quantum Physics and the Entanglement of Matter and Meaning*, Duke University Press.
Barad K (2009) "Matter feels, converses, suffers, desires, yearns and remembers": Interview with Karen Barad, in Dolphijn R and Tuin I van der (eds) (2009) *New Materialism: Interviews and Cartographies*, Open Humanities Press, 48–70.
Barash DP (1976) Male Response to Apparent Female Adultery in the Moutain Bluebird (*Sialia currucoides*): An Evolutionary Interpretation, *The American Naturalist*, 110(976) 1097–1101.
Bareis J and Katzenbach C (2022) Talking AI in Being: The Narratives and Imaginaries of National AI Strategies and Their Performative Politics, *Science, Technology, & Human Values*, 47(5), 855–881.
Barman D et al (2024) The Dark Side of Language Models: Exploring the Potential of LLMs in Multimedia Disinformation Generation and Dissemination, *Machine Learning with Applications*, 16, 100545.
Barron F (1955) The Disposition toward Originality, *Journal of Abnormal and Social Psychology*, 51, 478–485.
Barrow N (2024) Anthropomorphism and AI Hype, *AI and Ethics*, OnlineFirst.
Barth C (2014) Leibniz on Phenomenal Consciousness, *Vivarium*, 52(3/4), 333–357.
Barthes R (1953) The world as object, in Barthes R (1972) *Critical Essays*, Howard R (trans), Northwestern University Press, 3–12.
Barthes R (1972) *Critical Essays*, Howard R (trans), Northwestern University Press.
Barthes R (1974/[1973]) *S/Z*, R Miller (trans), Blackwell.
Barthes R (1977/[1967]) The Death of the author, in Barthes R (1977) *Image Music Text*, Heath S (trans), Fontana Press, 142–148.
Barthes R (1992/[1954]) *Michelet*, Howard R (trans), University of California Press.
Bataille (2022/[1976]) *The Limit of the Useful*, Knudson CA and Elliott T (ed and trans), MIT Press.
Bataille G (1933) The Notion of Expenditure, in Bataille (G) (1985) *Visions of Excess: Selected Writings, 1927–1939*, University of Minnesota Press, 116–129.
Bates HW (1862) Contributions to an Insect Fauna of the Amazon Valley. *Lepidoptera: Heliconidae*, *Transactions of the Linnean Society of London*, 23, 495–566.
Bates LA and Byrne RW (2007) Creative or Created: Using Anecdotes to Investigate Animal Cognition, *Methods*, 42, 12–21.
Bates LA and Proops L (2024) Elephant calves have been found buried – what does that mean? *The Conversation*, 15 March.
Bateson G (2000/[1972]) *Steps to an Ecology of Mind*, University of Chicago Press.
Bateson G (2002/[1979]) *Mind and Nature: A Necessary Unity*, Hampton Press.

Bateson P (2014) Play, Playfulness, Creativity and Innovation, *Animal Behavior and Cognition*, 1(2), 99–112.
Bateson P (2015) Playfulness and Creativity, *Current Biology*, 25(1), R12–R16.
Bateson P and Klopfer P (1973a) Preface, in Bateson P and Klopfer P (eds) (1973) *Perspectives in Ethology*, Springer, v–vi.
Bateson P and Klopfer P (eds) (1973b) *Perspectives in Ethology* [1], Springer.
Bateson P and Klopfer P (eds) (1987) *Perspectives in Ethology, Volume 7: Alternatives*, Plenum Press,
Baudelaire C (1853) A philosophy of toys, in Baudelaire C (1995/[1964]) *The Painter of Modern Life and Other Essays*, 2nd ed, Mayne J (trans), Phaidon, 198–204.
Baudry J-L (1974) Ideological Effects of the Basic Cinematographic Apparatus, Williams A (trans), *Film Quarterly*, 28(2), 39–47.
Beaulieu A et al (eds), *Deleuze and Metaphysics*, Rowman and Littlefield.
Beaussart ML et al (2013) Creative Liars: The Relationship between Creativity and Integrity, *Thinking Skills and Creativity*, 9, 129–134.
Becker JC et al (2021) Neoliberalism Can Reduce Well-Being by Promoting a Sense of Social Disconnection, Competition, and Loneliness, *British Journal of Social Psychology*, 60(3), 947–965.
Beckers R et al (1990) Collective Decision-Making through Food Recruitment, *Insectes Sociaux*, 37, 258–267.
Beckett S (1929) Dante... Bruno. Vico.. Joyce, in Beckett S et al (1972/[1929]) *Our Exagmination Round His Factification for Incamination of Work in Progress*, New Directions, 1–22.
Beebee TO (2021) Ahumanism, Art, Vampyroteuthis infernalis, and You, *Colloquia Germanica*, 52(3/4) 377–394.
Behler E (1993) *German Romantic Literary Theory*, Cambridge University Press, 165–170.
Bekoff M (2001) Social Play Behaviour: Cooperation, Fairness, Trust, and the Evolution of Morality, *Journal of Consciousness Studies*, 8(2), 81–90.
Bekoff M (2002) *Minding Animals: Awareness, Emotions, and Heart*, Oxford University Press.
Bekoff M (2003) Consciousness and Self in Animals: Some Reflections, *Zygon*, 38(2), 229–245.
Bekoff M (2006) *Animal Passions and Beastly Virtues: Reflections on Redecorating Nature*, Temple University Press.
Bekoff M (2009) Animal Emotions, Wild Justice and Why They Matter: Grieving Magpies, a Pissy Baboon, and Empathic Elephants, *Emotion, Space and Society*, 2, 82–85.
Bekoff M (2013) *Why Dogs Hump and Bees Get Depressed*, New World Library.
Bekoff M (2021) Do Dogs understand the consequences of their own actions? *Psychology Today*, 21 February.
Bekoff M and Byers JA (eds) (1998) *Animal Play: Evolutionary, Comparative, and Ecological Perspectives*, Cambridge University Press.
Bekoff M and Pierce J (2009) *Wild Justice: The Moral Lives of Animals*, The University of Chicago Press.
Bekoff M et al (eds) (2002) *The Cognitive Animal: Empirical and Theoretical Perspectives on Animal Cognition*, MIT Press.

Bell J and Nass M (eds) (2015), *Plato's Animals: Gadflies, Horses, Swans, and Other Philosophical Beasts*, Indiana University Press.
Bell RE (1991) *Women of Classical Mythology*, ABC-CLIO.
Bell RH (ed) (1993) *Simone Weil's Philosophy of Culture*, Cambridge University Press.
Belmonte A (2007) The Tangled Web of Self-Tying Knots, *Proceedings of the National Academy of Sciences of the United States of America*, 104(44), 17243-17244.
Benjamin W (1920) The concept of criticism in German romanticism, Lachterman D et al (trans), in Benjamin W (1996) *Walter Benjamin, Selected Writings: Volume 1, 1913-1926*, Bullock M and Jennings MW (eds), Harvard University Press, 116-200.
Benjamin W (1928) Toys and play, in Benjamin W (1999) *Walter Benjamin, Selected Writings: Volume 2, Part 1, 1927-1930*, Jennings MW et al (eds), Livingstone R et al (trans), Harvard University Press, 119-121.
Benjamin W (1930) Garlanded entrance: On the 'sound nerves' exhibition at the gesundheitshaus kreuzberg, A Bourneuf (trans), in Benjamin W (2008) *The Work of Art in the Age of its Technological Reproducibility, and Other Writings on Media*, Jennings MW et al (eds), Jephcott E et al (trans), Harvard University Press, 60-66.
Benjamin W (1935) The work of art in the age of mechanical reproduction, in Benjamin W (1999/[1955]) *Illuminations*, Zorn H (trans), Pimlico, 211-235.
Benjamin W (1936a) The storyteller, in Benjamin W (1999/[1955]) *Illuminations*, H Zorn (trans), Pimlico, 83-107.
Benjamin W (1936b) The work of art in the age of its technological reproducibility (Second Version), in Benjamin W (2002a) *Walter Benjamin, Selected Writings: Volume 3, 1935-1938*, Eiland H and Jennings MW (eds), Jephcott E et al (trans), Harvard University Press, 103-133.
Benjamin W (1939) The work of art in the age of its technological reproducibility (Third Version), in Benjamin W (2002b) *Walter Benjamin, Selected Writings: Volume 4, 1938-1940*, Eiland H and Jennings MW (eds), Jephcott E et al (trans), Harvard University Press, 251-283.
Benjamin W (1977/[1925]) *The Origin of German Tragic Drama*, J Osborne (trans), Verso.
Benjamin W (1996) *Walter Benjamin, Selected Writings: Volume 1, 1913-1926*, Bullock M and Jennings MW (eds), Harvard University Press.
Benjamin W (1999) *Walter Benjamin, Selected Writings: Volume 2, Part 1, 1927-1930*, Jennings MW et al (eds), Livingstone R et al (trans), Harvard University Press.
Benjamin W (2002a) *Walter Benjamin, Selected Writings: Volume 3, 1935-1938*, Eiland H and Jennings MW (eds), Jephcott E et al (trans), Harvard University Press.
Benjamin W (2002b) *Walter Benjamin, Selected Writings: Volume 4, 1938-1940*, Eiland H and Jennings MW (eds), Jephcott E et al (trans), Harvard University Press.
Benjamin W (2008) *The Work of Art in the Age of its Technological Reproducibility, and Other Writings on Media*, Jennings MW et al (eds), Jephcott E et al (trans), Harvard University Press.

Benjamin W (2010/[1935]) The Work of Art in the Age of Its Technological Reproducibility [First Version], Jennings MW (trans), *Grey Room*, 39, 11–38.

Benson EP (1975) The Quipu: "Written" Texts in Ancient Peru, *The Princeton University Library Chronicle*, 37(1), 11–23.

Bentham J (2007/[1789]) *An Introduction to the Principles of Morals and Legislation*, Dover Publications.

Berg S van der (2019) The Motivational Structure of Appreciation, *The Philosophical Quartlery*, 69(276), 445–466.

Berlyne DE (1960) *Conflict, Arousal, and Curiosity*, McGraw-Hill.

Berlyne DE (1966) Curiosity and Exploration, *Science*, 153(3731), 25–33.

Bernstein JM (2003) Introduction, in Bernstein JM (ed) (2003) *Classic and Romantic German Aesthetics*, Cambridge University Press, xxxii–xxxiii.

Bernstein JM (ed) (2003) *Classic and Romantic German Aesthetics*, Cambridge University Press.

Berridge KC and Kringelbach ML (2011) Building a Neuroscience of Pleasure and Well-Being, *Psychology of Well-Being: Theory, Research and Practice*, 1(1), article 3.

Berridge KC and O'Doherty JP (2014) From Experienced Utility to Decision Utility, in Glimcher PW and Fehr E (eds) (2014) *Neuroeconomics: Decision Making and the Brain*, 2nd ed, Academic Press, 335–351.

Berridge KC and Robinson TE (1998) What Is the Role of Dopamine in Reward: Hedonic Impact, Reward Learning, or Incentive Salience? *Brain Research Reviews*, 28, 309–369.

Berridge KC et al (2009) Dissecting Components of Reward: 'Liking', 'Wanting', and Learning, *Current Opinion in Pharmacology*, 9, 65–73.

Berry A (2019) Sympoetics of Place and the Red Dust of India, *Journal of Childhood Studies*, 44(2), 13–27.

Bertamini M (2018) *Programming Visual Illusions for Everyone*, Springer.

Bezemek C (2022) "The law works itself pure": Reflections on a cherished trope, in Bersier N et al (eds) (2022) *Common Law – Civil Law: The Great Divide?* Springer, 17–28.

Bilchitz D (2009) Moving beyond Arbitrariness: The Legal Personhood and Dignity of Non-human Animals, *South African Journal on Human Rights*, 25(1), 38–72.

Binswanger L (1963) *Being-in-the-World: Selected Papers of Ludwig Binswanger*, Needleman J (trans), Harper Torchbooks.

Birch J (2017) Animal Sentience and the Precautionary Principle, *Animal Sentience* 16(1), article 16.

Birch J (2018) Degrees of Sentience? *Animal Sentience*, 21(11), 143.

Birch J et al (2020) Dimensions of Animal Consciousness, *Trends in Cognitive Sciences*, 24(10), 789–801.

Birch J et al (2021) *Review of the Evidence of Sentience in Cephalopod Mollusc and Decapod Crustaceans*, The London School of Economics and Political Science (LSE)-LSE Consulting.

Bird C and Rhoads JW (2020) *Crafting Country: Aboriginal Archaeology in the Eastern Chichester Ranges, Northwest Australia*, Sydney University Press.

Bishop JM (2009) Why Computers Can't Feel Pain, *Minds and Machines*, 19, 507–516.

Bishop JM (2021) Artificial Intelligence Is Stupid and Causal Reasoning Will Not Fix It, *Frontiers in Psychology*, 11, 513474.
Blackstone W (1766) *Commentaries on the Laws of England, Volume II, Of the Rights of Things*, Oxford University Press.
Blattner CE (2019) The Recognition of Animal Sentience by the Law, *Journal of Animal Ethics*, 9(2), 121–136.
Blom I (2017) Video water, video life, videosociality, in Blom I et al (eds) (2017) *Memory in Motion: Archives, Technology and the Social*, Amsterdam University Press, 153–182.
Blom I et al (eds) (2017) *Memory in Motion: Archives, Technology and the Social*, Amsterdam University Press.
Blomley N (2005) The Borrowed View: Privacy, Propriety, and the Entanglements of Property, *Law and Social Inquiry*, 30, 617–661.
Blomley N (2016) The Boundaries of Property: Complexity, Relationality, and Spatiality, *Law & Society Review*, 50(1), 224–255.
Bloom L (2000) Intentionality and Theories of Intentionality in Development, *Human Development*, 43(3), 178–185.
Bloom L and Tinker E (2001) *The Intentionality Model and Language Acquisition: Engagement, Effort, and the Essential Tension in Development*, Blackwell.
Blute M (2022) Gabriel Tarde and the Cultural Evolution: The Consequence of Neglecting our Mendel, *Journal of Classical Sociology* [OnlineFirst].
Boddez Y et al (2019) Like What You See: Generalization of Social Learning Determines Art Appreciation, *Acta Psychologica*, 196, 18–25.
Boden M (ed) (1996) *The Philosophy of Artificial Life*, Oxford University Press.
Boden MA (2006) *Mind as Machine: A History of Cognitive Science, Volume I*, Clarendon Press.
Bolhuis JJ et al (2010) Twitter Evolution: Converging Mechanisms in Birdsong and Human Speech, *Nature Reviews: Neuroscience*, 11, 747–759.
Bolhuis JJ et al (2014) How Could Language Have Evolved? *PLoS Biology*, 12(8), 1–6.
Bonabeau E et al (1999) *Swarm Intelligence: From Natural to Artificial Systems*, Oxford University Press.
Borch C (2005) Urban Imitations: Tarde's Sociology Revisited, *Theory, Culture and Society*, 22(3), 81–100.
Borch C (2017) Tensional Individuality: A Reassessment of Gabriel Tarde's Sociology, *Distinktion: Journal of Social Theory*, 18(2), 153–172.
Borges JL (1941) The Library of Babel, Irby JE (trans), in Borges JL (1964) *Labyrinths: Selected Stories and Other Writings*, Yates DA and Irby JE (eds), New Directions, 51–58.
Borges JL (1945) The Aleph, Hurley A (trans), in Borges JL (2000) *The Aleph*, Hurley A (trans), Penguin, 118–133.
Borges JL (1960) Poem of the Gifts, Reid A (trans), in Borges JL (2010) *On Mysticism*, Kodama M (ed), Penguin.
Borofsky T et al (2020) Hive Minded: Like Neurons, Honey Bees Collectively Integrate Negative Feedback to Regulate Decisions, *Animal Behaviour*, 168, 33–44.
Boronat NSM (2016) Oasis of happiness: The play of the world and human existence, in MacLean M et al (eds) (2016) *Philosophical Perspectives on Play*, Routledge, 94–106.

Bose T et al (2017) Collective Decision-Making, *Current Opinion in Behavioral Sciences*, 16, 30–34.

Bostrom N and Yudkowsky E (2014) The ethics of artificial intelligence, in Frankish K and Ramsey WM (eds) (2014) *The Cambridge Handbook of Artificial Intelligence*, Cambridge University Press, 316–334.

Boulay R et al (2003) Colony Insularity through Queen Control on Worker Social Motivation in Ants, *Proceedings of the Royal Society B*, 270(1518), 971–977.

Bourgault S and Daigle J (eds) (2020) *Simone Weil: Beyond Ideology?* Palgrave Macmillan.

Bousquet AH et al (2011) Moving Calls: A Vocal Mechanism Underlying Quorum Decisions in Cohesive Groups, *Proceedings of the Royal Society B*, 278(1711), 1

Bradbury JW and Balsby TJ (2016) The Functions of Vocal Learning in Parrots, *Behavioral Ecology and Sociobiology*, 70, 293–312.

Bradbury M (1989/[1987]) *No, Not Bloomsbury*, Arena.

Bradley B (2022) Natural Selection According to Darwin: Cause or Effect? *History and Philosophy of the Life Sciences*, 44(2), article 13.

Bradshaw K (2020) *Wildlife as Property Owners: A New Conception of Animal Rights*, Chicago University Press.

Bradshaw M (2008) Hedgehog Theory: How to Read a Romantic Fragment Poem, *Literature Compass*, 5(1), 73–89.

Brancazio N and Segundo-Ortin (2020) Distal Engagement: Intentions in Perception, *Consciousness and Cognition*, 79, 102897.

Brandt R et al (1963) Wants as Explanations of Actions, *The Journal of Philosophy*, 60(15), 425–435.

Bräuer J (2020) Do animals plan for the future? *Psychology Today*, 18 March.

Brecht B (2000/[1932]), *Brecht on Film and Radio*, M Silberman (ed and trans), Bloomsbury.

Breton A (1929) Manifesto of surrealism, in Breton A (1972) *Manifestoes of Surrealism*, Seaver R and Lane HR (trans), Ann Arbor, 3–47.

Breton A (1972) *Manifestoes of Surrealism*, Seaver R and Lane HR (trans), Ann Arbor.

Brewster D (1855) *Memoirs of the Life, Writings, and Discoveries of Sir Isaac Newton, Vol II*, Edinburgh, T Constable & Sons.

Bridges AD and Chittka L (2019) Conformity and the Beginnings of Culture in an Insect, *Current Biology*, 29(5), R167–R169.

Brightman EG (1919) The Lisbon Earthquake: A Study in Religious Valuation, *The American Journal of Theology*, 23(4), 500–518.

Brooks HJB and Burghardt GM (2023) A -Review of Interspecific Play among Nonhuman Animals, *Neuroscience and Biobehavioral Reviews*, 151, 105232.

Brooks J and Yamamoto S (2021) Dog Stick Chewing: An Overlooked Instance of Tool Use? *Frontiers in Psychology*, 11, 577100.

Broom DM (2003) *The Evolution of Morality and Religion*, Cambridge University Press.

Broom DM (2014) *Sentience and Animal Welfare*, CABI.

Broom DM (2019) Sentience, in Choe JC (ed) (2019) *Encyclopedia of Animal Behavior*, 2nd ed, 131–133.

Brosnan SF (2011) An Evolutionary Perspective on Morality, *Journal of Economic Behavior & Organization*, 77, 23–30.

Brosnan SF and Waal F de (2003) Monkeys Reject Unequal Pay, *Nature*, 424, 297–299.

Brosnan SF et al (2015) Personality Influences Responses to Inequity and Contrast in Chimpanzees, *Animal Behaviour*, 101, 75–87.

Brower B (2016) On Animal Societies: Biology, Sociology, and the Class Struggle in France, *South Atlantic Quarterly*, 115(2), 331–349.

Brown C et al (2012) It Pays to Cheat: Tactical Deception in a Cephalopod Social Signalling System, *Biology Letters*, 8, 729–732.

Brown NO (1947) *Hermes the Thief: The Evolution of a Myth*, University of Wisconsin Press.

Brown RH (1992) The "Demonic" Earthquake: Goethe's Myth of the Lisbon Earthquake and Fear of Modern Change, *German Studies Review*, 15(3), 475–491.

Browning H and Birch J (2022) Animal Sentience, *Philosophy Compass*, 17, e12822.

Brucks D and Bayem AMP von (2020) Parrots Voluntarily Help Each Other to Obtain Food Rewards, *Current Biology*, 30, 292–297.

Brueggeman JA (1973) Parental Care in a Group of Free-Ranging Rhesus Monkeys, *Folia Primatology*, 20, 178–210.

Bruns GL (2016) The Invention of Poetry in Early German Romanticism, *The Wordsworth Cirlce*, 47(2–3), 110–114.

Bshary R et al (2014) Social Cognition in Fishes, *Trends in Cognitive Sciences*, 18(9), 265–271.

Buckner C (2013) Morgan's Canon, Meet Hume's Dictum: Avoiding Anthropofabulation in Cross-Species Comparisons, *Biology & Philosophy*, 28, 853–871.

Bugnyar T and Kotrschal K (2002) Observational Learning and the Raiding of Food Caches in Ravens, *Corvus Corax*: Is It 'Tactical' Deception? *Animal Behaviour*, 64, 185–195.

Bullough E (1912) "Psychical Distance" as a Factor in Art and an Aesthetic Principle, *British Journal of Psychology*, 5(2), 87–117.

Burgdorf J and Panksepp J (2006) The Neurobiology of Positive Emotions, *Neuroscience and Biobehavioral Reviews*, 30, 173–187.

Burghardt GM (1984) Ethology and Operant Psychology, *The Behavioral and Brain Sciences*, 7(4), 683–684.

Burghardt GM (1988) Anecdotes and Critical Anthropomorphism, *Behavioral and Brain Sciences*, 11(2), 248–249.

Burghardt GM (1998) The evolutionary origins of play revisited: lessons from turtles, in Bekoff M and Byers JA (eds) (1998) *Animal Play: Evolutionary, Comparative, and Ecological Perspectives*, Cambridge University Press, 1–26.

Burghardt GM (2005) *The Genesis of Animal Play: Testing the Limits*, MIT Press.

Burghardt GM (2007) Critical Anthropomorphism, Uncritical Anthropocentrism and Naïve Nominalism, *Comparative Cognition and Behavior Reviews*, 2, 136–139.

Burghardt GM (2015) Creativity, play, and the pace of evolution, in Kaufman AB and Kaufman JC (eds) (2015) *Animal Creativity and Innovation*, Academic Press, 129–159.

Burghardt GM (2020) Insights Found in Century-Old Writings on Animal Behaviour and Some Cautions for Today, *Animal Behaviour*, 164, 241–249.

Burghardt GM et al (2024) Animal Play and Evolution: Seven Timely Research Issues about Enigmatic Phenomena, *Neuroscience and Biobehavioral Reviews*, 160, 105617.
Burrell J (2016), How the Machine 'Thinks': Understanding Opacity in Machine Learning Algorithms, *Big Data & Society*, 3(1), 205395171562251.
Burrows RZ (1965) Deception as a Comic Device in the *Odyssey*, *The Classical World*, 59(2), 33–36.
Burwick F (2001) *Mimesis and Its Romantic Reflections*, Pennsylvania State University Press.
Butler J (2004) *Precarious Life: The Powers of Mourning and Violence*, Verso.
Butler S (1897) *The Authoress of The Odyssey* Longmans, Green, and Co.
Butler TL (1982) Can a Computer Be an Author – Copyright Aspects of Artificial Intelligence, *Hastings Communications and Entertainment Law Journal*, 4(4), 707–748.
Butlin P et al (2023) Consciousness in Artificial Intelligence: Insights from the Science of Consciousness, arXiv:2308.08708.
Buttel-Reepen H von (1900/[1917]) *Natural History of the Honeybee: Or, Are Bees Reflex Machines?* MH Geisler (trans), 2nd ed, The AI Root Company.
Byrne RW (1995) *The Thinking Ape: Evolutionary Origins of Intelligence*, Oxford University Press.
Byrne RW (2000) Changing views on imitation in primates, in Strum SC and Fedigan LM (eds) (2000) *Primate Encounters: Models of Science, Gender, and Society*, University of Chicago Press, 296–309.
Byrne RW (2007) Ape Society: Trading Favours, *Current Biology*, 17(7), R775–776.
Byrne RW (2015), The *What* as Well as the *Why* of Animal Fun, *Current Biology*, 25(1), R2–R4.
Byrne RW and Rapaport LG (2011) What Are We Learning from Teaching? *Animal Behaviour*, 82, 1207–1211.
Byrne RW and Whiten A (1992) Cognitive Evolution in Primates: Evidence from Tactical Deception, *Man*, 27(3), 609–627.
Byrne RW and Whiten A (eds) (1988) *Machiavellian Intelligence: Social Expertise and the Evolution of Intellect in Monkeys, Apes, and Humans*, Oxford University Press.
Caesar TP (1989) Joycing Parody, *James Joyce Quarterly*, 26(2), 227–237.
Cage J (1961) *Silence: Lectures and Writing*, Wesleyan University Press.
Caicoya AL et al (2023) Giraffes Make Decisions Based on Statistical Information, *Nature*, 13, 5558.
Cain P (2010) *Drawing: The Enactive Evolution of the Practitioner*, Intellect.
Calvino I (1953) The Argentine Ant, in Calvino I (1992/[1957]) *Adam, one Afternoon*, Minerva, 155–190.
Calvo P et al (2017) Are Plants Sentient? *Plant, Cell & Environment*, 40(11), 2858–2869.
Camazine S et al (2001) *Self-Organization in Biological Systems*, Princeton University Press.
Campbell T (2009) Vital Matters: Sovereignty, Milieu, and the Animal in Futurism's Founding Manifesto, *Annali d'Italianistica*, 27(A Century of Futurism: 1909–2009), 157–173.

Candea M (2010) "I Fell in Love with Carlos the Meerkat": Engagement and Detachment in Human-Animal Relations, *American Ethnologist*, 37(2), 241–258.
Candea M (2012) Different Species, One Theory: Reflections on Anthropomorphism and Anthropological Comparison, *The Cambridge Journal of Anthropology*, 30(2), 118–135.
Candea M (ed) (2016) *The Social After Gabriel Tarde*, 2nd ed, Routledge.
Canning G and Frere JG (1878a) The Loves of the Triangles, *The Anti-Jacobin*, 2(23), 16 April, 167–175.
Canning G and Frere JG (1878b) The Loves of the Triangles, *The Anti-Jacobin*, 2(23), 7 May, 274–280.
Cardoso DC et al (2024) Death Feigning in Ants, *Myrmecological News*, 34, 45–56.
Caro TM (1980) Effects of the Mother, Object Play and Adult Experience on Predation in Cats, *Behavioral and Neural Biology*, 29, 29–51.
Casacci LP et al (2013) Ant Pupae Employ Acoustics to Communicate Social Status in Their Colony's Hierarchy, *Current Biology*, 23, 323–327.
Casali S (2019) Crossing the borders: Vergil's intertextual Mercury, in Miller JF and Strauss Clay J (eds) (2019) *Tracking Hermes, Pursuing Mercury*, Oxford University Press, 173–190.
Cascone S (2016) New Rembrandt artwork created via 168,263 'Painting Fragments,' *ArtNet News*, 5 April.
Casey RA et al (2021) Dogs Are More Pessimistic If Their Owners Use Two or More Aversive Training Methods, *Nature*, 11, 19023.
Cassie B (1965) Rapper Knots from High Spen, *Folk Music Journal*, 1(1), 6–24.
Cassill DL et al (2008) Young Fire Ant Workers Feign Death and Survive Aggressive Neighbors, *Naturwissenschaften*, 95, 617–624.
Cavagna A and Giardina I (2010) Large-Scale Behaviour in Animal Groups, *Behavioural Processes*, 84, 653–656.
Ceccarelli FS (2022) Batesian mimicry, in Vonk J and Shackelford TK (eds) (2022) *Encyclopedia of Animal Cognition and Behavior*, Springer.
Ceccarelli FS and Cushing PE (2021) Myrmecomorphy, in Starr CK (ed) (2021) *Encyclopedia of Social Insects*, Springer, 609–612.
Cenni C et al (2020) Inferring Functional Patterns of Tool Use Behavior from the Temporary Structure of Object Play Sequences in a Non-Human Primate Species, *Physiology & Behavior*, 222, 112938.
Cervantes M (1613/[2008]) *The Dialogue of the Dogs*, Kipen D (trans), Melville House.
Cha YS (2017) *Decreation and the Ethical Bind: Simone Weil and the Claim of the Other*, Fordham University Press.
Chalmers D (1995) Facing up to the Problem of Consciousness, *Journal of Consciousness Studies*, 2(3), 200–219.
Chalmers D (2022) Could a Large Language Model Be Conscious? Address to the NeurIPS Conference, New Orleans, 28 November 2022.
Chamorro-Premuzic T (2023) How AI is making us more boring and less creative, *Fast Company*, 28 February.
Chang J et al (2021) Nest Choice in Arboreal Ants Is an Emergent Consequence of Network Creation Under Spatial Constraints, *Swarm Intelligence* 15(1–2) 7–30.
Chapman CB (1974) *The Flexner Report* by Abraham Flexner, *Daedalus*, 103(1), 105–117.

Chappell TDJ (1993) The Virtues of Thrasymachus, *Phronesis*, 38(1), 1–17.
Charlesworth A (2014) So who does own the copyright on a monkey selfie? *The Conversation*, 8 August.
Chemero A (2023) LLMs Differ from Human Cognition Because They Are Not Embodied, *Nature Human Behaviour*, 7, 1828–1829.
Chiesa LE (2017) Animal Rights Unraveled: Why Abolitionism Collapses into Welfarism and What It Means for Animal Ethics, *Georgetown Environmental Law Rview*, 28(4), 557–588.
Chijiiwa H et al (2015) Dogs Avoid People Who Behave Negatively to Their Owner: Third-Party Affective Evaluation, *Animal Behaviour*, 106, 123–127.
Chilton L (2023) Ed Sheeran threatens to quit music if he loses copyright trial, *Independent*, 3 May.
Chittenden J (1947) The Master of Animals, *Hesperia: The Journal of the American School of Classical Studies at Athens*, 16(2), 89–114.
Chittka L (2022) *The Mind of a Bee*, Princeton University Press.
Chittka L and Niven J (2009) Are Bigger Brains Better? *Current Biology*, 19, 995–1008.
Chittka L and Rossi N (2022) Social Cognition in Insects, *Trends in Cognitive Sciences*, 26(7), 578–592.
Choe JC (1999) *Secret Lives of Ants*, Leonard D (trans), The Johns Hopkins University Press.
Christensen A (2002) The Incan Quipus, *Synthese*, 133(1/2), 159–172.
Chrulew M et al (eds) (2018) *The Philosophical Ethology of Dominique Lestel*, Routledge.
Clare J (1835) The Skylark, in Clare J (1835) *The Rural Muse*, Whittaker & Co, 83.
Clark A and Chalmers D (1998) The Extended Mind, *Analysis*, 58(1), 7–19.
Clark CJ et al (2017) Making Punishment Palatable: Belief in Free Will Alleviates Punitive Distress, *Consciousness and Cognition*, 51, 193–211.
Clark PR et al (2020) Morphological Variants of Silent Bared-teeth Displays Have Different Social Interaction Outcomes in Crested Macaques (*Macaca nigra*), *American Journal of Biological Anthropology*, 173(3), 411–422.
Classen C (1992) The Odor of the Other: Olfactory Symbolism and Cultural Categories, *Ethos*, 20(2), 133–166.
Clay JS and Miller JF (2019) Introduction, in Miller JF and Strauss Clay J (eds) (2019) *Tracking Hermes, Pursuing Mercury*, Oxford University Press, 1–10.
Clifton M (2020) Cry Me A Cockroach: Valentine's Day Sadism and the San Antonio Zoo, *Animals 24–7*, 10 February.
Cochrane A (2018) *Sentientist Politics: A Theory of Global Inter-Species Justice*, Oxford University Press.
Cohen IB (1999) Some general aspects of the *Principia*, in Newton I (1687/[1999]) *The Principia: Mathematical Principles of Natural Philosophy*, IB Cohen et al (trans), University of California Press, Berkeley, 43–84.
Colditz IG (2020) A Consideration of Physiological Regulation from the Perspective of Bayesian Enactivism, *Physiology and Behavior*, 214, 112758.
Coleridge ST (1836) *The Literary Remains of Samuel Taylor Coleridge*, Coleridge HN (collected and edited), William Pickering.
Coletta WJ (1997) Writing Larks: John Clare's Semiosis of Nature, *The Wordsworth Circle*, 28(3), 192–200.

Collingwood RG (1958/[1938]) *The Principles of Art*, Oxford University Press.
Conley T (2009) From Antidote to Anecdote: Montaigne on Dissemblance, *SubStance*, 38(1), 5–15.
Conradt L et al (2019) Consensus Decisions, in Choe JC (ed) (2019) *Encyclopedia of Animal Behavior*, 2nd ed, 762–765.
Cooper JJ et al (2003) Clever Hounds: Social Cognition in the Domestic Dog (*Canis familiaris*), *Applied Animal Behaviour Science*, 81, 229–244.
Cornips L (2022) The Animal Turn in Postcolonial Linguistics: The Interspecies Greeting of the Dairy Cow, *Journal of Postcolonial Linguistics*, 6, 209–231.
Cornish WR (1995) Authors in Law, *The Modern Law Review*, 58(1), 1–16.
Cosmo L de (2022) Google engineer claims AI chatbot is sentient: Why that matters, *Scientific American*, 12 July.
Couzin ID (2007) Collective Minds, *Nature*, 445, 715.
Couzin ID (2009) Collective Cognition in Animal Groups, *Trends in Cognitive Sciences*, 13(1), 36–43.
Couzin ID and Krause J (2003) Self-Organization and Collective Behavior in Vertebrates, *Advances in the Study of Behavior*, 32, 1–75.
Couzin ID et al (2019) Group movement, in Choe JC (ed) (2019) *Encyclopedia of Animal Behavior: Volume 4*, 2nd ed, Academic Press, 775–783.
Cox M (2005) *The Pictorial World of the Child*, Cambridge University Press.
Crawford K (2021) *Atlas of AI: Power, Politics, and the Planetary Costs of Artificial Intelligence*, Yale University Press.
Creamer E (2023) Of Mice and Men first-draft fragment torn up by Steinbeck's dog goes to auction, *The Guardian*, 29 September.
Cronin AL (2012) Consensus Decision-Making in the ant *Myrmecina Nipponica*: House-hunters Combine Pheromone Trails with Quorum Responses, *Animal Behaviour*, 84, 1243–1251.
Cronin AL and Stumpe MC (2014) Ants Work Harder during Consensus Decision-making in Small Groups, *Journal of the Royal Society: Interface*, 11(98), 20140641.
Cropley AJ (2011) Definitions of creativity, in Runco MA and Pritzker SR (eds) (2011) *Encyclopedia of Creativity*, 2nd ed, Academic Press, 358–368.
Cropley DH (2011) The dark side of creativity, in Runco MA and Pritzker SR (eds) (2011) *Encyclopedia of Creativity*, 2nd ed, Academic Press, 351–357.
Cropley DH et al (2008) Malevolent Creativity: A Functional Model of Creativity in Terrorism and Crime, *Creativity Research Journal*, 20(2), 105–115.
Csata E et al (2020) Ant Foragers Compensate for the Nutritional Deficiencies in the Colony, *Current Biology*, 30, 135–142.
Cubitt S (2020) *Anecdotal Evidence: Ecocritique from Hollywood to the Mass Image*, Oxford University Press.
Cuéllar M-F (2019) A Common Law for the Age of Artificial Intelligence, *Columbia Law Review*, 119(7), 1773–1792.
Curtin P and Papworth S (2020) Coloring and Size Influence Preferences for Imaginary Animals, and Can Predict Actual Donations to Species-specific Conservation Charities, *Conservation Letters*, 13(4), e12723.
Czaczkes TJ (2022) Advanced Cognition in Ants, *Myrmecological News*, 32, 51–64.
D'Errico F and Poggi I (2016) "The Bitter Laughter": When Parody Is a Moral and Affective Priming in Political Persuasion, *Frontiers in Psychology*, 7, 1144.

Dacke M and Srinivasan MV (2008) Evidence for Counting in Insects, *Animal Cognition*, 11, 683–699.
Dadda M et al (2009) Spontaneous Number Representation in Mosquitofish, *Cognition*, 112(2), 343–348.
Dahl JL (2009a) Early Writing in Iran: A Reappraisal, *Iran*, 47, 23–31.
Dahl JL (2009b) The Marks of Early Writing, *Iran*, 50, 1–11.
Dahrendorf R (2022/[1968]) *Essays in the Theory of Society*, Routledge.
Dai X et al (2010), Wanting, Liking, and Preference Construction, *Emotion*, 10(3), 324–334.
Dalby A (2007) *Rediscovering Homer: Inside the Origins of the Epic*, WW Norton & Company.
Damasio A and Damasio H (2023) Sensing Is a Far Cry from Sentience, *Animal Sentience*, 33(16), 470.
Danto AC (1970) Foreword, in Tormey A (1971) *The Concept of Expression: A Study in Philosophical Psychology and Aesthetics*, Princeton University Press.
Darwin (1876) Sexual Selection in Relation to Monkeys, *Nature*, 15(2 November), 18–19.
Darwin C (1872/[1859]) *The Origin of Species, by Means of Natural Selection*, 6th ed, John Murray.
Darwin C (1873) Habits of Ants, *Nature*, 24 July, 244.
Darwin C (2004/[1879]) *The Descent of Man, and Selection in Relation to Sex*, 2nd ed, Penguin.
Davies A (2021) Advancing Mathematics by Guiding Human Intuition with AI, *Nature*, 600, 70–74.
Davies G et al (eds) (2021) *Copinger and Skone James on Copyright*, 18th ed, Sweet & Maxwell.
Davies S (2015) *The Artful Species*, Oxford University Press.
Davis KL and Panksepp J (2018) *The Emotional Foundations of Personality: A Neurobiological and Evolutionary Approach*, WW Norton & Company.
Dawkins MS (1993) *Through Our Eyes Only? The Search for Animal Consciousness*, WH Freeman.
Dawkins MS (2006) Through Animal Eyes: What Behaviour Tells Us, *Applied Animal Behaviour Science*, 100, 4–10.
Dawkins MS (2007) *Observing Animal Behaviour: Design and Analysis of Quantitative Data*, Oxford University Press.
Day CL (1950) Knots and Knot Lore, *Western Folklore*, 9(3), 229–256.
De la Mare W (1941) Tom's little dog, in De la Mare W (ed) (1941) *Bells and Grass*, Faber & Faber, 24.
Debord G (1957) Report on the construction of situations and on the international situationist tendency's conditions of organization and action, Knabb K (trans), in Knabb K (ed) (1981) *Situationist International Anthology*, Bureau of Public Secrets, 17–25.
Debord G and Wolman GJ (1956) Methods of détournement, Knabb K (trans), in Knabb K (ed) (1981) *Situationist International Anthology*, Bureau of Public Secrets, 8–14.
Decker et al (2019) Lying, deception, and the brain, in Meibauer J (ed) (2019) *The Oxford Handbook of Lying*, Oxford University Press, 83–92.

Deckha M (2021) *Animals as Legal Beings: Contesting Anthropocentric Legal Orders*, University of Toronto Press.
Deeks A (2019) The Judicial Demand for Explainable Artificial Intelligence, *Columbia Law Review*, 119(7), 1829–1850.
Deen M et al (2015) Playful identity in game design and open-ended play, in Frissen V et al (eds) (2015) *Playful Identities: The Ludification of Digital Media Cultures*, Amsterdam University Press.
Delahaye P (2019) *A Semiotic Methodology for Animal Studies*, Springer.
Deleuze G (1994/[1968]) *Difference and Repetition*, Patton P (trans), Columbia University Press.
Deleuze G and Guattari F (1987/[1980]) *A Thousand Plateaus: Capitalism and Schizophrenia*, Massumi B (trans), University of Minnesota Press, 239–240.
Delvendahl N et al (2022) Edible Insects as Food: Insect Welfare and Ethical Aspects from a Consumer Perspective, *Insects*, 13(2), 121.
Dempster MB (1998) *A Self-organizing Systems Perspective on Planning for Sustainability* (MA thesis), Environmental Stuides, University of Waterloo.
Dennett DC (1978) *Brainstorms: Philosophical Essays on Mind and Psychology*, 40th Anniversary ed, MIT Press.
Dennett DC (1983) Intentional Systems in Cognitive Ethology: The "Panglossian Paradigm" Defended, *Behavioral and Brain Sciences*, 6(3), 343–390.
Dennett DC (1988) Why Creative Intelligence Is Hard to Find, *Behavioral and Brain Sciences*, 11(2), 253.
Dennett DC (1996) *Kinds of Minds: Toward an Understanding of Consciousness*, Basic Books.
Dentith S (2005/[2000]) *Parody*, Routledge.
Derégnaucourt S and Bovet D (2016) The Perception of Self in Birds, *Neuroscience and Biobehavioral Reviews*, 69, 1–14.
Derrida J (1987) Before the law, Ronell A and Roulston C (trans), in Derrida J (1992) *Acts of Literature*, Attridge D (ed), Routledge, 181–220.
Derrida J (1991/[1987]) *Of Spirit: Heidegger and the Question*, G Bennington and R Bowlby (trans), The University of Chicago Press.
Derrida J (1992) *Acts of Literature*, Attridge D (ed), Routledge.
Derrida J (2000/[2005]) *On Touching – Jean-Luc Nancy*, C Irizarry (trans), Stanford University Press, Stanford.
Derrida J (2002) *Negotiations: Interventions and Interviews, 1971–2001*, E Rottenberg (trans), Stanford University Press.
Descartes R (1637) *Discours de la Méthode*, Maire; and Descartes R (1647) *Les Principes de la Philosophie*, C Picot (trans), Des-Hayes.
Descartes R (1644) *Principia Philosophiae (Principles of Philosophy)*, apud Ludovicum Elzevirium.
DeScioli P (2023) On the Origin of Laws by Natural Selection, *Evolution and Human Behavior*, 44(3), 195–209.
Desmond W (1995) *Being and the Between*, SUNY Press.
Despret V (2016/[2012]) *What. Would Animals Say If We Asked the Right Questions?* Buchanan B (trans), University of Minnesota Press.
Destrez A et al (2013) Chronic Stress Induces Pessimistic-like Judgment and Learning Deficits in Sheep, *Applied Animal Behaviour Science*, 148, 28–36.

Destrez A et al (2014) Repeated Exposure to Positive Events Induces Optimistic-like Judgment and Enhances Fearfulness in Chronically Stressed Sheep, *Applied Animal Behaviour Science*, 154, 30–38.
Deutchman P et al (2021) Punishment Is Strongly Motivated by Revenge and Weakly Motivated by Inequity Aversion, *Evolution and Human Behavior*, 42, 12–20.
Deutsch H (2009) Oranges, Anecdote and the Nature of Things, *SubStance*, 38(1), 31–55.
Dežman DV (2024) Promising the Future, Encoding the Past: AI Hype and Public Media Imagery, *AI and Ethics*, OnlineFirst.
Di Paolo EA et al (2010) Horizons for the enactive mind: Values, social interaction, and play, in Stewart J et al (eds) (2010) *Enaction: Toward a New Paradigm for Cognitive Science*, MIT Press, 33–87.
Diana LM (1967) The Peruvian Quipu, *The Mathematics Teacher*, 60(6), 623–628.
Dick PK (1968) *Do Androids Dream of Electric Sheep*, Doubleday.
Dickie G (1961) Bullough and the Concept of Psychical Distance, *Philosophy and Phenomenological Research*, 22(2), 233–238.
Dickie G (1964) The Myth of the Aesthetic Attitude, *American Philosophical Quarterly*, 1(1), 56–65.
Dietz C et al (eds) (2020) *A Jurisprudence of the Body*, Springer.
Dinets V et al (2015) Crocodilians Use Tools for Hunting, *Ethology Ecology & Evolution*, 27(1), 74–78.
Dobzhansky T (1962) *Mankind Evolving: The Evolution of the Human Species*, Yale University Press.
Doering EJ (2010) *Simone Weil and the Specter of Self-Perpetuating Force*, University of Notre Dame Press.
Dolphijn R and Tuin I van der (eds) (2009) *New Materialism: Interviews and Cartographies*, Open Humanities Press.
Donath J (2019) The robot dog fetches for whom? in Papcharissi Z (ed) (2019) *A Networked Self and Human Augmentics, Artificial Intelligence, Sentience*, Routledge, 10–24.
Donath J (2020) Ethical issues in our relationship with artificial entities, in Dubber MD et al (eds) (2020) *The Oxford Handbook of Ethics of AI*, Oxford University Press, Oxford, 53–73.
Dongen, J van (2021) String Theory, Einstein, and the Identity of Physics: Theory Assessment in the Absence of the Empirical, *Studies in the History and Philosophy of Science*, 89, 164–176.
Doomen J (2023) The Artificial Intelligence Entity as a Legal Person, *Information & Communications Technology Law*, 32(3), 277–287.
Dorey P (2010) A Poverty of Imagination: Blaming the Poor for Inequality, *The Political Quarterly*, 81(3), 333–343.
Douglas C et al (2012) Environmental Enrichment Induces Optimistic Cognitive Biases in Pigs, *Applied Animal Behaviour Science*, 139, 65–73.
Douglas HM et al (2018) A Possible Social Relative Reward Effect: Influences of Outcome Inequity between Rats during Operant Conditioning, *Behavioural Processes*, 157, 459–469.
Douglas M (1994/[1992] *Risk and Blame: Essays in Cultural Theory*, Routledge.

Doyle RE et al (2011) Measuring Judgement Bias and Emotional Reactivity in Sheep Following Long-term Exposure to Unpredictable and Aversive Events, *Physiology & Behavior*, 102, 503–510.

Drury N and Tudor K (2024) Radical Enactivism: A Guide for the Perplexed, *Journal of Theoretical and Philosophical Psychology*, 44(1), 1–16.

Du Bois WEB (1929) Postscript, *The Crisis*, 36(6), 203–204, 212–213.

Dubber MD et al (eds) (2020) *The Oxford Handbook of Ethics of AI*, Oxford University Press.

DuFour T (2023) Environmentality: A Phenomenology of Generative Space in Husserl, *Research in Phenomenology*, 53, 331–358.

Dugatkin LA (1999) *Cheating Monkeys and Citizen Bees: The Nature of Cooperation in Animals and Humans*, Free Press.

Duhamel G (1930) *Scènes de la vie future*, Mercure de France.

Duhamel G (1931/[1930]) *America, the Menace: Scenes from the Life of the Future*, Thompson CM (trans), Houghton Mifflin Company.

Duncan IJH (2006) The Changing Concept of Animal Sentience, *Applied Animal Behaviour Science*, 100, 11–19.

Dung L (2022) Why the Epistemic Objection against Using Sentience as Criterion of Moral Status Is Flawed, *Science and Engineering Ethics*, 28, article 51.

Eco E (1976) *A Theory of Semiotics*, Indiana University Press.

Editor (2023) Fragment of *Of Mice and Men* original manuscript sold for $13,000, Steinbeck's Sword for $3,500, *Fine Books & Collections*, 30 October.

Editorial (2015) A monkey's right to a selfie, *Deutsche Welle*, 22 September.

Editorial (2021a) Dog show: Pet pooches play more when humans are watching, *PhysOrg*, 10 February.

Editorial (2021b) A Patent Waiver on COVID Vaccines Is Right and Fair, *Nature*, 593, 478.

Edwards B (2024) Anthropic's Claude 3 Causes stir by Seeming to Realize When It Was Being Tested, *ArsTechnica*, 5 March.

Eichberg H (2016) *Questioning Play: What Play Can Tell Us about Social Life*, Routledge.

Eichberg H (2018) Play against Alienation? in Russell W et al (eds) (2018) *The Philosophy of Play as Life*, Routledge, 211–226.

Eliot L (2022) AI ethics lucidly questioning this whole hallucinating AI popularized trend that has got to stop, *Forbes*, 24 August.

Eliot L (2023) Some insist that generative AI ChatGPT is a mirror into the soul of humanity, vexing AI ethics and AI law, *Forbes*, 29 January.

Ellis S and Robinson EJH (2016) Inter-nest Food Sharing within Wood Ant Colonies: Resource Redistribution in a Complex System, *Behavioral Ecology*, 27, 660–668.

Ellis S et al (2017) Ecological Consequences of Colony Structure in Dynamic Ant Nest Networks, *Ecology and Evolution* 7(4) 1170–1180.

Ellul J (1979) Remarks on Technology and Art, D Hofstadter (trans), *Social Research*, 46(4), 805–833.

Ellwood CA (1901) The Theory of Imitation in Social Psychology, *The American Journal of Sociology*, 6(6), 721–41.

Emmert-Streib F et al (2020) Artificial Intelligence: A Clarification of Misconceptions, Myths and Desired Status, *Frontiers in Artificial Intelligence*, 3, 524339.

Enerson B (2004) Protecting Society from Patently Offensive Inventions: The Risks of Reviving the Moral Utility Doctrine, *Cornell Law Review*, 89, 685–720.
Epple A et al (eds) (2020) *Practices of Comparing: Towards a New Understanding of a Fundamental Human Practice*, Verlag-Bielefeld University Press.
Esperidiao-Antonio V et al (2017) Neurobiology of Emotions: An Update, *International Review of Psychiatry*, 29(3), 293–307.
Espinas A (1877) *Des sociétés animales*, Librairie Germer Baillière et Cie.
Esposito R (2007/[2012]) *Third Person*, Z Hanafi (trans), Polity.
Essinger J (2014) *Ada's Algorithm: How Lord Byron's Daughter Ada Lovelace Launched the Digital Age*, Melville House.
Essler JL et al (2017) Domestication Does Not Explain the Presence of Inequity Aversion in Dogs, *Current Biology*, 27, 1861–1865.
Etherington D (2020) MIT creates a soft-fingered robotic gripper that could eventually tie knots and sew stitches, *TechCrunch*, 13 July.
Evans M (1975) Mercury Versus Apollo: A Reading of *Love's Labor's Lost*, *Shakespeare Quarterly*, 26(2), 113–127.
Evrigenis ID (2010) The Power Struggle of *Republic* I, *History of Political Thought*, 31(3), 367–382.
Fadiman C (2000) Introduction, in Fadiman C and André B (eds) (2000) *Bartlett's Book of Anecdotes*, Rev ed, Little, Brown and Company, xiii–xxiv.
Faldalen JI (2013) Still Einstellung: Stillmoving Imagenesis, *Discourse*, 35(2), 228–247.
Fara P (2002) *Newton: The Making of Genius*, Columbia University Press.
Farrar BG et al (2021) Replications, Comparisons, Sampling and the Problem of Representativeness in Animal Cognition Research, *Animal Behavior and Cognition*, 8(2), 273–295.
Farrell BA (1950) Experience, *Mind*, 59(234), 170–198.
Fasel RN (2024) *More Equal Than Others: Humans and the Rights of Other Animals*, Oxford University Press.
Favareau D (2010) An evolutionary history of biosemiotics, in Favareau D (ed) (2010) *Essential Readings in Biosemiotics: Anthology and Commentary*, Springer, 1–77.
Feber RE et al (2017) Some Animals Are More Equal Than Others: Wild Animal Welfare in the Media, *BioScience*, 67(1), 62–72.
Fehr E and Fischbacher U (2004) Social Norms and Human Cooperation, *Trends in Cognitive Science*, 8, 185–190.
Fehr E and Schmidt KM (1999) A Theory of Fairness, Competition, and Cooperation, *The Quarterly Journal of Economics*, 114(3), 817–868.
Feng LC et al (2017) Why Do Animals Differ in Their Susceptibility to Geometrical Illusions? *Psychonomic Bulletin & Review*, 24, 262–276.
Fensch T (ed) (1988) *Conversations with John Steinbeck*, University Press of Mississippi.
Ferdinand M (2022) *Decolonial Ecology: Thinking from the Caribbean World*, AP Smith (trans), Polity.
Fernandez EJ (2022) Training as Enrichment: A Critical Review, *Animal Welfare*, 31, 1–12.
Ferrari GRF (1990) Plato and poetry, in Kennedy G (ed) (1990), *The Cambridge History of Literary Criticism*, Cambridge University Press, 92–148.
Fifield W (1982) *In Search of Genius*, Morrow.

Fineman J (1989) The history of the anecdote: Fiction and fiction, in Veeser HA (ed) (1989) *The New Historicism*, Routledge, 49–76.

Fineman MA (2020) Reasoning from the Body: University vulnerability and social justice, in Dietz C et al (eds) (2020) *A Jurisprudence of the Body*, Springer, 17–34.

Fink E (1957) Oasis of happiness: Thought toward an ontology of play, in Fink E (2016) *Play as Symbol of the World*, Moore IA and Turner C (trans), Indiana University Press, 14–31.

Fink E (2016) *Play as Symbol of the World*, Moore IA and Turner C (trans), Indiana University Press.

Flexner A (1908) *The American College: A Criticism*, The Century Co.

Flexner A (1910) *Medical Education in the United States and Canada*, The Carnegie Foundation for the Advancement of Teaching.

Flexner A (1921) *A Modern School*, General Education Board.

Flexner A (1939) The Usefulness of Useless Knowledge, *Harper's Magazine*, 179, 544–552.

Flexner A and Bachman FP (1918) *Public Education in Delaware*, General Education Board.

Flood A (2020) Isaac Newton notes almost destroyed by dog sell for £380,000, *The Guardian*, 9 December.

Floridi L (2020) AI and Its New Winter: From Myths to Realities, *Philosophy & Technology*, 33, 1–3.

Floridi L (2023a) AI as *Agency Without Intelligence*: on ChatGPT, Large Language Models, and Other Generative Models, *Philosophy & Technology*, 36, article 15.

Floridi L (2023b) *The Ethics of Artificial Intelligence: Principles, Challenges, and Opportunities*, Oxford University Press.

Flusser V (2002) *Writings*, A Ströhl (ed), E Eisel (trans), University of Minnesota Press.

Flusser V and Bec L (2012/[1987]) *Vampyroteuthis Infernalis: A Treatise, with a Report by the Institut Scientifique de Recherche Paranaturaliste*, VA Pakis (trans), University of Minnesota Press.

Flyn C (2021) What it's like to be an ant, *Prospect*, August–September.

Forbes P (2009) *Dazzled and Deceived: Mimicry and Camouflage*, Yale University Press.

Ford C (2020) Captured time: Simone Weil's vital temporality against the state, in Bourgault S and Daigle J (eds) (2020) *Simone Weil: Beyond Ideology?* Palgrave Macmillan, 161–184.

Foshay R (2017) Plato at the Foundation of Disciplines: Method and the *Metaxu* in the *Phaedrus*, *Sophist*, and *Symposium*, IAFOR *Journal of Arts and Humanities*, 4(2),15–23.

Francione GL (2010) Animal Welfare and the Moral Value of Nonhuman Animals, *Law, Culture and the Humanities*, 6(1), 24–36.

Francione GL (2021) *Why Veganism Matters: The Moral Value of Animals*, Columbia University Press.

Francione GL and Garner R (2010) *The Animal Rights Debate: Abolition or Regulation?* Columbia University Press.

Frankish K and Ramsey WM (eds) (2014) *The Cambridge Handbook of Artificial Intelligence*, Cambridge University Press.

Franklin EL and Franks NR (2012) Individual and Social Learning in Tandem-running Recruitment by Ants, *Animal Behaviour*, 84(2), 361–368.

Franks NR and Richardson T (2006) Teaching in Tandem-Running Ants, *Nature*, 439, 153.

Franks NR et al (1991) The Blind Leading the Blind in Army Ant Raid Patterns: Testing a Model of Self-Organization (*Hymenoptera: Formicidae*), *Journal of Insect Behavior*, 4, 583–607.

Franks NR et al (2021) Hide-and-Seek Strategies and Post-Contact Immobility, *Biology Letters*, 17, 20200892.

Fraser D (1995) Science, Values and Animal Welfare: Exploring the 'Inextricable Connection,' *Animal Welfare*, 4(2), 103–117.

Fraser D (2008) *Understanding Animal Welfare: The Science in Its Cultural Context*, Wiley-Blackwell.

Fraser D (2009) Animal Behaviour, Animal Welfare and the Scientific Study of Affect, *Applied Animal Behaviour Science*, 118, 108–117.

Frazer JG (1993/[1922]) *The Golden Bough: A Study in Magic and Religion*, Wordsworth.

Frederickson BL (1998) What Good Are Positive Emotions? *Review of General Psychology*, 2(3), 300–319.

Frey RG (1979) Rights, Interests, Desires and Beliefs, *American Philosophical Quarterly*, 16(3), 233–239.

Frey RG (1983) *Rights, Killing, and Suffering*, Blackwell.

Friedman DA and Søvik E (2021) The Ant Colony as a Test for Scientific Theories of Consciousness, *Synthese*, 198, 1457–1480.

Frissen V et al (eds) (2015) *Playful Identities: The Ludification of Digital Media Cultures*, Amsterdam University Press.

Froese T (2018) Searching for the conditions of genuine intersubjectivity, in Newen A et al (eds) (2020/[2018]) *The Oxford Handbook of 4E Cognition*, Oxford University Press, 163–186.

Frow J (1995) *Cultural Studies and Cultural Value*, Clarendon Press.

Frow J (1997) *Time and Commodity Culture*, Oxford University Press.

Frow J (2003) Invidious distinction: Waste, difference, and classy stuff, in Hawkins G and Muecke S (eds) (2003) *Culture and Waste: The Creation and Destruction of Value*, Rowman and Littlefield Publishers, 25–38.

Fuchs F (2023) *Civic Storytelling: The Rise of Short Forms and the Agency of Literature*, Zone Books.

Furniss D et al (2019) Exploring Structure, Agency and Performance Variability in Everyday Safety: An Ethnographic Study of Practices around Infusion Devices Using Distributed Cognition, *Safety Science*, 118, 687–701.

Gadamer H-G (1986) *The Relevance of the Beautiful and Other Essays*, Walker N (trans), Cambridge University Press.

Gadamer H-G (1992/[1960]) *Truth and Method*, Weinsheimer J and Marshall DG (trans rev) 2nd ed, Crossroad.

Gaffar H and Albarashdi S (2024) Copyright Protection for AI-generated Works: Exploring Originality and Ownership in a Digital Landscape, *Asian Journal of International Law*, 1–24. [OnlineFirst].

Galdikas BMF (1995) *Reflections of Eden: My Years with the Orangutans of Borneo*, Little, Brown and Company.

Galef BG (2015) Laboratory Studies of Imitation/field Studies of Tradition: Towards a Synthesis in Animal Social Learning, *Behavioural Processes*, 112, 114–119.

Gallardo Palacios JF et al (2011) Status of, and Conservation Recommendations for, the Critically Endangered Crested Black Macaque *Macaca nigra* in Tangkoko, Indonesia, *Oryx*, 46(2), 290–297.

Gallotti M and Frith CD (2013) Social Cognition in the We-mode, *Trends in Cognitive Sciences*, 17(4), 160–165.

Galpayage Dona HS and Chittka L (2020) Charles H Turner, Pioneer in Animal Cognition, *Science*, 370(6516), 530–531.

Galpayage Dona HS et al (2022) Do Bumble Bees Play? *Animal Behaviour*, 194, 239–251.

Gamillo E (2021) Why Cats Love to Sit in Boxes – Even Fake Ones, According to Science, *Smithsonian Magazine*, 11 May.

Gandz S (1930) The Knot in Hebrew Literature, or from the Knot to the Alphabet, *Isis*, 14(1), 189–214.

Gangadharbatla H (2021) The Role of AI Attribution Knowledge in the Evaluation of Artwork, *Empirical Studies of the Arts*, 40(2), 125–142.

Garcia-Pelegrin E et al (2022) Could It Be Proto Magic? Deceptive Tactics in Nonhuman Animals Resemble Magician's Misdirection, *Psychology of Consciousness: Theory, Research, and Practice*, 9(3), 267–284.

Gardner RA and Gardner BT (1969) Teaching Sign Language to a Chimpanzee, *Science*, 164, 664–672.

Gasché R (1991) Ideality in Fragmentation, Foreword to Schlegel F (1991/[1798–1800]) *Philosophical Fragments*, Firchow P (trans), University of Minnesota Press, vii–xxxii.

Gaster M (1914) Beads and Knots, *Folklore*, 25(2), 254–258.

Gaut B and Kieran M (eds) (2018) *Creativity and Philosophy*, Routledge.

Gaylord MM (2002) Cervantes' other fiction, in Cascardi AJ (ed) (2002) *The Cambridge Companion to Cervantes*, Cambridge University Press, 100–130.

Gebhardt Fearns VK (2019) Experiencing Tomorrow: The Importance of Immersive Scenarios for Climate Science Communication, *RCC Perspectives: Transformations in Environment and Society*, 4, 89–96.

Genette G (1979/[1992]) *The Architext*, JE Lewin (trans), University of California Press.

Genette G (1997/[1982]) *Palimpsests: Literature in the Second Degree*, Newman C and Doubinsky C (trans), University of Nebraska Press.

Genette G (1997/[1987]) *Paratexts: Thresholds of Interpretation*, Lewin JE (trans), Cambridge University Press.

Geraghty H (2023) Ed Sheeran warns he'll quit music if found guilty in copyright trial, *NME*, 2 May.

Gervais DJ (2020a) Is Intellectual Property Law Ready for Artificial Intelligence, *GRUR International*, 69(2), 117–118.

Gervais DJ (2020b) The Machine as Author, *Iowa Law Review*, 105(5), 2053–2106.

Ghidini G and Falce V (eds) (2022) *Reforming Intellectual Property*, Elgar.

Gibson J (2005) *Community Resources: Intellectual Property, International Trade, and the Protection of Traditional Knowledge*, Ashgate.

Gibson J (2006) *Creating Selves: Intellectual Property and the Narration of Culture*, Ashgate.

Gibson J (2008) The lay of the land: The geography of traditional cultural expression, in Graber CB and Murri-Nenova M (eds) (2008) *Intellectual Property and Traditional Cultural Expressions in a Digital Environment*, Elgar Publishing, 182–201.

Gibson J (2014) *The Logic of Innovation*, Routledge.

Gibson J (2019) An Aristocracy of Authors, *Queen Mary Journal of Intellectual Property*, 9(1), 1–2.

Gibson J (2020a) *Owned, an Ethological Jurisprudence of Property: From the Cave to the Commons*, Routledge.

Gibson J (2020b) Sine qua Non-Sense: Originality and the End of Copyright, *Queen Mary Journal of Intellectual Property*, 10(4), 411–417.

Gibson J (2021a) Artificial Intelligence and Patents: DABUS and Methods for Attracting Enhanced Attention to Inventors, *Queen Mary Journal of Intellectual Property*, 11(4), 401–408.

Gibson J (2021b) The Thousand-and-second Tale of NFTs, as Foretold by Edgar Allan Poe, *Queen Mary Journal of Intellectual Property*, 11(3), 249–269.

Gibson J (2022a) All words and no performance: A revolution in copyright through performance in sound, in Ghidini G and Falce V (eds) (2022) *Reforming Intellectual Property*, Elgar, 95–124.

Gibson J (2022b) Animals and property: A person possessed, in Graham N et al (eds) (2022) *The Routledge Handbook of Property, Law and Society*, Routledge, 297–311.

Gibson J (2022c) Temporal Parts and Free Space: An Anecdotal Explanation of Intellectual Property and the Metaverse, or, How I Met Bill Cornish, *Queen Mary Journal of Intellectual Property*, 12(4), 433–440.

Gibson J (2022d) The Man behind the Curtain: Developing Film's Double Exposure of Intellectual Property, in Morris PS (ed) (2022) *Intellectual Property and the Law of Nations, 1860–1920*, Brill, 207–241.

Gibson J (2023a) Living in the Pastiche: From Barbieland to *Computer World*, All the World's a Paste, *Queen Mary Journal of Intellectual Property*, 13(4), 379–391.

Gibson J (2023b) Page against the Machine: The Death of the Author and the Rise of the Producer? *Queen Mary Journal of Intellectual Property*, 13(3), 275–284.

Gibson J (2023c) The Authorial Fallacy: What Literary Theory, Roald Dahl, Donald Trump, and Artificial Intelligence Have in Common, *Queen Mary Journal of Intellectual Property*, 13(1), 1–10.

Gibson J (2023d) The Intellectual Property in Sustainable Fashion: Standards Are up to Mhe mark, *Queen Mary Journal of Intellectual Property* 13(2), 141–152.

Gibson J (2024a) People or Patents, Inventors or Owners: Why the Supreme Court Decision on Artificial Intelligence and Invention in *Thaler* Is Significance for All Intellectual Property, *Queen Mary Journal of Intellectual Property*, 14(1), 1–6.

Gibson J (2024b) Museum pieces or stealing the show? NFTs and the story of cinematic heritage in fragments, in Herman A-M (ed) *Mobile Heritage: Practices, Interventions, Politics*, Routledge (forthcoming).

Gibson J (2024c) "The pretension is nothing; the performing every thing": The origin of performers' rights and the creation of the performer as artist, in Morris SP (ed) (forthcoming) *The Silent Peacemaker: Intellectual Property Rights and the Interwar International Legal Order, 1919–1939*, Brill.

Gibson J (2025) *Made, the Nature of Intellectual Property: An Ethological Jurisprudence of Objects*, Routledge (forthcoming).
Gibson J et al (2015) *The Business of Being an Author*, ALCS.
Gibson JJ (1950) *The Perception of the Visual World*, Houghton Mifflin Company.
Gigliotti C (2022) *The Creative Lives of Animals*, New York University Press.
Gillick L (2016) *Industry and Intelligence: Contemporary Art Since 1820*, Columbia University Press.
Gino F and Wiltermuth SS (2014) Evil Genius? How Dishonesty Can Lead to Greater Creativity, *Psychological Science*, 25(4), 978–981.
Ginsburg J (2009) The Author's Place in the Future of Copyright, *Willamette Law Review*, 45, 381–394.
Gioia T (2006), *Work Songs*, Duke University Press.
Giurfa M and Brito Sanchez MG de (2020) Black Lives Matter: Revisiting Charles Henry Turner's Experiments on Honey Bee Color Vision, *Current Biology*, 30(20), R1235–R1239.
Giurfa M et al (2021) Charles Henry Turner and the Cognitive Behavior of Bees, *Apidologie*, 52(3), 684–695.
Glas R (2015) Breaking reality: Exploring pervasive cheating in foursquare, in Frissen V et al (eds) (2015) *Playful Identities: The Ludification of Digital Media Culture*, Amsterdam University Press.
Godfrey-Smith P (2020) *Metazoa: Animal Minds and the Birth of Consciousness*, William Collins.
Goetsch W (1957/[1953]) *The Ants*, Manheim R (trans), University of Michigan.
Gombrich EH (1977/[1960]) *Art and Illusion: A Study in the Psychology of Pictorial Representation*, 5th ed, Phaidon.
Gómez-Laplaza LLM et al (2018) Quantity Discrimination in Angelfish, *Pterophyllum scalare*: A Novel Approach with Food as the Discriminant, *Animal Behaviour*, 142, 19–30.
Goodin RE (1992) *Green Political Theory*, Polity Press.
Gossman L (2003) Anecdote and History, *History and Theory*, 42(2), 143–168.
Gould SJ (1978) Sociobiology: The Art of Storytelling, *New Scientist*, 80, 530–533.
Gould SJ (1990) Taxonomy as Politics, *Dissent*, 37(1), 73–78.
Gould SJ (1997) The Exaptive Excellence of Spandrels as a Term and Prototype, *Proceedings of the National Academy of Sciences USA*, 94, 10750–10755.
Gould SJ and Lewontin RC (1979) The Spandrels of San Marco and the Panglossian Paradigm: A Critique of the Adaptationist Programme, *Proceedings of the Royal Society B*, 205(1161), 581–598.
Goy N et al (2021) The Adaptive Value of Tandem Communication in Ants: Insights from an Agent-based Model, *Journal of Theoretical Biology*, 526, 110762.
Grace K (2023) AI is not an arms race, *Time Magazine*, 31 May.
Graham M (2023) ChatGPT can't lie to you, but you still shouldn't trust it, *The Conversation*, 9 March.
Graham P et al (2010) Animal Cognition: Multi-Modal Interactions in Ant Learning, *Current Biology*, 20(15), R639–R640.
Grebowicz M and Reyna ZL (2021) The Animality of Simone Weil, *Minnesota Review*, 97, 77–94.
Green GP and Kaufman JC (eds) (2015) *Video Games and Creativity*, Academic Press.
Gregg J (2022) *If Nietzsche Were a Narwhal*, Hodder & Stoughton.

Grialou P et al (eds) (2005) *Images and Reasoning*, Keio University Press.
Griend P van de (1996) A history of topological knot theory of knots, in Turner JC and Griend P van de (eds) (1996) *History and Science of Knots*, World Scientific, 205–260.
Griffin DR (1958) *Listening in the Dark*, Yale University Press.
Griffin DR (1976) *The Question of Animal Awareness: Evolutionary Continuity of Mental Experience*, The Rockefeller UP.
Griffin DR (1988) Subjective Reality, *Behavioral & Brain Sciences*, 11(2), 256.
Griffin DR (1999) Nonhuman Minds, *Philosophical Topics*, 27(1), 233–254.
Griffin DR (2001) *Animal Minds: Beyond Cognition to Consciousness*, University of Chicago Press.
Groos K (1898) *The Play of Animals*, EL Baldwin (trans), D Appleton and Company.
Gross M (2012) How ants Find Their Way, *Current Biology*, 22(16), R615–R618.
Gross M (2016) Could Plants Have Cognitive Abilities? *Current Biology*, 26(5), R181–R184.
Gross M (2020) Are -Numbers in Our Nature? *Current Biology*, 30(21), R1283–R1300.
Gross N (2019) Reading the Hive Mind, *Current Biology*, 29(20), R1055–R1058.
Grøtta M (2012–2013) Reading/Developing Images: Baudelaire, Benjamin, and the Advent of Photography, *Nineteenth-Century French Studies*, 41(1–2), 80–90.
Grøtta M (2015) *Baudelaire's Media Aesthetics: The Gaze of the Flâneur and 19th-Century Media*, Bloomsbury.
Gruber T et al (2015) Apes have culture but may not know that they do, *Frontiers in Psychology*, 6, article 91.
Guadamuz A (2017) Do Androids Dream of Electric Copyright? Comparative Analysis of Originality in Artificial Intelligence Generated Works, *Intellectual Property Quarterly*, 2, 169–186.
Guadamuz A (2018) Can the monkey selfie case teach us anything about copyright law? *WIPO Magazine*.
Guala F (2019) Preferences: Neither Behavioural Nor Mental, *Economics and Philosophy*, 35, 383–401.
Guérineau C et al (2022) Enrichment with Classical Music Enhances Affiliative Behaviours in Bottlenose Dolphin, *Applied Animal Behaviour Science*, 254, 105696.
Guilford JP (1950) Creativity, *American Psychologist*, 5(9), 444–454.
Guiney MS and Oberhauser KS (2008) Insects as Flagship Conservation Species, *Terrestrial Arthropod Reviews*, 1, 111–123.
Gullar F (1959) Theory of the Non-Object, Asbury M (trans and commentary), in Mercer K (ed) (2005) *Cosmopolitan Modernisms*, MIT Press, 168–189.
Guo D et al (2024) Concept-cognitive Learning Survey: Mining and Fusing Knowledge from Data, *Information Fusion*, 109, 102426.
Gurkaynak G et al (2016) Stifling Artificial Intelligence: Human Perils, *Computer Law & Security Review*, 32, 749–758.
Gutorow J (2008) The Moment of a Bird's Cry: A Note on Wallace Stevens and Simone Weil, *The Wallace Stevens Journal*, 32(2), 171–180.
Gutworth MB et al (2016) Creativity for Deliberate Harm: Malevolent Creativity and Social Information Processing Theory, *Journal of Creative Behavior*, 52(4), 305–322.

Gyori B et al (2010) Friend or Foe: Context Dependent Sensitivity to Human Behaviour in Dogs, *Applied Animal Behaviour Science*, 128, 69–77.
Hadamard J (1996/[1945]) *The Mathematician's Mind: The Psychology of Invention in the Mathematical Field*, Princeton University Press.
Hadley J (2015) *Animal Property Rights: A Theory of Habitat Rights for Wild Animals*, Lexington Books.
Hadley J (2019) *Animal Neopragmatism: From Welfare to Rights*, Palgrave Macmillan.
Haikonen PO (2012) *Consciousness and Robot Sentience*, World Scientific.
Hale, Sir Matthew (1677) *The Primitive Origination of Mankind, Considered and Examined According to the Light of Nature*, William Godbid.
Hall AR (1999) *Isaac Newton: Eighteenth-Century Perspectives*, Oxford University Press.
Hamm P et al (2023) Explanation Matters: An Experimental Study on Explainable AI, *Electronic Markets*, 33, article 17.
Hampton AJB (2023/[2019]) *Romanticism and the Re-Invention of Modern Religion*, Cambridge University Press.
Handy B (2020) Can kid art be real art? *The New Yorker*, 14 December.
Hannoosh M (1989) The Reflexive Function of Parody, *Comparative Literature*, 41(2), 113–127.
Haraway D (2016) *Staying with the Trouble: Making Kin in the Chthulucene*, Duke University Press.
Haraway DJ (2008) *When Species Meet*, University of Minnesota Press.
Hariman R (2008) Political Parody and Public Culture, *Quarterly Journal of Speech*, 94(3), 247–272.
Harnad S (2016) Animal Sentience: The Other-minds Pproblem, *Animal Sentience*, 1(1), article 1.
Harold J (2018) The Value of Fidelity in Adaptation, *British Journal of Aesthetics*, 58(1), 89–100.
Harrington KJ et al (2024) Innovative Problem Solving by Wild Falcons, *Current Biology*, 35, 190–195.
Harris J (1751) *Hermes, or A Philosophical Inquiry Concerning Universal Grammar*, H Woodfall.
Harrison E et al (2023) Sheeran releases new album *Subtract* after winning Marvin Gaye lawsuit, *Independent*, 5 May.
Harrison SH and Nurmohamed S (2023) Dirty Creativity: An Inductive Study of How Creative Workers Champion New Designs That Are Stigmatized, *Organizational Behavior and Human Decision Processes*, 175, 104224.
Hartigan Jr, John (2014) *Aesop's Anthropology: A Multispecies Approach*, University of Minnesota Press.
Hassija V et al (2024) Interpreting Black-Box Models: A Review on Explainable Artificial Intelligence, *Cognitive Computation*, 16, 45–74.
Hasslacher B and Tilden MW (1995) Living Machines, *Robotics and Autonomous Systems*, 15, 143–169.
Hatfield G (2019) Mind and psychology in descartes, in Nadler S et al (eds) (2019) *The Oxford Handbook of Descartes and Cartesianism*, Oxford University Press, 106–123.

Hawkins G and Muecke S (eds) (2003) *Culture and Waste: The Creation and Destruction of Value*, Rowman and Littlefield Publishers.

Hazel SJ et al (2015) 'Chickens Are a Lot Smarter Than I Originally Thought': Changes in Student Attitudes to Chickens Following a Chicken Training Class, *Animals*, 5, 821–837.

Healy M (2014/[2011]) *Shakespeare, Alchemy and the Creative Imagination*, Cambridge University Press.

Heidegger M (1968/[1954]) *What Is Called Thinking?* J Glenn Gray (trans), Harper & Row.

Heidegger M (2010/[1953]) *Being and Time*, Stambaugh J (trans), SUNY Press.

Held SDE and Špinka M (2011) Animal Play and Animal Welfare, *Animal Behaviour*, 81(5), 891–899.

Hénaff M (2009) The Anecdotal: Truth in Detail, J-L Morhange (trans), *SubStance*, 38(1), 97–111.

Henderson J (2006) Preface, in Plautus (2006) *Asinaria*, J Henderson (trans), the University of Wisconsin Press, Madison, vii–x.

Henderson TY (1970) In Defense of Thrasymachus, *American Philosophical Quarterly*, 7(3), 218–228.

Henning JSL et al (2022) Play and Welfare in Domestic Cats: Current Knowledge and Future Directions, *Animal Welfare*, 31, 407–421.

Herculano-Houzel S (2020) Remarkable, but not special: What human brains are made of, in Kaas JH (ed) (2020) *Evolutionary Neuroscience*, 2nd ed, Elsevier.

Herel D and Mikolov T (2024) Collapse of Self-trained Language Models, arXiv:2404.02305.

Herman LM (2012) Body and Self in Dolphins, *Consciousness and Cognition*, 21, 526–545.

Hern A (2022) Types and shutdowns: Robot "gives evidence" to Lords committee, *The Guardian*, 11 October.

Hernandez-Lallement J et al (2020), Harm to Others Acts as a Negative Reinforcer in Rats, *Current Biology*, 30(6), 949–961.

Herzfeld C (2016/[2012]) *Wattana: An Orangutan in Paris*, Martin OU and Martin RD (trans), University of Chicago Press.

Herzfeld C and Lestel D (2005) Knot Tying in Great Apes: Etho-Ethnology of an Unusual Tool Behaviour, *Social Science Information*, 44(4), 621–653.

Herzog D (2012) Aristocratic dignity? in Waldron et al (eds) (2012) *Dignity, Rank, and Rights*, Dan-Cohen M (ed), Oxford University Press, 99–118.

Hetzel A et al (2013) The Reception of the Mimetic Theory in the German-Speaking World, G Borrud (trans), *Contagion: Journal of Violence, Mimesis, and Culture*, 20(1), 25–76.

Heyes CM and Galef Jr BG (eds) (1996) *Social Learning in Animals: The Roots of Culture*, Academic Press

Heyman Y et al (2019) Ants Use Multiple Spatial Memories and Chemical Pointers to Navigate Their Nest, *iScience*, 14, 264–276.

Higgins J (2021) *Sentient: What Animals Reveal About Our Senses*, Picador.

Higgins J (2021), Cognising *with Others* in the We-Mode: A Defence of 'First-Person Plural' Social Cognition, *Review of Philosophy and Psychology*, 12, 803–824.

Higgs MJ et al (2020) Man's Best Friends: Attitudes towards the Use of Different Kinds of Animal Depend on Belief in Different Species' Mental Capacities and Purpose of Use, *Royal Society Open Science*, 7, 191162.

Hillman B (2009) In a house subcommittee on electronic surveillance, in Hillman B (ed) (2009) *Practical Water*, Wesleyan University Press, 48–49.

Hintikka J (1962) *Cogito, ergo sum*: Inference or Performance? *Philosophical Review*, 71(1), 3–32.

Hobson-West P and Davies A (2018) Societal Sentience, *Science, Technology, and Human Values*, 43(4), 671–693.

Hoehl S et al (2019) "Over-imitation": A Review and Appraisal of a Decade of Research, *Developmental Review*, 51, 90–108.

Hoffmann J (2015) Commentary on chapter 2: Creativity in the interaction, in Kaufman AB and Kaufman JC (eds) (2015) *Animal Creativity and Innovation*, Elsevier-Academic Press, Amsterdam, 42–44.

Hofstadter DR (1979) *Gödel, Escher, Bach: An Eternal Golden Braid*, Penguin.

Hofstadter DR (2023) Gödel, Escher, Bach, and AI, *The Atlantic*, 8 July.

Hölldobler B and Wilson EO (1990) *The Ants*, Harvard University Press.

Hölldobler B and Wilson EO (1994) *Journey to the Ants: A Story of Scientific Exploration*, Harvard University Press.

Hollingsworth C (2014) *Poetics of the Hive: Insect Metaphor in Literature,* University of Iowa Press.

Hollis KL and Nowbahari E (2013) Toward a Behavioral Ecology of Rescue Behavior, *Evolutionary Psychology*, 11(3), 647–664.

Holzinger A et al (2023) Toward Human-Level Concept Learning: Pattern Benchmarking for AI Algorithms, *Patterns*, 4(8), 100788.

Homer, (2008/[1974]) *The Iliad*, Fitzgerald R (trans), Oxford University Press.

Homer, (2008/[1980]) *The Odyssey*, Shewring W (trans) Oxford University Press.

Horowitz A (2009) Attention to Attention in Domestic Dog (*Canis familiaris*) Dyadic Play, *Animal Cognition*, 12, 107–118.

Horowitz A (2012/[2010]) *Inside of a Dog*, Simon & Schuster.

Horowitz A (2017) Smelling Themselves: Dogs Investigate Their Own Odours Longer When Modified in an "Olfactory Mirror" Test, *Behavioural Processes*, 143, 17–24.

Hourani GF (1962) Thrasymachus' Definition of Justice in Plato's Republic, *Phronesis*, 7(1), 111–120.

Huang J and Chang KCC (2024) Citation: A Key to Building Responsible and Accountable Large Language Models, arXiv:2307.02185v3.

Huang Y et al (2009) When Do Objects Become More Attractive? The Individual and Iinteractive Effects of Choice and Ownership on Object Evaluation, *Personality and Social Psychology Bulletin (PSPB)*, 35(6), 713–722.

Huber L et al (2022) Overimitation in Dogs: Is There a Link to the Quality of the Relationship with the Caregiver? *Animals*, 12(3), 326.

Huber MP (1820) *The Natural History of Ants*, Johnson JR (trans), Longman et al.

Hubinger E et al (2024) Sleeper Agents: Training Deceptive LLMs That Persist through Safety Training, arXiv:2401.05566v3.

Hughes J (1988) The Philosophy of Intellectual Property, *Georgetown Law Journal*, 77(2), 287–366.

Hull G (2009) Clearing the Rubbish: Locke, the Waste Proviso, and the Moral Justification of Intellectual Property, *Public Affairs Quarterly*, 23(1), 67–93.
Hume D (1969/[1739–1740]), *A Treatise of Human* Nature, Penguin.
Humphrey H (2022) *Sentience: The Invention of Consciousness*, Oxford University Press.
Humphreys RK and Ruxton GD (2018) A Review of Thanatosis (Death Feigning) as an Anti-Predator Behaviour, *Behavioral Ecology and Sociobiology*, 72, article 22.
Hunt T (2014) Reconsidering the Logical Structure of the Theory of Natural Selection, *Communicative and Integrative Biology*, 7(6), 3972848.
Hurka T (ed) *Games, Sports, and Play*, Oxford University Press.
Husserl E (1977/[1962]) *Phenomenological Psychology: Lectures, Summer Semester; 1925*, Scanlon J (trans), Martinus Nijhoff.
Husserl E (2002) *Natur und Geist: Vorlesungen Sommersemester 1919*, Weiler M (ed), Springer.
Hutcheon L (2000/[1985]) *A Theory of Parody: The Teachings of Twentieth-Century Art Forms*, University of Illinois Press.
Hutchins E (1995) *Cognition in the Wild*, MIT Press.
Hutson M (2018) How researchers are teaching AI to learn like a child, *Science*, 24 May.
Hutt C (1966) Exploration and play in children, in Jewell PA and Loizos C (eds) (1966) *Play, Exploration and Territory in Mammals, Symposia of the Zoological Society of London, 18*, Academic Press, 61–81.
Hutto DD and Myin E (2013) *Radicalizing Enactivism: Basic Minds Without Content*, MIT Press.
Hutton C (2019) *Serial Encounters: Ulysses and The Little Review*, Oxford University Press.
Huyssen A (1975) The Cultural Politics of Pop: Reception and Critique of US Pop Art in the Federal Republic of Germany, *New German Critique*, 4, 77–97.
Hven S (2022) *Enacting the Worlds of Cinema*, Oxford University Press.
Ianniello A (2021) Enactivism and Performance Art: Putting on Display our Perception, *Studia UBB Philosophia*, 66, 121–129.
Ilosvay TR (1953) Scientific Property, *The American Journal of Comparative Law*, 2(2), 178–197.
Imanishi K (1941/[2002]) *A Japanese View of Nature: The World of Living Things*, Asquith PJ et al (trans), Routledge.
Ingold T (2016/[2007]) *Lines: A Brief History*, Routledge.
Innis RE (1994) *Consciousness and the Play of Signs*, Indiana University Press.
Internationale Situationniste (1958) Contribution a une definition situationniste du jeu, *Internationale Situationniste*, 1. (Contribution to a Situationist Definition of Play, Thompson I (trans) https://isinenglish.com/1-6-contribution-to-a-situationist-definition-of-play/
Isaacs N (1918) The Schools of Jurisprudence: Their Places in History and Their Present Alignment, *Harvard Law Review*, 31(3), 373–411.
Jackson DE and Ratnieks FLW (2006) Communication in Ants, *Current Biology*, 16, R570–R574.
Jackson LA and Games AI (2015) Video games and creativity, in Green GP and Kaufman JC (eds) (2015) *Video Games and Creativity*, Academic Press, 3–38.

Jacobs IF and Osvath M (2015) The String-Pulling Paradigm in Comparative Psychology, *Journal of Comparative Psychology*, 129(2), 89–120.

Jacobsen LE (1983) Use of Knotted String Accounting Records in Old Hawaii and Ancient China, *The Accounting Histories Journal*, 10(2), 53–61.

Jakobson R and Halle M (1956) *Fundamentals of Language*, Mouton & Co.

James K et al (1999) Positive and Negative Creativity in Groups, Institutions, and Organizations: A Model and Theoretical Extension, *Creativity Research Journal*, 12(3), 211–226.

James W (1890a) *The Principles of Psychology, Volume I*, Henry Holt and Company.

James W (1890b) *The Principles of Psychology, Volume II*, Henry Holt and Company.

Jameson F (1991) *Postmodernism, or, The Cultural Logic of Late Capitalism*, Verso.

Jameson F (2003) Future City, *New Left Review*, 21, 65–79.

Janowitz A (1985) Coleridge's 1816 Volume: Fragment as Rubric, *Studies in Romanticism*, 24(1), 21–39.

Janowitz A (1998) The Romantic Fragment, in Wu D (ed) (1998/[2001]) *A Companion to Romanticism*, Blackwell, 442–451.

Janz BB (2019) Virtual place and virtualized place, in Champion E (ed) (2019) *The Phenomenology of Real and Virtual Places*, Routledge, 60–75.

Jeanson R (2012) Long-term Dynamics in Proximity Networks in Ants, *Animal Behaviour* 83, 915–923.

Jensen K (2010) Punishment and Spite, the Dark Side of Cooperation, *Philosophical Transactions of The Royal Society B*, 365, 2635–2650.

Jeong S (2015) Did PETA name the right macaque in its "Monkey Selfie" lawsuit? *Vice*, 28 September.

Jersáková J et al (2007) Mechanisms and Evolution of Deceptive Pollination in Orchids, *Biological Reviews*, 81(2), 219–235.

Jeschke JM and Tollrian R (2007) Prey Swarming: Which Predators Become Confused and Why? *Animal Behaviour*, 74(3), 387–393.

Johannsen K (2020) *Wild Animal Ethics: The Moral and Political Problem of Wild Animal Suffering*, Routledge.

Johansen RK (2010) Simone Weil's Ethic of the Other: Explicating Fictions through Fiction, or Looking through the Wrong End of the Telescope, *CrossCurrents*, 60(1), 70–88.

Johnson P (2024) Enhanced Distinctiveness and Why "Strong Marks" Are Causing Us All Confusion, *International Review of Intellectual Property and Competition Law*, 55, 185–212.

Johnson RI (1915) The Value of a Mistake, *The English Journal*, 4(5), 311–314.

Johnson S (2001) *Emergence: The Connected Lives of Ants, Brains, Cities and Software*, Scribner.

Johnston M et al (2023) Crows Flexibly Apply Statistical Inferences Based on Previous Experiences, *Current Biology*, 33(15) 3238–3243.

Jolles JW et al (2019) The Role of Individual Heterogeneity in Collective Animal Behaviour, *Trends in Ecology and Evolution*, 35(3), 278–291.

Jolley R (2010) *Children and Pictures: Drawing and Understanding*, Wiley-Blackwell.

Jones G (2005) Echolocation, *Current Biology*, 15(13), R484–R488.

Jordan MI (2019) Artificial Intelligence – The Revolution Hasn't Happened Yet, *Harvard Data Science Review*, 1(1), 1–9.

Jorgensen LM (2011) Mind the Gap: Reflection and Consciousness in Leibniz, *Studia Leibnitiana*, 43(2), 179–195.
Joseph GG (2011) *The Crest of the Peacock: Non-European Roots of Mathematics*, 3rd ed, Princeton University Press.
Jousse M (2015/[1981]) *The Oral Style*, Sienaert E and Whitaker R (trans), Routledge.
Joyce J (1922) *Ulysses*, Shakespeare & Company.
Joyce P (ed) (2014/[2002]) *The Social in Question: New Bearings in History and the Social Sciences*, Routledge, 117–132.
Jullien D (2009) Anecdotes, Faits Divers, and the Literary, *SubStance*, 38(1), 66–76.
Jünger E (2000/[1957]) *The Glass Bees*, L Rogan and E Mayer (trans), New York Review Books.
Jurgens A and Kirchhoff MD (2019) Enactive Social Cognition: Diachronic Constitution and Coupled Anticipation, *Consciousness and Cognition*, 70, 1–10.
Jürgens UM (2017) How Human-Animal Relations Are Realized: From Respective Realities to Merging Minds, *Ethics and the Environment*, 22(2), 25–57.
Kacelnik A (2009) Tools for Thought or Thought for Tools? *Proceedings of the National Academy of Sciences USA*, 106(25), 10071–10072.
Kant I (2002/[1790–1793]) *Critique of the Power of Judgment*, Cambridge University Press.
Kaplan G (2007) Elephants that paint, birds that make music: Do animals have an aesthetic sense? in Read CA (ed) (2007) *Cerebrum: Emerging Ideas in Brain Science*, The Dana Foundation, 137–150.
Kaplar ME and Gordon AK (2004) The Enigma of Altruistic Lying: Perspective Differences in What Motivates and Justifies Lie Telling within Romantic Relationships, *Personal Relationships*, 11(4), 489–507.
Karlsen J (2011) *Hot on the Tail of Hefty Atlantic Cod: An Interdisciplinary Study on the Behaviour at Ship Wrecks in the North Sea*, National Institute of Aquatic Resources.
Karlsson F (2018) Mobility, animals and the virtue of justice, in Cook N and Butz D (eds) (2018) *Mobilities, Mobility Justice and Social Justice*, Routledge, 217–229.
Kashyap R (2021) Artificial Intelligence: A Child's Play, *Technological Forecasting & Social Change*, 166(120555), 1–18.
Kaufman AB and Kaufman JC (eds) (2015) *Animal Creativity and Innovation*, Academic Press.
Kaufman AB and O'Hearn WJ (2017) Creativity in non-human animals, in Kaufman JC et al (eds) (2017) *The Cambridge Handbook of Creativity Across Domains*, Cambridge University Press, 492–506.
Kaufman JC and Glaveanu VP (2022) Making the CASE for Shadow Creativity, *Psychology of Aesthetics, Creativity, and the Arts*, 16(1), 44–57.
Kaufman JC et al (eds) (2017) *The Cambridge Handbook of Creativity Across Domains*, Cambridge University Press.
Kelly TAF (ed) (2007) *Between System and Poetics: William Desmond and Philosophy after Dialectic*, Routledge
Kenny K (2009) The Performative Surprise: Parody, Documentary and Critique, *Culture and Organization*, 15(2), 221–235.
Kerferd GB (1947) The Doctrine of Thrasymachus in Plato's Republic, *Durham University Journal*, 9, 19–27.

Kettering CF (1944) How Can We Develop Inventors? *Mechanical Engineering*, 66(4) 231–234.

Keyes O et al (2021) Truth from the Machine: Artificial Intelligence and the Materialization of Identity, *Interdisciplinary Science Reviews*, 46(1–2), 158–175.

Keynes M (1995) The Personality of Isaac Newton, *Notes and Records of the Royal Society of London*, 49(1), 1–56.

Kickmeier-Rust MD and Holzinger A (2019) Interactive Ant Colony Optimization to Support Adaptation in Serious Games, *International Journal of Serious Games*, 6(3) 37–50.

Kim D (2020) AI-generated Inventions: Time to Get the Record Straight? *GRUR International*, 69(5), 443–456.

Kim D et al (2023) How Should the Results of Artificial Intelligence Be Explained to Users? Research on Consumer Preferences in User-centered Explainable Artificial Intelligence, *Technological Forecasting & Social Change*, 188, 122343.

Kim J (2007) *Physicalism, or Something Near Enough*, Princeton University Press.

Kimmerer RW (2013) *Braiding Sweetgrass: Indigenous Wisdom, Scientific Knowledge and the Teachings of Plants*, Milkweed Editions.

King A (2016) Gabriel Tarde and Contemporary Social Theory, *Sociological Theory*, 34(1), 45–61.

King AJ and Cowlishaw G (2009) All Together Now: Behavioural Synchrony in Baboons, *Animal Behaviour*, 78(6), 1381–1387.

King AJ and Sumpter DJT (2012) Murmurations, *Current Biology*, 22(4), R112–R114.

King BJ (2013) *How Animals Grieve*, The University of Chicago Press.

King J (2023) My books were used to train AI, *The Atlantic*, 23 August.

Kingwell M (2020) Are Sentient AIs Persons? in Dubber MD et al (eds) (2020) *The Oxford Handbook of Ethics of AI*, Oxford University Press, 325–342.

Kiremidjian GD (1969) The Aesthetics of Parody, *The Journal of Aesthetics and Art Criticism*, 28(2), 231–242.

Klancher J (2013) *Transfiguring the Arts and Sciences: Knowledge and Cultural Institutions in the Romantic Age*, Cambridge University Press.

Klockmann V et al (2022) Artificial Intelligence, Ethics, and Intergenerational Responsibility, *Journal of Economic Behavior and Organization*, 203, 284–317.

Klopfer PH (1970) Sensory Physiology and Esthetics: Among Many Species Play Seems to Be a Guide for Conscious Action, *American Scientist*, 58(4), 399–403.

Knight J (2005a) Introduction, in Knight J (ed) (2005) *Animals in Person: Cultural Perspectives on Human-Animal Intimacies*, Berg, 1–13.

Knight J (ed) (2005b) *Animals in Person: Cultural Perspectives on Human-Animal Intimacies*, Berg.

Knight P (1978a) Introduction to *Maldoror*, in Comte de Lautréamont (1978) *Maldoror and Poems*, Penguin Books, 7–28.

Knight P (1978b) Introduction to *Poems*, in Comte de Lautréamont (1978) *Maldoror and Poems*, Penguin Books, 246–252.

Knoll E (1997) Dogs, Darwinism, and English sensibilities, in Mitchell RW et al (eds) (1997) *Anthropomorphism, Anecdotes, and Animals*, SUNY Press, 12–21.

Knutsson S and Munthe C (2017) A Virtue of Precaution Regarding the Moral Status of Animals with Uncertain Sentience, *Journal of Agricultural and Environmental Ethics*, 30, 213–224.

Kobylkov D et al (2023) Neural Coding of Numerousness, *BioSystems*, 232, 104999.

Koch C (2015) Intelligence without Sentience, *Scientific American Mind*, 26(4), 26–29.
Köhler W (1972/[1921]) *The Mentality of Apes*, 2nd ed, Winter E (trans), Random House.
Konopka A (2009) The Role of *umwelt* in Husserl's *Aufbau* and *Abbau* of the *Natur/ Geist* Distinction, *Human Studies*, 32(3), 313–333.
Konopka A (2015) Embodiment and *umwelt*: A Phenomenological Approach, *Social Imaginaries*, 1(2), 53–72.
Koralus P (2014) The Erotetic Theory of Attention: Questions, Focus and Distraction, *Mind & Language* 29(1), 26–50.
Kornblum A (1980) *Awkward Song*, Toothpaste Press, Iowa.
Kostelanetz R (2022/[2019]) *A Dictionary of the Avant-Gardes*, 3rd ed, Routledge.
Krause M and Robinson K (2017) Charismatic Species and Beyond: How Cultural Schemas and Organisation Routines Shape Conservation, *Conservation and Society*, 15(3), 313–321.
Krauss RE (1991/[1985]) *The Originality of the Avant-Garde and Other Modernist Myths*, MIT Press.
Kravets D (2015) Will the real monkey who snapped those famous selfies please stand up? *ArsTechnica*, 10 November.
Kriengwatana BP et al (2022) Music for Animal Welfare: A Critical Review and Conceptual Framework, *Applied Animal Behaviour Science*, 251, 105641.
Krusche P et al (2010) Quantity Discrimination in Salamanders, *Journal of Experimental Biology*, 213(11), 1822–1828.
Kubiak C (1994) Sowing Chaos: Discontinuity and the Form of Autonomy in the Fragment Collections of the Early German Romantics, *Studies in Romanticism*, 33(3), 411–449.
Küchler S (2003) Imaging the Body Politic: The Knot in Pacific Imagination, *L'Homme*, 165, 205–222.
Kulstad M (1981) Leibniz, Animals, and Apperception, *Studia Leibnitiana*, 13(1), 25–60.
Kumar PA et al (2022) Play and play spaces for global health, happiness, and well-being, in Deb S and Gerrard BA (eds) (2022) *Handbook of Health and Well-Being: Challenges, Strategies and Future Trends*, Springer, 129–154.
Kuta S (2024) Ten shipwrecks found off the coast of Greek Island, *Smithsonian Magazine*, 19 March.
Kwasny M (2012) Women and Nature, *The American Poetry Review*, 41(1), 33–37.
Lacoue-Labarthe P and Nancy J-L (1988/[1978]) *The Literary Absolute: The Theory of Literature in German Romanticism*, Barnard P and Lester C (trans), SUNY Press.
Lagercrantz S (1968) African Tally-Strings, *Anthropos*, 63, 115–128.
Laland KN (2017) *Darwin's Unfinished Symphony: How Culture Made the Human Mind*, Princeton University Press.
Laland KN and Galef BG (eds) (2009) *The Question of Animal Culture*, Harvard University Press.
Lancy DF (1982) Some Missed Opportunities in the Theories of Play, *Behavioral & Brain Sciences*, 5, 165–166.
Langlitz N (2020) *Chimpanzee Culture Wars: Rethinking Human Nature Alongside Japanese, European, and American Cultural Primatologists*, Princeton University Press.

Langton CG (1996) Artificial life, in Boden M (ed) (1996) *The Philosophy of Artificial Life*, Oxford University Press, 39–94.

Laskowski KL et al (2015) Predictors of Individual Variation in Movement in a Natural Population of Threespine Stickleback (*Gasterosteus aculeatus*), *Advances in Ecological Research*, 52, 65–90.

Latour B (2002) Gabriel tarde and the end of the social, in Joyce P (ed) (2014/[2002]) *The Social in Question: New Bearings in History and the Social Sciences*, Routledge, 117–132.

Latour B (2010) Tarde's idea of quantification, in Candea M (ed) (2016) *The Social After Gabriel Tarde*, 2nd ed, Routledge, 187–202.

Latour B (2011) Why Do Architects Read Latour? An Interview with Bruno Latour, Paris, France, March 19, 2010, *Perspecta*, 44, 64–69, 197.

Latour B and Lepinjay VA (2009) *The Science of Passionate Interests*, Prickly Paradigm Press.

Latour B and Woolgar S (1986/[1979]) *Laboratory Life: The Social Construction of Scientific Facts*, Princeton University Press.

Laumer IB et al (2024) Spontaneous Playful Teasing in Four Great Ape Species, *Proceedings of the Royal Society B*, 291, 20232345.

Laurier E et al (2006) Putting the Dog Back in the Park: Animal and Human Mind-in-action, *Mind, Culture and Activity*, 13(1), 2–24.

Lavik E (2014) Romantic authorship in copyright law and the uses of aesthetics, in Eechoud M van (ed) (2014) *The Work of Authorship*, Amsterdam University Press, 45–93.

Lawson A (2015) Monkey selfie is mine, UK photographer argues, *BBC News*, 24 September.

Le Fanu J (2004) Review: The Hand: A Philosophical Inquiry into Human Being, *Journal of the Royal Society of Medicine*, 27, 201–202.

Leadner K et al (2021) Evolution of Social Attentional Cues: Evidence from the Archerfish, *Cognition*, 297, 104511.

Leavens DA (2009) Animal Communication: Laughter Is the Shortest Distance between Two Apes, *Current Biology*, 19, R511–R513.

LeBoeuf AC (2017) Trophallaxis, *Current Biology*, 27, R1299–R1300.

Lee B (2023) Ed Sheeran cleared of infringing copyright in Marvin Gaye lawsuit, *The Guardian*, 4 May.

Lee M (2020) Why AI can't ever reach its full potential without a physical body, *The Conversation*, 5 October.

Lee P and Grisez G (2012) Total Brain Death: A Reply to Alan Shewmon, *Bioethics*, 26(5), 275–284.

Leeds JA (1989) The History of Attitudes Towards Children's Art, *Studies in Art Education*, 30(2), 93–103.

Lees CA and Overing GR (2019) *The Contemporary Medieval in Practice*, UCL Press.

Lefebvre H (1991/[1974]) *The Production of Space*, Nicholson-Smith D (trans), Blackwell.

Lefkowitz JB (2014), Aesop and animal fable, in GL Campbell (ed) (2014) *The Oxford Handbook of Animals in Classical Thought and Life*, Oxford University Press, 1–23.

Leibniz GW (1714a) Principles of nature and grace, in Leibniz GW (1934) *Philosophical Writings*, Parkinson GHR (ed), Morris M and Parkinson GHR (trans), JM Dent & Sons.

Leibniz GW (1714b) Monadology in Leibniz GW (1902) *Discourse on Metaphysics; Correspondence with Arnauld; Monadology*, Montgomery G (trans), Open Court.

Leibniz GW (1934) *Philosophical Writings*, Parkingson GHR (ed), Morris M and Parkinson GHR (trans), JM Dent & Sons.

Leibniz GW (1981) *The Political Writings of Leibniz*, Riley P (trans and ed), Cambridge University Press.

Leibniz GW (1985/[1710]) *Theodicy*, Huggard EM (trans), Open Court.

Leibniz GW (1989) *Philosophical Essays*, Ariew R and Garber D (trans and ed), Hackett.

Leibniz GW (1996/[1704]) *New Essays on Human Understanding*, Remnant P and Bennett J (trans and eds), Cambridge University Press.

Lenkei R et al (2021) Dogs (*Canis familiaris*) Recognize Their Own Body as a Physical Obstacle, *Nature*, 11, 2761.

Lents NH (2017) Why do humans make art? *Psychology Today*, 5 September.

Leroux G (1911) *The Phantom of the Opera*, Teixeira de Mattos A (trans) The Bobbs-Merrill Company.

Lesté-Lasserre C (2021) Playing dead really works to help insects avoid being eaten by birds, *New Scientist*, 3 March.

Lestel D (2011) What Capabilities for the Animal? *Biosemiotics*, 4, 83–102.

Lestel D (2018) Mirror effects, Chrulew M (trans), in Chrulew M et al (eds) (2018) *The Philosophical Ethology of Dominique Lestel*, Routledge, 47–57.

Lestel D and Herzfeld C (2005) Topological Ape: Knots tying and untying and the origins of mathematics, in Grialou P et al (eds) (2005) *Images and Reasoning*, Keio University Press, 147–162.

Lestel D and Herzfeld C (2016) How an Orangutan Became a Master of Tying Knots, *Live Science*, 21 May.

Lestel D et al (2014) The Phenomenology of Animal Life, *Environmental Humanities*, 5, 125–148.

Lewes GH (1877) Consciousness and Unconsciousness, *Mind*, 2(6), 145–167.

Li X et al (2023) Pre-Thinking and Recalling Enable ChatGPT to Self-Improve with Memory-of-Thoughts, arXiv:2305.05181.

Linardatos P et al (2021) Explainable AI: A Review of Machine Learning Interpretability Models, *Entropy*, 23(1), 18.

Lindig AM et al (2020) Musical Dogs: A Review of the Influence of Auditory Enrichment on Canine Health and Behavior, *Animals*, 10(1), 127.

Lispector C (1989/[1973]) *Agua Viva*, Lowe E and Fitz E (trans), University of Minnesota Press, 50.

Liu D et al (2009) Neural Correlates of Belief- and Desire-Reasoning, *Child Development* 80(4), 1163–1171.

Liu H and Sun F (2018) *Robotic Tactile Perception and Understanding: A Sparse Coding Method*, Springer.

Liu L (2022) AI is getting boring – and that's a good thing, *Forbes*, 22 April.

Lobo L et al (2018) The History and Philosophy of Ecological Psychology, *Frontiers in Psychology*, 9, 2228.

Locke D (1974) Reasons, Wants, and Causes, *American Philosophical Quarterly*, 11(3), 169–179.
Locke J (1689/[1988]) *Two Treatises of Government*, Cambridge University Press.
Locke LL (1912) The Ancient Quipu, A Peruvian Knot Record, *American Anthropologist*, 14(2), 325–332.
Lomellini V (2022) *Il 'lodo Moro': Terrorismo e ragion di Stato 1969–1986*, Laterza.
Long CP (2015) Who let the dogs out? Tracking the philosophical life among the wolves and dogs of the *Republic*, in Bell J and Nass M (eds) (2015), *Plato's Animals: Gadflies, Horses, Swans, and Other Philosophical Beasts*, Indiana University Press, 131–145.
Longman LD (1947) The Concept of Psychical Distance, *The Journal of Aesthetics and Art Criticism*, 6(1), 31–36.
Longo L et al (2024) Explainable Artificial Intelligence (XAI) 2.0: A Manifesto of Open Challenges and Interdisciplinary Research Directions, *Information Fusion*, 106, 102301.
Loo S and Sellbach U (2015) Insect Affects: The Big and Small of the Entomological Imagination in Childhood, *Angelaki: Journal of the Theoretical Humanities*, 20(3), 79–88.
Lopez U et al (2012) From behavioural analyses to models of collective motion in fish schools, *Interface Focus*, 2, 693–707.
Lorenc T (2012) Afterword: Tarde's pansocial ontology, in Tarde G (1895/[2012]) *Monadology and Sociology*, Lorenc T (ed and trans), re.press, 73–95.
Loretto M-C et al (2020) Contextual Imitation in Juvenile Common Ravens, *Corvus corax*, *Animal Behaviour*, 163, 127–134.
Lotman YM (1990) *Universe of the Mind: A Semiotic Theory of Culture*, Shukman A (trans), Indiana University Press.
Louâpre P et al (2010) Humans and Insects Decide in Similar Ways, *PLoS One*, 5(12), e14251.
Lovejoy M (1990) Art, Technology, and Postmodernism: Paradigms, Parallels, and Paradoxes, *Art Journal*, 49(3), 257–265.
Lovelace A (1843) Notes by the translator, in Taylor R (ed) (1843) *Scientific Memoirs, Selected from the Transactions of Foreign Academies of Science and Learned Societies*, Volume III, 691–731.
Luna D et al (2021) Do Domestic Pigs Acquire a Positive Perception of Humans through Observational Social Learning, *Animals*, 11(1), article 127.
Lund A (2014) Playing, Gaming, Working and Labouring: Framing the Concepts and Relations, *tripleC*, 12(2), 735–801.
Lund BD and Naheem KT (2024) Can ChatGPT Be an Author? A Study of Artificial Intelligence Authorship Policies in Top Academic Journals, *Learned Publishing*, 37(1), 13–21.
Lusseau D and Conradt L (2009) The Emergence of Unshared Consensus Decisions in Bottlenose Dolphins, *Behavioral Ecology and Sociobiology*, 63, 1067–1077.
Lyman SM and Scott MB (1967) Territoriality: A Neglected Sociological Dimension, *Social Problems*, 15(2), 236–249.
Lynch K (1990) *Wasting Away*, Sierra Club.
Lynch M (2016) Social Constructivism in Science and Technology Studies, *Human Studies*, 39(1), 101–112.
Lynn WT (1888) Newton and the Dog, *Notes and Queries*, 21 January, 41–42.

Lyon BE (2003) Egg Recognition and Counting Reduce Costs of Avian Conspecific Brood Parasitism, *Nature*, 422, 495–499.

Lyotard J-F (1984/[1979]) *The Postmodern Condition: A Report on Knowledge*, Bennington G and Massumi B (trans) University of Minnesota Press.

Lyotard J-F (1985/[1979]) *Just Gaming*, Godzich W (trans) University of Minnesota Press.

Maák I et al (2017) Tool Selection During Foraging in Two Species of Funnel Ants, *Animal Behaviour* 123, 207–216.

Macmillan F (2008) Is Copyright Blind to the Visual? *Visual Communication*, 7(1), 97–118.

Madden JR et al (2009) Calling in the Gap: Competition or Cooperation in Littermates' Begging Behaviour? *Proceedings of the Royal Society B*, 276, 1255–1262.

Maglieri V et al (2020) Levelling Playing Field: Synchronization and Rapid Facial Mimicry in Dog-Horse Play, *Behavioural Processes*, 174(104104), 1–8.

Maglieri V et al (2022) The Relaxed Open Mouth Is a True Signal in Dogs: Demonstrating Tinbergen's Ritualization Process, *Animal Behaviour*, 188, 65–74.

Mahon JE (2007) A Definition of Deceiving, *International Journal of Applied Philosophy*, 21(2), 181–194.

Maleki N et al (2024) AI Hallucinations: A Misnomer Worth Clarifying, arXiv:2401.06796v1.

Malouf C and White T (1953) Kutenai Calendar Records: A Study of Indian Record Keeping, *The Montana Magazine of History*, 3(2), 34–39.

Malvern SB (1995) Inventing "Child Art": Franz Cižek and Modernism, *British Journal of Aesthetics*, 35(3), 262–272.

Mandel GN (2011) To Promote the Creative Process: Intellectual Property Law and the Psychology of Creativity, *Notre Dame Law Review*, 86(5), 1999–2026.

Mangen A and Balsvik L (2016) Pen or Keyboard in Beginning Writing Instruction: Some Perspectives from Embodied Cognition, *Trends in Neuroscience and Education*, 5, 99–106.

Manger PR and Pettigrew JD (1995) Electroreception and the Feeding Behaviour of Platypus (*Ornithorhynchus anatinus: Monotremata: Mammalia*), *Philosophical Transactions: Biological Sciences*, 347(1322), 359–381.

Maran T (2017) *Mimicry and Meaning: Structure and Semiotics of Biological Mimicry*, Springer.

Marchesini R (2018/[2014]) Zoomimesis: Animal inspiration, Bussolini J (trans), in Bussolini J et al (eds) (2018), *The Philosophical Ethology of Roberto Marchesini*, Routledge, 179–201.

Margolis E and Laurence S (eds) (2015) *The Conceptual Mind: New Directions in the Study of Concepts*, MIT Press.

Margolis H (1993) *Paradigms and Barriers: How Habits of Mind Govern Scientific Beliefs*, University of Chicago Press.

Markl H (1985) Manipulation, Modulation, Information, Cognition: Some of the Riddles of Communication, *Fortschritte der Zoologie*, 31, 163–94.

Markus AF et al (2021) The Role of Explainability in Creating Trustworthy Artificial Intelligence for Health Care, *Journal of Biomedical Informatics*, 113, 103655.

Marlowe FW et al (2011) The 'Spiteful' Origins of Human Cooperation, *Proceedings of The Royal Society B*, 278, 2159–2164.

Marques MA (2021) Humour and politics: A discursive approach to humour, in Vanderheiden E and Mayer C-H (eds) (2021) *The Palgrave Handbook of Humour Research*, Palgrave Macmillan, 205–225.
Marsh LE et al (2019) Are You Watching Me? The Role of Audience and Object Novelty in Overimitation, *Journal of Experimental Child Psychology*, 180, 123–130.
Marshall A (2013/[1890]) *Principles of Economics*, Palgrave.
Marshall JAR and Reina A (2024) On Aims and Methods of Collective Animal Behaviour, *Animal Behaviour*, 210, 189–197.
Martin C (ed) (2009) *The Philosophy of Deception*, Oxford University Press.
Martins SB (2017) Passages: Ferreira Gullar, *ArtForum*, 55(8), 55.
Marx J (2004) Postcolonial literature and the Western literary canon, in Lazarus N (ed) (2004) *The Cambridge Companion to Postcolonial Literary Studies*, Cambridge University Press, 83–96.
Massumi B (2014) *What Animals Teach Us about Politics*, Duke University Press.
Matson WA (1976) *Sentience*, University of California Press.
Matthews D et al (2023) Using compulsory licences as a governance tool: the need for greater effectiveness and policy coherence, in Frankel S et al (eds) (2023) *Improving Intellectual Property*, Elgar Publishing, 61–74.
Matyja JR and Schiavio A (2013) Enactive Music Cognition, *Constructivist Foundations*, 8(3), 351–357.
Mautner M (2018) *Human Flourishing, Liberal Theory, and the Arts*, Routledge.
McClausland C (2014) The Five Freedoms of Animal Welfare are Rights, *Journal of Agricultural and Environmental Ethics*, 27, 649–662.
McClenachan L et al (2012) Extinction Risk and Bottlenecks in the Conservation of Charismatic Marine Species, *Conservation Letters*, 5(1), 73–80.
McCormick N (2023), Ed Sheeran's *Subtract* is a raw, powerful balm for suffering souls, *The Telegraph*, 5 May.
McCullough L (2012) Simone Weil's Phenomenology of the Body, *Comparative and Continental Philosophy*, 4(2) 195–218.
McFarland DT and Van Ness W (1987) Introduction, in Weil S (2010/[1987]) *Formative Writings, 1929–1941*, Routledge, 3–20.
McGetrick J and Range F (2018) Inequity Aversion in Dogs: A Review, *Learning & Behavior*, 46, 479–500.
McGhee PE (1982) Explaining the Evolutionary Significance of Intellectual Play: Are We Barking Up the Wrong Tree? *The Behavioral and Brain Sciences*, 5, 166–167.
McGill VJ (1966) Behaviorism and Phenomenology, *Philosophy and Phenomenological Research*, 26(4), 578–588.
McGrew WC (1992) *Chimpanzee Material Culture: Implications for Human Evolution*, Cambridge University Press.
McGrew WC (2009) Ten dispatches from the chimpanzee culture wars, plus postscript (Revisiting the Battlefronts), in Laland KN and Galef BG (eds) (2009) *The Question of Animal Culture*, Harvard University Press, 41–69.
McGrew WC and Marchant LF (1998) Chimpanzee Wears a Knotted Skin "Necklace," *Pan Africa News*, 5(1), 8–9.
McLaren RB (1993) The Dark Side of Creativity, *Creativity Research Journal*, 6, 137–144.

McMurtry TJ (2017) Has play changed? An essay comparing the communitarian and individualistic approaches to play and society, in Reid HL and Moore E (2017) *Reflecting on Modern Sport in Ancient Olympia*, Parnassos Press, 47–55.
Medawar P (1984) *The Limits of Science*, Oxford University Press.
Mehrkam LR and Wynne CDL (2021) Owner Attention Facilitates Social Play in Dog-Dog Dyads (*Canis lupus familiaris*): Evidence for an Interspecific Audience Effect, *Animal Cognition*, 24, 341–352.
Melillo ED (2014) Global Entomologies: Insects, Empires, and the "Synthetic Age" in World History, *Past & Present*, 223, 233–270.
Meling D (2021) Knowing Groundlessness: An Enactive Approach to a Shift From Cognition to Non-Dual Awareness, *Frontiers in Psychology*, 12, 696821.
Melitopoulos A and Lazzarato M (2012) Machinic Animism, *Deleuze Studies*, 6(2), 240–249.
Melnechuk T et al (1986) Round Table and Two Informal Presentations, Symposium on "Emotions and Psychopathology," Department of Psychology of Bowling Green State University, Ohio, 26–27 September, 1986, in Clynes M and Panksepp J (eds) (1988) *Emotions and Psychopathology*, Plenum Press, 279–308.
Meltzer F (1987) *Salome and the Dance of Writing: Portraits of Mimesis in Literature*, The University of Chicago Press.
Meltzer F (2001) The Hands of Simone Weil, *Critical Inquiry*, 27(4), 611–628.
Mendl M and Paul ES (2008) Do Animals Live in the Present? Current Evidence and Implications for Welfare. *Applied Animal Behaviour Science*, 113, 357–382.
Mengara O (2024) The Art of Deception: Robust Backdoor Attack Using Dynamic Stacking of Triggers, arXiv:2401.01537v1.
Merleau-Ponty M (1968/[1964]) *The Visible and the Invisible*, Lingis A (trans), Northwestern University Press.
Merleau-Ponty M (2003/[1995]) *Nature: Course Notes from the Collège de France*, D Séglard (comp), R Vallier (trans), Northwestern University Press.
Meske C et al (2022) Explainable Artificial Intelligence: Objectives, Stakeholders, and Future Research Opportunities, *Information Systems Management*, 39(1), 53–63.
Metz C (2022) AI is not sentient. Why do people say it is? *The New York Times*, 5 August (updated 22 June 2023).
Meurville M-P and LeBoeuf AC (2014) Trophallaxis: The Functions and Evolution of Social Fluid Exchange in Ant Colonies, *Myrmecological News*, 31, 1–30.
Meyer ED (2018) *Inner Animalities: Theology and the End of the Human*, Fordham University Press.
Michael M (2012) Anecdote, in Lury C and Wakeford N (eds) (2012) *Inventive Methods: The Happening of the Social*, Routledge, 25–35.
Michaelides-Nouaros G (1980) A New Evaluation of the Dialogue between Thrasymachus and Socrates, *Archives for Philosophy of Law and Social Philosophy*, 66(3), 329–345.
Michel AH (2023) Recalibrating assumptions on AI: Towards an evidence-based and inclusive AI policy discourse. Chatham House Research paper, 12 April.
Michel GF and Harkins DA (1985) Concordance of Handedness between Teacher and Student Facilitates Learning Manual Skills, *Journal of Human Evolution*, 14, 597–601.
Micheletta J et al (2015) Facial Expression Recognition in Crested Macaques (*Macaca nigra*) *Animal Cognition*, 18, 985–990.

Middelhoff F (2021) Thinking and Writing with Leaves: Poplar Sympoetics in Romanticism, *Green Letters: Studies in Ecocriticism*, 25(4), 356–376.

Midgley M (1998/[1983]) *Animals and Why They Matter*, The University of Georgia Press.

Mier T (2023) Ed Sheeran takes the stand in Marvin Gaye copyright trial, *Rolling Stone*, 25 April.

Mik E (2021) AI as a legal person? In Lee J-A et al (eds) (2021) *Artificial Intelligence and Intellectual Property*, Oxford University Press, 419–440.

Mikhalevich I and Powell R (2020) Minds without Spines: Evolutionary Inclusive Animal Ethics, *Animal Sentience*, 29(1), article 329.

Miles MC and Fuxjager MJ (2018) Animal Choreography of Song and Dance, *Animal Behaviour*, 140, 99–107.

Miletto Petrazzini ME and Wynne CDL (2016) What Counts for Dogs (*Canis lupus familiaris*) in a Quantity Discrimination Task? *Behavioural Processes*, 122, 90–97.

Milius S (2009) Dogs Strike over Unfair Treatment, *Science News*, 175(1), 13.

Millán-Zaibert E (2007) *Friedrich Schlegel and the Emergence of Romantic Philosophy*, SUNY Press.

Miller LJ (2017) Creating a Common Terminology for Play Behavior to Increase Cross-disciplinary Research, *Learning & Behavior*, 45, 330–334.

Miller LJ (2020) Behavioral Diversity as a Potential Indicator of Positive Animal Welfare, *Animals*, 10, 1211.

Miller P (2008) *The Power of Positive Dog Training*, Wiley.

Milton K (2002) *Loving Nature: Towards an Ecology of Emotion*, Routledge.

Miñarro M et al (2010) Role of Ants in Structuring the Aphid Community on an Apple, *Ecological Entomology*, 35(2), 206–215.

Minkowski E (2023/[1936]) *Vers une cosmologie: fragments philosophiques*, Éditions des compagnon d'humanité.

Minsky M (1988/[1986]), *The Society of Mind*, Simon & Schuster.

Mintline EM et al (2013) Play Behavior as an Indicator of Animal Welfare, *Applied Animal Behaviour Science*, 144(1–2), 22–30.

Miracchi L (2020) Updating the Frame Problem for AI Research, *Journal of Artificial Intelligence and Consciousness*, 7(2), 1–14.

Mitchell KS and Reiter-Palmon R (2023) Malevolent creativity: Personality, process, and the larger creativity field, in Kapoor H and Kaufman JC (eds) (2023) *Creativity and Morality*, Academic Press, 47–68.

Mitchell M (2020) On Crashing the Barrier of Meaning in Artificial Intelligence, *AI Magazine*, 41(2), 86–92.

Mitchell R and Singhorn K (2014) Why Do People Laugh during Dog-Human Play Interactions? *Anthrozoös*, 27(2), 235–250.

Mitchell RW (1986) A framework for discussing deception, in Mitchell RW and Thompson NS (eds) (1986) *Deception: Perspectives on Human and Nonhuman Deceit*, SUNY Press, 3–40.

Mitchell RW (1987) A comparative-development approach to understanding imitation, in Bateson P and Klopfer P (eds) (1987) *Perspectives in Ethology, Volume 7: Alternatives*, Plenum Press, 183–215.

Mitchell RW (2002) Kinesthetic-visual matching, imitation, and self-recognition, in Bekoff M et al (eds) (2002) *The Cognitive Animal: Empirical and Theoretical Perspectives on Animal Cognition*, MIT Press, 345–351.

Mitchell RW (2015) Creativity in the interaction: The case of dog-human play, in Kaufman AB and Kaufman JC (eds) (2015) *Animal Creativity and Innovation*, Elsevier-Academic Press, 31–42.
Mitchell RW (2017) Anecdote, in Vonk J and Shackelford TK (eds) (2017) *Encyclopedia of Animal Cognition and Behavior*, Springer, 259–265.
Mitchell RW and Thompson NS (eds) (1985) *Deception: Perspectives on Human and Nonhuman Deceit*, SUNY Press.
Mitchell RW et al (eds) (1997) *Anthropomorphism, Anecdotes, and Animals*, SUNY Press.
Mlot NJ et al (2011) Fire Ants Self-assemble into Waterproof Rafts to Survive Floods, *Proceedings of the National Academy of Sciences of the United States of America*, 108(19), 7669–7673.
Momigliano A (1993/[1971]) *The Development of Greek Biography*, Harvard University Press.
Mondémé C (2022) Why Study Turn-Taking Sequences in Interspecies Interactions? *Journal for the Theory of Social Behaviour*, 52(1), 67–85.
Mondémé C (2023) Sequence Organization in Human-animal Interaction, *Journal of Pragmatics*, 214, 73–88.
Mongillo P et al (2010) Selective Attention to Humans in Companion Dogs, *Canis familiaris*, *Animal Behaviour*, 80, 1057–1063.
Monmarché N et al (eds) (2010) *Artificial Ants*, Wiley.
Monro DB (1901) Relation of the Odyssey to the Iliad, in Monro DB (1901) *Homer's Odyssey: Books XIII-XXIV*, Clarendon Press, 324–339.
Monsó S and Osuna-Mascaró AJ (2020) Problems with Basing Insect Ethics on Individuals' Welfare, *Animal Welfare*, 29(8), article 337.
Moore A (2021) COVID vaccines: Why waiving patents won't fix global shortage, *The Conversation*, 4 May.
Moore JD and Swartout WR (1988) *Explanation in Expert Systems: A Survey*, No 228, Information Sciences Institute, University of Southern California.
Moore-Coyler R (2024) Claude 3 Opus has stunned AI researchers with its intellect and "self-awareness" – does this mean it can think for itself? *LiveScience*, 24 April.
Moravia A (1954) *Il disprezzo*, Bompiani.
Morawski S (1974) Expression, *The Journal of Aesthetic Education*, 8(2), 37–56.
Morell V (2016) Was Betty the crow a genius – or a robot? *Science*, 9 August.
Morgan CL (1894) *An Introduction to Comparative Psychology*, Walter Scott Ltd.
Morgan CL (1928) *Emergent Evolution*, Henry Holt & Company.
Morgan CL (1930) *The Animal Mind*, Edward Arnold.
Morice D (1988) *Wooden Nickel Art Project*, Happy Press.
Morice D (1997) Biographical entry, in Hedblad A (ed) (1997) *Something about the Author, Volume 93*, Gale, 140–142.
Morice D (2012) Interview, in Godstan D (2012) Interview with Dave Morice, *Pedagogical Arts*, 30 July.
Morice D and Hundreds of Co-authors (2009) *The Great American Fortune Cookie Novel: A Romance in Thousands of Fortunes*, Sackter House Media.
Morillo CR (1995) *Contingent Creatures: A Reward Event Theory of Motivation and Value*, Littlefield Adams.
Moro A et al (2023) Large Languages, Impossible Languages and Human Brains, *Cortext*, 167, 82–85.

Morris D (1962) *The Biology of Art*, Methuen & Co.
Morton ES et al (1978) On Bluebird 'Responses to Apparent Female Adultery, *The American Naturalis*, 112(987), 968–971.
Moscovice LR et al (2023) Spontaneous Helping in Pigs Is Mediated by Helper's Social Attention and Distress Signals of Individuals in Need, *Proceedings of the Royal Society B*, 290(2004), 20230665.
Mulhall S (2001) *Inheritance and Originality: Wittgenstein, Heidegger, Kierkegaard*, Clarendon Press.
Mullen RJ et al (2009) A Review of Ant Algorithms, *Expert Systems with Applications*, 36(6), 9608–9617.
Müller B (1997) Introduction, in Müller B (ed) (1997) *Parody: Dimensions and Perspectives*, Rodopi, 1–10.
Müller M and Wehner R (2010) Path Integration Provides a Scaffold for Landmark Learning in Desert Ants, *Current Biology*, 20, 1368–1371.
Muller SM (2022) Monkey Business in a Kangaroo Court: Reimagining *Naruto v Slater* as a Litigious Event, *Rhetoric & Public Affairs*, 25(1), 31–59.
Mulvey L (2012) *Le Mépris* (Jean-Luc Godard 1963) and its story of cinema: "A fabric of quotations," in MacCabe C and Mulvey L (eds) (2012) *Godard's Contempt: Essays from the London Consortium*, Wiley-Blackwell, 225–237.
Murphy M (2019) *Enacting Lecoq: Movement in Theatre, Cognition, and Life*, Springer Verlag. See further Lecoq J (1997/[2020]) *The Moving Body (Le Corps Poétique)*, D Bradby (trans), 3rd ed, Methuen.
Nad'o L and Kaňuch P (2015) Swarming Behaviour Associated with Group Cohesion in Tree-Dwelling Bats, *Behavioural Processes*, 120, 30–86.
Nadel J (2002) Imitation and imitation recognition: Functional use in preverbal infants and nonverbal children with autism, in Meltzoff AN and Prinz W (eds) (2002) *The Imitative Mind: Development, Evolution, and Brain Bases*, Cambridge University Press, 42–62.
Nagel T (1974) What Is It Like To Be A Bat? *The Philosophical Review*, 83(4), 435–450.
Nakarmi PK et al (2011) *CPU Scavenging through the Swarm Intelligence of Autonomous Agents*, Lambert Academic Publishing.
Nancy J-L (2002/[1997]) *Hegel: The Restlessness of the Negative*, Smith J and Miller S (trans), University of Minnesota Press.
Naqvi Z (2020) Artificial Intelligence, Copyright, and Copyright Infringement, *Marquette Intellectual Property Law Review*, 24(1), 15–51.
Nascimento DL et al (2024) The Underestimated Role of Leaf-cutting Ants in Soil and Geomorphological Development in Neotropical America, *Earth-Science Reviews*, 248, 104650.
Negus K and Pickering M (2004) *Creativity, Communication and Cultural Value*, SAGE.
Nelson XJ et al (2023) Joyful by Nature: Approaches to Investigation the Evolution and Function of Joy in Non-Human Animals, *Biological Reviews*, 98(5), 1548–1563.
Ness J et al (2009) Ants as mutualists, in Lach L et al (ed) (2009) *Ant Ecology*, 97–114.
Netanel NW (1996) Copyright and a Democratic Civil Society, *The Yale Law Journal*, 106(2), 283–387.

Newen A et al (2018) 4E cognition: Historical roots, key concepts, and central issues, in Newen A et al (eds) (2018) *The Oxford Handbook of 4E Cognition*, Oxford University Press, 3–15.

Newman L (2016) Cogito Ergo Sum, in Nolan L (ed) (2016) *The Cambridge Descartes Lexicon*, Cambridge University Press, 128–135.

Newport C (2021) Abstract Concept Learning in Fish, *Current Opinion in Behavioral Sciences*, 37, 56–62.

Ng Y-K (2022) *Happiness: Concept, Measurement and Promotion*, Springer.

Nguyen D et al (2021) Positive Affect: Nature and Brain Bases of Liking and Wanting, *Current Opinion in Behavioral Sciences*, 39, 72–78.

Nichols R (2014) Re-evaluating the Effects of the 1755 Lisbon Earthquake on Eighteenth-Century Minds: How Cognitive Science of Religion Improves Intellectual History with Hypothesis Testing Methods, *Journal of the American Academy of Religion*, 82(4), 970–1009.

Nicholson A (2014) *Why Homer Matters*, Henry Holt & Company.

Nieder A (2002) Seeing More Than Meets the Eye: Processing of Illusory Contours in Animals, *Journal of Comparative Physiology A*, 188, 249–260.

Nielsen C et al (2010) Ants Defend Aphids against Lethal Disease, *Biology Letters*, 6(2), 205–208.

Nishida T, Matsusaka T, and McGrew WC (2009) Emergence, Propagation or Disappearance of Novel Behavioral Patterns in the Habituated Chimpanzees of Mahale: A Review, *Primates*, 50, 23–36.

Nityananda V (2016) Attention-like Processes in Insects, *Proceedings: Biological Sciences*, 283(1842), 1–9.

North G (2015) The Biology of Fun and the Fun of Biology, *Current Biology*, 25(1), R1–R2.

Novalis (1903) *The Disciples at Saïs and Other Fragments*, FVMT and JCB (trans), Methuen & Co, 81.

Novalis (2011/[1791–1801]) Aphorisms and fragments, A Gelley (trans), in Willson AL (ed) (2011) *German Romantic Criticism: Novalis, Schlegel, Schleiermacher, and others*, Continuum, 62–83.

Nowroozi E et al (2024) Federated Learning Under Attack: Exposing Vulnerabilities Through Data Poisoning Attacks in Computer Networks, arXiv:2403.02983v1.

Nusbaum EC and Silvia PJ (2011) Are Intelligence and Creativity Really so Different? Fluid Intelligence, Executive Processes, and Strategy Use in Divergent Thinking, *Intelligence*, 39(1), 36–45.

Nussbaum MC (2023) *Justice for Animals: Our Collective Responsibility*, Simon & Schuster.

Nye A (1994) *Philosophia: The Thought of Rosa Luxemburg, Simone Weil, and Hannah Arendt*, Routledge.

O'Hear A (1995) Art and Technology: An Old Tension, *Royal Institute of Philosophy Supplements*, 38, 143–158.

O'Heare J (2017) *Aggressive Behavior in Dogs*, 3rd ed, BehaveTech Publishing.

O'Loughlin M (2006) *Embodiment and Education: Exploring Creatural Existence*, Springer.

Oberhauser FB et al (2020) Ants Resort to Heuristics When Facing Relational-Learning Tasks They Cannot Solve, *Proceedings of the Royal Society B*, 287(1932), 1–9.

Oberliessen L et al (2016) Inequity Aversion in Rats, *Rattus Norvegicus*, *Animal Behaviour*, 115, 157–166.
Ochse R (1990) *Before the Gates of Genius: The Determinants of Creative Genius*, Cambridge University Press.
Offenhuber D (2010) Visual Anecdote, *Leonardo*, 43(4), 367–374.
Ohkita M et al (2016) Owners' Direct Gazes Increase Dogs' Attention-getting Behaviors, *Behavioural Processes*, 125, 96–100.
Ohno T and Miyatake T (2007) Drop or Fly? Negative Genetic Correlation between Death-Feigning Intensity and Flying Ability as Alternative Anti-Predator Strategies, *Proceedings of the Royal Society B*, 274, 555–560.
Okediji R (2022) Is the Public Domain Just? Biblical Stewardship and Legal Protection for Traditional Knowledge Assets, *Columbia Journal of Law & Arts*, 45(4), 461–523.
Olcowicz S et al (2016) Birds Have Primate-like Numbers of Neurons in the Forebrain, *Proceedings of the National Academy of Sciences of the United States of America*, 113(26), 7255–7260.
Oliver K (2009) Duplicity makes the man: Or, can animals lie? In Martin C (ed) (2009) *The Philosophy of Deception*, Oxford University Press, 104–117.
Olkowicz S et al (2016) Birds Have Primate-like Numbers of Neurons in the Forebrain, *Proceedings of the National Academy of Sciences of the United States (PNAS)* 113(26), 7255–7260.
Olney JJ et al (2018) Current Perspectives on Incentive Salience and Applications to Clinical Disorders, *Current Opinion in Behavioral Sciences*, 22, 59–69.
Onions CT (ed) (1966) *Oxford Dictionary of English Etymology*, Oxford University Press.
Orth EW (2003) *Natur und Geist* in der Husserlschen Phänomenologie, *Phänomenologische Forschungen*, 23–37.
Osuna-Mascaró AJ et al (2023) Flexible Tool Set Transport in Goffin's Cockatoos, *Current Biology*, 33, 849–857.
Overall KL (2007) Why Electric Shock Is Not Behavior Modification, *Journal of Veterinary Behavior*, 2, 1–4.
Overall KL (2011) That Dog Is Smarter Than You Know: Advances in Understanding Canine Learning, Memory, and Cognition, *Topics in Companion Animal Medicine*, 26(1), 2–9.
Overall KL (2018) Beware the Misdirection Offense: The Truth about Shock, Aversives and Punishment, *Journal of Veterinary Behavior*, 25, iv–vi.
Oyston JW (2022) Molecular Phylogenies Map to Biogeography Better Than Morphological Ones, *Communications Biology*, 5, article 521.
Padberg B (2020) The Global Diversity of Institutes for Advanced Study, *Sociologica*, 14(1), 9839, 119–161.
Palace VM (2019) What If Artificial Intelligence Wrote This: Artificial Intelligence and Copyright Law, *Florida Law Review*, 71(1), 217–242.
Palmer C et al (2020) Exploring Dark Creativity: The Role of Power in an Unethical Marketing Task, *Economic Research*, 33(1), 145–159.
Panksepp J (1998) *Affective Neuroscience: The Foundations of Human and Animal Emotions*, Oxford University Press.
Panksepp J (2000) The Riddle of Laughter: Neural and Psychoevolutionary Underpinnings of Joy, *Current Directions in Psychological Science*, 9(6), 183–186.

Panksepp J (2005) On the Embodied Neural Nature of Core Emotional Affects, *Journal of Consciousness Studies*, 12(8–10), 158–184.
Panksepp J (2007) Neuroevolutionary Sources of Laughter and Social Joy: Modeling Primal Human Laughter in Laboratory Rats, *Behavioural Brain Research*, 182, 231–244.
Panksepp J and Biven L (2012) *The Archaeology of Mind: Neuroevolutionary Origins of Human Emotions*, WW Norton & Company.
Panksepp J and Burgdorf J (2003) "Laughing" Rats and the Evolutionary Antecedents of Human Joy? *Physiology and Behavior*, 79, 533–547.
Panksepp J and Wilson CG (2016) Brain SEEKING circuitry in neuroeconomics, in Reuter M and Montag C (eds) (2016), *Neuroeconomics*, Springer, 231–252.
Paolucci C (2021) *Cognitive Semiotics: Integrating Signs, Minds, Meaning and Cognition*, Springer.
Papcharissi Z (ed) (2019) *A Networked Self and Human Augmentics, Artificial Intelligence, Sentience*, Routledge.
Pargendler M (2012) The Rise and Decline of Legal Families, *The American Journal of Comparative Law*, 60(4), 1043–1074.
Park PS et al (2024) AI Deception: A Survey of Examples, Risks, and Potential Solutions, *Patterns*, 5(5), 100988.
Parker F (1962) Abraham Flexner, 1866–1959, *History of Education Quarterly*, 2(4), 199–209.
Parker ST and Gibson KR (eds) (1990) *"Language" and Intelligence in Monkeys and Apes: Comparative Developmental Perspectives*, Cambridge University Press.
Parsons T (1968/[1937]) *The Structure of Social Action: Volume II, Weber*, The Free Press.
Paterson TA and Welbourne TM (2019) I Am Therefore I Own: Implications of Organization-based Identity for Employee Stock Ownership, *Human Resource Management*, 59(2), 175–183.
Patry WF (2024) *Patry on Fair Use*, 2024 ed, Thomson Reuters.
Pavia W (2023) Ed Sheeran wins Marvin Gaye copyright lawsuit over 1973 hit, *The Times*, 4 May.
Pavis M (2021) Rebalancing Our Regulatory Response to Deepfakes with Performers' Rights, *Convergence*, 27(4), 974–998.
Peciña S et al (2003) Hyperdopaminergic Mutant Mice Have Higher "Wanting" But Not "Liking" for Sweet Rewards, *The Journal of Neuroscience*, 23(28), 9395–9402.
Pedoe D (1976/[1983]) *Geometry and the Visual Arts*, Dover Publications.
Pelacho M et al (2021) Science as a commons: Improving the governance of knowledge through citizen science, in Vohland K et al (eds) (2021) *The Science of Citizen Science*, Springer, 57–78.
Pence DE (2020) How Comparative Psychology Lost Its Soul: Psychical Research and the New Science of Animal Behavior, *Studies in History and Philosophy of Biology Biomedical Science*, 62, 101275.
Penguins (2004) *The Laws*, Saunders TJ (trans), Penguin.
Pérez Perozo VM (1946), Fables and Fable-Writers, *Books Abroad*, 20(4), 363–367.
Perkins D (2003) *Romanticism and Animal Rights*, Cambridge University Press.

Perry CJ and Baciadonna L (2017) Studying Emotion in Invertebrates: What Has Been Done, What Can Be Measured and What They Can Provide, *Journal of Experimental Biology*, 220, 3856–3868.

Peters G (2004) Dissymmetry and Height: Rhetoric, Irony and Pedagogy in the Thought of Husserl, Blanchot and Levinas, *Human Studies*, 27, 187–206.

Peterson AJ (2024) AI and the Problem of Knowledge Collapse, arXiv2404.03502.

Petit O and Bon R (2010) Decision-Making Processes: The Case of Collective Movements, *Behavioural Processes*, 84, 635–647.

Petridis A (2023) Ed Sheeran: *Subtract* review – easily his best ever album, *The Guardian*, 5 May.

Petter M et al (2009) Can Dogs (*Canis familiaris*) Detect Human Deception? *Behavioural Processes*, 82, 109–118.

Pham MHT (2017) Racial Plagiarism and Fashion, *QED: A Journal in GLBTQ Worldmaking*, 4(3), 67–80.

Phiddian R (1997) Are Parody and Deconstruction Secretly the Same Thing? *New Literary History*, 28(4), 673–696.

Piaget (1932) *The Moral Judgment of the Child*, Routledge & Kegan Paul.

Piazza J et al (2014) Cruel Nature: Harmfulness as an Important, Overlooked Dimension in Judgments of Moral Standing, *Cognition*, 131, 108–124.

Pick (2018) Vulnerability, in Gruen L (ed) (2018) *Critical Terms for Animal Studies*, University of Chicago Press, 410–423.

Pick A (2012) Turning to Animals Between Love and Law, *New Formations*, 2012(76), 68–85.

Pick A (2013) 'Some Small Discrepancy': Jean-Christophe Bailly's Creaturely Ontology, *Journal of Animal Ethics*, 3(2), 163–174.

Pika S et al (2018) Taking Turns: Bridging the Gap between Human and Animal Communication, *Proceedings of the Royal Society B*, 285, 20180598.

Pirruccello A (2002) Making the World My Body: Simone Weil and Somatic Practice, *Philosophy East and West*, 52(4), 479–497.

Plato (1951) *The Symposium*, Hamilton W (trans), Penguin.

Plato (1987) *The Republic*, Lee D (trans), 2nd ed (rev), Penguin.

Plato (1997) *The Laws*, in Cooper JM and Hutchinson DS (eds) *Plato: Complete Works*, Hackett.

Plato (2008) *Timaeus and Critias*, Lee D and Johanssen TK (trans), Penguin.

Plautus (2006) *Asinaria*, J Henderson (trans), University of Wisconsin Press.

Plotnik JM et al (2019) Elephants Have a Nose for Quantity, *Proceedings of the National Academy of Sciences of the United States (PNAS)*, 116(25), 12566–12571.

Poe EA (1845) The Purloined letter, in Poe EA (1988) *The Complete Illustrated Stories and Poems of Edgar Allan Poe*, Chancellor Press, 319–333.

Poincaré H (1910) Mathematical Creation, *The Monist*, 20(3), 321–335.

Poole A (1992) War and Grace: The Force of Simone Weil on Homer, *Arion: A Journal of Humanities and the Classics*, 2(1), 1–15.

Popova YB (2014) Narrativity and Enaction: The Social Nature of Literary Narrative Understanding, *Frontiers in Psychology*, 5, article 895.

Postoutenko K (2020) Preliminary typology of comparative utterances: A tree and some binaries, in Epple A et al (eds) (2020) *Practices of Comparing: Towards a New Understanding of a Fundamental Human Practice*, Verlag-Bielefeld University Press, 39–86.

Potocnik M (2024) Exposing gender bias in intellectual property law, in Jamar SD and Mtima L (eds) (2024) *Handbook of Intellectual Property and Social Justice: Access, Inclusion, Empowerment*, Cambridge University Press, 473–496.
Pound R (1912) The Scope and Purpose of Sociological Jurisprudence: III Sociological Jurisprudence, *Harvard Law Review*, 25(6), 489–516.
Povinelli DJ (2003) *Folk Physics for Apes: The Chimpanzee's Theory of How the World Works*, Oxford University Press.
Prager P (2013) Play and the Avant-Garde: Aren't We All a Little Dada? *American Journal of Play*, 5(2), 239–256.
Preiss DD et al (2020) *Creativity and the Wandering Mind: Spontaneous and Controlled Cognition*, Academic Press.
Premack D (1988) 'Does the chimpanzee have a theory of mind?' Revisited, in Byrne RW and Whiten A (eds) (1988) *Machiavellian Intelligence: Social Expertise and the Evolution of Intellect in Monkeys, Apes, and Humans*, Oxford University Press, 160–179.
Premack D and Woodruff G (1978) Does the Chimpanzee Have a Theory of Mind? *Behavioral & Brain Sciences*, 1(4), 515–526.
Preston E (2017) Sad "pigs" have been filmed apparently mourning a dead friend, *New Scientist*, 13 December.
Pretz K (2021) Stop Calling everything AI, machine-learning Pioneer says, *IEEE Spectrum*, 31 March.
Pritchard D et al (1972) Effects of Perceptions of Equity and Inequity on Worker Performance and Satisfaction, *Journal of Applied Psychology*, 56, 75–94.
Protzko J et al (2016) Believing There Is No Free Will Corrupts Intuitive Cooperation, *Cognition*, 151, 6–9.
Przytycki JH (1995) *Knots: A Combinatorial Approach to Knot Theory*, ICTP.
Puiu T (2021) Cats love to sit in boxes. Even invisible ones, *ZME Science*, 10 May.
Quaquebeke N van and Gerpott FH (2023) The Now, New, and Next of Digital Leadership: How Artificial Intelligence (AI) Will Take Over and Change Leadership as We Know It, *Journal of Leadership & Organizational Studies*, 30(3), 265–275.
Quinn S et al (2018) The Relationship between Symbolic Play and Language Acquisition: A Meta-analytic Review, *Development Review*, 49, 121–135.
Radder H (1993) Science, Realization and Reality: The Fundamental Issues, *Studies in the History and Philosophy of Science*, 24(3), 327–349.
Rahn J (2004) The Swerve and the Flow: Music's Relationship to Mathematics, *Perspectives of New Music*, 42(1), 130–148.
Ramage CJ (1922) Roman Law, *The Virginia Law Register*, 7(12) 881–886.
Ramanathan G (2020) *Kathleen Collins: The Black Essai Film*, Edinburgh University Press.
Ramsay MS and Teichroeb JA (2019) Anecdotes in Primatology: Temporal Trends, Anthropocentrism, and Hierarchies of Knowledge, *American Anthropologist*, 121(3), 680–693.
Rancière J (1994/[1992]) *The Names of History*, Melehy H (trans), University of Minnesota Press.
Range F et al (2009) The Absence of Reward Induces Inequity Aversion in Dogs, *Proceedings of the National Academy of Sciences of the United States (PNAS)*, 106(1), 340–345.

Range F et al (2011) Dogs Are Able to Solve a Means-end Task, *Animal Cognition*, 14, 575–583.
Ravignani A (2019) Rhythm and Synchrony in Animal Movement and Communication, *Current Zoology*, 65(1), 77–81.
Ravignani A et al (2019) Interactive Rhythms across Species: The Evolutionary Biology of Animal Chorusing and Turn-Taking, *Annals of the New York Academy of Sciences*, 1453, 12–21.
Ruyer R (2016/[1952]) *Neofinalism*, Edlebi A (trans), University of Minnesota Press.
Reed C (2024) *AI Fairness and Beyond*, Bloomsbury.
Rees A (2001) Anthropomorphism, Anthropocentrism, and Anecdote: Primatologists on Primatology, *Science, Technology, and Human Values*, 26(2), 227–247.
Rehn A and Cock C de (2009) Deconstructing creativity, in Rickards T et al (eds) (2009) *The Routledge Companion to Creativity*, Routledge, 222–231.
Reinhold AS et al (2019) Behavioral and Neural Correlates of Hide-and-seek in Rats, *Science*, 365(6458), 1180–1183.
Reznikova Z (2018) Ants – individual and social cognition, in Bueno-Guerra N and Amici F (eds) (2018) *Field and Laboratory Methods in Animal Cognition*, Cambridge University Press, 8–30.
Reznikova Z and Ryabko B (2011) Numerical Competence in Animals, with an Insight from Ants, *Behaviour*, 148(4), 405–434.
Ribeiro MT et al (2016) Why Should I Trust You? Explaining the Predictions of Any Classifier, *ArXiv*, 1602, 04938v3.
Richards DG (2002) The Ideology of Intellectual Property Rights in the International Economy, *Review of Social Economy*, 60(4), 521–541.
Richter A et al (2019) Storytelling for Narrative Approaches in Citizen Science: Towards a Generalized Model, *Journal of Science Communication*, 18(6), A02.
Ricketson S (1992) People or Machines: The Berne Convention and the Changing Concept of Authorship, *Columbia-VLA Journal of Law & the Arts*, 16(1), 1–38.
Rickles D (2014) *A Brief History of String Theory*, Springer.
Ricoeur P (1991/[1986]) *From Text to Action: Essays in Hermeneutics, II*, Blamey K and Thompson JB (trans), Northwestern University Press.
Rigby K (2020) *Reclaiming Romanticism: Towards an Ecopoetics of Decolonization*, Bloomsbury.
Risi V de (2007) *Geometry and Monadology: Leibniz's Analysis Situs and Philosophy of Space*, Springer.
Ristau C (1991a) Aspects of the cognitive ethology of an injury-feigning bird, the piping plover, in Ristau C (ed) (1991) *Cognitive Ethology: The Minds of Other Animals, Essays in Honor of Donald R Griffin*, Psychology Press, 91–126.
Ristau C (ed) (1991b) *Cognitive Ethology: The Minds of Other Animals, Essays in Honor of Donald R Griffin*, Psychology Press.
Ristau CA (1988) Deception: A Need for Theory and Ethology, *Behavioral and Brain Sciences*, 11(2), 262–263.
Riters LV et al (2019) Song Practice as a Rewarding form of Play in Songbirds, *Behavioural Processes*, 163, 91–98.
Rizzolatti G and Arbib MA (1998) Language within Our Grasp, *Trends in Neurosciences*, 21, 188–194.
Robinson EJG (2014) Polydomy: The Organisation and Adaptive Function of Complex Next System in Ants, *Current Opinion in Insect Science*, 5, 37–43.

Robinson J (2024) Are we rushing ahead with AI in the lab? *Chemistry World*, 2 May.
Robinson ME (1902) Originality, *International Journal of Ethics*, 12(4), 417–437.
Rogers CR (1954) Toward a Theory of Creativity, *ETC: A Review of General Semantics*, 11(4), 249–260.
Rogers CR (1967/[2020]) *On Becoming a Person*, Robinson.
Rogers SM and Simpson SJ (2014) Thanatosis, *Current Biology*, 24(21), R1031–R1033.
Rognstad O-A (2018) *Property Aspects in Intellectual Property*, Cambridge University Press.
Rollin BE (2000) Scientific Ideology, Anthropomorphism, Anecdote, and Ethics, *New Ideas in Psychology*, 18, 109–118.
Romanes GJ (1885) *Mental Evolution in Animals*, Kegan Paul, Trench, & Co.
Romanes GJ (1892) *Animal Intelligence*, D Appleton and Company.
Rooijen J van (2010) Do Dogs and Bees Possess a "Theory of Mind"? *Animal Behaviour*, 79, e7–e8.
Rooney N et al (2000) A Comparison of Dog-Dog and Dog-Human Play Behaviour. *Applied Animal Behaviour Science*, 66, 235–224.
Rooney N et al (2002) An Experimental Study of the Effects of Play Upon the Dog Human Relationship. *Applied Animal Behaviour Science*, 75, 161–176.
Rooney NJ and Bradshaw JWS (2006) Social Cognition in the Domestic Dog: Behaviour of Spectators towards Participants in Interspecific Games. *Animal Behaviour*, 72, 343–352.
Rose MA (1979) *Parody//Meta-Fiction: An Analysis of Parody as a Critical Mirror to the Writing and Perception of Fiction*, Croom Helm.
Rose MA (1993) *Parody: Ancient, Modern, and Post-Modern*, Cambridge University Press.
Rose MA (2011) *Pictorial Irony, Parody, and Pastiche: Comic Interpictoriality in the Arts of the 19th and 20th Centuries*, Aisthesis Verlag.
Rossi Federica (2023) The Failed Amnesty of the 'Years of Lead' in Italy: Continuity and Transformations between (De)politicization and Punitiveness, *European Journal of Criminology*, 20(2), 381–400.
Rossi Francesca (2019) Building Trust in Artificial Intelligence, *Journal of International Affairs*, 72(1), 127–134.
Rota G-C (1985) The Barrier of Meaning, *Letters in Mathematical Physics*, 10, 97–99.
Roughton A et al (2022), *Roughton, Johnson, and Cook on Patents*, 5th ed, Butterworths.
Rowe AK et al (2018) Collective Decision Making in Tibetan Macaques: How Followers Affect the Rules and Speed of Group Movement, *Animal Behaviour*, 146, 51–61.
Rozelle-Stone AR (2020) Simone Weil, Sarah Ahmed, and a politics of hap, in Bourgault S and Daigle J (eds) (2020) *Simone Weil, Beyond Ideology?* Palgrave Macmillan, 61–81.
Rudzite L (2022) Algorithmic Explainability and the Sufficient-Disclosure Requirement under the European Patent Convention, *Juridica International*, 31, 125–135.
Ruggieri M (2023) Ed Sheeran drowns in grief, then shoots up for air in profound new album *Subtract*, *USA Today*, 5 May.

Rumbaugh DA et al (2014) Language: Nonhuman Animals, *Reference Module in Biomedical Research*, Elsevier. doi:10.1016/B978-0-12-801238-3.05413-1

Runco MA and Jaeger GJ (2012) The Standard Definition of Creativity, *Creativity Research Journal*, 24(1), 92–96.

Ruskin J (1851) *The Stones of Venice, Volumes I and II*, John W Lovell.

Russ SW (2020) Mind wandering, fantasy, and pretend play: A natural combination, in Preiss DD et al (2020) *Creativity and the Wandering Mind: Spontaneous and Controlled Cognition*, Academic Press.

Russell S and Norvig P (2016) *Artificial Intelligence: A Modern Approach*, 3rd ed, Pearson.

Russell W et al (eds) (2018) *The Philosophy of Play as Life*, Routledge.

Russell YI (2016) Reciprocity and Reputation: A Review of Direct and Indirect Social Information Gathering, *The Journal of Mind and Behavior*, 37(3–4), 247–270.

Russon AE et al (1998) The comparative evolution of imitation, in Langer J and Killen M (eds) (2014/[1998]) *Piaget, Evolution, and Development*, Psychology Press, 103–143.

Rutz C and Webster MM (2021) *Ethology* Adopts the STRANGE Framework for Animal Behaviour Research, to Improve Reporting Standards, *Ethology*, 127(2), 99–101.

Ruxton GD et al (2018/[2004]) *Avoiding Attack: The Evolutionary Ecology of Crypsis, Warning Signals and Mimicry*, 2nd ed, Oxford University Press.

Ryall E et al (eds) (2013) *The Philosophy of Play*, Routledge.

Sabattini M (2019) *Zhu Guangaian and Benedetto Croce on Aesthetic Thought*, Brill.

Sachs D (1963) A Fallacy in Plato's Republic, *Philosophical Review*, 72(2), 141–158.

Sadler S (1999/[1998]) *The Situationist City*, MIT Press.

Sakaguchi K et al (2020) WinoGrande: An Adversarial Winograd Schema Challenge at Scale, *Proceedings of the AAAI Conference on Artificial Intelligence*, 34(5): AAAI Technical Tracks, 5, 8732–8740.

Samuel AL (1962) Artificial Intelligence: A Frontier of Automation, *The Annals of the American Academy of Political and Social Science*, 340, 10–20.

Samuelson P (1985) Allocating Ownership Rights in Computer-Generated Works, *University of Pittsburgh Law Review*, 47, 1185–1228.

San-Galli A and Bouret S (2015) Assessing Value Representation in Animals, *Journal of Physiology-Paris*, 109, 64–69.

Santos PE et al (2019) The Knowledge of Knots: An Interdisciplinary Literature Review, *Spatial Cognition & Computation*, 19(4), 334–358.

Sanz R (2019) Consciousness, Engineering, and Anthropomorphism, *APA Newsletter on Philosophy and Computers*, 19(1), 12–18.

Scaltsas T (1993) Fairness in Socratic Justice: 'Republic' I, *Proceedings of the Aristotelian Society*, 93, 247–262.

Schank JC et al (2023) Information and the *Umwelt*: A Theoretical Framework for the Evolution of Play, *Neuroscience and Biobehavioral Reviews*, 153, 105349.

Scharping N (2023) Citizen science observations are showing up in dozens of published research papers, *Discover*, 19 May.

Scheers P (2007) Towards a metaxological hermeneutics of plants and animals, in Kelly TAF (ed) (2007) *Between System and Poetics: William Desmond and Philosophy after Dialectic*, Routledge, 279–292.

Schiavio A and Høffding S (2015) Playing together without Communicating? A Pre-Reflective and Enactive Account of Joint Musical Performance, *Musicae Scientiae*, 19(4), 366–388.
Schlegel F (1800) On incomprehensibility, Firchow P (trans), in Bernstein JM (ed) (2003) *Classic and Romantic German Aesthetics*, Cambridge University Press, 297–307.
Schlegel F (1849) *The Aesthetic and Miscellaneous Works of Frederick von Schlegel*, Millington EJ (trans), Henry G Bohn.
Schlegel F (1968) *Dialogue on Poetry and Literary Aphorisms*, Behler E and Struc R (trans), Pennsylvania State University Press.
Schlegel F (1991/[1798–1800]) *Philosophical Fragments*, Firchow P (trans), University of Minnesota Press.
Schleidt WM and Shalter MD (2003) Co-Evolution of Humans and Canids – An Alternative View of Dog Domestication: Homo Homini Lupus? *Evolution and Cognition*, 9(1), 57–71.
Schmelz M et al (2011) Chimpanzees Know That Others Make Inferences, *Proceedings of the National Academy of Sciences of the United States (PNAS)*, 108(7), 3077–3079.
Schmitt A and Grammer K (1997) in Whiten A and Byrne RW (eds) (1997) *Machiavellian Intelligence II: Extensions and Evaluations*, Oxford University Press, 86–111.
Schöner G (2014) Embodied communication: Looking for systems that mean what they say, *Robohub*, 14 March.
Schopenhauer A (1903) *On The Fourfold Root of the Principle of Sufficient Reason, and On The Will in Nature: Two Essays by Arthur Schopenhauer*, K Hillebrand (trans), Rev ed, George Bell and Sons.
Schroeder T (2004) *Three Faces of Desire*, Oxford University Press.
Schyff D van der (2015) Music as a Manifestation of Life: Exploring Enactivism and the 'Eastern Perspective' for Music Education, *Frontiers in Psychology*, 6, article 345.
Scott K (2018) *Becoming Property: Art, Theory and Law in Early Modern France*, Yale University Press.
Seabright P (2010) *The Company of Strangers: A Natural History of Economic Life*, Princeton University Press.
Sebeok TA (1979) *The Sign and Its Masters*, University of Texas Press.
Sebeok TA (1981) *The Play of Musement*, Indiana University Press.
Sebeok TA (1986) *I Think I Am A Verb: More Contributions to the Doctrine of Signs*, Plenum Press.
Sebo J (2023) The Rebugnant Conclusion: Utilitarianism, Insects, Microbes, and AI Systems, *Ethics, Policy & Environment*, 26(2), 249–264.
Segundo-Ortin M and Calvo P (2019) Are Plants Cognitive? A Reply to Adams, *Studies in History and Philosophy of Science*, 73, 64–71.
Seligman MEP et al (1971) Unpredictable and uncontrollable aversive events, in Brush FR (ed) (1971) *Aversive Conditioning and Learning*, Academic Press, 347–400.
Seligman MEP (1972) Learned Helplessness, *Annual Review of Medicine*, 23, 407–412.
Serjeantson RW (2001) The Passions and Animal Language, 1540–1700, *Journal of the History of Ideas*, 62(3), 425–444.

Serres M (2008/[1985]) *The Five Senses: A Philosophy of Mingled Bodies*, Sankey M and Cowley P (trans), Continuum.
Serres M (2018/[2003]) *The Incandescent*, Burks R (trans), Bloomsbury.
Sevillano V (2020) Group Stereotypes: Human and Nonhuman, *Animal Sentience*, 27(15), 298.
Shaffi S (2023) 'It's the opposite of art': Why illustrators are furious about AI, *The Guardian*, 23 January.
Shakespeare W ([2004/1598]), Love's labour's lost, in Shakespeare W (2004) *The Complete Works of Shakespeare*, Bevington W (ed), 5th ed, Pearson Longman, 34–74.
Shanahan M (1997) *Solving the Frame Problem: A Mathematical Investigation of the Common Sense Law of Inertia*, Massachusetts Institute of Technology Press.
Shapiro D (2020) Does artificial intelligence design new drugs or discover them? *Forbes*, 26 November.
Shapiro HA (2019) Like mother, like son? Hermes and Maia in text and image, in Miller JF and Strauss Clay J (eds) (2019) *Tracking Hermes, Pursuing Mercury*, Oxford University Press, 13–29.
Shaviro S (2014) Thinking Blind, *Journal of the Fantastic in the Arts*, 25(2–3), 314–331.
Sheak WH (1917) Disposition and Intelligence of the Chimpanzee, *Proceedings of the Indiana Academy of Science*, 27, 301–310.
Sheak WH (1922) Disposition and Intelligence of the Orang-Utan, *Journal of Mammalogy*, 3(1), 47–51.
Sheak WH (1923) Anthropoid Apes I Have Known, *Natural History*, 23, 44–55.
Shen K (2019) (as Anson KS) Tactical Ant Media: Amplifying the Invertebrate Aesthetic of Ants Using Transversality as an Artistic Process, *Society & Animals*, 27(7) 678–696.
Shen K (2021) Turning around and upside down: The nomadic rhythms of rain ants in Sarayaku, in Lushetich N and Campbell I (eds) (2021) *Distributed Perception: Resonances and Axiologies*, Routledge, 31–48.
Shettleworth S (2010) *Cognition, Evolution, and Behavior*, Oxford University Press.
Shettleworth SJ (2012) Do Animals Have Insight, and What Is Insight Anyway? *Canadian Journal of Experimental Psychology*, 66(4), 217–226.
Shewan A (1913) Does the *Odyssey* imitate the *Iliad*? *The Classical Quarterly*, 7(4), 234–242.
Shewmon DA (1985) The Metaphysics of Brain Death, Persistent Vegetative State and Dementia, *Thomist*, 49(1), 24–80.
Shewmon DA (2006) "Brain Body" disconnection: Implications for the theoretical basis of "Brain Death," in Mattei R de (ed) *Finis Vitae: Is Brain Death Still Life*, Consiglio Nazionale delle Ricerche, 211–250.
Shik JZ et al (2021) Nutritional Niches Reveal Fundamental Domestical Trade-Offs in Fungus-Farming Ants, *Nature: Ecology & Evolution* 5, 122–134.
Shipley JT (ed) (1943) *Dictionary of World Literature: Criticism – Forms – Technique*, The Philosophical Library.
Shouse B (2002) Crows go the head of the class, *Science*, 9 August.
Shumailov I et al (2023) The Curse of Recursion: Training on Generated Data Makes Models Forget, Preprint arXiv:2305.17493, 1–14.

Shumaker RW et al (2011) *Animal Tool Behavior: The Use and Manufacture of Tools by Animals*, Rev & Updated Edition, Johns Hopkins University Press.

Siegel T (2018) "Monkey Selfie" film in the works at Conde Nast, *The Hollywood Reporter*.

Silbey J (2022) *Against Progress: Intellectual Property and Fundamental Values in the Internet Age*, Stanford University Press.

Silko LM (2010) *The Turquoise Ledge*, Viking, 183.

Simmel G (1994/[1909]) Bridge and Door, *Theory, Culture & Society*, 11(1), 5–10.

Simmons A (2001) Changing the Cartesian Mind: Leibniz on Sensation, Representation and Consciousness, *The Philosophical Review*, 110(1), 31–75.

Simmons A (2011) Leibnizian Consciousness Reconsidered, *Studia Leibnitiana*, 43(2), 196–215.

Simon HA (1968/[1996]) *The Sciences of the Artificial*, 3rd ed, MIT Press.

Singer JW (1988) Legal Realism Now, *California Law Review*, 76(2), 465–544.

Singer JW (2000) *Entitlement: The Paradoxes of Property*, Yale University Press.

Singer JW and Beermann JM (1993) The Social Origins of Property, *Canadian Journal of Law and Jurisprudence*, 6(2), 217–248.

Siniscalchi M (2022) Attention bias, in Vonk J and Shackelford TK (eds) *Encyclopedia of Animal Cognition and Behavior*, Springer, 548–550.

Sisario B (2023a) 6 Takeaways from Ed Sheeran's *Let's Get It On* copyright case, *The New York Times*, 5 May.

Sisario B (2023b) Ed Sheeran won his copyright trial. Here's what to know, The *New York Times*, 4 May.

Situationist International (1958) Contribution to a situationist definition of play, Thompson I and Keehan R (trans), *Internationale Situationniste* #1, at Internationale Situationniste in English [isinenglish.com]

Skinner BF (1979/[1990]) The Non-Punitive Society, *Japanese Journal of Behavior Analysis*, reprint of Commemorative lecture on the occasion of the award of honorary doctorate, Keio University, Japan, 25 September 1979.

Skinner BF (1983) *A Matter of Consequences: Part Three of an Autobiography*, Alfred A Knopf.

Skrbina D (2020) Panpsychism reconsidered: A historical and philosophical overview, in Seager W (ed) (2020) *The Routledge Handbook of Panpsychism*, Routledge, 103–115.

Slater DJ (2014) *Wildlife Personalities*, Blurb.

Smith C (2023) *Thoreau's Axe: Distraction and Discipline in American Culture*, Princeton University Press.

Smith G (2024) A man, a boat, and a goat – and a chatbot! *Mind Matters*, 15 May.

Smith GE et al (2021) If I Fits I Sits: A Citizen Science Investigation into Illusory Contour Susceptibility in Domestic Cats, (*Felis silvestris catus*) Applied Animal Behaviour Science, 240, 105338.

Smith H (2011) Can monkey who took grinning self-portrait claim copyright? *Metro*, 14 July.

Smith PK (1982) Does Play Matter? Functional and Evolutionary Aspects of Animal and Human Play, *The Behavioral and Brain Sciences*, 5, 139–184.

Smith W (1870) *Dictionary of Greek and Roman Biography and Mythology, Vol II*, Little, Brown, and Company.

Sneddon LU et al (2018) Fish Sentience Denial: Muddying the Waters, *Animal Sentience*, 21(1), article 115.
Sng Z (2020) *Middling Romanticism: Reading in the Gaps, from Kant to Ashbery*, Fordham University Press.
Snowdon CT et al (2015) Cats Prefer Species-Appropriate Music, *Applied Animal Behaviour Science*, 166, 106–111.
Sofri A (2004) On Optimism, L Cochrane (trans), *Critical Inquiry*, 739–770.
Solbu A and Frank MG (2019) Lie catchers: Evolution and development of deception in modern times, in Docan-Morgan T (ed) (2019) *The Palgrave Handbook of Deceptive Communication*, Palgrave Macmillan, 41–66.
Solli M and Netland T (2021) Enacting a Jazz Beat: Temporality in Sonic Environment and Symbolic Communication, *The British Journal of Aesthetics*, 61(4), 485–504.
Solomon O (2012) Doing, Being and Becoming: The Sociality of Children with Autism in Activities with Therapy Dogs and Other People, *The Cambridge Journal of Anthropology*, 30(1), 109–126.
Spencer H (1885) *The Principles of Psychology, Volume II*, D Appleton and Company.
Spier S (2007) Inside the Knot That Two Bodies Make, *Dance Research Journal*, 39(1), 49–59.
Spinelli E (2005/[1989]) *The Interpreted World*, 2nd ed, Sage.
Stadler B and Dixon AFG (2005) Ecology and Evolution of Aphid-Ant Interactions, *Annual Review of Ecology, Evolution, and Systematics*, 36, 345–372.
Stankowich T (2019) Defensive risk-taking in animals, in Choe JC (ed) (2019) *Encyclopedia of Animal Behavior, Volume 4*, 2nd ed, Academic Press, 340–348.
Steele MA et al (2008) Cache Protection Strategies of a Scatter-hoarding Rodent: Do Tree Squirrels Engage in Behavioural Deception, *Animal Behaviour*, 75, 705–714.
Stefanovska M (2009) Exemplary or Singular? The Anecdote in Historical Narrative, *SubStance*, 38(1), 16–30.
Stein MI (1953) Creativity and Culture, *The Journal of Psychology: Interdisciplinary and Applied*, 36(2), 311–322.
Stevens C (2003) Choreographic Cognition: The Time-course and Phenomenology of Creating a Dance, *Pragmatics & Cognition*, 11(2), 297–326.
Stolnitz J (1961) On the Origins of "Aesthetic Disinterestedness," *The Journal of Aesthetics and Art Criticism*, 20(2), 131–143.
Stone-Mediatore S (2013) Attending to Others: Simone Weil and Epistemic Pluralism, *Philosophical Topics*, 41(3), 79–95.
Stones G (1998) Parody and Imitation, in Wu D (ed) (1998/[2001]) *A Companion to Romanticism*, Blackwell, 355–363.
Stones G (1999) General Introduction, in Stones G (ed) (2016/[1999]) *Parodies of the Romantic Age: Volume I, The Anti-Jacobin*, Routledge, xiii–xliv.
Stones G (ed) (2016/[1999]) *Parodies of the Romantic Age: Volume I, The Anti-Jacobin*, Routledge.
Strauss Clay J (2019) Hide and go seek: Hermes in homer, in Miller JF and Strauss Clay J (eds) (2019) *Tracking Hermes, Pursuing Mercury*, Oxford University Press, 67–77.
Strawson G (2018) The consciousness deniers, *The New York Review of Books*, 13 March.
Strong CA (1922) *The Wisdom of the Beasts*, Houghton Mifflin Company.

Strum SC and Fedigan LM (eds) (2000) *Primate Encounters: Models of Science, Gender, and Society*, University of Chicago Press.
Stucki S (2020) Towards a Theory of Legal Animal Rights: Simple and Fundamental Rights, *Oxford Journal of Legal Studies*, 40(3), 533–560.
Su F (2020) *Mathematics for Human Flourishing*, Yale University Press.
Subbotsky E et al (2010) Watching Films with Magical Content Facilitates Creativity in Children, *Perceptual and Motor Skill*, 111(1), 261–277.
Suits B (2014/[1978]) *The Grasshopper: Games, Life, and Utopia*, 3rd ed, Broadview Press.
Suits (2019) Return of the grasshopper: Games and the end of the future, in Hurka T (ed) *Games, Sports, and Play*, Oxford University Press, 193–230.
Sullivan J (1929) Legend, Anecdote and History, *The Quarterly Journal of the New York State Historical Association*, 10(1), 29–44.
Sun L (2023) *The Liars of Nature and the Nature of Liars: Cheating and Deception in the Living World*, Princeton University Press.
Suzuki TN and Sugita N (2024) The 'after You' Gesture in a Bird, *Current Biology*, 34, R231–R232.
Suzuki TN et al (2016) Experimental Evidence for Compositional Syntax in Bird Calls, *Nature Communications*, 7, 10986.
Swain A and Fagan WF (2019) Group Size and Decision Making: Experimental Evidence for Minority Games in Fish Behaviour, *Animal Behaviour*, 155, 9–19.
Tallis R (1999/[1991]) *The Explicit Animal: A Defence of Human Consciousness*, Macmillan.
Tallis R (2003) *The Hand: A Philosophical Inquiry into Human Being*, Edinburgh University Press.
Tallis R (2004) *I Am: Philosophical Inquiry into First-Person Being*, Edinburgh University Press.
Tannenbaum J (1991) Ethics and Animal Welfare: The Inextricable Connection, *Journal of the American Veterinary Medical Association*, 198, 1360–1376.
Tarde G (1899) *Social Laws: An Outline of Sociology*, Warren HC (trans), Macmillan.
Tarde G (1900) Le droit comparé et la sociologie, in Société de Législation comparée (1905) *Congrès international de droit comparé: procès-verbeaux des séances et documents*, Librairie Générale de droit et de jurisprudence, 437–445.
Tarde G (1901) *L'opinion et la foule*, Félix Alcan.
Tarde G (1902) *Psychologie économique*, Félix Alcan.
Tarde G (1903) L'inter-psychologie, *Bulletin de l'institut general psychologique*, 2, 91–118.
Tarde G (1903/[1890]) *The Laws of Imitation*, Parsons EC (trans), Henry Holt & Co.
Tarde G (1905/[1896]), *Underground Man*, C Brereton (trans), Duckworth & Company.
Tarde G (1969) *On Communication and Social Influence*, TN Clark (ed), University of Chicago Press.
Tarde G (2004/[1873]) A Fragment on Difference, C Rol (trans), *Distinktion*, 9, 2004, 29–31.
Tarde G (2004/[1896]) *Underground (Fragments of Future Histories)*, L Gillick (update), M Lazzarato (introd), Les Maîtres de Forme Contemporains.
Tarde G (2007/[1902]) Economic Psychology, Toscano A (trans), *Economy and Society*, 36(4), 614–643.

Tarde G (2012/[1893]) *Monadology and Sociology*, Lorenc T (trans), Re-Press.
Tatham C (1977) Watt-Knots Enhance Endogenous Entropy, *Boundary 2*, 5(2), 351–362.
Tauginienė L et al (2020) Citizen Science in the Social Sciences and Humanities: The Power of Interdisciplinarity, *Nature-Palgrave Communications*, 6, article 89.
Tayler CK and Saayman GS (1973) Imitative Behaviour by Indian Ocean Bottlenose dolphins (*Tursiops aduncus*) in Captivity, *Behaviour*, 44, 286–298.
Taylor AH (2024) Darwin's Mischievous Hat Stealers Are Innovative Problem Solvers, *Current Biology*, 34, R16–R23.
Taylor KD (2010) Learned helplessness, in Mills DS et al (eds) (2010) *The Encyclopedia of Applied Animal Behaviour and Welfare*, CABI, 384.
Taylor T and Derclaye E (2021) Intellectual property rights and well-being: a methodological approach, in Calboli I and Montagnani ML (eds) (2021) *Handbook of Intellectual Property Research: Lenses, Methods, and Perspectives*, Oxford University Press, 654–670.
Tennie C et al (2009) Ratcheting up the -Ratchet: On the Evolution of Cumulative Culture, *Philosophical Transactions of the Royal Society of London B Biological Sciences*, 364(1528), 2405–2415.
Terranova T (2017) A neomonadology of social (Memory) production, in Blom I et al (eds) (2017) *Memory in Motion: Archives, Technology and the Social*, Amsterdam University Press, 287–305.
Thacker E (2013) Apophatic Animality: Lautréamont, bachelard, and the bliss of metamorphosis, *Angelaki: Journal of the Theoretical Humanities*, 18(1), 83–98.
Thomas A et al (2022) *UK Authors' Earnings and Contracts 2022*, CREATe.
Thomas N (2016) *Animal Ethics and the Autonomous Animal Self*, Palgrave Macmillan.
Thomson P and Jaque SV (2017) *Creativity and the Performing Artist: Behind the Mask*, Academic Press.
Thornton A and Raihani NJ (2008) The Evolution of Teaching, *Animal Behaviour*, 75, 1823–1836.
Timmons J (2024) Asian elephants seen burying their dead for the first time, *New Scientist*, 5 March.
Tinbergen N (1963) On Aims and Methods of Ethology, *Zeitschrift für Tierpsychologie*, 20, 410–433.
Tomasello M (1990) Cultural transmission in the tool use and communicatory signaling of chimpanzees? in Parker ST and Gibson KR (eds) (1990) *"Language" and Intelligence in Monkeys and Apes: Comparative Developmental Perspectives*, Cambridge University Press, 274–311.
Tomasello M (1999) Do apes ape? In Heyes CM and Galef Jr BG (eds) (1996) *Social Learning in Animals: The Roots of Culture*, Academic Press, 319–346.
Tonkin A (2019) Playing for a healthy brain, in Tonkin A and Whitaker J (eds) (2019) *Play and Playfulness for Public Health and Wellbeing*, Routledge, 20–33.
Tonkin A and Whitaker J (eds) (2019) *Play and Playfulness for Public Health and Wellbeing*, Routledge.
Tønnessen M and Beever J (2015) Beyond sentience: Biosemiotics as foundation for animal and environmental ethics, in Aaltola E and Hadley J (eds) (2015) *Animal Ethics and Philosophy: Questioning the Orthodoxy*, Rowman & Littlefield, 47–62.

Toomela A (ed) (2003) *Cultural Guidance in the Development of the Human Mind*, Ablex.
Tormey A (1971) *The Concept of Expression: A Study in Philosophical Psychology and Aesthetics*, Princeton University Press.
Townsend AK et al (2022) Infectious Disease and Cognition in Wild Populations, *Trends in Ecology and Evolution*, 37(10), 899–910.
Townsend M (2018) Throw your children's art away, *The Atlantic*, 16 September.
Trösch M et al (2020) Horses Feel Emotions When They Watch Positive and Negative Horse-Human Interactions in a Video and Transpose What They Saw to Real Life, *Animal Cognition*, 23(4), 643–653.
Troutt DD (2009) I Own Therefore I Am: Copyright, Personality, and Soul Music in the Digital Commons, *Fordham Intellectual Property, Media and Entertainment Law Journal*, 20(2), 373–452.
Tschinkel WR (2021) *Ant Architecture: The Wonder, Beauty, and Science of Underground Nests*, Princeton University Press.
Tse PU (2008) Symbolic thought and the evolution of human morality, in Sinnott-Armstrong W (ed) (2008) *Moral Psychology: The Evolution of Morality: Adaptations and Innateness*, MIT Press, 269–297.
Tuomela R (2006) Joint Intention, We-Mode and I-Mode, *Midwest Studies in Philosophy*, 30(1) 35–58.
Turing AM (1950) Computing Machinery and Intelligence, *Mind*, 59(236), 433–460.
Turner CH (1906) A Preliminary Note on Ant Behavior, *Biological Bulletin*, 12(1), 31–36.
Turner CH (1907) Do Ants form Practical Judgments? *Biological Bulletin*, 13(6), 333–343.
Turner CH (1907) The Homing of Ants: An Experimental Study of Ant Behavior, *The Journal of Comparative Neurology and Psychology*, 17(5), 367–435.
Turner CH (1907) *The Homing of Ants: An Experimental Study of Ant Behavior*, Dissertation, Ogden Graduate School of Science, The University of Chicago.
Turner CH (1914) An Experimental Study of the Auditory Powers of the Giant Silkworm Moths (*Saturniidae*), *Biological Bulletin*, 27(6), 325–332.
Turner JC and Griend P van de (eds) (1996) *History and Science of Knots*, World Scientific.
Tversky A and Kahneman D (1981) The Framing of Decisions and the Psychology of Choice, *Science*, 211(4481), 453–458.
Twain M (1913/[1905]) What Is Man? *The Monist* 23(2), 181–223.
Tyree E (2022) Let's make AI boring, *Technative*, 30 March.
Tzoulia E and Kalles D (2024) AI-Generated Subject Matter in the Light of IP Law: A sui generis Protection Regime as the Last Resort, *European Intellectual Property Review*, 46(3), 175–182.
Uexküll J von (1934) A stroll through the worlds of animals and men: A picture book of invisible worlds, CH Schiller (trans), in Schiller CH (ed) (1957) *Instinctive Behavior: The Development of a Modern Concept*, Methuen & Co, 5–80.
Uexküll J von (2010/[1934]) *A Foray Into the Worlds of Animals and Humans*, JD O'Neil (trans), University of Minnesota Press.
Uller C et al (2003) Salamanders (Plethodon cinereus) Go for More: Rudiments of Number in an Amphibian, *Animal Cognition*, 6(2), 105–112.

Urton G (1998) From Knots to Narratives: Reconstructing the Art of Historical Record Keeping in the Andes from Spanish Transciprtions of Inka Khipus, *Ethnohistory*, 45(3), 409–438.

Urton G (2003) *Signs of the Inka Khipu: Binary Coding in the Andean Knotted-String Records*, University of Texas Press.

Urton G (2005a) Khipu Archives: Duplicate Accounts and Identity Labels in the Inka Knotted String Records, *Latin American Antiquity*, 16(2), 147–167.

Urton G (2005b) String Theorist: Unraveling a Knotty Inca Puzzle (Interview), *Archaeology*, 58(6), 14.

Vámos TIF et al (2020) Numerical Ordinality in a Wild Nectivore, *Proceedings of the Royal Society B*, 287, 20201269.

Vanutelli ME et al (2024) Wild Laughs: Ontogenesis and Phylogenesis of Humour, *Neuroscience Letters*, 822, 137615.

Varela FJ et al (1993/[1991]) *The Embodied Mind: Cognitive Science and Human Experience*, MIT Press.

Varela FJ et al (2016) *The Embodied Mind: Cognitive Science and Human Experience*, Revised ed, MIT Press.

Vargas RA (2023) Ed Sheeran on copyright infringement lawsuit: 'Comes with the territory,' *The Guardian*, 7 May.

Varner G (2018) Sentience, in Gruen L (ed) (2018) *Critical Terms for Animal Studies*, The University of Chicago Press, Chicago, 356–369.

Vas J et al (2005) A Friend or an Enemy? Dogs' Reaction to an Unfamiliar Person Showing Behavioural Cues of Threat and Friendless at Different Times, *Applied Animal Behaviour Science* 94, 99–115.

Vaswani A et al (2017) Attention Is All You Need. 31st Conference on Neural Information Processing Systems (NIPS 2017), Long Beach, California.

Vats A (2020) *The Color of Creatorship: Intellectual Property, Race, and the Making of Americans*, Stanford University Press.

Vauclair J (2003) Would humans without language be apes? in Toomela A (ed) (2003) *Cultural Guidance in the Development of the Human Mind*, Ablex, 9–26.

Veblen T (2007/[1899]) *The Theory of the Leisure Class*, Oxford University Press.

Vehlken S (2019) *Zootechnologies: A Media History of Swarm Research*, Amsterdam University Press.

Vernitski A (2018) How maths can help us answer questions we haven't thought of yet, *The Conversation*, 3 September.

Vicino GA and Marcacci ES (2015) Intensity of Play Behavior as a Potential Measure of Welfare, *Zoo Biology*, 34(5), 492–496.

Vidal J-M et al (1996) Introducing Anthropomorphism, Discontinuities and Anecdotes to Question Them, *Behavioural Processes*, 35, 299–309.

Vilhauer M (2010) *Gadamer's Ethics of Play*, Lexington Books.

Vilhauer M (2013) Gadamer and the game of understanding: Dialogue-play and opening to the Other, in Ryall E et al (eds) (2013) *The Philosophy of Play*, Routledge, 74–86.

Vilone G and Longo L (2021) Notions of Explainability and Evaluation Approaches for Explainable Artificial Intelligence, *Information Fusion*, 76, 89–106.

Vohland K et al (eds) (2021) *The Science of Citizen Science*, Springer.

Volsche S et al (2022) Dogs Produce Distinctive Play Pants: Confirming Simonet, *International Journal of Comparative Psychology*, 35(1), 58492.

Voltaire (1900/[1759]) *Candide, and Other Romances*, Aldington R (trans), Murray's Book Sales.
Voltaire (2015/[1979]) *Candide ou l'Optimiste*, Librio.
Vossen B van der (2021) Property, the Environment, and the Lockean Proviso, *Economics and Philosophy*, 37(3), 395–412.
Voulgari-Kokota A et al (2023) Insects as Mini-livestock: Considering Insect Welfare in Feed Production, *NJAS: Impact in Agricultural and Life Sciences*, 95(1), 2191797.
Waal F de (2001) *The Ape and the Sushi Master: Cultural Reflections by a Primatologist*, Basic Books.
Waal F de (2016) *Are We Smart Enough to Know How Smart Animals Are?* Granta.
Waal F de and Bonnie KE (2009) In tune with others: The social side of primate culture, in Laland KN and Galef BG (eds) (2009) *The Question of Animal Culture*, Harvard University Press, 19–40.
Waal F de and Suchak M (2010) Prosocial Primates: Selfish and Unselfish Motivations, *Philosophical Transactions of the Royal Society B*, 365(1553), 2711–2722.
Walczyk JJ and Cockrell NF (2023) The nexus of morality and creativity vis-à-vis deception: a cognitive framework, in Kapoor H and Kaufman JC (eds) (2023) *Creativity and Morality*, Academic Press, 81–99.
Waldron J (2009) Dignity, rank, and rights (the Tanner Lectures), in Waldron et al (2012) *Dignity, Rank, and Rights*, Dan-Cohen M (ed), Oxford University Press, 13–76.
Walkley AB (1921) *Pastiche and Prejudice*, Alfred A Knopf.
Waller BM et al (2012) Evidence of Public Engagement with Science: Visitor Learning at a Zoo-Housed Primate Research Centre, *PLoS One*, 7(9), 344680.
Walters S (2013) Seeking, Playful Translators: Emotion, Difference, and Connection in Human-Animal Relations, *JAC*, 33(1/2), 336–351.
Wang J (2021) Is Artificial Intelligence Capable of Understanding? An Analysis Based on Philosophical Hermeneutics, *Cultures of Science*, 4(3) 135–146.
Wang Y and Zeng Y (2024) A Brain-Inspired Computational Model for Human-Like Concept Learning, arXiv:24-1.06471.
Ward M (1999) *Virtual Organisms: The Startling World of Artificial Life*, Macmillan
Wascher CAF (2023) Cognition: Crows Are Natural Statisticians, *Current Biology*, 33(15), R803–R810.
Washburn MF (1908) *The Animal Mind: A Textbook of Comparative Psychology*, MacMillan Co.
Wasserman EA et al (2013) Pigeons Learn Virtual Patterned-String Problems in a Computerized Touch Screen Environment, *Animal Cognition*, 16, 737–753.
Watiktinnakorn C et al (2023) Blurring the Lines: How AI Is Redefining Artistic Ownership and Copyright, *Discover Artificial Intelligence*, 3, article 37.
Watson S (2016) Philosophy Is also an Architecture of Signs, *Research in Phenomenology*, 46(1), 35–53.
Weber NA (1966) Fungus-Growing Ants, *Science* 153(3736), 587–604.
Webster J (2005) *Animal Welfare: Limping Towards Eden*, Blackwell.
Webster MM and Rutz C (2020) How STRANGE Are Your Study Animals? *Nature*, 582, 337–340.
Wehner R (2016) Early Ant Trajectories: Spatial Behaviour before Behaviourism, *Journal of Comparative Physiology A*, 202, 247–266.

Weil S (1929–1930) Science and perception in descartes, in Weil S (2010/[1987]) *Formative Writings, 1929–1941*, McFarland DT and Ness W van (eds and trans), Routledge, 31–88.
Weil S (1940) The *Iliad* or the poem of force, McCarthy M (trans), in Weil S and Bespaloff R (2005) *War and the Iliad*, New York Review Books, 1–37.
Weil S (1941a) Classical science and after, in Weil S (1968) *On Science, Necessity, and the Love of God*, Rees R (ed and trans), Oxford University Press, 3–43.
Weil S (1941b) Essay on the concept of reading, in Weil S (2015) *Late Philosophical Writings*, EO Springsted (ed), Springsted EO and Schmidt LE (trans), University of Notre Dame Press, 21–28.
Weil S (1942a) God in Plato, Springsted EO and Schmidt LE (trans), in Weil S (2015) *Late Philosophical Writings*, Springsted EO (ed), University of Notre Dame Press, 45–95.
Weil S (1942b) Reflections on quantum theory, in Weil S (1968) *On Science, Necessity, and the Love of God*, Rees R (ed and trans), Oxford University Press, 49–64.
Weil S (1942c) Reflections on the right use of school studies, in Weil S (1951/[1950]) *Waiting on God*, Craufurd E (trans), Routledge & Kegan Paul, 49–59.
Weil S (1943) Human personality, Rees R (trans), in Weil S (2015/[1962]) *Selected Essays: 1934–1943*, Wipf and Stock Publishers, 9–34.
Weil S (1951/[1950]) *Waiting on God*, Craufurd E (trans), Routledge & Kegan Paul.
Weil S (1959a) After the discovery of mind, in Weil S (1978/[1959]) *Lectures on Philosophy*, Price H (trans), Cambridge University Press, 90–128.
Weil S (1959b) Ethics and aesthetics, in Weil S (1978/[1959]) *Lectures on Philosophy*, Price H (trans), Cambridge University Press, 165–189.
Weil S (1959c) The materialist point of view, in Weil S (1978/[1959]) *Lectures on Philosophy*, Price H (trans), Cambridge University Press, 27–89.
Weil S (1962) *Selected Essays, 1934–1943*, Rees R (trans and ed), Wipf & Stock.
Weil S (1965) *Seventy Letters*, R Rees (trans), Wipf & Stock.
Weil S (1968) *On Science, Necessity, and the Love of God*, R Rees (trans and ed), Oxford University Press.
Weil S (1976/[1952]) *Intimations of Christianity Among the Greeks*, Geissbuhler EC (ed and trans), Routledge & Kegan Paul.
Weil S (1978/[1959]) *Lectures on Philosophy*, Price H (trans), Cambridge University Press.
Weil S (2001/[1955]) *Oppression and Liberty*, Will A and Petrie J (trans), Routledge.
Weil S (2002/[1947]) *Gravity and Grace*, Crawford E and Ruhr M von der (trans), Thibon G (ed), Routledge.
Weil S (2002/[1949]) *The Need for Roots*, Wills A (trans), Routledge.
Weil S (2009/[1951]) *Waiting for God*, Craufurd E (trans), Harper Perennial.
Weil S (2010/[1987]) *Formative Writings, 1929–1941*, McFarland DT and Ness W van (eds and trans), Routledge.
Weil S (2012/[1950]) *Awaiting God*, Jersak B (trans), Weil S(Sylvie) (introd), Fresh Wind Press.
Weil S (2015) *Simone Weil: Late Philosophical Writings*, Springsted EO and Schmidt LE (trans), University of Notre Dame Press.
Weil S (2015/[1970]) *First and Last Notebooks*, Rees R (trans), Wipf & Stock.
Weil S and Bespaloff R (2005) *War and the Iliad*, McCarthy M (trans), New York Review Books.

Weise C et al (2022) Paper Wasps form Abstract Concept of "Same and Different" *Proceedings of the Royal Society B*, 289(1979), 1–9.
Wellman C (2011) Touching Books: Diderot, Novalis, and the Encyclopedia of the Future, *Representations*, 114(1), 65–102.
Wells (1905) The empire of the ants, in Wells HG (ed) (1977) *The Empire of the Ants (and Other Stories)*, Scholastic, 1–28.
Wells HG (1945) *Mind at the End of Its Tether*, William Heinemann.
Welsh D (2023), Ed Sheeran claims he'll quit music if he loses *Thinking Out Loud* lawsuit, *HuffPost*, 2 May.
Wemelsfelder F (1997) The Scientific Validity of Subjective Concepts in Models of Animal Welfare, *Applied Animal Behaviour Science*, 53, 75–88.
West ML (1999) The Invention of Homer, *The Classical Quarterly*, 49(2), 364–382.
Weston P (2020) Sexy beasts: animals with 'charisma' get lion's share of EU conservation funds, *The Guardian*, 9 December.
Wheeler M (2018) Talking about more than heads: The embodied, embedded and extended creative mind, in Gaut B and Kieran M (eds) (2018) *Creativity and Philosophy*, Routledge, 230–250.
Wheeler WM (1910) *Ants: Their Structure, Development, and Behavior*, Columbia University Press.
Whipple T (2021) Human or robo-art? Spot the difference, *The Times*, 24 February.
Whitaker J and Tonkin A (2019) A place for play: Creating playful environments for health and wellbeing, in Tonkin A and Whitaker J (eds) (2019) *Play and Playfulness for Public Health and Wellbeing*, Routledge, 160–174.
White H (1984) The Question of Narrative in Contemporary Historical Theory, *History and Theory*, 23(1), 1–33.
White JM and Lidskog R (2022) Ignorance and the Regulation of Artificial Intelligence, *Journal of Risk Research*, 25(4), 488–500.
White SA (1995) Thrasymachus the Diplomat, *Classical Philology*, 90(4), 307–327.
White WF (1991/[1883]) *Ants and Their Ways*, Cornell University Library.
Whitehead AN (1933/[1967]) *Adventures of Ideas*, The Free Press.
Whiten A (1998) Origins of the mindreading system, in Langer J and Killen M (eds) (2014/[1998]) *Piaget, Evolution, and Development*, Psychology Press, 73–99.
Whiten A (2021) The Burgeoning Reach of Animal Culture, *Science*, 372(6537), 2 April, eabe6514.
Whiten A and Byrne RW (1988) Tactical Deception in Primates, *Behavioral and Brain Sciences*, 11(2), 233–273.
Whiten A and Byrne RW (eds) (1997) *Machiavellian Intelligence II: Extensions and Evaluations*, Oxford University Press.
Whiten A and Perner J (1991) Fundamental issues in the multidisciplinary study of mindreading, in Whiten A (ed) (1991) *Natural Theories of Mind: Evolution: Development and Simulation of Everyday Mindreading*, Basil Blackwell, 1–17.
Wickler W (1980) Vocal Dueting and the Pair Bond, *Zitschrift für Tierpsychologie*, 52, 201–209.
Wilkins A (2024) How AI mathematicians might finally deliver human-level reasoning, *New Scientist*, 10 April.
Wilkof N (2015) When History Is More about Patent Present Than Patent Past, *Journal of Intellectual Property Law and Practice*, 10(7), 487.

Williams DL (2016) Here's what Plato had to say about someone like Donald Trump, *The Washington Post*, 5 October.
Wilson EO (1965) Trail Sharing in Ants, *Psyche*, 72(1), 2–7.
Wilson EO (2020) *Tales from the Ant World*, Liveright.
Wilson JRS (1995) Thrasymachus and the Thumos: A Further Case of Prolepsis in Republic I, *The Classical Quarterly*, 45(1), 58–67.
Wimpenny JH et al (2009) Cognitive Processes Associated with Sequential Tool Use in New Caledonian Crows, *PLoS One*, 4(8), 36471.
Winch P (1978) Introduction, in Weil S (1978/[1959]) *Lectures on Philosophy*, Price H (trans), Cambridge University Press, 1–23.
Winch P (1989) *Simone Weil: "The Just Balance,"* Cambridge University Press.
Winner E and Drake JE (2022) *The Child as Visual Artist*, Cambridge University Press.
Wittgenstein L (1967/[1953]) *Philosophical Investigations*, GEM Anscombe (trans), 3rd ed, Blackwell.
Wittgenstein L (1978/[1956]) *Remarks on the Foundations of Mathematics*, GEM Anscombe (trans), 3rd ed, Blackwell.
Wittgenstein L (1993) *Philosophical Occasions, 1912–1951*, Klagge JC and Nordmann A (eds), Hackett.
Wolfe C (2007) Cognitive Science, Deconstruction, and (Post)Humanist (Non) Humans, *Oxford Literary Review*, 29, 103–125.
Wolfe C (2009) Human, All Too Human: "Animal Studies" and the Humanities, *PMLA*, 124(2), 564–575.
Wood L et al (2014) The Pet Factor: Companion Animals as a Conduit for Getting to Know People, Friendship Formation and Social Support, *PLoS One*, 10(4), e0122085.
Wood WJ (2011) Bunnies for Pets or Meat: The Slaughterhouse as Cinematic Metaphor, *JAC*, 31(1–2), 11–44.
Woodmansee M (1984) The Genius and the Copyright: Economic and Legal Conditions of the Emergence of the "Author," *Eighteenth-Century Studies*, 17(4), 425–448.
Woodmansee M and Jaszi P (eds) (1994) *The Construction of Authorship: Textual Appropriation in Law and Literature*, Duke University Press.
Wordsworth W (1807) The Green Linnet, in Wordsworth W (ed) (1815) *Poems, Vol I*, Longman, 243.
Worsley HK and O'Hara SJ (2018) Cross-species Referential Signalling Events in Domestic Dogs (*Canis familiaris*), *Animal Cognition*, 21(4), 457–465.
Wright HF et al (2017) Animals Can Assign Novel Odours to a Known Category, *Nature*, 7, 9019.
Wulf A (2022) *Magnificent Rebels: The First Romantics and the Invention of the Self*, Hachette.
Wynne C and Udell M (2020) *Animal Cognition: Evolution, Behavior and Cognition*, 3rd ed, Palgrave Macmillan.
Wystrach A (2013) We've been looking at ant intelligence the wrong way, *The Conversation*, 30 August.
Wystrach A et al (2020) Rapid Aversive and Memory Trace Learning during Route Navigation in Desert Ants, *Current Biology*, 30, 1–7.

Xu T et al (2021) A Trail Pheromone Mediates the Mutualism between Ants and Aphids, *Current Biology*, 31(21), 4738–4747, e4.

Yamamoto S (2017) Primate Empathy: Three Factors and Their Combinations for Empathy-related Phenomena, *Wiley Interdisciplinary Reviews: Cognitive Science*, 8(3), 1–11.

Yang X-S (ed) (2020) *Nature-Inspired Computation and Swarm Intelligence: Algorithms, Theory and Applications*, Academic Press.

Yang X-S and Karamanoglu M (2020) Nature-inspired computation and swarm intelligence: A state-of-the-art overview, in Yang X-S (ed) (2020) *Nature-Inspired Computation and Swarm Intelligence: Algorithms, Theory and Applications*, Academic Press, 3–18.

Yerkes RM and Sykes Child M (1927) Anthropoid Behavior, *The Quarterly Review of Biology*, 2(1), 37–57.

Yin S (2012) *Teaching Fido to Learn to Earn*, CattleDog Publishing.

Yong E (2022) *An Immense World: How Animal Senses Reveal the Hidden Realms Around Us*, Bodley Head.

York CA and Bartol IK (2016) Anti-predator Behavior of Squid throughout Ontogeny, *Journal of Experimental Marine Biology and Ecology*, 480, 26–35.

Zabelina DL (2018) Attention and creativity, in Jung RE and Vartanian O (eds) (2018) *The Cambridge Handbook of the Neuroscience of Creativity*, Cambridge University Press, 161–179.

Zaslavsky C and Crespo B (2000) The Inka Quipu: Positional Notation on a knotted Cord, *Mathematics Teaching in the Middle School*, 6(3), 164–166, 180–184.

Zednik C (2021) Solving the Black Box Problem: A Normative Framework for Explainable Artificial Intelligence, *Philosophy & Technology*, 34, 265–288.

Zentall TR (2022) *Learning and Motivation*, 80, 101844.

Zhang L et al (2021) Feline Communication Strategies When Presented with an Unsolvable Task: The Attentional State of the Person Matters, *Animal Cognition*, 24, 1109–1119.

Make a play

Index

accession 215; doctrine of 77, 215–216
Actualist Movement 152, 378
Actualists 153, 379
adaptation 27, 37, 124, 126, 135, 273, 282, 297, 311, 327, 331–332, 337, 348–351, 353, 361; epiphenomenal 143, 146; function of 275; functional rubric 152; fundamental 123; laws of 126; originality of 322; of phenomena 126; physical 34; processes of 290; sense of 348; social 223; theory of 329; value 24
adaptationist 125, 271; analysis 36; approach 124; conventions 143; imperative 175; interpretations 20, 277, 319; mode 320; narrative 289, 320, 323, 400; Panglossian paradigm 133; paradigm 24, 121, 124, 126, 143, 173, 205, 211; programme 121, 128; reasoning 283; reckoning 170; thinking 125
adaptive 136; advantage 99; behaviour 292; curiosities 288; explanation 317; fitness 220; intellectually 104; manner 250; purpose 170; resources 271; response 136, 171, 176, 322; value 272, 277
Adorno, T. W. 146
advocacy 11–12, 19, 177, 245, 296; personhood 128
Aesop 1, 11, 267, 348, 355
aesthetic 14, 37, 69, 104–105, 120, 142, 152, 224, 234–236, 289, 292, 294–296, 298, 316, 318, 350, 353, 364, 368–372, 374, 390, 405, 416–419; account 34, 369; achievements 120; activity 371, 374; of adornment 106; animal 22, 31, 405; appreciation 21; approach to artistic expression 213; approach to sentience 122; attention 236, 238, 364; attitude 295; behaviour 29; blindness 187; challenge 224; consciousness 295, 374; in design 18, 313–314; dimension 56, 150, 294–295, 317, 378; discourse 77; empathy 74; endeavour 24; engagements 358; enquiry 55; environmental 209; evidence 26; excess 141; experience 142, 146, 372; expression 363, 371; exuberance 273; fragment 315; of the intellect 69; interests 26; judgment 370–371, 408; knotmaking 104; labour 294; language 77; life 9, 10, 20; of movement 68; musical 18, 267; objects 77, 268, 369; or sentience 370; originality 314; of performance 68; personality 150; phenomena 28; of play 141, 272, 288, 295; play 267; pleasure 317; preference 317; pretensions to 17; production 267–268, 333, 405; science of 370; sense 5, 14–18, 27, 152, 208, 249, 268, 288, 294, 317, 370–371, 374; taste 234, 298; value 17, 32, 64, 178; wasteful 295
affect 135; expression of 289; positive 151, 173, 272, 289, 298; study of 138
affective 244; attitudes 73; community of play 238; computing 135; creativity 5; neuroscience 28; relationship 134; states 135, 138, 170
affiliation 26, 74, 362, 373, 408
affiliative 13, 70, 105, 150, 152, 166, 187, 212, 216, 275, 297–298, 337, 370; approach 318; behaviour 220,

362; capabilities 80; character 360; difference 362; dimension 400; dissensus 274; encounters 290; expression 377; formic individuals 182; function 13, 37, 58, 98, 267, 274; imitation 64; industry of play 140; kinship 38; knowledge 224, 249; learning 16, 75, 98; production 98; property 240; quality 36, 186, 274; relationship 221; sociality 273, 319; value 13, 37, 249, 271
affordance 76, 211
Agamben, G. 368
aggregation 238, 280, 328
aggression 272, 319
agriculture 168
Agua Viva (1973) 165
Ahmed, S. 213, 221
Ai-Da 20, 64, 79n29
alchemy 263; Hermetic 263; Newton's 263–264; popularity of 263
Alland, A. 15
allegory 1
American Psychological Association 140
Analytical Engine, The 144, 202
Andic, M. 244
anecdotes 4, 103, 104, 125, 153, 176, 223, 264, 287–288, 333, 349, 369, 373, 387–396, 398, 400–401, 403, 405–408
animal:activities (nonhuman animals) 24; aesthetic sense 17; artless 20; art-making 15–16, 21, 56, 77, 125, 136, 292, 367–368, 372, 403; authorship 10–11, 26, 90, 92, 137, 216–217, 285, 289, 371, 400, 418–419; behaviour 148, 174, 177, 178, 245, 388, 393; capabilities 101, 129, 176; capacities 54, 63; cognition 14, 16, 244, 323, 390, 391, 405; common sense 98; communication 365, 370; communities 95, 108; companion 220; consciousness 12, 66, 91, 279, 395; contamination 101; creativity 2, 6, 20, 61, 92, 201, 332, 347, 371–372; creators 36, 65; culture 14, 179; deception 312, 317, 320, 323; emotion 170; expression 64, 65; expressivity 187; feeling 171; function 24; human 16; husbandry 348; hypnosis 365; imitation 20; intelligence 176, 392; interests 126, 245; kingdom 179, 220; language 63–65; learning 174, 244; life 74; mathematical 107; mentality 14, 70; mentation 393; motivation 143; olfactory representations 67; operant conditioning 245; performing 102; personality 176; perspective 151; play 145, 375; play 249–250, 254, 273; population 29; protection 129; psychology 391; rights 51, 126, 130, 172, 322; sciences 63; semiotics 56; sentience 34, 125, 127, 138, 147, 172, 175, 377; social 14, 98; society 14, 180, 220, 246–247; sociology 177; studies 19, 56, 58, 63–64, 72, 127–128, 212, 278, 295, 403; subjective experience 250; territories 109, 210; theory of mind 59, 403, 405; thinking 172; welfare 10–11, 56, 127, 138, 150, 151, 207, 378; wellbeing 152, 397
animality 58, 74–75; domain of 58; of God (*zōē aiōnios*) 53; literal 1
anthropocentrism 1, 3, 5, 11–12, 25, 38, 55, 71–72, 77, 90, 130, 133, 136, 172, 174, 208–210, 218, 252, 268, 270–271, 279, 327–328, 403, 417
anthropodenial 30, 132, 368, 376
anthropofabulation 2
anthropology 10, 63, 377
anthropomorphism 1–2, 11, 15, 122, 136, 169, 174, 179, 207, 208, 289, 328–329, 417; critical 1, 244, 367; extreme 328; fantastical 405; frenetic 320; strategic 25, 93, 208, 245
antlions 366
ants 2, 3, 77, 107–108, 165–171, 173–181, 184, 186, 190, 250, 267–270, 280, 329, 331, 365, 388, 420; agricultural expertise of 168; behaviour of 330; capacity to learn 184; colonies of 6, 175; ethology of 168; fecundation of 184; fire 365; individual 169; intelligent species of 179; justice of the 269; Leaf-cutter 168; minute worlds of 5; mobilities 178; respect for 179; Simon's 173–179, 184; social lives of 179; spatial literacy of 184; swarming 181, 406; unemployed 170; winged 184; wisdom of 185; world of 169, 183; *see also* Turner, C. H.

Ants and the Grasshopper, The 267–268, 270
anxiety 35, 234, 263, 323, 359, 391, 417
aphorism 4, 318
Apollo 4
apperception 70, 145, 249
appetition 70, 275, 276
Argentine Ant, The (1953) 165
Aristotle 357
Armstrong, D. M. 15
art: children's 21; computer 21, 36; conceptual 24, 68; -making animal 15, 16, 21, 56, 77, 91, 125, 136, 152, 292, 367, 372, 403; nonhuman animals 21, 214; olfactory 209; performance 278, 405; photography 65, 216, 218, 237, 298, 332, 389, 405; sound 209; visual 18, 20, 65, 238, 369
artificial intelligence: aesthetic sense of 17, 328–329; anthropomorphism in 93, 122, 178, 207, 208, 328, 329, 405; anticipatory sociology of 32; authorship of 19, 31–32, 76, 133, 137, 144, 146, 208, 217, 319, 325, 417, 419–420; availability of 21; coercive imitation in 221; consciousness in 17, 31, 121; construction of 181; creative work of 5; cultural impact of 237; development of 19, 98–99, 174; errors repeated by 133; explainability in 29–32, 122, 375; extreme behaviourism of 136; generative 135, 397–398; inventorship of 19, 137, 146, 208, 217, 419; mythology of 17; optimistic view of 133; outputs of 31, 400; pattern-making of 182; personhood for 127, 137; potentialities of 398; productions of 13; sensation of 94; sentience in 17, 134, 329; socio-cultural limitation of 274–275; tools of 97
artificiality 1, 25
assemblage 100, 148, 184; self- 4
Atchison v Baty (1877) 72
attention: a certain kind of 6, 10, 70, 233, 240, 242, 244–245, 250; creative 6, 242, 252, 272; ethological 10, 76, 242, 243, 247; playful 235, 250, 252, 276; *see also* patience

attentive: attention 13, 210, 217, 243–244, 328, 333; distraction 298; ethical encounter 27; humans 249; inattention 263; inter- 96; listening 220; movement 211; perception 17; play 183, 251; quality 249; regard 348, 353, 363; salience 362; stewardship 419; system 221
attentive imitation 1, 5, 13, 28, 30, 34, 64, 70, 98, 182, 186–187, 220, 233, 242, 243, 246, 250–253, 272–273, 276, 298, 311, 328–330, 348, 350–355, 360–363, 368–369, 374, 399–401, 407; *see also* imitation; stereotypic imitation
attraction 28, 103, 248, 314, 328; force of 264; motivated 28
attribution 2, 13, 23, 28, 30, 32, 35–36, 187, 215, 239–242, 252–253, 274–275, 296, 298, 324, 326, 329–331, 335–336, 349, 353–354, 358–359, 375, 392, 398, 401–402
audience 4, 12, 18, 32, 35, 141–142, 147, 148, 233, 236, 249–250, 268, 331–332, 357, 360, 372, 391
auteur 18, 31, 65, 72, 76, 153, 334, 349, 377; *see also* author
author 1, 4, 6, 10, 17–24, 31, 97, 100, 119–120, 128, 130–131, 138–143, 145–146, 150, 153, 173, 187, 189, 206–207, 215, 218, 223, 237, 241, 265, 268, 270, 274–275, 279, 284–286, 288–290, 298, 316, 320, 324, 332, 336, 349, 356–359, 365, 370, 377–379, 399–401, 417–419,; as aristocrat 284–285; artificial intelligence 31, 400; as beggar 284, 295; consciousness of the 237; -construct 60, 130; copyright 143, 214, 234, 378; function 18; as god 352; incentives 392; mythology of the 236; nonhuman animal 51, 378; Romantic 352, 399; singular 20, 25, 65, 275, 349, 352, 372, 401; sovereign 61;starving 289; as tool of capitalism 283–284; wellbeing 419
authority 38, 60, 66, 209, 349, 352, 402
author's own intellectual creation 18, 37, 140–147, 215, 294, 313–314, 330, 372, 377
authorship: kinetic theory of 238; artificial authorship 92, 202, 285;

joint authorship 240, 334, 405; nonhuman animal authorship 11, 26, 217, 285, 293, 371, 408, 418–419
autonomy 22, 169, 398, 419; notion of 134; traditional 26
aversive salience 28
aversives 220–222
awareness 3, 17, 108, 129, 149, 150, 175, 177, 204, 317, 320, 360, 375; of awareness 128; bodily 149; dialogical 223; lack of 17; mental 393; personal 74; self- 14, 22, 129, 149; spatial 107

Babbage, C. 202
Bachelard, G. 4, 62, 68–69, 71–74, 165, 178, 179, 182–186, 201–204, 210, 395
Barad, K. 5
barriers 57, 60, 64, 65, 277; between 55; bisecting 55; concept of 274; language 65; logic of 207; object 77; play 59; *see also* language; species
Barthes, R. 35, 76–77, 401–402
Bataille, G 277, 283–287, 292, 295, 297
Bates, H. W. 330
Bateson, G. 325, 377–378
Bateson, P. 388, 392
Baudelaire C, 237, 295, 318
bees 149, 165, 170, 175, 180, 182, 188, 250, 322, 369, 393; glass 188; honey- 107; swarm of 188, 406
beggars and begging 232, 240, 284, 352; stupid 233, 284
behaviour 276, 295; communicative 220; education 337; explaining 176; human 332; injury-feigning 365; interpreting 220; maladaptive 10–11; motivated by 22; play 152; punishment of 219; repetitive 171; satirical 282; simple 174; unprincipled 187; wasteful 295
behavioural science 288, 393
behaviourism 109, 136, 179, 288, 323
Bekoff, M. 149; body-ness 149; i-ness 149; mine-ness 149
belief 1, 5, 15–16, 26, 28, 31–34, 61–63, 65–66, 68, 93, 98, 140, 212, 235, 276, 291, 316, 318–319, 323, 325, 375; anchors for 60; content of 404; different 291; dis- 351; evidence of 33; homogeneity of 315; imitation of 98, 276; magical 317; mistaken 324, 325; mutual 220; nonhuman animal 403; performance of 66; price of 28; psychologic; substantiation of 29; system of 6, 207; tribal 363; *see also* false belief
Benjamin, W. 4, 234–236, 238, 244, 249, 318, 335–336, 406
Bentham, J (2007/[1789]) 129, 157n69
Berg, S. van der 236
Berlyne, D. E. 272
Berne Convention 141
betweenness 58, 67; in- 55, 58–59, 248; *see also* duality; dualism; *metaxu*
bias 135, 243, 293, 329, 374; anthropocentric 5, 69, 170, 224, 252, 279; attention 238; calculated 126; cognitive 61, 222
bifurcation 285; of the art and science 57, 153; identifiable 239; implied 311; of losses and gains 61; of the natural world 206; of nature and culture 285, 395; of work and play 170
Binswanger, L. 148
biodiversity 29, 171
biologism 20
biosemiotics 147, 376
birds 37, 142, 291, 322, 333, 365–366, 368; African grey parrot 107; bluebird 319; coot 107; high-flying 367; hummingbirds 107; Japanese tit 369; nesting 180, 185, 367; plover 367; skylark 366–367; song 370
Bishop, J. M. 133
Blackstone, W. 215
Blom, I. 275
Borges, J. L. 397
boundaries 2, 51, 57–58, 62, 91, 109, 127, 165, 175–176, 203, 274, 289, 397; concepts 51, 274; disciplinary 5; disregard for 60; indecipherable 397; maintenance 372; -making 51, 122, 130, 274; marking 347; mental 392; motivated by 22; points 127; rational 172; war of 165
Bradbury, M. 364
Bradshaw, M. 396
Brecht, B. 285–286, 298, 314
Breton, A. 236, 269, 355, 370
British Broadcasting Company (BBC) 15, 16
Broom, D. M. 127

Burghardt, G. M. 171, 177, 179, 244–245, 393; *see also* play
Butler, S. 77
butterflies 333; Amazonian 330

Cage, J. 238, 240–241, 244, 334
Calvino, I. 165
Candea, M. 24
capacity 25–27, 34, 66–67, 69–70, 72–74, 107–108, 131–132, 141–142, 168, 172, 185, 212–213, 222, 242, 252, 288, 297, 317–318, 321–323, 325, 327, 333, 351, 363, 367, 369, 374, 392, 395, 403, 404, 417–419; of art 19; for attention 70; of authorship 28; -building 64; cognitive 405; creative 101, 325; for deception 322–323, 334–335; empty 184; expressive 150, 323; for imagery 318; for knowledge 69; for language 54, 63; limited 187; mental 92; nonhuman 288; potent 20; programmable 184; question of 129; sensory 135; subjective 129; to think 65–66; of vulnerability 67
capital 135, 150, 153, 169, 187, 217, 218, 284, 285, 372; circulation of 242, 286; cultural 169; drift of 61; of intellectual property objects 284; irredeemable 54; literary 131; models of sentience 5; predatory models of 5; preservation of 285; recuperation of 286; tool 285
capitalism 51–52, 206, 209–210, 253, 283–285
caricature 6, 203, 237, 282, 290, 332, 350–354, 356–357, 360, 375, 399
Cartesianism 59, 92, 377; anti- 73, 148, 183; contradiction in 58; criticism of 59; resilient 92; substance of 73; *see also* duality
categories 236, 292, 323, 360, 397; of art 17; base 171; capabilities in 67; human-animal distinction 53; of intellectual property 13; reasoning 67; of smells 67; thinking 56
cats 136, 250, 317–318, 322, 403
causality 55, 97, 123, 126, 129, 200–201, 203, 215, 218, 222, 245, 268, 275
celebrity 175, 239–241
Cervantes, M. 53

Chalmers, D. 31, 127
chatbot 134, 202
ChatGPT 135, 400
cheating 318
Chittka, L. 170, 180, 182
Choe, J. C. 168
choice 13, 24, 28, 34, 37, 141, 144–145, 208, 218–221, 313, 374
citation 32, 95, 274–275, 327, 337, 358, 396, 399
Civilisations (2018) 15, 91, 152, 175
Clare, J. 366–367
coercion 1, 12, 70, 187, 208, 220, 222, 223, 246, 251–253, 276, 328, 418; activity 418; binaries 296; consensus 58; cruel 418; force 253, 276; form of copying 13; imitation 221; monopoly 224; paradigm 220; potential 247; power 222; retelling 125; rule 187, 208; unreflective 13; usefulness 315; *see also* force
cognition: 4E 211; embedded 76, 328; embodied 10, 68, 71, 75–76, 92–94, 212, 291, 376, 377; enactive 404; extended 67, 76, 92, 144; *see also* enactivism; enaction
cognitive: ability 127, 395; agent 376; analysis 403; bias 61, 222; capacities 76, 404; creature 61; deficiency 252; enrichment 151; ethology 3, 66, 179, 388, 391, 394; evolution 68; function 96, 295; identity 376; model of value 139; processing 404; proficiencies 402; relevance 135; science 93, 135, 148, 173–174, 245, 286, 288, 335, 377; scientific thinking 212; semiotics 322; skills 16; studies 147, 376
Coleridge, S. T. 145, 318, 370
Coletta, W. J. 367
collaboration 12, 142, 178, 206, 207, 214, 253, 275, 405
collective 38, 107, 165, 180–181, 186–188, 238, 271, 315, 327, 328, 333, 349, 390; authorship 334; banality of 326; behaviour 181; character 126, 182; concept of the 38; critique of 177, 180; decision-making 180; enterprises 180; flourishing 222; functioning 181; glass 188; grand 38; hapless 188; homogeneous 125; homologous 398; indiscriminate 180; indistinctive 396; intelligence

180–181; inventive 181; limitations of 177; machine-like 327; mind 180–181; mindless 181; miscalculation of 188; monotonality of 267; motion 180; representations 58; of social production 181; social subject 146; species 25; summarising 101, 337; summation of the 390; tyranny of 285; unconscious 171; univocal 189; univocity of the 2; wisdom of the 187
Collingwood, R. G. 370–372
commercial flavour 204, 217, 219–220, 232, 246, 269, 276, 398
commodities 31, 168, 185, 238, 242, 419
communal property 2
communication 94, 97, 100, 105–106, 145, 147, 167, 181, 184, 185, 232, 273, 276, 318, 323–325, 334, 363, 394, 399; acts of 63, 276; bodily 323; catalyst for 97; commonality of 359; cooperative 290; of culture 14; dyadic 60; embodied 57, 73, 94, 181, 185, 291; embodiment of 97; expressive 148; failure of 203; functional 372; interpersonal 323; interplay of 96; interspecies 220; knotty 106; materials of 106; means of 58; meta- 75, 270, 325, 363; nonhuman animal 365, 370; perfect 325; representational 288; social 105–106, 275; symbolic 168, 177, 180–181, 185, 369; vocal 368
community 4, 18, 72, 76, 105, 107, 152, 153, 177, 179, 184, 206, 243, 246, 288, 289, 295, 316, 318, 326, 333; of authorial voices 349; authorship 138; creativity in 75; moral 129–130; play 238, 318; primatological 105; research 55; rhythm of 77; sociable 54
compassion 58, 173, 243, 273, 298, 397; fundamental basis for 273; intellectual property 151; relations 402; reservoir of 58
competition 6, 35, 54, 205, 206, 208, 232, 272, 323, 326, 355; damaging banalities of 3; false premise of 267; predatory drift of 205
complexity 5, 30, 56, 172, 174, 200, 271, 273, 293, 322, 332; cultural 98; of nonhuman wants 131

connections 2, 4, 6, 29, 183, 242, 281, 335, 348, 417, 419; of arguments 400; circulation of 289; human 281; impatient 140; important 64; proliferation of 352; requisite 360; willful 186
consensus 61, 98, 181, 351, 357, 407–408; -building 180; coercive 58; -decision making 181; -decision process 181; fallacious 187; social 171, 181; *see also* dissensus
consumer / consumption 18, 55, 123, 200, 204, 221, 223, 233, 243, 253, 268, 270, 277, 279, 283, 291, 296–297, 317–318, 331, 350; application 31; of art 236; articles of ordinary 216; behaviour 392; concept of conspicuous 296; human 123; of intellectual property 72; lack of 282; mass 146; passive 402; playful 297; production- 267; winter of 267–268; *see also* producer; user
contemplation 97, 234–235, 374
contradiction 58, 60, 66, 69, 77, 204, 223, 234; astonishing 66; essential 205; significant 17
control 22, 134, 176, 206, 216, 220, 222, 244, 251, 278, 282, 352, 357, 376, 391; environment 392; evidence of 278; exercise of 91; externalisation of 216; of the mind 186; potential 221; relationship of 10; *see also* force
co-production 178, 211, 214, 270, 367, 370, 372, 376, 402
copyright: actions 64; analogy 144; anthropocentrism of 77; attention bias 238; auteurism in 31; author 143, 234; automatic attachment of 143; claim of 9; context of 18, 29, 241; dilemmas 278; dispute 22; enforcement of 3; entitlement to 215; exceptionalism in 9; exploitation 418–419; expression in 68, 140, 276; framing problem 60; hegemony of 65; history of 9; infringement 23, 241, 283, 353; interest 22; lack of 26; language of 65; law 18, 27, 55, 141, 142, 146, 350, 356, 358, 372; legal fictions in 65; litigation 239, 241; mechanism of 200; narrative 97; objectivity in 146; objects of 2, 23; operation of 143; originality of 144,

146; paradox in 200; photographic 215; predatory drift of 61; protection 18, 23, 215, 282–283, 314; questions 25; recognition 19; system 62, 65, 284, 311, 326, 329, 350, 371, 418; violation 26; wants of 23; welfare principles in 278–279; work 20, 21, 64, 65, 72, 143, 243, 275, 282, 331, 351, 371
Copyright Act (1976) 23, 128
Copyright, Designs and Patents Act (1988) 352
Cornish, W. R. 144
correction 352–354, 364, 401, 407; connection 352; of an error 183; frenetic 406; literary 354; moral 358; or market failures 283; personal 389; process of 397; radical 399; of a sensory illusion 210
cost 29, 253
courtesy 219, 369
cows 168, 290
craft 1, 102, 104, 152, 210, 317, 318, 321, 371–372, 378
creative: accountancy 107, 142; act 35, 311; activity 17, 19, 72, 150; behaviour 140; capacity 101, 249; commodity 25; communities 38; deception 320; decisions 61; dissent 102; distinction 91; distraction 264, 417; endeavour 214; environment 253; expression 20, 37, 150, 220, 222; exuberance 34; freedom 37; inattention 6; industries 60, 138; intention 20, 21; lives 20; motivations 26; outputs 222; pattern 140; personality 140; potential 3; power 222; powers of the mind 23; process 21; production 200, 211, 294; quality 36; resource 185; transformation 60; work 5–6, 65, 72, 141, 150–151, 209, 216, 218, 220, 241, 281, 292, 311–312, 317, 325, 355, 374, 376, 405, 417, 419; workers 18; writing 20, 263
creativity: abundant 3; affective 5; affiliative function of 37; artificial intelligence; of authorship 254; capacity for 131; catalyst of 276; chaos of 327; collaborative 25; collapse 233; communal forms of 187; concepts of 142, 310;

constructive 273; contemporary 285; conventions around 120; critical value in 20; cultural complexity of 98; demonstration of 29, 152; differentiating systems of 6; dimension of 75; dirty 313; discourse on 94; disinterested 234; diversity of 136; embodied 211, 354; enforced environment for 220; evidence of 20; expressive mode of 146; extended 144; facility for 235, 254; gatekeeper of 151; imitative 1; incentives for 143, 251; inclusivity for 150; inconsequential 292; iterative 167; lack of 151; law's perspective on 5; loss of 220; malevolent 314; malign 311; marginalised forms of 25, 187; monadologicial approach to 4; motivation for 312, 332; movement of 76; multispecies 5, 419; narrative 146, 270; Naruto's 29; negative 8; nonhuman animal 2, 6, 22, 25, 37, 61, 120, 138, 143, 150–151, 178, 201, 209, 210, 219, 294, 332, 371–372; objects of 151; originality of 316; "othered" 209; over-regulation of 222; paths of 96; performer's 65; perspective on 277; play of 21; playful approach to 289; preclusion of 92; predisposition to 136, 248; presentations of 140; of pretence 4; process of 91; pseudo-biological narrative for 35; qualities of 6; recognising 22, 151, 312; research 312, 312; shadow 150–151; sociability of 37; social 20, 246, 273; sociology of 274; spontaneity of 136; stimulus for 109; stratification of 284; studies 233, 310; of swarms 3; utility 286; wants of 275; wasteful 272
credit 13, 34, 239–241, 270; *see also* attribution; stewardship
critical anthropomorphism *see* anthropomorphism
critical distance 237, 241, 276, 288, 322, 351, 355–356, 362, 374
crocodiles 291
Crump, B. 239, 241
culture 14–15, 17, 22, 56, 57, 95, 136, 168, 187, 221, 235, 271, 285, 292, 395, 401–402; acquisition of 238, 241, 316; animal culture 14;

behaviour 15; communication of 14; complex 168; concept of 14; cumulative 316, 406; domain of 56; exceptionalist 323; great ape 15; high 292; human 15, 91, 246; of impersonation 12; industry 146, 354; low 234, 292; material 292; nonhuman 15, 245; popular 171; vehicle of 14; wars 130
curation 35, 98, 141, 144, 153, 314, 400, 418
curiosity 10, 21–22, 27, 29, 34, 38, 68, 98, 103, 105, 141, 145, 207, 248–249, 272, 333, 389, 397, 401, 416; artificial 207–208, 254; dialectic of 248; imitation of 248; inventive 208; middling 60; Naruto's 28–29; playful 251; recognition of 248

Dadaism 236, 238
Dahrendorf, R. 203
dance 11–12, 96, 100, 142, 267, 369; choreography of 405; language of bees 180, 369; performance 294; swarm 182; *see also* bees
Dancing Monkeys, The 11–13, 331–332, 363–364
Danto, A. C. 149
Darwin, C. 55, 125–126, 172, 176, 178–179, 205–206, 288, 392, 394
Darwin, E. 413n118
Dawkins, M. S. 24, 139, 233
de Armado, A. 4
de la Mare, W. 200
de Volder, B. 57
death-feigning *see* thanatosis
Debord, G. 354
debt 90, 200–201, 253, 324, 349, 351; circulation of 200; cycle of 270; inescapable 269; intergenerational 240; ironic 349; legacy of 2; of stewardship 77
decapods 79n38, 193n86
deceit 322, 325, 337; absence of 320
deception 1, 6, 33–34, 75, 98, 103, 254, 291, 310, 312, 316–325, 327, 328, 331, 334–335, 337, 347, 348, 367–368, 373–374; achievements of 316, 323; animal 312, 323; apparent 373; artful 368; authorial 153, 310, 321, 348; capacity for 317, 322, 335; concept of 320; contradictory 317; creative 320; critical 1, 6; defensive 367; genuine 320; honest 325; innovation of the 61; intentional 4, 291, 320; nonhuman animal 317, 323; play of 321, 330, 335; principle of 351; purposive 33; strategy of 291, 317, 322, 325, 355, 387, 393; willful 316
Delahaye, P. 56
Deleuze, G. 148
Dennett, D. C. 61, 367, 394
Derrida, J. 2, 58
Descartes, R. 58, 66, 71, 74, 333
design 18, 121, 122, 135, 137, 207–208, 243, 282, 313–314, 320; common 334; experimental 147; law 314; protection 313; research 15, 17, 24, 170, 367
desire 9, 16, 24, 26, 37, 57, 61, 64, 68, 71, 98, 102, 135, 148, 173, 206–207, 212, 242, 244, 247–248, 267–268, 275–278, 280, 281, 284, 287, 297, 315, 318, 325
Desmond, W. 245
Despret, V. 342n124
détournement 290, 296, 330, 354–355, 358; *see also* Situationist International
development 19, 30, 31, 61, 98–99, 106, 127, 145, 174, 177, 244–245, 263, 271, 295, 326, 328, 330, 336, 388, 395, 396, 408; contemporary 76; cultural 146, 184; economic 295; evolutionary 223; legal 400–401; of maladaptive behaviour 10–11; personal 150; policy 10; principles of 208; scientific 72; social 14
Device for the Autonomous Bootstrapping of Unified Sentience (DABUS) 19, 217
dialectic 18, 68, 98, 203–204, 223, 248, 251, 270, 290, 322, 337, 397, 399, 407–408; critical 123; radical 334
dialogue 53–54, 100, 201, 203, 248, 251, 333, 335, 352, 355; embodied 290; honest 241; iterative 53; Platonic 249; of ruptures 53; Socratic 269
Dialogue of the Dogs, The 53
Diamond the dog (Isaac Newton) 263–265, 315
Dick, P. K. 328
diffraction 5, 264, 330

diffusion 35, 175, 183, 284, 348; cultural 250, 377; Tardean 330
digital 289–290, 316, 317; -based social theory 276; computers 326; environment 253, 290, 317; product 289, 371; property 75; realm 398
disguise 75, 98, 275, 327, 330, 335, 347, 365, 374; ambiguous coquetry of 73; authorship of 330; rhythm 69
disgust 171–172
dissensus 61, 98, 275, 327, 374, 407; affiliative 274; ironic 271
distance 234, 247, 324, 355–356, 359, 374–375, 390; dispassionate 236; intimate 71; loss of 276; play of 290; scientific 243; *see also* critical distance; *detournement*
distraction 6, 137, 233–236, 238, 240–242, 244, 272, 283, 290, 296, 298, 347, 354, 365, 367; clear 64; creative 264, 417; discussion of 296; disingenuous 242; display 365–367; drive to 233, 367; flushing 366; mischief of 254; of play 296; significance of 238; of strangeness 296; unproductive 19; useless 234; value of 263; wealth of 328; *see also* wandering
diversification 250, 279
Dobzhansky, T. 293, 294
doctrine of accession *see* accession, doctrine of
dogmatism 337
dogs 6, 16, 53, 56, 67, 76, 94, 107, 109, 149, 168, 222, 233, 249–250, 264, 273, 288, 290, 293, 321
dominion 71, 210, 213, 216, 220, 251
Donath, J. 129
Douglas, M. 10, 74
dreams 19, 328–329, 365–366
duality 57–60, 65, 90, 207, 356, 395; Cartesian 55, 57, 65, 92, 377; contrived 207; obstinate 279; phenomena of 313
Ducasse, I. 74, 353
Duflo, E. 295
Duhamel, G. 234, 236
Durkheim, É. 38, 59, 77, 126, 396

Eco, U. 321
ecological psychology 76, 211

economics 10, 28, 204, 206, 217, 296–297
effort 29, 31, 55, 102, 122, 176, 181, 183, 187, 208, 234, 237, 270, 275, 285, 393; active 250; constructive 102; creative 311; of discovery 69, 77; doctrine of 69; enterprising 108; equivalence in 213; muscular 244; negative 244; phenomenal 140; subjective experience of 140; wasted 277
Eichberg, H. 252
Einstein, A. 287
Ellul, J. 237
embodied cognition *see* cognition
embodied communication and expression 57, 64, 73, 94, 149, 181, 184, 289, 290
emergentism and emergent evolution 394–395
empathy 74, 108, 140, 242, 243, 273, 378
Empire of the Ants (1905) 167
enaction 71, 76, 377, 402
enactivism 76, 211, 376, 377, 402, 404
energy 74, 97, 212, 268; bundle of 97; -depleting 75; excess 277; of knots 99; productive 62; social 97; surplus 10; wasted 222
Engelhardt, A. 23
enrichment 10, 18, 23; cognitive needs 170; obstacles 177; pressures 317
entropy 6, 98, 271, 273, 280, 398
environmental: aesthetics 209; aspects 418; critiques 280; legislation 171; limitations 103; management 171, 224
epiphenomena 123, 126, 133, 135–136, 143, 146
epistemological: break 62, 183; obstacle 62, 64, 183, 201, 203; rupture 62
equilibrium 203; dynamic 203; economic 151; necessity of 295; Newtonian dis- 273; perceived 151
error 133, 135, 182, 269, 297, 321, 326–327; anthropomorphic 365; experimental 183; human 321; serious 70; trial and 101, 105, 169, 177; value of 183; *see also* mistake
Espinas, A. 180, 246
ethical 34, 151, 329, 408; attention 75; benefits 11; concerns 9, 172, 206,

216; consequences 36; dimension 28, 101, 233, 393; encounter 27; engagement 147, 149; issues 173, 329; limitations 18; parameters 206; questions 393; regard 10

ethological: account 181, 247, 328, 337–338; accountability 32; appreciation 400; approach 2, 6, 13, 26, 37–38, 58, 59, 65, 76, 103, 120, 147, 167, 176, 210–211, 233, 247, 273, 279, 287, 313, 315, 370–371, 377, 401, 408; attention 10, 76, 242, 243, 247, 253; authorship 69; context 211; dimension 151; enculturation 336; enquiry 3; ethic 402; expansion 55; experience 315; glow 178; insight 67; justice 336, 397; methodology 274; model 33, 274; perspective 25, 65, 107, 131, 153, 181, 186–187, 212, 222, 369, 417; properties 240; quality 274; sensibility 59; value 362

ethological jurisprudence 1–7, 12, 15, 32, 37, 39, 54, 62, 69, 70, 97, 101, 130, 150, 242–243, 274, 277, 408

ethology 6, 15, 32, 224, 244–245, 388, 393, 397, 402; of ants 168; cognitive 3, 66, 179, 388, 391, 394; of flourishing through cooperation 206; of imitation and innovation 37; of rhythms and assemblages 148; of the swarm 186

European Patent Convention 314

evolution: cognitive 68; of beings 126; emergent 395; of human language 91; of mind 395; theory of 391

exceptionalism 9, 60, 63, 119–120, 323, 392; absolute 56; bastion of 152; distinction of 72; doctrine of 55; human 5, 12, 54–55, 57, 77, 91–93, 119, 174, 175, 178–180, 205–207, 291, 408; of language 368; linguistic 92; mythical 71

expenditure 269, 277; concept of 297; expressive 234; personal 285; surplus 6; unconditional

experience 9, 14, 33, 62, 68, 69, 109, 134, 139–140, 142, 149, 173, 177, 181, 183, 186, 189, 208, 222, 244–245, 251, 253, 294–295, 312, 317, 336, 370, 374, 376, 389, 390, 402; actual 144; aesthetic 142, 146, 369, 372; aversive 173; -based learning 176; collaborative 372; creative 377; direct 235, 377; dynamic 147; embodied 148; emotional 139; ethological 315; familiar 240; harrowing 416; human 377, 394; of knowledge 68; manual 69; multisensory 210; Naruto's 33, 213; objective 139; perceptive 394; phenomenal 134, 401; real 109; relational 214; sensory 61; simultaneous 212; social 272; somatic 236; spectator's 235; subjective 30, 139–140, 147–149, 173, 182, 189, 237, 250, 263, 364, 370, 372, 376

explainability 30–33, 35, 144, 188, 275, 298, 337, 375, 401; artificial intelligence (XAI) 29–30, 32, 122; authorial trust 31; as a barrier 31; of intentionality 21; problem 5, 29–30, 32, 33, 90, 99, 122, 238, 375; question of 30; of sentience 252

exploration 1, 3, 64, 182, 272, 355, 389; diversive 272; of emotion 170; intentional 214; open-ended 272; of personhood 150; of relationship 355; scientific 14; specific 272; of truth 318

expression: active 367; aesthetic 363, 371; affiliative 377; artistic 106, 213; author's own intellectual creation 146, 377; bodily 139; communal 187; concept of 140; condition of 60; of consciousness 395; conventions of 316; copyright and 62, 68, 145, 276; creative 20, 36, 150, 220, 222; cultural 124, 138, 151, 170, 187, 201, 209–210, 242–243, 278, 372, 419; dichotomy 82n94; embodied 64, 149, 184, 289; enactive approach to 98; enduring forms of 65; ethological approach to 376; exemplary 185; field of 72; freedom of 10, 26, 28, 33, 220; happy 406; human 336; of humour 358; image-laden 406; individuality of 100; innovative 222; of intellectual creation 214, 378; of intentionality 93; nature of 76; nonhuman animal 64, 65, 284, 364, 408; object of 420; pastiche of 153; performative 408; physiognomic 106; playful 249; pleasurable 220; and purpose 68;

purposeful 371; rationalisation of 372; resources of 10; revelatory 183; sensory 370–372, 374; of sentience 188; shorter than short 389; spatial 290; specific 276; subjective 146–148; unfettered 12; world of 67

fables 1–2, 4, 11–12, 165, 175, 267–269, 331, 348, 355, 416
fair dealing 326, 353
fair use 326, 350, 352
fair(ness) 16, 29, 107, 109, 280, 288, 312, 314, 326, 350–351, 353, 361; associated 290; less than 201; means of foul 350; perceived un- 108; sense of 107; social 275; *see also* inequity aversion
false belief 33, 291, 320, 324
familiar production 1–3, 28, 37, 38, 59, 75, 106, 125, 141, 168, 175, 180, 182, 185–187, 247, 251, 271, 276, 289, 297, 315, 326, 333–334, 349, 388, 399, 405, 406
fans and fandoms 25, 31, 186, 188
Farrell, B. A. 139–140
fashion 105, 210, 235, 243–244, 314, 358, 372, 377, 404
Fifield, W. 263
film 236, 238, 241, 314, 349; producer 270; work 138; worlds 405
Fink, E. 290
fish 17, 149, 250, 291; angel- 104; mosquito- 107; stickleback 149
flair 416–417
Flexner, A. 272, 287; Report (1920) 287
Floridi, L. 134
Flusser, V. 171
force 28, 77, 165, 201, 205–209, 217–224, 246–247, 253, 264, 315, 318, 327, 336, 364, 398, 408; anthropocentric 204, 208; architecture of 221; of attraction 264; character of 204; of coercion 251; "commercial flavour" of 204; concept of 5, 220; creative 145; curative 312; of diffraction 264; direct 219; disciplinary circulation of 220; driving 251; dynamic of 219–220, 224; economics of 205; of enforcement 209; equilibrium of 224; excessive 206; fundamental 208; of habit 2, 126, 135, 140, 143, 279; harmonizing 126; historical 221; of imitation 276; instruments of 92; intensive qualities of 205; irreversibility of 204; mechanism of 204; narrative of 220; of nature 205; normative 132; perspectival 5; play of 249; positive 358; presenting 204; reversibility of 204, 233; show of 205–207; social order of 222; spent 218; subject to 205; threads of 201

fragment 6, 24, 30, 38, 51–52, 73, 95, 102, 241, 315, 333–337, 349, 352, 367, 395–402; aesthetic 315; concept of 398, 405; connections between 6; emergence of the 334; ethology of 402; historical instance in 389; integrity of the 399; legal 407; literary 95, 223, 237, 335–336, 397, 399; precious 369; romantic 334; of the Romantics 60, 397, 398; self-contained 2, 397; singularity of the 336; social 33; solitary 265; truth of the 334; unfinished 402; whole 396

framing 11, 21, 24, 30, 31, 56, 60–62, 72, 151, 209, 219, 222, 244, 288, 328, 347, 360, 388; *see also* boundaries
Fraser, D. 138
free will 219
freedom 10, 24, 141, 145, 213, 219, 253, 294, 336, 350, 359; of aesthetic expression 363; of choice 37; creative 37; desirable 350; of expression 12, 26, 28, 33, 220; five 10; principle of 141; from thinking 212; in thinking 394
free-riding 209
Freud, S. 288
Frey, R. G. 321
friendship 175
Frow, J. 284
frustration 10, 205, 216, 241, 268, 280–283, 295, 297
functionalism 16, 35, 99, 171, 176

Gadamer, H. -G. 27, 248, 250–252, 270, 294–295, 329
Gallotti, M. 404
games and gaming 34, 75, 95, 106, 168, 173, 236, 238, 269–270, 297, 351; of authorship 2; ball 297; children's 251; Navajo string 95; sociality of 238;

video 318; voluntary moral code of 222; *see also* play
Gangadharbatla, H. 21
Gasché, R. 335–336, 398
Gaye, M. 239, 240
Genette, G. 348, 359–360, 366
genius 189–190, 242, 352; artistic 61, 234; of authorship 122; creative 372; elusive quality of 263; musical 368; narrative 240; presentation of 241; romantic 239; singular 239, 352
genre 97, 237, 313, 359, 364, 398; conventions of a 276; fragmentary 335; narrative 388; obsession with 335; Romantic 335, 398; understanding of the 363
gesture 59, 94, 100, 146, 182, 288, 368–371, 406; aesthetic 368, 371; fluttering 369; Kiremidjian 369; Lyotard 407; referential 220; sensation of 369; of theatre 405
Gesunde Nerven 234
Ginsburg, J. 234
Glass Bees, The (1957) 188
global: north 282; south 295
goals 10, 28, 29, 34, 93, 178, 291, 315–316, 324; of authorship 10; imputing 10; -seeking 27
Godard, J. -L. 349
gods 348–349; capricious 283; divine providence of the 348; playful regard of the 349
Goetsch, W. 170
Gombrich, E. H. 106
Goodin, R. E. 138
Gossman, L. 407
Gould, S. J. 121, 125–126, 133, 135, 143, 146, 205, 319–320
Grant, U. S. 73–74, 76
gravity: fullness of 319; momentum for 352; moral 264
grief 16
Griffin, D. R. 14, 323, 365, 375, 393–394
Groos, K. 248–249
Guattari, F. 148
Guilford, J. P. 140

habit 55, 57, 62, 70, 135, 149, 170, 212–213, 221, 279; bad 207; breaking 62, 68; force of 2, 126, 135, 140, 143; ground-feeding 367; of justice 203, 207, 279; of objective knowledge 62; of perception 62; of rationality 207; renegotiation of 56; repertoire of 293; suppression of wants 58
habitat 9, 149, 210, 212; conservation 209; ground-nesting 367; preferences 374
hallucinations 321, 328, 365, 389, 398; AI 328; language of 328
handedness 91, 92, 209
hands 53, 55, 58, 77–78, 93–94, 204, 286, 291; changing 204; extension of 94; farm 216, 281; -shake 290; show of 91; *see also* touch
Hannoosh, M. 363
happiness 15, 18, 68, 102, 139, 142, 148, 153, 182, 186, 207, 214, 221, 275, 280, 297–298, 401; apparent 18; of authorial deception 318; of authorship 298; expressive potential of 182, 221; gift of 221; human 221; of parody 352, 359; playful 298; potential for 297; values of 274; in work 297, 350, 355, 370, 379
haptic *see* touch
Haraway, D. 30, 54, 95, 169, 243, 334, 406
Harris, J. 73
hedgehog 396–398
Heidegger, M. 58
Hermes *see* Mercury
Herzfeld, C. 99–101, 104–107
Hillman, B. 189
Hitch Hiker's Guide to the Galaxy, The (1986) 89; Deep Thought 89–90, 202; Dent, A. 89
Hobson-West, P. 56
Hofstadter, D. R. 238, 244–245
Hohfeld, W. N. 72
Hölderlin, F. 349–350
Hölldobler, B. 170
Homer 51, 347–349, 362; *Iliad* 204, 347, 348; legacy 348; *Odyssey* 51, 347–349, 362
homo: economicus 296, 326; *ludens* 296; *prodigi* 296, 298; *sapiens* 16
Horowitz, A. 220
horses 109, 273, 373
Huber, M. P. 168, 184, 185, 323
Hughes, J. 280
Hugo, V. 75, 182

human exceptionalism *see* exceptionalism
human rights 209, 285
humour 122, 145, 288, 334, 348, 350, 357–358, 377; attention to 288; expression of 358; ironic 367; jokes 34, 347, 388; sense of 288, 337; structure of 59
Husserl, E. 148
Hutcheon, L. 355, 361–362
Huyssen, A. 146

idea 13, 51, 105, 139, 142, 167, 180, 183, 212–214, 233, 240, 252, 280, 294, 310, 316, 334, 337, 354, 369, 377, 388, 398, 403, 406, 407; active 402; of animal reason 393; completion of 183; dichotomy of 62; dominant 176; exaggerated 202; false 354; fundamental 183; intellectual property world 123–125; intergenerational stewardship of 242; of a nonhuman animal author 51; particular 96; prevailing 176; of progress 354; of property 71; sequence of 234; stewardship of 326, 398; wasteful 287; *see also* expression
idolatry 327–328; Roman 327; self- 417
illusion 67, 245, 317–318, 329, 399; contours 317; notion of 317; optical 318; sensory 210; susceptibility to 317
image 1, 29, 54, 75, 212, 245, 276, 327, 337; -based works 18; capacity for 317; -laden expressions 406; memetic 276, 336; moving 76–77; of the project 57; uniquely patterned 96
imagination 67, 69, 91, 140, 145–146, 170, 183, 186, 212, 245, 316, 329, 394; act of 141; expressive 186; obstacles of 33, 91; play of 183; poetic 318; poverty of 295; strained 337
imitation: access to 253; affiliative 13, 37, 64; animal 20; banal 34; of beliefs 98, 276; coercive 221, 276; concept of 246; conscious 1, 247, 252, 273; consideration of 37; contagion of 181; creative 249, 330; cultures of 187; deliberate 1; detailed account of 6; dialectic of 337; differentiation of 13; ethological account of 247; ethological approach to 13; ethology of 37; evaluative 246, 328; expressive 12; false 327; familial 267; fecundity of 267; genuine 243, 246, 361; indentured 12; innovation 75, 180, 253, 275, 353; innovative reckonings of 13; inventive potential of 13; ironic 271, 351, 366, 374; laws of 59; movements of 77; of mutual interests 13; object of 98, 332; originality of 329, 352, 353; painstaking 98; perception of 332; in plagiarism 354; potential of 336; purposive 98; rays 4, 125, 240, 241, 336; relational 374; relationality of 32; rules-based 246, 328; secondary 253; of shared interests 13; sociable 13; social momentum of 33; social ties of 246–247; sociality of 237, 275, 294; society of 35; sociology of 13, 70; sophisticated 368; symbolic 368; theory of 32, 137, 284, 400; transformative impulsion of 13; universality of 13; unoriginal 34; vocal 368; *see also* attentive imitation; stereotypic imitation
impersonation 1, 12, 31
In a House Subcommittee on Electronic Surveillance (2009) 189
incentives 13, 28, 35–36, 124, 128, 136, 146, 150, 200–201, 203, 215, 218, 220, 222, 283, 417–420; author 392; banality of 37; calculation of 218; causality of 218; to creativity 251; doctrine of 35; economic 35, 140, 417; interrogation of 219; language of 124; narrative 36, 109, 200, 218, 292, 418; paradigm of 287, 417; punishment as an 218; rational 310; reconstruction of 143–144; salience 28, 233, 317, 389
individualism 37, 187–188, 206, 212, 404; of expression 100; psychological 404
inequity aversion 108–109
infinitesimal 126, 165, 390, 396; attention to the 179; in imitation 183; innovations 406; situations 388; sociology of the 59; *see also* miniature
Ingold, T. 95
injury-feigning *see* distraction, displays

innovation 1, 3–4, 12, 16, 20, 31, 37, 53, 61, 70, 76, 98–100, 106, 120, 123–124, 179–180, 205, 218, 220, 221, 237, 241, 246, 248, 253, 271, 274, 276, 285, 293, 310, 316, 317, 329–330, 353, 372, 394, 399, 406; agricultural 168; diffusion of 35; infinitesimal 406; inventor's 18; irreverent 224; key aspect of 271; model of 274; movement of 124; mythology 205; narrative 4, 123–124, 201, 310; of nonhuman animals 120; oversight of 314; paradigm of 124, 277; participatory 273; register of 377; relevance of 314; technical 106, 291; technological 310; traditional 292

insects 168, 170–172, 175, 182, 246, 288, 290; ambivalence around 172; concept learning in 177; concourse of 184; exclusion of 172; inclusion of 172; inner world of 182; limited species of 171; social 175–176; swarms of 6, 184; understanding 172

intellectual creation 101, 143–147, 187, 213, 214, 249, 285, 298, 311, 313–314, 321, 325, 328; apperception of the 145; attention to 187, 247, 419; author's own 18, 37, 140–142, 144–146, 215, 294, 314, 330, 372, 375, 377, 417–420; barrier of 207; capacity for 418; concept of 142; cultural complexities of 189; economic theory of 286; experience of 294; expression of 214, 378; expressivity of 206, 376; field of 371; fundamental quality of 145; fundamental test of 144; joy in 206; meaning of 354; nature of 144; originality in 351; particularisation of the 145; personal 144; process of 377; question of 419; recordings of 140; waste of 222, 286

intellectual property: anthropocentric 3, 213; application of 63; architecture of 188; assumptions of 175; attention in 28; authorship 18, 149; categories of 13; compassionate 151; consumers of 72; creation of 128; currency of 4; discourse 234; economic rationality of 28; ethological jurisprudence of 3, 39; explainability in 30; formal rules of 10; iconography of 122; institution of 6, 119; jurisprudence of 274; justice of 201; language of 209; law 58, 208, 270, 275; legal framework 75; logic of 55; mechanism of 284, 311; more-than-human 3, 55, 62, 336, 419; objects of 5, 97, 124, 147, 214, 242, 266, 278, 282, 284, 313, 371; operation of 38; paradigm 37, 123, 316; phenomenal 142; phenomenological 147; potential 31, 400; protection 137, 314, 315; purview of 4; relational property of 36; reorientation of 11; re-socialisation of 147; resolution of 208; rights 35, 141, 150, 218, 313, 418; scholarship 19; socio-cultural architecture of 150; solutions 18; stewardship of knowledge through 30; story of 5; structural emphasis in 3; sustainability of 206; system 55, 91, 124, 136, 138, 151, 167, 185, 188, 203, 206, 224, 232, 278–282, 287, 310–311, 420; world 123–125

intelligence 56, 62, 99, 102, 133, 134, 136, 167, 178, 180, 186, 207–208, 238, 244; animal 176, 391; campaign of 57; collective 180, 181; concept of 19, 56, 134; disobedience of 102; expressive 182; hierarchy 179; higher 291; human 136, 174, 207, 405; Machiavellian 387; machine 134, 173; of the maker 152, 378; narrative of 175; objective of 207; production 135; proof of 99; spatial 184–185; species hierarchy of 103; super- 122; swarm 168, 179–181, 185–187; technical 288; tests 135; *see also* artificial intelligence

intention 16, 21, 31, 61, 64, 72–73, 105, 121, 136, 138, 142–143, 173, 175, 177, 209, 219, 247, 284, 287, 313, 316–317, 321, 323, 328, 332, 335–336, 365, 401–404; act of deception 320; of aesthetic objects 77; attitude 336; authorial 291; causal narrative of 20; collective 404; creative 20, 21; of deception 4; deception 291; dialectical nature of 64; discussions of 27; emphasis on 20,

64; evidence of 316; explainability of 21; exploration 214; expression of 93; force 336; frame of 143; human 24; impossible question of 143; imputing 19; inductive 174; interactive 404; of knots 95, 99; of the machine 21; narrative 26; notions of 140; objects 147; obstacle 14; perceived 173; performance 367; perspective on 97; presumption of 19; requirement of 138; sense of 146; shared 404–405; stance 64, 121, 122, 134, 138, 208, 328, 367; states 291; strategy 138; surface play of 153; systematic 336; thinking 367; through play 6; totality 408; trajectory of 138; understanding of 243
intentionality 4, 6, 16, 19–21, 30, 61, 64, 72–73, 95, 97, 99, 121, 136, 140, 143–144, 153, 172, 209, 219, 247, 284, 287, 316, 328, 332; of aesthetic objects 77; authorial 291; causal narrative of 20; collective 404; of deception 4; discussions of 27; explainability of 21; expression of 93; human 24; imputed 20; inductive 174; presumption of 19; sense of 146; shared 404; supposed 401
interests 10, 26, 29, 33–34, 60, 65, 146, 171, 173, 203, 210, 214, 270–271, 277, 357; aesthetics 26; animal 245; dominant 136; equation of 67; of human exceptionalism 55; of humankind 9; layered 2; mutual 13, 27, 70, 99, 187, 246–247, 271, 274, 276; nonhuman animals 12, 26, 125, 149, 205, 209; ownership 36; separate 186; service of 34; shared 1, 10, 11, 13, 21, 27, 28, 38, 57, 70, 94, 98, 101, 108, 147–149, 165, 168, 169, 180, 181, 186–187, 189, 241, 246–247, 253, 271, 273, 274, 276, 297, 323, 334, 355, 403–405
inter-psychology 13, 32, 71, 177, 179, 223, 297, 390
invention 6, 13, 20, 60, 92, 101, 106, 120, 140, 144–145, 180, 202, 217, 274, 284, 310, 314, 327, 419; anecdote of 396; claims to 17; initial 353; ownership of 168; scientific 106; underlying 282; useful 120; value of 153

invertebrates 171–173, 288, 292, 365; social 170; underestimation of 175
irony 2, 5, 59, 122, 151, 319, 321, 334–335, 351–352, 355–358, 361, 365, 368, 399; of absolute reason 352; of authorship 319, 367; capacity for 325, 367; concept of 334, 336, 351; curious 58, 185; defensive 366; delectable 349; deployment of 366; ecstatic 319; iconic 367; interpretation of 351; in mockery 355; nonhuman capacity for 288; paradox of 71; of parody 361; play of 60, 71, 153; purposes of 351; relationship to 355; rich 349; Romantic 335, 351; semiotic 367; sociality of 358; Socratic 319, 335, 351, 365–367, 373, 396; spectacular 356; twisted 310; world of 351
Isaacs, N. 137

Jakobson, R. 362
James, W. 248
Jameson, F. 51–52, 360
Janz, B. B. 29
Jena Romanticism 333, 335, 350, 352, 354, 358, 367, 396, 406
Jordan, M. I. 133
Jousse, M. 273
joy *see* happiness
Joyce, J. 348, 362
Jünger, E. 188
Jurgens, A. 403
jurisprudence 32, 39, 72, 137, 274, 351, 356, 401; human rights 285; limited 356; property 72; sociological 138, 400; *see also* ethological jurisprudence
justice 38, 201, 203, 205, 207, 219, 221–222, 269, 273, 296, 336, 387, 406–407; access to 406; administration of 407; assimilation of 203; causality of 203; contract of 203; critical interrogation of 201; distributive 269; epistemological obstacle to 203; ethological 33, 336, 397; habits of 203; inconsistent definition of 201; narrative of 202; postjuridical 223; rationality of 224; sense of 269, 367; social 109, 150, 237, 274, 296, 390; spirit of 242; true meaning of 203; wild 203

Kant, I. 61, 370
Kashyap, R. 207
Kaufman, J. C. 150
Kettering, C. F. 141
khipu (*Quipu*) 96
Kimmerer, R. W. 206
King, A. 246
kinship 4, 21, 141, 403; creative 125; expressive 186; familial 333; imitative 38; relational 141
Kiremidjian, G. D. 369
Klopfer, P. H. 374, 388, 392
knots and knotting 52, 93–97, 99–107; energy of 99; essential 223; geometrical properties of 107; import of 94; intentionality of 95; magic 95; nautical 97; sequence of 96; strings of 95; tying of 93, 100–101, 107; Wattana's 99–101, 105, 186; see also world knot
Köhler, W. 102, 105
Kornblum, A. 152–153, 378
Krauss, R. E. 322
Kwasny, M. 189

Lacoue-Labarthe, P. 333, 335
landmarks and monuments 76, 174, 184, 390, 401
language: acquisition 73; aesthetic 77, 368; animal 63–65; anthropomorphic 245; of authorship 24, 143, 370; barrier 62–65, 92; biological narrative of 55; body 78, 370; capacity for 54; dance 180, 369; embodied 57, 90, 92, 93, 96, 107; of entitlement 72; everyday 359; of exclusion 62; functional 313; of hallucination 133, 320, 328; human 54–55, 63, 91–92, 368; literal 64; management of 65; meta- 363; musical 364; of obedience 219; origins 55; of personhood 25; problem 65; of protection in welfare 270; proto- 290; of rights 71–72; of selfhood 27; shared 240; studies 55; symbolic 64, 65, 67; of wants 10, 27, 28
Large Language Models (LLMs) 18, 98, 126, 135, 146, 187–188, 238, 280, 327–328, 337, 390–391
Latour, B. 71, 179, 276, 326, 363
Lautréamont, Comte de/ID 74, 354
Leakey, L. 105

Learn to Earn 219
learning 28, 60, 64, 98, 107, 135, 169, 184, 201, 208, 219, 222, 223, 236, 243, 249, 253, 273, 320, 364, 370, 397; abilities 176; affiliative 75, 98; animal 174, 244; associative 177, 250; avoidance 184; classical form of 20; concept 177, 180; cultural 332; embodied 94; experienced-based 176; human 244; in imitation 53; imitative 368; machine 31, 60, 94, 326; process 98; reinforcement 177; social 12, 16, 20, 70, 98, 126, 168, 180, 271, 273, 277, 296, 364
Lebenswelt 148
Lefebvre, H. 185, 210, 211
Leibniz, G. W. 4, 24, 59, 70–71, 90, 123, 125, 139, 143, 183, 206, 275, 327; concept of the monad 59, 70, 149, 271; criticism of Cartesianism 59; movement of mind 70; perceptions of perceptions 59; philosophy of mind 59, 70; theory of motion 97; theory of relations 181
Lents, N. H. 14
Leroux, G. 328
Lestel, D. 20, 101, 105–107
Lewes, G. H. 242
Lewontin, R. 121, 125–126, 133, 135, 143, 146, 205, 319
lifeworld (*Lebenswelt*) 148; see also *Umwelt*
Linguistic Society of Paris 55
Lion's Share Fund 37
Lispector, C. 165–166
Locke, J. 279–281, 283
Loo, S. 172
love 57, 58, 188, 219, 242, 244, 264, 311, 333, 337, 370; object of 337
Lovelace, A. 144, 202
lying 6, 73, 311, 318, 322–324; see also deception
Lynch, K. 280
Lynch, M. 363
Lyotard, J-F 407

Machiavellian 323, 387
machine learning 31, 60, 94, 168, 326
magic 95, 134, 317–318; proto 317; wanton 263
make believe 6, 33, 59, 75, 269, 324

Maldoror (*Les Chants de Maldoror*) 74–75
marginalisation 31, 38, 358
Markl, H. 323
Marques, M. A. 358
Massumi, B. 20, 56, 295
mathematics 90, 99, 107, 109, 276, 316
Matson, W. A. 73, 128, 136, 188, 326
Medawar, P. 141
Meltzer, F. 92
memetics 275
mentality 10, 34, 70, 90; animal 14, 70; inner 34; presence of 27; sense of 10
Mépris, Le (1963) 349
Mercury 1–4, 6, 263, 265, 347–349
Merleau-Ponty, M. 148
metacommunication 75, 270, 325, 363
metaphor 69, 92, 238, 246; of dominion 213; empty 74
metarepresentational abilities 14, 15
metaverse 75, 289, 371, 377
metaxu 58, 68, 71, 82n80, 91, 92, 109, 125, 152, 186, 235, 240, 251, 271, 274, 396
methodology 5, 59, 66, 288, 351, 359, 362, 372; of critical anthropomorphism 244; of doubt 66; ethological 274
middle and mediating 5, 55, 57, 60, 68, 202, 232, 243, 248, 347, 357
Midgley, M. 62
milieu 148–149
Millar v Taylor (1769) 387
Milton, K. 138
mimicry 12, 330–332, 356, 360; Batesian 330–331; effective 332; facial 273; nonhuman 331; vocal 368
Mind at the End of Its Tether (1945) 121
mind-body problem 5, 38, 90–91, 209
miniature 165, 183; mosaic 74
Minkowski, E. 185
Minsky, M. 377
minute perceptions 5, 59, 70, 353, 388
mirror 22, 245, 320, 327–328, 416–417; mirror test 135; misinformation of 388; olfactory 112n32, 159n114; problem 170, 417, 419; smelly 76; *see also* idolatry
mistake 34, 98, 135, 165, 272, 321, 324, 325, 327, 328, 406; *see also* error

Mitchell, R. 331, 375
mobility 34, 51, 167, 214
mockery 355–359, 362
model collapse 189
modernism 21, 336, 396
monad 57, 59, 70, 149, 271, 274–276, 315; aggregative 59; approach 4, 274, 276; closed 70; gregariousness of 57; impenetrable 271; neo- 37; open 71, 271; quality of 59, 76; renewed 271; sociology of 396
money 24, 146, 278, 286; *see also* capital
moral 1, 17, 267, 286; accountancy 109; agency 128; code of games 222; community 130; consideration 25, 129; correction 358; dimension of play 249; gravity 264; hostility 286; judgment 109; person 26; philosophy 207; practices 278; protection 131; qualification 127; question 218; reason 138; rights 24; sphere 65; standing 25, 33, 56, 109, 141, 173, 285; status 63, 65, 129–130, 147; thinking 109; utility 314; value 283, 286
morality 16, 95, 107, 202, 218, 222, 249, 251, 269, 273, 286, 314, 355, 358, 367
Morawski, S. 146
Morgan, C. L. 391–395
Morgan's canon 391–392, 395, 404
Morice, D. 153, 379
motivation 5, 10, 24, 26, 36, 37, 129, 133, 143, 200–201, 216, 233, 236, 238, 268–269, 332; approach 268; of avoidance 28; choreographies of 376; commercial 34; concept 28; creative 26; for creativity 312; of desires 5; economy 37; feedback loop 236; forces of 28; heterogeneity of 315; interpretation of 20; inverted 236; narrative of 28, 30; nonhuman animal 143; primary 312; social 170, 173
movement 31, 51, 57, 64, 67, 68, 70, 76, 97–98, 124, 142, 149, 179–181, 185, 210–212, 224, 241, 248, 354, 366, 369, 378, 389, 395, 399; aesthetic 68; assembly of 76; attentive 221; of authorship 124; complex 67, 91, 186; of creativity 76; of embodied sentience 5; expressive

378; of imitation 77; intellectual 354; kinaesthetic empathy of 74; music of 142; philosophical 334; productive 76; simple 91, 186; suggestion of 124
music 96, 142, 150, 168, 238–241, 329, 397, 405; commercial 240; copyright 239, 241; distraction 238, 241; epic 15; experience of 142; history of 240; industry 241; language of 364; listening to 238; logic of 239; -making 241; of movement 142; sociality of 240; streaming 75; threat to quit 239; traditions of 240; writing 239

Nagel, T. 14, 119
Nancy, J. -L. 94, 333–334
narration 16, 94
Naruto 7, 11, 12, 22, 27–39, 61, 65–66, 128, 130–131, 136, 143, 151, 171, 210, 213, 214, 216, 218–219, 236, 241, 247, 250, 278, 280, 297, 298, 322, 332, 374, 389, 394, 403–405, 418, 420
Naruto v Slater 11, 39n1
natural selection 121, 205, 222, 391, 395
Navajo 95
Negus, K. 292
neuroscience: affective 28
newness 310, 312–314, 390
Newton, I. 263–264, 271, 273
Next Friends relationship 11, 23
Nichols, R. 138
non-fungible tokens (NFTs) 242, 278
non-use 282
Nothing In Life Is Free (NILIF) 219
nouns, names and naming 24–25, 63, 72–74, 96, 101, 365
Novalis 397, 399
novelty 151, 202, 251, 310, 313–315, 325, 375, 394, 399
numeracy and counting 96, 107–108; *see also* mathematics
Nussbaum, M. C. 26, 129
Nye, A. 223

obedience 102, 219–220; dis- 102; *see also* training
object relations 38, 400
objectivity 55, 65, 77, 145–147, 173, 186, 242, 252, 282, 371, 389, 408
obsolescence 285

O'Hear, A. 238
ontogeny 245
openness 248–250, 273, 334, 392–394, 407
opportunism 209, 214
opposition 67, 124–126, 271, 273–274, 276, 297, 326, 327, 336, 361, 390
optimism 119, 122, 124–125, 138, 178, 222, 327, 389, 396
originality 1–2, 4, 18, 20, 27, 30, 33, 70, 140–142, 144, 146, 186–188, 202, 209, 215, 219, 237, 241, 251, 274, 311, 313–316, 322, 329–331, 335, 337, 349, 351–353, 359, 372, 396–397, 399–400, 407; *see also* author's own intellectual creation
Overall, K. L. 221
Owned, An Ethological Jurisprudence of Property 3, 5, 58–59, 108, 168, 219
owner 21, 200, 206, 214–218, 221, 232, 270, 281–283, 417–419
ownerless 36
ownership 4, 26, 35–36, 71, 75, 130, 131, 133, 142, 168, 208, 218, 241, 242, 281, 285, 313, 418

pain 129, 134, 152, 289; barrier 128; *see also* suffer
palimpsest 59, 188, 352, 353, 361, 401
Pangloss 119, 121–125, 142, 206, 283
Panglossian 38, 119, 123, 142, 149, 272, 273; attention 121; justification 128; paradigm 38, 119, 121, 125, 128, 133, 273, 319; parody 123; perspective 121; process 126; proper path of analysis 121, 133, 138, 143, 146, 285, 400; proportions 149; pseudo- 123–124; reasoning 133; stereotypes 126; tendrils 121
Panksepp, J. 139
Paolucci, C. 322
parasite 218
paratextuality 359
Paris Convention 282
parody 5, 6, 37, 60, 123, 237, 238, 267, 278, 282, 290, 316, 331–332, 348, 350–369, 373–375, 389, 396–399, 406
pastiche 4, 6, 153, 237, 278, 282, 290, 332, 334, 348–369, 374–375, 389, 396–399

patent 18, 30, 217, 282, 313, 314
patience 6, 97, 107, 165, 244, 245; *see also* rushing; speed
Pence, D. E. 393
People for the Ethical Treatment of Animals (PETA) 9, 23–26
perception 22, 31–33, 59, 62, 67, 68, 70, 76, 131, 152, 211, 212, 219, 275, 276, 315, 370, 371, 394, 402–404; action-based 402; active 152; of aesthetic value 31; attentive 212; of authorship 122; comprehensive 243; conscious 59; cultural 17; embodied 212, 402; fundamental 59; human 328; of imitation 332; of life 28; minute 5, 59, 70, 353, 388; of moral status 65; of perceptions 59; public 56; of reality 316; robotic 94; sensori-motor 76; tactile 92; theories of 211, 404; tiny 59; unconscious 59; of usefulness 313; visual 317
performance 6, 11–12, 21, 29, 31, 34–36, 63–66, 68, 73, 76, 77, 94, 96, 128, 131, 148, 149, 170, 200, 201, 209, 214, 232, 272, 278, 286, 289, 290, 292, 294, 328, 331, 332, 363, 367–369, 379, 395, 403, 405, 408, 419; aesthetic 68; of authorship 149; of belief 66; cosmological 95; of excess 270; human 95; intentional 367; literal 171; phenomena of 128; poetry as 153, 379; of property 176; relational 189; of relations 290; of sentience 6; of sociality 247; unrecorded 201; of value 12
performative excess 12, 136, 140, 173, 297; *see also* abundance; surplus; waste
performer 34, 96, 150–151, 239; creativity 65; rights 7n15
personality 12, 27, 100, 138, 149, 150, 176, 279, 361; aesthetic 150; animal 176; creative 140; differences 149; full expression of 217; generalisation of 103; individual 138; legal 131–132, 209; micro- 149; rights of the 217; studies 176
personhood 30, 60, 62, 64, 71–72, 77, 120–121, 127–133, 136–139, 147, 188, 204–205, 207, 209, 217, 221, 223, 245–247, 270, 277–279, 419; absence of 132; advocacy 128; agenda 130; analysis of 136; artificial 127, 188; attention of 217; of authorship 132, 139, 147; autonomy model of 26; barriers to 277; basis for 152; calculated 71; claim to 132; concept of 133, 207; context 26; cultural dimension to 246; discourse 128; discussion of 18, 130, 131, 133; exploration of 150; fundamental basis for 131; fundamental obstacle to 133; language of 25; legal 132; logic of 207; mantra of 72; matter of 246; meaning of 132; potential ethological 405; potential for 72; principles of 245; reckoning of 30; recognition of 137; risk 403; sensational threshold for 129; straw 128; synonym 129
perspective: animal 151; anthropocentric 17, 152, 174, 175, 209, 288, 370; artificial 106; authorial 249; behavioural 289; of commercial law 12; conceptual 389; conventional 12, 293; copyright 400; creative 277; critical 24, 72, 140, 142, 152, 313; disciplinary 15; diverse 20, 30, 63; dominant 123; embodied 369; ethological 25, 65, 107, 131, 153, 181, 186, 187, 212, 222, 369, 417; Eurocentric 370; fascinating 348; god-like 349; human 14, 135; individual's 147; juridical framing of 222; law's 5, 65, 311; multispecies 5; national 38; nonhuman animal 317; novel 251; othered 242; Panglossian 121; particular 38, 66, 400; policy 151, 311, 378; practical 233; presumed 404; presumptuous 63; proliferation of 183; radical shift in 419; range of 16; relational 97; relevant 325; reorientation of 277; scientific 138; shift in 172; situational 97; sociological 178; subjective experience of 189; -taking 41n56; technical 389
pessimistic 222, 389
phenomenal consciousness 140, 142, 144, 148, 172, 211, 250–251
phenomenological psychology 148
phenomenology 148, 183, 185
Philosopher, the Ants, and Mercury, The 1, 2, 348
photography *see* art

Piaget, J. 222
pigs 123, 250, 283
Pirruccello, A. 243
plagiarism 330, 353, 354; colonising impact of 241; potential 241; provenance in 353
plants 34, 127, 172; behaviour 34; exclusion of 127; kingdom 127; sentience 34
Plato 60; *Laws* 251; *Republic, The* 53, 78n16, 224n8, 225n24; *Symposium, The* 81n55; *see also* Thrasymachus
Platonic: dialogue 249; exchange 53; forum 53
Plautus, T. M. 54
play: and creativity 5, 29, 76, 273, 289, 295, 316, 318, 332, 334, 371; evolutionary fitness 277; and expression 10, 28, 33, 220, 249, 322, 377, 408; and morality and fairness 222, 249, 251, 269, 273, 355, 367; object 293; and phenomenal consciousness 142, 144, 251; and prolongation 68, 273, 276, 299n12, 318, 355, 396; social 271, 273; as welfare indicator 277, 295; -world 289; *see also* tools; toys
player 27, 34, 236, 249, 251, 273–274, 294, 295, 318
playfulness 21, 236, 248, 249, 361; intellectual 249
pleasure 10, 12, 28, 36, 107, 139, 145, 207, 218, 233, 236, 263, 287, 293, 315, 317–319, 331, 358, 362, 367, 370, 373, 375, 408
Pliny the Elder 106, 388
pluralism 126, 243
poeisis 141
poetry 141, 145, 152–153, 186, 318, 368, 378; epic 357; romantic 334
Poincaré, H. 144
political: agenda 234; complexities 244; demonstration 181; economy 296–297; entities 357; protestations 9; social ties 246; sociology 54; structures 134; theory 315
possession 71, 212, 284, 294; concept of 71; functional 168; intermediary of 71; philosophy 71; politics 71; reciprocal 70; social theories of 71; understanding of 71
Pound, R. 401

power 54, 64, 66–68, 70, 74–75, 101, 103, 184, 202, 204–206, 211, 219, 221–224, 246, 284, 298, 362; axiomatic 127; of boundary-making 51; coercive 222; colonial 221, 243; creative 23, 222; dialectic 204; of doubting 67, 74; economic 205, 206; economy of 37; enumerative 35; formalizing 68; harmonizing 126; impressive 184; intellectual 103; object of 222; preponderance of 204; registry of 135; of scent 416; struggle for 54; technical 27; of thinking 66, 75; tools 293–294; vital 20; *see also* force
precursors 4, 77, 97, 240, 275, 298, 348–349; acknowledged 4; ancient 54; Wattana's 101–105
predator 3, 184, 273, 325, 329–330, 365–367, 373; -distraction display 365
predatory: account 331; battle lines 290; behaviour 272; drift 3, 5, 24, 54, 61, 109, 123, 151, 174–175, 205–206, 218–219, 272, 329–330; models of authorship 6; models of capital 5; narrative 331
Premack, D. 324
pretence 4, 6, 17, 33–34, 60, 73, 75, 141, 144, 173, 201–202, 240, 252, 254, 290, 298, 316, 332, 347, 366, 375, 407
prey 291; dynamic 3; species 273
producer / production: aesthetic 267, 333, 405; affiliative 98; artificial 31; authorial 272, 286; coerced 27; collaborative 403; commanding 200; -consumption linearity 268; creative 201, 294; cultural 326, 403; of evidence 289; expressive 288; familiar 2, 3, 28, 37, 38, 59, 75, 106, 125, 168, 175, 180, 182, 185–187, 247, 251, 271, 276, 289, 297, 315, 326, 333–334, 349, 388, 399, 405, 406; gendered spaces of 210; as human 31; intellectual 185; intelligence 135; knowledge 167, 248, 287, 395; linear 399; literary 399; mass 125, 206, 237–238; nonhuman 13; process of 286–287, 289; reciprocal 271; relational 97; relentless 272; reversibility in 268; social 3, 37–38,

180, 181, 189, 271, 275, 315, 326, 337; of social memory 37; of space 182, 184, 189; space of 210; true 153; of wealth 267, 297
property: affiliative 240; application of 268; authorial 105; battle for 54; binary of 132; collaborative approach to 169; communal 2; conventions of 218; development 168; device of 29; digital 75; discourse on 174; dismantling of 213; double bind of 94; dynamic 150; ethological approach to 147; of exceptionality 150; functioning 28, 124; intangible 108, 216; intentional knot of 99; jurisprudence of 3, 5, 37, 242; law 58, 210, 215, 270, 403; objects of 108; performance of 131, 176; philosophies of 242; of play 76; predatory drift in 3, 54, 205; relational 36, 124, 144, 185, 219, 274, 281; relations 54, 97, 108, 168, 216; rivalrous 124, 214, 219; sensation of 94; sociability 124; social qualities of 37; subjective 148; systems 124; tangible 215; welfare 72, 247, 274; *see also* intellectual property
provenance 13, 23, 77, 109, 150, 188, 215, 217, 241, 282, 326, 353; *see also* attribution; stewardship
psychology 248, 297, 393, 397; animal 391; cerebral 32; comparative 177, 336, 391–392, 397; ecological 76, 211; economic 296; experimental 245; folk 375; inter- 13, 32, 71, 177, 179, 223, 237, 297, 390; mass 37; phenomenological 148; zoological 392
public domain 22, 36, 214, 245, 310, 317, 417, 419
punishment 109, 205, 209, 218–220, 222; concept of 218; narratives 109; use of 218–219

questions and asking 2, 5, 9–10, 22, 24–27, 30, 31, 71, 83, 89, 97, 107, 119, 127, 131–132, 135, 139, 143–144, 151, 168, 182, 190, 201–202, 216–217, 221, 234, 238, 240, 243–244, 249, 251–252, 274, 288, 314, 321, 331, 336, 352, 359, 364, 367, 389, 393–395, 401, 405, 416, 418; of attention 252; of authorship 19; catalysts for 51; commercial 36; complex 62, 73, 313; copyright 25; cultural 329; ethical 393; fundamental 5; intellectual property 19; jurisprudence 12; multifarious 211; of remuneration 151; semantic 63; serious 19; theological 53; wrong 26, 108, 151, 252, 388
quotation 282, 329–330, 349, 352; conventional 362; tissue of 401

rationality 63, 152, 204; economic 26, 28, 35, 37, 136, 143, 167, 217, 218, 254; habits of 207; irrational 207; of justice 224
rats 109, 218, 288; laboratory 139
reading 5, 60–61, 69, 77, 165, 179, 204, 210, 212, 236–237, 240–242, 273, 320, 367, 399, 405
reason 10, 35, 36, 62, 119, 120, 123, 125–127, 150, 152, 170–172, 179, 183, 184, 211, 214, 223, 243, 249, 292, 293, 295, 313, 317, 320, 326, 349, 351–353, 363, 391, 393–394, 404; decisive action of 184; good 35; missive of 4; moral 138; sufficient 119, 120, 123, 125, 133–137, 144; voice of 4
reciprocal 27, 54, 70, 97, 167, 247, 271, 276; concept of 246; creative 271; expectation of 108; possession 70
recursion: curse of 189
reflexivity 147, 356, 363; characteristic 356; self- 353
refrain 4, 11, 28–29, 51, 64, 119, 121, 135, 139, 239, 244, 328, 354, 361, 373; anticipatory 15; humorous 373; perceptible 361
relationality 28, 32, 59, 69–70, 72, 101, 216, 273–276, 281, 326, 330; of imitation 32; of opposition 276; problem 375; productive 273
relativism 353; banal 123
repetition 1, 53, 71, 126, 179, 187, 248, 249, 273–276, 336, 355, 356, 362, 395, 401
res familiaris 2, 58, 108, 241
reverberation (*retentissement*) 60, 184–185
reverie *see* dreams

reversibility 60, 204, 223, 233, 268, 313, 351; ir- 204
rewards 26, 37, 133, 200, 201, 203, 218–222, 253, 287, 292, 353
Ricketson, S. 142
Riehl, E. 99
Rigby, K. 334
rights: agenda 130; animal 51, 127, 130, 172, 321, 322; for artificial intelligence 90; author's 23, 131, 279; barrier to 152; -based approaches 207; discourse 11, 71, 127, 128, 132, 150, 217, 403; economic 150, 279; enforcing 30, 282; externalised 151; framework 218; human 209, 285; language of 71–72; moral 24; nature 29, 150, 204; nonhuman 125, 128; perpetual 387; personal 217; potential 72, 120; range of 4; reasons of 150; recognition of 152; rhetoric of 131; statutory 132; subject of 22; subsistence of 128; *see also* intellectual property
Ristau, C. 367, 368
rivalry 205; conventions of 232; property 124, 214, 219; relations 123
Rogers, C. R. 272–273, 312
Rollin, B. E. 393
Romanes, G. J. 101, 175, 176, 179
Romantic: author 352, 399; exigency 335; fragment 397, 398; German 145; irony 335, 351; literary ideal 335; Movement 145; period 145, 263, 395; philosophy 395, 396; theory of criticism 335; traditions 335
Romanticism 395, 396; Athenaeum 397; British 333, 336; German 4, 336, 350, 397, 399; Jena 335, 352, 358, 367
Rose, M. A. 357, 362
rushing 244
Ruskin, J. 237
Ruyer, R. 20

Sadler, S. 296
Saint-Hilaire, É. G. 101
salience 313; aversive 28, 362; incentive 28, 233, 317, 389–390
Samuel, A. L. 134
Samuelson, P. 36
Sanz, R. 328
say please 219, 221

scarcity 206; apprehension of 206; artificial 206, 253; contrived 283; of objects 253
Schlegel, F. 4, 5, 145, 319, 333–337, 351, 356–358, 361, 363, 364, 367–368, 373, 396, 398–399
Schopenhauer, A. 90, 183
Seabright, P. 175
Sebeok, T. A. 73, 74, 76–77, 369–370
seeking 21, 126, 236, 240, 242, 248, 276, 327; attention 210, 242; behaviour 10, 34; distraction 236; goal- 37; out 240; receptive 210
self 66, 73, 99, 149, 209, 312, 378; alchemical 3; -assemblage 3; -assured 68; -awareness 14, 22, 129, 149; bodyness of 376; complete 69; -consciousness 20, 25, 121, 138, 142, 208, 258, 314; -contained 136, 144; -criticism 363; -defeating 17, 403; -destruction 206; -directed 222; enacted 140; -esteem 299; -evident 202; exposition of the 145; -forming 334; government of the 37; -hood 22, 27, 74; -idolatry 417; -knowledge 335; -organizing 334; -parody 359, 360, 363, 364, 366, 397, 406; -perpetuating 219; -portrait 22; process of the 188; -promotion 19; realisation of 292; -recognition 17; -referentially 141, 349; -reflexivity 353; -representation 149; sense of 27, 130, 149; -sufficiency 188; -sustaining 334; -understanding 74; verbalisation of 74
selfie 21, 27, 213, 219; Monkey 9, 22, 23; Naruto's 27, 298
semiotics 321–322; animal 56; bio- 147, 376; cognitive 322; descriptive 56; general 322
sensation 33, 70, 94, 146, 210–211, 242, 243, 315, 368, 370
sense: aesthetic 5, 14, 16, 17, 19, 27, 152, 208, 249, 268, 288, 294, 317, 370, 374; of authorship 142; broadest 18, 121, 141, 171, 406; of coincidences 57; common 62, 98, 285, 368, 389; conceptual 146; of curiosity 27; -data epistemology 66; economic 297; evolutionary 374; of fairness 107; of humour 177; of intentionality 146; judgments 125;

of justice 269, 367; of language 57; making 94, 122, 147, 149, 170, 271, 276, 287, 290, 294, 318, 376, 400; material 72; of mentality 10; of occasion 148; of originality 70, 142; of place 96; practical 143; of the problem 201; of purpose 129; real 23; of self 27, 130, 149; significance 26; of utility 23; visual 211; wider 140, 206, 242, 281
sensori-motor: apprehension 69; cognition 68; perception 76; *see also* cognition
sentience: aesthetics 122, 369; anatomisation of 128; animal 127, 147, 175, 377; artefact of 29; artificial 129, 134; biological imperative in 131; of a chatbot 134; concept of 17, 19, 56, 65–66, 120, 127, 130–132, 144, 207, 396; debate 32; defining 129, 138; demonstration of 25, 152; deployment of 127; dilemma of 121; discourse of 134, 285; discussion 120, 136, 152, 283; embodied 5; emerging law on 5; evidence of 17, 127; examples of 17; existence of 129; fundamental barrier of 56; haptic 93; identity of 128; language of 143; machine 73, 144; mechanical 136; nonhuman animal 34, 121, 147, 279; notions of 17, 205; plant 34; potential for 90; question of 32; recruitment of 19; robotic 94; societal 56; theory of 98, 129, 136, 140, 144–145, 148, 402; threshold of 77; understanding 128, 131, 148
Serjeantson, R. W. 63
Serres M 38, 94, 125, 142
shadow creativity 150–151; *see also* creativity
Shakespeare, W. 4, 95
Shanahan, M. 62
shared interests 1, 10, 11, 13, 21, 27, 28, 57, 70, 94, 98, 99, 101, 108, 147–149, 165, 168, 169, 180, 181, 186–187, 189, 232, 246–247, 253, 271, 273, 274, 276, 297, 323, 334, 403–405
sharing 12, 29, 58, 107–108, 168, 206, 241, 269, 276, 316, 330, 395, 404
Shaviro, S. 135
Sheak, W. H. 102–103

sheep 231n177
Sheeran, E. 239–240
shipwreck 2, 3, 51–52, 55, 62, 121–122, 168, 234, 347, 348; catastrophic 119; copyright 279; Kasos 347
show 11, 12, 16, 35, 65–66, 69, 76, 91, 94, 103, 109, 138, 142, 145, 175, 200, 204–207, 210, 215, 222, 233, 235, 249–251, 271, 275, 289, 294, 295, 298, 317, 321, 323–324, 329, 336, 337, 369, 372, 375, 395, 398, 399
Silbey, J. 21
Silko, L. M. 253–254
Simmel, G. 178
Simon, H. A. 173–179, 184
Singer, J. W. 58
Singer, P. 128, 172
singularity 65, 284–285, 336, 352, 377, 390; of art 77; of authorship 130, 241, 333, 352, 372; of celebrity 241; of a copyright author 214; of the fragment 33; of the machine 188; persistent 181
situation 27, 61, 107, 132, 169, 178, 250, 278, 320, 323, 394, 407; awareness of the 108; concept of 57; in extension 57; of ownerlessness 36; reality of 291; welfare 10
Situationist International 290, 296, 330, 354; *see also détournement*
skill 145–146, 330, 366, 372, 416; human 93; inventive 16; judgement 330, 372; labour 29, 68, 93, 103, 140, 142, 170, 182, 221, 235, 238, 247, 268, 269, 279–281, 283, 294, 296, 330, 372, 417; test of 143
Skinner, B. F. 77, 253
Slater, D. J. 9, 22–23, 25, 27, 213–216, 298, 322, 332, 403
smell 64–65, 67, 76, 95, 181, 201, 252; olfactory 67, 209, 416; scent 32, 76, 95, 367, 417
sociability 28, 36–37, 68, 77, 91, 100, 124, 241, 313
social production 3, 37–38, 180, 181, 189, 271, 275, 315, 326, 337; *see also* familiar production
social tie 28, 240, 246–248, 253
socialisation 168, 169; re- 147
sociality 10, 13, 70, 92–93, 95, 108, 151, 168, 185, 216, 237–238, 240,

242, 247, 250, 274–275, 290, 294, 319, 325, 358, 398, 402; affective 244; affiliative 273, 297; attributive 271; of authorship 151; civilising 297; cooperative 322; embodiment of 95; fundamental 59; ideal 406; of irony 358; potential 206; pro- 70, 108, 109, 222, 271, 334; responsive 93; rich 184; substance of 70; theory of 404; vital 297, 325
societal failures 54
sociology 32, 59, 63, 126, 133, 137, 177–180, 271, 273, 276, 396; animal 177; anticipatory 32; classical 203; comparative 177; discipline of 348; human 180; of imitation 13, 70; micro- 37, 138, 390, 407; narratives of 407; nascent 177; optimism of 396; political 54; relational 271, 273, 327
Socrates 54, 201, 203
Socratic irony 319, 335, 351, 365–367, 373, 396; *see also* irony
sound 64–65, 67, 76, 184–185, 188, 209, 236, 239, 288, 324
space: aesthetic 418; authorial 214; of authorship 209–214; creative 288; of creativity 102; embodied 211; empty 210; engagement with 147; expressive 148, 288; generative measure of 148, 210; human 213, 223; infinite division of 97; inhabiting the 95; interaction with 176; judicial 408; of the knot 90; laboratory 178; making 147–150; Naruto's 29, 210; negative 74; obsession with 106; participatory moments of 184; personal character of 147; for play 64; production of 182, 184, 189, 210, 367; rendering of 106, 213; representation of 210; sense of 215; shaping of 184, 212; sounds of 184; subjective 148; tactile 106; use of 106, 149, 317; waste of 268
spandrels 273; of art 214; of artificial intelligence 285; of play 171; of San Marco's Basilica 121; *see also* Panglossian paradigm
species: barrier 14, 31, 35, 54–56, 59, 62, 65, 93, 152, 207, 289, 292; divide 2, 53, 56, 322
speech 4, 54, 63–64, 91, 321, 323, 368, 408; speaking 3, 21, 24, 25, 54, 64, 69, 77, 91, 99, 131, 168, 172, 200, 201, 242, 249, 279, 283, 286, 313, 316, 348, 354, 356, 370, 371, 377, 396, 406
speed 97, 181
Spencer, H. 374
spiders 330
standing 2, 25, 109, 150; concern 215; constitutional 9, 26; long- 349, 368; representational 26; statutory 26; visibly 150; *see also* moral standing; personhood
Stefanovska, M. 390
Steinbeck, J. 264–265; Toby the dog 264–265, 315
stereotypic imitation 5, 13, 34, 98, 173, 182, 186, 208, 243, 247, 253, 272, 276, 311, 328–329, 353, 360, 418; *see also* attentive imitation; imitation
stewardship 109, 239, 253, 296, 325, 326, 329, 330, 333–335, 349, 353, 398, 401, 417; basic 326; of citation 275; debt of 77; extra-legal norms of 241; genuine 241; of ideas 242, 399; of knowledge 4, 28, 30, 167, 188, 233, 241–242, 334, 349, 353, 419; in music 329
Stone-Mediatore, S. 243
Stones, G. 351, 354, 357
story: back 239; of attribution 23; of authorship 6; of creativity 165; critical part of the 39; diffusion of 348; legitimate 406; life 99; making 396; movement of 389; official 390; openness to 392; quality of 392; short 167, 357; simple 205; telling 95, 125, 336, 388, 390, 393, 401, 405
STRANGE framework 409n3
stranger 109, 153, 174–175, 201, 203, 205, 216, 251, 281, 284, 327, 352, 363, 420
string-pulling 16, 112n32, 229n135
Strong, C. A. 416
style 125, 243, 314, 315, 333, 336, 356, 359–360, 364, 399; attentional 250; Newtonian- 271; orangutan 93; personal 100
Su, F. 222
subjectivity 77, 294, 390; expressive 148; inter- 101, 358, 397
suffer 26, 67, 74, 90, 122, 128–130, 132, 151–152, 172–173, 221, 251, 276, 378

Suits, B. 269, 271, 272
surplus 34, 145, 270–271, 296; energy 10; expenditure 6; resources 271; value 270, 277, 282
surprise 288, 295, 317, 362; element of 28, 310; sense of 317; *see also* incentive, salience
survival of the fittest 3, 205–206, 223
swarm intelligence 168, 179–181, 185–187
symbiotic relationships 175
symbolic: communication 168, 177, 180–181, 185, 368, 369; language 64, 65, 67; thought 54, 62, 68, 72–73, 75, 323
sympathy 370; *see also* empathy
symphilosophy 333–334, 354
sympoeisis 228n81
sympoetry 333–334

tactical deception *see* deception
Tangkoko reserve 9, 22, 29
Tarde, G. 4, 13, 28, 33, 38–39, 69, 71, 74, 124–126, 148, 179–183, 212, 241, 246–248, 253, 271, 273, 275, 276, 278, 284, 296–298, 327–328, 336, 353, 379, 390, 396, 401, 405
taste 54, 64–65, 184, 286, 298, 416–418; aesthetic 234, 298; arbitration of 298, 314; service of 370
Terranova, T. 37, 326
territory 20, 37; inadmissible 54; overlapping 148; pretence of 366
testimony 24, 239, 336, 403; of authorship 403; ethological approach to 176; individual 38
textuality: archi- 359; hyper- 359; inter- 353, 359, 362; meta- 359; para- 359; trans- 359
thanatosis 365–366
theory of everything 208–209, 219, 223
third party evaluation 41n56; *see also* perspective
Thomson, P. 294
Thrasymachus 53–54, 201–204, 207, 219, 222, 233, 249; *see also* Plato
Tom's Little Dog (1941) 200, 219, 252
Tønnessen, M. 147
tools 51, 67–68, 74, 76, 92, 95, 98, 104–106, 211, 213–214, 223, 238, 288, 290–291, 293, 377, 394, 401, 407, 418; of artificial intelligence 97; artificial intelligence as 400; of authorship 290; behaviour 292; bodily 97; capital 285; of capitalism 283, 284; communicative 293; critical 296; crucial 331, 332; enrichment 10; expressive 362; of history 387; language 92; legitimate 235; manipulation 107, 290; methodological 387; novel 169; objects 169; for play 22; of play 318; playing the 290; policy 56, 120, 132, 285; power 293; powerful 271; primitive 95; research 393; social 275, 293; testing 169; two-limbed 223; understanding 211; use 16, 27, 101, 152, 168, 169, 291–294; welfare 25, 130, 418; *see also* toys and toying
Tormey, A. 147
Totemism 377
touch 57, 58, 64–65, 67, 92–94, 184–185, 210, 252, 287, 361; haptic 93–94, 97, 106; tactile 92, 94, 106, 116, 236
Townsend, E. 239, 240
toys 94, 106–107, 273, 318, 361–362
trade mark 18, 270, 282–283, 313–314
Trade-Mark Cases (1879) 22
traditional: cultural expressions 138, 151, 170, 187, 210, 242–243, 372, 419; knowledge 124, 151, 187, 209–210, 242, 278, 372
training 3, 168, 201, 219, 287; approaches to 221; context 220; data 328; discourse 219–220; dog 54, 253; hierarchy 103; intensive 133; literature 221; paradigm 220; by punishment 222; subjects 220; use of aversives 221; *see also* learning
trickery 60, 238, 322, 348, 366
trust 32, 100, 137, 173, 200–201, 207, 219, 316, 320, 389; authorial 31; consumer's 31; establishing 31; facilitation of 64; mis- 188; -worthy 32
truth 94, 106, 145, 202, 204, 219, 223, 242, 269, 318–323, 325, 326, 334, 354, 356, 364, 367, 373–374; contradictory 224; exemplary 390; exploration of 318; exterior 263; higher 224; infinite 405; opposing 223; spirit of 242; synthetic 128; in toying 318

Turner, C. H. 176–180, 186, 305, 323: Ant 176: *Turquoise Ledge, The* (2010) 253
turn-taking 53, 106, 290, 298, 354; acoustic 290; phenomenon of 290; *see also* fair(ness)

Umwelt 68, 147–149, 213, 219, 235, 271, 273, 317, 369, 372–374, 376–377, 403, 419
unconscious 59, 70, 187, 323, 325; collective 171; mind 70; obstacles 62; perceptions 59
unfinished 201, 237, 238, 253, 268–269, 276, 281, 334, 354, 396, 399, 405; fragment 401; nature of art 237; nature of work 33, 276
United Kingdom Intellectual Property Office 310
United States Copyright Act 214
Urton, G. 96
use: animal behaviour 174; animal cognition 390; artificial intelligence 19, 30; authorship through 124; aversives in training 220–222; beads 95; coercion 222; colloquy 53; commercial 133; contradiction 223; creativity 75; distraction 238; dogs' teeth 94; fair 326, 350, 352; force against force 218; hands 94; haptics 97; implements 167; interaction through 124; invaluable 125; lack of 281–283; language 92, 209, 313; material 106; nonhuman animals 29; perception of 315; photographs 23; plagiarism 330; punishment 218–219; social referencing by cats 250; space 106, 149, 185, 288, 317; terminology 132; transformative 332, 358; utility 23, 188, 267, 274, 281, 283, 286–287, 289, 314–315, 332, 363, 372, 389; *see also* tools
useless(ness) 75, 234, 248, 268, 270, 272, 273, 277, 284, 294–295, 356, 360, 363, 391, 394
user 18–19, 36, 124, 134, 186, 221, 232–233, 268, 270, 283, 284, 313, 402

value: adaptation 24; adaptive 272, 277; aesthetic 17, 64, 178; affiliative 37, 249, 271; art 30; of attribution 215; central 267, 329; circulation of 27; cognitive model of 139; commercial 31, 36, 137; co-production of 270, 372; cornerstone 28; critical 20, 216, 270; cult 236; cultural 13–14, 17, 31, 181, 209, 401, 419; of deceptive play 318; desired 329; dialogical 352; discrete 282; of distraction 263; of error 283; ethological 362; expressive 214; expropriation 29; fundamental 287; -generating 232, 277; high- 107; of historical reflection 177; intersection of 12; lack of 291; literary capital 131; manifest 29, 33; metacommunicative 277; monetary 287; moral 283, 286; objective 277, 297; of parody 364; performance of 12; personal 61; of play 277; productive 297; rationality of 167; real 240; redirection of 214; rhetorical 127; shifting 132; social 153, 181, 185, 240, 282–283, 315; socio-economic 32; strategic 318; surplus 270, 277, 282; theory of 138; transactional 108; transformative 332, 375; uncertain 314; waste as 286; to welfare 274
Varela, F. J. 377
Veblen, T. 296–297
verb 60, 69, 73–74, 77, 98, 186, 212, 276, 324; *see also* nouns, names and naming
vertebrates 170, 246, 365
virtual 27, 242, 289; environments 278
virtue 16, 90, 273, 293, 313, 324, 331, 398
visual 4, 65, 210, 252, 317, 330; account 65; acuity 317; anecdotes 394; arts 18, 20, 65, 238, 369; field 211; hegemony 4–5, 64–65, 252; landmarks 184; masterwork 65; material 280; memories 184; object classification 328; perception 317; primarily 211; regime 106; sense 211; sight 11, 184, 211, 325, 366, 377; tyranny 68
Voltaire 119, 138, 348
von Buttel-Reepen, H. 182
von Uexküll, J. 147, 148, 224, 291, 319
vulnerability 26, 27, 67, 129, 223

Waal, F. de 55
Wadge, A. 239

Waldron, J. 285
Walkley, A. B. 360–361, 363
wandering 213, 296, 347; distracted 263, 287; productive 182; purposeful 248
wants 10, 24, 26–27, 33–35, 57, 59, 64, 65, 70–71, 128, 148, 172, 173, 212, 236, 240, 247, 267, 269, 275, 312, 403; acquired 298; animal 233; attention to 24; of authorship 131, 170; basis of 34; comfort 10; complexity of nonhuman 131; copyright 23; creativity 275; curiosity 21; of curiosity 248; dimension of 27; evidence of 33; explainability of 31; food and water 10; freedoms from 10; frustration of 241, 280; good health 10; implicit theory of 10; impossible questions of 27; of innovation 276; issue of 36; language of 10, 27, 28; liminal relationship to 129; machine 209; mythical 315; narrative of 24; new 297; play 21; question of 27, 30, 332; recasting 151; relationality of 275; safety and security 10; seeking 21; suppressing 57; understanding of 10; wanting 10, 24–26, 28, 31, 34, 36, 54, 59, 73, 90, 128, 141, 175, 202, 232, 276, 325
waste 10, 12, 54, 170, 232, 234, 267–268, 270–271, 277, 279, 281–283, 286, 288–289, 292, 295–296; abundant 222; attention to 283; banal notion of 277; calculation of 282; of community 288; concept of 281–282; counterpoint of 6; discussion of 291; economy of 277; expressive 295; exuberance of 296, 297; glorious 145, 286; hostility towards 286; of the land 216; maddening 287; non- 280; notion of 278, 281; possible 282; preciousness of 296; preview 281; protection against 282; proviso 279–280; reconciliation of 6; of rights 282; social value in 282; of space 268; sublime 282; of time 170, 289, 295, 297, 405; as value 286; *see also* Locke, J
Wattana 99–101, 103, 105–108, 186
Webster, J. 138
Weil, S. 4–5, 24, 51, 57–61, 66–70, 73, 75–77, 91, 92, 129, 133, 140, 146, 148, 165, 170, 172, 181, 186–188, 204–206, 210–213, 216–222, 232, 241–244, 263, 275, 281, 285, 290, 297, 316, 319, 321, 327, 336, 351, 376, 379, 389; *see also* force; *metaxu*; reading
welfare 10, 26, 130, 173, 206, 208, 212, 247, 277–278, 420; animal 56, 127, 138, 149, 151, 207; of authors 150; as an authorship issue 11; -based strategies 130; catastrophes of social media 418; concept 274; concerns 120, 222, 278, 417; consequences 36, 56; context 11, 129, 131, 171, 277; of creators 11; decision 11; dialect 270; dimension 10, 150, 151, 253, 271, 280, 378, 419; dynamics 209; frameworks 130–131; good 10, 295; hostility towards 277; human 10, 151, 295; impact 139; indicators 277; individual 171, 420; interconnection of 11; issue 10, 151, 217, 295; laws 278; legislation 132, 151, 171, 278, 378; limitations 18; logic 232, 270; measure of 141; negative 10; nonhuman animal 10–11, 125, 205, 378; policy 130; poor 295; positive 26, 139; principles of 11, 72, 270, 277, 278; property 72, 247, 271; protection 72, 131, 172, 270; questions 11, 418; radical rethinking of 223; relationship 11, 270; rights 126; sense of 151; situation 10; tool 25, 130, 418; value 33, 274; violations 220; *see also* freedom, five
Wellman, C. 401
Wells, H. G. 121, 167
Wemelsfelder, F. 250
Wheeler, W. M. 169
White, S. A. 181
Whitehead, A. N. 139
Whiten, A. 325, 393
Wilson, E. O. 170
Winner, E. 21
Wittgenstein, L. 92, 108, 269
Wolfe, C. 403
wolves 168, 220
Wooden Nickel Art Project 153
Wordsworth, W. 333
work: labour 280–281; play relationship 221, 294; *see also* copyright

world building 10, 148, 281, 289, 337, 369, 396
world knot (*Weltknoten*) 52, 90–91, 209
writing 4, 32, 59–60, 77, 96, 128, 137, 178–179, 182, 187–188, 234, 237, 239, 242, 263, 269, 285, 288, 296, 333–334, 359, 363, 374, 388, 390, 397, 401–402; collective 334; creative 20, 263; historical 95, 390, 407; modern 95

Wynne, C. 233

Yerkes, R. M. 102

Zion, A. 21

For Product Safety Concerns and Information please contact our EU representative GPSR@taylorandfrancis.com
Taylor & Francis Verlag GmbH, Kaufingerstraße 24, 80331 München, Germany